A Hollow Remedy

By

Anant Kumar Tripati LLM, Merit

Published by:
SureShot Books Publishing LLC
P.O. Box 924
Nyack, New York 10960
www.sureshotbooks.com

Libarary of Congress Cataloging-in-Publication Data

A Hollow Remedy

This book has been published and made available as an e-book.

FOREWARD

This book has been painstakingly researched and written in hopes of enabling the basic humane treatment for all those incarcerated in the United States today and in the future.

THE AUTHOR

ANANT KUMAR TRIPATI LLM, Merit (2014)
UNIVERSITY OF LONDON
UNIVERSITY COLLEGE LONDON
QUEEN MARY UNIVERSITY OF LONDON

Mr. Tripati has specializations in Public International Law (2014), Public Law (2014), and European Law (2013).

TABLE OF CONTENTS

INTRODUCTION

Rightfully expecting state courts shall faithfully ensure the rights and guarantees secured by the constitution of the United States is abide by the states, Congress enacted federal habeas statutes, deferring to state courts and making it difficult for federal courts to set aside state convictions. The statute provided:

TITLE I—HABEAS CORPUS REFORM

SEC. 101. FILING DEADLINES.

Section 2244 of title 28, United States Code, is amended by adding at the end the following new subsection:
"(d)(1) A 1-year period of limitation shall apply to an application for a writ of habeas corpus by a person in custody pursuant to the judgment of a State court. The limitation period shall run from the latest of—

"(A) the date on which the judgment became final by the conclusion of direct review or the expiration of the time for seeking such review;

"(B) the date on which the impediment to filing an application created by State action in violation of the Constitution or laws of the United States is removed, if the applicant was prevented from filing by such State action;

"(C) the date on which the constitutional right asserted was initially recognized by the Supreme Court, if the right has been newly recognized by the Supreme Court and made retroactively applicable to cases on collateral review; or

"(D) the date on which the factual predicate of the claim or claims presented could have been discovered through the exercise of due diligence.

"(2) The time during which a properly filed application for State post-conviction or other collateral review with respect to the pertinent judgment or claim is pending shall not be counted toward any period of limitation under this subsection.".

SEC. 102. APPEAL.

Section 2253 of title 28, United States Code, is amended to read as follows:
"§2253. Appeal
"(a) In a habeas corpus proceeding or a proceeding under section 2255 before a district judge, the final order shall be subject to review, on appeal, by the court of appeals for the circuit in which the proceeding is held.

"(b) There shall be no right of appeal from a final order in a proceeding to test the validity of a warrant to remove to another district or place for commitment or trial a person charged with a criminal offense against the United States, or to test the validity of such person's detention pending removal proceedings.

"(c)(1) Unless a circuit justice or judge issues a certificate of appealability, an appeal may not be taken to the court of appeals from—

"(A) the final order in a habeas corpus proceeding in which the detention complained of arises out of process issued by a State court; or

"(B) the final order in a proceeding under section 2255.

"(2) A certificate of appealability may issue under paragraph (1) only if the applicant has made a substantial showing of the denial of a constitutional right.

"(3) The certificate of appealability under paragraph (1) shall indicate which specific issue or issues

1

satisfy the showing required by paragraph (2).".

SEC. 103. AMENDMENT OF FEDERAL RULES OF APPELLATE PROCEDURE

28 USC app. Rule 22 of the Federal Rules of Appellate Procedure is amended to read as follows:

"Rule 22. Habeas corpus and section 2255 proceedings

"(a) APPLICATION FOR THE ORIGINAL WRIT.—An application for a writ of habeas corpus shall be made to the appropriate district court. If application is made to a circuit judge, the application shall be transferred to the appropriate district court. If an application is made to or transferred to the district court and denied, renewal of the application before a circuit judge shall not be permitted. The applicant may, pursuant to section 2253 of title 28, United States Code, appeal to the appropriate court of appeals from the order of the district court denying the writ.

"(b) CERTIFICATE OF APPEALABILITY.—In a habeas corpus proceeding in which the detention complained of arises out of process issued by a State court, an appeal by the applicant for the writ may not proceed unless a district or a circuit judge issues a certificate of appealability pursuant to section 2253(c) of title 28, United States Code. If an appeal is taken by the applicant, the district judge who rendered the judgment shall either issue a certificate of appealability or state the reasons why such a certificate should not issue. The certificate or the statement shall be forwarded to the court of appeals with the notice of appeal and the file of the proceedings in the district court. If the district judge has denied the certificate, the applicant for the writ may then request issuance of the certificate by a circuit judge. If such a request is addressed to the court of appeals, it shall be deemed addressed to the judges thereof and shall be considered by a circuit judge or judges as the court deems appropriate. If no express request for a certificate is filed, the notice of appeal shall be deemed to constitute a request addressed to the judges of the court of appeals. If an appeal is taken by a State or its representative, a certificate of appealability is not required.".

SEC. 104. SECTION 2254 AMENDMENTS.

Section 2254 of title 28, United States Code, is amended— (1) by amending subsection (b) to read as follows:

"(b)(1) An application for a writ of habeas corpus on behalf of a person in custody pursuant to the judgment of a State court shall not be granted unless it appears that—

"(A) the applicant has exhausted the remedies available in the courts of the State; or

"(B)(i) there is an absence of available State corrective process; or

"(ii) circumstances exist that render such process ineffective to protect the rights of the applicant.

"(2) An application for a writ of habeas corpus may be denied on the merits, notwithstanding the failure of the applicant to exhaust the remedies available in the courts of the State.

"(3) A State shall not be deemed to have waived the exhaustion requirement or be estopped from reliance upon the requirement unless the State, through counsel, expressly waives the requirement.";

(2) by redesignating subsections (d), (e), and (f) as subsections (e), (f), and (g), respectively;

(3) by inserting after subsection (c) the following new subsection:

"(d) An application for a writ of habeas corpus on behalf of a person in custody pursuant to the judgment of a State court shall not be granted with respect to any claim that was adjudicated on the merits in State court proceedings unless the adjudication of the claim—

"(1) resulted in a decision that was contrary to, or involved an unreasonable application of, clearly established Federal law, as determined by the Supreme Court of the United States; or

"(2) resulted in a decision that was based on an unreasonable determination of the facts in light of the evidence presented in the State court proceeding.";

(4)   by amending subsection (e), as redesignated by paragraph (2), to read as follows:

"(e)(1) In a proceeding instituted by an application for a writ of habeas corpus by a person in custody pursuant to the judgment of a State court, a determination of a factual issue made by a State court shall be presumed to be correct. The applicant shall have the burden of rebutting the presumption of correctness by clear and convincing evidence.

"(2) If the applicant has failed to develop the factual basis of a claim in State court proceedings, the court shall not hold an evidentiary hearing on the claim unless the applicant shows that—

"(A) the claim relies on—

"(i) a new rule of constitutional law, made retroactive to cases on collateral review by the Supreme Court, that was previously unavailable; or

"(ii) a factual predicate that could not have been previously discovered through the exercise of due diligence; and

"(B) the facts underlying the claim would be sufficient to establish by clear and convincing evidence that but for constitutional error, no reasonable factfinder would have found the applicant guilty of the underlying offense."; and

(5) by adding at the end the following new subsections:

"(h) Except as provided in section 408 of the Controlled Substances Act, in all proceedings brought under this section, and any subsequent proceedings on review, the court may appoint counsel for an applicant who is or becomes financially unable to afford counsel, except as provided by a rule promulgated by the Supreme Court pursuant to statutory authority. Appointment of counsel under this section shall be governed by section 3006A of title 18.

"(i) The ineffectiveness or incompetence of counsel during Federal or State collateral post-conviction proceedings shall not be a ground for relief in a proceeding arising under section 2254.".

SEC. 105. SECTION 2255 AMENDMENTS.

Section 2255 of title 28, United States Code, is amended—

(1)   by striking the second and fifth undesignated paragraphs; and

(2)   by adding at the end the following new undesignatedparagraphs:

"A 1-year period of limitation shall apply to a motion under this section. The limitation period shall run from the latest of—

"(1) the date on which the judgment of conviction becomes final;

"(2) the date on which the impediment to making a motion created by governmental action in violation of the Constitution or laws of the United States is removed, if the movant was prevented from making a motion by such governmental action;

"(3) the date on which the right asserted was initially recognized by the Supreme Court, if that right has been newly recognized by the Supreme Court and made retroactively applicable to cases on collateral review; or

"(4) the date on which the facts supporting the claim or claims presented could have been discovered through the exercise of due diligence.

"Except as provided in section 408 of the Controlled Substances Act, in all proceedings brought under this section, and any subsequent proceedings on review, the court may appoint counsel, except as provided by a rule promulgated by the Supreme Court pursuant to statutory authority. Appointment of counsel under this section shall be governed by section 3006A of title 18.

"A second or successive motion must be certified as provided in section 2244 by a panel of the appropriate court of appeals to contain—

"(1) newly discovered evidence that, if proven and viewed in light of the evidence as a whole, would be sufficient to establish by clear and convincing evidence that no reasonable factfinder would have found the movant guilty of the offense; or

"(2) a new rule of constitutional law, made retroactive to cases on collateral review by the Supreme Court, that was previously unavailable.".

SEC. 106. LIMITS ON SECOND OR SUCCESSIVE APPLICATIONS.

(a) CONFORMING AMENDMENT TO SECTION 2244(a).—Section 2244(a) of title 28, United States Code, is amended by striking "and the petition" and all that follows through "by such inquiry." and inserting ", except as provided in section 2255.".

(b) LIMITS ON SECOND OR SUCCESSIVE APPLICATIONS.—Section 2244(b) of title 28, United States Code, is amended to read as follows:

"(b)(1) A claim presented in a second or successive habeas corpus application under section 2254 that was presented in a prior application shall be dismissed.

"(2) A claim presented in a second or successive habeas corpus application under section 2254 that was not presented in a prior application shall be dismissed unless—

"(A) the applicant shows that the claim relies on a new rule of constitutional law, made retroactive to cases on collateral review by the Supreme Court, that was previously unavailable; or

"(B)(i) the factual predicate for the claim could not have been discovered previously through the exercise of due diligence; and

"(ii) the facts underlying the claim, if proven and viewed in light of the evidence as a whole, would be sufficient to establish by clear and convincing evidence that, but for constitutional error, no reasonable factfinder would have found the applicant guilty of the underlying offense.

"(3)(A) Before a second or successive application permitted by this section is filed in the district court, the applicant shall move in the appropriate court of appeals for an order authorizing the district court to consider the application.

"(B) A motion in the court of appeals for an order authorizing the district court to consider a second or successive application shall be determined by a three-judge panel of the court of appeals.

"(C) The court of appeals may authorize the filing of a second or successive application only if it determines that the application makes a prima facie showing that the application satisfies the requirements of this subsection.

"(D) The court of appeals shall grant or deny the authorization to file a second or successive application not later than 30 days after the filing of the motion.

"(E) The grant or denial of an authorization by a court of appeals to file a second or successive application shall not be appealable and shall not be the subject of a petition for rehearing or for a writ of certiorari.

"(4) A district court shall dismiss any claim presented in a second or successive application that the court of appeals has authorized to be filed unless the applicant shows that the claim satisfies the requirements of this section.".

SEC. 107. DEATH PENALTY LITIGATION PROCEDURES.

(a) ADDITION OF CHAPTER TO TITLE 28, UNITED STATES CODE.— Title 28, United States Code, is amended by inserting after chapter 153 the following new chapter:

"CHAPTER 154—SPECIAL HABEAS CORPUS PROCEDURES IN CAPITAL CASES

"Sec.
"2261. Prisoners in State custody subject to capital sentence; appointment of counsel; require-
          ment of rule of court or statute; procedures for appointment.
"2262. Mandatory stay of execution; duration; limits on stays of execution; successive petitions.
"2263. Filing of habeas corpus application; time requirements; tolling rules.
"2264. Scope of Federal review; district court adjudications.
"2265. Application to State unitary review procedure.
"2266. Limitation periods for determining applications and motions.

"§2261. Prisoners in State custody subject to capital sentence; appointment of counsel; requirement of rule of court or statute; procedures for appointment

"(a) This chapter shall apply to cases arising under section 2254 brought by prisoners in State
custody who are subject to a capital sentence. It shall apply only if the provisions of subsections (b) and (c) are satisfied.
"(b) This chapter is applicable if a State establishes by statute, rule of its court of last resort, or by
another agency authorized by State law, a mechanism for the appointment, compensation, and
payment of reasonable litigation expenses of competent counsel in State post-conviction proceedings brought by indigent prisoners whose capital convictions and sentences have been upheld on direct appeal to the court of last resort in the State or have otherwise become final for
State law purposes. The rule of court or statute must provide standards of competency for the
appointment of such counsel.
          "(c) Any mechanism for the appointment, compensation, and reimbursement of counsel as
          provided in subsection (b) must offer counsel to all State prisoners under capital sentence
          and must provide for the entry of an order by a court of record—
                    "(1) appointing one or more counsels to represent the prisoner upon a finding that the
                    prisoner is indigent and accepted the offer or is unable competently to decide whether to
                    accept or reject the offer;
                    "(2) finding, after a hearing if necessary, that the prisoner rejected the offer of counsel
                    and made the decision with an understanding of its legal consequences; or
                    "(3) denying the appointment of counsel upon a finding that the prisoner is not indigent.
          "(d) No counsel appointed pursuant to subsections (b) and (c) to represent a State prisoner
          under capital sentence shall have previously represented the prisoner at trial or on direct ap-
          peal in the case for which the appointment is made unless the prisoner and counsel expressly
          request continued representation.
          "(e) The ineffectiveness or incompetence of counsel during State or Federal post-conviction
          proceedings in a capital case shall not be a ground for relief in a proceeding arising under sec-
          tion 2254. This limitation shall not preclude the appointment of different counsel, on the
          court's own motion or at the request of the prisoner, at any phase of State or Federal
          post-conviction proceedings on the basis of the ineffectiveness or incompetence of counsel in
          such proceedings.

"§2262. Mandatory stay of execution; duration; limits on stays of execution; successive petitions
          "(a) Upon the entry in the appropriate State court of record of an order under section
          2261(c), a warrant or order setting an execution date for a State prisoner shall be stayed upon
          application to any court that would have jurisdiction over any proceedings filed under section
          2254. The application shall recite that the State has invoked the post-conviction review pro-
          cedures of this chapter and that the scheduled execution is subject to stay.
          "(b) A stay of execution granted pursuant to subsection (a) shall expire if—
                    "(1) a State prisoner fails to file a habeas corpus application under section 2254 within

the time required in section 2263;

"(2) before a court of competent jurisdiction, in the presence of counsel, unless the prisoner has competently and knowingly waived such counsel, and after having been advised of the consequences, a State prisoner under capital sentence waives the right to pursue habeas corpus review under section 2254; or

"(3) a State prisoner files a habeas corpus petition under section 2254 within the time required by section 2263 and fails to make a substantial showing of the denial of a Federal right or is denied relief in the district court or at any subsequent stage of review.

"(c) If one of the conditions in subsection (b) has occurred, no Federal court thereafter shall have the authority to enter a stay of execution in the case, unless the court of appeals approves the filing of a second or successive application under section 2244(b).

"§2263. Filing of habeas corpus application; time requirements; tolling rules

"(a) Any application under this chapter for habeas corpus relief under section 2254 must be filed in the appropriate district court not later than 180 days after final State court affirmance of the conviction and sentence on direct review or the expiration of the time for seeking such review.

"(b) The time requirements established by subsection (a) shall be tolled—

"(1) from the date that a petition for certiorari is filed in the Supreme Court until the date of final disposition of the petition if a State prisoner files the petition to secure review by the Supreme Court of the affirmance of a capital sentence on direct review by the court of last resort of the State or other final State court decision on direct review;

"(2) from the date on which the first petition for postconviction review or other collateral relief is filed until the final State court disposition of such petition; and

"(3) during an additional period not to exceed 30 days, if—

"(A) a motion for an extension of time is filed in the Federal district court that would have jurisdiction over the case upon the filing of a habeas corpus application under section 2254; and

"(B) a showing of good cause is made for the failure to file the habeas corpus application within the time period established by this section.

"§2264. Scope of Federal review; district court adjudications

"(a) Whenever a State prisoner under capital sentence files a petition for habeas corpus relief to which this chapter applies, the district court shall only consider a claim or claims that have been raised and decided on the merits in the State courts, unless the failure to raise the claim properly is—

"(1) the result of State action in violation of the Constitution or laws of the United States;

"(2) the result of the Supreme Court's recognition of a new Federal right that is made retroactively applicable; or

"(3) based on a factual predicate that could not have been discovered through the exercise of due diligence in time to present the claim for State or Federal post-conviction review.

"(b) Following review subject to subsections (a), (d), and (e) of section 2254, the court shall rule on the claims properly before it.

"§2265. Application to State unitary review procedure

"(a) For purposes of this section, a 'unitary review' procedure means a State procedure that authorizes a person under sentence of death to raise, in the course of direct review of the judgment, such claims as could be raised on collateral attack. This chapter shall apply, as provided in this section, in relation to a State unitary review procedure if the State establishes by rule of its court of last resort or by statute a mechanism for the appointment, compensation, and payment of reasonable litigation expenses of competent counsel in the unitary review proceedings, including expenses relating to the litigation of collateral claims in the proceedings. The rule of court or statute must provide standards of competency for the appointment of such counsel.

"(b) To qualify under this section, a unitary review procedure must include an offer of counsel following trial for the purpose of representation on unitary review, and entry of an order, as provided in section 2261(c), concerning appointment of counsel or waiver or denial of appointment of counsel for that purpose. No counsel appointed to represent the prisoner in the unitary review proceedings shall have previously represented the prisoner at trial in the case for which the appointment is made unless the prisoner and counsel expressly request continued representation.

"(c) Sections 2262, 2263, 2264, and 2266 shall apply in relation to cases involving a sentence of death from any State having a unitary review procedure that qualifies under this section. References to State 'post-conviction review' and 'direct review' in such sections shall be understood as referring to unitary review under the State procedure. The reference in section 2262(a) to 'an order under section 2261(c)' shall be understood as referring to the posttrial order under subsection (b) concerning representation in the unitary review proceedings, but if a transcript of the trial proceedings is unavailable at the time of the filing of such an order in the appropriate State court, then the start of the 180-day limitation period under section 2263 shall be deferred until a transcript is made available to the prisoner or counsel of the prisoner.

"§2266. Limitation periods for determining applications and motions

"(a) The adjudication of any application under section 2254 that is subject to this chapter, and the adjudication of any motion under section 2255 by a person under sentence of death, shall be given priority by the district court and by the court of appeals over all noncapital matters.

"(b)(1)(A) A district court shall render a final determination and enter a final judgment on any application for a writ of habeas corpus brought under this chapter in a capital case not later than 180 days after the date on which the application is filed.

"(B) A district court shall afford the parties at least 120 days in which to complete all actions, including the preparation of all pleadings and briefs, and if necessary, a hearing, prior to the submission of the case for decision.

"(C)(i) A district court may delay for not more than one additional 30-day period beyond the period specified in subparagraph (A), the rendering of a determination of an application for a writ of habeas corpus if the court issues a written order making a finding, and stating the reasons for the finding, that the ends of justice that would be served by allowing the delay outweigh the best interests of the public and the applicant in a speedy disposition of the application.

"(ii) The factors, among others, that a court shall consider in determining whether a delay in the disposition of an application is warranted are as follows:

"(I) Whether the failure to allow the delay would be likely to result in a miscarriage of justice.

"(II) Whether the case is so unusual or so complex, due to the number of defendants, the nature of the prosecution, or the existence of novel questions of fact or law, that it is unreasonable to expect adequate briefing within the time limitations established by subparagraph (A).

"(III) Whether the failure to allow a delay in a case that, taken as a whole, is not so unusual or so complex as described in subclause (II), but would otherwise deny the applicant reasonable time to obtain counsel, would unreasonably deny the applicant or the government continuity of counsel, or would deny counsel for the applicant or the government the reasonable time necessary for effective preparation, taking into account the exercise of due diligence.

"(iii) No delay in disposition shall be permissible because of general congestion of the court's calendar.

"(iv) The court shall transmit a copy of any order issued under clause (i) to the Director of the Administrative Office of the United States Courts for inclusion in the report under paragraph (5).

"(2) The time limitations under paragraph (1) shall apply to— "(A) an initial application for a writ of habeas corpus;

"(B) any second or successive application for a writ of habeas corpus; and

"(C) any redetermination of an application for a writ of habeas corpus following a remand by the court of appeals or the Supreme Court for further proceedings, in which case the limitation period shall run from the date the remand is ordered.

"(3)(A) The time limitations under this section shall not be construed to entitle an applicant to a stay of execution, to which the applicant would otherwise not be entitled, for the purpose of litigating any application or appeal.

"(B) No amendment to an application for a writ of habeas corpus under this chapter shall be permitted after the filing of the answer to the application, except on the grounds specified in section 2244(b).

"(4)(A) The failure of a court to meet or comply with a time limitation under this section shall not be a ground for granting relief from a judgment of conviction or sentence.

"(B) The State may enforce a time limitation under this section by petitioning for a writ of mandamus to the court of appeals. The court of appeals shall act on the petition for a writ of mandamus not later than 30 days after the filing of the petition.

"(5)(A) The Administrative Office of the United States Courts   Reports. shall submit to Congress an annual report on the compliance by the district courts with the time limitations under this section.

"(B) The report described in subparagraph (A) shall include copies of the orders submitted by the district courts under paragraph (1)(B)(iv).

"(c)(1)(A) A court of appeals shall hear and render a final determination of any appeal of an order granting or denying, in whole or in part, an application brought under this chapter in a capital case not later than 120 days after the date on which the reply brief is filed, or if no reply brief is filed, not later than 120 days after the date on which the answering brief is filed.

"(B)(i) A court of appeals shall decide whether to grant a petition for rehearing or other request for rehearing en banc not later than 30 days after the date on which the petition for rehearing is filed unless a responsive pleading is required, in which case the court shall decide whether to grant the petition not later than 30 days after the date on which the responsive pleading is filed.

"(ii) If a petition for rehearing or rehearing en banc is granted, the court of appeals shall hear and render a final determination of the appeal not later than 120 days after the date on which the order granting rehearing or rehearing en banc is entered.

"(2) The time limitations under paragraph (1) shall apply to— "(A) an initial application for a writ of habeas corpus;

"(B) any second or successive application for a writ of habeas corpus; and

"(C) any redetermination of an application for a writ of habeas corpus or related appeal following a remand by the court of appeals en banc or the Supreme Court for further proceedings, in which case the limitation period shall run from the date the remand is ordered.

"(3) The time limitations under this section shall not be construed to entitle an applicant to a stay of execution, to which the applicant would otherwise not be entitled, for the purpose of litigating any application or appeal.

"(4)(A) The failure of a court to meet or comply with a time limitation under this section shall not be a ground for granting relief from a judgment of conviction or sentence.

"(B) The State may enforce a time limitation under this section by applying for a writ of mandamus to the Supreme Court.

Reports. "(5) The Administrative Office of the United States Courts shall submit to Congress an annual report on the compliance by the courts of appeals with the time limitations under this section.".

(b) TECHNICAL AMENDMENT.—The part analysis for part IV of title 28, United States Code, is amended by adding after the item relating to chapter 153 the following new item:

"154. Special habeas corpus procedures in capital cases ....2261.".

28 USC 2261 (c) EFFECTIVE DATE.—Chapter 154 of title 28, United States note. Code (as added by subsection (a)) shall apply to cases pending on or after the date of enactment of this Act.

SEC. 108. TECHNICAL AMENDMENT.

Section 408(q) of the Controlled Substances Act (21 U.S.C. 848(q)) is amended by amending paragraph (9) to read as follows:

"(9) Upon a finding that investigative, expert, or other services are reasonably necessary for the representation of the defendant, whether in connection with issues relating to guilt or the sentence, the court may authorize the defendant's attorneys to obtain such services on behalf of the defendant and, if so authorized, shall order the payment of fees and expenses therefor under paragraph (10). No ex parte proceeding, communication, or request may be considered pursuant to this section unless a proper showing is made concerning the need for confidentiality. Any such proceeding, communication, or request shall be transcribed and made a part of the record available for appellate review.".

However as shows in these pages this has not been so. States have not ensure that federal constitutional rights are protected and convictions are not obtained by misconduct.

In Arizona the office of the Arizona Atttorney General affirmatively condones the systemic practice of Arizona prosecutors to engage in misconduct to convict. Arizona state courts refuse to take ensue to ensure misconduct does not continue.

Federal judges decline to consider the systemic problems within the Arizona Criminal Justice system when resolving individual habeas corpus petitions.

Time has come for federal courts to prevent the State Of Arizona from benefiting from the provisions of the federal mhabeas corpus statutes until suchtime the State cleans house, examines ast convictions obtained by misconduct and ensures misconduct does not continue in future convictions.

The integrity of the United States Constitution demands no less.

MISTRIAL

JOHNNY RAY WASHINGTON, Petitioner - Appellant, v. CHARLES L. RYAN, Director, AZ Department of Corrections and STATE OF ARIZONA ATTORNEY GENERAL, Respondents - Appellees.No. 08-17039 UNITED STATES COURT OF APPEALS FOR THE NINTH CIRCUIT
(Text modified for emphasis)

THE POSITION OF THE COURT

Washington contends that the prosecutor in his first trial intended to provoke the defense into moving for a mistrial and that, consequently, his retrial violated the *Double Jeopardy Clause of the 5th Amendment*. Washington's contention is not supported by the record. Accordingly, the state court's decision was not contrary to, or an unreasonable application of, clearly established Supreme Court law, or an unreasonable determination of the facts in light of the evidence. *See 28 U.S.C. § 2254(d); see also Oregon v. Kennedy, 456 U.S. 667, 676, 102 S. Ct. 2083, 72 L. Ed. 2d 416 (1982)* ("[o]nly where the governmental conduct in question is intended to 'goad' the defendant into moving for a mistrial may a defendant raise the bar of double jeopardy to a second trial after having succeeded in aborting the first on his own motion").

REASONS WHY REMEDY IS HOLLOW

Arizona prosecutors with the help of state judges create situations in cases they know they may not prevail force defense counsel ask for mistrials. Though the Arizona Attorney general and courts know of this practice they decline to take any action.

DISCIPLINARY PROCEEDINGS

> **MATTHEW RONALD CREAMER, Petitioner - Appellant, v. CHARLES L. RYAN, Interim Director of ADOC and STATE OF ARIZONA ATTORNEY GENERAL, Respondents - Appellees.**
> **No. 09-16425 UNITED STATES COURT OF APPEALS FOR THE NINTH CIRCUIT**
> **(Text modified for emphasis)**

THE POSITION OF THE COURT

Creamer contends that because Arizona law does not provide for judicial review of prison disciplinary proceedings, he was not required to exhaust his claims in state court.

In Arizona, state court review of an inmate disciplinary decision may be obtained by filing a petition for special action. *See Rose v. Ariz. Dep't of Corrections, 167 Ariz. 116, 804 P.2d 845, 849 (Ariz. Ct. App. 1991).* Contrary to Creamer's argument, Arizona Revised Statutes ("A.R.S.") § 31-201.01(L) does not bar the initiation of a special action by a prisoner, because it only applies to tort claims. Likewise, A.R.S. § 12-302 does not prevent the filing of a special action by a prisoner. *See A.R.S. § 12-302(E)* (inability to pay filing fees does not prevent filing of an action).

Because Creamer did not challenge his disciplinary proceedings by filing a special action in state court, the district court properly dismissed his claims as unexhausted. *See 28 U.S.C. § 2254(b)(1)(A), (c).*

The district court did not abuse its discretion by denying Creamer's motion for reconsideration because he did not identify any new evidence, change in law, clear error, or manifest injustice in the court's order. *See Sch. Dist. No. 1J, Multnomah County, Or. v. ACandS, Inc., 5 F.3d 1255, 1262-63 (9th Cir. 1993)* (setting forth standard of review and grounds for reconsideration).

Finally, the district court did not abuse its discretion by denying Creamer's request for a stay. *See Jiminez v. Rice, 276 F.3d 478, 481 (9th Cir. 2001)* (district court may not grant a stay where the petition contains no exhausted claims).

REASONS WHY REMEDY IS HOLLOW

The Arizona Attorney general in proceedings in the Superior Court has made it a practice that relief by way of special action is not available. They however consistently deceive federal courts taking contrary positions, so as to defeat claims.

JUDICIAL CONFLICT

Jeffrey A. Herald, Petitioner, v. Charles L. Ryan, Arizona Attorney General, Respondents. No. CV 14-2188 PHX DLR (MEA) UNITED STATES DISTRICT COURT FOR THE DISTRICT OF ARIZONA
(Text modified for emphasis)

THE POSITION OF THE COURTS

A grand jury indictment returned September 17, 2008, charged Petitioner (using his own and an additional nine "aka" identities) with 39 counts of fraudulent schemes and artifices, class 2 felonies, and 39 counts of theft, class 2, 3, 4, 5, and 6 felonies (based upon the amount allegedly stolen). Thirteen of the counts, encompassing seven victims, involved Petitioner's "legal services" business and alleged he misrepresented to clients that he was a licensed attorney. The remaining counts pertained to a "loan origination" business.

Petitioner was initially represented in his criminal proceedings by retained counsel, who subsequently withdrew from representation. The state trial court thereafter appointed Mr. Wallin as Petitioner's defense counsel. On August 3, 2009, Petitioner sought to remove Mr. Wallin as counsel because he "considered [Petitioner] guilty without going through several boxes of evidence;" he had interviewed "several witnesses," including family members, but "came up with a total different story than reality;" and because he had "no clue about [Petitioner's] case." On December 29, 2009, Petitioner again moved to substitute counselThe state trial court denied these motions, finding that there was no legal basis to justify a change in defense counsel.

On May 18, 2010, Petitioner again sought to remove Mr. Wallin as counsel, asserting that Mr. Wallin had interviewed only one of Petitioner's proposed witnesses and that he had "corrupted the case" by interviewing state witnesses. Id., Exh. H. Petitioner filed two additional motions to remove Mr. Wallin. Mr. Wallin subsequently filed ten motions in limine, addressing multiple evidentiary issues. The trial court eventually granted Petitioner's motion to change counsel and directed that Mr. Wallin "meet and confer with the newly assigned attorney to discuss the history and progress of this case, its charges, and interviews thus far conducted."

On October 25, 2010, Ms. Shoemaker was appointed to represent Petitioner. On January 11, 2011, with the trial scheduled to begin on February 14, 2011, Ms. Shoemaker filed a motion pursuant to *Rule 11, Arizona Rule of Criminal Procedure*, requesting that Petitioner undergo a mental evaluation, although Petitioner had previously been found competent in July 2010. Ms. Shoemaker argued that she had personally witnessed Petitioner suffer extreme mood swings during legal visits and phone calls. The motion was granted, Petitioner was determined to be competent, and the trial was re-set for November 7, 2011. Ms. Shoemaker then re-urged all of Mr. Wallin's previously filed motions.

On May 2, 2011, Petitioner filed a "petition to compel," asking the state court to order defense counsel "to work with [Petitioner]." Petitioner avowed that he did not want to dismiss counsel, "as she seems capable to handle [his] case." Petitioner averred, however, that counsel had not visited him often enough and that counsel "[had] not moved forward on this case much at all to prepare for trial." Petitioner further alleged that he and his counsel suffered from a lack of communication and that he had not received certain documents he had requested from her. In a minute entry dated June 2, 2011, in response to Petitioner's request, the trial court stated that its practice was to avoid involvement in the attorney-client relationship unless there was a motion to change counsel before the court. Petitioner then avowed to the trial court that the issues raised in his motion to compel had been "satisfactorily resolved, except for an issue regarding counsel obtaining Petitioner's 'Quick Books.'"

On August 9, 2011, the parties averred they were ready for a trial commencing November 7, 2011. On August 26, 2011, a settlement conference was conducted, during which the settlement judge reviewed with Petitioner the charges against him and the potential sentences he faced if found guilty. At that time the state offered Petitioner a plea agreement that would allow Petitioner to plead guilty to three counts of fraudulent schemes as class 2 felonies with one prior conviction, with a sentencing range of 10 to 20 years on each count, with the court retaining discretion to decide whether the sentences would be concurrent or consecutive. The plea agreement also required Petitioner to plead guilty to five additional counts of fraudulent schemes and receive sentences of probation on those convictions, to be commenced after Petitioner served the terms of imprisonment. The court advised Petitioner at that time that, if he proceeded to trial and was convicted on most or all of the charges, he could potentially spend the rest of his life in prison.

Petitioner initially responded that he was legally innocent of the charges because he had run an "honest business" and that was merely the victim of a recession and clients who had falsified information. The prosecutor then summarized the evidence against Petitioner regarding both the legal services and loan businesses. Petitioner disputed the state's allegations and noted he had witnesses who said that he had actually closed some loans, thereby providing the agreed-upon services and arguing that, therefore, he could not be guilty of fraud. The judge (J. Schwartz) advised Petitioner that "the risk [was] huge" if Petitioner went to trial, particularly in light of his multiple prior felonies. Petitioner said "I'm totally innocent in this case," but stated that he and his lawyer would have to discuss the plea deal. He stated "it would be better if we could come down a little bit."

Petitioner brought "witnesses" with him to the settlement conference in an effort to bolster his argument that he had run a legitimate business and that he had not defrauded his clients. The prosecutor again summarized the evidence that would be presented against Petitioner, including the fact that he had previously been imprisoned for fraud schemes and theft. The prosecutor noted Petitioner had represented to his victims that he was a licensed attorney. The prosecutor delineated Petitioner's mortgage "scheme," noting that he had represented to victims that he could fund their multi-million dollar projects "in house" if he failed to acquire financing for the projects through third-parties. Petitioner again offered the "testimony" of an individual at the settlement conference who stated that they had given Petitioner $80,000 and he had returned the loan amount in full. Petitioner again asserted that he had "closed" the loans his victims complained of but that he had not done it in a sufficiently timely fashion or at an interest rate sufficiently low enough to keep his clients from asserting they had been defrauded.

The settlement conference was continued on September 16, 2011.

The court stated:

[O]bviously the worst case scenario is if the Judge gave a 23-year term and did three of them consecutively. That can add up to 69 years. I mean we have to have that possibility. But the best case scenario is a five year term on each count, all three of them to run concurrently. That's a five-year term.

Petitioner stated that he was 53 years of age and also noted the possibility that he could get "five times three which is 15 years." At the beginning of the settlement conference the court discussed with Petitioner potential sentencing judges, noting the parties had agreed that Judge Barton, who had been the assigned trial judge, would not sentence Petitioner. The prosecutor allowed that, if Petitioner would accept the plea agreement they would expand the "bottom" of the sentencing range in the plea agreement on each of the three counts to five years, and that she had "twisted arms" to get the five year "bottom".

After a recess to consult with his counsel and his wife, who was also present, and in the presence of the Deputy (because Petitioner was in custody), Petitioner agreed to the plea deal. At that time the parties agreed Petitioner would be sentenced by Judge Granville. Petitioner then entered a guilty plea.

The plea agreement, dated September 16, 2011, stipulated that Petitioner would plead guilty to Amended Counts 1, 3 and 5, charging fraudulent schemes and artifices as class 2 felonies with one prior felony conviction, and Counts 7 and 13, charging fraudulent schemes and artifices as class 2 felonies. Counts 1, 3 and 5 carried a presumptive sentence of 9.25 years, a minimum of 6 years (4.5 if the court made exceptional circumstances findings), and a maximum of 18.5 years.

The presentence report recommended Petitioner be sentenced to concurrent, presumptive terms of imprisonment on each count of conviction. The state's sentencing recommendation detailed Petitioner's history of arrests on fraud charges and eight felony convictions in four states since 1979.

Defense counsel filed a sentencing memorandum, which stated that the five guilty pleas involved legal practices counts that had already been resolved by the Arizona State Bar Association, and that the victims had received refunds of any fees paid to Petitioner. Counsel further stated that Petitioner took responsibility for misleading those victims. With regard to the counts involving the commercial loans, counsel averred Petitioner had "worked to get the loans funded," but that those clients "were not always happy with the loan terms."

Counsel cited two clients for whom Petitioner believed that he had earned the fees paid to Petitioner. Counsel also provided information on mitigating sentencing factors such as Petitioner's family support, mental health concerns, and remorse.

At Petitioner's sentencing on November 18, 2011, the state court (Judge Granville) heard from two character witnesses for Petitioner, then entered judgment on the five counts set forth in the plea agreement. The prosecutor made additional statements regarding Petitioner's conduct, including comments from victims. Petitioner responded that the prosecutor's facts were inaccurate and disputed the victims' comments. Petitioner asserted that the prosecutor could not "open my QuickBooks on the computer," which would have showed that he had refunded money on loan contracts. Petitioner stated that defense counsel "has the files" and "has gone through them," and that the court should look at his spreadsheet showing he had made partial payments of monies owed to his victims. Petitioner asked the court to follow the presentence report with regard to imposing sentence.

Defense counsel then spoke on Petitioner's behalf and averred she had acquired fifteen boxes of documents from Mr. Wallin, which documents were obtained from Petitioner's business office. She argued that Petitioner's company had actually tried to assist the victims, although the victims did suffer harm. Counsel noted the court had a list of victims whose money had been returned to them. She then noted Petitioner's medical problems and argued the presumptive term of imprisonment be imposed.

Before imposing sentence, the state court cited as mitigating factors Petitioner's age, that Petitioner had repaid many of the victims, his acknowledgment of responsibility, and health issues. The court then sentenced Petitioner to mitigated terms of eight years imprisonment on Counts 1, 3 and 5, with the term on Count 1 consecutive to Count 3 and the term on Count 5 concurrent with Count 3 and consecutive to Count 1. The court imposed a term of five years probation each on Counts 7 and 13, to begin after Petitioner's discharge from prison. Petitioner also received credit for 984 days of presentence incarceration. After sentence was imposed, Petitioner clarified with the court that the his aggregate sentence was 16 years.

On December 27, 2011, Petitioner filed a timely notice of post-conviction relief pursuant to *Rule 32, Arizona Rules of Criminal Procedure*, and counsel was appointed to represent him in his Rule 32 proceedings. On June 29, 2012, Petitioner's appointed counsel filed notice avowing that they had reviewed the record, transcripts, and correspondence from Petitioner, trial counsel's files, and a draft Rule 32 petition prepared by Petitioner, and that after doing so he was unable to find any colorable claims for relief to present in a Rule 32 petition.

Petitioner filed a pro per Rule 32 petition asserting he received ineffective assistance of counsel because counsel failed to obtain "full discovery," did not interview witnesses, and "never worked with Petitioner to prepare for trial." Petitioner also alleged his counsel failed to prepare mitigating factors at sentencing and gave Petitioner erroneous advice which prevented him from making an informed decision on whether to accept the plea agreement. Petitioner also argued that the state had violated his right to due process by failing to provide "full disclosure" and that the state trial court had violated his right to due process by failing to consider a motion to change counsel that he alleged was filed at sentencing.

The state trial court denied relief in Petitioner's *Rule 32* action in a decision entered January 11, 2013. The court concluded that relief was precluded pursuant to *Rule 32.2(a)(3), Arizona Rules of Criminal Procedure*, because Petitioner had waived the enumerated claims "when he validly entered into the plea agreement." The court found the *Rule 32* action was, therefore, subject to summary dismissal pursuant to Arizona Rule of Criminal Procedure 32.6.

Petitioner sought review of this decision by the Arizona Court of Appeals. Petitioner argued his trial counsel rendered ineffective assistance by failing to "get full discovery" from the state and by not meeting with him often enough. Petitioner alleged counsel failed to present mitigating evidence at sentencing and erroneously advised him that he would receive a term of no more than seven or eight years imprisonment if he entered into the plea agreement. Petitioner further alleged counsel lied when she provided the factual basis for the plea. Petitioner also asserted he was denied his right to the effective assistance of counsel because counsel appeared at sentencing even though he had "fired" her two weeks prior and because she failed to investigate facts and interview witnesses. Petitioner also alleged the state did not provide full disclosure and that the trial court erred because it failed to consider a motion for a change of counsel that was allegedly filed after Petitioner pled guilty. Petitioner also asserted that the trial judge should have recused himself because the judge allegedly knew Petitioner's uncle. Petitioner also argued he was innocent of the charges against him because there was insufficient evidence to support his convictions.

Attached to Petitioner's pleading to the Arizona Court of Appeals in his Rule 32 action, and offered as evidence in this habeas action, is a typescript of a "report" from Joseph Kalcantu of Houston, Texas, which avers that he was retained by a former Governor of Texas to investigate the bringing of criminal charges against Petitioner by Maricopa County. The letter avers that the fraud charges against Petitioner were the result of corporate materials stolen by Jeffrey Stallcup, a former employee, and provided to a Maricopa County detective "without a search warrant." The letter references taped telephone conversations from 2006 in which a Maricopa County investigator conveyed to Petitioner's clients that he was defrauding them. The letter averred it was "known" that Mr. Wallin and Ms. Shoemaker (Petitioner's plea and sentencing counsel) "made a deal with Ms. Van Wie [the prosecutor] on other clients in order to sacrifice Mr. Herald's case..." The letter concludes that, having been an FBI investigator on fraud cases for twenty-five years, Mr. Kalcantu had determined Petitioner had not committed fraud. The letter is signed as "signature on file," and is not notarized nor sworn.

The Arizona Court of Appeals granted review but denied relief. The appellate court found that Petitioner's ineffective assistance claims were without merit. The court also concluded Petitioner had waived any claim regarding the state's discovery when he pled guilty and that there was no evidence in the record regarding Petitioner's alleged motion to change counsel after sentencing. The Court of Appeals further determined that Petitioner had failed to support his judicial bias claim and that he had failed to demonstrate any potential prejudice. The court also determined Petitioner's insufficient evidence claim was without merit because Petitioner had provided a sufficient factual basis to support his guilty pleas on the counts of conviction.

On October 2, 2014, Petitioner filed the instant petition seeking a writ of habeas corpus. Petitioner asserts he is entitled to federal habeas relief because he was denied his right to the effective assistance of counsel and because he was subjected to an illegal search and seizure. Petitioner further argues he is entitled to relief because the prosecutor and defense counsel engaged in "corruption" and because there was "corruption and [a] major conflict of the sentencing judge".

E. Waiver of claims upon entry of guilty plea

Petitioner agreed to plead guilty to the charges against him in a written plea agreement. The United States Supreme Court limited the grounds upon which a state prisoner may seek habeas relief after entering a voluntary and intelligent guilty plea in *Tollett v. Henderson, 411 U.S. 258, 93 S. Ct. 1602, 36 L. Ed. 2d 235 (1973)* (holding that a knowing and voluntary guilty plea waives all non-jurisdictional defects occurring prior to the entry of the guilty plea). Other than a challenge to the voluntary and intelligent character of the plea itself, a defendant's guilty plea bars federal habeas relief based on pre-plea non-jurisdictional constitutional claims. See *Haring v. Prosise, 462 U.S. 306, 319-20, 103 S.Ct. 2368, 2376-77, 76 L. Ed. 2d 595 (1983)* ("Our decisions subsequent to Tollett make clear that a plea of guilty does not bar the review in habeas corpus proceedings of all claims involving constitutional violations antecedent to a plea of guilty"); *Moran v. Godinez, 57 F.3d 690, 700 (9th Cir. 1994)* (foreclosing pre-plea ineffective assistance of counsel claim); *Ortberg v. Moody, 961 F.2d 135, 137-38 (9th Cir. 1992)*; *Hudson v. Moran, 760 F.2d 1027, 1029-30 (9th Cir. 1985)* ("As a general rule, one who voluntarily and intelligently pleads guilty to a criminal charge may not subsequently seek federal habeas corpus relief on the basis of pre-plea constitutional violations."); *Mitchell v. Superior Court, 632 F.2d 767, 769 (9th Cir. 1980)*. Pre-plea error is considered "jurisdictional" when it implicates the government's power to prosecute the defendant. *United States v. Johnston, 199 F.3d 1015, 1019 n.3 (9th Cir.1999)*. See also *United States v. Broce, 488 U.S. 563, 574-76, 109 S.Ct. 757, 765, 102 L. Ed. 2d 927 (1989)*. For example, Tollett does not foreclose a claim that: a defendant was vindictively prosecuted, see *Blackledge v. Perry, 417 U.S. 21, 30-31, 94 S.Ct. 2098, 2103-04, 40 L. Ed. 2d 628 (1974)*, that the indictment under which a defendant pled guilty placed him in double jeopardy, see *Menna v. New York, 423 U.S. 61, 62, 96 S.Ct. 241, 242, 46 L. Ed. 2d*

195 (1975), or the statute under which the defendant was indicted is facially unconstitutional. See *United States v. Garcia-Valenzuela, 232 F.3d 1003, 1006 (9th Cir. 2000)*.

The federal courts have concluded that a plea colloquy must satisfy several requirements in order for a guilty plea to be considered voluntary and knowing. See, e.g., *Loftis v. Almager, 704 F.3d 645, 647-48 (9th Cir. 2012)*; *Tanner v. McDaniel, 493 F.3d 1135, 1146-47 (9th Cir. 2007)*. A guilty plea is not considered voluntary and knowing unless a defendant is informed of and waives his privilege against self-incrimination, his right to trial by jury, and his right to confront witnesses. *Tanner, 493 F.3d at 1147*, citing *Boykin v. Alabama, 395 U.S. 238, 243-44, 89 S. Ct. 1709, 1712-13, 23 L. Ed. 2d 274 (1969)*. A defendant must understand the consequences of his plea, including "the range of allowable punishment that will result from his plea." *Little v. Crawford, 449 F.3d 1075, 1080 (9th Cir. 2006)*.

The transcripts of the settlement hearings in this matter and Petitioner's plea colloquy indicate Petitioner's guilty plea was entered knowingly and voluntarily. At the time he entered his guilty plea the state court found the plea was knowing and voluntary. A state court's factual finding that a plea was voluntary and knowing is entitled to a presumption of correctness by a federal habeas court. See *Lambert v. Blodgett, 393 F.3d 943, 982 (9th Cir. 2004)*; *Cunningham v. Diesslin, 92 F.3d 1054, 1060 (10th Cir. 1996)*. Factual findings of a state court are presumed to be correct and can be reversed by a federal habeas court only when the federal court is presented with clear and convincing evidence. See *Miller-El v. Dretke, 545 U.S. 231, 125 S. Ct. 2317, 2325, 162 L. Ed. 2d 196 (2005)*; *Vega v. Ryan, 757 F.3d 960, 965 (9th Cir. 2014)*. Petitioner's after-the-fact conclusory allegations that he was incorrectly advised as to the consequences of his guilty plea are not clear and convincing evidence which can overcome the weight of his contemporaneous statements regarding his understanding of the plea agreement. A petitioner's contemporaneous statements carry substantial weight in determining if his entry of a guilty plea was knowing and voluntary. See *Blackledge v. Allison, 431 U.S. 63, 74, 97 S. Ct. 1621, 1629, 52 L. Ed. 2d 136 (1977)* ("Solemn declarations in open court carry a strong presumption of verity. The subsequent presentation of conclusory allegations unsupported by specifics is subject to summary dismissal, as are contentions that in the face of the record are wholly incredible"); *Doe v. Woodford, 508 F.3d 563, 571 (9th Cir. 2007)*; *Restucci v. Spencer, 249 F. Supp. 2d 33, 45 (D. Mass. 2003)* (collecting cases so holding).

Because Petitioner entered a knowing and voluntary guilty plea, federal habeas relief is precluded with regard to any pre-plea non-jurisdictional habeas claims, such as allegations of ineffective assistance of counsel which occurred prior to Petitioner's entry of a guilty plea and his allegation that he was denied his *Fourth Amendment* rights in the investigation of the alleged crimes.

F. Petitioner's claims for relief

1. Ineffective assistance of counsel

Petitioner argues that he was deprived of his right to the effective assistance of counsel because counsel did not meet with Petitioner often enough, counsel failed to get full discovery from the state, counsel failed to interview witnesses and investigate and pursue facts, and because counsel failed to present evidence of mitigating factors at Petitioner's sentencing. Petitioner also alleges counsel was lying when she provided the factual basis for the plea and that counsel provided erroneous information regarding the plea and the maximum sentence that could be imposed. Petitioner raised these claims before the Arizona Court of Appeals in his pro per petition in his state action for post-conviction relief pursuant to *Rule 32*, Arizona Rules of Criminal Procedure, and the Court of Appeals found the claims without merit. To the extent any of these claims are not precluded by the entry of Petitioner's guilty plea, they are without merit and the Arizona Court of Appeals' decision denying relief on Petitioner's allegation that he was denied his right to the effective assistance of counsel was not clearly contrary to nor an unreasonable application of federal law.

Petitioner was not prejudiced by what he asserts was his counsel's prediction of the sentences that might be imposed pursuant to the plea agreement because the state court clearly and repeatedly alerted Petitioner to the potential consequences of his guilty plea, including clarifying with Petitioner that he could be sentenced to a term of sixteen years imprisonment if the sentences were ordered to be served consecutively. See *Womack, 497 F.3d at 1003*, citing *Doganiere v. United States, 914 F.2d 165, 168 (9th Cir. 1990)* (holding that the petitioner "suffered no prejudice from his attorney's prediction because, prior to accepting his guilty plea, the court explained that the discretion as to what the sentence would be").

The record in this matter belies all of Petitioner's claims of ineffective assistance of counsel. Petitioner offers only vague and conclusory allegations with regard to any possible prejudice he might have suffered as a result of counsel's alleged inadequacies, as Petitioner faced a total sentence of 63 years imprisonment had he chosen to reject the plea agreement and proceed to trial. See *Greenway v. Schriro*, 653 F.3d 790, 804 (9th Cir. 2011) ("[Petitioner]'s cursory and vague [ineffective assistance of counsel claim] cannot support habeas relief."). Accordingly, the state court's decision that Petitioner was not denied his right to the effective assistance of counsel was not clearly contrary to nor an unreasonable application of *Strickland* and *Hill* and Petitioner is not entitled to federal habeas relief on this claim.

3. Petitioner contends he is entitled to habeas relief because the prosecutor and defense counsel engaged in "corruption."

Petitioner asserts that his counsel and the prosecutor "sacrificed" Petitioner in order to reach plea agreements in other criminal cases. Petitioner contends that an investigation undertaken at his behest by an alleged ex-FBI agent establishes that the Maricopa County prosecutor's office and the prosecutor assigned to his case engaged in prosecutorial misconduct. Petitioner arguably presented the factual basis for this claim to the Arizona Court of Appeals in his Rule 32 action, however, Petitioner presented the claim as one of ineffective assistance of trial counsel and, arguably, as a Brady claim, arguing to the court that the prosecutor had not supplied and his counsel had not reviewed nor propounded in his defense all of the evidence seized from his business.

Petitioner did not properly exhaust a prosecutorial misconduct claim in the state courts. Petitioner has not shown cause for nor prejudice arising from this procedural default. The letter proffered by Petitioner from the purported investigator is neither verified, notarized, nor even signed. Accordingly, Petitioner has not produced clear and convincing evidence from which the Court might find that Petitioner was prejudiced by the state court's "failure" to consider a claim of prosecutorial misconduct.

Additionally, any allegation of prosecutorial misconduct, i.e., that the prosecutor negotiated a plea deal with Petitioner's counsel in some fashion that was in some way nefarious or that the prosecutor withheld material in violation of Brady, would involve a non-jurisdictional pre-plea error which was waived by Petitioner's guilty plea pursuant to *Tollett*.

4. Petitioner alleges that the sentencing judge was corrupt and had a "major" conflict of interest.

In his habeas petition Petitioner contends that the sentencing judge and Petitioner's uncle were "great friends," a fact Petitioner alleges he did not know until after his sentencing, and that the judge "did some shady deal[s] at times and did some under handed favors for his friends." In support of this claim Petitioner proffers a letter alleged to be authored by Petitioner's uncle, which letter is addressed to the presiding judge of the Maricopa County Superior Court. The letter is not notarized nor accompanied by a sworn affidavit, and lists a return address in Houston, Texas. In the letter the uncle states that Judge Granville is an old friend and that Mr. Stallcup (which is the last name of Petitioner's ex-wife) convinced the sentencing judge to "throw the book" at Petitioner. Petitioner also attaches a sworn affidavit from his wife which states that, after the settlement judge and prosecutor left the settlement conference so that Petitioner could confer with his counsel, counsel informed Petitioner that he would receive a maximum sentence of eight years imprisonment if he agreed to the plea deal.

Petitioner alleged in his state action for post-conviction relief that the state sentencing judge had a conflict of interest. Petitioner filed a complaint against the sentencing judge after his sentencing, contending that the judge was extremely unprofessional during Petitioner's sentencing, primarily because the judge was making unwarranted derogatory comments about Petitioner and smiling at Petitioner and his wife during the sentencing proceedings. The Court of Appeals concluded that Petitioner had failed to support his judicial bias claim and and failed to demonstrate any potential prejudice. "Herald also claims the sentencing court should have recused itself because the court allegedly knew Herald's uncle. We deny relief on this issue because Herald offers no evidence the court knew Herald's unidentified uncle and he does not otherwise explain how he suffered any prejudice even if the court did know his uncle." Answer, Exh. XX.

The Arizona Court of Appeals' decision denying Petitioner's claim of judicial bias was not clearly contrary to nor an unreasonable application of federal law.

To succeed on a judicial bias claim, however, the petitioner must "overcome a presumption of honesty and integrity in those serving as adjudicators." *Withrow v. Larkin, 421 U.S. 35, 47, 95 S.Ct. 1456, 43 L. Ed. 2d 712, [] (1975)*. In the absence of any evidence of some extrajudicial source of bias or partiality, neither adverse rulings nor impatient remarks are generally sufficient to overcome the presumption of judicial integrity, even if those remarks are "critical or disapproving of, or even hostile to, counsel, the parties, or their cases." *Liteky v. United States, 510 U.S. 540, 555, 114 S.Ct. 1147, 127 L. Ed. 2d 474, [] (1994)*;

Larson v. Palmateer, 515 F.3d 1057, 1067 (9th Cir. 2008). On federal habeas review, the Court "must ask whether the state trial judge's behavior rendered the trial so fundamentally unfair as to violate federal due process under the United States Constitution." *Duckett v. Godinez, 67 F.3d 734, 740 (9th Cir. 1995)*. "To sustain a claim of this kind, there must be an 'extremely high level of interference' by the trial judge which creates 'a pervasive climate of partiality and unfairness.'" Id., quoting *United States v. DeLuca, 692 F.2d 1277, 1282 (9th Cir. 1982)*.

The Supreme Court held long ago that a "fair trial in a fair tribunal is a basic requirement of due process." *In re Murchison, 349 U.S. 133, 136, 75 S.Ct. 623, 99 L. Ed. 942, [] (1955)*. "Fairness of course requires an absence of actual bias in the trial of cases. But our system of law has always endeavored to prevent even the probability of unfairness." Id.; cf. *Mistretta v. United States, 488 U.S. 361, 407, 109 S.Ct. 647, 102 L. Ed. 2d 714, [] (1989)* ("The legitimacy of the Judicial Branch ultimately depends on its reputation for impartiality and nonpartisanship."). This most basic tenet of our judicial system helps to ensure both the litigants' and the public's confidence that each case has been adjudicated fairly by a neutral and detached arbiter.

"The *Due Process Clause of the Fourteenth Amendment* establishes a constitutional floor, not a uniform standard," for a judicial bias claim. *Bracy v. Gramley, 520 U.S. 899, 904, 117 S.Ct. 1793, 138 L. Ed. 2d 97, [] (1997)*. While most claims of judicial bias are resolved "by common law, statute, or the professional standards of the bench and bar," the "floor established by the *Due Process Clause* clearly requires a 'fair trial in a fair tribunal' before a judge with no actual bias against the defendant or interest in the outcome of his particular case." Id. at 904-05, 117 S.Ct. 1793 (quoting *Withrow v. Larkin, 421 U.S. 35, 46, 95 S.Ct. 1456, 43 L. Ed. 2d 712, [] (1975)*). The Constitution requires recusal where "the probability of actual bias on the part of the judge or decisionmaker is too high to be constitutionally tolerable." *Withrow, 421 U.S. at 47, 95 S.Ct. 1456*. Our inquiry is objective. *Caperton v. A.T. Massey Coal Co., 556 U.S. 868, 881, 129 S.Ct. 2252, 173 L. Ed. 2d 1208, [] (2009)*. We do not ask whether [the judge] actually harbored subjective bias. Id. Rather, we ask whether the average judge in her position was likely to be neutral or whether there existed an unconstitutional potential for bias. Id. "Every procedure which would offer a possible temptation to the average ... judge to forget the burden of proof required to convict the defendant, or which might lead him not to hold the balance nice, clear and true between the State and the accused, denies the [accused] due process of law." *Tumey v. Ohio, 273 U.S. 510, 532, 47 S.Ct. 437, 71 L. Ed. 749, 5 Ohio Law Abs. 159, 5 Ohio Law Abs. 185, 25 Ohio L. Rep. 236, [] (1927)*.

[Petitioner] need not prove actual bias to establish a due process violation, just an intolerable risk of bias.... Thus, we must ask "whether 'under a realistic appraisal of psychological tendencies and human weakness,' the [judge's] interest 'poses such a risk of actual bias or prejudgment that the practice must be forbidden if the guarantee of due process is to be adequately implemented.'" *Caperton, 556 U.S. at 883-84, 129 S.Ct. 2252* (quoting *Withrow, 421 U.S. at 47, 95 S.Ct. 1456*). Due process thus mandates a "stringent rule" that may sometimes require recusal of judges "who have no actual bias and who would do their very best to weigh the scales of justice equally" if there exists a "probability of unfairness." *Murchison, 349 U.S. at 136, 75*

S.Ct. 623. But this risk of unfairness has no mechanical or static definition. It "cannot be defined with precision" because "[c]ircumstances and relationships must be considered." Id.

...Non-pecuniary conflicts "that tempt adjudicators to disregard neutrality" also offend due process. *Caperton, 556 U.S. at 878, 129 S.Ct. 2252.* A judge must withdraw where she acts as part of the accusatory process, *Murchison, 349 U.S. at 137, 75 S.Ct. 623,* "becomes embroiled in a running, bitter controversy" with one of the litigants, *Mayberry, 400 U.S. at 465, 91 S.Ct. 499,* or becomes "so enmeshed in matters involving [a litigant] as to make it appropriate for another judge to sit," *Johnson v. Mississippi, 403 U.S. 212, 215-16, 91 S.Ct. 1778, 29 L. Ed. 2d 423, []* (1971).

Hurles v. Ryan, 752 F.3d 768, 788-90 (9th Cir. 2014).

The state court's decision denying Petitioner's claim of judicial bias was not clearly contrary to nor an unreasonable application of federal law. Petitioner asserted in the state court that the judge smiled and made unwelcome comments about Petitioner. These allegations fail to present a viable claim of constitutionally-impermissible judicial bias. See, e.g., *Alley v. Bell, 307 F.3d 380, 388 (6th Cir. 2002),* citing *Liteky, 510 U.S. at 555, 114 S.Ct. 1147.* Additionally, the letter proffered by Petitioner which purports to be from Petitioner's uncle and on it's face states that the uncle influenced Judge Granville to "throw the book" at Petitioner when sentencing him, is not notarized nor sworn and, as such, does not constitute "evidence" from which the Court could find that Petitioner's federal constitutional right to due process was violated by Judge Granville at sentencing.

REASONS WHY REMEDY IS HOLLOW

In Arizona prosecutors and defense counsel act in collusion with consent of the courts to convict and judges have conflicts hiding these. Courts refuse to do anything as to these issues and the Arizona Attorney General fails to disclose these systemic problems to the federal courts.

LEGAL ASSISTANCE

> **John Calvin Neuendorf II, Petitioner, v. Charles L. Ryan, et al., Respondents.**
> **No. CV-14-0176-PHX-DJH (DKD) UNITED STATES DISTRICT COURT FOR THE DISTRICT OF ARIZONA**
> **(Text modified for emphasis)**

THE POSITION OF THE COURT

Following his November 2009 indictment, Neuendorf entered a plea of guilty in Maricopa County Superior Court to one count of attempted aggravated assault, a class 4 felony, and one count of aggravated assault, a class 3 felony. During his change of plea, the Superior Court advised Neuendorf of all his pertinent constitutional rights and rights of review, and then took a recess to allow Neuendorf "the opportunity to read and review the entire plea agreement" before accepting his plea. On April 8, 2011, the Superior Court sentenced Neuendorf to an aggravated term of 10 years for the aggravated assault charge to be followed by a 4 year term of probation for the attempted aggravated assault charge.

First Rule 32 Proceeding. On March 6, 2012, nearly a year after his sentencing, Neuendorf filed a Petition for Post-Conviction Relief and, in March 9, 2012, he filed a Notice of Post-Conviction Relief and a second Petition. Together, these documents allege that he received ineffective assistance of counsel, his convictions and sentences were unconstitutional, and that newly discovered material facts would probably change the verdict or sentence. On March 30, 2012, the Superior Court found that he had failed to state a claim for which relief can be granted in an untimely Rule 32 proceeding and dismissed his post-conviction proceedingsFirst Habeas Petition. On April 10, 2012, Neuendorf filed a Petition for Writ of Habeas Corpus in this Court and, on July 27, 2012, he filed an Amended Petition. CV-12-755-PHX-RCB (DKD) at Docs. 1, 16. Neuendorf affirmatively alleged that he had not raised any of his claims to the Arizona Court of Appeals and so, on September 10, 2012, the Court dismissed the Amended Petition without prejudice for failure to exhaust state court remedies.

Successive Rule 32 Proceedings. On April 11, 2012, Neuendorf filed a Notice of Post-Conviction Relief alleging ineffective assistance of counsel and that the delayed filing was because he had been the victim of various assaults. On April 19, 2012, the Court dismissed his Notice because ineffective assistance of counsel claims cannot be raised in successive proceedings and because his explanation for the delay did "not present a situation where [Neuendorf was] without fault on his part for his late filings." On October 12, 2012, and again on November 23, 2012, Neuendorf petitioned the Court of Appeals to review the Superior Court's dismissal of his Rule 32 proceedings. On November 21, 2013, the Court of Appeals granted review and denied relief. Neuendorf's motion for reconsideration was denied on January 14, 2014, and he did not petition the Arizona Supreme Court for review.   In his October 12, 2012 Petition, Neuendorf wrote that he was requesting review of the Superior Court's April 18, 2012 decision, but he attached the Superior Court's September 18, 2012 minute entry. In his November 23, 2012 Petition, Neuendorf also wrote that he was requesting review of the Superior Court's April 18, 2012 decision but no minute entry was attached.

On August 20, 2012, Neuendorf filed a State Court Complaint in Maricopa County Superior Court alleging that his conviction and sentence violated the *Fourteenth Amendment*. The Court construed this filing as his third untimely Rule 32 Petition and, on September 18, 2012, dismissed it for failing to raise a claim for which relief can be granted in an untimely Rule 32 proceeding

On November 26, 2012, Neuendorf filed a Petition for Post-Conviction Relief in Maricopa County Superior Court and, on December 17, 2012, the Court summarily dismissed the Petition for failing to raise a claim for which relief can be granted in an untimely Rule 32 proceeding and because his claims either were or could have been raised in a prior Rule 32 proceeding

On February 27, 2013, Neuendorf filed a Notice of Post-Conviction Relief in Maricopa County Superior Court and, on April 4, 2013, the Court again summarily dismissed the Notice for failing to raise a claim for which relief can be granted in an untimely Rule 32 proceeding and because his claims either were or could have been raised in a prior Rule 32 proceeding.

On October 16, 2013, Neuendorf again filed a Notice of Post-Conviction Relief in Maricopa County Superior Court and, on October 30, 2013, the Court again summarily dismissed the Notice for failing to raise a claim for which relief can be granted in an untimely Rule 32 proceeding and because his claims either were or could have been raised in a prior Rule 32 proceeding. The Court also noted that Neuendorf was not entitled to relief under *Martinez v. Ryan, 132 S.Ct. 1309, 182 L. Ed. 2d 272 (2012)*, because the *Martinez* decision applied to federal, not state, post-conviction proceedings.

This Habeas Petition. On January 30, 2014, Neuendorf filed the Petition for Writ of Habeas Corpus under review in this case. His Petition argues that (1) he received ineffective assistance of trial counsel, (2) his sentence violated due process and the *Eighth Amendment*, (3) his plea was not knowingly or intelligently made, and (4) the State's failure to turn over impeachment evidence violated due process. (*Id.*) Respondents contend that his Petition is untimely and that he is not entitled to equitable tolling. The Court agrees and recommends that this Petition be denied and dismissed with prejudice.

Neuendorf's Petition is Untimely.

A state prisoner seeking federal habeas relief from a state court conviction is required to file the petition within one year of "the date on which the judgment became final by the conclusion of direct review or the expiration of the time for seeking such review." *28 U.S.C. § 2244(d)(1)(A)*. The period of limitations is statutorily tolled during the time in which a "properly filed application for State post-conviction or other collateral review with respect to the pertinent judgment or claim is pending" in the State courts. *28 U.S.C. § 2244(d)(2)*. If a defendant is convicted pursuant to a guilty plea, then the first post-conviction proceeding is considered a form of direct review and the conviction becomes "final" for purposes of *Section 2244(d)(1)(A)* when the *Rule 32* of-right proceeding concludes. *Pace v. DiGuglielmo, 544 U.S. 408, 414, 125 S. Ct. 1807, 161 L. Ed. 2d 669 (2005)* ("When a postconviction petition is untimely under state law, that is the end of the matter for purposes of § 2244(d)(2).") (internal quotation omitted); *Summers v. Schriro, 481 F.3d 710, 711 (9th Cir. 2007)* (conviction pursuant to plea agreement is final on expiration of the time for seeking Rule 32 relief).

Neuendorf was sentenced on April 8, 2011, and, when he did not timely initiate Rule 32 proceedings under *Arizona Rule of Criminal Procedure 32.4(a)*, his conviction became final on July 8, 2011. Thus, his one year clock for filing a habeas petition in this Court began on July 9, 2011, and ended on July 9, 2012.

Before July 9, 2012, Neuendorf had initiated two Rule 32 proceedings in Superior Court but these were both untimely. Because they were not "properly filed," they did not toll any time for *Section 2244(d)(2)*. *Pace, 544 U.S. at 413* (no AEDPA tolling from untimely state post-conviction petitions).

Before July 9, 2012, Neuendorf had also filed a habeas petition in this Court. But this did not toll any time because "an application for federal habeas corpus review is not an 'application for State post-conviction or other collateral review' within the meaning of *28 U.S.C. § 2244(d)(2)*." *Duncan v. Walker, 533 U.S. 167, 181, 121 S. Ct. 2120, 150 L. Ed. 2d 251 (2001)*. Moreover, Neuendorf's first habeas petition was dismissed because he had not exhausted his state court remedies. This means that he cannot relate this habeas petition to his earlier habeas petition because a "second habeas petition does not relate back to a first habeas petition when the first habeas petition was dismissed for failure to exhaust state remedies." *Green v. White, 223 F.3d 1001, 1003 (9th Cir. 2000)*.

None of Neuendorf's filings tolled any time and so his one year timeframe expired and, once expired, it could not be revived by subsequent filings. *Pace v. DiGuglielmo, 544 U.S. 408, 413, 125 S. Ct. 1807, 161 L. Ed. 2d 669 (2005)* (no AEDPA tolling from untimely state post-conviction petitions). Accordingly, his habeas petition, filed on January 30, 2014, was untimely.

Neuendorf is Not Entitled to Equitable Tolling.

Neuendorf's Petition is untimely unless he can show that he is entitled to equitable tolling. To make such a showing, Neuendorf must demonstrate both that he pursued his rights diligently and that some extraordinary circumstance prevented him from filing his petition. *Holland v. Florida, 560 U.S. 631, 649, 130 S. Ct. 2549, 177 L. Ed. 2d 130 (2010)*.

Neuendorf does not attempt to show either prong of this test. Instead, he argues that *Martinez v. Ryan, 132 S.Ct. 1309, 182 L. Ed. 2d 272 (2012)*, entitles him to file an untimely habeas petition. This argument is unpersuasive because *Martinez* does not address the limitations bar in *Section 2244(d)(2)* and it does not excuse an untimely habeas petition. *E.g., Madueno v. Ryan, 2014 U.S. Dist. LEXIS 69056, 2014 WL 2094189, at *7 (D.Ariz. May 20, 2014); Marshall v. Ryan, 2014 U.S. Dist. LEXIS 24666, 2014 WL 710954, at *5 (D.Ariz. Feb. 25, 2014); Moreno v. Ryan, 2013 U.S. Dist. LEXIS 182023, 2014 WL 24151, at *5 (D.Ariz. Jan. 2, 2014)*.

Neuendorf also seems to argue that his status as a pro se litigant entitles him to additional time. However, he is not entitled to equitable tolling because of his status as a pro se litigant, his lack of familiarity with the law, or the extent of his legal resources. *Rasberry v. Garcia, 448 F.3d 1150, 1154 (9th Cir. 2006)* ("a pro se petitioner's lack of legal sophistication is not, by itself, an extraordinary circumstance warranting equitable tolling").

REASONS WHY REMEDY IS HOLLOW

Aware that in Arizona PCR proceedings with appointed counsel are meaningless as counsel do not expend the resources to ensure claims are reviewed the Attorney General conceals this fact.

DEWEY DERALD GULLICK, Petitioner - Appellant, v. BOCK, Deputy Warden; STATE OF ARIZONA ATTORNEY GENERAL, Respondents - Appellees. No. 10-15409 UNITED STATES COURT OF APPEALS FOR THE NINTH CIRCUIT(Text modified for emphasis)

Gullick contends that the district court erred by denying equitable tolling of AEDPA's one-year statute of limitations. In light of Gullick's ability to file other petitions, represent himself at a hearing, and the reports on his mental condition during the relevant time period, Gullick has failed to demonstrate that his mental condition caused his untimely filing. *See Gaston v. Palmer, 417 F.3d 1030, 1034-35 (9th Cir. 2005), modified on other grounds, 447 F.3d 1165 (9th Cir. 2006)*. Further, any inadequate assistance Gullick received from other inmates is not an extraordinary circumstance that warrants equitable tolling. *See Chaffer v. Prosper, 592 F.3d 1046, 1049 (9th Cir. 2010)* (per curiam).

Finally, Gullick contends that, because the state courts incorrectly denied his state petitions as untimely, statutory tolling renders his federal petition timely. When a post-conviction petition is untimely under state law, that is the end of the matter for statutory tolling purposes. *See Pace v. DiGuglielmo, 544 U.S. 408, 414, 417, 125 S. Ct. 1807, 161 L. Ed. 2d 669 (2005).*

REASONS WHY REMEDY IS HOLLOW

Arizona does not have a law library and have a paralegal system made of paralegals, not able to afford inmates assistance. By their policies they forbid paralegals from assisting inmates in marshalling facts and arguments. However they argue in the course of federal proceedings that inmates have failed to comply with technical provisions of the rules. They obtain mental health from mental health practitioners who are willing to say anything to appease state authorities. Aware of this fact the Arizona Attorney general consistently misrepresents facts to the court to prevail.

DELAYED FILING

DEMONT OSHAUN HILL, Petitioner, v. CHARLES L. RYAN, TERRY GODDARD, Respondents. CIV 09-01597 PHX MHM (MEA) UNITED STATES DISTRICT COURT FOR THE DISTRICT OF ARIZONA
(text modified for emphasis)

THE COURTS DECISION

A Maricopa County grand jury indictment issued May 18, 1994, charged Petitioner and a co-defendant with conspiracy to commit armed robbery (Count I); first-degree murder (Count II); attempted armed robbery (Count III); and aggravated assault (Count IV). See Answer,. All of the offenses were alleged to occur on the same day and the murder victim was also a victim of the attempted armed robbery.

At the conclusion of a jury trial conducted in November of 1995 Petitioner was found guilty of conspiracy to commit armed robbery and guilty of attempted armed robbery. The jury found Petitioner not guilty of murder and not guilty of aggravated assault.

On January 12, 1996, after an aggravation and mitigation hearing, Petitioner was sentenced to a term of ten years imprisonment pursuant to his conviction for conspiracy to commit armed robbery (Count I). Petitioner was sentenced to a sentence of fifteen years imprisonment pursuant to his conviction on the charge of attempted armed robbery (Count III). The state trial court ordered that the sentence on Count III be served consecutively to the sentence imposed on Count I.

Petitioner took a direct appeal of his convictions and sentences.. Petitioner asserted he was denied his right to due process of law because the jury was given a "Pinkerton" instruction. Petitioner also asserted the imposition of consecutive sentences was not proper.

In a decision issued January 17, 1997, the Arizona Court of Appeals concluded that giving the instruction was error, but that the error was harmless because the jury had not convicted Petitioner based on the erroneous instruction.. The Court of Appeals further stated that the consecutive sentences were not improper. Petitioner sought review of this decision by the Arizona Supreme Court, arguing the jury had been instructed on a "nonexistent theory of criminal liability," which constituted a structural defect not amenable to harmless error analysis. The Arizona Supreme Court denied review in a decision issued May 28, 1997.

Petitioner filed an action seeking post-conviction relief pursuant to Rule 32, Arizona Rules of Criminal Procedure, on April 29, 2002. Petitioner re-asserted the claims stated in his direct appeal and also claimed that the government had committed perjury in Petitioner's direct appeal. Petitioner acknowledged his Rule 32 action was not timely but alleged he had not previously been aware of the availability of post-conviction relief or the time limitations regarding post conviction relief. Petitioner further asserted his recent awareness of the government's misstatements in its pleadings in his direct appeal constituted newly discovered evidence

In response to the assertion that his habeas petition was not timely filed, Petitioner again asserts that his constitutional rights have been violated and that he is, accordingly, entitled to relief. Petitioner maintains that he has exhausted his federal habeas claims in the state courts and that he has established cause and prejudice to excuse any procedural default of his habeas claims. Petitioner does not directly address the argument that his federal habeas petition was not filed within the deadline stated by the AEDPA. Petitioner asserts that, until he finished serving his sentence for conspiracy to commit armed robbery, he could not contest the validity of his sentence for attempted armed robbery without incriminating himself. Petitioner further contends that he has recently become innocent by completely serving his sentence for conspiracy to commit armed robbery because the sentence imposed for attempted armed robbery violates his federal constitutional rights, including his right to be free of double jeopardy.

REASON WHY REMEDY IS HOLLOW

Arizona courts refuse to afford relief for perjury and the Arizona Attorney General aware of this systemic problem in Arizona thwarts all attempts to obtain relief, thereby encouraging convictions on perjury.

**James E. Robinson, Petitioner, vs. Charles L. Ryan, et al., Respondents.
CIV 11-1383-PHX-GMS (MHB)UNITED STATES DISTRICT COURT FOR THE DISTRICT
OF ARIZONA   (Text modified for emphasis)**

THE POSITION OF THE COURT

On December 6, 2007, Petitioner pled guilty to one count of theft of a means of transportation As part of the plea, Petitioner admitted to having committed one historical prior felony offense. On December 20, 2007, the trial court sentenced Petitioner to a term of 6.5 years' imprisonment.

Nearly two years later, on September 22, 2009, Petitioner filed a notice of post-conviction relief alleging newly discovered evidence of actual innocence, stating:

> Defendant claims innocence in the matter of CR 2007-13870-001 DT. Defendant's belated post-conviction relief is due to discovery of [a] new material fact on August 28, 2009. Defendant, now, exercises due diligence to bring the matter forward to [the] court's attention, praying for relief under Arizona Rules of Criminal Procedure, Rule 32.

The trial court subsequently dismissed the petition as untimely filed, finding:

> This is Defendant's first Rule 32 notice. However, an "of right" Rule 32 notice must be filed within 90 days of sentencing. ... Because Defendant's notice was not filed within 90 days of sentencing, Defendant's notice is untimely.

The court further noted that despite Petitioner's claim of newly discovered evidence, the claim was nevertheless untimely because "Defendant [had] not set forth any facts in support of [his] claim." Petitioner did not file a petition for review in the Arizona Court of Appeals.

On April 28, 2010, the Arizona Court of Appeals declined to accept jurisdiction of Petitioner's request for special action jurisdiction.

On July 12, 2011, Petitioner filed the instant Petition for Writ of Habeas Corpus raising three grounds for relief. In Ground One, Petitioner claims that he was denied his *Fourteenth Amendment* right to have the state court judge review an affidavit that allegedly demonstrates that Petitioner was actually innocent of theft of a means of transportation. He notes that the order dismissing his notice of post-conviction relief did not mention the affidavit and incorrectly stated that Petitioner's claim of actual innocence was not supported by any facts. In Ground Two, Petitioner contends he was denied his *Sixth Amendment* right to "have fair trial court proceedings" because the state court judge did not review the affidavit. In Ground Three, he asserts that he is being incarcerated in violation of the *Eighth Amendment* because "[s]entencing an 'actually innocent' defendant to a prison term is illegal on its face."

DISCUSSION

In their Answer, Respondents contend that the habeas petition is untimely. As such, Respondents argue that Petitioner's habeas petition must be denied and dismissed.

In Arizona, post-conviction review is pending once a notice of post-conviction relief is filed even though the petition is not filed until later. See *Isley v. Arizona Department of Corrections, 383 F.3d 1054, 1056 (9th Cir. 2004).* An application for post-conviction relief is also pending during the intervals between a lower court decision and a review by a higher court. See *Biggs v. Duncan, 339 F.3d 1045, 1048 (9th Cir. 2003)* (citing *Carey v. Saffold, 536 U.S. 214, 223, 122 S. Ct. 2134, 153 L. Ed. 2d 260 (2002)).* However, the time between a first and second application for post-conviction relief is not tolled because no application is "pending" during that period. See *id.* Moreover, filing a new petition for post-conviction relief does not reinitiate a limitations period that ended before the new petition was filed. See *Ferguson v. Palmateer, 321 F.3d 820, 823 (9th Cir. 2003).*

The statute of limitations under the AEDPA is subject to equitable tolling in appropriate cases. See *Holland v. Florida,   U.S.   ,   , 130 S.Ct. 2549, 2560, 177 L.Ed.2d 130 (2010).* However, for equitable tolling to apply, a petitioner must show "'(1) that he has been pursuing his   rights diligently and (2) that some extraordinary circumstances stood in his way'" and prevented him from filing a timely petition. *Id. at 2562* (quoting *Pace, 544 U.S. at 418*).

Petitioner was sentenced under the plea agreement on December 20, 2007. Petitioner had 90 days to file an "of-right" petition for post-conviction relief pursuant to the Arizona Rules of Criminal Procedure. See *Ariz.R.Crim.P. 32.4(a).* He failed to file a petition within that time period and, thus, the statute of limitations began to run on March 20, 2008 -- one day after the 90-day period expired. The statute of limitations then expired one year later -- on March 20, 2009.

Petitioner filed an untimely notice of post-conviction relief on September 22, 2009 -- more than six months after the statute of limitations expired. Because the statute of limitations had passed by the time Petitioner filed his notice of post-conviction relief, the petition (or request for special action filed thereafter) did not toll the limitations period. See *Pace, 544 U.S. at 417* (holding that time limits for filing a state post-conviction petition are filing conditions which, if not met, preclude a finding that a state petition was properly   filed). An untimely state post-conviction petition does not restart an already expired statute of limitations. See *Jiminez v. Rice, 276 F.3d 478, 482 (9th Cir. 2001).* Petitioner filed the instant habeas petition on July 12, 2011 -- well over two years after the limitations period expired. The habeas petition is therefore untimely.

The Ninth Circuit recognizes that the AEDPA's limitations period may be equitably tolled because it is a statute of limitations, not a jurisdictional bar. See *Calderon v. United States Dist. Ct. (Beeler), 128 F.3d 1283, 1288 (9th Cir. 1997),* overruled in part on other grounds by *Calderon v. United States Dist. Ct. (Kelly), 163 F.3d 530, 540 (9th Cir. 1998).* Tolling is appropriate when "'extraordinary circumstances' beyond a [petitioner's] control make it impossible to file a petition on time." Id.; see *Miranda v. Castro, 292 F.3d 1063, 1066 (9th Cir. 2002)* (stating that "the threshold necessary to trigger equitable tolling [under AEDPA] is very high, lest the exceptions swallow the rule") (citations omitted). "When external forces, rather than a petitioner's lack of diligence, account for the failure to file a timely claim, equitable tolling of the statute   of limitations may be appropriate." *Miles v. Prunty, 187 F.3d 1104, 1107 (9th Cir. 1999).* A petitioner seeking equitable tolling must establish two elements: "(1) that he has been pursuing his rights diligently, and (2) that some extraordinary circumstance stood in his way." *Pace, 544 U.S. at 418.* Petitioner must also establish a "causal connection" between the extraordinary circumstance and his failure to file a timely petition. See *Bryant v. Arizona Attorney General, 499 F.3d 1056, 1060 (9th Cir. 2007).*

The circumstances in this case do not support a finding that Petitioner pursued his rights diligently or that extraordinary circumstances prevented him from filing a timely habeas petition. In his Traverse and memorandum in support thereof, Petitioner submits:

> It would take almost two years for Petitioner to find the whereabouts of witness who had [possession] of [the] motorcycle at the time Petitioner borrowed it, and for Petitioner to get [an] affidavit from him. ... Petitioner is aware that a lot of time had gone by from sentencing date and date he received evidence, but there was no way he could have predicted when or where he would find his witness.

Later in his pleading Petitioner states:

As evidence from the Petitioner has shown there was no way for the Petitioner to show evidence of innocence because there was no way to get [a hold] of his witness[;] the reason being was that witness Rosenthal was under conditions of release and could not be in contact with police for any reason.

The Court finds Petitioner's reasoning specious and contradictory. While he may not have had Rosenthal's affidavit in hand, Petitioner has undoubtedly been aware of the essential facts presented in the affidavit since the date of his arrest. Further, although a review of the affidavit suggests that Petitioner knew Rosenthal (in that Petitioner merely "borrowed" his motorcycle), Petitioner, nevertheless, failed to meet the state court deadlines for seeking review of his case contending that it took two years to find him. Within the same pleading Petitioner states that Rosenthal was under conditions of release and there was no way to get in contact with him. Petitioner filed an untimely notice of post-conviction relief, and after that proceeding was dismissed, failed to seek appellate review of the dismissal by filing petition for review -- even after he claims to have acquired the evidence   at issue. The Court additionally notes that the record is void of any requests for extensions of time. This is not a case where Petitioner has been diligently pursuing his rights, and Petitioner has not described any extraordinary circumstance which prevented him from filing a timely habeas petition.

Despite the Court finding that Petitioner has not been diligently pursuing his rights and has failed to establish extraordinary circumstances, Petitioner contends that the "actual innocence gateway" of *Schlup v. Delo*, 513 U.S. 298, 115 S. Ct. 851, 130 L. Ed. 2d 808 (1995), applies to him and warrants equitable tolling. A credible claim of actual innocence can constitute an equitable exception to the AEDPA's limitations period. See *Lee v. Lampert*, 653 F.3d 929, 932 (9th Cir. 2011) (*en banc*). However, in order to present otherwise time-barred claims to a federal habeas court under Schlup, Petitioner has the heavy burden of producing "new reliable evidence -- whether it be exculpatory scientific evidence, trust-worthy eyewitness accounts, or critical physical evidence -- that was not presented at trial" that so strongly shows his actual innocence "that it is more likely than not that no reasonable juror would have convicted him   in light of the new evidence." *Id.* at 938 (quoting *Schlup*, 513 U.S. at 324, 327). The Court finds that Petitioner lacks such evidence.

As previously indicated, Petitioner attempts to support his claim of actual innocence with an affidavit, which appears to be penned by Petitioner and signed by Howard Rosenthal. The affidavit states the following:

On June 13, 2007, I was in [the] process of purchasing a 2003 Triumph motorcycle, with 1100CC capacity, and black in color. On June 14, 2007, the motorcycle was in my garage at my residence ... awaiting final transaction. When Mr. James Robinson arrived at my house, while I was asleep, he asked my room[m]ate ... if he could use the motorcycle in question to facilitate purchasing food; he assumed the motorcycle belong[ed] to me -- therefore, with no illegality attached to it. Subsequent to Robinson's return, my home was raided by Phoenix police [and] Robinson was arrested and charged for "theft -- means of transportation." Neither I nor Robinson had any knowledge [that] said motorcycle was stolen. In fact, initial police investigation at the scene did not reveal the motorcycle was stolen. Robinson was unaware of any illegality, if it in fact existed   and he used it for legitimate purposes. I further offer my full cooperation to state authorities to resolve this matter, in any way necessary, for Mr. Robinson is completely innocent of this crime. I am writing this of sound mind and under no duress or threats of any sort.

Initially, the Court notes that affidavits alone are not a promising way to demonstrate actual innocence. Though sworn, affidavits are not convincing evidence of innocence because "the affiants' statements are obtained without the benefit of cross-examination and an opportunity to make credibility determinations." *Herrera v. Collins*, 506 U.S. 390, 417, 113 S. Ct. 853, 122 L. Ed. 2d 203 (1993). In addition to the inherent weakness of an affidavit, the affidavit at issue is particularly unhelpful and does not have the indicia of reliability sufficient to make out a claim of actual innocence in that the statements set forth therein are based on layers of hearsay, opinions, inference, and conclusory assertions -- not particularized facts. Moreover, actual innocence evidence "must be considered in light of the proof of Petitioner's guilt at trial." *Id. at 418.* Where, as in this case, Petitioner pled guilty, such admission of culpability mitigates strongly   against a subsequent finding of actual innocence, particularly given the unreliable nature of the evidence submitted by Petitioner. See id. (finding "troubling" petitioner's failure to offer an explanation as to why he, "by hypothesis an innocent man, pleaded guilty").

The Court finds that the Rosenthal affidavit simply fails to qualify as "exculpatory scientific evidence, trustworthy eyewitness accounts, or critical physical evidence," such that it would establish a gateway actual innocence claim as contemplated by Schlup. Accordingly, Petitioner is not entitled to equitable tolling and his habeas petition is untimely.

REASONS WHY REMEDY IS HOLLOW

Arizona has a history of convicting innocent people and the Attorney General fails to disclose this to the federal court.

ARTIS GIPSON, Petitioner - Appellant, v. CHARLES RYAN and STATE OF ARIZONA ATTORNEY GENERAL, Respondents - Appellees. No. 10-15792 UNITED STATES COURT OF APPEALS FOR THE NINTH CIRCUIT
(Text modified for emphasis)

THE POSITION OF THE COURT

The parties agree that AEDPA's one-year statute of limitations began to run on July 13, 2006, when Gipson's 90-day window for petitioning the U.S. Supreme Court for certiorari expired. *See 28 U.S.C. § 2244(d)(1).* Gipson is correct that he is entitled to statutory tolling while he pursued timely state post-conviction relief -- that is, from when Gipson's conviction became final on July 13, 2006 until October 25, 2007, when the time for Gipson to file a petition for review for post-conviction relief (after receiving one extension of time) expired. *See id. § 2244(d)(2).* Gipson filed his federal habeas petition one year and 122 days later, on February 23, 2009.

Gipson argues that he is entitled to equitable tolling of that one year and 122 days based on (1) the state trial court's inexplicable decision to forward Gipson's pro se transcript request to his appointed counsel, with whom Gipson allegedly could not communicate, and (2) the state trial court's miscalculation of his filing deadline and concomitant denial of his second request for an extension of time to file a petition for review for post-conviction relief.

A petitioner is entitled to equitable tolling only when he shows "'(1) that he has been pursuing his rights diligently, and   (2) that some extraordinary circumstance stood in his way' and prevented timely filing." *Holland v. Florida, 130 S. Ct. 2549, 2562, 177 L. Ed. 2d 130 (2010)* (citation omitted).

Here, even if Gipson had pursued his rights diligently, the state trial court's errors did not prevent him from filing a timely federal habeas petition. First, with respect to the miscommunication about Gipson's transcript request, Gipson has failed to identify anything in the transcript that was necessary for him to be able to file his federal habeas petition. Furthermore, Gipson received the transcript on October 3, 2008, more than three weeks before AEDPA's limitations period ran, but has failed to show that it was impossible for him to file his petition within those three weeks. And second, with respect to the denial of the extension of time as a result of the miscalculated filing deadline, even after Gipson exhausted his state appeals of that denial, he still had five months left on AEDPA's limitations period to timely file his petition. Alternatively, as the Supreme Court has noted, Gipson could have filed a "protective" petition with the district court and asked it to "stay and abey the federal habeas proceedings until state remedies are exhausted." *Pace v. DiGuglielmo, 544 U.S. 408, 416, 125 S. Ct. 1807, 161 L. Ed. 2d 669 (2005).* Accordingly, Gipson has not met his burden to show that extraordinary circumstances made it impossible for him to file a timely habeas petition.

Thus, because Gipson filed his § 2254 petition 122 days after AEDPA's one-year limitations period expired, and because he is not entitled to equitable tolling, we affirm the district court's dismissal of his petition as untimely. We therefore need not address Gipson's argument that the state court's denial of his motion for a second extension of time amounted to an inadequate state procedural bar.

REASONS WHY REMEDY IS HOLLOW

It is very common in Arizona for courts to forward records to the wrong person and miscalculate times. Though aware of this fact the Attorney General conceals this from the court.

SENTENCES

> Robert Earl Johnson, Petitioner, vs. Charles Ryan, et al., Respondents. No. CV11-0780-PHX-SRB
> UNITED STATES DISTRICT COURT FOR THE DISTRICT OF ARIZONA
> (text modified for emphasis)

THE COURTS DECISION

Petitioner argues that he was improperly sentenced in state court pursuant to *A.R.S. § 13-604(A)* and *(B)*, when he should have been sentenced pursuant to *A.R.S. § 13-702.02*. Petitioner claims this sentencing error violates the *Fifth, Eighth* and *Fourteenth Amendments to the United States Constitution*. In Ground Two, Petitioner argues that he received illegal sentences in state court in violation of the *Fifth, Eighth* and *Fourteenth Amendments* because the prior felony conviction used to enhance his sentence did not qualify as a historical prior felony conviction under Arizona law.

The Magistrate Judge issued his Report and Recommendation on October 24, 2011 recommending that the Petition be denied because Petitioner argued that his sentences were imposed in violation of Arizona law and such state law claims are not cognizable on federal habeas corpus review. The Magistrate Judge also concluded that Petitioner's reference to the *Fifth, Eighth* and *Fourteenth Amendments to the United States Constitution* do not transform his state law claims into federal ones

REASON WHY REMEDY IS HOLLOW

Arizona courts consistently refuse to afford relief for erroneous sentences and the Attorney General impedes the attempts by victims to be correctly sentenced.

> David Martinez Ramirez, Petitioner, vs. Charles L. Ryan, et al., Respondents.
> No. CV-97-1331-PHX-JAT UNITED STATES DISTRICT COURT FOR THE DISTRICT OF ARIZONA
> (Text modified for emphasis)

THE POSITION OF THE COURT

In Petitioner's briefing in support of cause and prejudice, he alleges that certain pretrial, trial, and sentencing events prevented his post-conviction counsel from raising Claim 34 in a timely manner. In pretrial proceedings, on September 28, 1989, Petitioner filed a motion for appointment of experts, requesting an independent psychiatric evaluation, a child psychologist, a mitigation specialist, a fingerprint examiner, a jury consultant, a serologist, and a pathologist. In the motion, Petitioner cited *Ake v. Oklahoma, 470 U.S. 68, 105 S. Ct. 1087, 84 L. Ed. 2d 53 (1985)*, and requested, without explanation, that an independent psychiatrist be appointed to assess his sanity at the time of the crime. He summarily requested the appointment of the other experts. Subsequently, the court appointed an investigator to assist Petitioner, who at that point was representing himself with advisory counsel. The following week, the court denied the remainder of the expert requests without prejudice, allowing for reconsideration after Petitioner had an opportunity to consult with his investigator. At an ex parte proceeding, Petitioner's investigator asserted that a child psychologist was important to help determine Petitioner's social upbringing and to collaborate with a mitigation specialist. A mitigation specialist was needed to work with the investigator, Petitioner, and mental health professionals in order to prepare a complete mitigation presentation. Advisory counsel explained that the mental health experts were requested for mitigation purposes in the event Petitioner was found guilty, not to evaluate his competency to stand trial. The court denied the request for a mitigation specialist but indicated that it would be reconsidered if Petitioner was convicted. It appears the Court appointed a serologist.

Subsequently, prior to trial, there was a change of judge ordered, with Maricopa County Superior Court Judge Thomas W. O'Toole, presiding over the case. After jury selection, Petitioner requested that advisory counsel be appointed to represent him going forward, and the court granted the request. After the jury found Petitioner guilty on both murder counts, Petitioner's counsel informed the court that previously she had requested a mitigation specialist; when the judge asked if she was referring to Arizona Rule of Criminal Procedure 26.5, which provides for presentence mental health examinations, counsel answered, "Well, so to speak." The court appointed the mental health expert proposed by Petitioner, Dr. McMahon, "to test and evaluate the defendant's curre." The court authorized compensation in the amount of $500, but that additional fees and expenses could be obtained with "prior written approval of the court." Petitioner made no other requests for the appointment of experts prior to sentencing.

In his sentencing memorandum, Petitioner's counsel relied on Dr. McMahon's August 18, 1990, evaluation to support assertion of *A.R.S. § 13-703 (G)(1)* statutory mitigating circumstance--that his ability to appreciate the wrongfulness of his conduct or conform his conduct to the law was significantly diminished. Dr. McMahon concluded that Petitioner's capacity to appreciate the wrongfulness of his conduct or conform his conduct to the requirement of law was significantly diminished due to his psychological condition and his drug and alcohol intoxication on the night of the crimes. (ROA-PCR 160 at 8.) Dr. McMahon's psychological evaluation also measured Petitioner's intelligence quotient ("IQ"), utilizing the Peabody Picture Vocabulary Test ("PPVT"). Dr. McMahon reported: "The defendant obtained a PPVT IQ of 94, which is well within the average range of intelligence and in no way indicative of any form of mental retardation."

At sentencing, the judge found three aggravating circumstances: Petitioner had two prior violent felony convictions (*A.R.S. § 13-703(F)(2)*); Petitioner committed the murders in an especially cruel, heinous, or depraved manner (*A.R.S. § 13-703 (F)(6)*); and Petitioner committed multiple homicides during the same episode (*A.R.S. § 13-703(F)(8)*). The judge found one statutory mitigating circumstance and seven non-statutory circumstances, but determined they were not sufficiently substantial to warrant leniency, and sentenced Petitioner to death on both murder counts. The Arizona Supreme Court affirmed Petitioner's convictions and sentences on direct appeal. *State v. Ramirez, 178 Ariz. 116, 871 P.2d 237 (1994)*.

Prior to filing his post-conviction relief ("PCR") petition, Petitioner did not request any investigative or expert resources. In his PCR petition, Petitioner raised a claim of ineffective assistance of counsel ("IAC"), alleging that counsel did not have a cohesive defense strategy at trial or with regard to mitigation. With respect to IAC at sentencing, Petitioner alleged that counsel did not have a clear strategy, which was evidenced by counsel's attempt to use Petitioner's alleged gang membership in mitigation. The PCR court ruled that Petitioner failed to raise a colorable claim of ineffective assistance and denied relief. The Arizona Supreme Court denied review.

Petitioner initiated federal habeas proceedings, raising both conviction and sentencing claims. Subsequently, the Court stayed Petitioner's sentencing claims so that he could file a successive PCR petition in state court asserting that he is mentally retarded and ineligible for capital punishment pursuant to *Atkins v. Virginia, 536 U.S. 304, 122 S. Ct. 2242, 153 L. Ed. 2d 335 (2002)* (recognizing that the *Eighth Amendment* prohibits a state from sentencing to death or executing a mentally retarded person). In state court, the Court limited Petitioner's counsel, the Federal Public Defender ("FPD"), to the *Atkins* litigation. In April 2005, Petitioner initiated an *Atkins* claim in successive PCR proceedings. In response to this Court's Order, Respondents provided a complete copy of the state court record of Petitioner's *Atkins* litigation to the Court for its review.

Subsequently, also in April 2005, a private attorney "conducted an initial *pro bono* review" of Petitioner's case and filed a separate successive state PCR notice attempting to litigate five non-Atkins claims, including Claim 34, an allegation of ineffective assistance of counsel for failing to conduct a complete mitigation investigation, obtain, and present available mitigation evidence at sentencing. The PCR court summarily dismissed this action as unexceptional, rendering it subject to timeliness rules that required all PCR claims be filed during a petitioner's initial PCR proceeding. Based on the PCR court's ruling, for Claim 34 to be timely and considered on the merits, Petitioner was required to have raised it during his initial PCR proceeding. Petitioner did not raise Claim 34 during his initial PCR proceeding. This Court has concluded that Claim 34 was procedurally defaulted according to an adequate and independent state procedural rule and will not be considered on the merits apart from a showing of cause and prejudice or a fundamental miscarriage of justice.   Due to his alleged mental retardation, Petitioner contends that the Court should relax the procedural rules regarding cause and prejudice and fundamental miscarriage of justice. In *Tacho v. Martinez, 862 F.2d 1376, 1381 (9th Cir. 1988)*, the court considered and concluded that the petitioner's mental condition did not constitute cause. Furthermore, the Court further notes that Petitioner had counsel during all of his post-conviction proceedings. *See id.* The Court addresses *infra* Petitioner's argument regarding allegations of mental retardation and whether they constitute an excuse in the context of a fundamental miscarriage of justice.

Cause and Prejudice

In *Coleman v. Thompson, 501 U.S. 722, 750, 111 S. Ct. 2546, 115 L. Ed. 2d 640 (1991)*, the Court made explicit that if a state prisoner has procedurally defaulted a federal claim in state court pursuant to an independent and adequate procedural rule, "federal habeas review of the claim[] is barred unless the prisoner can demonstrate cause for the default and actual prejudice as a result of the alleged violation of federal law[.]" Ordinarily "cause" to excuse a default exists if a petitioner can demonstrate that "some objective factor external to the defense impeded counsel's efforts to comply with the State's procedural rule." *Id. at 753*. Objective factors constituting cause include interference by officials which makes compliance with the state's procedural rule impracticable, a showing that the factual or legal basis for a claim was not reasonably available to counsel, and constitutionally ineffective assistance of counsel. *Murray v. Carrier, 477 U.S. 478, 488, 106 S. Ct. 2639, 91 L. Ed. 2d 397 (1986); see also Amadeo v. Zant, 486 U.S. 214, 222, 108 S. Ct. 1771, 100 L. Ed. 2d 249 (1988)* (cause is established if unavailable evidence was the reason for the default). "Prejudice" is actual harm resulting from the alleged constitutional error or violation. *Magby v. Wawrzaszek, 741 F.2d 240, 244 (9th Cir. 1984)*. To establish prejudice resulting from a procedural default, a habeas petitioner bears the burden of showing not merely that the errors at his trial or sentencing constituted a possibility of prejudice, but that they worked to his actual and substantial disadvantage, infecting the entire proceeding with errors of constitutional dimension. *United States v. Frady, 456 U.S. 152, 170, 102 S. Ct. 1584, 71 L. Ed. 2d 816 (1982)*.

Discussion

Petitioner asserts that he has cause and prejudice to excuse his failure to present the claim because the trial court, thru interrelated failures, prevented PCR counsel from timely presenting it. Specifically, the trial court failed to authorize funding for a mitigation specialist, failed to fund a mental health expert until sentencing proceedings, and then inadequately funded the court-appointed mental health expert, Dr. Mickey McMahon, Ph.D. These failures also prevented sentencing counsel from obtaining an adequate social history of Petitioner to provide to Dr. McMahon, which caused Dr. McMahon to conclude that Petitioner was not mentally retarded. (*Id.* at 10-11.) Dr. McMahon's allegedly inaccurate mental retardation conclusion caused PCR counsel not to actively investigate Petitioner's mental health and present Claim 34 during his initial PCR proceeding. *See id.* at 11 (citing *Forman v. Smith, 633 F.2d 634, 641 (2d Cir.1980)* (observing in *dicta* that an official's intentional or inadvertent misleading statement "that obscures the opportunity to develop a federal constitutional violation" may constitute cause to excuse a procedural default)).

State Official Interference

Cause may be established by demonstrating interference by state officials that made compliance with the state procedural rule impracticable. *Coleman, 501 U.S. at 753*. The external impediment, whether it be government interference or the reasonable unavailability of the factual basis for the claim, must have prevented petitioner from constructing or raising the claim. *See Murray, 477 U.S. at 492*.

In this case, nothing prevented Petitioner from presenting Claim 34 during his initial PCR proceeding. Even though Petitioner argues that the trial court's interrelated failures made compliance with the state procedural rule impracticable, the sentencing record shows otherwise. Counsel submitted a sentencing memorandum specifically discussing that at the age of 9 and 12, Petitioner's IQ was tested, and that he recorded low IQ scores of 70 and 77 respectively. Counsel presented Petitioner's scores in the context of possible mental retardation and borderline intellectual functioning. Counsel's sentencing memorandum chronicled Petitioner's major difficulties progressing thru different grades in   school, and that at age 14, when he took the California Achievement Grade Point Test, he scored 3-4 grade levels below his schoolmates. Petitioner's presentence report also described him as below average intelligence and socially immature.

Based on this sentencing record, the trial court's actions did not keep Petitioner's low intelligence from being discovered, documented and further investigated as a mental health issue. Rather, counsel presented it as mitigation at sentencing. Counsel's presentation of Petitioner's low intelligence and possible mental retardation at sentencing put PCR counsel on notice that his mental health was at issue and warranted further investigation. PCR counsel was also on notice that Arizona required that all allegations of ineffective assistance be brought during the initial PCR proceeding. *Ariz. R. Crim. P. 32.5*. Where the petitioner had access to the information necessary to state the claim, the failure to develop and present the claim will not constitute cause. *See Murray, 477 U.S. at 486* (citing *Engle v. Isaac, 456 U.S. 107, 133-34, 102 S. Ct. 1558, 71 L. Ed. 2d 783 (1982)* ("the mere fact that counsel failed to recognize the factual   or legal basis for a claim, or failed to raise the claim despite recognizing it, does not constitute cause for a procedural default")). On this record, the trial court's alleged failures did not impede or prevent PCR counsel from complying with the state procedural rule.

Next, Petitioner alleges that Dr. McMahon's official interference establishes cause. Petitioner contends that Dr. McMahon was a state actor and that his inaccurate testing and reporting of Petitioner's IQ impeded PCR counsel from asserting Claim 34 at his initial PCR proceeding. (Doc. 215 at 10-12, 17-18.) Petitioner argues that because Dr. McMahon was authorized by the court, paid by the State to evaluate his mental health, and provide a report to the court, his actions are attributable to the state and constitute "official interference" if adverse to Petitioner. (*Id.* at 10.) The Court disagrees.

The Court need not decide whether Dr. McMahon was a state actor under these circumstances because there is no constitutional right implicated even if the State did provide an ineffective psychologist at sentencing for purposes of presenting mitigation. *See Harris v. Vasquez, 949 F.2d 1497, 1517-18 (9th Cir. 1991)* (rejecting   the argument that petitioner had a constitutional right to a competent mental health expert at trial or sentencing); *see also Coleman, 501 U.S. at 753* (stating that only when counsel is constitutionally required may attorney error constitute cause and be imputed to the State) Thus, any alleged misdiagnosis by Dr. McMahon regarding Petitioner cannot constitute cause.

Furthermore, Dr. McMahon's alleged failures did not impede or prevent PCR counsel from complying with the state procedural rule. As the Court has already discussed, the sentencing record gave PCR counsel notice that Petitioner's mental health was at issue and warranted additional investigation. Where the petitioner had access to the information necessary to state the claim, the failure to develop and present the claim will not constitute cause. *See Murray, 477 U.S. at 486.*

Petitioner relies on *Parkus v. Delo, 33 F.3d 933 (8th Cir. 1994)*, to argue that state officials prevented PCR counsel from raising Claim 34. In *Parkus*, the habeas petitioner had an extensive history as a mentally disturbed man who had been raised in state institutions since the age of four. *Id. at 934*. Trial counsel made a request for   his childhood mental health records, but was told by the records custodian that the records had been destroyed. *Id. at 936*. As a result, Parkus's mental health expert was unable to testify at trial or at sentencing that Parkus suffered from a mental disease or defect. *Id.* He was convicted of first-degree murder and received the death penalty. Parkus failed to raise an IAC claim during post-conviction proceedings. *Id. at 937*. During habeas proceedings, however, Parkus obtained his childhood mental health records (which had not, in fact, been destroyed) and, based on those records, his mental health expert submitted an affidavit attesting that Parkus suffered from a mental disease or defect. *Id. at 936*. Due to the missing mental health records, the court concluded that Parkus did not have notice of his trial counsel's ineffectiveness and therefore had adequate cause not to present the claim. *Id. at 938*. The Eighth Circuit decided that there was "some" official interference which made compliance with the procedural rule impracticable and ordered an evidentiary hearing. *Id. at 938-39.*

The lack of notice counsel had in *Parkus* is distinguishable from the facts at issue here. Unlike *Parkus*, in this case, there are no missing records. Based on the sentencing record, PCR counsel was on notice that Petitioner had two IQ tests documenting low intelligence and another test demonstrating he was behind his peers in educational development. PCR counsel was also on notice that the presentence report indicated that Petitioner displayed low intelligence and emotional immaturity. Even though Dr. McMahon reported that Petitioner was not mentally retarded, PCR counsel was still on notice of the contrast between Dr. McMahon's report and the low IQ scores being reported, as well as the mental health deficiencies counsel presented as mitigation at sentencing. PCR counsel was also on notice of his need to investigate mental health because in Arizona a "slow, dull and brain-damaged" mental impairment may have a significant mitigating effect as it may evidence an inability of the defendant to control his conduct. *See, e.g., Walton v. Arizona, 159 Ariz. 571, 588, 769 P.2d 1017, 1034 (1989)*. Thus, unlike in *Parkus*, there was no official interference preventing PCR counsel from obtaining the factual basis for an IAC sentencing claim for presentation during the PCR proceeding.

Petitioner also argues that *Perkins v. LeCureux, 58 F.3d 214, 218 (6th Cir. 1995)* supports his contention that PCR counsel did not have the factual basis to raise Claim 34 due to Dr. McMahon's report. In *Perkins*, a pre-AEDPA case, the court held that petitioner had cause to bring a new habeas claim in a successive petition because the facts underlying his new claim did not arise until years after his initial habeas proceeding had been concluded. *Perkins, 58 F.3d at 218*. Petitioner compares his case to *Perkins*, arguing that due to Dr. McMahon's misdiagnosis, the factual basis of Petitioner's mental retardation was unavailable to PCR counsel. The Court disagrees.

The availability of the factual basis of Claim 34 was established by the sentencing record. The sentencing record contained multiple records of low intelligence and possible mental retardation. These records put PCR counsel on notice that Petitioner's mental health warranted further investigation for possible IAC allegations during PCR proceedings. *See Williams v. Taylor, 529 U.S. 420, 438-39, 444, 120 S. Ct. 1479, 146 L. Ed. 2d 435 (2000)* (discussing the availability of a potential *Brady* claim since state habeas counsel was on notice of a psychiatric report, its possible materiality and the need for further investigation). *Perkins* is inapposite.

The Court concludes that neither the trial court's actions nor Dr. McMahon's report prevented PCR counsel from investigating and timely presenting Claim 34 during his initial PCR proceeding.

Ineffective Assistance of Sentencing Counsel

Next, Petitioner contends sentencing counsel's ineffectiveness constitutes cause to excuse the procedural default. Petitioner alleges that counsel was ineffective due to his failure to properly provide background information to Dr. McMahon prior to his psychological evaluation, which resulted in Dr. McMahon improperly concluding that Petitioner was not mentally retarded. Specifically, counsel should have provided Dr. McMahon with Petitioner's educational, vocational, and medical records prior to his evaluation.

Before ineffective assistance of counsel may be utilized as cause to excuse a procedural default, the particular ineffective assistance allegation must first be submitted and exhausted before the state courts as an independent claim. *See Murray, 477 U.S. at 489-90; Tacho, 862 F.2d at 1381*. A petitioner is not entitled to bring an ineffective assistance claim as cause to excuse a procedural default when that particular ineffective assistance allegation itself is defaulted. *See Edwards v. Carpenter, 529 U.S. 446, 451-53, 120 S. Ct. 1587, 146 L. Ed. 2d 518 (2000)*. Here, PCR counsel did not fairly present this particular IAC allegation in state court. Therefore, it cannot serve as cause to excuse the procedural default of Claim 34.

Inadequacy of Arizona's Post-Conviction Process/IAC of PCR Counsel

Alternatively, Petitioner argues cause to excuse his default because Arizona's post conviction process was inadequate to protect his rights due to its failure to ensure he was appointed competent counsel and because PCR counsel performed ineffectively.

Although Petitioner contends that Arizona's PCR process failed to ensure he was appointed competent counsel, Petitioner cites no case, and the Court has found none which holds that a state is required by the federal constitution to provide counsel in PCR proceedings. The fact that a state may, "as a matter of legislative choice," *Ross v. Moffitt, 417 U.S. 600, 618, 94 S. Ct. 2437, 41 L. Ed. 2d 341 (1974)*, provide for counsel in discretionary appeals following a first appeal of right does not extend the *Sixth Amendment's* guarantee of effective counsel to discretionary appeals. *See Evitts v. Lucey, 469 U.S. 387, 394, 397 n.7, 105 S. Ct. 830, 83 L. Ed. 2d 821 (1985); Pennsylvania v. Finley, 481 U.S. 551, 559, 107 S. Ct. 1990, 95 L. Ed. 2d 539 (1987)* (where a state provides a lawyer in a state post-conviction proceeding, it is not "the Federal Constitution [that] dictates the exact form such assistance must assume," rather, it is in a state's discretion to determine what protections to provide). Further, the Ninth Circuit has held explicitly that "ineffective assistance of counsel in [state] habeas corpus proceedings does not present an independent violation of the *Sixth Amendment* enforceable against the states through the *Due Process Clause of the Fourteenth Amendment." Bonin v. Calderon, 77 F.3d 1155, 1160 (9th Cir. 1996).* Since Petitioner's PCR proceeding took place after his appeal of right, it was a discretionary proceeding that did not confer a constitutional right to the effective assistance of counsel. Thus, even assuming that PCR counsel's performance did not conform to minimum standards, it did not violate the federal constitution and cannot excuse the procedural default.

As to Petitioner's argument that PCR counsel's ineffectiveness establishes   cause, IAC can represent sufficient cause only when it rises to the level of an independent constitutional violation. *Coleman, 501 U.S. at 755.* When a petitioner has no constitutional right to counsel, there can be no constitutional violation arising out of ineffectiveness of counsel. *Id. at 752.* There is no constitutional right to counsel in state PCR proceedings. *See Finley, 481 U.S. at 555; Murray v. Giarratano, 492 U.S. 1, 7-12, 109 S. Ct. 2765, 106 L. Ed. 2d 1 (1989)* (the Constitution does not require states to provide counsel in PCR proceedings even when the putative petitioners are facing the death penalty); *Bonin v. Vasquez, 999 F.2d 425, 429-30 (9th Cir. 1993)* (refusing to extend the right of effective assistance of counsel to state collateral proceedings).

In the context of IAC of PCR counsel, the Ninth Circuit has considered and rejected the argument that cause exists to excuse a procedural default where PCR counsel failed to assert a claim during PCR proceedings. *See Ortiz v. Stewart, 149 F.3d 923, 932 (9th Cir. 1998); Nevius v. Sumner, 105 F.3d 453, 460 (9th Cir. 1996); Moran v. McDaniel, 80 F.3d 1261, 1271 (9th Cir. 1996); Bonin, 77 F.3d at 1158-59.*[6] Therefore, PCR counsel's alleged ineffectiveness does   not constitute cause. *Manning v. Foster, 224 F.3d 1129 (9th Cir. 2000)* is not to the contrary. In *Manning*, the Ninth Circuit reiterated that the actions or omissions of PCR counsel cannot constitute cause to overcome a procedural default. *Id. at 1133* (stating that "any ineffectiveness of Manning's attorney in the post-conviction process is not considered cause for the purposes of excusing the procedural default at that stage"). In *Manning*, rather, the court held that where direct appeal counsel actually interfered with the petitioner's ability to initiate post-conviction proceedings, such conduct by constitutionally-entitled counsel may constitute cause to excuse a procedural default.

The Court has denied all of Petitioner's argument regarding cause. Because Petitioner has not established cause to excuse the procedural default, the Court need not analyze prejudice. *See Boyd v. Thompson, 147 F.3d 1124, 1127 (9th Cir.1998).*

Discovery

Petitioner contends that he has produced enough colorable evidence of cause to warrant discovery or an evidentiary hearing. Specifically, Petitioner requests discovery in support of his cause arguments: that sentencing counsel   failed to obtain and provide his necessary social history records to Dr. McMahon, the failure of the trial court to properly fund and timely appoint an independent mental health expert or mitigation specialist, Dr. McMahon's misleading diagnosis, the inadequacies of Arizona's post-conviction relief system, including funding limitations and the appointment of post conviction counsel. Petitioner also contends that he is entitled to conduct discovery regarding deceased PCR counsel, including his bar records, depositions of those who worked with him, and expert testimony on the duties of post-conviction counsel.

The Court first notes that Petitioner is not requesting discovery in the context of an exhausted claim. *See, e.g., Bracy v. Gramley, 520 U.S. 899, 117 S. Ct. 1793, 138 L. Ed. 2d 97 (1997)* (discussing good cause for discovery in the context of an exhausted claim). Rather, discovery is sought to support Petitioner's various contentions of cause to excuse the procedural default of Claim 34. However, to demonstrate cause, the petitioner must demonstrate some external factor external to the defense impeded his efforts to comply with the state procedural rule. *See Robinson v. Ignacio, 360 F.3d 1044, 1052 (9th Cir. 2004)*   (internal citation and quotation omitted). The Court has already considered and concluded that none of Petitioner's contentions constituted an external impediment that excused his failure to raise Claim 34 in a timely manner. Hence, Petitioner cannot justify his discovery requests as his cause contentions have been rejected. *See Campbell v. Blodgett, 997 F.2d 512, 524 (9th Cir. 1992)* (stating that an evidentiary hearing is not necessary to allow a petitioner to show cause and prejudice if the court determines as a matter of law that he cannot satisfy the standard). Therefore, Petitioner's requests for discovery are denied.

Fundamental Miscarriage of Justice

If a petitioner cannot meet the cause and prejudice standard, the Court still may hear the merits of procedurally defaulted claims if the failure to hear the claims would constitute a "fundamental miscarriage of justice." *Sawyer v. Whitley, 505 U.S. 333, 339, 112 S. Ct. 2514, 120 L. Ed. 2d 269 (1992)*. The fundamental miscarriage of justice exception is also known as the "actual innocence" exception. "[A] claim of actual innocence is not itself a constitutional claim, but instead a gateway through which a habeas petitioner must pass to have his otherwise barred constitutional claim considered on the merits." *Herrera v. Collins, 506 U.S. 390, 404, 113 S. Ct. 853, 122 L. Ed. 2d 203 (1993)*. There are two types of claims recognized under this exception: 1) that a petitioner is "innocent of the death sentence," or, in other words, that the death sentence was erroneously imposed; and 2) that a petitioner is actually innocent of the capital crime. *See Calderon v. Thompson, 523 U.S. 538, 559-60, 118 S. Ct. 1489, 140 L. Ed. 2d 728 (1998)*. To be innocent of the crime itself, the petitioner must show that "a constitutional violation has probably resulted in the conviction of one who is actually innocent[.]" *Schlup v. Delo, 513 U.S. 298, 327, 115 S. Ct. 851, 130 L. Ed. 2d 808 (1995)*. The requisite probability requires a showing "that it is more likely than not that no reasonable juror would have found petitioner guilty beyond a reasonable doubt." *Id.* To be innocent of a death sentence, the petitioner must show by clear and convincing evidence that, but for a constitutional error, no reasonable juror would have found the existence of an aggravating circumstance or some other condition of eligibility for the death sentence under the applicable state law. *Sawyer, 505 U.S. at 336, 345.* Under this standard, a showing of actual innocence refers to those state-law requirements that must be satisfied to impose the death penalty. *Id. at 348.*

In *Atkins, 536 U.S. 304, 122 S. Ct. 2242, 153 L. Ed. 2d 335*, the Supreme Court altered the death penalty landscape by prohibiting states from sentencing to death or executing a mentally retarded person. The *Atkins* Court specifically reserved to the states how mental retardation would be defined and proven. *536 U.S. at 317; State v. Grell, 212 Ariz. 516, 521, 135 P.3d 696, 701 (2006).* In the context of a fundamental miscarriage of justice challenge, clear and convincing proof that the petitioner is mentally retarded under state law forecloses a condition of eligibility for imposition or continued imposition of a death sentence. *See Sasser v. Norris, 553 F.3d 1121, 1126 n.4 (8th Cir. 2009)* (applying Arkansas law and stating that a petitioner is "actually innocent" and thus ineligible for the death penalty where he demonstrates that he is mentally retarded).

Actual Innocence of the Death Penalty

Petitioner contends that his mental retardation renders him ineligible and actually innocent of the death penalty. Because fundamental miscarriage of justice is a federal issue, Petitioner contends that this Court is not bound by the fact finding or the disposition of his *Atkins* hearing in state court that he is not mentally retarded. On the other hand, Petitioner concedes that determining actual innocence of the death penalty is determined by reference to Arizona law.

Both state and federal law are involved in this Court's fundamental miscarriage of justice analysis. Under *Sawyer*, innocence of the death penalty requires a proper showing by petitioner that he does not meet some condition of eligibility for the death penalty under state law. *Sawyer, 505 U.S. at 345.* Under *Atkins*, it is up to the states to develop "appropriate ways to enforce the constitutional restriction" upon the execution of the mentally retarded. *Atkins, 536 U.S. at 317.* Thus, both *Sawyer* and *Atkins* point this Court to state law to determine as a condition for eligibility of the death penalty whether Petitioner is mentally retarded. Yet, it is under *Sawyer* that this Court evaluates, based on the state court record, whether Petitioner has demonstrated that he is mentally retarded. *See Sawyer, 505 U.S. at 348; Winston v. Kelly, 600 F.Supp.2d 717, 735-36 (W.D. Va. 2009), vacated and remanded on other grounds, 592 F.3d 535 (4th Cir. 2010)* (evaluating whether petitioner demonstrated that was actually innocent of the death penalty due to mental retardation in the context of the fundamental miscarriage of justice exception). Under *Sawyer*, the Court is not undertaking a *de novo* review of Petitioner's *Atkins* hearing; rather, the Court is undertaking a limited review of the record to assess whether Petitioner demonstrated by clear and convincing evidence that no reasonable factfinder would have determined that he is not mentally retarded.

Arizona's Mental Retardation Statute

In Arizona, similar to *Sawyer's* burden of proof, the statutory scheme requires that the petitioner prove mental retardation to the trial court by clear and convincing evidence. *Grell, 212 Ariz. at 524, 135 P.3d at 704* (concluding that Arizona's burden of proof is not unconstitutional); *A.R.S. § 13-703.02(G) (West 2005)*. Under Arizona law, a petitioner establishes mental retardation by proving that he meets the statutory definition, which is "a mental deficit that involves significantly subaverage general intellectual functioning, existing concurrently with significant impairment in adaptive behavior, where the onset of the foregoing conditions occurred before the [petitioner] reached the age of eighteen." *A.R.S. § 13-703.02(K)(2)*. To establish mental retardation, a petitioner must prove all three elements, the intellectual functioning prong, the adaptive behavior prong, and onset before the age of eighteen. *See State v. Roque, 213 Ariz. 193, 227-28, 141 P.3d 368, 402-03 (2006)*. Arizona's current statute for mental evaluations for capital defendants is codified at *A.R.S. § 13-753*.

Under the intellectual functioning prong, "'[s]ignificantly subaverage general intellectual functioning' means a full scale intelligence quotient of seventy or lower." *A.R.S. § 13-703.02(K)(4)*. The court is further directed to "take into account the margin of error for the test administered." *Id*. In *Roque*, the Arizona Supreme Court reiterated that the statute does not refer to individual IQ sub-tests, but rather employs a single intelligence quotient, the full scale IQ score. *Roque, 213 Ariz. at 228, 141 P.3d at 403*. Because mental retardation is generally a static mental condition, full scale IQ testing is relevant both before and after the age of eighteen. *State v. Arellano, 213 Ariz. 474, 479-80, 143 P.3d 1015, 1020-21 (2006)*.

The standard error of measurement means that an IQ score can overestimate or underestimate a person's true level of intellectual functioning. *See Ledford v. Head, No. 02-CV-1515, 2008 U.S. Dist. LEXIS 21635, 2008 WL 754486 at *8 (N.D. Ga. March 19, 2008)*. However, it may be speculative to conclude that IQ scores receive either a downward adjustment or an upward adjustment. *See Walton v. Johnson, 440 F.3d 160, 178 (4th Cir. 2006)* (noting that petitioner could only speculate that the standard error of measurement would lower his IQ score). Moreover, measurement error is more of a factor when only one IQ test is given. *See Ledford, 2008 U.S. Dist. LEXIS 21635, 2008 WL 754486 at *8*. When more than one IQ test is given and the scores corroborate each other, the possibility of measurement error is substantially reduced. *Id*.

Under the adaptive behavior prong, the statute requires an overall assessment of the petitioner's ability to meet society's expectations of him; it does not require a finding of mental retardation based solely on proof of specific deficits in only a couple of areas. *Grell, 212 Ariz. at 529, 135 P.3d at 709*. The statute defines adaptive behavior as "the effectiveness or degree to which the defendant meets the standards of personal independence and social responsibility expected of the defendant's age and cultural group." *A.R.S. § 13-703.02(K)(1)*. In *Arellano, 213 Ariz. at 478-80, 143 P.3d at 1019-21*, the Arizona Supreme Court clarified that behavior after age eighteen is relevant to the adaptive behavior inquiry, even if the behavior under review comes from within a prison context. In *Arellano*, the court reversed a trial court ruling precluding Arizona Department of Correction officials from testifying at a mental retardation hearing regarding the petitioner's present adaptive behavior in prison. *Id. at 480, 143 P.3d at 1021*. In *Grell*, the court reiterated that the statute requires a showing of current impairment in adaptive ability and that an assessment based on recent interviews is persuasive. *Grell, 212 Ariz. at 527-28, 135 P.3d at 707-08*. Finally, the statute requires the onset of mental retardation to occur before the age of eighteen. *A.R.S. § 13-703.02(K)(2)*.

Petitioner's Atkins Proceeding

In support of his claim of innocence of the death penalty, Petitioner filed numerous exhibits from his 2005 *Atkins* proceeding where he sought post-conviction relief.

In 2005, Petitioner filed a successive PCR petition alleging that he is mentally retarded. He supported his petition with scores from two full scale IQ tests given to him at school, where his IQ was reported at 70 and 77. Petitioner also attached to his petition a declaration from Dr. Ricardo Weinstein, Ph.D., a psychologist who opined that he was mentally retarded.

Under the statute, if a petitioner's IQ is tested at 75 or less, the court appoints additional experts to eval-uate the petitioner and will hold a subsequent hearing to determine whether petitioner is mentally retarded. *See A.R.S. § 13-703.02(D), (G); State ex rel Thomas v. Duncan, 222 Ariz. 448, 451, 216 P.3d 1194, 1197 (App. 2009).* In a post-trial evaluation of mental retardation, each party selects one psychological expert to evaluate and report to the court their findings on whether the petitioner is mentally retarded. *See A.R.S. § 13-703.02(D); State v. Canez, 205 Ariz. 620, 626, 74 P.3d 932, 938 (2003)* (because the statutory procedures focus on a pre-trial mental retardation evaluation, in a post-trial setting, courts utilize the statutory proce-dures as applicable). In addition, the statute allows appointment of a third psychologist, appointed   on be-half of the court, not the state or the petitioner. The PCR court appointed Dr. Ricardo Weinstein for Petition-er, Dr. Sergio Martinez for the State and Dr. John Toma, on behalf of the court.

On November 25, 2005, Dr. Toma submitted his report to the court. (*Id.* at 1875-1884.) Regarding intel-lectual functioning, Dr. Toma administered the Wechsler Adult Intelligence Scales-Third Edition ("WAIS III") to Petitioner on November 9, 2005. Petitioner's full scale IQ for the test was 77. Regarding adaptive behavior, Dr. Toma used the Adaptive Behavior Scale--Residential and Community: Second Edition ("ABS-RC:2"). Dr. Toma reviewed all of Petitioner's childhood records but also focused on Petitioner's current level of functioning and concluded that he showed no significant deficits in adaptive functioning. Dr. Toma concluded that Petitioner did not meet the statutory definition for mental retardation.

On January 20, 2006, Dr. Martinez submitted his report to the court. Regarding intellectual functioning, Dr. Martinez administered WAIS III to Petitioner on January 11, 2006, reporting   a full scale IQ score of 87. Dr. Martinez also administered the Reynolds Intellectual Assessment Scales ("RIAS") to Petitioner, with a score of 91. Regarding adaptive behavior, Dr. Martinez utilized the Adaptive Behavior Assessment System-II ("ABAS-II"). (*Id.* at 2405.) Based on Petitioner's self-report and an extensive review of background materials, Dr. Martinez concluded that Petitioner demonstrated low average scores, not significant impairment scores in adaptive functioning testing. Dr. Martinez concluded that Petitioner did not meet the statutory definition of mental retardation.

On February 14, 2006, Dr. Weinstein submitted his report to the court. Regarding intellectual functioning, Dr. Weinstein administered the WAIS III to Petitioner on July 29, 2004, with a full scale IQ score of 70. On No-vember 11, 2004, Dr. Weinstein administered the Woodcock-Johnson Intelligence Test-Third Edition (W-J III) to Petitioner, with a full scale IQ score of 71. Dr. Weinstein also reported that Petitioner's two school-age IQ tests utilized the Wechsler Intelligence Scale for Children   ("WISC"), scoring a 70 in 1967 and a 77 in 1969. Dr. Weinstein also utilized the ABAS-II to evaluate adaptive behavior. Dr. Weinstein had Richard Garcia, Peti-tioner's step-father, rate Petitioner's adaptive behavior utilizing the ABAS-II. Dr. Weinstein identified a num-ber of childhood adaptive behavior deficits based upon other interviews and declarations from Petitioner's family and friends regarding his formative years. Dr. Weinstein identified deficits in conceptual, social, and practical adaptive behavior skills. Additionally, he found deficits in Petitioner performing major activities for daily living. Dr. Weinstein concluded that Petitioner met the statutory definition of mental retardation.

Although not appointed by the court, on February 24, 2006, Dr. Marc Tasse, a recognized mental retarda-tion expert, submitted a report on behalf of Petitioner. Dr. Tasse did not administer an IQ test to Petitioner, but reviewed the intelligence testing that had been done. Dr. Tasse opined that the RIAS test utilized by Dr. Martinez was unreliable, that there would be a significant   practice effect on the last WAIS III test adminis-tered by Dr. Martinez due to the short eight week duration between the last time that Petitioner had taken the same test, and that when all scores are adjusted for the "Flynn Effect," Petitioner meets the statutory definition of significant subaverage intellectual functioning. Dr. Tasse utilized the ABAS II to administer an adaptive behavior test to Petitioner. Dr. Tasse concluded that Petitioner was significantly impaired in adaptive functioning, with onset before the age of eighteen. Finally, Dr. Tasse concluded that Petitioner was mentally retarded under the statutory definition.   According to the Flynn Effect theory, the passage of time inflates full scale IQ test scores by approximately one-third to two-thirds of a point per year since the normalization of the particular test in question. The premise of the Flynn Effect theory is that IQ tests that are not renormed to take rising IQ scores into account will overstate a test taker's score. Once calculated, these amounts are subtracted from the full scale IQ score before applying the standard margin of error. *See, e.g.,* *In re Salazar, 443 F.3d 430, 433 (5th Cir. 2006).*

The PCR court conducted an eight-day evidentiary hearing. Dr. Weinstein and Dr. Tasse testified on behalf of Petitioner. Dr. Martinez testified for the State, and Dr. Toma testified on behalf of the court. The following persons also testified, Petitioner's Aunt, Eloise Arce, and Phoenix School District Psychologists Sidney Wilson and Gloria McConkey. Petitioner formally waived his right to be present at the hearing before the PCR court.

Intellectual Functioning

At the hearing, the experts testified that the WAIS III was the most widely used IQ test. The third edition of the test is a 1997 revision of the second edition. It is an individually administered test designed to assess the intelligence of individuals ranging in age from 16 to 89 years. Three experts tested Petitioner utilizing the WAIS III. Dr. Tasse testified that it was appropriate to adjust the WAIS III administered by Dr. Martinez by five points downward due to practice effect because he administered the test to Petitioner within one year of the previous time that WAIS III was administered. Dr. Martinez alternatively administered the RAIS, but Dr. Tasse discounted its use because it is a fairly new test and not as comprehensive as WAIS III. Dr. Tasse testified that the following full scale IQ scores were valid: 70, 77, 70, 71, 77 and 82 (after receiving the five point reduction for practice effect).

The PCR court throughly reviewed and discussed the evidence regarding the intellectual functioning prong, as follows:

> Full Scale I.Q. Testing   The Defendant has failed to establish by clear and convincing evidence or by a preponderance of the evidence that he suffers from "significantly sub average general intellectual functioning" which means a "full scale intelligence quotient (IQ) of seventy or lower." A.R.S. § 13-703.02(G), (K)(2) & (4).
>
> Beginning in February of 1967, when he was 9 years of age, through January of 2006, when he was 38 years of age, the Defendant has been given six full-scale IQ tests, as well as several less thorough IQ tests. The six tests included two WISC tests, a Woodcock-Johnson, 3rd edition test (W-J III) and three WAIS III tests. In each test, except for the WAIS-III test administered by Dr. Martinez on January 11, 2006, where the practice effect skewed and raised the score to 87, the Defendant's IQ was determined to be 70, 77, 70, 71 and 77. . . . Applying the accepted "margin of error for the tests administered," it is 95 percent certain that the Defendant's full scale IQ is within the range of 63 to 82. This consistency in IQ test scores over [more than a] 38 year period of time, especially on the "gold standard" WISC and WAIS III tests, compels the conclusion that the Defendant has failed to establish by clear and convincing evidence or by a preponderance of the evidence that his IQ is 70 or lower. The court agrees with Dr. Marc Tasse that these tests were properly administered and scored.
>
> DFlynn Effect:
>
> Though it has considered the "Flynn Effect" in determining the defendant's IQ, the Court is not persuaded that it is required to apply it to adjust downward each of the six full scale test IQ scores for alleged test obsolescence. See exhibits 223 and 210, where the Flynn Effect is and is not applied to the various IQ test scores. As shown by Exhibit 223, the defendant's expert, Dr. Marc Tasse, applies the Flynn Effect, as well as the practice effect to the January 11, 2006 test, in finding that the Defendant's IQ is 70 or lower (these Flynn Effect adjusted scores are 64, 70, 69, 74 and 78 respectively). Although the 2005 AAMR User's Guide, Exhibit 59, directs that the Flynn Effect, standard error of measurement and practice effect, all be used when scoring the WAIS-III test to determine a person's IQ, the Court concludes that use of the Flynn Effect is not mandated by the statute and is not part of the "current community, nationally, and culturally accepted . . . psychological and intelligence testing procedures" that must be used when scoring all full scale IQ tests. A.R.S. § 13-703.02(E)   . Although the Flynn Effect was widely known when A.R.S. § 13-703.02 was enacted in 2001, and when *Atkins* was decided in 2002, it was not adopted or discussed by either. Recently, some appellate courts have directed that the trial court consider it

when determining a person's IQ, *Green v. Johnson, [No. CIVA 2:05CV340, 2006 U.S. Dist. LEXIS 90644, 2006 WL 3746138 (E.D. Va. Dec. 15, 2006)]; Walton v. Johnson, 440 F.3d 160, 176-178 (4th Cir. 2006)* and *Walker v. True, 399 F.3d [3]15, 322-328 (4th Cir. 2005)*, while other courts have rejected its application absent statutory authorization. *See Bowling v. Kentucky, 163 S.W.3d 361, 375 (2005)* and cases cited therein.

In fact, Dr. Weinstein, a defense expert, did not adjust the full-scale IQ score for the Flynn Effect in his 2004 Declaration and in his 2006 report to the court. In addition, Dr. Toma, the court-appointed expert, did not use the Flynn Effect in scoring his testing of the defendant and testified that such was not required for those tests.

In addition, the Flynn Effect is not part of the "margin of error . . ." calculation that *A.R.S. § 13-703.02(K)(4)* and the current WAIS Scoring Manual require to be used in scoring the WAIS-III tests administered in 2004, 2005 and 2006, and was not used when the WISC tests were given to the Defendant as a child in 1967 and 1969. Instead the manual merely directs that a standard error of measurement of ± 7 be applied in scoring the 1967 and 1969 WISC tests, and that a standard error of measurement of ± 5 be applied for W[AIS]-III tests given in 2004, 2005 and 2006.

In sum, the defendant has failed to show by clear and convincing evidence or a preponderance of evidence that he possesses "significant sub average general intellectual functioning," as defined and required by *A.R.S. § 13-703.02(G) & (K)(2) & (4)*. If the Flynn Effect was required to be used in scoring these tests, the court finds that the defendant has proved by a preponderance of the evidence that his full scale IQ is 70 or lower.

Intellectual Functioning Discussion

Under *Sawyer*, the Court's limited review is to assess whether Petitioner demonstrated by clear and convincing evidence that no reasonable fact finder would have determined that he is not mentally retarded. According to Dr. Tasse's testimony at the evidentiary hearing, there were six valid full scale IQ scores posted for Petitioner, 70, 77, 70, 71, 77 and 82. (*Id.* at 5250-51.) These full scale IQ scores are represented in the following chart.

Date of Administration	IQ Test and Administrator	Results Obtained
2/14/1967	WISC (Wilson)	FSIQ = 70
10/6/1969	WISC (McConkey)	FSIQ = 77
7/29/2004	WAIS-III (Weinstein)	FSIQ = 70
11/11/2004	W-J III (Weinstein)	GIA = 71
11/9/2005	WAIS-III (Toma)	FSIQ = 77
1/11/2006	WAIS-III (Martinez)	FSIQ = 82 (after 5 point deduction)

Date of Administration	Standard Margin of Error
2/14/1967	63 to 77
10/6/1969	70 to 84
7/29/2004	65 to 75
11/11/2004	67 to 75
11/9/2005	72 to 82
1/11/2006	77 to 87

The PCR court utilized the following margin of error calculations for the IQ tests--a standard error of measurement of ± 7 for scoring the 1967 and 1969 WISC tests, and a standard error of measurement of ± 5 for scoring the WAIS III tests. Excluding any correction for the alleged Flynn Effect, Dr. Tasse testified that the margin of error range for the WJ-III test was 67 to 75.

Based on the evidence, Petitioner had two full scale IQ scores that met the statutory requirement for mental retardation and four scores that did not meet the statutory requirement. A reasonable factfinder could easily find Petitioner's four IQ scores over 70 more persuasive than his two scores of 70 or below. *See Winston, 600 F. Supp.2d at 736* (concluding that the petitioner failed to establish mental retardation in the context of a fundamental miscarriage of justice inquiry because his three scores over 70 were more persuasive than his one score below 70).

When accounting for margin of error, as this Court has already noted, it is necessarily speculative to conclude that Petitioner's IQ scores should receive either a downward adjustment or an upward adjustment. *See Walton, 440 F.3d at 178* (stating that petitioner could only speculate that the standard error of measurement would lower his IQ score); *see also Winston, 600 F. Supp.2d at 729* ("there is no basis in practice for using [standard error of measurement] to find that an individual's true IQ falls in the range below the earned score on a given IQ test because it was equally likely that the test-taker's true IQ could fall in the range above the earned score."). In review of Dr. Tasse's testimony he made the same point at the evidentiary hearing. During cross-examination about Petitioner's IQ score on WJ-III, Dr. Tasse reiterated his contention that Petitioner's full scale IQ score of 71 should be adjusted downward for the Flynn Effect to 69. Dr. Tasse was then questioned about margin of error and its effect on Petitioner's IQ score.

> **State's Attorney**: This test doesn't establish that his IQ falls below 70?
>
> **Dr Tasse**: Yes, it does, in my opinion. . . . The Woodcock-Johnson III, it established his IQ is below 70.
>
> **State's Attorney**: The range is 65 to 74; correct?
>
> **Dr. Tasse**: Yes.
>
> **State's Attorney**: Okay. Explain your position?
>
> **Dr. Tasse**: The GIA is 69; that is below 70.

Based on the testimony of Petitioner's own expert, Dr. Tasse agreed with what this Court previously recognized--that the most important number in the range is the earned full scale IQ score. A reasonable factfinder could reject the factual assertion that Petitioner's full scale IQ scores should be adjusted downward based on standard margin of error. *See Winston, 600 F. Supp.2d at 736.*

Petitioner contends, however, that the Court should disregard the state court's conclusion regarding the Flynn Effect, utilize it to adjust downward his full scale IQ scores, and conclude that he has adequately proven mental retardation.

Dr. Tasse indicated that there were six valid full scale IQ scores posted for Petitioner, 70, 77, 70, 71, 77 and 82. (*Id.* at 5250-51.) According to Dr. Tasse, the full scale IQ scores should be further reduced for the Flynn Effect, recommending the six scores be reduced to, 64, 70, 69, 67, 74 and 78. Drs. Toma and Martinez disagreed with Dr. Tasse's testimony regarding whether the Flynn Effect should be applied to reduce individual full scale IQ scores. Drs. Toma and Martinez both testified that it is not their clinical practice to reduce full scale IQ scores for the Flynn Effect.

For a number of reasons, the Court concludes that there is fair support in the record not to factor in the Flynn Effect to reduce Petitioner's full scale IQ scores. First, Arizona's mental retardation statute does not indicate that the Flynn Effect should be applied to full scale IQ scores. Second, there is no Arizona precedent indicating that the Flynn Effect should be applied. Third, in Dr. Tasse's testimony, he conceded that the WAIS III administrative manual does not recommend deducting points from an IQ test to factor in for the Flynn Effect. Fourth, the experts at the hearing did not all agree that individual IQ scores should be adjusted downward for the Flynn Effect. Finally, other courts have arrived at the same conclusion that the Flynn Effect need not be factored in to reduce a full scale IQ score. *See, e.g., Winston, 600 F. Supp.2d at 736* (stating that a reasonable factfinder could reject the factual assertion that full scale IQ scores should be adjusted downward for the Flynn Effect).

Under *Sawyer*, Petitioner has failed to establish by clear and convincing evidence that no reasonable fact-finder would have determined that his full scale IQ is not 70 or lower.   Therefore, he has failed to establish the significant subaverage general intellectual functioning prong of the mental retardation statute. *See A.R.S. § 13-703.02(K)(2)*. Even though Petitioner must establish all three prongs of the statute in order to be found mentally retarded, the Court will proceed to discuss the adaptive behavior prong and onset before age 18.

Adaptive Behavior

In Petitioner's fundamental miscarriage of justice arguments, although he generally alleged that his mental retardation renders him actually innocent of the death penalty, his only specific argument regarding adaptive behavior was that neither Dr. Toma nor Dr. Martinez utilized established diagnostic methods to assess adaptive behavior.

The PCR court throughly reviewed and discussed the evidence regarding Petitioner's adaptive behavior, as follows.

> The court further finds that the Defendant has proved by a preponderance of the evidence, but not by clear and convincing evidence, that throughout his childhood and adult life he has suffered from significant impairment in adaptive behavior in meeting the standards of personal independence and social responsibility expected of a person of his   age and cultural group. *A.R.S. 13-703.02(K)(1)*. All experts agreed that the AAMR [American Association on Mental Retardation] Users Guide, 2002 edition, provides the "current community, nationally, and culturally accepted...procedure"for evaluating a person's adaptive behavior, as required by *A.R.S. 13-703.02(E)*. In essence, this requires that the experts investigate and determine a defendant's conceptual, social and practical adaptive behavior and skills in the context of his or her behavior in the community. However, the court can also consider a defendant's institutional behavior in determining whether he has significant adaptive behavior deficits. *See State v. Arellano (Appelt) [sic], 213 Ariz. 474, PP 14-23 (2006)*, where the court held that, pursuant to *A.R.S. 13-703.02(K)*, the trial court has the discretion to consider defendant's adult institutional behavior, including his communication, social and interpersonal skills, and work, leisure and health habits, in determining the existence of adaptive behavior deficits. This behavior is especially relevant in this case, where the defendant has spent nearly his entire his adult life in prison before and after he committed these murders in 1989. Finally, the experts agree that the Adaptive Behavior Assessment System, 2d edition, (ABAS-II) test is the most appropriate and accepted formal assessment tool for determining whether the Defendant has significant adaptive behavior deficits.

> Viewed in this context, the Court agrees in part with the findings of Drs. Weinstein and Tasse, that the Defendant has significant adaptive behavior deficits as defined by *A.R.S. 13-703.02(K)(1)*, particularly in the area of conceptual, social, and practical skills. As detailed in their reports and testimony, both experts investigated all aspects of the defendant's life before and after turning 18 years of age, including his institutional behavior. In addition to reviewing the testimony of the mitigation witnesses at the 1990 aggravation and mitigation hearing, they also interviewed several family members who were close to the Defendant in his formative years when he grew up in Phoenix and in southern California. They also considered sworn declarations from individuals who were familiar with the Defendant's behavior in non-institutional and institutional settings. The defendant also presented the testimony of Eloise Arce, an aunt who cared   for him for about 18 months until age three and who also observed him in his youth, about his maladaptive conduct during his childhood years in Phoenix. This information confirmed, as detailed in the testimony and reports of Drs. Weinstein and Tasse, that although the Defendant as a young boy was a good care giver to his younger siblings in the absence of their alcoholic mother, he showed many symptoms of very slow and delayed development of conceptual, social and practical skills. Finally, Dr. Tasse, unlike Drs. Toma and Martinez, correctly administered the ABAS-II test, the most appropriate adaptive behavior test, to the Defendant and Richard Garcia, his stepfather from approximately 1966 to 1973. This test, together with the

independent evidence of the defendant's non-institutional behavior, establishes probable cause to believe that since childhood the Defendant has displayed significant adaptive behavior impairments in conceptual, social and practical skills.

The Court is unable to conclude, however, that there is clear and convincing evidence that the defendant has significant adaptive behavior deficits. A more complete picture of his conduct in his formative years as a child   and teenager, as well as his conduct in prison over nearly all of the last twenty-six years, shows that the defendant has regularly shown adequate personal independence and social responsibility expected of a person of his age and cultural group, including proper conceptual, social and practical skills. In contrast to numerous hearsay declarations of Richard Garcia and others, and the somewhat conflicting and unreliable testimony of Eloise Arce about certain adaptive behavior deficits of the defendant, the testimony at the October 19, 1990 and November 30, 1990 sentencing mitigation hearing of Erlinda Martinez, his aunt and the sister of the defendant's mother, and of two of the defendant's immediately younger sisters, shows that when the defendant grew up in Phoenix he exercised personal independence and proper conceptual, social and practical skills for a person of his age and cultural group. Before he became a teenager, and in the frequent absence of his alcoholic mother, he was described as the "man of the family," who did most of the cooking, cleaning and caring for his younger siblings. In addition, they attributed his poor school performance and being "kept back" in school   to his frequently missing school and constantly changing schools due to his mother being regularly on the move around Phoenix. This nomadic existence is corroborated by the school records and Joint Chronology timeline submitted by the parties, which shows that over a seven-year time frame from September of 1963 to September of 1970, the defendant attended at least ten different schools, was regularly absent and was twice held back. Most of the critical fact witnesses relied on by the defendant's experts were not called to testify and thus not subjected to cross-examination.

In 1971, at approximately the age 14, the defendant moved to El Monte, California with his mother and her husband, Richard Garcia. Three years later the defendant and his mother returned to Arizona without Richard. The defendant then married and fathered two sons, and was gainfully employed as a cook and dishwasher at various locations before being sent to prison for the first time in April of 1979.

The defendant's conduct in prison, where he has been since April of 1979 except for only two short periods of release, further compels the conclusion that the defendant has failed to show by clearing [sic] and convincing   evidence that he has significant adaptive behavior deficits. Department of Corrections officers who supervised the defendant from 1987 to 1989 at Florence, testified that the defendant worked as a porter in the officers dining room and prepared and served food to DOC officers. His supervisors described him as a self-starter, who was polite, acted with responsibility, and was trusted and skilled. At one point, he was promoted and put in charge of running the morning shift at the dining room.

In concluding that the defendant has failed to show by clear and convincing evidence that he has significant adaptive behavior deficits, the court agrees with Dr. Toma's opinion that the defendant does not suffer from significant adaptive behavior deficits and that as an adult the defendant has consistently displayed the ability to engage in independent and self-directed thinking, planning and conduct. Although Dr. Toma did not fully administer the ABAS-II test to formally determine if the defendant had significant impairment in adaptive behavior, his opinion is credible because it is based on numerous contacts with the defendant during interviews and I.Q. testing, and his evaluation of the defendant's   well documented conduct during nearly 26 years in prison from 1979 to 1989 and then from 1991 to 2006.   This conduct is portrayed in the voluminous prison and inmate records he reviewed, exhibits 138-209 not in evidence.

In sum, although the conflicting evidence shows by a preponderance of the evidence that the defendant has significant adaptive behavior deficits, the court is unable to conclude that the evidence of these deficits is clear and convincing.

Adaptive Behavior Discussion

The Court's limited *Sawyer* review evaluates whether Petitioner established by clear and convincing evidence that no reasonable factfinder would have determined that he lacks significant adaptive behavior deficits. In *Apelt, 213 Ariz. at 478-80, 143 P.3d at 1019-21*, the Arizona Supreme Court clarified that it is proper to consider a petitioner's institutional behavior in determining whether he has significant adaptive behavior deficits. Further, the controlling statute defines mental retardation as including current impairment in adaptive ability. *See A.R.S. § 13-703.02(K); Grell, 212 Ariz. at 527, 135 P.3d at 707.*

Dr. Toma concluded, based on his interview with Petitioner, and his review of Petitioner's institutional records as well as childhood records, that Petitioner does not have significant adaptive behavior deficits. Dr. Toma further concluded that as an adult Petitioner had consistently displayed the ability to engage in independent, self directed thinking, citing his ability to utilize the prison library, maintaining correspondence with pen pals, defending his rights in prison based on prison regulations, dealing with monies in his prison account, and other various correspondence with the prison. Dr. Martinez concluded, based on a current interview and assessment of Petitioner's adaptive behavior, that Petitioner did not have significant adaptive behavior deficits. In contrast, both Dr. Tasse and Dr. Weinstein focused on Petitioner formative and early teen-age years in concluding that he did have significant adaptive behavior deficits.

The PCR court reviewed all of the evidence taken from the *Atkins* hearing and from Petitioner's mitigation hearing prior to sentencing and concluded that Petitioner did not have significant adaptive behavior deficits. Based on this evidence, a reasonable fact finder could conclude that Petitioner does not currently have significant adaptive behavior deficits. *See Winston, 600 F. Supp.2d at 736* (concluding that Petitioner failed to establish adaptive behavior deficits due in part to differing expert testimony).

Petitioner's main argument against this conclusion is that neither Dr. Toma nor Dr. Martinez utilized established diagnostic methods to assess his adaptive behavior. Petitioner is referring to Dr. Toma utilizing an adaptive behavior scale that was not specifically designed to assess mental retardation and Dr. Martinez, although properly utilizing the ABAS-II, only relying on Petitioner's self report of his adaptive behavior, and not conducting independent interviews dating back to Petitioner's non-institutional behavior.

The PCR court reviewed this contention and discounted the opinions of Drs. Toma and Martinez regarding Petitioner's pre-institutional adaptive behavior. Citing agreement with the reports of Drs. Weinstein and Tasse, the court found that Petitioner, in his formative years as a child and teenager displayed significant adaptive behavior deficits. (*Id.*) However, under the statute, adaptive behavior is measured by an overall assessment of the Petitioner's abilities; it is not based only on administration of adaptive behavior scales. *See Grell, 212 Ariz. at 529, 135 P.3d at 709*. The *Grell* court also emphasized that the statute defines mental retardation as including current impairment in adaptive ability. *Id. at 527, 135 P.3d at 707* (stating that assessments based on recent interviews of the petitioner are persuasive).

After reviewing all of the adaptive behavior evidence, both pre-institutional and institutional behavior, Dr. Toma and Dr. Martinez concluded that Petitioner did not currently have significant adaptive behavior deficits. Concurring, the court concluded that "as an adult the [petitioner] has consistently displayed the ability to engage in independent and self-directed thinking, planning, and conduct." After reviewing all of this evidence, under *Sawyer*, Petitioner has failed to establish by clear and convincing evidence that no reasonable fact finder would have determined that he lacks significant adaptive behavior deficits. Petitioner raised no argument regarding the statutory requirement that onset of adaptive behavior deficits occur before the age of eighteen. The PCR court concluded that Petitioner established by a preponderance of the evidence that onset of adaptive behavior deficits occurred before he reached the age of eighteen, citing *A.R.S. § 13-703.02(K)(2).* (Doc. 228 at 3833.)

Conclusion

Under *Sawyer*, Petitioner cannot demonstrate that no reasonable juror would have found him ineligible for the death penalty due to his mental retardation. Accordingly, his claim of actual innocence of the death penalty cannot excuse the procedural default of Claim 34.

Actual Innocence of the Capital Crime

Petitioner argues that a fundamental miscarriage of justice will occur if Claim 34 is not resolved on the merits because he is actually innocent of the capital crime due to new evidence of brain damage demonstrating that he would be unable to premeditate, an essential element of his first degree murder charge.

In *Schlup*, the Court discussed the fundamental miscarriage of justice exception in the context of a claim of actual innocence of the capital crime. *513 U.S. at 324-27.* In *Schlup*, the petitioner accompanied his actual innocence evidence with an assertion of constitutional error at trial. *Id. at 315.* The *Schlup* Court ruled that if a petitioner "presents evidence of innocence so strong that a court cannot have confidence in the outcome of the trial unless the court is also satisfied that the trial was free of nonharmless constitutional error, the petitioner should be allowed to pass through the gateway and argue the merits of his underlying claims." *Id. at 316.* To establish the requisite probability, the petitioner must prove with "new reliable evidence" that "it is more likely than not that no reasonable juror would have found petitioner guilty beyond a reasonable doubt." *Id. at 324, 327.*

However, even if Petitioner does have new evidence indicative of brain damage, "Arizona does not allow evidence of a defendant's mental disorder short of insanity either as an affirmative defense or to negate the *mens rea* element of a crime." *State v. Mott, 187 Ariz. 536, 541, 931 P.2d 1046, 1051 (1997).* A defendant cannot present evidence of mental disease or defect to show that he was *incapable* of forming a requisite mental state for a charged offense. *Id. at 540, 931 P.2d at 1050;* see *Clark v. Arizona, 548 U.S. 735, 126 S. Ct. 2709, 165 L. Ed. 2d 842 (2006)* (upholding the constitutionality of the *Mott* rule and finding that the exclusion of expert testimony regarding diminished capacity does not violate due process); *see also Cook v. Schriro, 538 F.3d 1000, 1029 (9th Cir. 2008)* (holding that in the context of a fundamental miscarriage of justice challenge, evidence of voluntary intoxication cannot negate premeditation under Arizona law). Thus, because Petitioner's new evidence of brain damage would not negate premeditation, Petitioner's actual innocence of the capital crime claim fails; it is not more likely than not that no reasonable juror would have convicted him of the crime in light of the new evidence.

Finally, Petitioner argues that all of the new mitigation evidence that he obtained at his *Atkins* hearing should be considered to determine whether on the basis of the additional mitigation, he has established the fundamental miscarriage of justice exception. This argument was specifically rejected in *Sawyer*. The *Sawyer* Court rejected the argument that the fundamental miscarriage of justice exception should be extended beyond the elements of eligibility for a capital   sentence to the existence of additional mitigating evidence. *505 U.S. at 345.* The Court reasoned:

> A federal district judge confronted with a claim of actual innocence may with relative ease determine whether a submission, for example, that a killing was not intentional, consists of credible, noncumulative, and admissible evidence negating the element of intent. But it is a far more difficult task to assess how jurors would have reacted to additional showings of mitigating factors, particularly considering the breadth of those factors that a jury under our decisions must be allowed to consider. . . . the "actual innocence" requirement must focus on those elements that render a defendant eligible for the death penalty, and not on additional mitigating evidence that was prevented from being introduced as a result of a claimed constitutional error.

Sawyer, 505 U.S. at 345-46, 347.

REASONS WHY REMEDY IS HOLLOW

Arizona prosecutors hire experts who testify   falsely as to the mental competence of defendants and the judiciary allow this to sentence the incompetent.

Michael Apelt, Petitioner, v. Charles L. Ryan, et al., Respondents.
No. CV-98-00882-PHX-ROS UNITED STATES DISTRICT COURT FOR THE DISTRICT OF ARIZONA
(Text modified for emphasis)

THE POSITION OF THE COURT

In an order dated September 1, 2015, the Court denied all but one of Apelt's remaining habeas claims. With respect to Claim 12, alleging ineffective assistance of counsel at sentencing, the Court found the state court's rejection of the claim was unreasonable under *28 U.S.C. § 2254(d)(1)*. The Court directed the parties to file supplemental briefs addressing whether an evidentiary hearing was necessary to determine if Apelt is entitled to habeas relief on the claim. On September 15, Respondents filed a motion asking the Court to reconsider its analysis of Claim 12. On September 18, the parties filed their supplemental briefs, each stating that an evidentiary hearing was unnecessary.

As set forth below, the Court will deny the motion for reconsideration and grant relief on Claim 12.

1. Motion for Reconsideration is Denied

Respondents move for reconsideration pursuant to Rule 7.2(g) of the Local Rules of Civil Procedure. Motions for reconsideration are disfavored and should be denied "absent a showing of manifest error or of new facts or legal authority." L.R. Civ. P. 7.2(g). A motion for reconsideration may not repeat arguments made in support of or in opposition to the motion that resulted in the Order for which the party seeks reconsideration. *Id.*

The state PCR court denied Claim 12 on procedural grounds and, alternatively, on the merits. This Court reviewed the state court's ruling under *28 U.S.C. § 2254(d)* and found the state court's denial of the claim was contrary to and an unreasonable application of *Strickland v. Washington, 466 U.S. 668, 104 S. Ct. 2052, 80 L. Ed. 2d 674 (1984)*.

Respondents contend the Court committed manifest error by applying *Martinez v. Ryan, 132 S. Ct. 1309, 182 L. Ed. 2d 272 (2012)*, to excuse the procedural default of Claim 12. As Apelt notes, however, the Court did not apply *Martinez* to excuse the default but instead reviewed the state court's alternative merits ruling. The Court noted *Martinez*, but only in the context of reassessing its earlier determination that Claim 12 was procedurally defaulted and barred from federal review. The Court concluded, citing *Clabourne v. Ryan, 745 F.3d 362, 382 (9th Cir. 2014)*, that the state court's alternative merits ruling was subject to review under *§ 2254(d)*. Respondents believe the Court has overlooked one of their arguments. Respondents believe Claim 12 was procedurally defaulted and, given the state court's alternative merits ruling, the procedural default must be enforced. Under this argument, *Martinez* is not available to excuse the procedural default of any claim where an alternative merits ruling is also issued. In *Martinez* itself, the Arizona Attorney General's Office argued on remand that the presence of an alternative merits ruling meant that alternative ruling had to be reviewed under a deferential standard. CV-08-0785-JAT, Doc. 31 at 40-44. That is, the Arizona Attorney General's Office claimed the alternative merits ruling *was* subject to review under the deferential standard of review required by AEDPA. While the Arizona Attorney General's Office is not bound to take the same position in every case regarding the meaning of *Martinez*, it has not offered any explanation for its evolving interpretation of *Martinez* in effectively identical situations. More importantly, the Ninth Circuit appears to have addressed the exact situation presented here. In a post-*Martinez* opinion--also litigated by the Arizona Attorney General's Office--the Ninth Circuit noted the Arizona state court had held a claim was procedurally defaulted but had also addressed the claim on its merits. *Clabourne v. Ryan, 745 F.3d 362, 383 (9th Cir. 2014)*. The Ninth Circuit held "AEDPA deference applie[d] to th[e] alternative holding on the merits" and concluded the state court's alternative merits ruling "was not contrary to, nor an unreasonable application of federal law." *Id.* Accordingly, rather than overlooking one of Respondents' arguments, the Court considered it and rejected it as barred by clear precedent. Even now, Respondents have not clearly explained how this Court could have committed error by following the sequence explicitly set forth by the Ninth Circuit in *Clabourne*.

Respondents further contend the Court committed manifest error in its application of *§ 2254(d)* and *Strickland*. Specifically, Respondents argue the Court erred in its assessment of *Strickland*'s prejudice prong by failing to reweigh the totality of the mitigating evidence against the aggravating factors. Here, Respondents repeat arguments made previously which is cause for denial under L.R. Civ. P. 7.2(g). In any event, the arguments are without merit.

The Court found that Apelt was prejudiced by sentencing counsel Villareal's deficient performance because "[t]he magnitude of the difference between the mitigating evidence that was presented at sentencing and the evidence that could have been presented through a competent investigation is sufficient to undermine confidence in the outcome." In making that determination, the Court necessarily took into account the aggravating factors as well as the totality of the mitigating evidence. There was no error.

Respondents' motion to reconsider will be denied.

2. Apelt is Entitled to Habeas Relief

In its prior order, the Court noted it was unclear whether an evidentiary hearing was required or appropriate. In making that observation, the Court also pointed out that an evidentiary hearing would give Respondents the opportunity to "challenge the veracity of Apelt's evidence." Respondents have declined an evidentiary hearing because "the existing record, including the extensive record from the state-court *Atkins v. Virginia* . . . hearing, is sufficient to resolve Claim 12." Respondents also state they "have interviewed Villareal" and he "would offer testimony generally consistent with the multiple affidavits he has presented in this case and the facts that are readily apparent from the record." Given that Apelt agrees no evidentiary hearing is needed, one will not be held. The Court notes, however, an evidentiary hearing would have been especially useful to assess whether Villareal's performance was, in fact, deficient. But Respondents do not argue Villareal performed competently. Accordingly, the Court will focus only on the issue of prejudice.

In 2002 the Court stayed the habeas proceedings to allow Apelt to pursue a claim under *Atkins v. Virginia, 536 U.S. 304, 321, 122 S. Ct. 2242, 153 L. Ed. 2d 335 (2002)* (holding the *Eighth Amendment* prohibits the execution of intellectually disabled prisoners). The state court held an evidentiary hearing in 2007 and determined Apelt did not meet his burden of showing intellectual disability. The Court previously discussed the deficiencies of Villareal's performance at sentencing. Villareal did almost nothing to investigate and present evidence of Apelt's social background and mental health history. He did not collect relevant records, interview potential mitigation witnesses, contact a mental health professional, or present a single witness at the sentencing hearing. *See, e.g., Robinson v. Schriro, 595 F.3d 1086, 1108-09 (9th Cir. 2010)*. His performance fell well below "prevailing professional norms." *Strickland, 466 U.S. at 688*.

The Court noted that Villareal's case in mitigation omitted evidence directly contradicting the argument that Apelt's childhood was "normal" as presented to the trial court at sentencing. This evidence, presented to the state court by PCR counsel, was of extreme poverty, physical abuse, developmental delays, and mental health problems. PCR counsel also presented evidence that as a child Apelt had been sexually assaulted twice by older men, once at knife point.

The record developed since the PCR court's denial of Claim 12 strengthens Apelt's allegation of prejudice. As argued by Apelt, the record details "a uniquely brutal and sadistic upbringing" and history of developmental delays.

Through affidavits of friends and family, and in testimony from the *Atkins* hearing, Apelt has offered the evidence that follows in support of Claim 12. He was conceived when his father, Rudi Sr., raped his mother, Lieselotte Schmidt. Lieselotte experienced a difficult labor, which resulted in Petitioner suffering anoxia, or oxygen deprivation. Lieselotte had an IQ of 66 and was likely intellectually disabled.

Apelt's family was poor. They lived in an unheated three-room apartment with Rudi Sr., Lieselotte, seven children, a grandmother, an aunt, and two cousins.

Rudi Sr. beat Apelt on the head with sticks, a coal oven iron, and his fists. Apelt and his brother Rudi suffered the worst beatings because they were the youngest. The beatings resulted in multiple concussions. On another occasion, when Rudi Sr. discovered that Apelt had gotten a tattoo on his arm, he burned the tattoo off with a red-hot iron.

Rudi Sr. was cruel to his children. He killed the family dog simply to show his children what he was capable of doing. He drugged the children to control their behavior, sedating them so that he did not have to provide supervision.

Rudi Sr. also sexually abused his children, including raping Apelt's sister. Rudi Sr. and other men wearing dark uniforms took Apelt and Rudi into the basement, tied them up, and struck their genitals with canes.

On several occasions during his childhood and adolescence, Apelt attempted suicide and was hospitalized. His mother and siblings also attempted suicide.

Apelt suffered extreme stress as a result of his father's abuse. He was unable to control his bowels until the first or second grade. When he soiled himself, his father would rub his pants in his face.

Dr. Moran, the State's expert at the *Atkins* hearing, conceded Apelt's father was "sadistic" and "possibly psychotic." He characterized Apelt's childhood as "psychosocially deprived" and "astoundingly bad."

Apelt's childhood development was delayed. He brought his pacifier to school when he was seven or eight and continued to use it until he was ten or eleven. By age ten, he could barely speak and often confused letters. Before that, he communicated through hand signals and noises. Once he did learn to speak, he stuttered, spoke in short sentences, and used a limited vocabulary. During his developmental years, Apelt had difficulty maintaining his hygiene and dressing appropriately.

Apelt attended a special education school for learning disabled and mentally retarded children. When he reached the ninth grade, he left school.

Apelt had a difficult time maintaining employment and worked in unskilled labor. Although in Germany even intellectually disabled people attended vocational school and completed an apprenticeship, Apelt never successfully finished the training "even for fairly simple professions." Instead, he failed his apprenticeship and worked in part-time positions.

In 1983, Apelt was discharged from compulsory service in the German armed forces for "mental inadequacy." The next year, at age 21, he was sent to a psychiatric institution after a suicide attempt. He experienced nightmares, memory loss, and depression. He also suffered severe stress, resulting in "shortness of breath, vertigo, and pain in the left arm." Such attacks caused Apelt to seek emergency treatment on numerous occasions. In 1986, Apelt was hospitalized for five months. Before that, he had been on disability for seven to eight months.

None of this evidence was presented at sentencing. As a result, the court was given a picture of Apelt's background that bore "no relation" to the picture that could have been presented if sentencing counsel had performed competently. *Rompilla v. Beard, 545 U.S. 374, 392-93, 125 S. Ct. 2456, 162 L. Ed. 2d 360 (2005)*. In circumstances like these, where such "classic" mitigation has been omitted, courts have consistently found ineffective assistance of counsel. *Hamilton v. Ayers, 583 F.3d 1100, 1131 (9th Cir. 2009)*.

In *Hamilton*, the sentencing jury heard only that Hamilton had been placed temporarily in foster care due to unspecified problems at home, that he was kind to stray animals and people, and that he loved his children. *Id.* Counsel failed to present evidence of "the indisputably horrific treatment Hamilton and his siblings suffered at the hands of his mother, father, and various extended family members. It did not hear that Hamilton had been diagnosed with mental health problems as early as age twelve, and that he had ongoing depression and suicidal thoughts through trial." *Id.* In *Rompilla, 545 U.S. at 390-93*, the Supreme Court found prejudice where counsel failed to discover and present evidence that the defendant was raised in a slum, beaten by his parents, witnessed his father's frequent abuse of his mother, quit school at sixteen, had no indoor plumbing, and may have had schizophrenia or another mental disorder. In *Williams v. Taylor, 529 U.S. 362, 369-70, 120 S. Ct. 1495, 146 L. Ed. 2d 389 (2000)*, the Court found prejudice where counsel failed to investigate and present evidence that the defendant had been abused and neglected during his childhood, was borderline mentally retarded, had suffered repeated head injuries, and might have mental impairments organic in origin. *See also Douglas v. Woodford, 316 F.3d 1079, 1088 (9th Cir. 2003)* (finding prejudice where counsel failed to discover and present evidence that defendant was abandoned as a child and raised by foster parents, including an abusive alcoholic foster father who frequently locked him in a closet; rarely had enough food; and was beaten and raped in jail at the age of fifteen); *Karis v. Calderon, 283 F.3d 1117, 1139 (9th Cir. 2002)* (finding prejudice where counsel failed to present evidence of the substantial abuse suffered by defendant whose father and stepfather "viciously beat" him and his mother on a regular basis).

Respondents contend the three aggravating factors outweigh the totality of the mitigating evidence. They argue that the aggravating factors are "compelling," that the evidence of an abusive childhood would be entitled to "minimal" weight because it was unconnected to the crime, and that rebuttal evidence about Apelt's anti-social personality disorder would have been "devastating." The trial court at sentencing found that

Apelt procured the murder with the promise of pecuniary gain, committed the murder with the expectation of pecuniary gain, and committed the murder in an especially cruel, heinous or depraved manner. *Apelt, 176 Ariz. 349, 367, 861 P.2d 634, 652 (1993)*.

"In establishing prejudice under *Strickland*, it is not necessary for the habeas petitioner to demonstrate that the newly presented mitigation evidence would necessarily overcome the aggravating circumstances." *Correll v. Ryan, 539 F.3d 938, 951-52 (9th Cir. 2008)* (citing *Williams, 529 U.S. at 398*); *see also Rompilla, 545 U.S. at 393* (explaining "although we suppose it is possible that [the sentencer] could have heard it all and still decided on the death penalty, that is not the test"). Instead, the court "evaluate[s] whether the difference between what was presented and what could have been presented is sufficient to 'undermine confidence in the outcome' of the proceeding." *Lambright v. Schriro, 490 F.3d 1103, 1121 (9th Cir. 2007)* (quoting *Strickland, 466 U.S. at 694*).

As the Ninth Circuit noted in *Lambright*, "both this court and the Supreme Court have consistently held that counsel's failure to present readily available evidence of childhood abuse, mental illness, and drug addiction is sufficient to undermine confidence in the result of a sentencing proceeding, and thereby to render counsel's performance prejudicial." *Id.* In Apelt's case, the omitted evidence of childhood deprivation, pervasive physical and sexual abuse, and delayed intellectual development is sufficient to undermine confidence in the outcome of the sentencing, notwithstanding the three aggravating factors. *See, e.g., Ainsworth v. Woodford, 268 F.3d 868, 878 (9th Cir. 2001)* ("Defense counsel failed to investigate, develop and present the wealth of evidence available concerning Ainsworth's troubled background and his emotional stability and what led to the development of the person who committed the crime."); *Wharton v. Chappell, 765 F.3d 953, 978 (9th Cir. 2014)* (finding a reasonable probability of a different sentence if counsel has presented testimony of sexual abuse); *Correll, 539 F.3d at 952* (finding prejudice where counsel failed to develop and present classic mitigation evidence of substance abuse and family dysfunction).

Respondents' arguments to the contrary are not persuasive. First, though three aggravating factors were found, under Arizona law the pecuniary gain and procuring factors are not both entitled to "full weight." *State v. Carlson, 202 Ariz. 570, 48 P.3d 1180, 1191 (2002)*. In addition, "the Supreme Court has made clear that counsel's failure to present mitigating evidence can be prejudicial even when the defendant's actions are egregious." *Stankewitz v. Woodford, 365 F.3d 706, 717-18 (9th Cir. 2004)* (finding prejudice where defendant attacked a 70-year-old man, shot at a police officer, attacked a counselor, stabbed a fellow inmate, and attacked several officers at a police station). "Evidence of mental disabilities or a tragic childhood can affect a sentencing determination even in the most savage case." *Lambright, 241 F.3d at 1208*; *see Earp v. Ornoski, 431 F.3d 1158, 1180 (9th Cir. 2005)* (finding prejudice where 18-month old victim died from multiple head blows or shaking, and had severe rectal and vaginal injuries consistent with sexual assault); *Mak v. Blodgett, 970 F.2d 614, 620-22 (9th Cir. 1992)* (finding prejudice despite the presence of exceedingly horrific circumstances of the crime in which the defendant slaughtered thirteen people in the course of one night to eliminate all witnesses to an armed robbery). Finally, the Ninth Circuit has recognized "prejudice is 'especially likely'" where the aggravating factors are based on the circumstances of the crime. *Earp, 431 F.3d at 1180* (quoting *Lambright, 241 F.3d at 1208*). Here, the three aggravating factors are related to the facts of the murder.

Respondents discount the significance of the omitted mitigating evidence by arguing no connection exists between the poverty and abuse Apelt experienced as a child and the murder he committed at age 25. They also contend the mitigating value that Apelt suffers from mental impairment, including intellectual deficits, would be offset by rebuttal evidence diagnosing him with anti-social personality disorder These arguments are not persuasive.

While it is true the absence of a causal connection between the mitigating circumstance and the crime may be a factor in assessing the weight of the mitigation, *see State v. Hampton, 213 Ariz. 167, 185, 140 P.3d 950, 968 (2006)*, it is established that "evidence about the defendant's background and character is relevant because of the belief, long held by this society, that defendants who commit criminal acts that are attributable to a disadvantaged background, or to emotional and mental problems, may be less culpable than defendants who have no such excuse." *Penry v. Lynaugh, 492 U.S. 302, 319, 109 S. Ct. 2934, 106 L. Ed. 2d 256 (1989)*, *abrogated by Atkins v. Virginia, 536 U.S. 304, 122 S. Ct. 2242, 153 L. Ed. 2d 335 (2002)* (quotation omitted). The evidence of Apelt's allegedly horrific childhood is "the kind of troubled history we have declared relevant to assessing a defendant's moral culpability." *Wiggins, 539 U.S. at 535.*

Respondents overstate their argument with the assertion that evidence of antisocial personality disorder would have been "devastating." "[T]he Arizona Supreme Court has made it clear that an antisocial personality disorder (sociopathic disorder) is a mitigating factor" and "there can be no doubt that the trial court must consider that personality defect when it is present in a case." *Smith v. Stewart, 140 F.3d 1263, 1270 (9th Cir. 1998).*

In addition, whatever impact the diagnosis would have on the other mental health evidence, it would have no effect on the new mitigation evidence that Apelt allegedly was raised in an environment of extreme poverty and dysfunction and suffered horrific physical and sexual abuse. "Given the nature and extent of the abuse, there is a reasonable probability that a competent attorney, aware of this history, would have introduced it at sentencing, and that a [sentencer] confronted with such mitigating evidence would have returned with a different sentence." *Wiggins, 539 U.S. at 513; see, e.g., Wharton, 765 F.3d at 977* ("Childhood sexual abuse can be powerful evidence in mitigation, particularly when it is not an isolated event."); *Karis, 283 F.3d at 1140* (explaining there was "no risk in putting on evidence of the wrenching abuse of Karis and his mother" and omission of such "highly relevant information of an abusive childhood" was prejudicial).

3. Conclusion

Villareal's representation at sentencing was inadequate and prejudiced Apelt. If Villareal had performed a competent mitigation investigation, there is a reasonable probability that Apelt would not have been sentenced to death. Villareal's deficient performance, which resulted in the near-total omission of classic mitigation evidence, undermines confidence in the sentencing decision. Apelt is entitled to relief on Claim 12.

REASONS WHY REMEDY IS NOT HOLLOW

It is the norm for Arizona prosecutors and judges not to follow state law as to sentencing and this is the rare case where relief was granted.

Boy White, Petitioner, v. Charles Ryan, Arizona Attorney General, Respondents. CIV 11-02126 PHX GMS (MEA)UNITED STATES DISTRICT COURT FOR THE DISTRICT OF ARIZONA

(Text modified for emphasis)

A grand jury indictment returned July 12, 2006, charged Petitioner with three counts of fraudulent schemes and artifices, class 2 felonies (counts 1, 5, and 8), seven counts of burglary in the second degree (counts 2, 4, 6, 7, 9, 10, and 11), and one count of theft (count 3). See Answer, Exh. A.

In a written plea agreement signed by Petitioner on February 16, 2007, Petitioner agreed to plead guilty to one count of theft (count 3), with one prior felony conviction; one count of burglary in the second degree (count 6); and one count of burglary in the second degree (count 9). The plea agreement provided, inter alia, that, with regard to the sentence to be imposed on count 3, the charge of theft, the crime carried a "presumptive sentence of 6.5 years; a minimum sentence of 4.5 years (3.5 years if the Court makes an exceptional circumstances finding); and a maximum sentence of 13.0 years (16.25 years if the trial court makes an exceptional circumstances finding)", and that Petitioner would serve "not less than 6.5 years in the Department of Corrections.

At a change of plea proceeding, the trial court reviewed the plea agreement with Petitioner and advised him of the range of possible sentences.. Petitioner's counsel advised the court at the beginning of the proceeding that Petitioner was illiterate and could not read nor write English. The court informed Petitioner that the maximum sentence he could receive based on a guilty plea to count 3 was 13 years imprisonment, which could be increased to a term of 16 years upon a finding of special circumstances. The court noted that Petitioner would not be sentenced to less than 6.5 years imprisonment.

At the change of plea proceeding   Petitioner told the court the plea agreement had been read to him and that his lawyer had explained the plea agreement to Petitioner. Petitioner was told he was waiving his right to a jury trial and to have a jury find him guilty beyond a reasonable doubt. Petitioner stated that he had not consumed any drugs or alcohol prior to entering the plea. Petitioner admitted the factual basis for the crimes to the court.

On April 12, 2007, the trial court entered judgment pursuant to Petitioner's guilty plea, and sentenced Petitioner to an aggravated term of eleven years imprisonment pursuant to his conviction for theft (count 3). The court suspended imposition of sentence on the other two counts and ordered that Petitioner be placed on concurrent terms of probation for four years upon his discharge from prison.

On May 9, 2007, Petitioner filed a petition for post-conviction relief, seeking a reduction in his sentence, in which he alleged:

> Defendant was told by his attorney that upon a plea of guilty, Defendant would receive a sentence of 6.5 years. When the Court sentenced Defendant to 11 years and Defendant asked his counsel why he didn't get the 6.5 years sentence   promised by counsel, counsel snidely remarked, "Be glad you didn't get 13 (years)." Defendant signed off on the plea and initialed each paragraph only because counsel explained it meant a 6.5 year sentence. Defendant signed where counsel indicated--because Defendant is illiterate! A test administered by the Arizona Dept. of Corrections 5 days after sentencing indicates Defendant reads at a sub-first grade level and that his language skills are at a first grade level. The words and language of the plea are far too technical for a 6 year old (--or first grader) mind to comprehend. Defendant signed and initialed where counsel indicated after counsel said it meant a 6.5 year sentence. Based on the facts of this case, it is clear that the Plea was coerced and/or induced by counsel and that it was not knowingly and intelligently entered by Defendant in violation of his constitutional rights where defendant received an 11 year sentence after being promised a 6.5 year sentence. The facts also appear to raise the argument that Defendant also was denied effective assistance of counsel.

Petitioner was appointed counsel to represent   him in his Rule 32 proceedings. On August 10, 2007, Petitioner's appointed counsel informed the state court that she was unable to find any claims for relief to raise on Petitioner's behalf. The state Superior Court ordered counsel to remain in an advisory capacity and granted Petitioner 45 days in which to file a pro per petition for post-conviction relief.

On October 31, 2007, the state trial court dismissed Petitioner's Rule 32 proceedings because Petitioner had failed to file a petition for post-conviction relief by the deadline imposed by the court. Petitioner did not seek review of this decision by the Arizona Court of Appeals.

On July 10, 2008, Petitioner initiated a second action for state post-conviction relief pursuant to *Rule 32, Arizona Rules of Civil Procedure.* In attempting to justify the successive and untimely nature of the action Petitioner claimed "newly-discovered material facts exist which probably would have changed the verdict or sentence"; "the defendant's failure to file a timely notice of post-conviction relief ... was without fault on the defendant's part"; and "there has been   a significant change in the law that would probably overturn the conviction or sentence." Petitioner asserted in the second Rule 32 action that:

> 1. Defendant is illiterate and requires assistance as he cannot read or write and was put in solitary confinement with no assistance when he previously filed a "NOTICE of POST-CONVICTION Relief." Defendant received legal mail from the Court and an attorney but could not read it and waited months for legal assistance. Defendant has recently been moved to a new unit (Santa Rita) at ASPC Tucson, where help is available.
>
> 2. Stokes v. Schrio, Apprendi, Blakely, State v. Honorable Michael J Brown and the statutory changes to *A.R.S. 13-702* prescribe the factors used by a judge to aggravate his sentence must be determined by "trier of fact" (jury) first.
>
> 3. A new witness has been located.

On July 25, 2008, the state Superior Court dismissed Petitioner's second Rule 32 action because he failed to demonstrate that he was entitled to an exception under *Rule 32.1(f)*; he failed to demonstrate a significant change in the law; he had waived his right to a jury determination of aggravating factors in his plea agreement; and he had not demonstrated that newly-discovered material facts exist that would probably have changed the verdict or sentence. Petitioner did not seek review of this decision by the Arizona Court of Appeals.

On March 13, 2009, Petitioner filed a third notice of post-conviction relief, seeking review based on newly-discovered evidence. The Superior Court found that Petitioner had sufficiently raised a claim to allow an untimely filing, and gave Petitioner 60 days in which to file a pro per petition for post-conviction relief. Petitioner's pro per Rule 32 petition, filed January 4, 2010, alleged:

> The appointed legal advocate, Scott Allen, requested a mitigation hearing. Theresa Sanders, the sentencing judge, refused.
> Petitioner is diagnosed schizophrenic. He was untreated at the time of the burglary giving rise to the imprisonment. He was diagnosed and put on medication while awaiting trial.

On March 29, 2010, the state trial court dismissed Petitioner's third Rule 32 action, determining he had failed to show any colorable claim for relief pursuant to *Rule 32.1 of the Arizona Rules of Criminal Procedure*. Petitioner sought review of this decision by the Arizona Court of Appeals, which rejected the petition as untimely filed.

On February 25, 2011, Petitioner filed another notice of post-conviction relief which alleged:

> Defendant is illiterate, and an inmate reviewing his "plea agreement" saw that the stipulated sentence was not followed. Defendant was diagno[s]ed as schizophrenic, which contributed to his lack of understanding of the plea and sentencing process. His counsel was ineffective, and did not follow through on the stipulated sentence, nor did he bring a m[i]tigating specialist. His Rule 32 counsel was ineffective, and did not evaluate defendant's illiteracy, mental condition, and the sentence stipulation. Defendant respectfully requests that a lawyer be appointed to review this case and represent him in a post-conviction relief.

On March 28, 2011, the state Superior Court dismissed Petitioner's fourth Rule 32 action as untimely, finding that Petitioner had "failed to state a claim for which relief could be granted in an untimely Rule 32 proceeding." Petitioner sought review of this decision by the Arizona Court of Appeals, which dismissed the petition for review as untimely filed.

On August 11, 2011, Petitioner filed another notice of petition for post-conviction, alleging:

> Defendant/Petitioner White was sentenced in 2007. He is illiterate. Another inmate at the [illegible] unit looked at his time comp, release date does not compute. He should have been given credit for more days served in Maricopa County Jail. Petitioner respectfully requests that this court appoint an attorney to help correct this error.

On September 2, 2011, the state Superior Court dismissed the petition on the merits, stating: "the defendant is not being held beyond the expiration of his sentence.". Petitioner did not seek review of this decision.

In his federal habeas petition Petitioner asserts he is entitled to relief because he was denied his right to the effective assistance of counsel because his counsel allowed Petitioner, who is illiterate, to sign a plea agreement understanding that the agreement provided for a maximum sentence of 6.5 years and Petitioner received a sentence of eleven years. Petitioner also alleges counsel was ineffective because he did not assert Petitioner's incompetence; Petitioner avers he was diagnosed as schizophrenic two years after his legal proceedings. Petitioner contends he did not knowingly and voluntarily enter the plea agreement. Petitioner alleges he was heavily medicated at the time the plea agreement was explained to him by his counsel. Petitioner asks, as relief, that his sentence be reduced to the 6.5 years specified in the plea agreement. Attached to the pleadings is a form dated April 17, 2007, and a letter dated September 15, 2008, indicating Petitioner does not have a GED or high school diploma and that Petition has learning disabilities as a result of schizophrenia because his medications interfere with his focus.

II Analysis

A. Statute of limitations

The petition seeking a writ of habeas corpus is barred by the applicable statute of limitations found in the Antiterrorism and Effective Death Penalty Act ("AEDPA"). The AEDPA imposed a one-year statute of limitations on state prisoners seeking federal habeas relief from their state convictions. See, e.g., *Espinoza Matthews v. California, 432 F.3d 1021, 1025 (9th Cir. 2005); Lott v. Mueller, 304 F.3d 918, 920 (9th Cir. 2002).*

Petitioner's conviction became final ninety days after the date the state court entered his conviction and sentenced Petitioner. Prior to this date, Petitioner filed a timely state action for post-conviction relief, which tolled the applicable statute of limitations until October 31, 2007, when the state trial court dismissed Petitioner's Rule 32 proceedings because Petitioner had failed to file a petition for post-conviction relief by the deadline imposed by the court. Petitioner did not seek review of this decision by the Arizona Court of Appeals.

Accordingly, the one-year statute of limitations with regard to Petitioner's habeas action began on or about November 30, 2007, and expired on November 29, 2008, unless it was tolled by a "properly filed" application for state post-conviction relief. *Pace v. DiGuglielmo, 544 U.S. 408, 414, 125 S. Ct. 1807, 161 L. Ed. 2d 669 (2005).* See also *Allen v. Siebert, 552 U.S. 3, 5-7, 128 S. Ct. 2, 169 L. Ed. 2d 329 (2007)* (holding that the rule announced in Pace applies even where there are exceptions to the state-court filing deadlines, and reaffirming that a state court's rejection of a petition as untimely is "the end of the matter" for determining whether a petitioner is entitled to tolling under *§ 2244(d)(2)*);

Petitioner's second state action for post-conviction relief, filed and dismissed in July of 2008 did not toll the statute of limitations because they were not "properly filed". See *Laws v. Lamarque, 351 F.3d 919, 922 (9th Cir. 2003); Ferguson v. Palmateer, 321 F.3d 820, 823 (9th Cir. 2003); Jiminez v. Rice, 276 F.3d 478, 482 (9th Cir. 2001); Webster v. Moore, 199 F.3d 1256, 1259 (11th Cir. 2000).* See *Zepeda v. Walker, 581 F.3d 1013, 1018 (9th Cir. 2009)* (rejecting contention that state must prove that rules concerning time bars are "firmly established and regularly followed before noncompliance will render a petition improperly filed for AEDPA tolling"). See also *White v. Martel, 601 F.3d 882 (9th Cir. 2010)* (per curiam) (relying on Zepeda to reject petitioner's claim that state timeliness requirement was not regularly applied, stating, "the adequacy analysis used to decide procedural default issues is inapplicable to the issue of whether a state petition was 'properly filed' for purposes of *section 2244(d)(2)*").

The one-year statute of limitations for filing a habeas petition may be equitably tolled if extraordinary circumstances beyond a prisoner's control prevent the prisoner from filing on time. See *Holland v. Florida, 130 S. Ct. 2549, 2554, 2562, 177 L. Ed. 2d 130 (2010); Bills v. Clark, 628 F.3d 1092, 1096-97 (9th Cir. 2010).*   A petitioner seeking equitable tolling must establish two elements: "(1) that he has been pursuing his rights diligently, and (2) that some extraordinary circumstance stood in his way." *Pace v. DiGuglielmo, 544 U.S. 408, 418, 125 S. Ct. 1807, 1814-15, 161 L. Ed. 2d 669 (2005).* See also *Waldron-Ramsey v. Pacholke, 556 F.3d 1008, 1011-14 (9th Cir. 2009).*

The Ninth Circuit Court of Appeals has determined equitable tolling of the filing deadline for a federal habeas petition is available only if extraordinary circumstances beyond the petitioner's control make it impossible to file a petition on time. See *Chaffer v. Prosper, 592 F.3d 1046, 1048-49 (9th Cir. 2010); Waldron-Ramsey, 556 F.3d at 1011-14 & n.4; Harris v. Carter, 515 F.3d 1051, 1054-55 & n.4 (9th Cir. 2008); Gaston v. Palmer, 417 F.3d 1030, 1034 (9th Cir. 2003),* modified on other grounds by *447 F.3d 1165 (9th Cir. 2006).* Equitable tolling is only appropriate when external forces, rather than a petitioner's lack of diligence, account for the failure to file a timely habeas action. See *Chaffer, 592 F.3d at 1048-49; Waldron-Ramsey, 556 F.3d at 1011; Miles v. Prunty, 187 F.3d 1104, 1107 (9th Cir. 1999).* Equitable tolling is also available if the petitioner establishes their actual innocence of the crimes of conviction. See *Lee v. Lampert, 653 F.3d 929, 933-34 (9th Cir. 2011).*

Equitable tolling is to be rarely granted. See, e.g., *Waldron-Ramsey, 556 F.3d at 1011*; *Jones v. Hulick, 449 F.3d 784, 789 (7th Cir. 2006)*; *Steed v. Head, 219 F.3d 1298, 1300 (11th Cir. 2000)*. Equitable tolling is inappropriate in most cases and "the threshold necessary to trigger equitable tolling [under AEDPA] is very high, lest the exceptions swallow the rule." *Miranda v. Castro, 292 F.3d 1063, 1066 (9th Cir. 2002)*. Petitioner must show that "the extraordinary circumstances were the cause of his untimeliness and that the extraordinary circumstances made it impossible to file a petition on time." *Porter v. Ollison, 620 F.3d 952, 959 (9th Cir. 2010)*. It is Petitioner's burden to establish that equitable tolling is warranted in his case. See, e.g., *Espinoza Matthews v. California, 432 F.3d 1021, 1026 (9th Cir. 2004)*; *Gaston, 417 F.3d at 1034*.

A petitioner's pro se status, ignorance of the law, and lack of legal representation during the applicable filing period do not constitute circumstances justifying equitable tolling because such circumstances are not "extraordinary."   See, e.g., *Chaffer, 592 F.3d at 1048-49*; *Waldron-Ramsey, 556 F.3d at 1011-14*; *Rasberry v. Garcia, 448 F.3d 1150, 1154 (9th Cir. 2006)*; *Shoemate v. Norris, 390 F.3d 595, 598 (8th Cir. 2004)*. Equitable tolling may be available when a petitioner can establish they are so mentally ill that they are incompetent. Compare *Laws v. Lamarque, 351 F.3d 919, 923 (9th Cir. 2003)*, with *Bills, 628 F.3d at 1098*. Alleged errors by a petitioner's appellate counsel do not per se constitute an "extraordinary circumstance" warranting equitable tolling. See *Randle v. Crawford, 604 F.3d 1047, 1058 (9th Cir.)*, cert. denied sub nom., *Randle v. Skolnik, 131 S. Ct. 474, 178 L. Ed. 2d 301 (2010)*; *Ramirez v. Yates, 571 F.3d 993, 998 (9th Cir. 2009)*. It is not sufficient that counsel was negligent; only representation that meets the extraordinary misconduct standard can be a basis for applying equitable tolling. See *Porter, 620 F.3d at 959*.

Respondents assert:

> In this case, Petitioner has not demonstrated grounds for equitable tolling. Although petitioner claims to be "illiterate," and claims to have been diagnosed as "schizophrenic," he has not demonstrated either that the foregoing constituted "extraordinary circumstances," or that they made it "impossible" for him to file his Petition within the statutory period, notwithstanding his "diligence." See *Steel v. Ryan, 468 Fed. Appx. 659, 2011 U.S. App. LEXIS 24333, 2011 WL 6093378 (9th Cir. 2011)*; *Bills v. Clark, 628 F.3d 1092 (9th Cir.2010)* (condition must be so "severe" that either the "petitioner was unable rationally or factually to personally understand the need to timely file" or "unable personally to prepare a habeas petition"). Indeed, the record reveals that Petitioner--who was convicted in September 2002--was more than capable of filing a timely federal petition, but instead elected to pursue five state petitions for post-conviction relief, with the result that the statutory period expired on November 30, 2008, over 2 1/2 years before Petitioner filed his federal petition. See *Gaston v. Palmer, 417 F.3d 1030, 1034-35 (9th Cir. 2005)*. Having failed to demonstrate that "extraordinary circumstances beyond his control" made it "impossible" for Petitioner to file a timely federal petition, equitable tolling is not available. *Lambert, 465 F.3d at 969*; see also *United States v. Marcello, 212 F.3d 1005, 1010 (7th Cir. 2000)* (upholding dismissal of petition filed 1 day after limitations period expired).

Allowing   that Petitioner's diagnosis of mental illness and the fact that he diligently pursued post-conviction remedies warrants equitable tolling, the Magistrate Judge will consider Respondents' argument that Petitioner failed to properly exhaust his federal habeas claims in the state courts. Respondents contend that the claims for relief are also barred by the doctrine of exhaustion and procedural default.

D. Fundamental miscarriage of justice

Review of the merits of a procedurally defaulted habeas claim is required if the petitioner demonstrates review of the merits of the claim is necessary to prevent a fundamental miscarriage of justice. See *Dretke v. Haley, 541 U.S. 386, 393, 124 S. Ct. 1847, 1852, 158 L. Ed. 2d 659 (2004)*; *Schlup v. Delo, 513 U.S. 298, 316, 115 S. Ct. 851, 861, 130 L. Ed. 2d 808 (1995)*; *Murray v. Carrier, 477 U.S. 478, 485-86, 106 S. Ct. 2639, 2649, 91 L. Ed. 2d 397 (1986)*. A fundamental miscarriage of justice occurs only when a constitutional violation has probably resulted in the conviction of one who is factually innocent. See *Murray, 477 U.S. at 485-86, 106 S. Ct. at 2649*;   *Thomas v. Goldsmith, 979 F.2d 746, 749 (9th Cir. 1992)* (showing of factual innocence is necessary to trigger manifest injustice relief). To satisfy the "fundamental miscarriage of justice" standard, a petitioner must establish by clear and convincing evidence that no reasonable fact-finder could have found him guilty of the offenses charged. See *Dretke, 541 U.S. at 393, 124 S. Ct. at 1852; Wildman v. Johnson, 261 F.3d 832, 842-43 (9th Cir. 2001)*.

Petitioner does not contend that he is actually innocent of the crimes of conviction, accordingly, no fundamental miscarriage of justice will occur absent a consideration of the merits of Petitioner's habeas claims.

Additionally, even if Petitioner's mental disabilities constitute cause for his procedural default of his habeas claims, Petitioner cannot show prejudice arising from the procedural default of his claims.

The "clearly established Federal law, as determined by the Supreme Court of the United States" at issue in this case is the test for ineffective assistance of counsel claims set forth in *Strickland v. Washington, 466 U.S. 668, 104 S. Ct. 2052, 80 L. Ed. 2d 674, [] (1984)*, and in *Hill v. Lockhart, 474 U.S. 52, 106 S. Ct. 366, 88 L. Ed. 2d 203, [] (1985)*. Under Strickland, to establish a claim of ineffective assistance of counsel, the petitioner must show (1) grossly deficient performance by his counsel, and (2) resultant prejudice. *466 U.S. at 687, 104 S. Ct. 2052*. In Hill, the Supreme Court adapted the two-part Strickland standard to challenges to guilty pleas based on ineffective assistance of counsel, holding that a defendant seeking to challenge the validity of his guilty plea on the ground of ineffective assistance of counsel must show that (1) his "counsel's representation fell below an objective standard of reasonableness," and (2) "there is a reasonable probability that, but for [his] counsel's errors, he would not have pleaded guilty and would have insisted on going to trial." *474 U.S. at 57-59, 106 S. Ct. 366*.

Womack v. McDaniel, 497 F.3d 998, 1002 (9th Cir. 2007).

To establish deficient performance, a person challenging a conviction must show that counsel's representation fell below an objective standard of reasonableness. A court considering a claim of ineffective assistance must apply a strong presumption that counsel's representation was within the wide range' of reasonable professional assistance. The challenger's burden is to show that counsel made errors so serious that counsel was not functioning as the "counsel" guaranteed the defendant by the *Sixth Amendment*.

Premo v. Moore, 131 S. Ct. 733, 739, 178 L. Ed. 2d 649 (2011) (internal citations and quotations omitted), citing *Harrington, 131 S. Ct. at 788* ("The question is whether an attorney's representation amounted to incompetence under 'prevailing professional norms,' not whether it deviated from best practices or most common custom."). Counsel's performance is not deficient nor prejudicial when counsel "fails" to raise an argument that counsel reasonably believes would be futile. See *Premo, 131 S. Ct. at 741; Harrington, 131 S. Ct. at 788*.

Furthermore, to succeed on a claim that his counsel was constitutionally ineffective regarding a guilty plea, a petitioner must show that his counsel's advice as to the consequences of the plea was not within the range of competence demanded of criminal attorneys. See, e.g., *Hill v. Lockhart, 474 U.S. 52, 58, 106 S. Ct. 366, 369, 88 L. Ed. 2d 203 (1985)*. Although the Court may proceed directly to the prejudice prong when undertaking the Strickland analysis, the Court may not assume prejudice solely from counsel's allegedly deficient performance. See *Jackson v. Calderon, 211 F.3d 1148, 1155 n.3 (9th Cir. 2000)*.

Petitioner has not established that his counsel's performance was deficient, or that any alleged deficiency prejudiced Petitioner. The plea agreement was beneficial to Petitioner and Petitioner indicated both in the written plea agreement, which was read to him, and at the plea colloquy that he understood the terms of the plea agreement and was pleading guilty voluntarily and knowingly. Petitioner has not demonstrated that, but for counsel's advice with regard to the plea agreement, Petitioner would have chosen to go forward to trial on all of the counts charged in the indictment. Nowhere in his pleadings does Petitioner contend that he could not be found guilty of the other charges stated in the indictment and Petitioner fully understood that, if convicted of the other charges in the indictment, Petitioner faced a lengthy sentence.

Petitioner's unsupported statements in his federal habeas pleadings that his guilty plea was not voluntary do not supply the "clear and convincing evidence" standard necessary for the Court to conclude that Petitioner's plea was not knowing or voluntary. Petitioner's contemporaneous statements regarding his understanding of the plea agreement carry substantial weight in determining if his entry of a guilty plea was knowing and voluntary. See *Blackledge v. Allison, 431 U.S. 63, 74, 97 S. Ct. 1621, 1629, 52 L. Ed. 2d 136 (1977)* ("Solemn declarations in open court carry a strong presumption of verity. The subsequent presentation of conclusory allegations unsupported by specifics is subject to summary dismissal, as are contentions that in the face of the record are wholly incredible"); *Doe v. Woodford, 508 F.3d 563, 571 (9th Cir. 2007); Restucci v. Spencer, 249 F. Supp. 2d 33, 45 (D. Mass. 2003)* (collecting cases so holding).

REASONS WHY REMEDY IS HOLLOW

Arizona uses its prisons to incarcerate the mentally incompetent and illiterate and state courts allow this practice. The Arizona Attorney General fails to bring this o the attention of federal courts.

> **RODOLFO ROMERO, Petitioner, v. CHARLES RYAN and ARIZONA ATTORNEY GENERAL, Respondents. CIV 08-02020 PHX SRB (MEA) UNITED STATES DISTRICT COURT FOR THE DISTRICT OF ARIZONA (Text modified for emphasis)**

THE POSITION OF THE COURT

A Maricopa County grand jury indictment returned June 21, 1988, charged Petitioner and a co-defendant, Mr. Conde, with one count of first-degree murder, one count of burglary in the first-degree, five counts of armed robbery, one count of attempted armed robbery, and three counts of aggravated assault. The charges arose from a bank robbery occurring on May 27, 1988, in Phoenix, Arizona. police officer was shot and killed as he attempted to stop the fleeing robbers. The following is taken from the Arizona Court of Appeals' decision in Mr. Conde's appeal:

> The evidence at trial showed that [Mr. Conde] and an accomplice entered a bank armed with handguns which they pointed at customers and bank personnel. Conde leaped on the top of a counter and ordered a teller to place money in a plastic bag. He then ordered a customer to surrender her car keys so that he and his accomplice could escape. They obtained their getaway vehicle in the bank parking lot by taking it from its driver at gunpoint. At this juncture, the police officer, working off-duty as a bank security guard, opened fire on Conde and his accomplice. In the exchange of shots the officer was killed.
>
> The robbers fled the scene in the stolen car. During the next half-hour, they commandeered two other vehicles at gunpoint. When police located Conde and ordered him to stop, he fired at them. He was wounded and was eventually taken into custody.

Arizona v. Conde, 174 Ariz. 30, 31, 846 P.2d 843, 844 (1992). See also Conde v. Flanagan, CIV 02-2034 PHX SRB GEE (D. Ariz).

At a pretrial conference in Petitioner's case the state indicated its theory of Petitioner's case was that Mr. Conde actually shot the bullet that killed the police officer; the charge of murder against Petitioner was predicated on acccomplice liability.

Petitioner's co-defendant was taken into custody the day the crimes occurred. Petitioner left the United States after the crimes occurred. Petitioner's co-defendant was tried and convicted by a jury of the charges stated in the indictment in late 1989, and was sentenced to an aggregate in excess of 200 years imprisonment.

In May of 1996, eight years after the indictment was issued, the Arizona Attorney General submitted an extradition request to the United States Department of Justice, asking for Petitioner's extradition in the event that law enforcement authorities could locate Petitioner in Mexico. Approximately four years later, in June of 2000, Petitioner was arrested by Mexican authorities in Mexico.

On February 20, 2001, a Mexican district court approved the United States' request to extradite Petitioner to Arizona. On March 15, 2001, Mexico's Secretary of Foreign Relations formally granted the extradition request. Before Petitioner could be brought to the United States, however, on October 2, 2001, the Mexico Supreme Court concluded that the sentence of life imprisonment constituted cruel and unusual punishment and could not be imposed on a Mexican national by any court. Accordingly, Petitioner subsequently successfully moved a Mexico federal court to set aside the grant of extradition because one of the offenses charged by Arizona, i.e., first degree murder, was punishable by life imprisonment. The Mexican federal court's opinion setting aside the approval of extradition allowed Mexico's Secretary of Foreign Relations to file a pleading addressing whether Petitioner's extradition was barred by the possible imposition of a life sentence.

Accordingly, on October 18, 2001, Mexico's Secretary of Foreign Relations requested assurances from the United States that Petitioner "[would] not be subject to imprisonment for life for murder..." if extradited to Arizona. Referencing the governing extradition treaty between the United States and Mexico, the American ambassador responded *inter alia* that, in the event of Petitioner's conviction, "the State of Arizona [would not] seek or recommend a penalty of 25 years to life imprisonment at the sentencing phase of the judicial proceeding in this case," but that instead the State of Arizona would recommend imposition of a sentence of "50 to 60 years' imprisonment." Regarding the possibility that the Arizona trial court might impose a life sentence upon Petitioner's conviction, notwithstanding the above-referenced recommendation, the United States ambassador informed Mexico that, should that circumstance arise, "the State of Arizona will take appropriate action to formally request that the court reduce such sentence to a term of years." The ambassador acknowledged that, nonetheless, "[i]t would then be for the court to decide whether to accept the executive authority's determination."

On November 28, 2001, Mexico granted the United States' request to extradite Petitioner on every requested charge except the charge of burglary. The opinion approving the extradition noted the agreement complied with the relevant treaty in that Petitioner was not facing a death sentence and also noted the exchange of diplomatic notes regarding Mexico's insistence that Petitioner be sentenced to a term of years, rather than an indeterminate sentence, i.e., a sentence of life imprisonment. On March 21, 2002, Mexico extradited Petitioner to Arizona. Mexico did not extradite on this charge because the Mexican criminal code lacked an offense equivalent to second degree burglary.

Just prior to trial, Petitioner's counsel moved the court to reduce the charge of first-degree murder to second-degree murder, citing the extradition treaty and agreement between Mexico and the United States. After the matter was fully pled, the trial court heard argument on the motion November 18, 2002. The trial court denied the motion at that time.

Petitioner's jury trial on the 1988 charges began on November 18, 2002. Due to unavailability of witnesses, the trial court granted the state's motion to dismiss one count of armed robbery and one count of aggravated assault. Without any objection from the defense, the jury was instructed as to the lesser-included offense of second-degree murder. Defense counsel told the jury during closing argument that Petitioner was "only guilty of Second Degree Murder."

The jury found Petitioner guilty of one count of first-degree murder, one count of burglary, four counts of armed robbery, one count of attempted robbery, and three counts of aggravated assault.

During the trial, and after Petitioner was convicted but prior to sentencing, his defense counsel notified the Mexican government of Petitioner's trial and conviction on the charge of first degree murder.. The Mexican government responded that it was not in favor of the imposition of a life sentence. A letter from a Mexican diplomat states:

> I reiterate that the government of Mexico is interested in seeing that the aforementioned reassurance of no application of life sentence on the accused, is complied with, this in case he is found guilty in the legal process being pursued against him in the United States of America, he is handed down a sentence of a determined number of years and not a life sentence, without concern for how these assurances are complied with by the United States government...

Petitioner's trial counsel filed a motion for a new trial asserting Petitioner could not be convicted of murder in the first degree or burglary because the charges were precluded by the extradition agreement. Defense counsel also moved to dismiss both these charges. At a hearing on February 7, 2003, the parties stipulated to dismissal of the conviction for burglary.

In response to Petitioner's post-trial motion to dismiss, the state offered to reduce the murder charge; however, Petitioner wanted dismissal of the count on the basis that jurisdiction was not proper. On March 19, 2003, the state moved the trial court to reduce Petitioner's conviction from guilty of first-degree murder to guilty of second-degree murder, which would allow for a sentence of less than life imprisonment. The motion states it was "made to satisfy extradition agreement between the governments of the   United States and Mexico. Defendant and defense counsel are aware of this motion and have no objection thereto." The trial court granted the motion on March 21, 2003.

The trial court conducted an aggravation and mitigation hearing on March 21, 2003, at which hearing Petitioner spoke on his own behalf. At that time the court imposed an aggravated term of 20 years incarceration pursuant to Petitioner's conviction on the charge of second-degree murder. The trial court found as aggravating circumstances the fact that the victim was a police officer who acted in his official capacity by trying to prevent the bank robbery, and the severe emotional harm to the officer's family. The state court also found as aggravating circumstances the presence of an accomplice, Petitioner's flight from the scene, and Petitioner's failure to self-surrender. The trial court found as other aggravating circumstances the fact that the murder occurred "in the immediate flight from a robbery to prevent detection" and Petitioner's decision to arm himself with assault rifles equipped with "banana-clips" and high-powered ammunition to ensure   that he was "not apprehended at all costs." Stating that "the aggravating factors far, far outweigh the mitigating factors," the trial court indicated it would have imposed the same sentence even if it had disregarded the victim's status as a police officer and the pecuniary motive of the underlying armed robbery. The trial court also stated the sentence was warranted by the aggravating factors, which outweighed Petitioner's youthfulness and lack of a prior criminal record at the time of the crime.

The trial court imposed aggravated prison terms on the remaining convictions based upon the presence of an accomplice, flight from the scene, and the fact that the murder committed in immediate flight to prevent detection. The aggregate length of Petitioner's sentences is 106 years.

Petitioner took a direct appeal of his convictions and sentences, arguing:

> The trial court erroneously replaced Defendant's first-degree murder conviction with a second-degree murder conviction because the conviction for that crime is not expressly allowed by the controlling extradition agreement between the United States and Mexico. And,   the *Supremacy Clause* requires that the first-degree murder conviction be vacated because it conflicts with the controlling extradition agreement.

. Petitioner argued the State of Arizona had violated the extradition agreement between the United States and Mexico and the "doctrine of specialty" by reducing the charge after conviction and by imposing consecutive sentences. In his direct appeal Petitioner also argued that the trial court violated his *Sixth Amendment* right to a jury trial by enhancing his sentence using facts that were neither admitted by Petitioner nor found to be true beyond a reasonable doubt by a jury.

The Arizona Court of Appeals affirmed Petitioner's convictions and sentences in a decision issued August 16, 2005. The Court of Appeals noted that Mexico had agreed to extradite Petitioner on a charge of first-degree murder. The Court of Appeals noted Mexico had agreed to extradite Petitioner on that charge if the State of Arizona agreed to oppose the imposition of a life sentence if convicted. Additionally, the Arizona Court of Appeals reiterated the fact that, after Petitioner   was convicted, his counsel notified the Mexican government of Petitioner's conviction.. The Mexican government responded that it was not in favor of the imposition of a life sentence.

The Arizona Court of Appeals held that Petitioner's extradition, trial, and conviction on the charge of first degree murder was not in violation of the extradition agreement because the agreement specifically provided

Petitioner could be extradited to face that charge. The appellate court concluded that the means used to bring the sentence mandated by the extradition agreement into compliance with Arizona law did not deprive Petitioner of any substantive right. Additionally, the Arizona Court of Appeals concluded that relief based on the application of the doctrine of specialty would depend on the wishes of Mexico, which country had indicated only a desire that Petitioner not be sentenced to life imprisonment if convicted of first-degree murder.

The Arizona Court of Appeals also determined that, if there had been any violation of the specialty doctrine, the error was invited by Petitioner because there was no contemporaneous objection to the state's motion for diminution of the murder count and because prior to trial and in closing argument Petitioner himself had argued for conviction on the lesser-included offense of second-degree murder.

Petitioner did not seek review of the Court of Appeals' decision in his direct appeal by the Arizona Supreme Court.

Petitioner initiated an action for state post-conviction relief pursuant to Rule 32, Arizona Rules of Criminal Procedure, on October 25, 2005.. This action was dismissed on Petitioner's motion on November 14, 2005.

Petitioner filed another Rule 32 action on December 2, 2005. Id., Exh. KK. Petitioner was appointed counsel, who informed the state trial court on October 10, 2006, that she could not find any colorable claims to raise in a Rule 32 petition.. Petitioner filed a pro per petition for relief, reasserting the claims raised in his direct appeal. The state trial court denied relief and the Arizona Court of Appeals denied review in a decision issued September 26, 2008.

Petitioner asserts he is entitled to relief from his convictions because the trial court's reduction of the first-degree murder conviction to second-degree murder was, he contends, erroneous. Petitioner asserts that "the conviction for that [second-degree murder] is not expressly allowed by the controlling extradition agreement between the United States and Mexico." Accordingly, he argues, "the *Supremacy Clause* requires that the first-degree [murder conviction] be vacated because it conflicts with the extradition agreement". Petitioner also contends his sentences must be vacated because the trial court aggravated his sentence based on facts not found by the jury, in violation of his *Sixth Amendment* rights.

Respondents maintain the petition must be denied and dismissed. Respondents assert that Petitioner's challenge to the reduction of his first-degree murder conviction to second-degree murder is procedurally barred because the Arizona Court of Appeals found that Petitioner invited any error by requesting the challenged reduction in charge. Respondents also contend this claim may be denied because the Arizona Court of Appeals' ruling on the merits was neither contrary to, nor an unreasonable application of, United States Supreme Court precedent. Respondents assert the second claim for relief must be denied because Arizona Court of Appeals' rejection of Petitioner's *Sixth Amendment* challenge was neither contrary to, nor an unreasonable application of, Supreme Court precedent.

II Analysis
The principles of exhaustion of claims and the presence of an "adequate and independent" state law basis for denial of habeas corpus relief on the merits of the claim

Respondents argue that the Court should not review the merits of Petitioner's extradition-based claim regarding the propriety of his conviction for first-degree murder and the reduction in his conviction to second-degree murder because the state court's decision denying his specialty doctrine claim in Petitioner's direct appeal rested on an adequate and independent basis for barring federal habeas relief. Respondents contend the adequate and independent state basis for rejecting Petitioner's claim is that Petitioner waived the objection by inviting any error. Respondents cite to cases indicating the rule was clear, consistently applied, and well-established at the time of Petitioner's direct appeal.

Some federal courts have concluded that a state's common law "invited error" rule is an independent and adequate state law that is sufficient to bar federal habeas review of a claim for relief. See *Leavitt v. Arave, 383 F.3d 809, 832-33 (9th Cir. 2004)* (stating "[t]here is no reason that we should treat the invited error rule differently from other state procedural bars"); *Wilson v. Ozmint, 357 F.3d 461, 467 (4th Cir. 2004); Coleman v.*

O'Leary, 845 F.2d 696, 699-701 (7th Cir. 1988); Francois v. Wainwright, 741 F.2d 1275, 1282 (11th Cir. 1984); Tillman v. Cook, 25 F. Supp. 2d 1245, 1274-76 (D. Utah 1998).

However, it is at least arguable whether the Arizona Court of Appeals' decision denying this claim in Petitioner's direct appeal rested on the bar of invited error. The appellate court did begin discussion of the specialty doctrine claim by noting Petitioner had repeatedly sought the outcome achieved, i.e., conviction on second degree, rather than first degree, murder. After then thoroughly discussing the doctrine of specialty and applicable federal law and the merits of the claim, the Arizona Court of Appeals summarily stated that, "even if" Petitioner's conviction on second-degree murder had violated the specialty doctrine, any error was invited error and, accordingly, not reversible.

Because the claim may be denied on the merits and it is arguable if the state court decision may be affirmed based on the "adequate and independent" state bar, it is necessary to discuss whether the Court of Appeals' denial of the claim on the merits of the claim was clearly contrary to established federal law.

Violation of extradition agreement

Petitioner contends that the trial court violated the extradition treaty between the United States of America and Mexico by convicting him of first degree murder because, Petitioner argues, the governing treaty did not allow for a Mexican national's extradition for prosecution on an offense which could result in life imprisonment. Petitioner also contends that reducing the conviction from first-degree murder to second-degree murder violates the specialty doctrine, i.e., the doctrine that one can only be tried for the offense specified in the extradition agreement.

Petitioner raised these issues in a pre-trial motion. The motion was denied by the state trial judge after briefing and oral argument regarding the diplomatic note, the relevant treaty, the current status of the interpretation and extension of the treaty, the circumstance of Petitioner's case, including the exchange of notes between   Mexican and United States officials regarding Petitioner's extradition agreement, and Arizona law.

The Arizona Court of Appeals denied the extradition-based claims on the merits when presented in petitioner's direct appeal. The Court of Appeals determined:

> The doctrine of specialty provides that a state that has obtained extradition of a person is prohibited from prosecuting that person "for any offense other than that for which the surrendering state agreed to extradite." *United States v. Andonian, 29 F.3d 1432, 1434-35 (9th Cir. 1994)* (internal citations omitted).
>
> An extradited person may be tried for offenses other than those for which the person was surrendered if the extraditing country consents. The proceedings did not violate the doctrine of specialty. Romero was extradited for first-degree murder, all in compliance with the extradition agreement and the doctrine of specialty. The subsequent reduction to the lesser-included offense of second-degree murder in order to comply with the sentencing provisions of the agreement does not mandate reversal of Romero's conviction.
>
> ***
>
> Extradition treaties are construed liberally to effect their purpose of surrendering   fugitives to be tried for their alleged offenses. *United States v. Wiebe, 733 F.2d 549, 554 (8th Cir. 1984).* Under these circumstances, the reduction of Romero's conviction to a lesser-included offense constituted a reclassification contemplated by the treaty. Romero does not contest that the charge of second-degree murder, as a lesser included offense of first-degree murder, was based on the same factual allegations as those established in the request for extradition based on first-degree murder, or that the punishment for second degree murder provided for a sentence of less than life imprisonment. Therefore, the treaty itself permitted a conviction for second-degree murder.

In "*United States v. Rauscher, 119 U.S. 407, 7 S. Ct. 234, 30 L. Ed. 425 (1886),* and *Johnson v. Browne, 205 U.S. 309, 27 S. Ct. 539, 51 L. Ed. 816 (1907),* the Supreme Court set forth principles for interpreting extradition

treaties and analyzed the effect of limitations on what offenses may be punished by the extraditing country."
Rodriguez Benitez v. Garcia, 495 F.3d 640, 643 (9th Cir. 2007). The Arizona Court of Appeals' decision denying
Petitioner's claim was not an objectively unreasonable application of the holdings   in these cases.

> Rauscher established the doctrine of specialty, which provides that an extradited defendant
> may not be prosecuted for any offense other than that for which the surrendering country
> agreed to extradite.[].
>
> ...
>
> In Browne, a defendant who was convicted in the United States of conspiracy to defraud the
> government fled the country and was extradited from Canada under a treaty which did not cov-
> er conspiracy. [] Because of the treaty's limitations, Canadian authorities surrendered the de-
> fendant for another offense but not for the conspiracy charge. [] The Supreme Court, looking to
> the agreed-upon terms of extradition and to the relevant treaty language, refused to uphold a
> reinstated conviction on the conspiracy charge.

Rodriguez Benitez, 495 F.3d at 643-44 (internal citations and quotations omitted).

Similar to the circumstance of the petitioner in *Rodriguez Benitez*, the terms of the agreement regarding
the Petitioner's extradition indicated Mexico's concern about the sentence which could be imposed on Petitioner and not the degree of murder on which Petitioner could be tried. The Arizona trial court's reduction of
the crime of conviction, which was supported by the evidence adduced   at trial and which reduction was not
contemporaneously opposed by Petitioner, did not deprive Petitioner of a substantive constitutional right. Cf.
United States v. Campbell, 300 F.3d 202, 211 (2d Cir. 2002) (recognizing a difference between extradition
terms limiting what sentence could be entered by the receiving state's courts and what sentence the receiving state could force the prisoner to serve).

The Ninth Circuit Court of Appeals concluded in Rodriguez Benitez that, because Supreme Court precedent, i.e., Rauscher and Browne, addressed limitations on charged offenses and the case before them involved limitations on the petitioner's sentence, it could not be said that the state court's opinion was contrary
to clearly established federal law because to decide otherwise would have required an extension of the specialty doctrine. See *495 F.3d at 644*. "Only if the refusal to extend Rauscher's and Browne's holdings was objectively unreasonable must Benitez be granted a writ." Id. "Refusing to extend Supreme Court holdings governing limitations on charged offenses to unilaterally imposed sentencing conditions was not objectively unreasonable, and therefore AEDPA requires us to leave   the decision of the California court undisturbed." *Id.*
Similarly, the Arizona court's decision regarding Petitioner's claims based on the specialty doctrine and the
reduction of Petitioner's conviction was not objectively unreasonable and Petitioner is not entitled to habeas
relief on this claim.

Sixth Amendment sentencing claim

Petitioner asserts his aggravated prison terms violate his *Sixth Amendment* rights and the doctrine of
Blakely v. Washington because the trial court, rather than a jury, found the existence of the six circumstances
used to aggravate his sentence for second-degree murder.

In rejecting relief on this claim, the Arizona Court of Appeals applied the Arizona Supreme Court's decision
in *Arizona v. Martinez, 210 Ariz. 578, 115 P.3d 618 (2005)*, interpreting Blakely. The appellate court concluded
that, pursuant to Martinez, Petitioner's constitutional rights were not violated because Petitioner had conceded at least one aggravating circumstance, i.e., the presence of an accomplice. The Court of Appeals reiterated the holding of Martinez that, once it was established that a single Blakely-compliant aggravating factor
existed, i.e., a jury had found   or the defendant had admitted the existence of an aggravating factor, the defendant's rights were not violated because the trial judge found additional aggravating factors.

The Arizona courts have interpreted Blakely to allow for the imposition of an aggravated sentence
founded partially on facts not found by a jury if at least one aggravating factor is compliant with Blakely, i.e.,
found by a jury or admitted by the defendant. See *Arizona v. Martinez, 210 Ariz. 578, 115 P.3d 618 (2005)*;
Arizona v. Henderson, 210 Ariz. 561, 115 P.3d 601 (2005). The sentencing scheme iterated in Martinez was

upheld upon review by the United States Supreme Court. See *Martinez v. Arizona, 546 U.S. 1044, 126 S. Ct. 762, 163 L. Ed. 2d 592 (2005)*.

Arizona's response to Blakely as explained in Martinez has been found to be not clearly contrary to federal law. See *Cunningham v. California, 549 U.S. 270, 294 n.17, 127 S. Ct. 856, 871 n.17, 166 L. Ed. 2d 856 (2007)* (finding California's sentencing process unconstitutional and analyzing the Colorado Supreme Court's response to Blakely in *Colorado v. Lopez, 113 P.3d 713, 716 (Colo. 2005)*; Colorado's Lopez decision is materially similar to the Arizona Supreme Court's Martinez opinion); *Stokes v. Schriro, 465 F.3d 397, 402-03 (9th Cir. 2006)* (holding "the Arizona state courts' interpretation of these [sentencing] provisions does not contradict clearly established federal law"). Accordingly, the Arizona court's decision denying this claim in Petitioner's direct appeal was not clearly contrary to federal law and Petitioner is not entitled to relief on this claim.

REASONS WHY REMEDY IS HOLLOW

Arizona as a matter of course violates treaties as in this case and as it did in Martinez finds ways to water down the effect of Blakely. The Arizona courts allow this and the Attorney General fails to bring this systemic problem to the federal court's attention.

DISBARRED PROSECUTORS

Martin Soto Fong, Petitioner, vs. Charles Ryan, et al., Respondents.No. CV 04-68-TUC-DCB
UNITED STATES DISTRICT COURT FOR THE DISTRICT OF ARIZONA
(text modified for emphasis)

THE COURTS DECISION

At 10:15 p.m. on June 24, 1992, police were dispatched to the El Grande Market in response to a 911 call. There, they found the bodies of Fred Gee, Ray Arriola, and Zewan Huang, all employees of the market.[3] Gee had been shot in the head and torso with a .25 caliber handgun. Arriola and Huang had been shot in the head with a .38 caliber weapon and in the torso with a .25 caliber weapon.

Shortly thereafter, police found an abandoned car that was parked out of place several blocks from the market. Tire tracks indicated an abrupt stop, and the engine was still warm. Christopher McCrimmon's fingerprint was found on the driver's side window. The car belonged to David Durbin, who had lent it to his girlfriend, Queen E. Ray. The morning after the shootings Ray initially told Durbin it had been impounded for unpaid parking tickets. She told the lead homicide investigator, Tucson Police Detective Joseph Godoy, that she had driven a friend to some apartments, experienced mechanical problems, and abandoned the car. Months later, on the eve of a preliminary hearing for McCrimmon and Andre Minnitt, Godoy confronted Ray about the truthfulness of her statement and told her she would be charged with perjury if she lied on the witness stand. At the hearing, Ray testified that on the night of the market shooting, she had loaned McCrimmon the car in return for money. She said that McCrimmon, Minnitt, and a third person, whom she knew as Martinez, left McCrimmon's apartment with the car around 10:00 p.m. and that about an hour later the three returned without the car. McCrimmon gave Ray $30 and the car keys. During trial, Ray, who had seen pictures of Petitioner on television following his arrest, identified Petitioner as "Martinez."

At the time of the murders, the market was in the process of closing. Two registers had been cleared, leaving only one open. The body of the manager, Fred Gee, was found at the open register at the liquor counter. The register had a $1.69 sale rung up on it, and nearby on the counter were produce bags containing a cucumber and three lemons. Petitioner's fingerprints were found on each bag. On the floor near Gee's body were two crumpled $1 food stamps, not yet stamped with the market's name. Petitioner's fingerprints were also found on one of these food stamps. At least $175.52 was missing from the store. Testimony at trial indicated that Gee routinely permitted known customers through the iron security gate after the store's 9:00 closing time.

The investigation took a significant turn on August 31, 1992, when Detective Godoy received a tip from an anonymous caller and obtained information from a confidential informant working with Gang Unit Sergeant Zimmerling. From these sources, Godoy gleaned the name "Martin Soto," along with that of Christopher McCrimmon. A background check revealed that Soto and Fong were the same person. Godoy also learned from the Gee Family that Martin Fong was a former market employee.

Around this same time, Tucson Police Detective Fuller began investigating an August 26, 1992, robbery and non-fatal shooting at   Mariano's Pizza. McCrimmon became a potential suspect after forensic evidence linked him to the crime scene. Fuller discovered that Minnitt also may have been involved in the robbery and relayed this information to Godoy on September 1. At that point, McCrimmon was already a suspect for the market murders. With the additional information connecting McCrimmon and Minnitt, Godoy considered Minnitt a possible suspect. Moreover, according to Fuller, McCrimmon and Martin Soto Fong were close friends. On September 2, McCrimmon and Minnitt were arrested for the pizzeria robbery and in the days that followed Godoy tried to locate Petitioner.

Also in late August, Keith Woods, a close friend of McCrimmon's, was released from prison. On August 30, Tucson police arrested him on drug charges. Because Woods was already a three-time felon, and possessing drugs was a parole violation subjecting him to a possible twenty-five year prison sentence, he agreed to become an informant in exchange for release and dismissal of the drug charges. On September 8, following an initial 30 to 45-minute untaped conversation, Godoy created a ruse to move Woods into a wired room. While being surreptitiously recorded,   Woods told Godoy that on the day he was released from prison McCrimmon and Minnitt told him they committed the El Grande murders along with a third person, Cha-Chi, a Mexican guy, who had worked at the market and set up the robbery. Woods also said they told him Cha-Chi went into the store by himself "masked down or whatever," someone rebelled, and Cha-Chi shot them with a .25 caliber gun. McCrimmon and Minnitt then ran in, and the latter shot two of the victims after they were already down. Woods initially denied ever meeting or knowing Cha-Chi but in a later statement to Godoy on November 20 Woods said Cha-Chi was a guy named Martin, who was Betty Christopher's boyfriend. There was no dispute at trial that Petitioner was Betty Christopher's boyfriend.

Using an outstanding juvenile runaway complaint filed by Petitioner's mother, police finally found, arrested, and fingerprinted Petitioner on September 9, the day after Woods made his initial statement. In response to questioning, Petitioner denied any involvement in the crime, claiming that he had last been in the store about two weeks before the murders to buy beer. The next day, Godoy learned of Petitioner's   fingerprint match to items found at the crime scene, and Petitioner was re-arrested.

Petitioner's trial took place before that of his co-defendants. The prosecution theorized that Fong was recognized by market employees, permitted to enter the store during closing, filled plastic bags with lemons and a cucumber, and paid Gee at the liquor counter register with two $1 food stamps before the shooting began. The defense theory was one of mistaken identity: Petitioner claimed Cha-Chi was Martin Garza, another acquaintance of McCrimmon's. The defense also maintained that investigators improperly handled the forensic evidence, making the fingerprints inherently unreliable. Further, the defense called Keith Woods as a witness to support the theory that Detective Godoy improperly coerced both Woods and Ray to implicate Fong.

Co-Defendant Retrials

After their convictions were reversed due to juror coercion, the trial court severed the retrials of McCrimmon and Minnitt. Minnitt's initial retrial resulted in a hung jury. *See State v. Minnitt, 203 Ariz. 431, 433, 55 P.3d 774, 777 (2002).* He was tried again in 1999, found guilty of all charges, and resentenced to death for the murders.

On appeal,   the Arizona Supreme Court determined that Minnitt's third trial should have been barred by principles of double jeopardy resulting from prosecutorial misconduct at the first two trials. *Id.* Specifically, the court found that the prosecutor, Kenneth Peasley, knowingly elicited false testimony from Detective Godoy concerning how and when McCrimmon, Minnitt, and Fong became suspects in the market murders. The court recounted the following relevant facts:

In all three Minnitt trials and in both McCrimmon trials, the state's case depended heavily on Keith Woods' credibility. Importantly, as of September 2, the police had identified Soto-Fong, McCrimmon, and Minnitt as suspects in the El Grande crimes and had interviewed them. But according to Godoy, police had yet to interview anyone who could provide direct evidence linking any of the three to the crimes. Woods was not interviewed until September 8, six days after the McCrimmon and Minnitt interviews. Godoy claimed to have received his first knowledge of any involvement by McCrimmon and Minnitt from his interview with Woods. This was the information the police were seeking - that McCrimmon and Minnitt had implicated themselves in the murders   and that a witness would so testify.

Woods' credibility was tenuous. He was a convicted felon and drug addict who entered into an agreement with the state to provide testimony to avoid a lengthy prison sentence. The state had no plausible explanation why Godoy conducted the untaped interview with Woods. The defense strategy in the Minnitt and McCrimmon trials was to show that Godoy was the source of Woods' information about Minnitt's and McCrimmon's involvement in the case, and that during the untaped interview, he fed that information to Woods. If Godoy was indeed the source, Woods' testimony would not have helped the state. Similarly, without Woods, the state's case would be significantly weakened because no direct or physical evidence connected Minnitt to the crime, and the credibility of the remaining witnesses was questionable.

Id. at 434-35, 55 P.3d at 777-78.

Peasley was aware Godoy had begun investigating McCrimmon, Minnitt, and Fong before Godoy first met with Woods. Nonetheless, during the initial 1993 joint trial, Peasley repeatedly told the jury and elicited from Godoy information to the contrary--that police did not have the suspects' names until after Godoy interviewed Woods   on September 8, 1992--thus bolstering Woods's credibility. Peasley repeated this conduct during Minnitt's 1997 retrial, asking the detective "a series of questions designed to erase any doubt that the source of Godoy's information could have been anyone but Woods." *Id. at 436, 55 P.3d at 779*. One week after the jury in Minnitt's initial retrial failed to reach a verdict, McCrimmon's retrial began. By this time McCrimmon's defense counsel had learned of Godoy's false testimony and vigorously pursued the issue. During McCrimmon's trial, Godoy admitted he testified falsely at Minnitt's trial because he feared causing a mistrial by revealing information obtained from a confidential informant. The jury ultimately acquitted McCrimmon on all charges.

Based on his misconduct in the McCrimmon and Minnitt trials, Peasley was later disbarred from the practice of law. *In Re Peasley, 208 Ariz. 27, 90 P.3d 764 (2004).*

Postconviction Proceedings

On direct appeal, Fong was represented by his trial attorney, James Stueringer. After the Arizona Supreme Court denied appellate relief on August 19, 1996, Stueringer sought certiorari in the United States Supreme Court. That petition was denied on May 19, 1997. *Soto-Fong v. Arizona, 520 U.S. 1231, 117 S. Ct. 1826, 137 L. Ed. 2d 1033 (1997)*. In February 1998, Stueringer's son was arrested in Ohio for various criminal offenses. (Doc. 46, Ex. 61.) Stueringer asked Peasley, the prosecutor in Fong's case, for assistance, and Peasley ultimately wrote a letter to an Ohio judge in June 1998 urging probation for Stuehringer's son. Around this same time, Stuehringer, acting *pro bono,* wrote a letter defending Peasley against charges of ethical misconduct lodged with the state bar by McCrimmon's defense lawyer. On December 17, 1998, the Arizona Supreme Court issued its mandate in Petitioner's case and appointed new counsel to represent him in postconviction proceedings. In May 2000, the State Bar of Arizona filed a formal complaint against Peasley and the Pima County Attorney hired Stueringer to defend Peasley in the disciplinary proceeding.

On August 20, 1999, Petitioner filed his first state PCR petition raising numerous claims, including prosecutorial misconduct based on alleged perjured testimony from Detective Godoy concerning his investigation of Petitioner. He also raised several claims of ineffective assistance of counsel (IAC), challenging *inter alia* Stueringer's failure to retain an identification expert, failure to call Petitioner as a witness, failure to challenge Godoy's testimony both during trial and on appeal, and decision to call Keith Woods as a witness. In supplemental filings dated November 13, 2000, and July 9, 2001, Petitioner added claims alleging conflict of interest arising from Stueringer's representation of Peasley in the state bar proceedings and a violation of *Brady v. Maryland* from the prosecutor's failure to disclose one of Godoy's reports. All told, Petitioner raised 35 claims in his PCR petition.

In August 2000, the State Bar of Arizona sought clarification concerning Stuehringer's representation of Peasley in light of Stuehringer's role as Petitioner's trial counsel. In January 2001, the state bar hearing officer found no conflict because the allegations in Peasley's disciplinary case arose from his conduct in the trials of McCrimmon and Minnitt, not Petitioner.

The officer further ordered that Stuehringer could not be called as a witness and that it was unclear how any confidential communications between Petitioner and Stuehringer could relate to Peasley's conduct in prosecuting McCrimmon and Minnitt.

In January and August 2001, Pima County Superior Court Judge Gordon Alley, serving in place of the deceased trial judge, held evidentiary hearings on Petitioner's ineffectiveness claims. Because Godoy was under indictment for perjury stemming from the McCrimmon and Minnitt trials, he invoked his rights under the *Fifth Amendment* and refused to testify. Stuehringer testified as to his defense strategy, and the court also heard testimony from several other witnesses, including Peasley, regarding the alleged *Brady* and prosecutorial misconduct violations.

Judge Alley unexpectedly died prior to ruling on Petitioner's claims. Judge Clark Munger was reassigned to the case, and the parties agreed that approximately half of Petitioner's claims could be decided without further evidentiary development. In June 2002 the state court issued a 34-page ruling addressing those claims. At Petitioner's request the court held another evidentiary hearing in August 2002 on the remaining claims. However, Petitioner did not present any new witnesses. Stuehringer, Peasley, and two other witnesses provided testimony substantially similar to that given at the 2001 hearing. Although no longer under indictment, Godoy was not called as a witness. In October 2002, the court issued a 29-page ruling rejecting the remaining claims.

Following this Court's order staying federal habeas proceedings pending resentencing in light of *Roper* and exhaustion of new claims relating to actual innocence and a Vienna Convention violation, Petitioner's federal habeas counsel were appointed as counsel for Petitioner by the state court and filed a second PCR petition raising (and re-raising) numerous claims. The actual innocence claim was based primarily on a January 2005 article from *The New Yorker* magazine which contained a summary of a statement by an alleged new witness, Carole Grijalva-Figueroa, who claimed she was the "lookout" during the El Grande Market robbery and that Petitioner, McCrimmon, and Minnitt were not involved. In mid-2005, the state court vacated Petitioner's death sentence, summarily dismissed the majority of Petitioner's successive PCR claims on procedural grounds, and directed Petitioner to obtain an affidavit from Grijalva-Figueroa to substantiate the innocence allegation. In January 2006, the court denied relief when Petitioner failed to produce any supporting evidence. The Arizona Court of Appeals affirmed. *State v. Soto-Fong*, No. 2 CA-CR 2006-0091 & No 2 CA-CR 2006-0056-PR (consolidated) (Ariz. App. May 3, 2007) (unpublished memorandum decision).

Subsequently, Petitioner filed a third PCR petition in state court, again asserting an actual innocence claim and requesting leave to conduct discovery. In May 2009, the PCR court denied discovery and dismissed the petition, finding the claims precluded because they had been addressed previously. Accepting a discretionary petition for review, the court of appeals denied relief. *State v. Soto-Fong*, No. 2 CA-CR 2009-0294-PR, 2010 Ariz. App. Unpub. LEXIS 467, 2010 WL 1138956 (Ariz. App. Mar. 25, 2010) (unpublished memorandum decision).

I. CLAIM A: PROSECUTORIAL MISCONDUCT

Petitioner asserts that his rights under the *Fifth*, *Sixth*, *Eighth*, and *Fourteenth Amendments* were violated by prosecutorial misconduct. He divides the specific allegations underlying this claim into three categories: (1) Testimonial Evidence; (2) Physical Evidence; and (3) Confrontation, Abuse of Process & Other Misconduct. Each of these categories contain multiple allegations. Petitioner also asserts deprivation of his rights based on the cumulative effect of the alleged misconduct.

REASON WHY REMEDY IS HOLLOW

Arizona prosecutors as a matter of routine engage in this type of misconduct and courts refuse to afford relief.

DENIAL OF COMPLETE DEFENSE

FRANK ROQUE, Petitioner, v. CHARLES L. RYAN and ARIZONA ATTORNEY GEN-ERAL, Respondents. CIV 08-02154 PHX PGR (MEA)UNITED STATES DISTRICT COURT FOR THE DISTRICT OF ARIZONA (Text modified for emphasis)

THE POSITION OF THE COURT

I Procedural History

On September 25, 2001, a Maricopa County grand jury indicted Petitioner on one count of first-degree murder in the death of Mr. Balbir Singh Sodhi on September 15, 2001 (Count 1). Petitioner was also charged with three counts of drive-by shooting, involving a Mobil gas station (Count 6), the shooting of Mr. Sodhi in front of a Chevron gas station (Count 2), and a shooting at a private residence in Mesa previously owned by Petitioner (Count 7). The grand jury further indicted Petitioner on three counts of attempted first-degree murder, naming as victims Anwar Khalil (Count 3), Leali Chamseddine (Count 4), and Ali Khein (Count 5). The indictment also charged Petitioner with three counts of reckless endangerment, naming as victims Louis Ledesma (Count 8), Jesus Ledesma (Count 9), and Jose Valencia (Count 10

The state subsequently filed a notice of intent to seek the death penalty if Petitioner was convicted of first-degree murder in the death of Mr. Sodhi. Two of the attempted murder counts and two of the reckless endangerment counts were later dismissed. The amended indictment on which Petitioner was tried was comprised of Count 1, the first-degree murder of Mr. Sodhi; Count 2, the drive by shooting at the Chevron station; Count 3, the attempted first degree murder of Mr. Khalil; Count 4, the drive by shooting at the Mobil; Count 5, the drive by shooting at the private residence; Count 6, the reckless endangerment of Mr. Ledesma.

Prior to trial, on March 22, 2002, Petitioner's counsel filed a motion pursuant to Rule 11, Arizona Rules of Criminal Procedure, requesting a hearing to evaluate Petitioner's mental competence to stand trialThe prosecution and the defense subsequently stipulated that the trial court could determine Petitioner's competency to stand trial based upon the reports of two appointed experts, Dr. Jack Potts and Dr. Michael Colfield. At the time Petitioner requested a competency determination, he had been prescribed and was being medicated with Zyprexa, an anti-psychotic medication.

Both experts found Petitioner competent to stand trial. After reviewing the experts' reports, on May 28, 2002, the state trial court concluded that Petitioner understood the proceedings and was able to assist counsel with his defense. Accordingly, the state trial court determined Petitioner was mentally competent to stand trial, citing *Arizona Revised Statutes § 13--4510(B)*.

The presentation of evidence to the jury in Petitioner's trial began on or about September 2, 2003. Mr. Ledesma, a witness to the shooting of Mr. Sodhi, testified that he was in front of the Chevron station showing Mr. Sodhi a problem with a landscaping water line when he heard tires squealing. Mr. Ledesma testified he then heard Mr. Sodhi say "Don't shoot me", and then he heard gunshots. Mr. Ledesma testified that he was more or less kneeling on the ground about one and a half feet from Mr. Sodhi at the time the shots were fired. Mr. Ledesma testified that, after the first shot was fired, he saw that Mr. Sodhi had been shot in the stomach. Mr. Ledesma testified that he then flung himself prone onto the ground. Mr. Ledesma testified that Mr. Sodhi fell to the ground after the second or third gunshot. Mr. Ledesma testified that when he looked up he saw a black truck speeding away. Mr. Ledesma testified that he did not see the individual who fired the gunshots which struck Mr. Sodhi.

A witness to the shooting of Mr. Sodhi at the Chevron station testified that between one and three in the afternoon he was in his vehicle on a street adjacent to the Chevron station when he heard three gunshots and saw Mr. Sodhi fall to the ground. The witness testified that the shots appeared to come from a black Chevrolet S10 truck at a distance from Mr. Sodhi of twenty or thirty feet, and that the truck sped off after Mr. Sodhi was shot.

Mr. Ahmed Sahak, who had purchased a house in Mesa from Petitioner in late 1998, testified that around 3 p.m. on September 15, 2001, he and his wife were about to leave their house when they heard gunshots.

Mr. Sahak testified he looked outside through a window and saw a man in a dark pick-up truck putting down a weapon in the truck. Mr. Sahak testified that he did not recognize the man in the truck as Petitioner and that Petitioner had a beard on September 15, 2001, but did not have a beard in 1998 when Mr. Sahak had purchased the house.

Several witnesses, including Mr. Anwar Khalil, testified that at approximately 2:45 p.m. on Saturday, September 15, 2001, a man in a black truck fired from the truck into a combination Mobil gas station and sandwich shop on University Drive at Val Vista in   Mesa, Arizona. (testimony of Ms. Andrews) & 70-72 (testimony of Ms. Benchley), (testimony of Mr. Khalil). Mr. Khalil testified that he was injured by glass fragmented from a light fixture by the shooting.

The state offered evidence from police detectives, crime scene investigators, and a ballistics expert, that the bullets which struck Mr. Sodhi and the bullets that were fired into the Mobil station and at the house in Mesa were fired from weapons found in Petitioner's house and that shell-casings from the guns found in the house were found in Petitioner's black Chevrolet S10 truck, which Petitioner was seen driving on September 15, 2001.

The government's case in chief focused on establishing that the murder of Mr. Sodhi was premeditated. The government presented testimony that Petitioner was very upset by the events of September 11, 2001. Several witnesses testified Petitioner had expressed animus towards the ethnic group he believed responsible for the events of September 11, 2001. Several of Petitioner's co-workers testified   regarding Petitioner's emotional response to the events of September 11, 2001. The state also offered testimony from two of Petitioner's co-workers that Petitioner had told them he had "a hard time" with a man who worked at a gas station on Broadway who was "probably Indian". The government also presented a witness who worked at an Applebee's restaurant visited by Petitioner on September 11, 2001, who testified that on that date Petitioner, who was extremely upset, had used the derogatory term "towelhead" to refer to people of Middle Eastern heritage. (testimony of Mr. Sewell). The government also presented witnesses who encountered Petitioner at three different bars on the date of the crime, i.e., the Wild Hare, Famous Sam's, and the Papillon Too.

Defense counsel was successful in discrediting some of the prosecution's evidence of premeditation. A police detective, Steve Casillas, testified that when he had interviewed Ms. Baldenegro she told him she did not see Petitioner get in his truck and   leave the Wild Hare on September 15, 2001, contradicting her testimony on the stand at the trial.. Upon questioning by defense counsel, Detective Casillas testified that he had garnered Petitioner's Mobil, Chevron, and Discover credit card records and that, within the six months prior to the date of the crimes, there was no evidence Petitioner had purchased gasoline at either the Mobil station or the Chevron station where the crimes occurred on September 15, 2001. This evidence contradicted the coworker's statement that Petitioner had told him he had trouble with a person who wore a turban that worked in a gas station Petitioner patronized. The detective testified that, although there was no evidence Petitioner had purchased gasoline at either of the stations involved in the crimes within that six month time period, Petitioner had used his Mobil and Chevron credit cards at other Chevron and Mobil stations in that area during that time period. Additionally, the detective testified he first contacted Petitioner at about 9 p.m. on September 15, 2001, and that he was with Petitioner until about 11:30 p.m.,   and that during that time period he saw no sign of intoxication.

At the close of the state's case Petitioner's counsel moved for a judgment of acquittal on the charge of reckless endangerment with regard to Mr. Ledesma (Count 6 of the amended indictment), asserting the state had failed to present sufficient evidence to sustain the charge against Petitioner. The motion was denied.

In addition to challenging the legal sufficiency of the state's evidence with regard to Count 6, Petitioner presented a defense of guilty-except-insane. In support of this defense Petitioner introduced evidence from his sister and his brother that their mother suffered from and had been hospitalized for schizophrenia. Petitioner's sister and his brother both testified they had observed behavior indicating Petitioner also suffered from mental illness from the time he was an adolescent.. Petitioner's brother testified that he spoke with Petitioner by telephone on September 15, 2001, and that on that day his brother was incoherent and so emotionally unstable that Petitioner's brother   contacted police because he feared Petitioner would harm himself. Petitioner's daughter also testified as to her father's state of mind the week of September 11, 2001, and his uncharacteristic extreme agitation on September 15, 2001.

The defense presented the testimony of two psychological experts, Dr. Philip Barry and Dr. Richard Rosengard, regarding Petitioner's mental condition at the time of the crimes. Dr. Barry, a psychologist, testified that prior to examining Petitioner in May of 2003 he had reviewed the reports of Dr. Scialli and Dr. Rosengard. Dr. Barry testified he had administered, *inter alia*, the MMPI (Minnesota Multi-phasic Personality Inventory) to Petitioner, by reading the questions to Petitioner and recording his answers, which was not the standard methodology for performing that test. Dr. Barry testified he had administered an IQ test and that Petitioner's IQ was below average.

Dr. Barry testified his testing indicated Petitioner had a "schizotypal" personality disorderDr. Barry testified that Petitioner had experienced a "psychotic episode" on the day of the crimes, which episode was precipitated by the events occurring on September 11, 2001.

Dr. Rosengard testified he had examined Petitioner in February and March of 2002. Dr. Rosengard, a forensic psychiatrist, disagreed with Dr. Barry's diagnosis, and testified Petitioner suffered from major affective disorder with psychotic features. Dr. Rosengard agreed with Dr. Barry that Petitioner was not legally responsible for his crimes at the time of the crimes.

An independent forensic psychological expert, Dr. Potts, called by the prosecution in rebuttal, testified that in his opinion Petitioner was legally sane at the time of the crimes. Dr. Potts examined Petitioner in 2003 on two separate occasions for two hours each time. Dr. Potts averred Petitioner told him that, on September 13, 2001, Petitioner had heard a voice telling him to "kill the devils. Dr. Potts testified this statement was consistent   with what Petitioner had told Dr. Scialli and Dr. Rosengard, i.e., Petitioner told these individuals he heard a voice telling him to "kill the devils" on September 13.

Dr. Toma, a psychologist, testified he had performed a second MMPI-2 test on Petitioner in August of 2003. Id., Exh. O. Dr. Toma testified he had been asked to administer the test to Petitioner because of the arguable validity of the first MMPI test administered by Dr. Barry. Dr. Toma testified some mental health experts believed the test should not be administered by the expert reading the test to the subject and recording their answers.

Dr. John Scialli, a medical expert called by the state, testified at Petitioner's trial that he had examined Petitioner twice in 2002. Dr. Scialli testified that shortly after Petitioner was incarcerated in the Madison Avenue Jail pending his trial, Petitioner was prescribed Zyprexa by a different doctor, i.e., the physician attending the inmates at the jail. Dr. Scialli testified that, when he examined Petitioner in 2002, Petitioner did not appear to be psychotic at that time.. This expert   witness opined Petitioner did not fit the medical diagnosis to warrant prescribing Zyprexa, i.e., that Petitioner did not suffer from schizophrenia or manic episodes with grandiose behavior as those terms are represented in the DSM IV.

Dr. Scialli testified that, in his opinion Petitioner did not suffer from bipolar disorder with psychosis. Dr. Scialli testified Petitioner did not need to be on Zyprexa. Dr. Scialli did allow that Petitioner had said he heard voices.

Dr. Scialli further testified that, at the time of the crimes, the only disorder Petitioner suffered from was alcohol dependence, with possibly an adjustment disorder with depressed mood. Dr. Scialli opined Petitioner had committed the crimes while suffering a strong reaction to a situational "stressor", i.e., the events of September 11, 2001.. Dr. Scialli opined that, at the time of the crimes, Petitioner was not having hallucinations.

Dr. Scialli also testified that Petitioner knew that what he was doing was wrong, as evidenced by his subsequent evasiveness, i.e., speeding away in his car after committing   crimes.. The doctor stated: "Someone who's delusional doesn't have a particular reason to get away." Additionally, Dr. Scialli noted in his testimony that Petitioner did not start talking about having "command" hallucinations until conversations with investigators at the end of September.

Dr. Scialli disagreed with Dr. Barry that Petitioner suffered from schizotypal personality disorder. Dr. Scialli also disagreed with Dr. Rosengard's diagnosis of recurring major depressive disorder. Dr. Scialli gave detailed testimony as to why he had concluded Petitioner was not suffering from a definable mental disorder and these disorders specifically. Dr. Scialli testified that, at the time of the crimes, Petitioner did not fall within the legal definition for insanity. Additionally, Dr. Scialli testified he thought it was possible Petitioner was faking or exaggerating any mental disease.

Ms. Amy Woods, a counselor at the jail where Petitioner was incarcerated pending his trial, testified she interviewed Petitioner on September 17, 2001. She stated Petitioner did not complain of hearing voices at that time. Ms. Woods testified Petitioner denied he had said he heard voices coming from a television set.

The jury was instructed, *inter alia,* that it was Petitioner's burden to establish his insanity at the time of the crimes by clear and convincing evidence, stating Petitioner bore the burden of providing evidence it was "highly probable that the defendant was insane. This is a lesser standard of proof than beyond a reasonable doubt." The jury was dismissed to begin deliberations on the afternoon of September 29, 2003. The jury returned with a verdict at approximately 11:45 a.m. on September 30, 2003, having deliberated that morning since 9 a.m.

The jury found Petitioner guilty of the murder of Mr. Sodhi, guilty on one count of attempted murder, and guilty on one count of reckless endangerment. Id., Exh. P. The jury also found Petitioner guilty on three counts of drive-by shooting. Additionally, the jury found that the government had established that the murder, attempted murder, and drive-by shootings were all dangerous offenses. The jury also found the existence of another aggravating factor, i.e., a grave risk of death to Mr. Ledesma. As stated supra, Mr. Ledesma was next to Mr. Sodhi but closer to the ground, i.e., kneeling on the ground while Mr. Sodhi stood, when Mr. Sodhi was shot. Mr. Ledesma testified at Petitioner's trial that he was not injured during the shooting.

A hearing regarding Petitioner's sentences for his capital crime was conducted on October 7 and October 8, 2003. The jury determined that the evidence offered in mitigation was insufficient to call for leniency with regard to the sentence to be imposed for the murder conviction. Accordingly, on October 9, 2003, Petitioner was sentenced to death pursuant to his conviction for the murder of Mr. Sodhi. The trial court subsequently imposed aggravated sentences as to each of the other counts of conviction. At the hearing regarding the remaining sentences to be imposed, the state asked the trial court to aggravate the sentences because the victims were targeted based on their race or religion. The state also asked for aggravation on Count 2 because that drive-by shooting resulted in the death of Mr. Sodhi. The state asked for aggravation on Petitioner's conviction on the charge of endangerment because the commission of that crime involved the use of a weapon.

The state trial court concluded the sentences on Counts 2 and 6 could be aggravated by the fact of conviction on Counts 3, 4, and 5. The court determined that Counts 3 and 4 could be aggravated based on the fact of Petitioner's convictions on Counts 1, 2, 5, and 6.

Petitioner took a direct appeal of his convictions and sentences to the Arizona Supreme Court. In his direct appeal Petitioner alleged that the state wrongfully discriminated in choosing a jury by using a peremptory strike on a prospective African American jury venireman. Petitioner also argued the trial court should have precluded Dr. Ben Porath's testimony regarding the ultimate issue of Petitioner's insanity, based on the state's failure to disclose the scope of the expert's testimony.

Additionally, Petitioner asserted that the admission of certain videotaped statements violated the *Confrontation Clause*. Petitioner further maintained that there was insufficient evidence to support the jury's finding of the "grave risk of death" aggravating factor with regard to the charge of reckless endangerment of Mr. Ledesma. Petitioner also alleged the trial court abused its discretion by allowing a juror to remain on the panel after contact with a media outlet.

The Arizona Supreme Court affirmed all of Petitioner's convictions and the non-capital sentences in a lengthy decision issued August 14, 2006. See also *Arizona v. Roque, 213 Ariz. 193, 141 P.3d 368 (2006)* (en banc). Reviewing Petitioner's capital sentence pursuant to his conviction for murder, the Arizona Supreme Court exercised its discretion to independently review the aggravating circumstances and the mitigation evidence. Upon conclusion of this review, the Arizona Supreme Court reduced Petitioner's sentence on the murder conviction from death to life imprisonment without the possibility of release.

On September 6, 2006, Petitioner initiated an action for state post-conviction relief pursuant to Rule 32, Arizona Rules of Criminal Procedure. In his Rule 32 action Petitioner raised fifty claims for relief including, *inter alia,* that his rights were violated by the use of a stun belt during his trial. Petitioner also asserted there was prosecutorial and juror misconduct during his trial. Petitioner further argued he was denied his right to the effective assistance of trial counsel and appellate counsel, and also alleged his convictions should be vacated because he was forced to take anti-psychotic medication during his trial. Petitioner did not seek appointment of counsel in his Rule 32 action but averred to the state court that he wished to proceed *pro se* in that matter.

On May 18, 2007, the state trial court summarily dismissed Petitioner's post-conviction action pursuant to *Rule 32.6(c), Arizona Rules of Criminal Procedure*. The Superior Court concluded Petitioner had failed to raise a colorable issue of fact or law entitling him to relief or warranting further proceedings. Petitioner appealed this decision to the Arizona Court of Appeals, which denied relief on March 14, 2008. Petitioner sought review by the Arizona Supreme Court, which denied review on June 13, 2008. This   subsection provides:

> Summary Disposition. The court shall review the petition within twenty days after the defendant's reply was due. On reviewing the petition, response, reply, files and records, and disregarding defects of form, the court shall identify all claims that are procedurally precluded under this rule. If the court, after identifying all precluded claims, determines that no remaining claim presents a material issue of fact or law which would entitle the defendant to relief under this rule and that no purpose would be served by any further proceedings, the court shall order the petition dismissed. If the court does not dismiss the petition, the court shall set a hearing within thirty days on those claims that present a material issue of fact or law. If a hearing is ordered, the state shall notify the victims, upon the victims' request pursuant to statute or court rule relating to victims' rights, of the time and place of the hearing.

In his amended petition for habeas relief before the District Court, filed February 5, 2009, Petitioner asserts:

1. The state violated his right to due process of law by withholding exculpatory evidence regarding his blood alcohol level at the   time of the offenses;

2. His right to due process of law and his right to a fair trial were violated when the state failed to fully disclose the content of an expert witness' rebuttal testimony;

3. He was denied a fair trial as a result of juror misconduct;

4. He was incompetent to stand trial *inter alia* because he was on anti-psychotic medication at the time of trial;

5. His constitutional right to confront the witnesses against him was violated;

6. He was denied the ability to assist and confer with his defense counsel because he was required to wear a stun belt during his trial;

7. His constitutional right to due process of law was violated by the introduction of autopsy photographs as evidence;

8. His right to due process of law was violated by the introduction of evidence regarding a prior conviction;

9. He was subjected to 22 specific instances of prosecutorial misconduct, the cumulative effect of which was to violate his right to a fair trial;

10. He was denied a fair trial as a result of testimony by Dr. Jack Potts;

11. His trial and appellate counsel were both unconstitutionally ineffective, in violation of his *Sixth Amendment* rights;

12. The indictment was defective because it failed   to allege aggravating factors and because the prosecution was granted a sixty-day continuance to consult the government of India regarding its opinion on imposition of the death penalty;

13. There was insufficient evidence presented at trial to support Petitioner's convictions for drive-by shooting and the finding of premeditation on the charge of attempted first-degree murder;

14. His rights were violated because the state failed to prove the aggravating factors beyond a reasonable doubt.

Respondents allow that the *section 2254* habeas petition is timely filed. Respondents assert that Petitioner did not properly exhaust all of his federal habeas claims in the state courts. See Docket No. 20. Respondents argue that because Petitioner did not present nine of his habeas claims to the Arizona Supreme Court in his action for post-conviction relief, Petitioner has procedurally defaulted those claims. Respondents maintain that, to fully exhaust these claims, Petitioner was required to raise the claims to the state Supreme Court in addition to the state Court of Appeals because Petitioner was originally sentenced to death, rather than life imprisonment. Respondents allow that,   at the time Petitioner's post-conviction action was heard by the Arizona Court of Appeals, Petitioner stood sentenced to life imprisonment.

In reply to the answer to his habeas petition, Petitioner asserts that there was no proper evidence that he was intoxicated at the time of the crimes and that, at the time of the crimes, he heard "voices from God telling him to kill devils." Petitioner asserts that, at the time of the crimes, he was "suffering severe decompesation (sic) due to 9-11 events". Petitioner re-argues and characterizes the evidence and testimony presented at his trial. Petitioner notes evidence presented at trial indicated his mother was a schizophrenic and that Petitioner suffered from mental illness prior to reaching adulthood. Petitioner states: "Both defense experts concluded Petitioner was legally insane at the time of the offenses."

Petitioner further argues that his fourteenth claim for relief includes the allegation that his sentence violates the holding of Blakely v. Washington. Petitioner contends he has "suffered 'cause and prejudice'", citing Dretke v. Haley and Teague v. Lane. Petitioner alleges that he was improperly sentenced   to aggravated terms of imprisonment on Counts 1 through 6 pursuant to a preponderance of the evidence standard, rather than having the aggravating factors found by a jury. Accordingly, Petitioner argues, the holding of Blakely dictates a finding of prejudice. Petitioner also alleges that he has exhausted his tenth, eleventh, and thirteenth grounds for habeas relief by raising these claims to the Arizona Supreme Court in a supplemental brief filed February 13, 2006. Petitioner also asserts he exhausted grounds 2, 5, 7, 9, and 10 through 14 of his federal habeas petition by raising them in his direct appeal.

With regard to the exhaustion of claims raised in his state action for post-conviction relief, Petitioner contends the state trial court's "denial to review the 50 claims raised on P.C.R. does not specifically state a procedural default for failure to fairly present the claim." Petitioner asserts that *Rule 32.2(a)(3) of the Arizona Rules of Criminal Procedure* is not an adequate and independent basis for denying federal habeas relief and that this rule is not regularly enforced.   *Arizona Rule of Criminal Procedure 32.2(a)(3)* precludes post-conviction relief based on any   ground "waived at trial, on appeal, or in any previous collateral proceeding." Claims predicated on "a significant change in the law that if determined to apply to defendant's case would probably overturn the defendant's conviction or sentence," *Ariz. R. Crim. P. 32.1(g)*, are excluded from the general rule of preclusion under certain circumstances, *Ariz. R. Crim. P. 32.2(b)*.

Arizona v. Shrum, 220 Ariz. 115, 116, 203 P.3d 1175, 1176 (2009).

II Analysis

D. Petitioner's claims for relief

1. Petitioner asserts the state violated his right to due process of law by withholding exculpatory evidence regarding his blood alcohol level during the offenses.

Petitioner argues his constitutional rights were violated by the state's failure to disclose evidence regarding his blood alcohol level during the offenses. Petitioner contends the prosecutor did not disclose that a police detective had determined that Petitioner's blood alcohol content would have been below the legal limit for driving while intoxicated after the consumption of two Fosters beers three and one half hours prior to the crime. Petitioner contends the failure to disclose this evidence prior to trial violated his rights pursuant to Brady v. Maryland. Regardless of any failure to fully or properly exhaust   this claim, it may be denied on the merits.

In Brady v. Maryland the United States Supreme Court held that a defendant's right to due process of law is violated when the government fails to disclose evidence that is material to the defendant's guilt or innocence, including impeachment evidence. See *373 U.S. 83, 86-87, 83 S. Ct. 1194, 1196-97, 10 L. Ed. 2d 215 (1963); Schad v. Ryan, 595 F.3d 907, 915 (9th Cir. 2010)*. The state violates this obligation and denies a criminal defendant due process of law if "(1) the evidence in question was favorable to the defendant, meaning that it had either exculpatory or impeachment value; (2) the state 'willfully or inadvertently' suppressed the evidence; and (3) the defendant was prejudiced by the suppression." *Schad, 595 F.3d at 915*, quoting *Strickler v. Greene, 527 U.S. 263, 281-82, 119 S. Ct. 1936, 1948, 144 L. Ed. 2d 286 (1999)*. See also *Horton v. Mayle, 408 F.3d 570, 578 (9th Cir. 2005)* (holding the government's failure to disclose a leniency deal with a witness was reversible error).

Petitioner's state of intoxication, or not, at the time of the crimes, and whether Petitioner had a preexisting alcohol consumption issue, were disputed during testimony. The inferences that Petitioner was intoxicated at the time of the crimes was countered by testimony that signs of intoxication could have resulted from allergies or extreme mental agitation. Petitioner's counsel elicited testimony from the employees of the restaurant and sports bar who had contact with Petitioner on the day of the crimes that they regularly called taxis for people who were obviously intoxicated and that they did not think it necessary to call a taxi for Petitioner. *Inter alia*, Petitioner's brother testified he believed Petitioner had a problem with alcohol prior to the events of September 11, 2001. Petitioner's brother testified that Petitioner was so incoherent when he spoke with him by telephone on September 15, 2001, that the brother initially surmised Petitioner was intoxicated. The record indicated that Petitioner had purchased two beers and consumed at least one of them at the Wild Hare bar at approximately 11:30 on the morning of September 15, 2001.

Any undisclosed evidence regarding Petitioner's blood alcohol level at the time of the crimes could not have been exculpatory because evidence that Petitioner's blood alcohol level was below the legal limit for driving while intoxicated would not necessarily prove or disprove Petitioner's affirmative defense of insanity. No prejudice resulted from the alleged "failure" to disclose this evidence because in Arizona a defendant's voluntary intoxication is not a defense to a charge of murder, assault with a deadly weapon, or drive-by shooting. *Arizona v. Kiles, 222 Ariz. 25, 33, 213 P.3d 174 & n.10, 222 Ariz. 25, 213 P.3d 174, 182 & n.10 (2009)* ("The statute unambiguously provides that intoxication is a defense only against the culpable mental state of intentionally."); *Arizona v. Lavers, 168 Ariz. 376, 389, 814 P.2d 333, 346 (1991)* (concluding that voluntary intoxication is not defense to knowing first degree murder). Accordingly, this claim for federal habeas relief may be denied on the merits of the claim. "The legislature amended the statute in 1994 to eliminate intoxication as a defense 'for any criminal act or requisite state of mind.' *A.R.S. § 13-503 (2001)*; 1993 Ariz. Sess. Laws, ch. 256, §§ 2, 3 (1st Reg. Sess.)."

2. Petitioner contends his right to due process of law and his right to a fair trial were violated when the state failed to fully disclose the content of an expert witness' rebuttal testimony and when that expert witness made inconsistent statements.

Petitioner raised this *federal habeas* claim in his direct appeal. The en banc Arizona Supreme Court denied relief on this claim:

> At trial, the defense called Drs. Rosengard and Barry to testify regarding Roque's mental condition at the time of the crimes. Before the defense rested, the State called Dr. Ben-Porath out of order in rebuttal. The State had disclosed to the defense only that Dr. Ben-Porath would testify regarding the validity of the administrations of the MMPI-2. However, on the stand, Dr. Ben-Porath began to interpret the results of Roque's MMPI-2 tests. The defense immediately objected that the doctor's testimony fell outside the scope of disclosure, pointing out that the State had neither disclosed any written report from Dr. Ben-Porath nor outlined his opinion. Citing *Arizona Rule of Criminal Procedure 15.1(a)(3)*, the defense asserted that the State was obligated to disclose "an overview" of the expert's testimony, including an "outline" of his opinion or a "written report."
>
> The judge concluded that the State would have had to disclose any written report generated by Dr. Ben-Porath, but did not have to create an overview of his testimony. The judge therefore found no disclosure violation, but nonetheless proposed giving the defense the remainder of the afternoon, commencing at approximately 3:15 p.m., to interview Dr. Ben-Porath. The de-

fense attorney declined, saying that he could not effectively challenge Dr. Ben-Porath's expanded testimony on such short notice. The judge ruled that Dr. Ben-Porath could continue to testify, and the doctor proceeded to analyze Roque's MMPI-2 results in detail.

Dr. Ben-Porath then began to analyze the results of the M-FAST that Dr. Barry had administered to Roque. The defense again objected, this time because Dr. Ben-Porath was testifying regarding a diagnostic tool other than the MMPI-2. The judge overruled the objection. Dr. Ben-Porath proceeded to opine on the critical questions of whether the MMPI-2 results indicated that Roque had mental disorders and whether the M-FAST results indicated malingering.

The prosecutors conceded below that they had not revealed to the defense that Dr. Ben-Porath would testify to anything other than the proper administration of the MMPI-2. Recognizing that their failure to disclose the scope of Dr. Ben-Porath's testimony might create an appellate issue, the lead prosecutor said, "I don't suppose an appellate court cares whether I'm sorry about something but I think we had ... a miscommunication." The prosecutor then said he would not object if the defense had to hire another expert to rebut Dr. Ben-Porath's testimony because of the "miscommunication."

213 Ariz. 193, 206, 141 P.3d 368, 381. The state court continued: "We therefore conclude, under these facts, that the trial court erred in ruling that *Rule 15.1(a)(3)* requires that only a 'written report or statement' need be disclosed." *Id., 213 Ariz. at 209, 141 P.3d at 384*.

The Arizona Supreme Court further found:

Dr. Ben-Porath's testimony far exceeded a discussion of the validity of an oral administration of the MMPI-2 followed three months later by a paper administration of the test. Dr. Ben-Porath analyzed several of Roque's scores from both test administrations, such as those indicating bizarre mentation. *Indeed, Dr. Ben-Porath testified to the ultimate question in dispute, opining that Roque's MMPI-2 scores did not indicate that Roque had any of several mental conditions about which the prosecutor questioned him. On this critical issue, Dr. Ben-Porath was the only expert to find no evidence of mental illness.* Dr. Ben-Porath also testified that Roque's M-FAST score indicated malingering, and he offered a general psychological opinion in response to a juror's question.

Id., 213 Ariz. at 209, 141 P.3d at 384 (emphasis added).

Accordingly, the court held: "The State's failure to fully and fairly disclose to the defense the results of Dr. Ben-Porath's assessment of Roque's mental health, the critical issue in this capital case, violated *Rule 15.1(a)(3)*." *Id., 213 Ariz. at 210, 141 P.3d at 385*. Citing state law, the Arizona Supreme Court found the state trial court had fashioned an appropriate sanction for the prosecution's improper conduct, notwithstanding defense counsel's refusal to accept the trial court's proffered sanction. Therefore, the Arizona Supreme Court held, the failure to preclude the testimony was not reversible error. *Id., 213 Ariz. at 211, 141 P.3d at 386*, citing *Arizona v. Tucker, 157 Ariz. 433, 441, 759 P.2d 579, 587 (1988)* (observing that, without reversal, counsel may consider admonition only a "verbal spanking").

A federal court is limited in conducting habeas review to deciding whether a conviction violates the Constitution, laws, or treaties of the United States. *28 U.S.C. § 2254(a); Estelle v. McGuire, 502 U.S. 62, 67-68, 112 S. Ct. 475, 480, 116 L. Ed. 2d 385 (1991)*. A state court's evidentiary ruling does not provide a basis for habeas relief unless the ruling infringed upon a specific federal constitutional right or deprived the petitioner of a fundamentally fair trial as guaranteed by the right to due process of law. See *Pulley v. Harris, 465 U.S. 37, 41-42, 104 S. Ct. 871, 874-75, 79 L. Ed. 2d 29 (1984); Briceno v. Scribner, 555 F.3d 1069, 1076-77 (9th Cir. 2009)*. The violation of a state rule of criminal procedure does not, by itself, constitute a violation of a defendant's federal constitutional rights, including their right to procedural due process.

To be entitled to habeas relief on this type of claim, the petitioner must establish that the admission of the evidence was so arbitrary or prejudicial that it rendered their trial fundamentally unfair. See *Walters v. Maass, 45 F.3d 1355, 1357 (9th Cir. 1995)* (stating this in the context of a claim that the improper admission of the fact of a prior conviction violated the petitioner's federal constitutional right to due process of law). "In essence, the inquiry comes down to the question, whether absent the constitutionally-forbidden evidence, honest and fair-minded jurors might very well have brought in not-guilty verdicts." *Burns v. Clusen, 798 F.2d 931, 943 (7th Cir. 1986).* Typically, the federal courts require other evidence of guilt to be overwhelming before concluding a constitutional error was harmless. See *Mauricio v. Duckworth, 840 F.2d 454, 459 (7th Cir. 1988).*

The state court's conclusion that any violation of Petitioner's rights in admitting the testimony of Dr. Ben Porath was harmless is not clearly contrary to federal law as established by the United States Supreme Court.

> With regard to expert testimony, we recently noted that we have found no cases "support[ing] the general proposition that the Constitution is violated by the admission of expert testimony concerning an ultimate issue to be resolved by the trier of fact." *Moses v. Payne, 543 F.3d 1090, 1105 (9th Cir. 2008).* "Although '[a] witness is not permitted to give a direct opinion about the defendant's guilt or innocence .... an expert may otherwise testify regarding even an ultimate issue to be resolved by the trier of fact.'" *Id.* at 1106 (quoting *United States v. Lockett, 919 F.2d 585, 590 (9th Cir. 1990)* [*51] (alteration in original)). We found this "not surprising," id., in light of the well-established rule permitting opinion testimony on ultimate issues, see *Hangarter v. Provident Life & Accident Ins. Co., 373 F.3d 998, 1016 (9th Cir. 2004).*

Briceno, 555 F.3d at 1077-78.

Because the state court's decision regarding this claim was not clearly contrary to nor an unreasonable application of federal law, Petitioner is not entitled to habeas relief on the merits of this claim.

5. Petitioner maintains his *Sixth Amendment* right to confrontation was violated by the introduction of statements made by his wife to a police investigator.

In his amended habeas petition Petitioner asserts that a videotape of his wife being interviewed by police was introduced as evidence at Petitioner's trial. Petitioner argues that, because his wife did not testify at trial and because she made statements on the videotape regarding Petitioner's mental health, the introduction of the tape violated his *Sixth Amendment Confrontation Clause* rights, i.e., his right to confront witnesses against him. Petitioner also alleges that his rights were violated by the introduction at trial of testimony by a police detective as to statements made to the detective by Petitioner's wife.

Petitioner's wife could not be located by the prosecution and, accordingly, was not subpoenaed to testify at Petitioner's trial. The primary issue at trial was Petitioner's sanity at the time the crimes were committed. Conflicting testimony was presented regarding whether or not Petitioner exhibited signs of mental illness, such as hallucinations, prior to the date of the crimes and on the date of the crimes. The trial court admitted a videotape of police detectives telling Petitioner about statements made by his wife in the course of their investigation of the crimes committed on September 15, 2001, at which time Petitioner was a suspect in those crimes. The admission of out-of-court statements by Petitioner's wife, who was not available to testify, to a police detective investigating the crimes regarding Petitioner's mental condition, would arguably violate the holding in Crawford.

Respondents assert Petitioner is factually mistaken in claiming that the jury viewed a videotape of the police interviewing his wife. The record indicates that, during Petitioner's trial, portions of a videotape of two police investigators interviewing Petitioner were played for the jury. Defense counsel objected to the introduction of this evidence. The videotape was recorded shortly after Petitioner was taken into custody. In the videotape the investigators tell Petitioner that his wife has told them certain facts about Petitioner.

Additionally, the jury was shown a portion of a videotape in which Petitioner and his wife are talking at the police station after Petitioner was interviewed by the investigators. Petitioner's counsel objected to the introduction of the videotape, asserting it was hearsay and also arguing that it violated marital privilege. [*60] The trial judge overruled defense counsel's objection to the admission of the videotape, concluding that the statements in the tape were not being offered for the truth of the asserted facts.

The videotape of Petitioner speaking with his wife was introduced during Dr. Scialli's testimony, and was offered as the best evidence regarding Petitioner's mental state at a time close to the time of the crimes, as compared to the examinations of mental health experts weeks, months, or years after the crimes. Dr. Scialli had reviewed the tapes and believed it supported his conclusion that Petitioner was not unable to understand his circumstance or what had occurred at the time of the crimes.

The trial judge instructed the jury that the videotapes were offered only to establish the context of Petitioner's statements as relied upon by Dr. Scialli when he rendered his expert opinion regarding Petitioner's mental state and that the jury was not to accept the truth of what the detectives said on the videotape or the truth of what Petitioner's wife had said on the videotape.

Petitioner raised the first portion of his fifth federal habeas claim in his direct appeal, asserting that the trial court improperly admitted as evidence a videotape of Petitioner's wife being interviewed by police. Petitioner argued that the police interviewers testified at his trial as to his wife's statements about Petitioner's mental state at the time of the crimes.

In denying this claims, the Arizona Supreme Court concluded:

> During the videotaped interrogation of Roque after the shootings, the police detectives told Roque that his wife, Dawn, had made statements to them incriminating Roque. Dawn refused to testify at trial. Roque asserts that the admission of the videos at trial violated the *Sixth Amendment's Confrontation Clause* as interpreted in *Crawford v. Washington*, 541 U.S. 36, 124 S. Ct. 1354, 158 L. Ed. 2d 177, [] (2004), because the detectives used Dawn's statements in questioning Roque and Roque had no opportunity to cross-examine Dawn.

> The trial court's admission of the videos did not violate the *Confrontation Clause*. Crawford establishes that the *Sixth Amendment* right to confront witnesses attaches to testimonial witness statements made to a government officer to establish some fact. See *541 U.S. at 68, 124 S. Ct. 1354*. In this case, however, there was no evidence presented that Dawn actually made the statements that the detectives used in questioning Roque. *The detectives' report of what Dawn said was not being offered at trial for the truth of the matters allegedly asserted by Dawn and therefore did not constitute hearsay.* Instead, the detectives were using an interrogation technique to elicit a confession from Roque. The judge instructed the jury, in watching the interrogation videos, not to consider the detectives' statements for their truth. Because the statements allegedly made by Dawn were never introduced for their truth, they were not testimonial hearsay statements barred by the *Confrontation Clause*. See *id. at 59 n.9, 124 S. Ct. 1354*. The admission of the videotaped statements therefore did not violate Roque's rights under the *Confrontation Clause*.

213 Ariz. at 213-14, 141 P.3d at 388-89 (emphasis added).

In addition to the videotape, the prosecution introduced testimony relating to a police interview between Petitioner's wife and police detective Donald Vogel. Petitioner's defense counsel objected to this testimony, arguing that it was hearsay. The prosecutor responded that it was not hearsay because it was not being offered for the truth of the matter asserted, but rather to impeach previous testimony regarding claims that Petitioner had heard voices prior to the offense.. The trial court overruled the objection, and instructed the jury that the testimony was not being offered to prove or disprove the matter asserted or the truth of any matter not asserted by a person who was speaking outside of the courtroom, i.e., Petitioner's wife. On cross-examination, Detective Vogel admitted that he did not ask Petitioner's wife specific questions about Petitioner's mental health, and that he did not ask her whether Petitioner had heard voices the week prior to the offense.

In *Crawford v. Washington*, 541 U.S. 36, 124 S. Ct. 1354, 158 L. Ed. 2d 177 (2004), the United States Supreme Court held that the *Sixth Amendment* right to confront witnesses attaches to testimonial witness statements made to a government officer to establish some fact. However, non-testimonial statements do not implicate the *Sixth Amendment's* core concerns. *Id., 541 U.S. at 51, 124 S. Ct. at 1364*. See also *United States v. Earle, 488 F.3d 537, 543 (1st Cir. 2007)* (describing categories of statements which have been held to be testimonial).

Detective Vogel's testimony was not offered for the truth of the matter asserted, i.e., that Petitioner had told his wife he heard voices or that he did not, but rather to impeach prior testimony regarding the assertion that Petitioner had heard voices prior to the date of the crimes. Because this testimony was not introduced for the truth of the matter asserted but instead was impeaching, it did not involve testimonial hearsay statements barred by the *Confrontation Clause*. See *Crawford, 541 U.S. at 59, 124 S. Ct. at 1369*. Because the state court's decision in this regard was not clearly contrary to federal law, i.e., the United States Supreme Court's decision in Crawford, Petitioner is not entitled to relief on this claim.

In Crawford, issued in 2004 while Petitioner's case was on appeal, the United States Supreme Court held that the admission at trial of a wife's out-of-court statements to police officers investigating her husband's complicity in felony crimes violated the husband's *Confrontation Clause* rights. Accordingly, to the extent Petitioner asserted in his direct appeal that or his post-convictions proceedings that the trial court improperly admitted evidence   of his wife's statements to police officers, a state court decision denying this claim on the merits of the claims would be contrary to established federal law.

Assuming that such a claim was properly exhausted and wrongly decided by the state courts, however, Petitioner is still not entitled to federal habeas relief on this claim.

> Under AEDPA, even where the state court has committed constitutional error under § 2254(d), habeas relief may still be denied absent a showing of prejudice. ... To determine prejudice, we apply the harmless-error standard from Brecht. Under this standard, we grant relief where we believe the error "had substantial and injurious effect or influence in determining the jury's verdict." *Brecht, 507 U.S. at 623, 113 S.Ct. 1710* (quoting *Kotteakos v. United States, 328 U.S. 750, 776, 66 S.Ct. 1239, 90 L. Ed. 1557[] (1946)* (internal quotation marks omitted)). As the Supreme Court has explained, under the Brecht standard, we ask, "Do I, the judge, think that the error substantially influenced the jury's decision." *O'Neal v. McAninch, 513 U.S. 432, 436, 115 S.Ct. 992, 130 L. Ed. 2d 947, [] (1995)*. In a case where the record is so evenly balanced that a "conscientious judge is in grave doubt as to the   harmlessness of an error," the petitioner must prevail. *Id. at 438, 115 S. Ct. 992*. Thus, in the course of a Brecht inquiry, the state bears the "risk of doubt." See *Valerio v. Crawford, 306 F.3d 742, 762 (9th Cir. 2002)* (en banc).

Gautt v. Lewis, 489 F.3d 993, 1016 (9th Cir. 2007) (some internal citations and quotations omitted).

To be entitled to federal habeas relief, the Court must independently conclude that Petitioner's constitutional rights were violated and that the violation was not harmless error.

Confrontation Clause violations are subject to harmless error analysis. See, e.g., *Lilly v. Virginia, 527 U.S. 116, 140, 119 S. Ct. 1887, 1901-02, 144 L. Ed. 2d 117 (1999)*; *Winzer v. Hall, 494 F.3d 1192, 1201 (9th Cir. 2007)* ("Violation of the *Confrontation Clause* is trial error subject to harmless-error analysis ... because its effect can be 'quantitatively assessed in the context of other evidence presented' to the jury." (citation omitted)).

The entire record submitted by the parties in this matter having been thoroughly reviewed, the Magistrate Judge concludes that any error in admitting the videotape of the interview of Petitioner's wife by the police detective at Petitioner's trial was harmless   error. In light of all of the evidence presented at Petitioner's trial, including the testimony of psychiatric experts, police detectives, Petitioner's daughter and brother, and the people who observed Petitioner on the date of the crimes, the admission of any testimonial statements by Petitioner's wife could not have influenced the jury's decision. Accordingly, habeas relief may be denied on this claim.

6. Petitioner was denied the ability to assist and confer with defense counsel because he was required to wear a stun belt during trial. Petitioner contends wearing the belt inhibited his ability to confer with his defense attorney.

Petitioner contends that the shock belt hampered his ability to assist his defense counsel because he was afraid any quick movement would result in a shock and because prongs in the shock belt kept him in constant pain and he could not lean back. Petitioner alleges the trial judge found the use of the device was at the sole discretion of the detention officers and that the trial judge did not make a record regarding any necessity for the belt. Petitioner raised this claim in his state action for post-conviction relief, in which relief was summarily denied   by the state courts.

All of the federal cases which discuss habeas relief based on a shackling claim state that, to succeed on this type of claim, the petitioner must show that the physical restraints 'had substantial and injurious effect or influence in determining the jury's verdict..." *Rhoden v. Rowland, 172 F.3d 633, 636 (9th Cir. 1999)*. See also *Holbrook v. Flynn, 475 U.S. 560, 568-69, 106 S. Ct. 1340, 1345, 89 L. Ed. 2d 525 (1986)*. To be entitled to habeas relief on this claim the District Court must conclude that the jury saw or was aware of the restraint and that the restraint was not justified by state interests. See *Ghent v. Woodford, 279 F.3d 1121, 1132 (9th Cir. 2002)*. Additionally, for unjustified restraint to rise to the level of a constitutional trial error, Petitioner must establish that he suffered prejudice as a result of the restraint. See id.; *Williams v. Woodford, 384 F.3d 567, 592-93 (9th Cir. 2004)*; *Gonzalez v. Pliler, 341 F.3d 897, 903 (9th Cir. 2003)*. See also *Dyas v. Poole, 317 F.3d 934, 936-37 (9th Cir. 2003)*.

Petitioner has not established that the jury saw the stun belt. See *Williams, 384 F.3d at 592-93*; *Packer v. Hill, 291 F.3d 569, 583 (9th Cir. 2002)* (concluding no prejudice   resulted from the defendant's leg brace when no juror interviewed after trial remembered seeing a leg brace on the defendant); *Rich v. Calderon, 187 F.3d 1064, 1069 (9th Cir. 1999)*. Petitioner's defense counsel has conceded that the jury was never aware of any such device. Moreover, although Petitioner claims that the stun belt inhibited his ability to participate in his defense, unlike the defendant in *Gonzalez*, there is nothing in the record to support this assertion. The record is devoid of any complaints, comments, or objections on the part of Petitioner regarding the device. In an unpublished opinion which is, therefore, not precedential but is indicative of the reasoning of the Ninth Circuit Court of Appeals, that court stated:

> Despite this violation of his constitutional rights, we cannot grant habeas relief. In the habeas context, [harmless error analysis] means that the petitioner must show that the physical restraints had substantial and injurious effect or influence in determining the jury's verdict. *Gonzalez, 341 F.3d at 903* (internal quotation marks and citations omitted). There is no evidence that the belt was visible to the jury. Berg's speculative   claims that the jury's perception of him was distorted by the React belt and the fear and anxiety that it provoked in both him and his trial counsel do not show substantial and injurious effect or influence where the jury was also presented with significant and strong evidence of Berg's guilt. In the light of this evidence, it is unlikely that the React belt and its effects on Berg's comportment and demeanor had a substantial influence on the jury's determination of his guilt. Further, the evidence tendered in this case was insufficient to establish that Berg could not communicate with his counsel because of the use of the React belt.

Berg v. Runnels, 198 Fed. Appx. 672, 673 (2006).

8. Petitioner asserts his right to due process of law was violated by the introduction of evidence regarding a prior conviction.

In his direct appeal Petitioner asserted the trial court erred by allowed the fact of a prior conviction to be introduced to the jury. In denying this claim, the Arizona Supreme Court concluded:

> Here, however, the judge permitted an expert to testify regarding his reliance on the conviction in assessing Roque's mental health. Roque does not contest that evidence of his previous conviction is the type of evidence reasonably relied upon by experts in making mental health assessments. Under the Rules of Evidence, therefore, the evidence may be disclosed as forming the basis of an opinion without regard to its independent admissibility. See Ariz. R. Evid. 703. Roque claims, however, that the mention of the conviction was so unduly prejudicial that it outweighed the probative value of the evidence.
>
> We agree that Roque's 1983 attempted robbery conviction   had only minimal probative value in showing a lack of mental illness because the State did not produce evidence that the

attempted robbery was alcohol-induced or that it was motivated by racism, which were its theories at trial. Nor did Dr. Scialli's testimony demonstrate the relevance of the 1983 conviction to his assessment of Roque's mental health. See *Ex parte Vaughn, 869 So.2d 1090, 1097, 1099 (Ala. 2002)* (finding probative value of prior bad acts substantially outweighed by prejudice where state 'presented nothing to indicate that the prior acts committed by [defendant] were relevant to his mental state during the shooting that occurred ... many years later').

But if the probative value of the conviction was minimal, so was any prejudicial effect. The jury heard of the conviction from at least two other experts, Dr. Potts and Dr. Rosengard, who testified that because of the age of the conviction and lack of violence involved, it did not affect their assessments of Roque's mental health. Moreover, Roque admitted doing the acts that constituted the crimes for which he was charged in this trial, so the jury did not rely on the prior conviction to conclude that Roque may have acted in conformity with it in committing the present crimes. Finally, we note that the trial judge offered to give a limiting instruction advising the jurors to consider the conviction only as information relied upon by the expert, but Roque declined the offer.

213 Ariz. at 209, 211-12, 141 P.3d at 386-87.

This conclusion was not contrary to clearly established federal law because the Court of Appeals correctly identified the governing rule and its application of the rule to the facts of the case was not unreasonable. See *Inthavong v. Lamarque, 420 F.3d 1055, 1061 (9th Cir. 2005).*

The Supreme Court has established a general principle that the admission of evidence which is extremely unfair to the defendant, including the fact of a prior conviction, may violate the defendant's right to due process. See *Dowling v. United States, 493 U.S. 342, 352, 110 S. Ct. 668, 674, 107 L. Ed. 2d 708 (1990); Alberni v. McDaniel, 458 F.3d 860, 864 (9th Cir. 2006).* However, a state court's evidentiary rulings can form the basis for federal habeas relief under the *due process clause* only when they were so conspicuously prejudicial or of such magnitude as to fatally infect the trial and deprive the defendant of due process. See *Parker v. Bowersox, 94 F.3d 458, 460 (8th Cir. 1996).* The improper admission of unduly prejudicial evidence violates a defendant's right to due process only when there were no permissible inferences the jury could have drawn from the evidence. See *Windham v. Merkle, 163 F.3d 1092, 1103 (9th Cir. 1998).*

Even assuming that the evidence was unduly prejudicial, the jury could draw permissible inferences from the fact of Petitioner's prior conviction, i.e., that the fact of the conviction did or did not weigh in favor of a particular expert's opinion regarding Petitioner's mental state at the time of the crimes. Accordingly, the state court's decision denying relief on the merits of the claim was not clearly contrary to nor an unreasonable application of federal law and Petitioner is not entitled to relief on the merits of the claim.

9. Petitioner alleges that he was subjected to prosecutorial misconduct.

Petitioner raised twenty-eight specific claims of prosecutorial misconduct in his direct appeal. The state Supreme Court thoroughly addressed these claims, stating:

> Roque asserts that twenty-eight incidents of prosecutorial misconduct occurring throughout the guilt and sentencing proceedings denied him a fair trial. We have addressed fifteen of the alleged incidents elsewhere in this opinion, and, of those, only the State's failure to disclose the scope of Dr. Ben-Porath's testimony warrants inclusion here. Roque also alleges thirteen additional incidents, which we now address.

213 Ariz. at 228, 141 P.3d at 403. "After reviewing each incident for error," the state court assessed "whether the incident should count toward [Petitioner's] prosecutorial misconduct claim." After the specific incidents contributing to a finding of misconduct were identified, the court went on to "evaluate their cumulative effect on the trial." *213 Ariz. at 230, 141 P.3d at 405.*

The state Supreme Court then concluded:

> Under the Hughes test, we cannot say that the cumulative effect of the misconduct here so permeated the entire atmosphere of the trial with unfairness that it denied Roque due process.

[] We recognize in particular that the prosecutors' failure to disclose the scope of Dr. Ben-Porath's testimony was improper and potentially prejudicial, but the defense did not make a good faith effort to resolve that discovery dispute. As a result, we cannot now assess the prejudice the defendant may ultimately have suffered. The cumulative effect of   the incidents of misconduct in this case thus does not warrant reversal.

213 Ariz. at 230, 141 P.3d at 405.

Only those specific acts of the prosecutor alleged to be instances of prosecutorial misconduct that were exhausted in state court would be properly considered in this habeas action. The undersigned concludes the state court's determination that the asserted instances of prosecutorial misconduct did not deprive Petitioner of his right to procedural due process of law was not clearly contrary to federal law.   Petitioner contends the prosecutor committed misconduct by introducing the testimony of Dr. Ben Porath; by telling the jury Petitioner had said he had a preexisting conflict with Mr. Sodhi; by calling Petitioner a terrorist and comparing Petitioner to Osama Bin Laden; by discrediting the defense experts with harassment and innuendo; by being insolent and dismissive about Dr. Toma's qualifications; by calling the defense experts "so called medical experts presented by the defense" and calling Dr. Potts a "so called" psychiatrist; by saying he was using the term "doctor" "loosely" with regard to the defense experts; by telling the jury they could not consider Petitioner's IQ   or any mental impairment because it did not excuse his conduct. Petitioner further asserts prosecutorial misconduct because, he asserts, the prosecution's statement that he was urging them not to accept the "distorted" story told via the expert witnesses testifying as to what Petitioner had said to them constituted a comment on Petitioner exercising his right to remain silent. Petitioner additionally argues the prosecutor committed misconduct by eliciting testimony from Dr. Scialli that he had previously worked with Petitioner's defense counsel and by repeatedly telling the jury that Petitioner was a drunk, an alcoholic, and a racist. Petitioner notes his defense counsel moved for a mistrial based on the prosecutor's misconduct, which motion was denied.

A habeas petitioner is not entitled to federal habeas relief based on a prosecutor's improper statements unless the statements infected the entire proceeding and rendered it fundamentally unfair in violation of defendant's right to due process of law. See *Darden v. Wainright, 477 U.S. 168, 181, 106 S. Ct. 2464, 2471, 91 L. Ed. 2d 144 (1986)*, quoting *Donnelly v. DeChristoforo, 416 U.S. 637, 643, 94 S. Ct. 1868, 1871, 40 L. Ed. 2d 431 (1974); Davis v. Woodford, 384 F.3d 628 (9th Cir. 2004).*

> On   a petition for a writ of habeas corpus, the standard of review for a claim of prosecutorial misconduct is the narrow one of due process, and not the broad exercise of supervisory power. *Darden v. Wainwright, 477 U.S. 168, 181, 106 S. Ct. 2464, 91 L. Ed. 2d 144, [] (1986)* (quoting *Donnelly v. DeChristoforo, 416 U.S. 637, 642, 94 S. Ct. 1868, 40 L. Ed. 2d 431, [] (1974)*). Thus, to succeed, [the petitioner] must demonstrate that it so infected the trial with unfairness as to make the resulting conviction a denial of due process. *Donnelly, 416 U.S. at 643, 94 S. Ct. 1868.*

Renderos v. Ryan, 469 F.3d 788, 799 (9th Cir. 2006).

> Thus, we must examine the entire proceedings to determine whether the prosecutor's remarks so infected the trial with unfairness as to make the resulting conviction a denial of due process. Before granting relief, we must also determine that any constitutional error was not harmless. Specifically, we must find that the error had substantial and injurious effect or influence in determining the jury's verdict. Only if the record demonstrates that the jury's decision was substantially influenced by the error or there is grave doubt about whether an error affected a jury will [the petitioner] be entitled to   relief.

Sechrest v. Ignacio, 549 F.3d 789, 807-08 (9th Cir. 2008) (internal citations and quotations omitted).

To be entitled to relief on this claim, Petitioner must demonstrate that the prosecutor's comments "had [a] substantial and injurious effect or influence in determining the jury's verdict." *Brecht v. Abrahamson, 507 U.S. 619, 623, 113 S. Ct. 1710, 1714, 123 L. Ed. 2d 353 (1993)*, quoting *Kotteakos v. United States, 328 U.S.*

750, 776, 66 S. Ct. 1239, 1253, 90 L. Ed. 1557. In making this determination, the Court must look at the nature of the prosecutor's comments, the nature and quantum of the evidence before the jury, the arguments of opposing counsel, the judge's charge, and whether the alleged errors were isolated or repeated. See *Billings v. Polk, 441 F.3d 238, 250 (4th Cir. 2006).*

The United States Supreme Court has concluded that habeas relief on this type of claim is not appropriate unless the prosecutor manipulated or misstated the evidence or implicated other specific rights of the defendant, such as his right to counsel or his right to remain silent. See *Darden, 477 U.S. at 181-82, 106 S. Ct. at 2471-72.* A prosecutor's statements might satisfy the standard if they are racially motivated or if they attempt to establish guilt by association. See *United States v. Wolfswinkel, 44 F.3d 782, 787 (9th Cir. 1995).*

The complained of statements were not racially motivated insofar as they did not disparage Petitioner because of his race or his associations. The prosecutor did not manipulate the evidence or wrongfully implicate Petitioner's invocation of his right to counsel. The statement alleged by Petitioner to have implicated his right to remain silent did not explicitly do so, instead it encouraged the jury not to accept the version of events proffered by the defense expert witnesses, based on what Petitioner had told them. Neither did the prosecutor explicitly implicate Petitioner had exercised his right to remain silent after his arrest. Additionally, Petitioner's counsel successfully argued to limit the effect of the improper statements by the prosecutor and to challenge the prosecutor's characterization of factual evidence.

The contested statements made by Petitioner's prosecutor reflected emotional reactions and attempts to elicit emotional responses to the evidence from the jury, which, even if classified as improper, undesirable, or even universally condemned, did not violate Petitioner's right to due process. See *Darden, 477 U.S. at 180-81, 106 S. Ct. at 2470-71; Hovey v. Ayers, 458 F.3d 892, 923 (9th Cir. 2006); Allen v. Woodford, 395 F.3d 979, 997 (9th Cir. 2005).*

The Magistrate Judge concludes the statement of the prosecutor did not so infect the trial with unfairness as to make the resulting conviction a violation of due process. See *Williams v. Borg, 139 F.3d 737, 745 (9th Cir. 1998); Thompson v. Borg, 74 F.3d 1571, 1576-77 (9th Cir. 1996)* (denying habeas relief based on a due process claim regarding a prosecutor's comments in closing argument because, in part, the jury returned a verdict of second degree murder rather than first degree murder). Accordingly, the state courts' decision that Petitioner was not deprived of a constitutional right by the prosecutor's challenged comments was not clearly contrary to federal law and Petitioner is not entitled to federal habeas relief on the merits of this claim.

10. Petitioner contends he was denied a fair trial as a result of testimony by Dr. Jack Potts.

In his amended habeas petition Petitioner contends Dr. Potts committed perjury by testifying Petitioner had told him Petitioner had been to one of the gas stations the day or week before the events of September 15, 2001. See Docket No. 14. Petitioner has arguably not exhausted this claim for relief. In his state action for post-conviction relief Petitioner argued Dr. Potts committed perjury by stating Petitioner was intoxicated at the time of the crimes. This is a different factual premise for the asserted perjury claimed in the habeas petition. However, regardless of any failure to fully exhaust this claim, the claim may denied on the merits. Petitioner is not entitled to relief based on a single alleged instance of perjury unless it rendered his trial fundamentally unfair. See *Estelle, 502 U.S. at 67-68, 112 S. Ct. at 479-80.* Although Dr. Potts did testify that Petitioner had told Dr. Potts he had been to one of the gas stations involved in the crimes prior to September 15, 2001, this testimony did not render Petitioner's trial fundamentally unfair. Defense counsel did an admirable job of eliciting testimony contradicting the prosecution's assertion that Petitioner had been to one or both of the gas stations prior to the date of the shootings and that Petitioner had previously had negative interactions with Mr. Sodhi. Accordingly, habeas relief on this claim may properly be denied.

11. Petitioner contends his trial and appellate counsel were both unconstitutionally ineffective.

Petitioner raised ineffective assistance of counsel claims in his state action for post-conviction relief pursuant to Rule 32, Arizona Rules of Criminal Procedure. The state court determined that Petitioner was not entitled to relief from his convictions and sentences based on these claims.

In his action for state post-conviction relief pursuant to Rule 32, Arizona Rules of Criminal Procedure, Petitioner alleged he was denied his right to the effective assistance of trial counsel because his counsel failed to submit or request adequate jury instructions regarding the insanity defense. Petitioner also asserted his counsel was ineffective because he did not object to Petitioner being forced to wear a stun belt during the trial. Petitioner further alleged his rights were violated because his counsel did not object to Petitioner's being forced to take anti-psychotic medications during his trial. Petitioner further alleged his trial counsel's performance was deficient because counsel failed to adequately cross-examine the state's key expert witness. Petitioner argued his trial counsel was incompetent because he failed to object to Dr. Ben Porath's inconsistent statements. Additionally, Petitioner asserted his trial counsel's performance was unconstitutionally deficient because he failed to secure a change of venue.

Petitioner also maintains his counsel was ineffective because he failed to move for a competency hearing close to the date of the trial and because he did not move for a Willits jury instruction. Petitioner alleges his trial counsel was ineffective because he failed to challenge the admission of a prior conviction from 1983 as not authenticated. Petitioner also asserts his trial counsel was ineffective because he did not object to the admission of the autopsy photographs and because he did not object to prosecutorial misconduct.

With regard to his appellate counsel, Petitioner asserted counsel failed to argue there was insufficient evidence to convict Petitioner of first degree murder and insufficient evidence to convict Petitioner of drive-by shooting at the gas stations, and insufficient evidence to convict Petitioner of drive-by shooting at the Mesa residence. Petitioner also alleged his appellate counsel was ineffective for failing to argue a violation of Petitioner's right to be free of double jeopardy caused by the charge of attempted murder and drive by shooting at the Mobil gas station. Additionally, Petitioner asserted his appellate counsel was ineffective for failing to contend that being forced to wear a stun belt at his trial and being forcibly medicated during his trial violated Petitioner's constitutional rights, warranting reversal of his convictions.

The state trial court summarily denied the ineffective assistance of counsel claims raised in Petitioner's Rule 32 action. The Arizona Court of Appeals and the Arizona Supreme Court declined to review or reverse this decision. The entire record in this matter having been thoroughly reviewed, including the recording of oral argument in Petitioner's direct appeal proceedings, the Magistrate Judge concludes the state courts' resolution of Petitioner's ineffective assistance of counsel claims was not contrary to federal law.

To state a claim for ineffective assistance of counsel, a petitioner must show that his attorney's performance was deficient and that the deficiency prejudiced the petitioner's defense. See *Strickland v. Washington, 466 U.S. 668, 687, 104 S. Ct. 2052, 2064, 80 L. Ed. 2d 674 (1984).* The petitioner must overcome the strong presumption that counsel's conduct was within the range of reasonable professional assistance required of attorneys in that circumstance. See *id., 466 U.S. at 687, 104 S. Ct. at 2064.* To establish prejudice, the petitioner must establish that there is "a reasonable probability that, but for counsel's unprofessional errors, the result of the proceeding would have been different." *Strickland, 466 U.S. at 694, 104 S. Ct. at 2068.* See also, e.g., *Martin v. Grosshans, 424 F.3d 588, 592 (7th Cir. 2005).* Additionally, prejudice from counsel's allegedly deficient performance is less likely when the case against the defendant is strong. See, e.g., *Avila v. Galaza, 297 F.3d 911, 924 (9th Cir. 2002)* (collecting the cases so holding).

To prevail on the merits of a habeas claim of ineffective assistance of counsel, it is the habeas applicant's burden to show that the state court applied Strickland to the facts of his case in an objectively unreasonable manner. "An unreasonable application of federal law is different from an incorrect application of federal law." *Woodford, 537 U.S. at 25, 123 S. Ct. at 360, 154 L. Ed. 2d 279* (internal quotations omitted). Vague or conclusory claims do not establish evidence sufficient to conclude the state court's decision was clearly contrary to federal law. See *Jones v. Gomez, 66 F.3d 199, 205 (9th Cir. 1995); James v. Borg, 24 F.3d 20, 26 (9th Cir. 1994).*

The Strickland prejudice requirement applies to claims of ineffective assistance of appellate counsel:

> The *Sixth Amendment* right to effective assistance of counsel includes the right to effective appellate counsel. However, appellate counsel need not advance every possible argument, even those that are non-frivolous, and should instead concentrate his advocacy on winnowing out weaker arguments on appeal and focusing on one central issue if possible, or at most on a few key issues. The two-part Strickland test, which the Court has used in evaluating claims of ineffec-

tive assistance of trial counsel, supra, also guides an analysis of claims of ineffective assistance of appellate counsel.

Davis v. Singletary, 853 F. Supp. 1492, 1549 (M.D. Fl. 1994) (internal quotations and citations omitted).

To succeed on an assertion his counsel's performance was deficient because counsel failed to raise a particular argument, either in his trial proceedings or in his appeals, the petitioner   must establish the argument was likely to be successful, thereby establishing that he was prejudiced by his counsel's omission. See *Tanner v. McDaniel, 493 F.3d 1135, 1144 (9th Cir. 2007); Weaver v. Palmateer, 455 F.3d 958, 970 (9th Cir. 2006)*. The appropriate inquiry is not whether raising a particular issue on appeal would have been frivolous, but whether there is a reasonable probability raising the issue would have led to the reversal of Petitioner's conviction. See *Miller v. Keeney, 882 F.2d 1428, 1434 (9th Cir. 1989)*. If Petitioner had only a remote chance of obtaining reversal based upon' a specific issue, neither element of the Strickland test is satisfied.

A defendant's counsel's decisions regarding jury instructions are fairly construed as a strategic decision. See *Scott v. Elo, 302 F.3d 598, 607 (6th Cir. 2002)*. "[S]trategic choices made after thorough investigation of law and facts relevant to plausible options are virtually unchallengeable; and strategic choices made after less than complete investigation are reasonable precisely to the extent that reasonable professional judgments support the limitations on investigation." *Strickland, 466 U.S. at 690-91, 104 S. Ct. at 2066.*

Under   AEDPA, we apply Strickland to each individual case, irrespective of whether the precise fact pattern at issue has been considered previously by the Supreme Court. See *Williams, 529 U.S. at 391, 120 S. Ct. 1495* (That the Strickland test "of necessity requires a case-by-case examination of the evidence . . . obviates neither the clarity of the rule nor the extent to which the rule must be seen as 'established' by this Court."). "[B]ecause the Strickland standard is a general standard, a state court has even more latitude to reasonably determine that a defendant has not satisfied that standard." *Knowles v. Mirzayance,   U.S.   , 129 S.Ct. 1411, 1420, 173 L. Ed. 2d 251, [] (2009) []*. We do not, however, afford the state courts a blank check to determine, at their whim, whether an attorney's conduct was reasonable or unreasonable. . .

Where counsel's failure to investigate was both objectively unreasonable and prejudicial, and where the state court acted unreasonably in finding to the contrary, we will grant a petition for habeas corpus.

Richter v. Hickman, 578 F.3d 944, 951-52 (9th Cir. 2009).

The Arizona state court's decision in Petitioner's Rule 32 proceedings, that Petitioner was not denied his right to the effective assistance of counsel, was not clearly contrary to nor an unreasonable application of federal law and Petitioner is not entitled to federal habeas relief on his claim that he was deprived of the effective assistance of counsel. Compare *Jones v. Ryan, 583 F.3d 626, 640 (9th Cir. 2009)* (holding counsel was ineffective for (1) failing to secure the appointment of a mental health expert; (2) failure to timely move for neurological and neuropsychological testing; and (3) failure to present additional mitigation witnesses and evidence).

REASONS WHY REMEDY IS HOLLOW

Arizona prosecutors have mastered the art of obtaining convictions by misconduct to include falsifying evidence, concealing evidence, destroying evidence and the Arizona Attorney general has failed to notify federal courts of this issue. State courts decline to take remedial action.

George Russell Kayer, Petitioner, vs. Charles L. Ryan, et al., Respondents.
No. CV 07-2120-PHX-DGC UNITED STATES DISTRICT COURT FOR THE DISTRICT OF ARIZONA

THE POSITION OF THE COURT

In 1997, a jury in Yavapai County convicted Petitioner of first degree murder for taking the life of Delbert L. Haas. The following facts concerning the circumstances of the crime and Petitioner's trial are derived from the opinion of the Arizona Supreme Court affirming Petitioner's conviction and sentence, *State v. Kayer, 194 Ariz. 423, 427-30, 984 P.2d 31, 35-38 (1999),* and from this Court's review of the record.

On December 3, 1994, two couples searching for Christmas trees on a dirt road in Yavapai County discovered a body, later identified as that of Delbert L. Haas. Haas had been shot twice, once behind each ear. On December 12, 1994, Yavapai County Detective Danny Martin received a phone call from Las Vegas police officer Larry Ross. Ross told Martin that a woman named Lisa Kester had approached a security guard at the Pioneer Hotel in Laughlin, Nevada, and said that her boyfriend, Petitioner, had killed a man in Arizona. Kester also indicated that a warrant had been issued for Petitioner's arrest in relation to a different crime, a fact Las Vegas police officers later confirmed. Kester gave Las Vegas officers the gun she said was used to kill Haas and led them to credit cards belonging to Haas that were found inside a white van in the hotel parking lot.

During her interaction with the officers, Kester appeared agitated. She told them she had not come forward sooner because she feared Petitioner would kill her, and asked to be placed in the witness protection program. Kester described Petitioner's physical appearance and agreed to accompany an officer to the police station.

Hotel security guards and Las Vegas police officers soon spotted Petitioner leaving the hotel. The officers arrested Petitioner and took him to the police station for questioning. Kester had already been arrested for carrying a concealed weapon. Detectives Martin and Roger Williamson flew to Las Vegas on December 13 to interrogate Kester and Petitioner. Kester gave a complete account of the events that led to Haas's death. Petitioner spoke briefly with the detectives before invoking his right to counsel.

Kester's statements to Detectives Martin and Williamson formed the basis of the State's prosecution of Petitioner. She said Petitioner continually bragged about a gambling system he had devised to beat the Las Vegas casinos, but neither Petitioner nor Kester had money with which to gamble. Petitioner earned some money selling t-shirts, jewelry, and knickknacks at swap meets. His only other income came from using fake identities to bilk the government of benefits. Petitioner learned that Haas had recently received money from an insurance settlement. He and Kester visited Haas at his house near Cordes Lakes late in November 1994. Kester said that Petitioner convinced Haas to go gambling with them. On November 30, 1994, Petitioner, Kester, and Haas left for Laughlin, Nevada, in Petitioner's van.

The three stayed in the same hotel room in Laughlin. After the first night of gambling, Petitioner claimed to have "won big." Haas agreed to loan Petitioner about $ 100 of his settlement money so that Petitioner could further utilize his gambling system. Petitioner's system proved unsuccessful and he lost all of the money Haas had given him. Petitioner again told Haas that he had won big, but claimed that someone had stolen his winnings. Kester asked Petitioner what they were going to do now that they were out of money. Petitioner said he was going to rob Haas. When Kester asked how Petitioner was going to get away with robbing someone he knew, Petitioner replied, "I guess I'll just have to kill him."

The three left Laughlin to return to Arizona on December 2, 1994. On the road, all three consumed alcohol, especially Haas. Petitioner and Haas argued over how Petitioner was going to repay Haas. The van made several stops for bathroom breaks and to purchase snacks. At one of these stops, Petitioner took a gun that he stored under the seat of the van and put it in his pants. Petitioner asked Kester if she was "going to be all right with this." Kester said she wanted Petitioner to warn her before he killed Haas.

Petitioner traveled on a series of back roads that he claimed would be a shortcut to Haas's house. Eventually, he stopped the van near Camp Wood Road in Yavapai County. At this stop, Kester said Haas exited the van and began urinating behind it. Kester started to climb out of the van as well, but Petitioner motioned to her with the gun and pushed her back into the vehicle. The van had windows in the rear and on each side through which Kester viewed what occurred next. Petitioner walked quietly up to Haas from behind while he was urinating and shot him behind the ear at point-blank range. He dragged the body off the side of the road to the bushes where it was eventually found, then returned to the car carrying Haas's wallet, watch, and jewelry.

Petitioner and Kester began to drive away in the van when Petitioner realized that he had forgotten to retrieve Haas's house keys. He turned the van around and returned to the murder scene. Kester and Petitioner both looked for the body. Kester spotted it and then returned to the van. Petitioner returned to the van, too, and asked for the gun, saying that Haas did not appear to be dead. Kester said Petitioner approached Haas's body and that she heard a second shot.

Petitioner and Kester then drove to Haas's home. Petitioner entered the home and removed several guns, a camera, and other items of personal property. He attempted unsuccessfully to find Haas's PIN number in order to access Haas's bank accounts. Petitioner and Kester sold Haas's guns and jewelry at pawn shops and flea markets over the course of the next week, usually under the aliases of David Flynn and Sharon Hughes. They then traveled to Laughlin where Petitioner used the proceeds from selling Haas's property to test his gambling system again and to pay for a room at the Pioneer Hotel. Kester approached the Pioneer Hotel security guard and reported the shooting.

On December 29, 1994, a grand jury indicted Petitioner and Kester on several charges, including premeditated first degree murder and felony first degree murder. In February 1995, the State filed a notice that it would seek the death penalty against both Petitioner and Kester. In September 1995, Kester entered into a plea agreement with the State. In exchange for her truthful testimony, the original charges would be dropped and Kester would be charged with several lesser counts including facilitation to commit first degree murder.

Petitioner was tried in March 1997. His defense centered on the claim that Kester alone had killed Haas and was now framing Petitioner for the murder. The State presented evidence that corroborated Kester's testimony and discredited Petitioner's testimony. The jury convicted Petitioner of all charges, finding him guilty of first degree murder under both premeditated and felony murder theories.

At sentencing, the trial judge, Yavapai County Superior Court Judge William T. Kiger, found two aggravating factors: that Petitioner had previously been convicted of a serious offense, pursuant to *A.R.S. § 13-703(F)(2)*, and that the murder was committed for pecuniary gain under *§ 13-703(F)(5)*. Dkt. 36, Ex. A. Judge Kiger found that Petitioner had failed to establish any statutory mitigating factors and had proved only one nonstatutory mitigator. *Id.* After weighing the aggravating and mitigating factors, the judge sentenced Petitioner to death.

The Arizona Supreme Court affirmed the convictions and sentences. *Kayer, 194 Ariz. 423, 984 P.2d 31.* Petitioner filed a petition for postconviction relief ("PCR") with the trial court. PCR Pet., filed 6/6/05. Judge Kiger dismissed a number of claims as precluded and, following an evidentiary hearing on Petitioner's claims of ineffective assistance of counsel, denied the PCR petition. Dkt. 36, Exs. B, C. Petitioner filed a petition for review ("PR"), PR doc. 9, which the Arizona Supreme Court denied. An earlier PCR notice had been vacated when initial PCR counsel failed to file a timely petition (Case No. CR-02-0048-PC). Counsel withdrew, new counsel were appointed, and a new PCR notice was filed (Case No. CR-07-0163-PC).

PROCEDURAL ANALYSIS

Petitioner has raised 30 claims. Respondents contend that only five of the claims are properly exhausted.. For the reasons set forth below, the Court finds that Claims 1(B)(1), 1(B)(2), 1(B)(3), 1(B)(5), 13-21, 24, and 26 are procedurally barred and will not be considered on the merits. The Court will address procedural issues with respect to the remaining claims as necessary.

Claim 1

Petitioner raises five subclaims alleging ineffective assistance of counsel during the guilt and penalty phases of his trial. Respondents concede that subclaim 1(B)(4), alleging ineffective assistance at sentencing, is exhausted, but contend that the remaining subclaims were not exhausted in state court and are procedurally barred.

In subclaims 1(B)(1), 1(B)(2), and 1(B)(3), Petitioner alleges, respectively, that he was denied effective assistance of counsel because his attorneys failed to conduct an immediate and thorough investigation; his first lead counsel failed to seek second counsel in a timely manner and second counsel, when appointed, undertook little work on Petitioner's behalf; and neither of his lead attorneys was qualified to defend a capital case. In subclaim 1(B)(5), Petitioner alleges that he was denied effective assistance of counsel during death qualification of the jury.

In his PCR petition, Petitioner raised two claims of ineffective assistance of counsel, alleging that counsel failed to conduct an adequate mitigation investigation and that counsel performed ineffectively during voir dire. PCR Pet. at 32, 37. In his petition for review to the Arizona Supreme Court, Petitioner included only the claim that counsel's performance was ineffective with respect to mitigation. PR doc. 9. In neither filing did

Petitioner raise a claim that his rights were violated by counsel's performance at the guilt stage of trial as alleged in Claims 1(B)(1), 1(B)(2), or 1(B)(3). If Petitioner were to return to state court and attempt to exhaust these claims, the claims would be found waived and untimely under Rules 32.2(a)(3) and 32.4(a) of the Arizona Rules of Criminal Procedure because they   do not fall within an exception to preclusion. *See* Ariz. R. Crim. P. 32.2(b); 32.1(d)-(h). Therefore, subclaims 1(B)(1), 1(B)(2), and 1(B)(3) are "technically" exhausted but procedurally defaulted because Petitioner no longer has an available state remedy. *Coleman, 501 U.S. at 732, 735 n.1*. Petitioner does not attempt to show cause and prejudice or a fundamental miscarriage of justice.

Claim 1(B)(5) is also procedurally defaulted. In Arizona, fair presentation requires that capital petitioners present their allegations not only to the PCR court but also to the Arizona Supreme Court upon denial of relief. *See O'Sullivan, 526 U.S. at 848; Swoopes v. Sublett, 196 F.3d 1008 (9th Cir. 1999)* (per curiam) (capital petitioners must seek review in Arizona Supreme Court to exhaust claims). In his petition for review, Petitioner did not include his claim regarding counsel's performance during voir dire. *See* PR doc. 9. Therefore, he did not fairly present the claim to the Arizona Supreme Court. Petitioner may not exhaust the claim now because he does not have an available state court remedy. Petitioner does not assert that cause and prejudice or a fundamental miscarriage of justice excuse the default   of these subclaims. Therefore, subclaims 1(B)(1), 1(B)(2), 1(B)(3), and 1(B)(5) are denied as procedurally barred.

Claims 13-21, 26

Petitioner raised these claims for the first time in his PCR petition. Judge Kiger denied them as "[p]recluded by Rule 32.2(a)(3)."

Rule 32.2(a)(3) constitutes a regularly followed and adequate state procedural bar. *See Ortiz, 149 F.3d at 932*. Petitioner nonetheless argues that the PCR ruling "was ambiguous and therefore insufficient to constitute a clear express invocation of a state procedural rule permitting preclusion." Dkt. 40 at 49. According to Petitioner, it is not clear whether the PCR court believed the claims should have been raised on direct appeal or in his prior PCR petition. *Id.* at 45-46. Petitioner cites no authority for the proposition that this alleged ambiguity renders the invocation of Rule 32.2(a)(3) inadequate as a procedural bar, and the Court is unconvinced. There is no ambiguity either in the PCR court's citation to Rule 32.2(a)(3) as the sole basis for finding the claims precluded or in the language of the Rule itself, which states that a claim is precluded if it was waived "at trial, on appeal,   or in any previous collateral proceeding." Nothing in the rule requires the state court to specifically identify the proceeding in which the waiver occurred. Moreover, given that the first PCR notice was vacated before a petition was filed, there is no question that the PCR court's ruling referred to Petitioner's failure to raise the claims on direct appeal.

As cause for the default of Claims 13, 14, 16, 17, 19, and 20, Petitioner asserts ineffective assistance of appellate counsel. Ineffective assistance of counsel may constitute cause for failing properly to exhaust claims in state court and excuse procedural default. *Ortiz, 149 F.3d at 932*. To meet the "cause" requirement, however, the ineffective assistance must amount to an independent constitutional violation. *Id.; see also Coleman, 501 U.S. at 755* ("We reiterate that counsel's ineffectiveness will constitute cause only if it is an independent constitutional violation."). As explained below with respect to Claim 22, Petitioner has failed to show that appellate counsel performed at a constitutionally ineffective level. Therefore, he cannot establish cause for the default of the claims. Claims 13-21 and   26 are denied as procedurally barred.

Claim 24

Petitioner alleges that the State improperly withheld exculpatory and impeachment evidence in violation of *Brady v. Maryland*. As Respondents note, Petitioner never presented this claim in state court.   Because no state remedies remain, the claim is technically exhausted but procedurally defaulted. Petitioner does not allege cause and prejudice or a fundamental miscarriage of justice. Claim 24 is denied as procedurally barred.

MERITS ANALYSIS

Claim 1(B)(4):

Petitioner alleges that he was denied effective assistance of counsel at sentencing because his attorneys failed to conduct an immediate and thorough mitigation investigation.

Background

Pretrial, trial, and sentencing

Petitioner was indicted on December 29, 1994. On January 6, 1995, Linda Williamson was appointed to represent him. RT 1/6/95 at 3. Williamson was under a contract with Yavapai County to represent indigent defendants and had been an attorney for nearly five years with significant experience in criminal law, although she had not tried a capital murder case.

Williamson asked James Bond, an experienced criminal attorney, to serve as second chair, with the intent that he would focus on mitigation and sentencing. When Bond agreed to serve as second-chair, he understood that the trial would not occur for a long time; his involvement in the case was minimal. Although Williamson never focused on the sentencing phase of trial, she spoke with Petitioner about mitigation in a general way.

Williamson filed a number of pretrial motions, including one requesting a Rule 11 pre-screening psychiatric examination of Petitioner. The court appointed Dr. Daniel Barack Wasserman to conduct the examination. Dr. Wasserman concluded that Petitioner did not suffer from an identifiable mental illness or defect, although some test results were suggestive of a "paranoid or depressive disorder." Based on Dr. Wasserman's evaluation, the trial court found Petitioner competent to stand trial and no further evaluations took place.

After investigating leads and interviewing witnesses, Williamson concluded that the case would be difficult to win. She believed that delay was her best option, hoping that Kester, the State's key witness, who was pregnant with Petitioner's child, would begin using drugs again, abscond, or otherwise become unavailable to testify.

In June 1996, Petitioner sought to remove Williamson and replace her with Bond as lead counsel. The State wanted the case to proceed to trial, the trial court wanted to schedule a firm July trial date, and Bond was adamant that he could not be appointed lead counsel due to his heavy case load. Two days later, after further discussion, the court allowed Williamson to withdraw, directed Bond to remain as second-chair, and appointed David Stoller, the next contract attorney in line for capital cases, as lead counsel.

At the time of his appointment, Stoller had been practicing criminal law for nearly 30 years, both as a prosecutor and a defense attorney. As a prosecutor, he had taken 50 felony cases to jury trial, including one capital case.

In August, the trial court allowed Bond to withdraw. Petitioner subsequently requested that Marc Victor be appointed to replace Bond. Victor had represented Petitioner on another criminal matter. He was appointed as second counsel. At the time, he had about two years of experience as a lawyer.

In January 1997, defense counsel filed a number of motions, including an *ex parte* application for funds to further investigate the crime and to conduct a mitigation investigation. At the time of Petitioner's trial, requests for certain defense expenses were required to be made to the Yavapai County presiding judge. Judge Weaver, the presiding judge, granted additional funds for the crime investigation but deferred ruling on the request for funds relating to mitigation. Judge Weaver stated that he would wait to see if there was a conviction before he would authorize funds for a mitigation investigation.

The trial began on March 5, 1997. The jury returned its verdict on March 26. The court scheduled the aggravation/mitigation hearing for May 27, with a sentencing date of June 17, 1997.

On April 8, 1997, at Stoller's request, Judge Weaver authorized $ 6,000 for mitigation specialist Mary Durand to begin an investigation. The order provided that the amount was not to be exceeded without prior authorization. *Id.* Counsel subsequently argued that Durand needed additional time to conduct her mitigation investigation; the court continued the aggravation/mitigation hearing to June 24, and set sentencing for July 15, 1997.

The court held a status conference on June 6. Defense counsel Victor informed the court that Durand had met twice with Petitioner, but that she needed an additional three to six months to complete her investigation. Victor also told the court that Petitioner objected to such a continuance, explaining that Petitioner "understands exactly what is going on. He understands the nature of putting the mitigation case on. He understands that that would be to some extent compromised, if myself and Mr. Stoller are not able to push back the date." Next, lead counsel Stoller, who wanted to make a "good record" of the issue, indicated that Petitioner understood Durand's position that potentially significant areas of mitigation needed to be explored. Petitioner, however, "simply didn't want to wait in the county jail and have that kind of diet and not have access to things to read and television, and things of that nature." Based in part upon this "life-style choice," and against Stoller's "best advice" and "strong recommendation," Petitioner had informed counsel that he would not waive time to allow Durand to complete her investigation. Stoller appeared at the hearing telephonically.

The court next addressed Petitioner directly. Petitioner detailed his reasoning as follows:

> In speaking with Mary Durand, I had no idea what a mitigation specialist was before I sat down and talked to her. Didn't know what they looked for, didn't know what she was looking for in this case with me or with my life. We talked as has been indicated on two separate occasions for several hours. There isn't any major areas of investigation that are open or available to her that her and I have discussed [sic].
>
> These areas that Mr. Stoller brings out that he is calling substantial evidence, from what I understand in my conversation with Mary Durand, she is talking about a fetal alcohol syndrome that possibly existed. She hasn't had the opportunity to investigate it, and some minor areas and details in my life that I personally can't see how they would relate to mitigation in this case.
>
> So it's with reservations when Mr. Stoller talks about vital areas and evidence that can be used in mitigation. It's a personal difference, and certainly of opinion [sic]. I'm saying I don't see anything here of substantial value. Obviously, Mr. Stoller is saying that he does.

Petitioner also explained that Durand had told him that she would testify at the aggravation/mitigation hearing and do her best even if she was unable to complete her investigation. Petitioner then continued to detail his rationale for objecting to a further continuance:

> I don't think that -- I don't think that some people understand exactly where I'm at. It certainly hasn't been presented here, and I don't want to turn this into a mitigation hearing, but I feel that there's a few things that need to be said today in view of where we're at.
>
> One of them is that I don't have a death wish. I'm not trying to manipulate the Court to such a position that they have no alternative but to decide to give me the death penalty. I don't feel the lack of Mary Durand's mitigation is going to be a major factor in the decision.

Judge Kiger, explaining that he would look favorably on a request for an additional 30 days "or something like that," though not a continuance of 90 or 180 days, directly asked Petitioner if he wished to continue the June 24 aggravation/mitigation hearing. Id. at 20-21. Petitioner responded that he understood the court's position but was "not in favor of any more continuances." Petitioner explained, "Believe me, if I thought that -- that Miss Durand had valid evidence that should be presented to this Court, I'd be scratching and clawing and asking for 180 days."

Citing Petitioner's waiver of a continuance and its effect on their ability to represent him, counsel moved to withdraw. The court denied the motion. At the end of the hearing, at defense counsel's request, the court rescheduled the aggravation/mitigation hearing for July 8 while maintaining the sentencing date of July 15.

Counsel filed a sentencing memorandum on Petitioner's behalf. In arguing against a death sentence, counsel offered one statutory mitigating factor and several nonstatutory circumstances: intoxication causing an inability to appreciate the wrongfulness of one's conduct under A.R.S. § 13-703(G)(1); intoxication not rising to the level of the (G)(1) factor; Petitioner's military record; the disparity in sentences between Petitioner and Kester; Petitioner's poor physical health; his intelligence and ability to contribute to society; and his devotion to his mentally disabled son.

At the July 8 aggravating/mitigation hearing, defense counsel called four witnesses: a corrections officer who testified briefly about Petitioner's non-disruptive conduct and his work with other inmates in the law library; Petitioner's mother and sister; and Mary Durand. Petitioner and his son also made statements to the court.

Sherry Rottau, Petitioner's mother, testified that his father, an aeronautical engineer, died when Petitioner was in kindergarten. Rottau remarried when Petitioner was in high school. When Petitioner was 15 the family relocated to Arkansas for a year before moving back to California where he graduated from high school. In school Petitioner earned Bs and Cs and some As. He was an "ambitious" child who earned money by mowing lawns and shining shoes. Rottau testified that Petitioner was sick a lot as a child with colds, the flu, and earaches; he was also hyperactive and had trouble sleeping.

After high school Petitioner joined the Navy and got married. He began exhibiting manic depressive behavior following his military service. He would work for 24 hours straight and then sleep for a long period of time; he would start projects only to abandon them and become depressed. Rottau was concerned about these cycles of happiness and depression.

Rottau also testified that Petitioner had a history of heart problems. Finally, she testified about the close relationship between Petitioner and his son, Tayo.

Jean Hopson, Petitioner's older sister, testified that his father had drinking and gambling problems and that Petitioner suffered difficulties in those areas as well. Hopson described Petitioner's mental state as consisting of highs and lows and testified that he had been diagnosed as bipolar, had experienced a nervous breakdown, and been treated with lithium. She also described a loving relationship between Petitioner and Tayo.

Mary Durand testified about the role of a mitigation specialist, which is to develop a social history of the defendant "in order to determine family dynamics, . . . mental, medical, emotional, familial, nutritional, and social factors, and behaviors that the defendant has been involved in and exposed to throughout the course of his life." Durand explained that a mitigation specialist investigates "social and educational, medical, marital, sexual, any kind of issue that presents itself that gives us an idea of who the client is that we're dealing with, specifically to look at impairment." She testified that the average number of hours needed to complete a mitigation investigation is "ideally" between 2,500 and 5,000, but as a practical matter "between 1,000 and 1,500 hours . . . begins to approach a competent test and reliability." According to Durand, a mitigation specialist must "attempt to get every piece of information you can," including medical and mental health records, military records, school records, and court documents.

Durand testified that she met with Petitioner twice for a total of six or seven hours. She also met with his mother twice, his sister once, his uncle twice, and his son once. She reviewed the presentence reports from Petitioner's criminal cases. Durand did not obtain any of Petitioner's psychiatric, medical, school, or military records because Petitioner was "not interested in having the world know about his life." Concerning Petitioner's reluctance to allow a full-scale mitigation investigation, Durand explained:

> We talked for an extraordinarily long period of time, just about the issue of allowing me the time I needed to do an appropriate, complete and reliable mitigation on his behalf. He had very, very strong feelings where -- the fact that he had been in jail two years and . . . five months at that time, and was not willing to wait another year.
>
> I was very direct with him, and I told him I couldn't do it in three weeks or six weeks or eight weeks, or three months, and he is very concerned about his emotional health, his physical health, and catching a new case, if you will, being in this particular environment for that period of time.
>
> He was very concerned about putting his family through any emotional, public hearing. He was concerned about his son. His mother is 76 and not in good health and has serious memory lapses, and he was concerned that he would add to her already fragile medical state, and he just didn't want to put anybody through this process. He felt like they've been through enough, and he didn't want to add to that.

Petitioner did sign a waiver for the release of his military records, but at the time of the hearing Durand had not yet received them. Durand then testified that if Petitioner had been willing to allow additional time she would have investigated several areas of potential mitigation, foremost among them the issue of Petitioner's mental health. Durand stated that "there's definitely very serious indications   of serious psychiatric difficulties," including a diagnosis of bipolar disorder and an incident in which he was hospitalized with "suicide ideation." Durand also testified, citing reports of alcohol abuse in Petitioner's family background, that she would have investigated the issue of alcoholism and poly-substance abuse. Finally, she would have further investigated Petitioner's physical health based on reports that his mother experienced a difficult pregnancy and labor and that Petitioner was a sickly child. Durand indicated that Petitioner's "educational record does appear to be good in that there are areas in which he clearly is quite brilliant and very, very well-spoken."

Durand reiterated that Petitioner did "not want to talk about" the proposed areas of mitigation. She concluded that, in addition to Petitioner's unwillingness to spend additional time in the county jail and his reluctance to expose his mother and son to further legal proceedings, he did not wish to pursue a mitigation investigation due to his "pride," "dignity," and desire not to "relive" his past.

At the conclusion of the aggravation/mitigation   hearing, after listening to Durand's testimony, the trial court engaged in the following colloquy with Petitioner:

> Court: Change your mind about what you told me last time as far as go ahead with sentencing on the 15th of July? Do you want more time? By asking you the question, I'm basically saying if you tell me right now that you've considered it, and you want more time, I'm prepared to give you more time.
>
> But I think you're an intelligent individual. You know what she's just testified to. I believe strongly that an individual ought to have the ability to make some decisions on their own, if they have gotten all the information and have the requisite intelligence.
>
> You got the information, you got the intelligence, you've talked to your counsel, you've heard Ms. Durand. Your call.
>
> Petitioner: I appreciate your patience and your concern in this, and I have not changed my feeling. Thank you.

In addition to the testimony from the aggravation/mitigation hearing, Judge Kiger, in sentencing Petitioner, reviewed information contained in the presentence report. The report discussed Petitioner's mental health, describing an incident when "he became extremely depressed,   had near suicide attempts [and] in September of 1989, he had been diagnosed as Manic Depressive at the Phoenix VA Hospital"; it further indicated that Petitioner had been prescribed lithium. The report also noted Petitioner's substance abuse history, including the fact that he was a "heavy abuser of alcohol."

The trial court also reviewed, along with Dr. Wasserman's Rule 11 report, the results of a mental status examination prepared in 1990 by Dr. Jeffrey Penney, a psychiatrist from Prescott. Dr. Penney reported that Petitioner described experiencing symptoms of mania and depression with "intermittent suicidal ideation"; Petitioner indicated that he was presently taking lithium and an anti-depressant. Dr. Penney noted that drug and alcohol use were often associated with the manic episodes described by Petitioner. Petitioner reported a "history of heavy alcohol usage throughout his life" and informed Dr. Penney that he currently drank "3 six-packs a week" and would drink more if he could afford to do so. Id. Dr. Penney observed that Petitioner experienced "notable" gaps in his memory and that his "[i]nsight   seemed mildly impaired and judgment impaired based on his continued alcohol abuse with depression and with symptoms consistent with some alcohol-induced memory dysfunction." Dr. Penney also reported that Petitioner carried a cyanide pill with him at all times, including during the evaluation, in the event he wanted to commit suicide. Dr. Penney diagnosed Petitioner with amphetamine, marijuana, and alcohol abuse, as well as depression probably secondary to alcohol intake. Because Petitioner would not authorize the release of his medical records, Dr. Penny reached a "rule out" diagnosis of Bipolar Affective Disorder.

At the sentencing hearing on July 15, the court engaged in another colloquy with Petitioner, explaining that "if you told me you wanted more time, as your attorneys were requesting, as Miss Durand had requested, to find additional information and evidence to present to me, . . . I would certainly grant it." Judge Kiger next outlined the applicable provisions of the death penalty statute and indicated that he was prepared to find two aggravating circumstances. The court then asked Petitioner if, with that information in   mind, he wished to proceed with sentencing. While Petitioner consulted with counsel, the court elaborated:

> This is a very, very important decision, and I want Mr. Kayer to make it based upon discussion with counsel and reflection, and I want him to have as much information as possible. I hope he understands what I have just reviewed with him, and if there is any question about that, I'd be happy to respond.
>
> Before I officially get into the sentencing of this matter, if that's -- I will tell you this, if Mr. Kayer, after review, still wants to go ahead with sentencing today, I'm ready to proceed. On the other hand, if Mr. Kayer believes that he needs to ask for additional time, I am willing to do it that way.

The court took a recess to allow further consultation. *Id.* at 6. After the recess Petitioner indicated that he understood the information provided by the court, but that he wished to proceed with sentencing. In his special verdict, Judge Kiger found that "the intentional and knowing decisions and actions of the defendant have blocked the attempts by his trial counsels [sic] to fully pursue mitigation pursuant to 13-703(G)(1) and the court is unable to   find that any such factor has been proven by a preponderance of the evidence." The court found that no statutory mitigating circumstances existed. The court then "considered" Petitioner's proffered nonstatutory mitigating circumstances, finding that Petitioner had proved that he was "an important figure in the life of his son." The court found that the remaining nonstatutory circumstances had not been proved, explaining, in relevant part:

> 2. The defendant was apparently diagnosed and treated for a time for a mental condition referred to as a bipolar or manic/depressive problem. The court can speculate as to a possible relationship between such a condition and the murder; the court cannot find a relationship by a preponderance of the evidence.
>
> . . . .
>
> 4. The defendant has apparently had some level of addiction to both gambling and alcohol. There is no dispute that the defendant consumed several beers on the trip from Laughlin to the place where the murder took place. As with #2 above, there may be some possible connection between such a condition and the murder such that it effected [sic] the defendant's ability or capacity to conform his conduct   with the requirements of the law. It would be at best speculation by the court and is not found by a preponderance of the evidence.
>
> 5. The Rule 11 evaluation conducted by Dr. Wasserman in 1995 found some unusual results in the MMPI and some possible problems with paranoia. As with #2 above, there may be some possible connection between such a condition and the murder such that it effected [sic] the defendant's ability or capacity to conform his conduct with the requirements of the law. It would be at best speculation by the court and is not found by a preponderance of the evidence.
>
> 6. There have been references to the defendant having suicide thoughts. Apparently at one time, the defendant carried a cyanide pill to the office of a doctor who was performing a mental health evaluation. His explanation was that he would use the pill if he decided it was needed. The court has considered the possibility that the defendant has determined to block the attempts by his attorneys to present mitigation as a way of now bringing about his death. This too is speculation by the court and does not rise to the point of proof by a preponderance of the evidence.

Judge Kiger concluded that "[s]ince these factors have not been proven, the court cannot find these factors applicable to the sentencing structure called for in 13-703. These factors as considered have essentially no weight to balance against the aggravating factors."

On appeal, the Arizona Supreme Court agreed with the trial court's assessment of the mitigating evidence:

> Defendant's alleged mental impairment on the day he murdered Haas, whether attributed to historical substance abuse or a mental disorder, also must be considered as a nonstatutory mitigating circumstance.
>
> . . . .
>
> But the record shows that the existence of impairment, from any source, is at best speculative. Further, in addition to offering equivocal evidence of mental impairment, defendant offered no evidence to show the requisite causal nexus that mental impairment affected his judgment or his actions at the time of the murder. Thus, we conclude that the trial court ruled correctly that impairment was not established as a nonstatutory mitigating factor by a preponderance of the evidence.

Kayer, 194 Ariz. at 438, 984 P.2d at 46 (citations omitted).

Postconviction proceedings

In March 2006, Judge Kiger held an evidentiary hearing on Petitioner's ineffective assistance claims. The hearing lasted nine days. Petitioner called 17 witnesses, including each of the attorneys who had represented him at trial, along with Ms. Durand and his current mitigation specialist. He also presented expert testimony from a clinical neuropsychologist, a forensic psychiatrist, and a physician specializing in addiction medicine. Finally, several family members and a friend testified about Petitioner's family background, problems with alcohol abuse and gambling, and mental health issues. In addition, Larry Hammond, a local attorney with capital case experience, testified as an expert on the *Strickland* standard. In his opinion, Petitioner's trial counsel performed at a constitutionally ineffective level.

Lead counsel Stoller testified that the defense plan was to obtain mitigating information and present a full mitigation case, including mental health evidence, through Durand's investigation; she would gather the information and submit it to the appropriate experts. Petitioner, however, did not want the continuance necessary to allow such an investigation, nor did he want to explore issues concerning his metal health because, as Durand informed Stoller, "he felt they would cause him to be viewed as weak and vacillating in prison." Petitioner also "thought it wouldn't make any difference." In addition, he believed that his "living conditions" would improve in prison because he would have "smoking and television privileges." Thus, Stoller testified, the defense team was prevented from developing more mitigation by Petitioner's waiver of a continuance. Nevertheless, Stoller went to Phoenix to visit Petitioner's mother, son, and sister, and later had contact with other family members. He asked Petitioner's mother for a history of Petitioner's life. *Id.* at 165. Later, Stoller discussed mitigation with Petitioner's mother and explained that "bad is good" for purposes of mitigation.

Second-chair Victor testified that he and Stoller had intended to pursue Petitioner's mental health as mitigating evidence. Victor tried to "disabuse" Petitioner of the notion that to pursue mitigation was tantamount to admitting guilt. Victor testified that he spoke in "great detail" with Petitioner until he was assured that Petitioner understood the nature and purpose of mitigation evidence.. Petitioner explained to Victor why he did not wish to delay sentencing in order to pursue mitigation: first, he was very close to his mother and son and thus "he was very adverse [sic] to having things about his past . . . brought out in front of them, and so he was very adverse [sic] to having them exposed to that information and he was not willing to cooperate with mitigation." Petitioner also cited the fact that he had been in the county jail for an extended period and he looked forward to the benefits of prison, primarily television and smoking privileges; he "perceived that whatever time he had to spend in the Department of Corrections would be more pleasurable than the time he had been spending in the Yavapai County Jail." Victor argued "as persuasively as I could, on many occasions" to convince Petitioner to allow an investigation. He was also hopeful that Durand would be able to change Petitioner's mind by outlining the scope of a full mitigation investigation and explaining that in his case persuasive mitigation information   existed. Victor adamantly opposed Petitioner's decision to waive a continuance, but "believe[d] Mr. Kayer understood things and had a rational position and didn't want to put his family through mitigation."

Mary Durand testified that Petitioner was motivated to waive a continuance based on fear for his emotional and physical well being in the county jail. According to Durand, he "wanted desperately to get out." Nevertheless, despite his reluctance to pursue mitigation, Petitioner provided contact information for family members and executed some releases for documentary evidence. Durand explained the purpose of mitigation to Petitioner, who became upset that counsel had waited so long to begin an investigation. Notwithstanding their conversations, Durand felt Petitioner had only a "minimal understanding of [the] scope and breadth and depth of mitigation."

Keith Rohman, Petitioner's post-conviction mitigation specialist, testified that a mitigation investigation should begin immediately, in part because it is necessary to "educate the client" and overcome his initial reluctance to present mitigating evidence.   Rohman testified that Petitioner's decision not to "cooperate with the mitigation investigation" was based on several factors: "he did not have a clear understanding of mitigation," about which his lawyers had failed to educate him; "he was very concerned about the situation at the Yavapai Jail"; "he was frustrated with his attorneys for having waited so long"; he believed that the presentation of mitigation was an admission of guilt; and he thought that offering mitigating evidence would be futile. Rohman testified that there were four areas of mitigation that trial counsel omitted or left insufficiently developed: Petitioner's bipolar disorder, alcoholism, pathological gambling, and his transient living situation as a child. Rohman then outlined his findings with respect to each of these areas. *Id.* Finally, Rohman testified about the violent, overcrowded conditions of the Yavapai County Jail. He also noted that the jail failed to provide Petitioner with the special diet recommended for his heart condition.

Petitioner presented testimony from a number of experts. Dr. Anne Marie Herring, a clinical neuropsychologist, testified that   Petitioner had an average IQ (102) and that, with one exception, the results of the tests she administered were normal. The exception was one of the card sorting tests, designed to measure complex problem solving abilities, on which Petitioner achieved a low-average or borderline score.   This result was indicative of a cognitive deficit. According to Dr. Herring, such a deficit would be consistent with various etiologies, including chronic heavy substance abuse, bipolar disorder, and traumatic brain injury.

Dr. Barry Morenz, a forensic psychiatrist, diagnosed Petitioner with the following conditions: bipolar type 1, hypomanic; alcohol dependence; personality disorder with schizotypal, narcissistic, and antisocial features; and, citing Dr. Herring's test results, cognitive disorder not otherwise specified. Dr. Morenz testified that Petitioner's cognitive disorder interfered with his capacity to address his other conditions, impairing his ability to recover from his alcohol and gambling addictions. At the time of the murder, according to Dr. Morenz, all of these conditions   were manifesting themselves and combined to make Petitioner "very, very impaired."

Dr. Morenz further testified that Petitioner was enjoying his life in prison, where he had completed and published one book and was working on two others. He enjoyed receiving fan mail for his writing. *Id.* His laundry and trash were picked up and his meals were provided. Dr. Morenz characterized Petitioner's positive state of mind as unrealistic and a function of his hypomania.

Dr. Michel Sucher, a physician specializing in addiction medicine, diagnosed Petitioner with alcohol dependence, polysubstance abuse, and pathological gambling.

Several lay witnesses testified, including Petitioner's sister, two cousins, an aunt, and a friend. Their testimony indicated that several of Petitioner's relatives also suffered from mental health issues, including manic and depressive episodes. According to this testimony, Petitioner's maternal cousin was institutionalized in a psychiatric facility, where she was initially diagnosed with schizophrenia and later with manic depressive disorder. Her mother had also experienced severe   mood swings. Petitioner's maternal aunt had a history of hearing voices, as did her grandfather and sister. Petitioner's other maternal aunt suffered from depression.

The testimony of these witnesses further indicated that Petitioner had longstanding issues with substance abuse and gambling, as did other family members. Pete Decell, a friend and coworker with whom Petitioner had committed a series of residential burglaries, testified that Petitioner had been a heavy drinker. He also stated that Petitioner did not like to work and had gotten a "rush" from committing the burglaries.

Judge Kiger, presiding over the PCR proceedings, rejected Petitioner's claim of ineffective assistance of counsel at sentencing. Judge Kiger determined "at the time of sentencing, the defendant voluntarily prohibited his attorneys from further pursuing and presenting any possible mitigating evidence." He ruled that Petitioner had failed to demonstrate deficient performance, explaining that "trial counsel did not fall below the *Strickland* standard for effective representation concerning   potential mitigation." This finding was based on the judge's "own observations of the defendant during trial and the sentencing phase" and the Arizona Supreme Court's determination that Petitioner was competent when he waived a further mitigation investigation and that the waiver was knowing and voluntary.

Judge Kiger also found that Petitioner had not shown that he was prejudiced by counsel's performance:

> This court further concludes that if there had been a finding that the performance prong of the *Strickland* standard had been met, that no prejudice to the defendant can be found. In stating this conclusion the court has considered the assertion of mental illness, jail conditions, childhood development, and any alcohol or gambling addictions.

Analysis

Petitioner contends that the PCR court's rejection of this claim constituted an unreasonable application of clearly established federal law and was based on an unreasonable determination of the facts. The Court does not agree.

The clearly established federal law governing claims of ineffective assistance of counsel is set forth in *Strickland v. Washington, 466 U.S. 668, 104 S. Ct. 2052, 80 L. Ed. 2d 674 (1984)*. To prevail under   *Strickland,* a petitioner must show that counsel's representation fell below an objective standard of reasonableness and that the deficiency prejudiced the defense. *466 U.S. at 687-88.*

In assessing whether counsel's performance was deficient under *Strickland,* the test is whether counsel's actions were objectively reasonable at the time of the decision. *Id. at 689-90.* A petitioner must overcome "the presumption that, under the circumstances, the challenged action might be considered sound trial strategy." *Id. at 689.* The question is "not whether another lawyer, with the benefit of hindsight, would have acted differently, but 'whether counsel made errors so serious that counsel was not functioning as the counsel guaranteed the defendant by the *Sixth Amendment.*'" *Babbitt v. Calderon, 151 F.3d 1170, 1173 (9th Cir. 1998)* (quoting *Strickland, 466 U.S. at 687*).

While trial counsel has "a duty to make reasonable investigations or to make a reasonable decision that makes particular investigations unnecessary, . . . a particular decision not to investigate must be directly assessed for reasonableness in all the circumstances, applying a heavy measure of deference to counsel's judgments." *Id. at 691.*   In making this assessment, the court "must conduct an objective review of [counsel's] performance, measured for reasonableness under prevailing professional norms, which includes a context-dependent consideration of the challenged conduct as seen from counsel's perspective at the time." *Wiggins v. Smith, 539 U.S. 510, 523, 123 S. Ct. 2527, 156 L. Ed. 2d 471 (2003)* (citation and quotation marks omitted). The Supreme Court has instructed that "[i]n judging the defense's investigation, as in applying *Strickland* generally, hindsight is discounted by pegging adequacy to 'counsel's perspective at the time' investigative decisions are made" and by applying deference to counsel's judgments. *Rompilla v. Beard, 545 U.S. 374, 381, 125 S. Ct. 2456, 162 L. Ed. 2d 360 (2005)* (quoting *Strickland, 466 U.S. at 689*).

With respect to *Strickland's* second prong, a petitioner must affirmatively prove prejudice by "show[ing] that there is a reasonable probability that, but for counsel's unprofessional errors, the result of the proceeding would have been different. A reasonable probability is a probability sufficient to undermine confidence in the outcome." *Strickland, 466 U.S. at 694.* The *Strickland* Court explained that "[w]hen a defendant challenges a death sentence . . . the   question is whether there is a reasonable probability that, absent the errors, the sentencer . . . would have concluded that the balance of aggravating and mitigating circumstances did not warrant death." *466 U.S. at 695*. In *Wiggins, 539 U.S. at 534*, the Court noted that "[i]n assessing prejudice, we reweigh the evidence in aggravation against the totality of available mitigating evidence." The totality of the available evidence includes "both that adduced at trial, and the evidence adduced in the habeas proceeding." *Id. at 536* (quoting *Williams v. Taylor, 529 U.S. at 397-98*).

Under the AEDPA, this Court's review of the state court's decision is subject to another level of deference. *Bell v. Cone, 535 U.S. 685, 698-99, 122 S. Ct. 1843, 152 L. Ed. 2d 914 (2002); see Knowles v. Mirzayance, 129 S. Ct. 1411, 1420, 173 L. Ed. 2d 251 (2009)* (noting that a "doubly deferential" standard applies to *Strickland* claims under AEDPA). Therefore, to prevail on this claim, Petitioner must make the additional showing that the state court's ruling that counsel was not ineffective constituted an objectively unreasonable application of *Strickland. 28 U.S.C. § 2254(d)(1)*.

In reviewing Petitioner's allegations of ineffective assistance, this Court further notes that the judge who presided over Petitioner's trial and sentencing also presided over the PCR proceedings. Thus, in considering Petitioner's ineffective assistance claims, Judge Kiger was already familiar with the record and the evidence presented at trial and sentencing. This familiarity with the record provides the Court an additional reason to extend deference to the state court's ruling. *See Smith v. Stewart, 140 F.3d 1263, 1271 (9th Cir. 1998)*. As the Ninth Circuit explained in *Smith,* when the judge who presided at the post-conviction proceeding is the same as the trial and sentencing judge, the court is considerably less inclined to order relief because doing so "might at least approach 'a looking-glass exercise in folly.'" *Id.* (quoting *Gerlaugh v. Stewart, 129 F.3d 1027, 1036 (9th Cir. 1997)*).

Finally, because an ineffective assistance of counsel claim must satisfy both prongs of *Strickland,* the reviewing court "need not determine whether counsel's performance was deficient before examining the prejudice suffered by the defendant as a result of the alleged deficiencies." *466 U.S. at 697* ("if it is easier to dispose of an ineffectiveness claim on the ground of lack of sufficient   prejudice . . . that course should be followed").

Petitioner is not entitled to relief because Judge Kiger did not apply *Strickland's* second prong in an unreasonable manner when he determined that Petitioner failed to prove that he was prejudiced by counsel's performance. First, under *Schriro v. Landrigan, 550 U.S. 465, 127 S. Ct. 1933, 167 L. Ed. 2d 836*, Petitioner cannot show prejudice because he waived an extension of the sentencing date and thereby waived presentation of the full-scale mitigation case that defense counsel and mitigation specialist Durand had intended to develop and present. Next, Petitioner cannot show prejudice because the evidence produced during the PCR proceedings, which was the product of an exhaustive mitigation investigation, was largely cumulative of the evidence presented at sentencing and fell short of the type of mitigation information that would have influenced the sentencing decision. *See id. at 481*. Finally, the reasonableness of the PCR court's rejection of this claim is buttressed by the fact that Judge Kiger had presided over Petitioner's trial and sentencing and was therefore "ideally situated," *Landrigan, 550 U.S. at 476*, to gauge the validity of Petitioner's waiver and to weigh   the totality of the mitigating evidence against the evidence presented at sentencing. *See Gerlaugh, 129 F.3d at 1036*.   Because this claim is more readily resolved on the basis of lack of prejudice, *see Strickland, 466 U.S. at 697*, the Court makes no finding regarding the alleged deficiency of trial counsel's performance at sentencing.

In *Landrigan,* the petitioner refused to allow defense counsel to present the testimony of his ex-wife and birth mother as mitigating evidence. He also interrupted as counsel tried to proffer other evidence and told the Arizona trial judge that he did not wish to present any mitigating evidence and to bring on the death penalty. The court sentenced him to death and the sentence was affirmed on direct appeal. *State v. Landrigan, 176 Ariz. 1, 859 P.2d 111 (1993)*. The PCR court rejected Landrigan's request for a hearing and denied his claim that counsel was ineffective for failing to conduct further investigation into mitigating circumstances, finding that he had instructed counsel at sentencing not to present any mitigating evidence at all. Landrigan then filed a federal habeas petition. The district court denied the petition and refused to grant an evidentiary hearing because Landrigan could not make out a colorable claim of ineffective assistance of counsel. A panel of the Ninth Circuit affirmed the denial. *Landrigan v. Stewart, 272 F.3d 1221 (9th Cir. 2001)*. The en banc Ninth Circuit reversed, holding that counsel's performance at sentencing was ineffective. *441 F.3d 638 (9th Cir.*

2006). According to the court, Landrigan's "last-minute decision could not excuse counsel's failure to conduct an adequate investigation prior to sentencing." *Id. at 647.* The court then reiterated its view "that a lawyer's duty to investigate [mitigating circumstances] is virtually absolute, regardless of a client's expressed wishes." *Id.*

The Supreme Court reversed. *Schriro v. Landrigan, 550 U.S. 465, 127 S. Ct. 1933, 167 L. Ed. 2d 836.* The Court held that the district court did not abuse its discretion in failing to hold an evidentiary hearing on Landrigan's claim of sentencing-stage ineffectiveness and that the court was within its discretion in denying the claim based on Landrigan's unwillingness to present mitigation evidence.

Landrigan compels the conclusion that Petitioner is not entitled to habeas relief. *Landrigan* establishes the standard for evaluating a sentencing-stage ineffective assistance   claim brought by a petitioner who directed counsel not to pursue a case in mitigation. "If [the petitioner] issued such an instruction, counsel's failure to investigate further could not have been prejudicial under *Strickland." Id. at 475; see Owens v. Guida, 549 F.3d 399, 406 (6th Cir. 2008)* ("a client who interferes with her attorney's attempts to present mitigating evidence cannot then claim prejudice based on the attorney's failure to present that evidence"); *see also Wood v. Quarterman, 491 F.3d 196, 203 (5th Cir. 2007)* ("Neither the Supreme Court nor this court has ever held that a lawyer provides ineffective assistance by complying with the client's clear and unambiguous instructions to not present evidence."); *Lovitt v. True, 403 F.3d 171, 179 (4th Cir. 2005)* ("Lovitt is correct to insist that a client's decision in this regard should be an informed one. At the same time, Lovitt's lawyers were hardly ineffective for incorporating their client's wishes into their professional judgment."); *Rutherford v. Crosby, 385 F.3d 1300, 1313-14 (11th Cir. 2004)* ("[U]nder *Strickland* the duty is to investigate to a reasonable extent . . . and that duty does not include a requirement to disregard   a mentally competent client's sincere and specific instructions about an area of defense and to obtain a court order in defiance of his wishes."); *Jeffries v. Blodgett, 5 F.3d 1180, 1198 (9th Cir. 1993)* ("[C]ounsel for Jeffries had been prepared to present evidence in mitigation and had discussed with Jeffries the ramifications of failing to present the evidence. Accordingly, counsel did not deprive Jeffries of effective assistance in acquiescing in the latter's considered decision.").

In Petitioner's case, prior to his conviction, counsel performed only a limited investigation into mitigating evidence. When funding for a mitigation specialist was authorized, Mary Durand began a full-scale investigation. Counsel planned to use the information she gathered to retain further experts, including mental health professionals. While Durand's investigation was still in its early stages, Petitioner indicated that he did not wish to delay the sentencing date. His waiver of a continuance -- a continuance the trial court was prepared to grant -- was based on several factors, including an unwillingness to involve his family in an investigation into his background and a belief that no valuable information   could be obtained. By the date of sentencing, when he was offered a final opportunity to rescind his waiver and allow additional investigation, Petitioner was fully informed of the nature, scope, and purpose of mitigating information, having spoken with counsel and Durand and having heard Durand's detailed testimony at the aggravation/mitigation hearing. After being afforded several opportunities by the judge to obtain a continuance, Petitioner chose to proceed to sentencing without a complete mitigation investigation.

Despite Petitioner's position, the defense investigation continued until the date of the aggravation/mitigation hearing, which had been extended at counsel's request. At the hearing, counsel presented testimony concerning Petitioner's childhood, alcohol dependence, gambling addiction, mental health history, and positive character traits and conduct.

Given all of these circumstances, Petitioner's claim for relief is even less persuasive than Landrigan's. Petitioner's waiver of a continuance was neither equivocal nor last-minute. The record demonstrates that he was fully aware of the consequences of his decision and persisted in that decision even after counsel's attempts   to change his mind, exposure to Durand's testimony detailing the elements and potential benefits of a full-scale mitigation investigation, and repeated opportunities afforded by the court to reconsider his decision. His waiver did not prevent counsel from investigating and presenting a mitigation case within the parameters Petitioner had set. Therefore, under the clearly-established law set forth in *Landrigan,* Petitioner is not entitled to relief.

The second factor dictating a conclusion that Petitioner has not demonstrated prejudice is the nature of the new mitigating information. At Petitioner's sentencing, counsel offered what amounted to an outline of the mitigation case presented during the PCR proceedings. The information later presented by PCR counsel supported the mitigating circumstances proffered at sentencing, including Petitioner's alcohol dependence, gambling addiction, and bipolar disorder. It also added a new diagnosis that Petitioner suffers from a cognitive deficit affecting his complex reasoning skills.

In his special verdict, Judge Kiger found that several of the nonstatutory mitigating factors advanced by defense counsel, including Petitioner's alcohol and gambling problems and his bipolar condition, had not been proved and therefore were not weighty. In his PCR order, Judge Kiger considered all of the new evidence, but determined that Petitioner had not been prejudiced by counsel's performance at sentencing. To obtain relief, Petitioner must show that Judge Kiger's determination was not merely incorrect, but "unreasonable-a substantially higher threshold." *Landrigan, 550 U.S. at 473.*

The reasonableness of Judge Kiger's ruling is supported by several considerations. First, most of the new mitigating evidence, while more detailed than the information offered at sentencing, duplicated the evidence already presented. *See Babbitt, 151 F.3d at 1176* (no prejudice where evidence omitted at sentencing was "largely cumulative of the evidence actually presented"). Thus, it did not alter the basic sentencing profile originally provided to the judge. *See Strickland, 466 U.S. at 699-700; see also Henley v. Bell, 487 F.3d 379, 387-88 (6th Cir. 2007)* (no prejudice resulting from counsel's failure to call a psychiatric expert to testify during sentencing phase of capital murder trial that defendant had learning disabilities, had dropped out of school, and at the time of the offense was depressed and acting out of character). To the extent that the new evidence supported a diagnosis that Petitioner suffered from a cognitive deficit, that diagnosis was the product of a single test result, which was the only indication that Petitioner was not within the normal range with respect to brain function. Moreover, Dr. Herring, who performed the test, did not herself make a diagnosis of cognitive deficit; nor could she say whether any such deficit was in place at the time of the murder, more than 10 years earlier. Therefore, the only new category of mitigating information was of limited impact.

Thus, in contrast to cases such as *Rompilla, Wiggins,* and *Williams,* where counsel's failure to investigate mitigating evidence prejudiced the defendant, the omitted mitigation evidence about Petitioner's background and mental health was relatively "weak." *Landrigan, 550 U.S. at 481.* For example, in *Rompilla,* counsel failed to present evidence that his client was beaten by his father with fists, straps, belts, and sticks; that his father locked him and his brother in a dog pen filled with excrement; and that he grew up in a home with no indoor plumbing and was not given proper clothing. *545 U.S. at 391-92.* In *Wiggins,* counsel failed to present evidence that the defendant suffered consistent abuse during the first six years of his life, was the victim of "physical torment, sexual molestation, and repeated rape during his subsequent years in foster care," was homeless for portions of his life, and had diminished mental capacities. *539 U.S. at 535.* In *Williams,* counsel failed to discover "records graphically describing Williams's nightmarish childhood," including the fact that he had been committed at age 11, had suffered dramatic mistreatment and abuse during his early childhood, and was "borderline mentally retarded." *529 U.S. at 370-71, 395. See also Stankewitz v. Woodford, 365 F.3d 706, 717-19 (9th Cir. 2004)* (prejudice existed where omitted evidence showed that Stankewitz was exposed to extreme deprivation and abuse from his family and in a variety of foster homes, was borderline retarded, and suffered from significant brain dysfunction). In *Landrigan* itself, the Court described as "poor quality," and therefore not supportive of a colorable claim of ineffective assistance, omitted mitigating evidence indicating that the petitioner suffered from fetal alcohol syndrome with attendant cognitive and behavioral defects, was abandoned by his birth mother, was raised by an alcoholic adoptive mother, began abusing alcohol and drugs at an early age, and had a genetic predisposition to violence. *550 U.S. at 480.*

By contrast, the evidence presented to the PCR court simply corroborated Petitioner's alcohol dependence, gambling addiction, and bipolar disorder, while adding a diagnosis of cognitive deficit that was neither significant nor well supported. It was not unreasonable for Judge Kiger to find that this evidence was not persuasive enough to have produced a different sentence. *See id.; see also Hill v. Mitchell, 400 F.3d 308, 319 (6th Cir. 2005)* ("to establish prejudice, the new evidence that a habeas petitioner presents must differ in a substantial way -- in strength and subject matter -- from the evidence actually presented at sentencing"). In sum, the mitigation case presented during the PCR proceedings "establishes at most the wholly unremarkable fact that with the luxury of time and the opportunity to focus resources on specific parts of a made record, post-conviction counsel will inevitably identify shortcomings in the performance of prior counsel." *Turner v. Crosby, 339 F.3d 1247, 1279 (11th Cir. 2003)* (quoting *Waters v. Thomas, 46 F.3d 1506, 1514 (11th Cir. 1995)).*

Finally, the reasonableness of Judge Kiger's ruling is supported by the fact that he had presided at Petitioner's sentencing and was familiar with the record and the efforts of trial counsel. During the PCR proceedings, the judge was presented with the results of an exhaustive mitigation investigation. He denied relief, again finding that Petitioner had waived additional mitigation and failed to show prejudice. The Ninth Circuit has commented on the appropriate review of cases where the judge considering a claim of ineffective assistance was also the judge who presided over trial and sentencing. In *Gerlaugh,* the court denied an ineffective assistance claim and rejected the petitioner's request for an evidentiary hearing in state court, explaining:

> The trial and sentencing judge has already considered *all* of this information in the post-conviction hearing and has held that none of it would have altered his judgment as to the proper penalty for Gerlaugh. And, the Arizona Supreme Court looked at the substance and results of the post-conviction proceeding and affirmed the trial judge in all respects. In effect, petitioner has already had what he is asking for -- consideration in a formal hearing of this evidence.

Gerlaugh, 129 F.3d at 1036; see Smith, 140 F.3d at 1271.

Petitioner likewise was able to discover and present all available mitigating evidence to the sentencing judge during the PCR proceedings. Petitioner received a comprehensive mitigation investigation, carried out by a full complement of investigators and experts, followed by a hearing at which all of the mitigating information was presented. Judge Kiger heard and considered the evidence and determined that if it had been presented at sentencing it would not have altered his decision to sentence Petitioner to death. This Court cannot classify as objectively unreasonable Judge Kiger's assessment of the evidence and its impact on his sentencing determination.

Conclusion

The PCR court, in rejecting Petitioner's claim of ineffective assistance of counsel at sentencing, did not apply *Strickland* in an objectively unreasonable manner. Under *Landrigan,* Petitioner's waiver of additional mitigation evidence forecloses relief. In addition, Judge Kiger did not unreasonably determined that the omitted mitigation evidence was not sufficient to result in a reasonable probability of a different sentence.

In *Owens,* the Sixth Circuit, citing *Landrigan,* cautioned that "[a] defendant cannot be permitted to manufacture a winning [ineffective assistance of counsel] claim by sabotaging her own defense, or else every defendant clever enough to thwart her own attorneys would be able to overturn her sentence on appeal." *549 F.3d at 412.* That principle applies equally to Petitioner's case. Claim 1(B)(4) is denied.

Claim 2

Petitioner alleges that the trial court violated the *Eighth Amendment* prohibition against arbitrary and capricious sentencing in capital cases when it allowed Petitioner, over his counsel's objection, to determine that a continuance of the mitigation hearing was unnecessary. He further alleges that the court violated his *Sixth Amendment* right to counsel by ignoring defense counsel's "learned decision" that additional time was necessary to prepare mitigation in favor of Petitioner's uninformed desire to proceed to sentencing. Respondents concede that the claim is exhausted to the extent it was raised on direct appeal.

Background

As explained above, Petitioner opposed a continuance of the sentencing proceedings and thereby foreclosed a complete mitigation investigation by the defense team. On direct appeal, Petitioner contended that the trial judge improperly allowed him to waive the presentation of mitigation evidence against the advice of counsel. Opening Br. at 26. The Arizona Supreme Court rejected Petitioner's argument. *Kayer, 194 Ariz. at 434-37, 984 P.2d at 42-45.* The court held that its jurisprudence does not preclude a defendant from refusing to cooperate with a mitigation specialist, explaining that a competent defendant can waive counsel altogether and that "[a] defendant's right to waive counsel includes the ability to represent himself or herself at the sentencing phase of a case that could result in the death penalty." *Id. at 436, 984 P.2d at 44*. Therefore, according to the court, "[a]n anomaly would exist were we to accept defendant's argument that counsel exclusively controls the presentation of all mitigation evidence: a defendant could waive counsel at sentencing and thereby have exclusive control over the presentation of all mitigation evidence; yet if a defendant accepts counsel, he would have no input on what mitigating factors to offer." *Id. at 436-37, 984 P.2d at 44-45*. The court also noted that "[t]he United States Supreme Court has upheld a defendant's right to waive all mitigating evidence." *Id.* (citing *Blystone v. Pennsylvania, 494 U.S. 299, 306, 110 S. Ct. 1078, 108 L. Ed. 2d 255 & n. 4 (1990))*. The court then explained:

> [O]ur case law allows defendant the freedom not to cooperate with a mitigation specialist and thereby potentially limit the mitigation evidence that is offered. Significantly, defendant stressed to the trial judge that he wanted Durand to advocate on his behalf at the mitigation hearing. Defendant also wanted his attorneys to argue other mitigating evidence. Consequently, seven mitigating circumstances were offered. Durand testified on defendant's behalf, albeit without defendant's full cooperation. Defendant was not conceding defeat; he wanted advocacy in all areas except the psychological areas that Durand wanted to explore. . . .

> We conclude that the trial court properly allowed defendant not to cooperate with the court-appointed mitigation specialist, given the repeated warnings of the consequences of this decision and the factual record before us.

Id. at 437, 984 P.2d at 45 (citation omitted).

Analysis

Petitioner contends that the state courts violated his constitutional rights by allowing him to waive the presentation of additional mitigation and that the courts erred in finding that the waiver was knowing and voluntary. The Court disagrees.

First, as the Arizona Supreme Court noted, citing *Blystone v. Pennsylvania*, there is no dispute that a defendant may waive the presentation of mitigating evidence. In *Blystone*, the United States Supreme Court held that no constitutional violation occurred when a defendant was allowed to waive all mitigation evidence after repeated warnings from the judge and advice from counsel. *494 U.S. 299, 306, 110 S. Ct. 1078, 108 L. Ed. 2d 255 & n.4*. That principle was buttressed by the holding in *Landrigan*, which denied an ineffective assistance claim based on the defendant's refusal to allow the presentation of a mitigation case. *550 U.S. at 475*. Therefore, the fact that the trial court accepted Petitioner's waiver of a more detailed mitigation case does not, by itself, establish a constitutional violation.

Petitioner asserts that his waiver was not knowing and voluntary because he did not understand the consequences of his decision. This argument is unavailing on both legal and factual grounds. In *Landrigan*, the Supreme Court explained that it had "never imposed an 'informed and knowing' requirement upon a defendant's decision not to introduce evidence" and has "never required a specific colloquy to ensure that a defendant knowingly and intelligently refused to present mitigating evidence." *Landrigan, 550 U.S. at 479*.

In Petitioner's case, nonetheless, the state courts reasonably found that his waiver was informed and voluntary. Judge Kiger afforded Petitioner repeated opportunities to reconsider his decision to limit the mitigation defense, ensured that Petitioner discussed the matter fully with counsel, determined that Petitioner had discussed the matter at length with his mitigation specialist, and afforded Petitioner an opportunity to reconsider the decision after he had heard the testimony at his own mitigation hearing. The judge determined that Petitioner "voluntarily prohibited his attorneys from further pursuing and presenting any possible mitigating evidence."

The judge was "ideally situated" to make this assessment, and his factual findings are presumed correct. *Landrigan, 550 U.S. at 474, 476; see 28 U.S.C. § 2254(e)(1)*. Petitioner has not met his burden of rebutting that presumption with clear and convincing evidence. By the time of the sentencing hearing, when Petitioner again waived a continuance, he was fully aware of the nature and purpose of a mitigation investigation and its significance to his case. Durand's testimony at the aggravation/mitigation hearing alone was adequate to apprise Petitioner of the ramifications of his waiver. And Petitioner's colloquies with Judge Kiger further support a finding that his decision to limit the mitigation case was informed and voluntary.

The ruling of the Arizona Supreme Court rejecting this claim was neither contrary to nor an unreasonable application of clearly established federal law, nor was it based on an unreasonable determination of the facts. Therefore, Claim 2 is denied.

Claim 3

Petitioner alleges that he was denied effective assistance of counsel because trial counsel labored under a conflict of interest. Petitioner concedes that the claim is unexhausted because he failed to include it in his petition for review   to the Arizona Supreme Court. He contends, however, that he has an available state court remedy under *Rule 32.2* because his waiver of the claim was not knowing, voluntary, and intelligent, and he requests a stay of these proceeding so that he may return to state court and exhaust the claim. *Id.* The Court concludes that the claim, regardless of its procedural status, is plainly without merit. *See 28 U.S.C. § 2254(b)(2); Rhines v. Weber, 544 U.S. 269, 277, 125 S. Ct. 1528, 161 L. Ed. 2d 440 (2005).*

Analysis

To establish an ineffective assistance of counsel claim based on a conflict of interest, it is not sufficient to show that a "potential" conflict existed. *Mickens v. Taylor, 535 U.S. 162, 171, 122 S. Ct. 1237, 152 L. Ed. 2d 291 (2002).* Rather, "until a defendant shows that his counsel actively represented conflicting interests, he has not established the constitutional predicate for his claim of ineffective assistance." *Cuyler v. Sullivan, 446 U.S. 335, 350, 100 S. Ct. 1708, 64 L. Ed. 2d 333 (1980).* An actual conflict of interest for *Sixth Amendment* purposes is one that "adversely affected counsel's performance." *Mickens, 535 U.S. at 171.* Petitioner has not established that his attorneys actively represented conflicting interests or that any conflict of interest affected their performance.

At trial, lead counsel Stoller cross-examined the victim's widow, Wilma Haas. Near the conclusion of her testimony, Stoller asked for a sidebar conference. He informed the court, the prosecutor, and Kayer that after observing Haas testify, he believed he may have represented her son by a prior marriage a few years earlier on DUI charges in Phoenix. The prosecutor and Stoller questioned Haas outside the presence of the jury. She confirmed that Stoller had represented her son, but stated that they had no contact regarding this case.. Under these circumstances, Petitioner has not established that an actual conflict existed based on Stoller's prior representation of the victim's widow's son. Nor does Petitioner explain how Stoller's prior representation adversely affected his performance.

Petitioner contends that second counsel Victor was burdened with a conflict of interest based on his representation of an inmate named Pierce. Prior to Kester's testimony, the State filed a motion in limine to preclude the admission of various acts to impeach Kester. One of those acts concerned an altercation between Kester and   Pierce in the women's dorm of the Yavapai County Jail. *Id.* Later, while discussing the motion in court, the judge noted that Victor had represented Pierce on a different matter.

Contrary to Petitioner's assertion that "Victor's loyalty to his prior client . . . prevented him from being able to use such information to impeach Kester," Victor forcefully argued that the dorm incident should be admissible to impeach Kester on cross-examination by showing that she was not the weak and submissive individual portrayed by the State. The court disagreed and precluded use of the incident. *Id.* at 6-7, 170-74. Petitioner therefore has failed to demonstrate that Victor's representation of Pierce affected his performance as Petitioner's counsel.

Claim 3 is without merit and will be denied.

Claim 4

Petitioner alleges that his right to trial by an impartial and representative jury under the *Sixth* and *Fourteenth Amendments* was violated when the trial court death-qualified his jury. Respondents concede that this claim is exhausted.

Prior to trial Judge Kiger informed the parties that during voir dire he would explain to the jurors that the death penalty was a possible sentence, but that the judge, not the jurors, determined the sentence. After providing such information the judge would then ask if the juror could still be fair and impartial. Judge Kiger overruled defense counsel's "vehement" objection to this process.

Judge Kiger questioned the jurors in groups of three, asking each juror, "knowing what your duty as a juror is, do you believe that this kind of a case [a potential death penalty case] would be such that you could not be a fair and impartial juror?" Upon receiving confirmation that a particular juror would be fair and impartial, the judge asked no further questions regarding the death penalty. During this process, Stoller asked each of the potential jurors their views about the role of the jury in a criminal trial, with his questions focusing on the guilt rather than sentencing phase of the trial.

On direct appeal, the Arizona Supreme Court, relying on its own precedent as well as *Wainwright v. Witt*, *469 U.S. 412, 424, 105 S. Ct. 844, 83 L. Ed. 2d 841 (1985)*, and *Adams v. Texas, 448 U.S. 38, 45, 100 S. Ct. 2521, 65 L. Ed. 2d 581 (1980)*, held that "voir dire questioning related to a juror's views on capital punishment is permitted to determine whether those views would prevent or substantially impair the performance of the juror's duties to decide the case in accordance with the court's instructions and the juror's oath." *Kayer, 194 Ariz. at 431, 984 P.2d at 39* (quoting *State v. Martinez-Villareal, 145 Ariz. 441, 449, 702 P.2d 670, 678 (1985)*).

The Arizona Supreme Court reasonably applied clearly established federal law, which holds that the death-qualification process in a capital case does not violate a defendant's right to a fair and impartial jury. *See Lockhart v. McCree, 476 U.S. 162, 178, 106 S. Ct. 1758, 90 L. Ed. 2d 137 (1986)*; *Witt, 469 U.S. at 424*; *Adams, 448 U.S. at 45 (1980)*; *see also Ceja v. Stewart, 97 F.3d 1246, 1253 (9th Cir. 1996)* (death qualification of Arizona jurors not inappropriate). The fact that the trial court death-qualified the venire does not establish a federal constitutional violation. Petitioner is not entitled to relief on Claim 4.

Claim 5

Petitioner alleges that his right to trial by an impartial and representative jury under the *Sixth* and *Fourteenth Amendments* was violated when the trial court dismissed a juror because of his views concerning the death penalty. Respondents concede that the claim is exhausted.

Background

Only one juror was excused as a result of the death-qualification questioning described above. In response to inquiries by Judge Kiger, juror Ed DeMar indicated that he had "reservations" about a proceeding that involved the potential of a death sentence. Rather than have DeMar explain further, Judge Kiger asked him to step outside so that questioning could continue with the two jurors who had not expressed concern regarding the death penalty. DeMar was then brought before the judge and the parties, and the following exchange took place:

> Court: So we are talking about whether or not you had any personally-held beliefs, philosophical opinions, or religious convictions that would get in the way and make it difficult or impossible for you to be a fair and impartial juror knowing that the death penalty was a possibility.
> DeMar: Yes. That would be a -- I would have reservations about an action in which the death penalty might be imposed or could be imposed.
> Court: Let me emphasize, again, though, your duty as a juror is to -- and there is a specific instruction that I'm going to give these jurors, do not consider the possible punishment in making your deliberations.
> DeMar: Well, that would put me in a sort of difficult position.
> Court: That's why I'm asking the question.
> . . . .
> DeMar: I'm not opposed to the death penalty, but I -- it would depend on the conditions involving questions of premeditation, of stalking, of cruelty, of a particularly heinous crime, of

multiple deaths, things of the sort that would tend to follow the Federal application of the death penalty rather than the State application.

And that's what would perhaps give me some difficulty. If I -- and also the question of degree, whether it's first degree, second, third, or manslaughter. Those things would be considerations that I think would affect my impartiality, if I knew that the State had stated that it might seek the death penalty, not knowing those other conditions.

In other words, conditionally, I would not necessarily be against the death penalty, but I would be looking toward the kinds of things that I told you that would -- would perhaps affect that decision.

. . . .

Court: And I guess -- and listen carefully. I'm going to try to summarize what you're telling me so that I can understand it. And if I'm missing the point, I'll trust that you will try to help me. But what you're saying to me seems like knowing that there is that possibility of the death penalty out there would be bumping into your thoughts on, making it -

DeMar: Yes. I would need to know more, really, and it doesn't mean that I'd be against it, but it means that under certain conditions I would, and not knowing those other factors would trouble me somewhat.

Court: And would it get in your way, then, of being a fair and impartial juror as the process continued?

DeMar: It might, again depending on what -- how much of a factor became evidence in testimony and what have you.

Court: Okay.

DeMar: But it would not be -- be a hands-down opposition to the death penalty as such.

Court: I understand what you're saying, and of course at this point we are looking for whether or not you can work in this trial as a fair and impartial juror to both defendant and the State.

DeMar: I understand.

Court: Let me -- let me try it this way, to -- knowing what you know right now, knowing your personal opinions and beliefs and what you know the job of the juror to be, because this is a possibility of a death penalty case at this point, would you like me to excuse you from jury duty in this case?

DeMar: I think that probably would be fair to the -- to the State and to the defense, both really, since that reservation is honestly held.

Court: Okay. Okay. Mr. DeMar, I'm going to accept what you tell me. I'm going to thank you for spending now a day and a half with us and putting up with all of our questioning, and I'm going to excuse you from jury duty in this case, with our sincere appreciation.

Neither party challenged DeMar for cause or objected to his excusal.

On direct appeal, Petitioner argued that DeMar's dismissal was not supported by a finding that his views on the death penalty would prevent him from performing his duties as a juror. The Arizona Supreme Court rejected this claim, explaining:

[T]he judge was willing to allow DeMar to continue as a potential juror upon a simple assurance that DeMar could be fair and impartial. Because DeMar could not give such an assurance, he accepted the court's decision that he be excused from the jury panel in order to be fair to both the defendant and the State.

Similarly, our case law is clear that a trial judge must excuse any potential jurors who cannot provide assurance that their death penalty views will not affect their ability to decide issues of guilt. See Detrich, 188 Ariz. at 65, 932 P.2d at 1336 (urging as "imperative" the dismissal of any juror who cannot assure impartiality on guilt issues because of views regarding the death penalty (citing State v. Hyde, 186 Ariz. 252, 921 P.2d 655 (1996))). Thus, the trial court did not err in asking DeMar questions regarding the death penalty, nor did the court err in allowing

DeMar to be excused from jury service given the presence of "honestly held" reservations regarding the death penalty that might have affected DeMar's ability to carry out his oath with respect to issues of guilt.

Kayer, 194 Ariz. at 431-32, 984 P.2d at 39-40.

Analysis

Clearly established Supreme Court law provides that, when selecting a jury in a capital case, jurors cannot be struck for cause "because they voiced general objections to the death penalty or expressed conscientious or religious scruples against its infliction." *Witherspoon v. Illinois, 391 U.S. 510, 522, 88 S. Ct. 1770, 20 L. Ed. 2d 776 & n.21 (1968)* (noting that exclusion for cause is appropriate if views on the death penalty would "prevent them from making an impartial   decision as to the defendant's guilt"). Therefore, "[a] juror may not be challenged for cause based on his views about capital punishment unless those views would prevent or substantially impair the performance of his duties as a juror in accordance with his instructions and his oath." *Adams v. Texas, 448 U.S. at 45; see Wainwright v. Witt, 469 U.S. at 424.*

In Petitioner's case, the record indicates that DeMar was not challenged for cause. Instead, at the end of a colloquy in which he consistently expressed reservations about his ability to sit as a fair and impartial juror in a death penalty case, the judge asked him if he would prefer to be excused. He stated that he would, in fairness to both parties, and neither Petitioner nor the State objected. Under these circumstances, Petitioner cannot demonstrate that the Arizona Supreme Court unreasonably applied *Witherspoon* in rejecting this claim.   During the PCR evidentiary hearing, both Stoller and Victor testified that they did not want DeMar on the jury.

Even assuming that DeMar was struck for cause, under *Uttecht v. Brown, 551 U.S. 1, 127 S. Ct. 2218, 167 L. Ed. 2d 1014 (2007)*, Petitioner would not be entitled to relief. In *Uttecht*   the prosecution struck for cause a panel member referred to as "Juror Z." Juror Z initially indicated that he could impose the death penalty in "severe situations"- for example, if a defendant would inevitably re-offend if released. When informed by defense counsel that the defendant would never be released from prison, Juror Z expressed uncertainty about his ability to impose a death sentence. Pressed by the prosecution, he continued to equivocate regarding his willingness to consider the death penalty in the circumstances of the case before him, though he generally stated "that he could consider the death penalty or follow the law." The prosecution challenged Juror Z for cause, citing his confusion about the proper circumstances for the imposition of a death sentence. The defense indicated that it had no objection, and the trial court excused the juror. The Ninth Circuit granted habeas relief on the grounds that the state courts had not made a finding that the juror was "substantially impaired" and that "the transcript unambiguously proved Juror Z was not substantially impaired." The Supreme Court reversed, holding that the record   established that Juror Z "had both serious misunderstandings about his responsibility as a juror and an attitude toward capital punishment that could have prevented him from returning a death sentence under the facts of this case." As illustrated above, DeMar in his colloquy with Judge Kiger demonstrated similar characteristics -- confusion about his role as a juror and an attitude toward the death penalty suggesting that he might have been unable to serve as a fair and impartial juror. Indeed, DeMar himself stated that he thought his excusal from the jury would be fair to the State and the defense.

In addition, if, as Petitioner contends, Judge Kiger dismissed DeMar for cause after finding that his ability to be fair and impartial was substantially impaired due to his beliefs about the death penalty, then the judge's determination was "based in part on [DeMar's] demeanor" and is "owed deference by reviewing courts." Judge Kiger had "broad discretion" to dismiss DeMar after conducting a "diligent and thoughtful voir dire" that revealed "considerable confusion" on the part of the juror.

Petitioner notes that DeMar indicated that he was not unambiguously   opposed to the death penalty and would vote to apply it in certain circumstances. But "such isolated statements indicating an ability to impose the death penalty do not suffice to preclude the prosecution from striking for cause a juror whose responses, taken together, indicate a lack of such ability or a failure to comprehend the responsibilities of a juror." *Morales v. Mitchell, 507 F.3d 916, 941 (6th Cir. 2007).*

The Arizona Supreme Court did not unreasonably apply clearly established federal law in rejecting this claim on appeal. Therefore, Claim 5 is denied.

Claim 25

Petitioner alleges that his convictions were obtained in violation of his right to a fair trial and to due process of law under the *Fifth, Sixth, Eighth*, and *Fourteenth Amendments* because Lisa Kester's plea agreement contained an unenforceable "consistency" provision. Respondents concede that the claim is exhausted.

As Petitioner's trial approached, Kester entered into a plea agreement with the State. The agreement required Kester to verify "that all prior statements made to [Yavapai County Detectives] Danny Martin and Roger Williamson were truthful." It also required Kester to "appear at any proceeding including trial upon the request of the State and testify truthfully to all questions asked" and to "cooperate completely with the State of   Arizona in the prosecution of" Petitioner. The State was allowed to dishonor the agreement if Kester violated any of its terms.

The Arizona Supreme Court rejected Petitioner's claim that the plea agreement contained a consistency provision in violation of his due process rights. *Kayer, 194 Ariz. at 430-31, 984 P.2d at 38-39*. Because Petitioner did not object to the agreement at trial, and in fact used the agreement to attack Kester's credibility, the court reviewed the claim only for fundamental error and found none. *Id.* The court did not reach a conclusion as to whether the agreement actually contained a consistency provision. *Id. at 431 n.1, 984 P.2d at 39*.

Even if the plea agreement had contained a consistency provision, Petitioner would not be entitled to relief on this claim. Petitioner has not cited, nor has the Court identified, any Supreme Court authority addressing the due process implications of consistency agreements. As the Ninth Circuit observed in *Cook v. Schriro*, "there is no Supreme Court case law establishing that consistency clauses violate due process or any other constitutional provision." *538 F.3d 1000, 1017 (9th Cir. 2008)*. The Ninth Circuit   [*124] concluded that, "[b]ecause it is an open question in the Supreme Court's jurisprudence, we cannot say 'that the state court unreasonably applied clearly established Federal law'" by rejecting Petitioner's claim. *Id.* (quoting *Musladin, 549 U.S. at 77*) (internal quotations omitted). Claim 25 is denied.   The federal appellate courts do not appear to have addressed the issue directly, although they have consistently held that "[a]n agreement that requires a witness to testify truthfully in exchange for a plea is proper so long as 'the jury is informed of the exact nature of the agreement, defense counsel is permitted to cross-examine the accomplice about the agreement, and the jury is instructed to weigh the accomplice's testimony with care.'" *Allen v. Woodford, 395 F.3d 979, 995 (9th Cir. 2005)* (quoting *United States v. Yarbrough, 852 F.2d 1522, 1537 (9th Cir. 1988))*. Nor is Petitioner's claim supported by state law. In *State v. Rivera, 210 Ariz. 188, 191, 109 P.3d 83, 86 (2005)*, the Arizona Supreme Court held that the co-defendants' plea agreements, which required truthful testimony and avowals that prior statements were true, were not impermissible "consistency agreements."

REASONS WHY REMEDY IS HOLLOW

The Attorney General concealed from the court that in Arizona defense lawyers have the tendency not to investigate cases thoroughly.

ANGEL MENDOZA LOPEZ, Petitioner, v. CHARLES L. RYAN and ARIZONA ATTORNEY GENERAL, Respondents.CIV 09-0536 PHX NVW (MEA) UNITED STATES DISTRICT COURT FOR THE DISTRICT OF ARIZONA
(Text modified for emphasis)

THE POSITION OF THE COURT

In June 2004, an Arizona Department of Corrections ("ADOC") officer searched Petitioner's prison cell. The officer discovered a prison-made weapon, or "shank," encased in two socks under Petitioner's mattress toward the middle of the bunk. The ADOC officer who discovered the shank testified at Petitioner's trial that Petitioner's bunk was approximately six feet from the bars of Petitioner's cell.. Petitioner stated to an   ADOC investigator that he was "responsible for everything in his cell." Petitioner testified on his own behalf at his trial, asserting the shank was not his and that someone else must have placed the shank in his cell. A jury found Petitioner guilty of promoting prison contraband, and the trial court sentenced Petitioner to a term of 15.75 years imprisonment, to be served consecutively to the sentence Petitioner was serving at the time the shank was discovered.

Petitioner took a direct appeal of this conviction and sentence. Petitioner argued that the trial court erred in denying his motion for a directed verdict, i.e., that the state presented insufficient evidence for rational jurors to find him guilty. Petitioner alleged the ADOC officer who testified it was six feet between the edge of Petitioner's mattress to the bars of his cell committed perjury by so testifying.

Petitioner also argued that the state violated his constitutional rights as established by Brady v. Maryland by failing to disclose the distance between the bars of Petitioner's cell and his bunk. Appended to his opening brief on appeal was an affidavit and diagram of Petitioner's cell, indicating the distance between the cell bars and his bunk was far shorter than shown by the evidence presented by the prosecution at his trial and inferring that the shank could have been planted by someone outside Petitioner's cell.

The Arizona Court of Appeals reviewed Petitioner's Brady claim for fundamental error because Petitioner failed to raise the issue at his trial, and affirmed Petitioner's conviction and sentence.. The appellate court concluded Petitioner knew of the "evidence" at the time of his trial and, accordingly, that the state had no duty to "disclose" this information.. Petitioner sought review of this decision by the Arizona Supreme Court, which denied review.

Petitioner initiated an action for state postconviction relief pursuant to Rule 32, Arizona Rules of Criminal Procedure. Petitioner was appointed counsel to represent him in his Rule 32 proceedings. In his petition for post-conviction relief Petitioner argued that his trial counsel was ineffective because he failed to produce evidence to support Petitioner's theory of the case, i.e., counsel failed to establish that Petitioner's bunk was 22 inches from the cell bars and that the socks in which the shank was found were not standard prison-issue socks, although they were available at the prison store. Petitioner also asserted counsel failed to properly cross-examine the ADOC officer who discovered the shank. Additionally, Petitioner alleged his trial counsel failed to emphasize to the jury that ADOC personnel had not found any of the materials used to make the shank in Petitioner's cell. Petitioner also alleged his conviction was obtained through perjured testimony, in violation of the United States and Arizona Constitutions.   The shank was constructed of thick gauge steel wire with a handle manufactured from masking tape.

The state trial court conducted an evidentiary hearing. The trial court concluded that, even assuming that counsel's performance was deficient, Petitioner failed to demonstrate there was a reasonable probability that the verdict would have been different. The trial court noted the "overwhelming" circumstantial evidence, including the fact that Petitioner had been confined to his cell for 23 out of 24 hours per day for the two months preceding the discovery of the shank.

Petitioner sought review of this decision by the Arizona Court of Appeals, which granted review but denied relief Petitioner did not seek review of this decision by the Arizona Supreme Court.

In his section 2254 petition, Petitioner argues that his right to due process was violated because the state withheld allegedly exculpatory evidence. Petitioner also alleges that he was denied his *Sixth Amendment* right to effective assistance of trial counsel. Respondents allow that the petition is timely and that Petitioner exhausted his Brady claim in the state courts. Respondents contend Petitioner did not properly exhaust his ineffective assistance of counsel claim because he failed to present the claim to the Arizona Supreme Court in his Rule 32 action.

Petitioner's ineffective assistance of counsel claim

To state a claim for ineffective assistance of counsel, a petitioner must show that his attorney's performance was deficient and that the deficiency prejudiced the petitioner's defense. See *Strickland v. Washington, 466 U.S. 668, 687, 104 S. Ct. 2052, 2064, 80 L. Ed. 2d 674 (1984).* The petitioner must overcome the strong presumption that counsel's conduct was within the range of reasonable professional assistance   required of attorneys in that circumstance.

To prevail on the merits of a habeas claim of ineffective assistance of counsel, "it is the habeas applicant's burden to show that the state court applied Strickland to the facts of his case in an objectively unreasonable manner. An unreasonable application of federal law is different from an incorrect application of federal law." *Woodford, 537 U.S. at 25, 123 S. Ct. at 360* (internal quotations omitted). "A fair assessment of attorney performance requires that every effort be made to eliminate the distorting effects of hindsight, to reconstruct the circumstances of counsel's challenged conduct, and to evaluate the conduct from counsel's perspective at the time." *Strickland, 466 U.S. at 689, 104 S. Ct. at 2065*. Indeed, "strategic choices made after thorough investigation of law and facts relevant to plausible options are *virtually unchallengeable ....*" *Id., 466 U.S. at 690-91, 104 S. Ct. at 2066* (emphasis added).

To succeed on an assertion his counsel's performance was deficient because counsel failed to raise a particular argument the petitioner must establish the argument was likely to be successful, thereby establishing that he was prejudiced by his counsel's omission. See *Tanner v. McDaniel, 493 F.3d 1135, 1144 (9th Cir.),* cert. denied, *552 U.S. 1068, 128 S. Ct. 722, 169 L. Ed. 2d 565 (2007); Weaver v. Palmateer, 455 F.3d 958, 970 (9th Cir. 2006),* cert. denied, *552 U.S. 873, 128 S. Ct. 177, 169 L. Ed. 2d 120 (2007)*. A defendant has no constitutional right to compel counsel to raise particular objections if counsel, as a matter of professional judgment, decides not to raise those objections. See *Jones v. Barnes, 463 U.S. 745, 751, 103 S. Ct. 3308, 3312, 77 L. Ed. 2d 987 (1983)* (declining to promulgate "a per se rule that the client, not the professional advocate, must be allowed to decide what issues are to be pressed").

Petitioner raised a claim of ineffective assistance of trial counsel in his state action for post-conviction relief. After conducting an evidentiary hearing, the state trial court concluded that Petitioner's trial counsel's performance was arguably deficient with regard to his cross-examination of the ADOC officer who found the shank in Petitioner's cell. The state trial court concluded that, nonetheless, the amount of circumstantial evidence against Petitioner was overwhelming and, accordingly, that even if counsel's performance was deficient in this regard the deficiency was not prejudicial. The state Court of Appeals affirmed this decision.

The state courts' decisions denying Petitioner's ineffective assistance of counsel claim was not clearly contrary to federal law. Although counsel may not have sufficiently cross-examined the ADOC officer regarding the distance between the bars of the cell and the edge of Petitioner's mattress, Petitioner's theory of the case was otherwise presented to the jury. Petitioner testified that he did not know the shank was in his cell and that he did not place the shank under his mattress. The jury heard this testimony and testimony that Petitioner had been housed alone in the cell for two months, that Petitioner was in the cell for all but one hour a day, and that Petitioner had admitted that he was "responsible" for what was present in his cell.

Because the state court could reasonably conclude that any failure to more strenuously cross-examine the ADOC officer was not prejudicial given the circumstantial evidence against Petitioner, the state court's decision was not an unreasonable application of Strickland and Petitioner is not entitled to habeas relief on this claim.

REASONS WHY REMEDY IS HOLLOW

It is a very common practice in Arizona for defense lawyers not to investigate the case. In the Arizona Prison System it is a very common practice for prison officials to plant evidence in inmate cells. It is very common for prosecutors to misrepresent the facts of the case. With proper investigation the results would be different. The Arizona Attorney General with knowledge of this deficiency fails to disclose this to the courts.

Charles Anthony McDonald, Petitioner, vs. Charles L. Ryan, et al., Respondents. No. CV-10-1513-PHX-DGC (LOA) UNITED STATES DISTRICT COURT FOR THE DISTRICT OF ARIZONA (Text modified for emphasis)

POSITION OF THE COURTS

A. Charges, Trial and Sentencing

On January 29, 2004, the State of Arizona filed an indictment in the Arizona Superior Court, Maricopa County, charging Petitioner with burglary in the second degree, a Class 3 felony, and possession of burglary tools, a Class 6 felony. The State amended the indictment to allege 23 historical prior felony convictions, commission of the offenses while released from confinement, and aggravating circumstances other than prior convictions.

Following a mistrial, on December 8, 2004, a second trial commenced on December 9, 2004. On December 14, 2004, the jury found Petitioner guilty as charged. The jury subsequently found that the State had established several aggravating circumstances beyond a reasonable doubt. On March 2, 2005, the trial court sentenced Petitioner as a repetitive offender to an aggravated 20-year term of imprisonment on the second-degree burglary conviction and an aggravated concurrent 4.5-year term of imprisonment on the possession of burglary tools conviction.

1   The Honorable John A. Buttrick presided.
2   The Honorable Gregory H. Martin presided.

B.   Direct Appeal

Petitioner timely appealed. Appellate counsel filed a brief pursuant to *Anders v. California, 386 U.S. 738, 87 S. Ct. 1396, 18 L. Ed. 2d 493 (1967)*. Thereafter, Petitioner filed a *pro se* brief asserting that: (1) the trial court denied Petitioner the right to self-representation; (2) the trial court considered improper aggravating circumstances when sentencing Petitioner; (3) the trial court improperly admitted a victim impact statement during sentencing; (4) the trial court denied Petitioner the opportunity to review the pre-sentence report; and (5) the trial court imposed an excessive sentence.

On March 2, 2006, the Arizona Court of Appeals affirmed Petitioner's convictions and sentences. Petitioner filed a motion for reconsideration which the appellate court denied. Petitioner filed a petition for review in the Arizona Supreme Court, which was summarily denied on August 17, 2006. Petitioner did not petition the United States Supreme Court for a *writ of certiorari*.

C. Post-Conviction Review

On August 25, 2006, Petitioner, proceeding *pro se*, filed a notice of post-conviction relief in the   trial court pursuant to Ariz.R.Crim.P. 32. Petitioner filed a petition for post-conviction relief, raising the following claims:

1. Trial counsel was ineffective for failing to request a mistrial based on juror bias.
2. Trial counsel was ineffective for failing to properly advise Petitioner on the merits of a plea offer.
3. Trial counsel was ineffective for failing to object to statements made by the prosecution on behalf of the victim's son at the sentencing hearing.
4. Trial counsel was ineffective for failing to effectively cross-examine state witnesses.
5. Trial counsel was ineffective for failing to adequately investigate and interview corroborating witnesses.
6. Trial counsel was ineffective for failing to present meaningful mitigation evidence at the sentencing hearing.

After the petition was fully briefed, the trial court conducted an evidentiary hearing on the issue of counsel's failure to adequately advise Petitioner of the strength and weaknesses of his case in association with a plea offer. At the conclusion of the evidentiary hearing, on May 21, 2008, the court denied the petition.

Petitioner   petitioned the Arizona Court of Appeals for review of the denial of post-conviction relief. The appellate court summarily denied review on November 24, 2009. On December 18, 2009, the Arizona Supreme Court likewise denied review.

D. Federal Petition for Writ of Habeas Corpus

Thereafter, Petitioner filed a timely   Petition for Writ of Habeas Corpus pursuant to *28 U.S.C. § 2254* in this District Court. Petitioner raises the following claims for relief:

1. The trial court denied Petitioner his right to self-representation.

2. Petitioner's sentence violated the *Sixth Amendment* because the court submitted improper aggravating circumstances to the jury and the trial court considered an aggravating factor not submitted to the jury.

3. Petitioner's aggravated sentences violate the *Eighth Amendment*.

4. Trial counsel was ineffective for failing to advocate on Petitioner's behalf at sentencing.

5. Trial counsel was ineffective for failing to conduct reasonable pretrial investigation.

6. Trial counsel was ineffective for failing to raise the issue of juror bias.

7. Trial counsel was ineffective for failing to properly advise Petitioner regarding   the merits of a plea offer.

8. Petitioner's right to due process was violated during post-conviction proceedings.

The Court previously dismissed Ground 8 and directed Respondents to answer the remaining grounds for relief. Respondents have filed an Answer to the Petition, to which Petitioner has replied. For the reasons set forth below, the Petition should be denied.

A. Ground One - Right to Self-Representation

In Ground One, Petitioner argues that he was denied the right to represent himself at trial. Respondents concede that this claim is properly before the Court on habeas corpus review.

Prior to trial, Petitioner filed a motion to proceed in *propria persona*. Before Petitioner filed that motion, his trial had been continued from May to June 2004. On June 2, 2004, the continuance panel granted a second extension and continued the trial to July 20, 2004. Petitioner moved to proceed in *propria persona* on June 30, 2004. The trial court scheduled oral argument for July   9, 2004. During the July 9, 2004 hearing, Petitioner informed the court that he lacked confidence in trial counsel, wanted the assistance of advisory counsel, and needed an additional 90 to 180 days to prepare for trial. The trial court advised Petitioner that his simultaneous request to proceed in *propria persona* and for an extension of time weighed against granting Petitioner's request to represent himself. The court also informed Petitioner that it could not grant a continuance, but that Petitioner would have to return to the continuance panel to renew his request. The trial court then inquired whether Petitioner was prepared to proceed to trial on July 20, 2004. Petitioner stated he was not ready to proceed on July 20, 2004 by himself. Petitioner explained that he thought the trial court could continue the trial date. The trial court reiterated that it lacked the authority to grant a continuance and that Petitioner would have to seek a continuance from the continuance panel. The trial court   proposed substituting counsel and Petitioner responded that he would "be willing to try that." The trial court denied the motion without prejudice, withdrew the Office of the Public Defender from further representation of Petitioner, and appointed the Office of the Legal Defender. The court emphasized that Petitioner retained the right to represent himself and could "decide to try to exercise that [right] at a later time."

On direct appeal, Petitioner argued that the trial court had denied his right to self-representation. Petitioner argued that the trial court used a "threat tactic" to deny Petitioner's right to self-representation by stating that it could not continue the trial date. The appellate court found that the trial court had not threatened Petitioner, but had simply informed him that he would be held to the same standard as an attorney, and would not necessarily be granted a continuance of the trial date. The appellate court found that the trial court did not deny Petitioner his right to self-representation by advising   him of the disadvantages of self-representation. The appellate court noted that the trial court had clarified that Petitioner retained the right to self-representation and could renew his request. The court also noted that nothing in the record indicated that Petitioner had ever renewed his request to represent himself. The appellate court concluded that the trial court did not violate Petitioner's right to self-representation.

As Respondents argue, Petitioner has not shown that the State court's decision was contrary to, or an unreasonable application of, federal law, or that it was based on an unreasonable determination of the facts. *28 U.S.C. § 2254(e)(1)*. Under the *Sixth Amendment*, criminal defendants have a right to be represented by counsel. The right to counsel has been interpreted to include "an independent constitutional right" of the accused to represent himself at trial, and thus waive the right to counsel. *Faretta v. California, 422 U.S. 806, 95 S. Ct. 2525, 45 L. Ed. 2d 562 (1975)*. A defendant who seeks to represent himself "must 'knowingly and intelligently'" waive the right to counsel by being "made aware of the dangers and disadvantages of self-representation, so that the record will establish that 'he knows what he is doing and his choice is made with eyes open.'" *Id.* at 835 (quoting *Johnson v. Zerbst, 304 U.S. 458, 464-65, 58 S. Ct. 1019, 82 L. Ed. 1461 (1938)); see also, Iowa v. Tovar, 541 U.S. 77, 88, 124 S. Ct. 1379, 158 L. Ed. 2d 209 (2004)*. A criminal defendant's request for self-representation must also be unequivocal, timely, and not for purposes of delay. *Faretta, 422 U.S. at 835; United States v. Erskine, 355 F.3d 1161, 1167 (9th Cir. 2004); see also United States v. Arlt, 41 F.3d 516, 519 (9th Cir. 1994)*. Courts consider three factors to determine whether a request for self-representation is unequivocal: "the timing of the request, the manner in which the request was made, whether the defendant repeatedly made the request." *Stenson v. Lambert, 504 F.3d 873, 882 (9th Cir. 2007)*. In applying these factors, the court gives significant deference to the state court's factual findings. *Id., 504 F.3d at 882* (citing *28 U.S.C. § 2254(e)(1)* (state court's factual findings "shall be presumed to be correct").

Here, during the *Faretta* hearing, the trial court advised Petitioner of the responsibilities and disadvantages of self-representation. Petitioner agreed to the trial court's to substitute counsel. Petitioner's request to represent himself was not unequivocal when he simultaneously requested advisory counsel, a continuance of the trial date, and conceded that he was not prepared to proceed on the trial date. The matter proceeded to trial in December 2004. Petitioner did not renew his request to represent himself, even though the trial court had advised him that he could do so at any time.

The record supports the State court's finding that Petitioner's right to self-representation was not violated. Petitioner has not shown that the State court's rejection of this claim was based on an unreasonable determination of the facts, or was contrary to, or based on an unreasonable application of, controlling Supreme Court precedent. *Taylor v. Maddox, 366 F.3d 992, 999 (9th Cir. 2004)* ("[A] federal court may not second-guess a state court's fact-finding process unless . . . it determines that the state court was not merely wrong, but actually unreasonable."). Accordingly, Petitioner is not entitled to habeas corpus relief on this claim. *28 U.S.C. § 2254(d)*.

B. Ground Two - Aggravating Circumstances

In Ground Two, Petitioner argues that his *Sixth Amendment* rights, as articulated in *Blakely v. Washington, 542 U.S. 296, 124 S. Ct. 2531, 159 L. Ed. 2d 403 (2000)*, were violated when the trial court asked the jury to consider an improper aggravating circumstance at sentencing. Petitioner asserts that the aggravating circumstance, "use, threatened use, or possession of a deadly weapon," was improperly submitted to the jury because Petitioner was not charged with those circumstances and use of a weapon was not a fact reflected in the guilty verdict. Petitioner further argues that the trial court improperly considered a victim impact statement as an aggravating circumstance because it was not submitted to the jury for consideration. Respondents concede that Petitioner's sentencing claims are properly before the Court.

Before trial, the State filed an allegation of aggravating circumstances other than prior convictions alleging that:

> 1. The offense(s) involved the use, threatened use or possession of a deadly weapon or dangerous instrument during the commission of a crime, specifically a gun.
> 2. The defendant committed the offense(s) as consideration for the receipt, or in the expectation of the receipt, of of pecuniary value.
> 3. The offense(s) caused emotional harm to the victim.
> 4. At least one victim of the offense was sixty-five or more years of age or was a disabled person.

After the jury found Petitioner guilty, the aggravation phase began. The jury considered whether the State proved the aggravating circumstances beyond a reasonable doubt. With regards to the burglary conviction, the jury considered whether: (1) the offense involved the use of a weapon, (2) Petitioner committed the offense for pecuniary gain, (3) the offense caused emotional harm to the victim, and (4) whether one of the victims was at least 65 years old or disabled. The jury found that the State had failed to prove that a weapon was used in the commission of the offense, but found the existence of the other three aggravating factors beyond a reasonable doubt. Before sentencing Petitioner, the trial court found the allegation that Petitioner had 23 historical prior felony convictions was established beyond a reasonable doubt. The trial court sentenced Petitioner to an aggravated term of 20 years' imprisonment on the second-burglary conviction.

With regards to the possession of burglary tools conviction, the jury considered whether: (1) the offense involved the use of a weapon, and (2) whether Petitioner committed the offense for pecuniary gain. The jury found beyond a reasonable doubt that Petitioner committed the offense for pecuniary gain. The jury further found that the State had failed to prove that the offense involved the use of a weapon. The trial court sentenced Petitioner as a repetitive offender to an aggravated 4.5-year term of imprisonment.

On direct appeal, Petitioner raised the issue of improper aggravating circumstances. The appellate court found that the trial court did not consider the objectionable aggravating circumstance in sentencing Petitioner.

With regards to the "victim impact statement," during the sentencing hearing, the prosecutor relayed several statements from the victims' son, who lived out of state, was not present during the sentencing hearing, and had not written a letter to the court. The prosecutor stated that the victims' son, Patrick, was staying with his parents during the incident. The victims' son was concerned that the incident had hastened the death of his mother who was ill at the time of burglary and died several months later. The prosecutor advised the court that the victim's son felt the maximum sentence was appropriate . Petitioner did not object to the prosecutor's statements at the sentencing hearing. On direct appeal, Petitioner argued that those statements unfairly influenced that the court in imposing a maximum, rather than the presumptive, sentence.

The appellate court found that the "form and method in which [the] statement was presented" to the trial court might have been improper, but that its admission was not fundamental error because Petitioner's sentence was within the statutory range, several aggravating factors were present, and there was no evidence that the trial court's sentencing determination was influenced by the victim impact statement. Petitioner has not shown that the State court's ruling was to, or an unreasonable application of, clearly established Supreme Court precedent. *28 U.S.C. § 2254(d)(1).*

Before *Blakely v. Washington, 542 U.S. 296, 124 S. Ct. 2531, 159 L. Ed. 2d 403 (2000)*, in *Apprendi v. New Jersey, 530 U.S. 466, 120 S. Ct. 2348, 147 L. Ed. 2d 435 (2000)*, the Supreme Court held "[o]ther than the fact of a prior conviction, any fact that increases the penalty for a crime beyond the prescribed statutory maximum must be submitted to a jury, and proved beyond a reasonable doubt." *530 U.S. at 490.* The Supreme Court specifically carved out an exception for prior convictions. *Id.; United States v. Castillo-Rivera, 244 F.3d 1020, 1025 (9th Cir. 2001)* (holding the district court could consider a defendant's prior conviction in imposing a sentence enhancement even though such conduct had not been charged in the indictment, presented to the jury, and proved beyond a reasonable doubt); *United States v. Pacheco-Zepeda, 234 F.3d 411, 415 (9th Cir. 2001)* (noting *Apprendi* held all prior convictions are exempt under *Apprendi's* new rule, therefore, district court properly considered prior convictions in sentencing).

As previously stated, under *Blakely*, any factor which lead to a sentence greater than that which would be imposed based on the jury's finding of guilt must be found by the jury beyond a reasonable doubt. *542 U.S. at 301. Blakely* reaffirmed the exemption for prior convictions and reiterated that they may serve as aggravating factors without further proof. *United States v. Quintana-Quintana, 383 F.3d 1052, 1053 (9th Cir. 2004)* (citing *Blakely, 542 U.S. at 303*). *Blakely* also clarified that the "statutory maximum" sentence is initially the presumptive term and is the "maximum sentence the judge may impose solely *on the basis of the facts reflected in the jury verdict or admitted by the defendant.* In other words, the relevant 'statutory maximum' is not the maximum sentence a judge may impose after finding additional facts, but the maximum he may impose without any additional findings." *Blakely, 542 U.S. at 303-04* (emphasis in original). The *Blakely* Court concluded that, before a trial court can impose a sentence above the statutory maximum, a jury must find beyond a reasonable doubt, or defendant must admit, all facts *"legally essential* to punishment." *Id., 542 U.S. at 313* (emphasis added).

With respect to Petitioner's second-degree burglary conviction on Count 1, the jury found, beyond a reasonable doubt, the following   aggravating factors: (1) Petitioner committed the offense for pecuniary gain, (2) the offense caused emotional harm to the victim, and (3) one of the victims was over 65 years old or disabled. The jury found that the State had failed to prove an additional aggravating factor regarding use of a weapon during com-mission of the offense. Contrary to Petitioner's argument, there is no evidence that the trial court considered that factor in sentencing Petitioner. Rather, in sentencing Petitioner on Count 1, the court noted that the jury had found "three aggravators: You committed the offense for pecuniary gain, the emotional harm to the victim, and then at least one of the victims was 65 or more years of age or was a disabled." The Court found that there were sufficient aggravating factors to justify a sentence in excess of the presumptive. (*Id.*) Moreover, [HN24] the existence of one *Blakely*-complaint factor - such as a prior conviction, facts admitted by defendant, or found beyond a reasonable doubt by the jury - is sufficient support for the imposition of "a sentence anywhere within the statutory range." *Jones v. Schriro, 2006 U.S. Dist. LEXIS 44578, 2006 WL 1794765, * 3 (D.Ariz. June 27, 2006)*   (stating that "once a jury finds or a defendant admits a single aggravating factor, the *Sixth Amendment* permits the sentencing judge to find and consider additional factors relevant to the imposition of a sentence up to the maximum prescribed in that statute.'" *2006 U.S. Dist. LEXIS 44578, [WL] at * 2* (quoting *State v. Martinez, 210 Ariz. 578, 585, 115 P.3d 618 (2005)*).

Likewise, with respect to Petitioner's conviction for possession of burglary tools, the jury found, beyond a reasonable doubt, that Petitioner committed the offense for pecuniary gain. The jury further found that the State had failed to prove beyond a reasonable doubt that the offense involved the use of a weapon. Nothing in the record suggests that the State court relied on the unproven aggravating factor - use of a weapon - when sentencing Petitioner. Indeed, the Court noted that the jury found the pecuniary gain aggravating factor and that it was sufficient "to justify a sentence in excess of the presumptive term . . . ."

Petitioner further argues that the trial court's alleged consideration of the victim impact statement violated *Blakely*. Nothing in the record indicates that the court   considered the prosecutor's statements made on behalf of the victim's son when imposing the sentences. However, assuming the trial court considered the victim impact statement in sentencing Petitioner, it could do so even if the jury did not find the victim impact statement proven beyond a reasonable doubt. Once a single *Blakely*-compliant or *Blakely*-exempt aggravating factor was found, the court could consider other factors in determining Petitioner's sentence. *Jones, 2006 U.S. Dist. LEXIS 44578, 2006 WL 1794765, * 3.*

Finally, the trial court did not violate *Blakely* by considering Petitioner's prior convictions when sentencing him. In *Apprendi*, the Supreme Court specifically carved out an exception for prior convictions. *Apprendi, 530 U.S. at 490; United States v. Maria-Gonzalez, 268 F.3d 664, 670 (9th Cir. 2001)* (holding prior aggravated felony conviction did not constitute an element of the offense where base sentence for illegally reentering the United States following deportation is enhanced if deportation was subsequent to conviction for aggravated felony). *United States v. Castillo-Rivera, 244 F.3d 1020, 1025 (9th Cir. 2001)* (holding the district court could consider defendant's prior   conviction in imposing sentence enhancement even though such conduct had not been charged in the indictment, presented to the jury, and proved beyond a reasonable doubt). *Blakely* confirmed that exception. *Blakely, 542 U.S. at 301.*

Because the sentences imposed comported with the *Sixth Amendment* as construed in *Blakely*, Petitioner is not entitled to habeas corpus relief on his sentencing claims.

C. Ground Three - Disproportionate Sentence

In Ground Three, Petitioner argues that the sentences are disproportionate to other sentences imposed for the same conduct. The jury found Petitioner guilty of burglary in the second-degree, a Class 3 felony, and possession of burglary tools, a Class 6 felony. The convictions were based on Petitioner's nighttime entry into an elderly couple's home. The jury found, beyond a reasonable doubt, the existence of three aggravating factors pertaining to the burglary conviction, and one aggravating factor pertaining to the possession of burglary tools conviction. Before sentencing Petitioner, the trial court determined that Petitioner had 23 historical prior felony   convictions. The court imposed an aggravated term of 20 years' imprisonment on the burglary conviction and sentenced Petitioner as a repetitive offender to an aggravated concurrent 4.5-year term on the possession of burglary tools conviction.

On direct appeal, Petitioner argued that the trial court imposed an excessive sentence based on the improper consideration of an aggravating factor not found by the jury, the improper consideration of the victim impact statement, and Petitioner's lack of opportunity to review and challenge inaccuracies in an untimely disclosed pre-sentence report. The appellate court found that Petitioner's sentence fell within the statutory guidelines, and that imposition of a maximum sentence was supported by the aggravating circumstances found by the jury and by Petitioner's prior convictions as determined by the trial court. Petitioner has not shown that the State court's ruling is contrary to, or involves an unreasonable application of, clearly established federal law, as determined by the Supreme Court. *28 U.S.C. § 2254(d)(1)*

The *Eighth Amendment* provides that "[e]xcessive bail shall not be required, nor excessive fines imposed, nor cruel and unusual punishment inflicted." *Harmelin v. Michigan, 501 U.S. 957, 1001, 111 S. Ct. 2680, 115 L. Ed. 2d 836 (1991)*. A sentence that is "grossly disproportionate" to the crime for which a defendant was convicted may violate the *Eighth Amendment. Harmelin, 501 U.S. at 1001 (1991)*. "[O]utside of the context of capital punishment, successful challenges to the proportionality of particular sentences [are] exceedingly rare . . . . Reviewing courts, of course, should grant substantial deference to the broad authority that legislatures necessarily possess in determining the types and limits of punishments for crimes, as well as to the discretion that trial courts possess in sentencing convicted criminals." *Solem v. Helm, 463 U.S. 277, 289-90, 103 S. Ct. 3001, 77 L. Ed. 2d 637 (1983)* (citations omitted). Petitioner is correct that the Supreme Court has noted that a proportionality analysis under the *Eighth Amendment* should consider the following criteria, including: "(i) the gravity of the offense and the harshness of the penalty; (ii) the sentences imposed on other criminals in the same jurisdiction; and (iii) the sentences imposed for commission of the same crime in other jurisdictions." *Id., 463 U.S. at 292.* The Supreme Court, however, has not uniformly applied this three step analysis. *See, e.g., Harmelin, 501 U.S. at 1005; Rummel v. Estelle, 445 U.S. 263, 285, 100 S. Ct. 1133, 63 L. Ed. 2d 382 (1980).*

In an effort resolve this inconsistency, the Supreme Court has identified what constitutes "clearly established federal law" in its *Eighth Amendment* jurisprudence for the purpose of habeas review. Specifically, in *Lockyer v. Andrade, 538 U.S. 63, 72, 123 S. Ct. 1166, 155 L. Ed. 2d 144 (2003)*, after conceding that its "precedents in this area have not been a model of clarity," the Supreme Court held that "one governing legal principle emerges as 'clearly established' under § 2254(d)(1): A gross disproportionality principle is applicable to sentences for terms of years." *Id., 538 U.S. at 72; see also Gonzalez v. Duncan, 551 F.3d 875, 879 (9th Cir. 2008).* In so holding, the Court did not refer to a constitutional imperative requiring courts to make the various intra- and inter-jurisdictional comparisons recommended by the *Solem* court. *Lockyer, 538 U.S. at 72.* Rather, the Supreme Court held that "the only relevant clearly established law amenable to the 'contrary to' or 'unreasonable application of' framework is the gross disproportionality principle, the precise contours of which are unclear, applicable only in the 'exceedingly rare' and 'extreme' case." *Id. at 73.*

When analyzing an *Eighth Amendment* proportionality challenge, a court determines whether a "comparison of the crime committed and the sentence imposed leads to an inference of gross disproportionality." *United States v. Bland, 961 F.2d 123, 129 (9th Cir. 1992)* (citing *Harmelin, 501 U.S. at 1001*) (finding that sentence of life imprisonment without possibility of parole did not raise inference of disproportionality when imposed on a felon in possession of a firearm.); *see also Harris v. Wright, 93 F.3d 581, 583-85 (9th Cir. 1996)* (holding that a mandatory sentence of life imprisonment without possibility of parole did not raise inference of disproportionality when imposed on convicted murderer). A court generally will not overturn a sentence on *Eighth Amendment* grounds provided it does not exceed statutory limits. *United States v. Zavala-Serra, 853 F.2d 1512, 1518 (9th Cir. 1988)* (upholding sentence of ten years' imprisonment for conspiracy to possess and distribute 2,000 grams of cocaine where sentence was within statutory range.)

Here, Petitioner's sentences, totaling 20 years imprisonment, are not grossly disproportionate to his convictions for second degree burglary and possession of burglary tools. The jury found aggravating circumstances - Petitioner committed the offenses for pecuniary gain, the offense caused emotional harm to the victim, and one of the victims was over 65 years old or disabled. Additionally, Petitioner had an extensive criminal history consisting of 23 prior felonies, involving kidnaping and similar offenses of burglary and armed robbery. *See Ewing v. California, 538 U.S. 11, 30, 123 S. Ct. 1179, 155 L. Ed. 2d 108 (2003)* (finding that sentence of 25 years to life in prison, imposed for felony grand theft under the three strikes law, is not grossly disproportionate and therefore does not violate the *Eighth Amendment's* prohibition against cruel and unusual punishment. And stating, that "Ewing's sentence is a long one. But it reflects a rational legislative judgment, entitled to deference, that offenders who have committed serious or violent felonies and who continue to commit felonies must be incapacitated."); *Nunes v. Ramirez-Palmer, 485 F.3d 432, 439 (9th Cir. 2007)* (finding that sentence of 25 years to life imprisonment for shoplifting $114.40 worth of tools was not grossly disproportionate in view of defendant's "extensive felony record" dating back almost sixty years).

Petitioner's sentences do not raise an inference of gross disproportionality. Petitioner has not shown that the State court's determination that his sentences do not violate the *Eighth Amendment* is contrary to, or rests on an unreasonable application of, federal law. *28 U.S.C. § 2254.* Accordingly, he is not entitled to habeas corpus relief.

D. Ground Four - Ineffective Assistance of Counsel

In Ground Four, Petitioner contends that trial counsel was ineffective for failing to advocate on his behalf and present mitigating evidence at sentencing. Petitioner specifically argues that counsel failed to object to statements the prosecutor made on behalf of the victims' son, who was not present during the sentencing hearing. During sentencing, the prosecutor stated that the victims' son was afraid for his parents during the time Petitioner was inside the house with them, and speculated that the incident had hastened his mother's death several months later. Petitioner further argues that trial counsel was ineffective for failing to present unspecified mitigating evidence. Petitioner raised these claims on during post-conviction review. The State court rejected these claims without discussion. Although the State court did not explain its decision, *Section 2254(d)* applies to this summary denial of Petitioner's claim. *Richter, 562 U.S. at , 131 S. Ct. at 786.*

Respondents argue that Petitioner is not entitled to habeas corpus relief because there is no clearly established federal governing the assistance of counsel during non-capital sentencing. Respondents correctly note that the Supreme Court has not articulated a standard which applies to ineffective assistance of counsel claims in the context of non-capital sentencing noting that, in *Strickland*, the Supreme Court declined to "consider the role of counsel in ordinary sentencing which . . . may require a different approach to the definition of constitutionally effective assistance." *Strickland, 466 U.S. at 686. See also Cooper-Smith v. Palmateer, 397 F.3d 1236, 1244 (9th Cir. 2005).*[HN28] "Where the Supreme Court has not addressed an issue in its holding, a state court adjudication of the issue not addressed by the Supreme Court cannot be contrary to, or an unreasonable application of, clearly established federal law." *Stenson v. Lambert, 504 F.3d 873, 881 (9th Cir. 2007); see also Wright v. Van Patten, 552 U.S. 120, 124-26, 128 S. Ct. 743, 169 L. Ed. 2d 583 (2008).* In other words, if habeas corpus relief depends on the resolution of an "open question in [Supreme Court] jurisprudence,' § 2254(d)(1) precludes relief." *Crater v. Galaza, 491 F.3d 1119, 1123 (9th Cir. 2007)* (quoting *Musladin, 549 U.S. at 76*) (stating that "[g]iven the lack of holdings from this Court regarding the potentially prejudicial effect of spectators' courtroom conduct of the kind involved here, it cannot be said that the state court 'unreasonably applied clearly established federal law.'"). Thus, as a threshold matter, Petitioner is not entitled to habeas relief under *28 U.S.C. § 2254(d)(1)* because there is no clearly established Supreme Court precedent in the noncapital sentencing context. *Davis v. Grigas, 443 F.3d 1155, 1158 (9th Cir. 2006); Cooper-Smith, 397 F.3d at 1244.* Even if the *Strickland* standard for capital cases applied to this noncapital sentencing, Petitioner's claims asserted in Ground Four fail.

The relevant federal law governing claims of ineffective assistance of counsel is *Strickland v. Washington, 466 U.S. 668, 104 S. Ct. 2052, 80 L. Ed. 2d 674 (1984),* which requires a showing of "both deficient performance by counsel and prejudice." *Knowles v. Mirzayance, 556 U.S. 111, 129 S.Ct. 1411, 1420, 173 L. Ed. 2d 251 (2009).* "'Surmounting *Strickland's* high bar is never an easy task.'" *Richter, 131 S.Ct. at 788* (quoting *Padilla v. Kentucky, 559 U.S. , 130 S.Ct. 1473, 1485, 176 L. Ed. 2d 284 (2010)).* "The question is whether an attorney's representation amounted to incompetence under 'prevailing professional norms,' not whether it deviated from best practices or most common custom." *Richter, 131 S. Ct. at 788* (quoting *Strickland, 466 U.S. at 690*). Establishing that a state court's application of *Strickland* was unreasonable under *§ 2254(d)* is even more difficult, because both standards are "highly deferential," *466 U. S. at 689*, and because *Strickland's* general standard has a substantial range of reasonable applications. The issue under *§ 2254(d)* is not whether counsel's actions were reasonable, but whether there is any reasonable argument that counsel satisfied *Strickland's* deferential standard. *Richter, 131 S. Ct. at 788*. The Supreme Court recently addressed the reasons for a "most deferential" standard for judging counsel's performance:

> Unlike a later reviewing court, the attorney   observed the relevant proceedings, knew of materials outside the record, and interacted with the client, with opposing counsel, and with the judge.

Premo v. Moore,   U.S.   , 131 S. Ct. 733, 739-40, 178 L. Ed. 2d 649 (2011). Mindful of these principles, the Court will consider whether the state court unreasonably applied *Strickland* to the facts of this case. *28 U.S.C. § 2254*.

1. Failure to Object to Victim Impact Statement

Even if the statement of the victims' son was not presented to the sentencing court in the appropriate manner, Petitioner cannot show that he was prejudiced. As the court of appeals noted, there is no evidence that the trial court was improperly influenced by the victim impact statement in sentencing Petitioner. The aggravated sentence that the trial court imposed was based on Petitioner's extensive criminal history, and the aggravating circumstances found by the jury. At sentencing, the court stated:

> All right. Well, I remember your testimony. I remember your defense. The jury didn't buy it, and I don't either.
>
> Now you are here as a repetitive offender with two priors. That said, you have 20 prior convictions. I understand a lot of them are in the same case,   but you really cover it. You got a possession for sale conviction, you've got - - 17 counts of burglary, armed robbery, and kidnapping out of one of our matters some time ago.
>
> My recollection is that you had a big prison sentence in that case. You also got a conviction for armed robbery. So your record remains aggravating even with the fact that you are a repetitive offender.
>
> The jury found on Count 1 the existence of . . . three aggravators: You committed the offense for pecuniary gain, the emotional harm to the victim, and then at least one of the victims was 65 or more years of age or was a disabled person; and then aggravators two and three, if you -- well, the pecuniary gain aggravator was also found on . . . the second count.
>
> I think certainly there are sufficient aggravating factors in this case and your record to justify a sentence in excess of the presumptive term on each count. And I think [the probation officer's] recommendation is well taken, frankly. I mean you could justify the absolute maximum.
>
> I am going to give you the maximum sentence on both counts. It is the judgment and sentence of the Court on Count 1 that the defendant be imprisoned for 20 years, on Count 2 for 4 and   a half years.

The trial court's statements at sentencing indicate that it did not rely on the victim impact statement - as conveyed by the prosecutor - when sentencing Petitioner. Rather, the court relied on the aggravating factors and Petitioner's extensive criminal history. Accordingly, Petitioner has not shown that trial counsel was ineffective at sentencing for failing to object to the statements of the victims' son as conveyed by the prosecutor.

2. Failure to Present Mitigating Evidence at Sentencing

Petitioner also argues that trial counsel was ineffective for failing to present mitigating evidence at sentencing. Petitioner presented this claim on post-conviction review. Petitioner, however, did not identify what evidence counsel should have presented at sentencing. The post-conviction court summarily rejected Petitioner's claim. Although the State court did not explain its decision, *Section 2254(d)* applies to this summary denial of Petitioner's claim. *Richter, 562 U.S. at   , 131 S. Ct. at 786.* Petitioner has not shown that the state court's rejection of this claim was contrary to, or based on an unreasonable application   of, controlling federal law.

To the extent that Petitioner argues that trial counsel should have called witnesses to testify at the sentencing hearing, Petitioner's failure to identify such witness is fatal to his claim. [HN30] "[C]omplaints of uncalled witnesses are not favored in federal habeas corpus review because allegations of what the witness would have testified are largely speculative . . . . In addition, for [a petitioner] to demonstrate the requisite *Strickland* prejudice, [he] must show not only that [the] testimony would have been favorable, but also that the witness would have testified at trial." *Evans v. Cockrell, 285 F.3d 370, 377 (5th Cir. 2002)* (citations omitted); *see also United States v. Harden, 846 F.2d 1229, 1231-32 (9th Cir. 1988)* (rejecting the claim of ineffective assistance based on counsels' failure to call a witness who would have taken responsibility for a gun found in defendant's possession because, *inter alia,* "[t]here is no evidence in the record which establishes that Washington would testify in [petitioner's] trial."). Petitioner has not presented any factual or legal arguments in support of his claim that trial counsel was ineffective for failing to present   mitigating evidence at sentencing. Petitioner's conclusory allegations are not sufficient to support a claim of ineffective assistance of counsel. *Villafuerte v. Stewart, 111 F.3d 616 (9th Cir. 1997).*

The record reflects that Petitioner's counsel advocated for Petitioner and argued for the presumptive, or a mitigated term, at the sentencing hearing. Counsel discussed Petitioner's intelligence, recent employment history, and family support. Petitioner personally addressed the sentencing court and apologized for intruding on the victims' property. The sentencing court found that aggravated sentences were warranted because of Petitioner's extensive criminal history and the aggravating factors found by the jury. Petitioner does not present any specific evidence that counsel should have presented to have mitigated his sentence. Petitioner has failed to show that the trial court's rejection of this claim was contrary to, or an un-reasonable application of, federal law.

E. Ground Five - Failure to Investigate

In Ground Five, Petitioner argues that trial counsel was ineffective for failing to conduct an adequate pre-trial   investigation to locate witnesses who could have supported Petitioner's defense. Petitioner contended that he entered the victims' home because he was looking for Danny Miller, who was giving him a ride home and had left him in the car after telling Petitioner he "had business in the [victims'] home." Petitioner asserts that, when Miller did not return to the car in a reasonable time, Petitioner went in search of him. Petitioner claims that he entered the victims' home through an open door, then went inside the bathroom. While he was using the bathroom, police entered the house and discovered Petitioner. Petitioner asserts that counsel should have located and interviewed Danny Miller, conducted a latent print comparison with the fingerprints found at the scene, and investigated discrepancies in the witness' description of the man he saw and described to the 911 operator.

Petitioner presented this claim on post-conviction review, which was rejected without discussion. Although the State court did not explain its decision, *Section 2254(d)* applies to this summary denial of Petitioner's claim. *Richter, 562 U.S. at   , 131 S. Ct. at 786.*

"Counsel   has a duty to make reasonable investigations or to make a reasonable decision that makes a particular investigations unnecessary." *Strickland, 466 U.S. at 691.* Additionally, "a particular decision not to investigate must be directly assessed for reasonableness in all circumstances." *Id.*

> A court deciding an actual ineffectiveness claim must judge the reasonableness of counsel's challenged conduct on the facts of the particular case, viewed at the time of counsel's conduct. A convicted defendant making a claim of ineffective assistance must identify the acts or omissions of counsel that are alleged not to have been the result of reasonable professional judgment. The court must then determine whether, in light of all the circumstances, the identified acts or omissions were outside the wide range of professionally competent assistance. In making that determination, the court should keep in mind that counsel's function, as elaborated in pre-

vailing professional norms, is to make the adversarial testing process work in the particular case. At the same time, the court should recognize that counsel is strongly presumed to have rendered adequate assistance and made all significant decisions the exercise of reasonable professional judgment.

Strickland, 466 U.S. at 690.

To assess Petitioner's claim that counsel was ineffective for failing to investigate, the evidence presented at Petitioner's trial is relevant. The evidence indicated that Petitioner stepped out from behind the door in the master bathroom in the victims' home as a police officer approached the bathroom to search it. Petitioner struggled as he was arrested and never told police that he was looking for someone inside the house. Police officers found a Leatherman's tool on Petitioner's person. Police officers on the scene also found that: (1) the light bulb had been removed from the motion sensor over the back door and placed on the ground; (2) there were pry marks on the back window; (3) a gym bag containing a purse and a jewelry box were on the ground outside the patio door; and (4) there was a flashlight near the door to the master bedroom. Officers also observed a picture or painting, and a wrapper of some kind in the middle of the floor of the walk-in closet of the master bedroom, which seemed out of place. A file cabinet in a spare bedroom had been pried open. Three houses away from the victims' home, police officers found an unoccupied vehicle with the engine running, and a window partially open. The car was registered to a person named Lamar Ellis. The police did not find anyone else in the backyard, alley, or inside the house.

This evidence undermines Petitioner's assertion that he was merely present at the house looking for a person named Danny Miller and rendered the investigation that Petitioner claims counsel should have undertaken unnecessary. Additionally, Petitioner testified at trial and presented his theory of defense. Petitioner explained that Danny Miller was driving him home and stopped at the victims' house. After waiting in the car for a while, Petitioner "went looking for [Miller.]" Petitioner testified that he walked to the house, and entered through the back door. He continued to walk through the house looking for Miller and then decided to use the bathroom. While he was using the bathroom, Petitioner heard people talking, then opened the door, and saw the police. Petitioner testified that a police officer directed him to "hit the floor, which [he] did." Petitioner testified that he never saw Danny Miller inside the house. He also testified that Danny Miller "was shot in a police gun battle," some time before trial. The record reflects that Petitioner did not tell police that he was inside the victims' home looking for Danny Miller, and nothing at the scene suggested the presence of a second person. Police officers did not see another person near the victims' home. The victims' son saw the shadow of one person rummaging through his parents' bed-room with a flashlight. A single flashlight was recovered by the door to the master bedroom. The car in which Petitioner had allegedly been a passenger was found three houses away from the victims' home. Nothing in the car connected it to Danny Miller.

Based on the foregoing, counsel's strategic decision not to investigate the whereabouts of Danny Miller was not ineffective assistance. On post-conviction review, defense counsel testified that Petitioner's "story was simply   beyond belief." According to Petitioner, Danny Miller died before trial and could not have testified on Petitioner's behalf. At trial, Petitioner presented his theory of defense - that he was inside the victims' home because he was looking for Danny Miller. Aside from Petitioner's testimony, evidence showed that Petitioner was in the victims' home when the burglary was in progress. He had on his person a Leatherman's Tool containing pliers. The police officers' testimony confirmed that Petitioner was found at the scene of the burglary. Finally, Petitioner did not argue that Danny Miller committed the offense, but that he was merely looking for Danny Miller who was inside the house because he had "some business" therein. In view of the foregoing, Petitioner has not shown that there is a reasonable probability that, but for counsel's failure to investigate the presence of Danny Miller, the result of the trial would have been different.

Petitioner also argues that counsel was ineffective for failing to investigate and present testimony regarding the discrepancies between the description of the intruder the victims' son gave to the 911 operator and Petitioner's appearance. Any discrepancies between Petitioner's appearance and the description of the intruder given by the victims' son is explained by the son's brief opportunity to observe the intruder in the dark. The victims' son, Patrick, testified that he woke up in the middle of the night and went to the kitchen to get some water. He noticed the backdoor was open and saw his "dad's tennis bag with jewelry boxes and whatnot in it" on the ground. Patrick testified that he returned to the kitchen and noticed a flashlight coming from his parents' bedroom. He walked to the bathroom and "walked up on somebody that didn't belong there." Patrick testified that he saw the person in his parents' darkened bedroom from "the back . . . [l]ong enough to see what was going on and to get out of there." He testified that the person appeared to be a man by "the build." Patrick further testified that he did not see the person's face, and "couldn't really say" what type of clothing the intruder was wearing. Thus, any discrepancies between Petitioner's appearance and the description of the intruder that Patrick gave the 911 operator was explained by Patrick's own testimony that he only caught a glimpse of the back of the intruder in the dark. Moreover, the intruder's description was not an issue because police found Petitioner in the victims' home.

Petitioner also argues that counsel was ineffective for failing to investigate for latent fingerprints Police officers were unable to recover fingerprints from the flashlight that was found near the master bedroom. Police officers recovered two latent fingerprints from the file cabinets in the second bedroom, and submitted them for testing. Petitioner was excluded as a match for one of the prints and the other could not be identified. Officers did not try to recover prints from a wooden dresser in the bedroom because the "grain structure" is "too rough to be able to see the tiny ridges on your finger." Officers did not try to recover fingerprints from the light bulb from the motion sensor. The fingerprints available to defense counsel -those taken by the police officers the night of the burglary - were exculpatory because they were not Petitioner's. Evidence regarding the fingerprints was presented at trial. Petitioner has not shown how additional investigation into the fingerprints would have benefitted his defense. Moreover, Petitioner has not shown that he was prejudiced by counsel's failure to investigate latent fingerprints when the fingerprint evidence presented at trial was exculpatory.

For the reasons set forth above, Petitioner is not entitled to habeas corpus relief on his claim that trial counsel was ineffective for failing to investigate.

F. Ground Six - Juror Bias and Inadequate Cross-Examination

In Ground Six, Petitioner argues that counsel was ineffective for failing to investigate the improper communication between the trial judge, his judicial assistant, and an impaneled juror. Petitioner asserts that trial counsel should have requested a mistrial based on juror bias. Petitioner presented this claim on post-conviction review. The trial court rejected it without discussion. Although the State court did not explain its decision, *Section 2254(d)* applies to this summary denial of Petitioner's claim. *Richter, 562 U.S. at , 131 S. Ct. at 786.*

Petitioner's case proceeded to trial on December 9, 2004. At the outset, the trial judge introduced his staff, including his judicial assistant, who was not present in the courtroom. The trial judge stated:

> Let me go ahead and introduce everyone. My name is Greg Martin. I am a judge on the Superior Court. Again, my court reporter is Melinda Setterman, the lady to my right. Elaine Hill is my deputy clerk for today.
>
> Greg Paduganan - you already met Greg. Deputy Patterson is here to the left. She is usually in the courtroom as well. Also a part of my staff but not usually in the courtroom is my judicial assistant, Ann Kaites. If you are one of the 14 people, it is likely you will meet her. She is in the outer officer, and she's . . . my judicial assistant.
>
> By chance, does anybody know either me or somebody here on the staff at all? Okay.

When the court next convened, the trial court notified the parties that his judicial assistant, who had not been in the courtroom during *voir dire*, knew one of the jurors. The juror was the mother of a someone with whom the judicial assistant had attended school. The judicial assistant had not seen the juror in 20 years. When asked whether anyone on the jury panel knew the judicial assistant, Ann Kaites, the juror did not respond because she did not know the judicial assistant by that last name. The trial court had the following discussion with the juror on the record:

> The Court: Okay. This is juror 4. I understand you know Ann?
>
> The Juror: Yes, I do.
>
> The Court: Okay. And when I said her name, I said her married name of course. You probably know her as Ann Peralta?
>
> The Juror: Yes.
>
> The Court: The fact that she's my judicial assistant, is that going to make it hard for you to be a fair and impartial juror in this case?
>
> The Juror: No.
>
> The Court: Any questions?
>
> Ms. Kay: None from the State.
>
> Ms. Todd: None from the defense, your Honor.

The *Sixth Amendment's* right to a jury trial "guarantees a criminally accused a fair trial by a panel of impartial, indifferent jurors." *Irvin v. Dowd, 366 U.S. 717, 722, 81 S. Ct. 1639, 6 L. Ed. 2d 751 (1961).*The bias or prejudice of a single juror denies a defendant the right to a fair trial. *Tinsley v. Borg, 895 F.2d 520, 523-24 (9th Cir. 1990); United States v. Eubanks, 591 F.2d 513, 517 (9th Cir. 1979).* The test for determining whether a juror is biased is whether the juror had such fixed opinions that he or she could not judge the guilt of the defendant impartially. *Patton v. Yount, 467 U.S. 1025, 1035, 104 S. Ct. 2885, 81 L. Ed. 2d 847 (1984).* A trial judge's finding that a particular juror was not biased has been regarded as a factual finding subject to the statutory presumption of correctness, because "resolution [of the juror impartiality issue] depends heavily on the trial court's appraisal of witness credibility and demeanor." *See Thompson v. Keohane, 516 U.S. 99, 111, 116 S. Ct. 457, 133 L. Ed. 2d 383 (1995); Wainwright v. Witt, 469 U.S. 412, 428-29, 105 S. Ct. 844, 83 L. Ed. 2d 841 (1985); Patton, 467 U.S. at 1038.* Petitioner has not meet his burden of adducing clear and convincing evidence to overcome this presumption. *See 28 U.S.C. § 2254(e)(1).*

The attenuated relationship between the judicial assistant and the juror in this case does not support a claim of implied bias. The judicial assistant was not in the courtroom during *voir dire* and the juror at issue did not recognize her current last name. The trial court was immediately notified when the juror and the judicial assistant realized they knew each other. The trial court notified counsel for both sides and conducted an examination of that juror to determine whether she could remain impartial. The juror confirmed that she could remain impartial. Nothing suggested that the juror's response was not truthful. Counsel for the State and the defense were permitted, but declined, to ask questions. Defense counsel had no reason to infer improper communication or juror bias from this incident. Petitioner has not shown that trial counsel was ineffective for failing to further pursue the issue of juror bias.

In Ground Six, Petitioner also argues that trial counsel was ineffective for failing to adequately cross-examine the State's witnesses. Petitioner argues that defense counsel's cross-examination of the State's witnesses, including the alleged victim and three police officers who responded to the scene, was "of no significance." He specifically argues that counsel was ineffective for failing to question "Stacy Hubbard, a technician with the Phoenix Police Department crime lab" about whether she compared the latent prints found at the scene with exemplars from Danny Miller.

There is a strong presumption that counsel's conduct falls within the wide range of reasonable professional assistance. *Strickland, 466 U.S. at 689.* Here, Petitioner's defense was that he was merely present in the victims's house looking for Danny Miller who was giving him a ride home, but had stopped at the victims' house to conduct some business. The record reflects that counsel pursued that defense. On cross-examination of the victims' son, Patrick, defense counsel called into question his ability to identify Petitioner as the intruder. Counsel emphasized that Patrick's identification of Petitioner was based "upon when [he] saw the police bring [Petitioner] out of the house . . . ." Counsel further elicited testimony from Patrick that his identification of Petitioner "was not based on the intruder in the house," because he only had a limited sighting of the intruder in the dark.

Defense counsel's cross-examination of the police officers, who responded at the scene, focused on the fact that the description of the intruder given to the 911 operator that did not match Petitioner's features or his clothing, that officers did not find a baseball cap the intruder was reportedly wearing, that Petitioner had a substantial sum of money - over $650.00 - in his wallet that did not belong to the victims, and that officers did not attempt to obtain latent prints from the light bulb that had been removed from the motion sensor. Defense counsel did not cross-examine Stacy Hubbard, the latent print examiner, who testified on direct that Petitioner was excluded from one of the fingerprints she examined and that she did not match the second print to any known exemplars.

During closing argument, defense counsel argued that the State had not established beyond a reasonable doubt that Petitioner was in the home to commit a burglary. Counsel reiterated that the State had not presented any fingerprint evidence connecting Petitioner to the crime, that the fingerprint evidence presented excluded Petitioner, and that the police officers had not attempted to take fingerprints from the light bulb of the motion sensor. Counsel further argued that police had not tried to match the pry marks on the window with the Leatherman Tool found on Petitioner. Defense counsel also argued that description of the intruder given to the 911 operator did not match Petitioner's appearance, and argued that it did not make sense that Petitioner would commit the robbery when he had nearly $650.00 in cash on his person.

The record reflects that Petitioner's trial counsel adequately cross-examined the State's witnesses. His cross-examination focused on Petitioner's mere-presence defense, and the weaknesses in the State's case - including the lack of fingerprints connecting Petitioner to the crime scene, and the discrepancies between the description of the intruder given to the 911 operator and Petitioner's appearance. Petitioner has not shown that the State court's rejection of his claim of ineffective assistance of counsel based on counsel's failure to cross-examine witness is contrary to, or based on an unreasonable application of, Supreme Court precedent.

G. Ground Seven - Failure to Adequately Advise on Merits of Plea Offer

In Ground Seven, Petitioner argues that counsel was ineffective for failing to properly advise him of a plea offer, and failing to adequately inform him of risks of going to trial and his sentencing exposure

Petitioner raised this claim during post-conviction proceedings and the State court conducted an evidentiary hearing. At the evidentiary hearing, trial counsel testified that the State had extended several plea offers but that the first, mandating a term of 7 years' imprisonment, was withdrawn by the State shortly after it was extended. The plea was withdrawn on March 22, 2004 after the police detective investigating the case objected to the plea offer as too lenient. A second plea offer was extended for a sentencing range of 10 to 13 years imprisonment, but Petitioner rejected that offer after informing counsel that he had given a free-talk in a murder case that the State could not prove without his testimony, and he thought the State would extend a better offer. Petitioner told defense counsel that he was telling the truth, that he wanted to go to trial, and that he thought he would be acquitted. (*Id.* at 28, 30) Petitioner asked counsel about the substantial difference in the proposed sentences between the two offers and asked what had happened to the offer for a term of 7-years' imprisonment.

Defense counsel testified that she explained the terms of the plea offer to Petitioner, discussing the impact of his 20-plus prior felony convictions on the sentencing range, and informed Petitioner that he would be subject to "an extremely aggravated sentence" if convicted at trial, "which was much worse than we get under the plea offer." Defense counsel also explained that the plea offer was for a sentencing range of not less than 10 years and no more than 13 years, and that it "was better than what he was going to get from [the trial judge]." Petitioner never conveyed to counsel that he interpreted the sentencing range to be an additional 13-year sentence. Defense counsel testified that she reviewed the merits of the case with Petitioner, and informed him that his version of the events could not be corroborated and that she "didn't think the jury was going to believe his story. His story was simply beyond belief. Defense counsel confirmed with the prosecutor and the previous defense attorney that Petitioner had had discussions with the State about testifying in a murder case. The State offered Petitioner an "8 to 11-year" plea offer if Petitioner cooperated in the murder case. Petitioner rejected the offer, stating that it was "still too much time." Counsel further testified that, on the first day of trial which ended in a mistrial, Petitioner gave counsel the name of a woman he said would corroborate his story. Counsel called the woman, but she hung up the phone once counsel explained the nature of her call. After the mistrial, the attorneys talked to the jurors who conveyed that they did not believe Petitioner's version of the events. After speaking to the jurors, the State notified defense counsel that it would re-extend the "10 to 13-year" plea offer, but that Petitioner would have to accept it immediately. Defense counsel conveyed the jurors' impressions to Petitioner, and Petitioner stated that he did not care and wanted to select a new jury. Defense counsel told Petitioner that the State had re-extended the "10 to 13-year" plea offer. Defense counsel's discussion with Petitioner was brief focused on the length of the sentence offered. Petitioner rejected the plea offer because the sentence was too long

At Petitioner's first trial, when the court decided that it would grant a mistrial, the judge asked the prosecutor how quickly she could retry the case. The prosecutor responded that Petitioner could accept the plea offer, or the trial would commence the following day. The court asked about the terms of the plea offer and defense counsel stated that it was a "10 to 13-year" plea. As the parties discussed an additional term of the plea offer, defense counsel interrupted and stated, "my client just informed me that he's continuing to reject that offer." The jury returned to the courtroom and the trial court declared a mistrial.

At the evidentiary hearing on Petitioner's petition for post-conviction relief, Petitioner testified that he first became aware of a plea offer including a 7-year term of imprisonment after he received the file from appellate counsel. Petitioner also stated that he did not hear about the "10 to 13-year" plea offer until a mistrial was declared. Petitioner stated that he and counsel had a brief conversation about the plea offer at the defense table and it was the only conversation he ever had with counsel about that plea offer. Petitioner testified that he understood the "10 to 13-year" plea offer to mean that the trial court could "give [him] up to 13 plus years" or "the top was 13 and aggravated meant that [the court] could go over the 13 and give [him] a few years on top of it."

At the conclusion of the evidentiary hearing, the post-conviction court found that Petitioner had not met his burden of establishing that trial counsel rendered ineffective assistance. The State court explained:

> The testimony from Ms. Todd (defense counsel) indicates that she did in fact, have a conversation with Mr. McDonald in the jail regarding the plea agreement, that she had the plea agreement with her, that she advised the defendant of the stipulations in the plea agreement for an aggravated term of 10 to 13 years and that there was some discussion regarding the 7 years being withdrawn.
>
> So it sounds like based on her testimony, Mr. McDonald also knew about the   seven-year offer and I don't need to reach the second prong unless I find that counsel's performance was deficient.
>
> I find that the defendant has not proved by a preponderance that defense counsel's performance was deficient and he was aware of the offer and communicated to him in the jail and communicated again to him after the mistrial, as reflected in the transcript and the resuscitation of the conversation between the prosecutor, the Court and defense counsel on page 12 of Mr. Beene's response [to the petition for post-conviction relief.]
>
> Petition for Post-Conviction Relief is dismissed.

Petitioner has not shown that the State court's ruling was contrary to, or an unreasonable application of, federal law. The relevant federal law governing ineffective assistance of counsel claims is *Strickland v. Washington, 466 U.S. 668, 104 S. Ct. 2052, 80 L. Ed. 2d 674 (1984)*, which requires a showing of "both deficient performance by counsel and prejudice." *Knowles v. Mirzayance, 556 U.S. 111, 129 S.Ct. 1411, 1420, 173 L. Ed. 2d 251 (2009)*. The *Sixth Amendment* guarantees a criminal defendant effective assistance of counsel during all critical stages of the criminal process, including plea negotiations. *Hill v. Lockhart, 474 U.S. 52, 57, 106 S. Ct. 366, 88 L. Ed. 2d 203 (1985)*;   *United States v. Leonti, 326 F.3d 1111, 1116 (9th Cir. 2003)*. Thus, *Strickland's* two-prong test applies to ineffectiveness claims in connection with the plea process. *Hill, 474 U.S. at 57*. The first part of the inquiry is whether counsel's performance was "within the range of competence demanded of attorneys in criminal cases." *Id.* (quoting *McMann v. Richardson, 397 U.S. 759, 771, 90 S. Ct. 1441,*

25 L. Ed. 2d 763 (1970)). The second part focuses on whether counsel's deficient performance affected the outcome of the plea process. *Id., 474 U.S. at 59.* Petitioner must establish that he was prejudiced by counsel's deficient performance, *i.e.,* that "there is a reasonable probability that, but for counsel's unprofessional errors, the result of the proceeding would have been different." *Id. at 694.* A reasonable probability is a probability sufficient to undermine confidence in the outcome. *Id.*

"'Surmounting *Strickland's* high bar is never an easy task.'" *Richter, 131 S. Ct. at 788* (quoting *Padilla v. Kentucky, 559 U.S. , 130 S.Ct. 1473, 1485, 176 L. Ed. 2d 284 (2010)).* "The question is whether an attorney's representation amounted to incompetence under 'prevailing professional norms,' not whether it deviated from best practices or most common custom." *Richter, 131 S. Ct. at 788* (quoting *Strickland, 466 U.S. at 690*). Establishing that a state court's application of *Strickland* was unreasonable under § 2254(d) is even more difficult, because both standards are "highly deferential," *466 U. S. at 689,* and *Strickland's* general standard has a substantial range of reasonable applications. The issue under § 2254(d) is not whether counsel's actions were reasonable, but whether there is any reasonable argument that counsel satisfied *Strickland's* deferential standard. *Richter, 131 S. Ct. at 788.* The Supreme Court recently addressed the reasons for a "most deferential" standard for judging counsel's performance:

> Unlike a later reviewing court, the attorney observed the relevant proceedings, knew of materials outside the record, and interacted with the client, with opposing counsel, and with the judge.

Premo v. Moore, U.S. , 131 S.Ct. 733, 739-40, 178 L. Ed. 2d 649 (2011). The Court also recognized that[HN37] "[p]lea bargains are the result of complex negotiations suffused with uncertainty, and defense attorneys must make careful strategic choices in balancing opportunities and risks" of a plea. *Id. at 741.* Considerations surrounding these strategic choices in the pre-trial context "make strict adherence to the *Strickland* standard all the more essential when reviewing the choices an attorney made at the plea bargain stage." *Id.* Mindful of these principles, the Court will consider whether the State court unreasonably applied *Strickland* to the facts of this case. *28 U.S.C. § 2254.*

A. Whether Counsel's Performance was Deficient

To establish a claim of ineffective assistance of counsel under *Strickland,* a petitioner must establish that his counsel's errors were so serious that counsel was deficient, and that counsel's "deficient performance prejudiced the defense." *Strickland, 466 U.S. at 687.* To be deficient, counsel's representation must have fallen "below an objective standard of reasonableness," *Id., 466 U.S. at 688,* and there is a "strong presumption" that counsel's representation is within the "wide range" of reasonable professional assistance. *Id. at 689; see also Kimmelman v. Morrison, 477 U.S. 365, 381, 106 S. Ct. 2574, 91 L. Ed. 2d 305 (1986)* (quoting *Strickland, 466 U.S. at 689*). *Strickland* mandates a "strong presumption of competence." *Cullen v. Pinholster, U.S. , 131 S.Ct. 1388, 1407, 179 L. Ed. 2d 557 (2011).* This Court must "'give [counsel] the benefit of the doubt." *Id.* (citations omitted). As stated above, the post-conviction court found that there was no evidence that trial counsel's performance was deficient. During the evidentiary hearing on post-conviction review, the trial court found that counsel discussed the plea offers with Petitioner. On habeas corpus review, this Court defers to the State court's factual findings.

The State court record establishes that the State extended several plea offers in this case and that Petitioner was aware of the offers. The State court's record further establishes that Petitioner rejected the plea offers because the sentences were too long and he thought he would be acquitted. (Respondents' Exh. N) Petitioner has not met his high burden of establishing that the State court's conclusion that trial counsel's performance was not deficient was based on an unreasonable determination of the facts, or was contrary to, or an unreasonable application of, clearly established federal law. Moreover, as discussed below, even assuming counsel's performance was deficient, Petitioner has not established prejudice.

B. Prejudice

Even if counsel's performance was constitutionally deficient, Petitioner is not entitled to habeas corpus relief because he fails to demonstrate prejudice. *Strickland, 466 U.S. at 687*. Petitioner must "show that there is a reasonable probability that, but for counsel's unprofessional errors, the result of the proceeding would have been different." *Id., 466 U.S. at 694*. "A reasonable probability is a probability sufficient to undermine confidence in the outcome." *Id*. "That requires a 'substantial,' not just 'conceivable,' likelihood of a different result." *Pinholster, 131 S.Ct. at 1403* (quoting *Richter, 562 U.S. , 131 S. Ct. at 791*).

The United States Supreme Court has not specifically addressed what constitutes prejudice when a criminal defendant rejects a plea offer and proceeds to trial. The parties' briefing does not specifically address this issue. Rather, Petitioner appears to argue that, to establish prejudice, he must establish a reasonable likelihood he would have accepted a plea offer. Respondents appear to agree with this statement of the law.

The Supreme Court has held that *Strickland* applies in the context of plea bargaining. *Hill v. Lockhart, 474 U.S. 52, 106 S. Ct. 366, 88 L. Ed. 2d 203 (1985)*. However, the Supreme Court has not addressed the specific question of what constitutes prejudice when a petitioner rejects a plea offer and proceeds to a fair trial. The Supreme Court has interpreted the *Sixth Amendment's* right to effective assistance of counsel as ensuring a criminal defendant receives a fair trial. *Strickland, 466 U.S. at 687*. The Supreme Court reiterated in *Pinholster* that, "'the purpose of the effective assistance guarantee of the *Sixth Amendment* is not to improve the quality of legal representation . . . [but] simply to ensure that criminal defendants receive a fair trial.'" *Pinholster, 131 S.Ct. at 1403* (quoting *Strickland, 466 U.S. at 689*). The Supreme Court has never held that a defendant who foregoes a plea bargain and is later convicted after a fair trial has suffered a constitutional violation. *See Nunes v. Mueller, 350 F.3d 1045, 1052-53 (9th Cir. 2003)*. Rather, the Supreme Court's cases interpreting the *Sixth Amendment* in the context of plea bargaining have involved cases where the petitioner waived the right to a fair trial by accepting a plea offer, not a case where the petitioner rejected a plea and exercised his right to a fair trial. *Premo v. Moore, 562 U.S. , 131 S.Ct. 733, 737-40, 178 L. Ed. 2d 649 (2011); Wright v. Van Patten, 552 U.S. 120, 124-25, 128 S. Ct. 743, 169 L. Ed. 2d 583 (2008); Hill v. Lockhart, 474 U.S. 52, 59, 106 S. Ct. 366, 88 L. Ed. 2d 203 (1985); McMann v. Richardson, 397 U.S. 759, 760-66, 90 S. Ct. 1441, 25 L. Ed. 2d 763 (1970)*. Although circuit courts, including the Ninth Circuit, have discussed *Strickland's* prejudice prong in the context of a rejected plea offer, the lack of any Supreme Court holding on that issue precludes a finding that the State court's decision in this case was contrary to, or an unreasonable application of, clearly established Supreme Court precedent. [4] *Pinholster, 131 S.Ct. at 1399* "State court decisions are measured against [the United States Supreme Court's] precedents as of the 'time the state renders its decision.'") (quoting *Lockyer v. Andrade, 538 U.S. 63, 71-72, 123 S. Ct. 1166, 155 L. Ed. 2d 144 (2003)); Ponce v. Felker, 606 F.3d 596, 604 (9th Cir. 2010)* ("If Supreme Court cases 'give no clear answer to the question presented,' the state court's decision cannot be an unreasonable application of clearly established federal law.") (quoting *Van Patten, 552 U.S. at 126); Moses v. Payne, 555 F.3d 742, 754 (9th Cir. 2009)* ("In light of *Musladin, Panetti,* and *Van Patten,* we conclude that when a Supreme Court decision does not 'squarely address[] the issue in th[e] case' or establish a legal principle that 'clearly extend[s]' to a new context to the extent required by the Supreme Court in these recent decisions . . . , it cannot be said, under [the] AEDPA, there is 'clearly established' Supreme Court precedent addressing the issue before us, and so we must defer to the state court's decision.") (quoting *Van Patten, 552 U.S. 120, 125, 128 S. Ct. 743, 169 L. Ed. 2d 583 (2008)* (alterations in original); *see also Earp v. Ornoski, 431 F.3d 1158, 1184 n. 23 (9th Cir. 2005)* (describing habeas petitioner's reliance on circuit-court authority as "futile" because, "post-AEDPA[,] only Supreme Court holdings are binding on state courts.") (citing *Lambert v. Blodgett, 393 F.3d 943, 974 (9th Cir. 2004))*. The Supreme Court has recently granted certiorari to determine, "What remedy, if any should be provided for ineffective assistance of counsel during plea bargain negotiations if the defendant was later convicted and sentenced pursuant to constitutionally adequate procedures?" *Lafler v. Cooper, U.S. , 131 S.Ct. 856, 178 L. Ed. 2d 622 (January 7, 2011)*.Nevertheless, for purposes of analyzing Petitioner's claim, the Court will consider Ninth Circuit authority. The Ninth Circuit has held that to establish prejudice from incorrect advice resulting in rejection of a plea offer, Petitioner "must show that there is a reasonable probability that he would have accepted the plea agreement had he received accurate advice from his attorney." *Hoffman v. Arave, 455 F.3d 926, 941-942 (9th Cir. 2006), judgment vacated in part on other grounds by Arave v. Hoffman, 552 U.S. 117, 128 S. Ct. 749, 169 L. Ed. 2d 580 (2008); see also Nunes, 350 F.3d at 1052.* However, as discussed below, while the Ninth Circuit has discussed *Strickland's* prejudice prong in the context of a rejected plea offer, the lack of any Supreme Court holding on that issue precludes a finding that the State court's decision in this case was contrary to, or an unreasonable application of, clearly established Supreme Court precedent. *Pinholster, 131 S.Ct. at 1399* ("State court decisions are measured against [the United States Supreme Court's] precedents as of the 'time the state renders its decision.'") (citations omitted).

Undoubtedly, Petitioner would prefer a lesser sentence than the one he received. The Court, however, must look to Petitioner's statements and beliefs at the time of the trial to determine whether there is a reasonable probability that Petitioner would have pled guilty absent counsel's alleged deficient performance. The record here reflects that Petitioner was committed to his defense that he was merely present at the scene and did not commit any crimes. When discussing plea offers with his trial counsel, Petitioner expressed his belief that he thought he would be acquitted. Before and during his trial, during his post-conviction proceedings in State court, and in this Petition, Petitioner has consistently maintained that he was merely present at the scene and did not commit any crimes. Additionally, the record reflects that Petitioner felt that the plea offers were for too much time. Petitioner does not offer any support for his contention that he would have accepted a plea offer. The Ninth Circuit has stated that such self-serving statements are viewed with skepticism:

> [The petitioner's] self-serving statement, made years later, that [defense counsel] told him that 'this was not a death penalty case' is insufficient to establish that [the habeas petitioner] was unaware of the potential death verdict. If the rule were otherwise, every rejection of a plea offer, viewed perhaps with more clarity in the light of an unfavorable verdict, could be relitigated upon   the defendant's later claim that had his counsel better advised him, he would have accepted the plea offer.

Turner v. Calderon, 281 F.3d 851, 881 (9th Cir. 2002) (internal citations omitted).

Petitioner's consistent belief that he was merely present at the scene and had not committed a crime, does not support his contention that he would have accepted any plea offer. *See Smith v. United States, 348 F.3d 545, 552 (6th Cir. 2003)* (stating that, although not dispositive, "[p]rotestations of innocence throughout trial are properly a factor" in determining whether a defendant would have accepted a plea agreement).

In sum, Petitioner has not shown that the State court's rejection of his claim of ineffective assistance of counsel was contrary to, or an unreasonable application of, clearly established federal law, or that it was based on an unreasonable determination of the facts. *28 U.S.C. § 2254.* Thus, Petitioner is not entitled to habeas corpus relief on this claim.

REASONS WHY REMEDY IS HOLLOW

The Attorney general concealed from the federal court that in Arizona counsel routinely do not investigate the case and refuse to investigate and present mitigating evidence.

MICHAEL MARTIN SANDERS, Petitioner - Appellant, v. CHARLES L. RYAN; DORA B. SCHRIRO; ARIZONA ATTORNEY GENERAL, Respondents - Appellees. No. 09-17088 UNITED STATES COURT OF APPEALS FOR THE NINTH CIRCUIT
        (Text modified for emphasis)

THE POSITION OF THE COURT

Michael Martin Sanders appeals the district court's denial of his *28 U.S.C. § 2254* habeas petition challenging his Arizona convictions for first-degree felony murder, first-degree burglary, unlawful imprisonment, and aggravated assault. Sanders's convictions arose out of an incident where he and four associates invaded a house. A gunfight between Sanders and an occupant   of the house resulted in the deaths of two people inside. By convicting Sanders of burglary and felony murder, the jury found that Sanders invaded the house with the intent to commit a robbery, and rejected his claim that he entered the house with the intent to apprehend a bail absconder.

Because Sanders filed his petition after April 24, 1996, the Antiterrorism and Effective Death Penalty Act ("AEDPA") of 1996 governs review of his claims. Under AEDPA, *28 U.S.C. § 2254(d)*, our review is highly deferential. *Harrington v. Richter, 131 S. Ct. 770, 785, 178 L. Ed. 2d 624 (2011)*. We will not grant habeas relief unless Sanders can show that the state court's last reasoned adjudication of his federal claims resulted in a decision that (1) "was contrary to, or involved an unreasonable application of, clearly established Federal law, as determined by the Supreme Court of the United States," or (2) "was based on an unreasonable determination of the facts in light of the evidence presented in the State court proceeding." *28 U.S.C. § 2254(d)*.

Sanders's primary contention is that trial counsel was ineffective for not arguing at trial and in post-trial proceedings that Sanders's entry into the house was justified under *Arizona Revised Statutes § 13-3892*, which provides that a private person may enter a building to arrest someone who commits a felony in the private person's presence. *See Ariz. Rev. Stat. § 13-3892*. The state court concluded in post-conviction proceedings that counsel was not ineffective, and this conclusion was not an unreasonable application of the facts. The person Sanders claimed committed a felony in his presence was not in the house during the invasion, and the § 13-3892 defense was thus inapplicable. *See Juan H. v. Allen, 408 F.3d 1262, 1273 (9th Cir. 2005)* ("[T]rial counsel cannot have been ineffective for failing to raise a meritless objection."). The state court's alternative finding that the verdict would not have been different had trial counsel presented the § 13-3892 defense was also not unreasonable, because the jury rejected Sanders's argument that the invasion was for legitimate bail enforcement purposes. *See Strickland v. Washington, 466 U.S. 668, 694, 104 S. Ct. 2052, 80 L. Ed. 2d 674 (1984)*.

Sanders further maintains that trial counsel was ineffective for not offering expert testimony concerning the tactics that bail enforcement agents employ when entering a house to apprehend a bail absconder. The state court's rejection of this claim of ineffective assistance was not unreasonable. Sanders does not identify the exculpatory evidence that any purported expert would have provided. *See Grisby v. Blodgett, 130 F.3d 365, 373 (9th Cir. 1997)*. Moreover, the state court's finding that the verdict would have been the same had counsel proffered expert testimony on bail enforcement tactics was not unreasonable, because evidence that Sanders complied with the standards governing bail enforcement agents would have been irrelevant. Such evidence would have been irrelevant since Sanders could have entered the house with the sole intent to commit a robbery, yet executed the robbery using tactics that were consistent with bail enforcement standards.

Sanders also contends that appellate counsel was ineffective for not asserting on direct appeal that the jury instructions constituted fundamental error under *Sullivan v. Louisiana, 508 U.S. 275, 113 S. Ct. 2078, 124 L. Ed. 2d 182 (1993)*. An examination of the record reveals, however, that appellate counsel did raise this argument on direct appeal, and, in any event, the substance of the claim is meritless. The state court's conclusion that appellate counsel was not ineffective was thus not unreasonable.

Sanders also contends that various evidentiary rulings by the state court violated his constitutional rights. The state court's denial of these claims on direct appeal was not unreasonable. Sanders has not established that the trial court's rulings rendered his trial fundamentally unfair or denied him a meaningful opportunity to present a complete defense. *See Brecht v. Abrahamson, 507 U.S. 619, 637-38, 113 S. Ct. 1710, 123 L. Ed. 2d 353 (1993); Crane v. Kentucky, 476 U.S. 683, 690, 106 S. Ct. 2142, 90 L. Ed. 2d 636 (1986)*. The trial court's evidentiary rulings did not prevent him from arguing to the jury that he entered the house with the intent to arrest a bail absconder rather than to commit a robbery, an argument the jury rejected.

Sanders further contends that the State violated his right to counsel by interfering with the attorney-client relationship. The state courts rejected these claims in Sanders's motion to vacate the judgment and in post-conviction relief proceedings. The state courts' rejection of these claims was not unreasonable. Sanders has not established that the State's alleged interferences with the attorney-client relationship were prejudicial. *See Williams v. Woodford, 384 F.3d 567, 584-85 (9th Cir. 2004)* (noting that government interference "with the confidential relationship between a criminal defendant and defense counsel . . . violates the *Sixth Amendment* right to counsel if it substantially prejudices the criminal defendant").

Sanders finally contends that the record the district court reviewed was inadequate to consider his claims. Sanders, however, would not be entitled to habeas relief even if all disputes regarding the record were resolved in his favor. *See Harrington, 131 S. Ct. at 786-87.* The habeas record is thus sufficient to fully consider his claims, and remand to the district court for further development of the record is unnecessary. *See Hart v. Stagner, 935 F.2d 1007, 1011 (9th Cir. 1991).*

REASONS WHY REMEDY IS HOLLOW

In Arizona it is a common practice for counsel to not argue all the necessary issues and for witnesses for the state not to disclose exculpatory convictions. The state courts decline to ensure these breaches do not happen and the Arizona Attorney General conceals this during federal habeas proceedings.

ANDREW J. ALLERDICE, Petitioner - Appellant, v. CHARLES L. RYAN, Director of the Arizona Department of Corrections, and ARIZONA ATTORNEY GENERAL, Respondents - Appellees. No. 08-17281 UNITED STATES COURT OF APPEALS FOR THE NINTH CIRCUIT

(text modified for emphasis)

THE POSITION OF THE COURT

Allerdice first argues that his trial counsel's stipulations constituted ineffective assistance of counsel. To prevail on an ineffective assistance claim, a petitioner must show that his counsel's performance was deficient and that the deficient performance prejudiced the defense. *Strickland v. Washington, 466 U.S. 668, 687, 104 S. Ct. 2052, 80 L. Ed. 2d 674 (1984).* Allerdice argues that prejudice should be presumed, because his lawyer failed to subject the state's case to "meaningful adversarial testing." *United States v. Cronic, 466 U.S. 648, 659-60, 104 S. Ct. 2039, 80 L. Ed. 2d 657 (1984).* For prejudice to be presumed, counsel's failure must be complete. *Bell v. Cone, 535 U.S. 685, 696-98, 122 S. Ct. 1843, 152 L. Ed. 2d 914 (2002).* Here, although counsel stipulated to certain facts, he also obtained stipulations from the state regarding defense exhibits, offered evidence, cross-examined witnesses, elicited favorable testimony, and presented a coherent if ultimately unsuccessful defense in closing argument. This is not a complete failure to test the State's case. Thus, *Strickland,* rather than *Cronic,* governs assessment of Allerdice's ineffective assistance of counsel claim.

Counsel was not ineffective. Strategic choices as to how to defend a case are "virtually unchallengeable." *Strickland, 466 U.S. at 690.* Counsel chose a strategy of defending on lack of intent to defraud, bolstered by claims of poor police work, after an adequate investigation; given the facts, the choice fell within a "wide range of reasonable professional assistance." *Id. at 689.* Moreover, Allerdice cannot show that he was prejudiced, as his claim that the State was unprepared to prove its case absent the stipulations is speculative. The Mohave County Superior Court's rejection of Allerdice's ineffective assistance of counsel claim was not objectively unreasonable. *Williams, 529 U.S. at 409.*

Allerdice next contends that the stipulations, entered over his express objection, constituted the "practical equivalent of a plea of guilty." *Brookhart v. Janis, 384 U.S. 1, 86 S. Ct. 1245, 16 L. Ed. 2d 314 (1966).* A plea of guilty is not just an admission of guilt, but an agreement that no further proof by the prosecution is required; there is nothing to do but impose judgment. *Boykin v. Alabama, 395 U.S. 238, 242, 89 S. Ct. 1709, 23 L. Ed. 2d 274 (1969).*

The Arizona court did not unreasonably reject this claim. First, it was not fairly presented in state court. *Picard v. Connor, 404 U.S. 270, 275-76, 92 S. Ct. 509, 30 L. Ed. 2d 438 (1971).* Instead of relying on *Brookhart,* Allerdice framed his claim as an ineffective assistance of counsel claim, predicated on a failure to reasonably inform. This was inadequate to alert the state court to the controlling legal principles that he now relies on. *Anderson v. Harless, 459 U.S. 4, 6, 103 S. Ct. 276, 74 L. Ed. 2d 3 (1982) (per curiam); Rose v. Palmateer, 395 F.3d 1108, 1111-12 (9th Cir. 2005), cert. denied, 545 U.S. 1144, 125 S. Ct. 2971, 162 L. Ed. 2d 896 (2005); see also Picard, 404 U.S. at 277* (rejecting as procedurally defaulted an equal protection claim that "entered this case only because the Court of Appeals injected it"). Accordingly, Allerdice did not exhaust this claim. *Id. at 275.* Because the time for Allerdice to raise this claim in state court has expired, *Ariz. R. Crim. P. 32.4, 32.1*, he has procedural-ly defaulted it, and federal habeas relief is unavailable absent cause   and prejudice or a fundamental miscar-riage of justice, which Allerdice has not attempted to demonstrate. *Engle v. Isaac, 456 U.S. 107, 125 n.28, 129, 102 S. Ct. 1558, 71 L. Ed. 2d 783 (1982); Beaty v. Stewart, 303 F.3d 975, 987 (9th Cir. 2002).*

Second, even if not procedurally defaulted, Allerdice's claim lacks merit. The stipulations did not compare to a guilty plea. Defense counsel still vigorously contested the state's evidence, especially with respect to Al-lerdice's mental state. Moreover, counsel's conduct in Allerdice's trial was more like that in *Florida v. Nixon, 543 U.S. 175, 188?89, 125 S. Ct. 551, 160 L. Ed. 2d 565 (2004),* than it was like that in *Brookhart.* In *Nixon,* counsel conceded his client's guilt in order to preserve his credibility to argue mitigation at the penalty phase. The *Nixon* court determined that there was no *Brookhart* violation, and that counsel's actions did not violate the defendant's constitutional rights.

Allerdice's original claim of failure to reasonably inform was equally unmeritorious. The record demon-strated that counsel began negotiating the stipulations, with Allerdice's knowledge, six months before trial. Further, although Allerdice objected to the stipulations, he simultaneously rejected any plea deal. He did not show lack of consultation or prejudice. However denominated, the Mohave County Superior Court reasonably rejected Allerdice's claim.

REASONS WHY THE REMEDY IS HOLLOW

Both the Arizona Courts and Attorney General are aware that in Arizona prosecutors determine how the defendant shall defend his/her case. They act in concerto with defense counsel to deny a meaningful defense and courts decline to take any action as to this systemic problem.

Sanjay Babulal Gohel, Petitioner -vs- Charles L. Ryan, Respond-ent.CV-10-0001-PHX-FJM (JFM)
UNITED STATES DISTRICT COURT FOR THE DISTRICT OF ARIZONA
(text modified for emphasis)

THE COURTS DECISION

A. FACTUAL BACKGROUND

As summarized by the Arizona Court of Appeals on direct appeal, evidence at trial showed that on four separate occasions, Petitioner tried to hire someone to kill his wife, Jaimini. The first three attempts fell through, but in June 1997 Petitioner asked co-indictee Falcon, a frequent shopper in Petitioner's grocery store, to kill her. Falcon offered to find someone else to commit the murder for the $8000 offered by Peti-tioner. This person was Falcon's co-worker Munoz, known as "El Gato." Over the next month, Petitioner made periodic payments to Falcon and Munoz, drove them to both his home in Peoria and his wife's place of busi-ness, showed them his wife's car, invited Munoz to his grocery store at a time his wife would be there so Munoz could identify her, and provided Munoz with the handheld remote for entry to his wife's   car.

In the early morning of July 31, 1997, Munoz used the remote control to enter Petitioner's wife's car, which was parked in the driveway of Petitioner's home. He then hid under a coat in the back seat, provided by Petitioner for this purpose. When Petitioner's wife entered the vehicle to drive to work, she began backing out of the driveway. Munoz shot her twice in the head, killing her. A neighbor called 9-1-1 after hearing the noise and witnessing a Hispanic male run from the scene.

B. PROCEEDINGS AT TRIAL

Falcon and Petitioner were eventually   indicted for their parts in the crime. Falcon entered into a plea agreement and pled guilty to one count of manslaughter.

Munoz was never located, and Petitioner filed, *inter alia*, a successful Motion in Limine to prevent Falcon from testifying to statements by Munoz.

After selection of a jury, Petitioner proceeded to trial on September 27, 2000. The trial included the fol-lowing testimony:

Benny Hays -- Mr. Hays testified that he was a neighbor of Petitioner, and on the morning of the shooting he was outside having coffee at about 5:30 a.m. when he heard a loud noise, walked to the end of his drive and back and heard another loud noise a minute or two later. He then saw a man, 20-25 years old, running down the street.

Then, a neighbor came and told him a lady had driven a car through a short block fence. He called 911, to report the accident. He and the neighbor, Hank, walked to the scene and saw that the car had backed across the street into the fence. The front passenger door was open, and the lady was slumped over in the driver's seat. They decided not to try to move the victim to avoid injuring her.

They went to Petitioner's house and he answered the door in his night clothes. Petitioner said he recognized the car and they walked across the street. He did not see Petitioner try to assist the driver. An officer arrived in a few minutes, and he told the officer his story. He did not think either loud noise sounded like a gunshot. He did not see any blood on the victim, and did not look closely at her. He is not familiar with the sound of gunfire, and was not certain about the elapsed time.

Neil Morse -- Officer Morse testified that he responded to the scene of the shooting, and created a diagram of the scene. The car had backed across the street into a block wall. There was minimal damage to the vehicle suggesting a low impact speed. The car was in line with the driveway across the street. The victim had already been removed when he arrived. Although he responded at 6:00 a.m., he was first patrolling the neighborhood and did not arrive at the scene for several hours. (Supp. Exhibit I, R.T. 9/27/00 at 77-87.)

Mary Stephaniak -- Officer Stephaniak testified that she was called to the scene at about 5:30 a.m., and was the first responder. About five people were standing around the car, and Petitioner flagged her down. She approached Petitioner and he said "She's my wife." Petitioner appeared concerned but not upset, and was not crying. The front passenger door was open. She checked the victim for a pulse, found a slight pulse and saw a large amount of blood. The victim's purse was on the passenger side floorboard, and appeared undisturbed. A bag of fruit was on the passenger seat. She called for the fire department. She asked Petitioner if identification would be in the victim's wallet, and she noticed the wallet was in the purse on the top with the clasp closed. She and another officer removed the victim from the car and began CPR. Then the fire department arrived and transported her to the hospital. As they moved her and did CPR, blood spattered on the pavement and outside the car.

She spoke with Petitioner who told her the victim was going to work, and had said goodbye, but he had fallen back to sleep, until the neighbor knocked on the door. Petitioner said he had not heard anything.

The victim had a gold colored bracelet on her right wrist. She looked for a wound, but couldn't find it because of the blood matted in the victim's hair. The other officer found a bullet hole in the driver's side windshield. So, she checked the victim's hands and around her for signs that the wound was self-inflicted. She found nothing, and there was no weapon in the car.

When she first responded to the scene, she did not believe there was an emergency. Petitioner's hair was disheveled. She couldn't determine the location or nature of the victim's wound because of the blood. They did not determine the victim had been shot until the other officer arrived. Petitioner had been pacing around the car, and had not been told the victim had been shot. She requested the fire department twice, and the other officer had done so once. Petitioner had asked where the ambulance was. Petitioner had started to assist them in removing the victim, but Stephaniak stopped him. She questioned Petitioner while the ambulance crew worked on the victim, but he was unresponsive. Petitioner's father offered to answer her questions. Petitioner and his father both said they had not heard anything.

The victim was transported by helicopter. When she was put on the gurney, Petitioner began to cry, and his father had to restrain him from going to his wife. Petitioner's legs began to buckle and they sat him on the sidewalk.

Petitioner was in a T-shirt and shorts. When she told him it looked like the victim had been shot, his demeanor did not change.

Douglas Maurer - Mr. Maurer testified that his grandmother shopped at the Wittmann grocery store owned by Petitioner's father. His grandmother bought on credit, and he would borrow money from Petitioner. His sister-in-law worked for Petitioner, and he installed gravel and put in a security light for Petitioner. He had felony convictions and had problems with drugs. In late 1996, Petitioner approached him and asked what would happen if he put nitroglycerin in someone's drink, whether it would kill them. Petitioner mentioned his wife had been in a car accident and had seizures. Maurer didn't know, but agreed to find out. Petitioner later got angry with him when Petitioner heard that he was asking around about nitroglycerin.

In February, 1997, Petitioner approached him about putting a hit on his wife, because he wanted out of the marriage. Maurer suggested some ways Petitioner could kill her, and Petitioner talked about staging a robbery in Las Vegas, or hiding in her car and cutting her throat or shooting her. Petitioner brought the subject up again a week later, and they discussed Maurer following them to Las Vegas on a bus, and killing her with a knife at a motel. Petitioner was going to pay him in cash and credit. He agreed to do it for money for drugs. He talked about the plan with his brother's current wife, Tammy, and decided it wasn't smart.

In March, 1997, Maurer asked Deputy Baker about who would be believed if a businessman hired a drug addict to kill their wife. He told the officer the businessman was Petitioner, who had asked him to kill Petitioner's wife. He told defense counsel he had not identified Petitioner to Deputy Baker. The officer did not believe him. His criminal problems would have been helped by being an informant when he talked to Deputy Baker about Petitioner.

He had talked with Deputy Baker about being an informant about drug suppliers, and assumed they paid informants. But Baker's supervisors wouldn't let him become an informant. He did not think he would be paid for telling about the conversations with Petitioner.

In the spring of 1997, he was facing a criminal prosecution for escape, and a potential probation violation on a prior Georgia conviction. He had escaped from a police car, and eventually turned himself into Deputy Baker on April 22, 1997 because officers had told his grandmother he would be shot.

Later, Petitioner brought up the subject again, suggesting Maurer use a gun, and asked him to test fire a gun. Maurer got the gun from Petitioner in May, 1997. He was supposed to kill the victim in Arizona. He was to be paid the same amount. Maurer test fired the gun and then traded the gun for drugs, telling Petitioner that he had ditched it because an officer was following him.

Petitioner found out about the gun, and banned Maurer from the store. On a later occasion, Maurer was walking past the store and he and Petitioner got in an argument over Maurer owing him for the gun. Petitioner claimed Maurer had stolen the gun.

On June 23, 1997, he was placed on probation. Within a couple of days he went on a crystal meth binge with Tammy Goad, in violation of his probation. He was home on drugs on July 2nd and July 4th, but went and bought shoes and applied for a job on July 3rd. The purchase and application documented his whereabouts on July 3, the date of the murder. He was arrested on July 7th on a probation violation, and Peoria police interviewed him, and he told them the same information. . The police officers interviewed him on July 9th and twice on July 23. Between the two conversations on the 23rd they had inspected his sneakers and when they told him they matched the imprint in the car, he refused to talk further. When he spoke with Peoria police he referred to Petitioner as a "sand nigger." In the time period he was talking with Petitioner, he would wear camouflage clothing.

He is 5 feet, 9 inches tall, and at the time of the murder he weighed about 135 pounds.

He was using crystal methamphetamine and marijuana in 1996, but only methamphetamine by late 1996, and in increasing amounts through the summer of 1997. He was suffering from anxiety, depression, and hearing voices at the time, and had attempted suicide. He was discharged from the Navy due to a personality disorder, but eventually received a disability. He would hear voices when he had been without sleep for weeks at a time.

Tammy Goad was a drug addict, and had relationships with Maurer and his brother, and would be with Maurer when he had money for drugs. She eventually married his brother.

During one of his conversations with Petitioner, Maurer recorded the conversation. He didn't take the tapes to the police because he planned to blackmail Petitioner. Tammy stole the tape recorder and tape. Tammy told him she listened to the tape and didn't hear anything incriminating on it. They had planned for him to escape to avoid his criminal problems, and Tammy would handle the blackmail. The tapes of Petitioner had recorded, but were erased by Tammy's brother.

Maurer testified he was losing money by testifying at trial. The drugs did not affect his memory, and Petitioner asked him to kill his wife in 1996 and 1997. At the time, he did not care what happened to him, whether his probation was violated. His attitude changed in 1998 when his grandmother died. He completed intensive probation, graduated college, and got into a drug treatment program.

Maurer testified he had nothing to do with the victim's murder. His conversations with Deputy Baker about the killing did not have any effect on his pending charges.

Isidro Falcon -- Mr. Falcon testified that in 1997 he weighed 199, and was five feet and five or six inches tall. He lived two blocks from Wittmann grocery. Alfonso Munoz, known as El Gato, lived 60 feet from the store, with his sister-in-law, Paula Hernandez. He had known Petitioner for about eight years, having met him at the store they owned in Surprise. He cannot read, and completed the sixth grade, and worked in agriculture and landscaping, and was working at a golf course.

About three weeks before the murder, Petitioner had started a conversation about having his wife killed. Falcon had been buying groceries on credit. Petitioner said he had a job for Falcon, who thought it was for landscaping. Petitioner said he wanted his wife killed, Falcon responded that he didn't want to do it. Petitioner asked if he knew someone who could do it. He offered $2,000, but Falcon told him the trigger man wanted more, so they discussed $8,000, $2,000 down and payments.

When he first talked with Petitioner about wanting to have his wife killed, Petitioner told him it was because she spent a lot of money when she went to California. Falcon couldn't believe he wanted to kill her. Petitioner said his wife had a disease and blamed him for giving it to her, and that he had it but blamed her.

After talking with Petitioner, he asked El Gato who claimed to have killed for money in Mexico. They discussed $2,000, but El Gato wanted $8,000. The next day, he told Petitioner that El Gato would do it. Petitioner knew El Gato.

About a week before the murder, El Gato told him that the victim was going to be killed soon. Petitioner had told him that he wanted her killed before their anniversary, when they had a trip planned to go to California.

Petitioner gave him $2,000 in cash in a white envelope, and a gun, a .380 chrome pistol with a brown handle in a holster. That same day, which was a couple of days before the murder, he gave the pistol to El Gato, and he didn't see it again. He gave El Gato the pistol to commit the murder. He gave El Gato $1,000 and Petitioner was supposed to make payments through Colin Head for the balance.

Falcon had never been to Petitioner's house. The first plan was to kill her in the parking lot at her workplace, Del Webb Hospital. Petitioner drove Falcon and El Gato there. Falcon translated for El Gato, who did not speak any English. Petitioner then decided he wanted her killed in front of his house, because he had been "burned" by Doug Maurer and Colin, who he had given stuff to kill her but they hadn't followed through. Petitioner wanted to watch through the window. He told Falcon and El Gato this while driving them to his house the Friday before the murder.

They had arranged to meet at Peter Piper Pizza in Peoria, where Falcon was taking his family. Petitioner and El Gato got him out of the restaurant, and they drove to Petitioner's house. Petitioner told them the days his wife worked, and what time she left, which was early in the morning, around 5:00 or 5:30. Petitioner gave Falcon a remote to the victim's car. Falcon gave the remote to El Gato, and Petitioner showed him how to use it. El Gato was to cover himself up with a coat in the floor of the back of the car, and kill her with the gun.

Three days before the murder, Petitioner arranged for the victim to come to the store, and then called Falcon on pretense of reviewing landscaping plans. Falcon and El Gato went to the store and saw the victim. Petitioner showed Falcon her car. Petitioner knew El Gato was to be the one to actually murder the victim.

On July 3, 1997 he got a ride to work from El Gato, arrived at 4:20 and left at about 1:00 or 1:30. On the day of the murder, El Gato was dressed in two pair of army pants, an army shirt, and had sweats and a sweatshirt on. He was wearing white tennis shoes.

He rode home with another worker. He loaned his car to El Gato and expected him to pick him up, but he never arrived. He saw El Gato later that day when it was getting dark, and El Gato said "he had done what he had to do."

The car, a 1976 Toyota, had been bought by Petitioner, and Falcon was driving it to decide whether to buy it. A week before they first discussed the murder, Petitioner sold him the car for $1,000, to be paid $100 every two weeks. Petitioner gave him the car, the key and the title. He took it to Flagstaff but it didn't have enough power so he told Petitioner he didn't want it. Petitioner insisted on the sale. In between, they discussed Petitioner wanting his wife murdered. He never paid anything on the car. El Gato had never borrowed his car before. After the murder, he told Petitioner he did not want the car because it had been used in a murder. Petitioner told him to keep it and start making the payments. He eventually sold the car.

He got another $1,000 in a white envelope from Colin, which he delivered to El Gato. El Gato threatened to come after Falcon if   he ever got caught. He told El Gato that Petitioner wanted the murder done before his anniversary.

After the murder, one of Petitioner's employees, Don Mecham, took him to get the car. He paid him $5 for gas. El Gato said something to him so he knew where to find his car after the murder. The car was parked two blocks from Petitioner's house on a residential street. The car wouldn't start, so they had to jump it. The key was in the ignition. There was a white envelope in the car. He took the car home. When he went to pick up the car after the murder, the windows were down and the key was in the ignition.

He went to talk to Petitioner the next day. Petitioner asked if everything was fine, and he said yes. He said he didn't know they were going to use his car, and he didn't want it. Petitioner told him to do whatever he wanted with it. He sold the car a couple of days later.

With the money he got, he bought his kids some clothes and put a down payment on some land. He did not finish paying for it because he was arrested on the murder in December, 1997. He was charged with murder and conspiracy to commit murder, and pled guilty to manslaughter. He was awaiting sentencing, in a range of 7 to 18 years. He agreed to testify and assist in the investigation as part of the plea agreement.

After he told Colin Head to take away the envelope with money after the murder, he did not receive anything further from Petitioner. A couple of days after the murder, El Gato came to his house and asked for money to go to Mexico. He told El Gato he had no money and he should go talk to Petitioner. He has not seen El Gato since then.

At the time of the events, he was drinking 12 to 18 beers per evening, and would smoke marijuana on a nightly basis. Before his plea agreement he was facing charges for murder and conspiracy to commit murder, and the state had filed a notice of intent to seek the death penalty.

He told his friend Ron Wallace about the murder, but discovered that Wallace had been wearing a wire and had set him up.

William Moore -- Mr. Moore testified that he had lived in Wittman, Arizona, and knew Petitioner since 1991 or 1992. Petitioner owned Wittman Grocery. Moore bought from the store and did work for Petitioner as a sign maker. He knew Petitioner's father who ran the liquor store. Moore was in prison for three years in Nevada on possession   of a stolen vehicle.

In February of 1997, Moore's nephew, who worked for Petitioner, told Moore that Petitioner wanted to see him about some signs. Don Mecham lived with Moore. Petitioner asked about Moore's legal troubles in Nevada, and then asked him "what if I needed somebody to disappear." Moore responded that nothing could be that bad.

Moore knew Isidro Falcon. In June of 1997, he saw Falcon talking with Petitioner at the store. Later in June, he saw Petitioner talking to Falcon outside by Petitioner's truck.

In December, 1997 he had a conversation with Petitioner about rumors surrounding the murder. Moore denied talking about Petitioner, and Petitioner said the rumors were told by Leslie. Moore had heard Leslie say that Petitioner had gotten Falcon to kill his wife. Moore asked Petitioner why he didn't just divorce his wife. Petitioner responded that he would lose everything if he had. Petitioner expressed a lack of trust in Falcon, and concern if Falcon was arrested and said anything, Petitioner would be harmed. He offered Moore $10,000, $5,000 for Moore and $5,000 for somebody from Nevada, to kill Falcon. Moore expressed dissatisfaction that Petitioner had involved Don Mecham,   by having him take Falcon to the scene to pick up the car.

He was aware at the time of this conversation in December that the victim had been murdered, although he was in California when it occurred.

He did not report any of this to law enforcement until two weeks later, in December, 1997 when he was in jail on class two felony charges of fraudulent schemes and artifices arising in Tucson. Those charges arose out of a $100 deposit he had taken as a licensed sign painter and hadn't done the job. He expected it to be dropped to a misdemeanor, with six months sentence. He had his wife contact Detective Lopez' office. He was aware at that time that Petitioner and Falcon had been arrested. If convicted he faced the possibility of a substantial prison sentence because of his extensive prior criminal history. Those charges were dismissed after a request by the prosecutor in Petitioner's case in exchange for testimony from Moore.

In addition, theft charges from Maricopa County were dismissed along with the Tucson charges when Detective Lane said that it should be dismissed because of his cooperation. Also, a seven year old charge in Mohave County was dismissed.

At the time of trial, Moore faced probation violations in Kingman and Maricopa County. He pled guilty to another theft charge in Kingman, and was awaiting sentencing to prison or reinstatement on probation. A good word from the prosecutor in this case would be helpful to him.

He had been convicted on two counts of theft in Maricopa County, each class three felonies, and placed on probation. He faced sentencing on violation of that probation, either by reinstatement or prison sentences of up to two 8.5 year consecutive sentences. He had a total of eleven prior convictions.

He got good deals in exchange for his agreement to testify in another conspiracy/murder for hire case in Pima County. There was a verdict in that case. He violated his probation because he received a threat on his life.

He had no agreements about his current cases concerning his testimony in this case.

In March, 1998 he had a conversation with Detective Lopez about the conspiracy with regard to the Petitioner, and contrasted it to the situation in Pima County.

He believed Petitioner approached him about killing his wife and Falcon because Petitioner knew about his extensive criminal history, and he knew people who could do something like that.

Mark Fischione -- Dr. Fischione, an employee of the medical examiner's office, testified that he had performed the autopsy on the victim, and determined that her death was a homicide, the result of two gunshot wounds to the back of her head. One shot was in an upward, right to left trajectory, hit the top of the skull and bounced back within the brain. The second shot was in the same general trajectory, but only grazed across the scalp without penetrating into the scalp. The two gunshots appeared to be from some distance other than direct contact. The soot and stippling which could indicate the range would have been caught by the victim's hair. The hair was sent for examination, but he did not do the testing or get the results.

Lewis Roane -- Mr. Roane, a crime scene technician with the Peoria police department, testified that he responded to the scene. He took various pictures as directed by a detective.

Robert Sanders -- Sergeant Sanders, of the Peoria police department, testified that he responded to the scene of the murder which he first believed to be the scene of an injury accident. He arrived at 5:39 a.m., and saw a vehicle that had backed into and over a small block fence. The vehicle was running and the front passenger door was open. The driver's window was halfway down, and the radio station was playing extremely loudly. Officer Stefaniak was present.

He spoke with Benny Hays and then instructed units to circulate in the area to look for a person running from the scene, giving a description of a Hispanic male wearing a green military jacket, blue pants and a white shirt, five-seven, 160 pounds.

He could see blood on the right side of the victim's head. Officer Stefaniak reported that the victim still had a pulse. They removed the victim from the car and placed her on the ground, and began performing life-saving efforts.

He noticed a bullet hole in the windshield and advised Stefaniak that they might have a gunshot victim. The bullet hole was made from the inside out. There was brain matter, hair, tissue, and blood on the inside of the windshield and dashboard. There were no signs of forced entry into the vehicle.

The fire department arrived after 15 to 18 minutes.

He looked for a gun in the vehicle, but found none. He found a charcoal black sweatshirt with silver cuffs and a sunscreen in the back of the car. In the front, there was a black purse on the front passenger floorboard, and a plastic baggie of fruit on the passenger seat. In the rear of the car there was a key and a remote control for a keyless entry or car alarm behind the passenger seat. Behind the driver's seat there was a shell casing. The purse did not look ransacked. He did not find a second shell casing.

When he first looked in the car, the victim was slumped over to the right side. When he looked in the car after determining there was a bullet hole in the windshield, he saw a lot more blood. At first he thought the bullet hole was bird droppings, and that the blood was from the victim hitting her head on the windshield.

Kenneth Kowalski -- Mr. Kowalski, a criminalist with the Arizona Department of Public Safety, testified that he examined shoeprints found on the rear door panel of the vehicle with tennis shoes provided by Detective Rock. He determined that the shoeprints could have been made by the shoes.

He examined a spent shell casing from a .380 auto cartridge case. He also examined   fragments from a spent, jacketed bullet, that could have been from a .380 or 9mm bullet. The casing was from an auto-ejecting pistol, and had an ejector mark.

Colin Head -- Mr. Head testified that in 1997 he lives in Wittmann, and worked for Petitioner at his store for seven or eight years. He was not paid a regular wage, but would as for money if he needed it or get food or drink from the store. He stocked, swept, and mopped. He had met the victim at the store.

Head denied telling police or defense counsel that Petitioner had approached him about killing someone, and that he was afraid of Petitioner. He had told Petitioner he thought his girlfriend was cheating on him and that he would hurt her if he found it was true. Petitioner told him that was not right.

He had known Isidro Falcon for several months as of July 3, 1997. He had seen Falcon talking to Petitioner. He had delivered a white enveloped to Falcon sometime after July 3, 1997, as he had been told to do by Cynthia who had been contacted by Petitioner. He delivered it to Falcon outside the store. He told Falcon it was from Petitioner. The envelope was thin and did not feel like it had   a wad of money in it.

He had purchased two vehicles from Petitioner, one in 1996 and one in 1997. Petitioner would give him money to go to the doctor or for gas. Head continued working for Petitioner's father at the store until it closed in 1998 or 1999 when the highway was widened. He was at the store when Petitioner was arrested on December 15.

He did not know an El Gato or an Alfonso Munoz.

Petitioner did not come into the store until a month and a half after the murder. Head was taken into custody at the same time as Petitioner.

His statements to the police were while he was in custody, had been threatened with prison, and was scared. While he was being questioned, Falcon came in and told him that Petitioner had paid him to kill his wife, and that Head should tell the police what he knew. He told police that Petitioner had asked him to kill his wife. At first Head asserted he lied to police, but eventually claimed he told the police the truth.

Don Mecham -- Don Mecham testified that he suffered from cerebral palsy, had relocated from Wittmann to Oregon, and knew Petitioner from the Wittmann Grocery store. He had been working for Petitioner for   about three years stocking shelves and backing, and was paid hourly wages.

He saw the victim at least once when she brought Petitioner lunch. He had known Indio Falcon for several months before the murder. He saw Falcon speaking with Petitioner.

He recognized the brown Toyota car that Falcon got from Petitioner. After July 3, 1997, Petitioner asked him to take Falcon to get the car because it had run out of gas. Petitioner and Mecham were both at the store at the time. He took Falcon to Peoria to get the car on a residential street. He did not know whether it was close to Petitioner's residence. Falcon showed him the way. Falcon started the car and drove away. He did not see Falcon use or have a key to start the car. He had taken Falcon other places.

He did not see Falcon come to the store any more after the murder.

He had seen a chrome pistol in the draw of Petitioner's desk at the store. He did not remember seeing it after the murder. After the murder, Petitioner told him to drive around town and tell him if he saw any undercover police officers or detectives. He told Petitioner that he saw new cars in town, but didn't think they were undercover cops.

After the murder, Falcon showed him   a lot near Wittmann that he had purchased.

He didn't know an "El Gato." Petitioner told him he married his wife to keep his store.

He knew William Moore ("Tony") who he had visited in prison in California and Nevada. Tony had a daughter who died. He liked Tony.

Later, he took an officer to show him where the picked up the car, and then identified the car at an impound yard. When he spoke with the officer he took to where the car had been parked, he knew Petitioner and Colin had been arrested. He didn't remember the officer telling him anything about Tony.

Ruby Maribella -- Ruby Maribella testified that her sister Grace was married to Petitioner's brother Ume Gohel. She was friends with Petitioner since 1990, prior to his marriage to the victim, and for at least a little while after the murder. Petitioner visited Maribella almost every weekend. She would help him buy food for his store in Wittman. They would eat together. He would come to her apartment. He had sold her cars and loaned the money for the cars to her. She paid Petitioner back on the car loans and had borrowed several hundred dollars for her mom.

In May, 1997, Petitioner called her while she was in Colorado and said he had received a letter saying his wife was having an affair. She would reach Petitioner by paging him. She would call him at the grocery store but not at home. She paged and called him daily.

Petitioner told her that the victim said that if he wouldn't sleep with her, that she would find someone else to sleep with and there was a guy named Jose at work who was interested in her. He told Maribella this after the phone call in Colorado.

Aiche Jasser -- Aiche Jasser testified that she was a clinical pharmacist at Del Webb hospital, where she worked with the victim who was a staff pharmacist. They would eat lunch together. She liked her, and they would discuss personal matters. She saw Petitioner come to the hospital once. The victim introduced him to her.

She visited the victim at home in Peoria after she was in an accident in California, which made the victim miss more than a month of work.

There was a pharmacy technician named Jose Munoz who worked at the hospital. He would walk her to her car after work.

The victim had been distraught, but just prior to the murder, the victim seemed in good spirits. She was going traveling with her husband, and seemed in good spirits in conversations about purchasing a new home.

Lupe Gonzales -- Lupe Gonzales testified that she worked as a pharmacy technician at Del Webb Hospital in 1997, and knew the victim and Jose Munoz, an IV technician. The victim and Munoz were inseparable, would follow each other around the pharmacy, he would wait for her after work, and when she returned from lunch they would be sitting talking. She saw them giving each other a good bye kiss in the parking lot.

In May, 1997, she wrote a letter to Petitioner at his store telling him that his wife was seeing someone in the hospital. She didn't sign the letter or put a return address on it. She didn't think what the victim and Munoz were doing was right. She didn't write a letter to Munoz's wife because a friend spoke to Munoz.

She had met Petitioner at the hospital when he could visit the victim. He and the victim would have lunch together. The victim treated him nicely. They seemed glad to see each other. He had visited there once or twice.

She liked the victim and went and talked to her and said she should be careful about what she was doing at the hospital.

Tammy Maurer-Goad -- Tammy Maurer testified that she was formerly Tammy Goad. She knows Doug Maurer and is married to his brother Dan. In 1997 she lived in Wittman, and new Doug Maurer for about two years prior to the murder. She knew Petitioner, who ran the Wittman Grocery, where she traded a lot. Doug Maurer was often in the store and would talk to Petitioner.

Indio or Isidro Falcon was her next door neighbor. He normally drove a truck, but in June of 1997 had an additional vehicle. She talked more with his wife, Catalina. Indio drank a lot.

If they didn't have money for food, Petitioner would let them get food and pay him later. They would always pay him back.

She saw Doug Maurer with a gun. He had it for about a week.

A week after she saw Doug Maurer with the gun, Petitioner told her that Doug had stolen his gun that day. She knew it wasn't that day because she had seen Maurer with the gun. She and her boyfriend Danny told Petitioner to call the police, but he said he couldn't because the gun was not registered. Petitioner seemed nervous, and had brought up the subject of the gun.

About two to four months prior to the murder, she and her husband   confronted Petitioner and told him that Doug Maurer was telling people that Petitioner was trying to get his wife killed. Petitioner denied it and smiled.

At that period of time, Doug Maurer was doing drugs, but didn't have problems with his memory. He gave her a tape recorder and told her to listen to it. It was inaudible, but she is deaf in one ear. She could hear male voices but couldn't tell who they were or what they were saying. She gave it to Danny who took it to work and recorded over the tape. Doug was angry when he found out.

She applied for a job at a mobile home park on July 3, 1997. She was with Doug Maurer on that day. He also applied for a job there. They went shopping on that day, and Doug bought some shoes. It may also have been the day she got a tattoo.

She was seeing both Doug and Danny in 1997. She was addicted to crystal methamphetamine at the time. She and Doug would do drugs together. Doug had gotten out of jail in June, 1997, and they were doing a lot of drugs together.

Robert Tavernaro -- Robert Tavernaro, a latent print examiner for Arizona Department of Public Safety, testified that he examined fingerprints in a black   pickup truck at the scene and a blue Toyota Camry vehicle at the DPS facility, including objects in the vehicles. He also assisted with photographs, including shoeprints.

He compared the latent prints to prints of the victim, Petitioner, Babula Gohel, Doug Maurer, and Isidro Falcon. On Falcon, he had comparison prints of his entire hand, including fingertips and edges of the hand. No prints of Falcon or any other known person were found in the Camry. Some prints possibly from gloves were found on the outside driver's door.

He also examined a car alarm remote, and there were no identifiable prints on it. There were no identifiable prints on any of the door handles. No prints of Falcon or Maurer were found anywhere in or on the vehicle. The failure to find a person's prints does not mean they were not in the vehicle.

He only examined the exterior of the black pickup, because that is all Detective Lopez asked him to examine. Though the comparison prints he had for Maurer were not "major case prints" he did have good enough prints to not need additional prints to eliminate Maurer.

The   only identification made on the black pickup was Petitioner's print.

Jose Munoz -- Jose Munoz testified that he was employed as an IV technician at Del Webb Hospital in 1997. He worked in the same department and same hours as the victim, who was a pharmacist. He also worked with Aiche Jasser, a pharmacist, and Lupe Gonzales a technician. He became friends with the victim, but only at work. They would talk about her marriage. They would talk about the pharmacy and problems she had at home. He would hold her hand when she was upset, and perhaps when he walked her to her car. They would meet when she was on her way to the parking lot and he was on break. He never kissed her, but she kissed him once on the cheek. Perhaps they touched cheek to cheek in the parking lot.

The Peoria police asked if he was having an affair with the victim. He was not and never got close to it. He met the Petitioner in the Pharmacy two or three months before the murder. The victim was upbeat about trips to California with her husband over July 4th and to Tanzania to her family. The victim and Petitioner appeared to be getting closer to each other in the time shortly before   her death, and sent flowers to each other.

He knew Lupe Gonzales prior to becoming friends with the victim. After he became friends with the victim, Lupe Gonzales became more quiet toward both of them.

The victim and Aiche Jasser were friends. He was aware of the victim's car accident in California in November, 1996.

Ella McKinney -- Ella McKinney testified that she has lived in Wittmann for 20 years, and knew Petitioner who ran the grocery store. Around June 26, 1997, she sold a 1984 brown Toyota Camry to Petitioner because she needed the money. She cancelled the insurance two days after she sold the car. She sold it for 500 in cash and 200 in credit for groceries. Petitioner had given her credit at the store before, and she had paid it off.

Petitioner told her to leave the title open because he did not want it in his name. She had a door key and a gas key. Petitioner said he was buying the car for Don, and planned to sell it. She talked about it with Petitioner for about a week before selling it.

Bobby Garcia -- Bobby Garcia testified that he live in Wittmann in July of 1997, and worked at Trail Ridge Golf Course in Sun City West. He knew Isidro Falcon, but never met Alfonso Munoz or El Gato.

He bought a brown 1984 Toyota from Falcon for $1700 at the end of July, 1997. The title was in the name of Ella McKinney. He paid the full price in payments to Falcon at work or at his house, with $500 down and $200 per month. He got only one key to the vehicle. Eventually the police seized the vehicle for three days. He got it back and sold it in 1998. It was running when he sold it.

William Laing -- Officer William Laing, of the Peoria Police Department, testified that he responded to the vicinity of the scene of the murder and conducted a canvas of the neighbors and interviewed Benny Hays. When he canvased the neighborhood of the scene, he was looking for someone based on a description from Benny Hays of a Hispanic male, 20 to 25 years of age. Five seven, five eight, 160 to 170 pounds. Black hair. Wearing a pale olive green army jacket with a white T-shirt underneath, and white tennis shoes. Neat looking and possibly clean shaven. The person was in a dead run. No description of any pants was given by Hays.

He then went to the hospital to talk to Petitioner. Petitioner related that he was awake but in bed as the victim was leaving that morning. She gave him a kiss on the cheek before she left. Their normal routine was to set the alarm for 4:00 a..m. for the victim, but he usually remained in bed and left for work or the gym between 6:30 and 7:00 a.m. The victim was the primary user of the Toyota Camry vehicle she was murdered in. Her normal work days were Wednesdays off and rotating weekends.

Petitioner and the victim had gone out Wednesday night, July 2, 1997, celebrating their second wedding anniversary. The victim's sister, Bijal, went with them. The victim cooked dinner at the house and they went out to see a movie. They went in the Toyota Camry. In anticipation of a trip to California that weekend, they had the tires on the car rotated and it had been washed at a car wash.

Petitioner related that he found out about the murder when he heard the doorbell ring and answered the door to find two men who asked him if it was his vehicle and to tell him that there was a woman inside that was hurt. Petitioner said they had no children, that the victim had been hurt in a serious accident, but they planned to try to have a child within the next   year.

Petitioner denied any problems with vandalism around the house. He said he was away from home most of the time.

Petitioner described the car as having an automatic transmission, and the doors automatically locked once the vehicle was started. They had an after market alarm installed on the vehicle. The victim usually kept the doors of the car locked. The day before they had used Petitioner's keys, but the victim had driven the car the prior day, and he didn't know if the doors were locked or not at the time she got in the vehicle.

On December 15, and December 16, 1997, Laing interviewed Don Mecham. His interview with Don Mecham was to find out the route he had taken. Mecham told him he had given Indio a ride only one time and that was to go get Indio's car. Mecham never mentioned Petitioner being part of the arrangements to take Indio to his car. But Laing never asked him about any involvement by Petitioner. On the 15th, they went for a ride and Mecham showed him a route from Wittmann to near Petitioner's home, on Palo Verde. He took Mecham to the impound yard, and Mecham identified a brown car as the one that had been on Palo Verde.

Laing went to the morgue on July 3, 1997 to view   the body of the victim. He examined the wounds, including a laceration on the side of her head, and an entrance wound at the back of the head. He impounded her clothing and jewelry.

Laing admitted that his report did not reflect Petitioner saying the men at his door told him about the victim being hurt. Petitioner told him that their alarm system on the car was not the most reliable, and sometimes did not work.

There was a tape recording of the interview with Petitioner that was misplaced. His written report was based on his notes during the conversation.

Laing interviewed Ruby Garcia with Sergeant Stall on about July 9, 1997. The initial interview with Ruby Garcia was at her employment, but they went to her residence.

He participated in the execution of a search warrant at the residence of Ethel Maurer in Glendale. She was the mother of Doug Maurer. They found a pair of army camouflage pants and other items that appeared to belong to a younger man rather than an older woman. .

Detective Lopez was the primary investigating officer, but task assignments were made by Sergeant Stall.

Eric Stall -- Sergeant Eric Stall, of the Peoria Police Department,   testified that he responded to the scene of the murder at 6:30 in the morning, and took charge of the scene. He interviewed Petitioner.

Petitioner said the victim normally left for work at 5:30 a.m., except on Wednesdays, and was employed as a pharmacist at Del Webb Hospital. He said they had a good relationship. He couldn't understand how this could happen and had no idea who did it. Petitioner showed him his truck and it was locked. Petitioner opened it to show him something.

There was nothing to suggest that the victim's car had been broken into or that a car-jacking had been attempted.

He interviewed Lupe Gonzales, Ruby Garcia, and Colin Head. He contacted Colin Head on December 15, 1997, and took him to the Peoria Police Department to be interviewed. Head did not want to answer questions, and he was very direct with him to elicit responses, but was not rude or abrasive. Indio Falcon was brought into confront Head. At that point, Head put his head down and cried. He then answered Stall's questions. The interview was videotaped, but only the audio actually recorded.

Detective Lopez was the lead investigator on the case. Lopez looked to Stall as the sergeant for assistance and advice.

When   he interviewed Petitioner, he asked about guns. Petitioner gave him a 9mm gun from his truck.

When he interviewed Lupe Gonzalez, the interview lasted 90 minutes and was not entirely amicable and he was direct with her. When he interviewed Ruby Garcia, it was first at her employment, then at the police station, and then at her apartment. Those interviews occurred on July 9, 1997.

On November 22, 1997, they received an anonymous phone call concerning the case which resulted in him checking into an organization called the Fourth Reich Skin Heads, and three individuals, but that information lead to nothing.

Colin Head was arrested and taken to the Peoria Police Department. Stall wanted to have Head corroborate statements from Falcon that Petitioner had approached Head about killing the victim, and Petitioner had Head deliver an envelope to Falcon. Head initially denied any involvement. Stall asked him to be truthful and got confrontational with Head, including screaming at him, cursing at the subject matter but not at Head, and raising his voice. He called Head a liar and told him he thought he was involved in the murder, even though Stall had no information that Head was directly involved.   He told Heat that he could do eight years in prison

No recording was made of his pre-Miranda discussions with Head, which included the confrontation by Indio Falcon, Stall getting confrontational, and Head crying. Those discussions occurred over a half hour period and took a total of about 15 minutes, all prior to the Miranda warnings and tape recordings.

In that time period, he left to confirm with Indio Falcon his story. He asked Falcon to repeat his claims to Head. Falcon did so, and Head put his head down and appeared to cry. Stall then turned the recorder on, and gave Head his Miranda rights. Head then told him that Petitioner had asked him to murder his wife, and Petitioner had him deliver an envelope to Falcon.

He brought Falcon in to Head so Head would know Stall was not speculating or making up the story about Head's involvement.

He didn't record the pre-Miranda conversation because it would not be admissible. Although Head was a suspect, Stall was not certain whether Head would be a witness or a defendant. Head was released later that night. Stall had concluded there was not significant evidence of Head's involvement with the conspiracy to commit homicide.

William Sparpana -- Officer William Sparpana, of the Peoria Police Department, testified that he was asked to assist with surveillance via electronic listening device of conversations between Isidro Falcon and a confidential informant. Detective Lopez was interacting with Falcon. A recording was made of the conversation between Falcon and a confidential informant while they were in a trailer, and later that day in an abandoned old house. This occurred on December 11th.

On December 15th, Sparpana participated in the arrest of Petitioner at the Wittman Grocery.

Thomas Stewart -- Detective Stewart, of the Peoria Police Department, testified that in this case he collected evidence, interviewed witnesses, assisted in searches and seizures, and attended the autopsy. He did not interview Petitioner.

He arrived at the scene of the murder at about 7:45. He collected evidence from the Camry, including a purse from the right front passenger seat. Some items in the purse were removed and separately impounded. The purse did not appear to have been disturbed.

He seized out of the back of the car an Excalibur car remote, a black sweater, and a Winchester 380 caliber auto shell casing. A 380 is a 9mm short round. He seized the key from the car.

He seized shoes from the property of Doug Maurer at the Maricopa County Jail. He had the treads compared at DPS and went to a Payless Shoe Store in Glendale where Doug Maurer claimed he purchased the shoes in the morning hours of July 3, 1997. He got a receipt signed by the store manager, reflecting purchase on July 3, 1997 at 10:24 a.m. He did not take the shoes to the store, but the manager was able to confirm the shoes from a four digit code on the shoes.

When he got to the scene, the Camry was backed up to a wall across the street from the victim's house, and the doors were opened. There was a bullet hole through the front windshield. There was broken glass on the driveway. He did not examine the glass to determine whether it was windshield glass.

At the autopsy, he impounded projectile fragments removed from the victim's head.

He participated in the search of Petitioner's home on July 17, 1997 pursuant to a search warrant. They seized various items, including a bag with brochures from Caesar's Palace in Las Vegas. There were two Excalibur car remotes that had been seized from the victim's car, one in the back and one on her key chain.

He interviewed the manager of the Payless Shoe Store and Ella McKinney. He went to Three Fountains Mobile Home Park and got a job application submitted by Doug Maurer dated July 3, 1997.

He and Detective Lopez interviewed Doug Maurer on July 9, 1997. They had a discussion for about 30 to 45 minutes, and then began recording the interview. They returned on July 23, 1997, but Mr. Maurer refused to talk to them. They executed the warrant on the shoes the next day, July 24, 1997.

A brown Toyota Camry was seized from Bob Garcia and was taken to the impound lot, perhaps to see if certain keys worked in it.

The receipt from Payless Shoe Store was timed from 10:24 a.m. through 10:46 and the job application was dated 10:30 a.m. The Payless Shoe Store was approximately a quarter mile from the trailer park where Maurer had applied.

Juan Lopez -- Detective Juan Lopez, of the Peoria Police Department, testified that he was assigned as the case agent, and arrived at the scene at 7:00 a.m. He participated in the investigation of the scene with Officer Stewart. He observed the bullet hole in the windshield, and blood spatter, and residual particles of glass in the driveway of the home.

He observed a weapon in Petitioner's truck. It was a black, semi-automatic handgun, either 9mm or .380 caliber.

The victim had been shot in the back of the head, the car left running, keys in the car, radio on, purse undisturbed with nothing appearing to have been taken, and no indication the car had been broken into, either the doors or the trunk. There was minimal scraping damage to the car from running into the little wall. All four doors were open.

The day before his testimony he tested the remote found in the back seat of the victim's car, and the one found in the ignition, and found that they both would unlock the car. The remote found in the house would not unlock the car.

On December 16, 1997, he tested the key found in the back of the victim's car and it operated the ignition in the brown Toyota Camry sold by Isidro Falcon to Bobby Garcia, as well as opening the passenger door and hatchback door. It did not open the driver's door which appeared to be faulty.

On July 8, 1997, he received a phone message from Deputy Baker. They arranged to meet at the substation and Baker told him information about something Doug Maurer had previously told him. He then went and interviewed Doug Maurer with Detective Stewart on July 9, 1997.

He also received information on December 8, 1997 from Detective Baker about a man named Ron Wallace. He contacted Wallace and set him up with a body wire and monitored conversations he had on December 11, 1997 with Isidro Falcon. The conversations occurred at two separate locations, and concerned the murder and Petitioner. Tapes of the conversations were made.

Wallace picked up Falcon and took him to an old mobile home that had a hard wire installed.

Wallace told Lopez where the brown Toyota Camry could be found. Lopez went to find it, but couldn't see the license plate. He went back later and confirmed the license number. It was at the home of Bob Garcia.

He interviewed Isidro Falcon on December 15, 1997. The interview was audio and video taped.

He interviewed Paula Hernandez at her home in Wittmann, Arizona on December 15, 1997, to attempt to locate her brother-in-law, Alfonso Munoz, otherwise known as El Gato. She provided a phone number in Juarez, Mexico. He tried the number then and a week before trial, and never got an answer at the number. An address was given to the U.S. Customs Service and the Border Patrol, provided photographs to them, to try to locate Munoz in Juarez, Mexico or around El Paso, Texas. Lopez did not try going to the address. They had information that Munoz might be returning to the northwest Phoenix area. The information has not panned out. No one has reported seeing Munoz around Hernandez's residence.

Paula Hernandez also provided an address for her mother, the mother-in-law to Alfonso Munoz. He could not have gotten permission to go look for Munoz in Mexico, from his department, the government of Mexico, or the United States government.

Lopez spoke with Cattie Falcon, wife of Isidro, outside her apartment in Wittmann.

He spoke with Doug Maurer with Detective Stewart. He met with him on July 9th and 23rd. After the meeting on the 9th, he got a warrant to get Maurer's shoes. Maurer was at one point considered a suspect because of shoe impressions found in the victim's car.

Although Maurer had originally waived his Miranda rights and agreed to talk with them, when Maurer expressed fear of Petitioner, started getting upset and asked why they weren't investigating Petitioner and if they were going to book him, Maurer refused to answer more questions.

Lopez later obtained information from Detective Stewart about Maurer's purchase of the shoes, and no longer considered Maurer a suspect. He believed Maurer had thrown his old shoes away.

He interviewed William Moore, Aiche Jasser, Tammy Goad Maurer, and Richard Tan, concerning the investigation. He was present for the search of Petitioner's residence. He spoke with other people as well, took inked prints from Falcon, and spoke with Petitioner.

He spoke with Petitioner on July 3, 1997. Petitioner was not arrested or in custody prior to December 15, 1997. In between those dates, Petitioner wanted to talk to him and would call. Three phone conversations were transcribed, two on July 4th and one on July 9th or 10th. The conversations were discussions. Petitioner was seeking information about what may have happened to his wife, and about her remains.

In a phone conversation on July 4, 1997, Petitioner said the doors in the victim's car did not automatically lock when you put the car in gear. There were two alarms on the car, one installed by the manufacturer, and one installed after market by someone named Joe. He said it didn't always work. There was a kill switch that would cause the engine to die a short time after someone tampered with the car. Petitioner said the victim had been in a car accident in California about a year before. Petitioner said he opened the store only one day per week, but he would arrive between 7:00 and 8:00. Unless he closed, he would leave between five and six p.m. for the 45 minute drive home. When he closed, he would not leave until 10:00 p.m. Petitioner said he worked a lot of hours at the store, and gave credit to people there.

He interviewed Petitioner once at the police station on July 3, 1997. They met at Petitioner's home and they rode together in the police car. Petitioner was not in custody and was not even particularly a suspect at that time. Petitioner answered his questions voluntarily. Video and audio recordings were made of the interview. Petitioner was given his Miranda warnings.

Petitioner told him the victim left around 5:30 a.m. every morning except Wednesdays and weekends. She worked as a pharmacist at Del Webb Hospital. They had been married about two years. He said he and his wife had a near perfect marriage. He said he had no idea who might have harmed his wife.

He drove Petitioner back home and they talked about Petitioner contacting him and about dealing with the media.

He spoke with Petitioner by phone on July 7, 1997, and Petitioner said services for the victim had been dealt with and said that a good friend of the victim's from her work, Jose, might have some information. Detective Helen Rock interviewed Jose later that day.

Lopez and Petitioner continued to have conversations until July 11, when Petitioner retained counsel.

Lopez did a search of the Wittmann Grocery Store on December 17, 1997, finding papers reflecting the extension of credit by the store, primarily to store employees. Some just reflected first names.

Petitioner denied hearing any rumors about his wife, other than that he heard around town that people said he had a hit on his wife. He didn't inquire further, and didn't remember who told him that.

Petitioner told him he met the victim at a function at the East Indian dance festival. He had a prior, brief, arranged marriage. His marriage to the victim was not arranged. The victim was of a higher caste than Petitioner, and that caused problems on both sides. They had eloped and married in Las Vegas, Nevada, and then she returned to California, and he to Arizona. Only later did they tell their families and have a marriage in their culture. The second marriage ceremony was a year later. They then moved in with Petitioner's parents. Petitioner was devoted to his father, and as the eldest son was responsible for taking care of his parents in their culture.

Petitioner mentioned to Lopez that he had noticed that when he would ride in the victim's vehicle that the passenger seat would be pushed all the way back and sometimes reclined back. It seemed to bother him. The discussed the possibility that the victim was going out on him, and Petitioner said it crossed his mind, but he didn't believe she would do that. He said his heart also told him maybe, but he threw that feeling away, and he didn't want to talk about it.

Petitioner had heard rumors that someone wanted to car jack his truck. He had a hard time in the business at first because of his skin color, but eventually got to know everybody in town and made a lot of friends. Some got angry when he wouldn't sell to them on credit.

Based on Lopez's reconstruction of the scene and the autopsy, he believed the shooter was behind the victim, in the backseat compartment   of the car, close to the center console. A second 380 casing was found in the car when it was at the impound lot, on December 15, 1997, when the driver's seat was removed. It was impounded by Detective Rock. It was found under the driver's seat, closer to the rear floorboard, on the same side of the car as the other casing.

There were TV station vans at Petitioner's home on July 3, 1997, and there was newspaper and television coverage of the murder. Channel 12 did a silent witness re-enactment. There was print coverage when Petitioner was arrested. And Silent Witness circulated flyers, using the victim's drivers license photo. When Lopez handed three of the flyers to Petitioner on November 20, 1997, Petitioner laid them face down on his desk. Petitioner put some of the flyers up in his store. The police department did some media releases through their Public Information Officer.

Lopez interviewed different people about potential motives. It was suggested that there was an inability to divorce in Petitioner's culture. Lopez did not know if Petitioner had obtained a religious divorce to end his religious marriage to his first wife. There was information that the victim was a spendthrift,   but Lopez could not corroborate that claim. There was information that there was some insurance policy, but the only one located was the one through the victim's employer in a relatively small amount. There was information about a prenuptial agreement, but the existence of such an agreement could not be substantiated. Although Falcon had told defense counsel that the victim having an affair was a motive, Falcon did not relate such a claim to Lopez. In the interim, police reports had been read to Falcon.

The taped interviews of witnesses did not contain discussions of the criminal or substance abuse histories of the witnesses.

The day before Lopez interviewed Donnie Mecham, he had talked with his close family friend, William Moore, who he referred to as his uncle. During the pre-taping discussions with Donne Mecham, Lopez did not suggest that Mecham helping in the investigation could benefit Moore. They discussed Petitioner agreeing to Mecham taking Falcon to get his car. That was different from what Mecham had previously told Detective Lang, and Lopez.

He also had pre-taping conversations with Catalina Falcon, Cynthia Gragg, Ron Wallace, and Ron Moore. On the tape, he recapped what had told him and she assented to it. Lopez disagreed that it would be better to tape all but the introductions, because witnesses are reluctant to talk on a recording until they know what they are going to be asked. He always asks witnesses to let him know if they remember anything else. Most people don't.

He was aware that Petitioner and the victim had assets which included three pieces of property in Maricopa County, her car, her insurance policy, and jewelry seized from a Bank of America vault in a search. Property settlements are commonly parts of divorces.

Catalina Falcon -- A video deposition of Catalina Falcon was played for the jury on stipulation of the parties. A transcript has not been provided. (Supp. Exhibit P, R.T. 10/12/00 at 42-44.) In the prosecution's closing argument, the testimony was described as relating that Catalina had been called by El Gato to pick him up the morning of the murder, after he left the car.

Bijal Chollera -- The victim's sister, Bijal Chollera, testified that she was around the victim and Petitioner in July, 1997. Their family is in Mwanza, Tanzania, where they were born. Their ethnic origin is East Indian. They both came to the United States in September, 1986, settled in Phoenix and went to Phoenix College. The victim had a doctor of pharmacy degree from the University of Southern California.

Chollera had known Petitioner as an acquaintance since 1991, four years before he married the victim. She met him at a religious cultural function, his wedding reception with his first wife. She, the victim and Petitioner were Hindu, and of Indian ethnic origin. Petitioner's first wife was Indian as well.

She was aware the Petitioner and the victim had eloped and gotten married after Petitioner left his first wife. In their tradition, a divorce was integrated with western culture, and involved signing papers. If there is no civil marriage, then the parties call their families together, tell them it's not working out and they can take their daughter and her possessions back. They might do it in front of someone within the hierarchy of the society, or the cultural organization to be a witness. In the Hindu tradition, it is disfavored. It was disfavored for a woman to go with a man who left his first wife, as the victim did.

After they eloped in May, 1994, they announced their engagement. The victim was finishing her degree in California, and a year later on July 2, 1995 they got married under Hindu rituals. They then started living together. There were 6 to 8 years difference in age between Petitioner and the victim.

Petitioner and the victim lived with his parents, consistent with Indian traditions that the eldest son take care of the parents.

Chollera was in their home many times. There was one whole room of the house dedicated to Hindu rituals.

In early 1996, the victim was in an accident on Grand Avenue with a drunk driver. She injured her knee, had trouble walking, and needed therapy. She was working in Phoenix at the Veterans Hospital in a pharmacy internship and residency at the time. She recovered and was physically fine. She did not have seizures.

She obtained a settlement that she used to pay off some credit card debts she had accumulated. She then began paying for most things by cash. She was not a spendthrift, but continued to shop, buy jewelry, go to California and buy things. She loved shopping and if she liked something she got it. She had good taste, and if it cost a lot she would buy it. She especially liked Indian jewelry, which was usually 22 carat gold. She had traditional Indian jewelry when she got married.

In the summer of 1996, Petitioner presented the victim with a Lincoln Mark V. Chollera didn't know how the car was paid for or who bought it. The victim didn't want a vehicle that large. So they bought the Camry involved in this case, using the victim's credit.

In July, 1996, the victim went to work at Del Webb Hospital, and was in an accident in November, 1996 in Los Angeles. She was hit head on, had a head injury, lost her memory for three or four days, and was having seizures. She was hospitalized for a few days. Petitioner was the first person from Arizona to get to the hospital, and rented a car to driver her and Chollera back to Arizona.

Afterwards, the victim would lose her balance, needed support to walk, and had seizures. Chollera saw her have one of these seizures at home. She would have spit coming out of her mouth and her muscles were pulling. She was disabled from the accident for about three months. She took seizure medications. She improved with therapy that lasted about a month. But, she lost weight, lost energy, and was easily angered and seemed dazed. She was off work for three months. She had full medical coverage, and may have had paid time off.

During this time, Petitioner stopped paying as much attention to her and stopped spending time with her. He stopped taking her to therapy, and relied on his parents to take her. He was always at the store in Wittman. The victim preferred to have Chollera take her to therapy.

By March and April the victim was back to work, and released to drive. The victim was back to her normal self, energetic, positive, active, pleasant and nice to Petitioner. She and Petitioner began doing things more on weekend nights. Chollera would sometimes join them. The victim went to work at 5:30 or 6:00 in the morning and would get home in the middle of the afternoon. But Petitioner was gone on the weekdays and weekday evenings and weekend days. The store was open from about 7:00 a.m to 10:00 p.m., but Petitioner only worked a few evenings. They would go out in the evenings to dinner or the movies. The last month or two before she was killed, the victim was lively and vibrant.

The victim would help her mother in law in the afternoons with her catering business.

In June, 1997, Chollera noticed some kind of tenseness. They would still go out, but Petitioner would have Chollera drive and would sit in the back of her two-door car by himself. Petitioner would come home tense, and said he was stressed from work.

On July 2, 1997, Chollera had taken the victim to get her car from Discount Tire that afternoon so Petitioner and the victim could take it on a trip. The victim had prepared dinner. Then the three of them went out to go to the movies. Petitioner asked the victim to drive her car, the blue Toyota Camry. The victim seemed surprised and happy to get to drive and had to go back in to get her keys. Chollera asked him about it because it was their anniversary. Petitioner said he was tired and just wanted to sit in the back. He rode in the back seat by himself, behind Chollera.

When they returned, the victim parked the car on the left side, in front of the car port, which was filled with two cars. A truck was parked to the right. Chollera mistakenly took the victim's sunglasses, and the victim kiddingly scolded her and asked her to put them back in the car. The victim had given Petitioner the keys and remote and he unlocked the car for Chollera. She opened the door, put the glasses back in the car, and closed the door. Petitioner clicked again and she heard the doors lock. The sounds of the car locking and unlocking were different. The remote did not make any sound Petitioner went in and put the keys that the victim had been using to drive with on the kitchen dining cabinet. When interviewed by defense counsel, she did not mention Petitioner locking the car. Petitioner and the victim each had their own sets of keys. Chollera didn't know if Petitioner had a set of keys to the car that evening. She did not recall Petitioner mentioning before the murder having problems with the remote, but he did mention it after the murder. She did not remember seeing both sets of keys the day before the murder.

The victim asked her to spend the night that evening, July 2nd, but Chollera wasn't able to.

The victim was anticipating a trip Petitioner had planned to Mexico via San Diego for their anniversary. It was to start on July 4th.

The victim was planning on a trip to Africa around August. It was the first time she had gone back home. Chollera had helped her with her passport. Her passport and ticket arrived the day she passed away. Chollera handled getting a refund.

Their Indian tradition calls for 13 days of hymns and mourning. Chollera only saw Petitioner cry on two occasions. Otherwise, his reaction to her death seemed to be quiet, deep thinking, dazed. On the ritual days, Petitioner would sit for a little bit where the victim's picture and a candle were.

Petitioner went through the victim's things and found a box of pictures. He only wanted the picture on the dresser from when they eloped. That disturbed Chollera. Petitioner left the picture on the dresser. The mother-in-law wanted to keep their wedding pictures. The Hindu tradition was to put a single picture of the deceased in the prayer room. The father-in-law put in the shrine a large picture of the victim from her wedding day. The picture had arrived the night before her death.

After Petitioner and the victim were married in 1994, they sent to Las Vegas from time to time for the weekend. Petitioner said they stayed at Circus Circus.

Chollera had nothing against Petitioner, but objected to the victim seeing him, and to their eloping without discussing it with her family. She responded to the news of their marriage by saying "you're so stupid, how could you." She objected because Petitioner had been married before, the victim was five years younger, the victim had a higher education, and Petitioner's family was from a lower caste in India. No one in the victim's family had ever married outside of their caste.

Chollera spent a lot of time at the Petitioner and victim's house, but did not live there. She was usually there three to four days a week, sometimes for more than several hours. Some of the time Petitioner was gone, but she would have dinner with them. Petitioner and his family had a sense of humor and were fun. In the week or ten days prior to the murder, she was there almost all of the time, but not constantly. She would spend some nights there.

She was aware that Petitioner and the victim had purchased some investment land in the spring and early summer of 1997, and were looking at buying a home for themselves.

Chollera graduated from Western International in June of 1997, and Petitioner and the victim had a graduation party at their home. She planned to move to Los Angeles.

Joyot Paul Chaudhuri -- Dr. Chaudhuri, professor of political science at Arizona State University, testified that he was born and educated in India until 1952, was from a Hindu background, and wrote articles and functioned as an expert in issues of Hindu and Indian culture and heritage.

Chaudhuri testified that although there is associated regret, and family pressure against it, Hindus do get divorced. There is no religious objection, but the wife usually returns to her family with different settlements being made. The caste system was used to divide people into different social functions, and eventually developed a hierarchy. It is not a legal distinction, but one of family and inter-family relationships.

Oldest sons have ritual obligations, such as cremation of the father. They have special obligations to both parents by custom. Oldest sons of oldest sons have great expectations placed on them.

Hindu families often have shrines in their homes, with different features dependent upon their sect. The rituals for different sects and castes would vary.

Marriage ceremonies may include a ceremony at the bride's home, a parade to the husband's home, and a ceremony at the husband's. Usually the bride will go to live with the husband's family. Arranged marriages are common, although increasingly the husband and wife will have met each other before the marriage.

Indian's often take their customs and Hinduism with them and continue them in a foreign country.

Daily prayer is a common tradition, but it is not ostentatious.

It is common when a death occurs to keep just a few pictures of the deceased out. The notion of death is that life goes on.

Stipulation re Reward -- The parties stipulated that the $11,000 reward offered consisted of $10,000 from the Chollera family, and $1,000 from the Silent Witness program.

Conclusion - Petitioner was convicted by the jury of first degree murder and conspiracy to commit first degree murder.

After an aggravation/mitigation hearing the trial court found the existence of an aggravating factor but declined to impose the death penalty, instead sentencing Petitioner to life in prison without possibility of parole on the murder charge, and life with possibility of parole after 25 years on the conspiracy charge.

D. PROCEEDINGS ON POST-CONVICTION RELIEF

On February 11, 2004, Petitioner filed an Application for Leave to File Delayed Notice of Postconviction Relief , noting that his PCR notice was due by December 31, 2003, and seeking leave to filed a delayed notice. Petitioner eventually filed, on May 13, 2005, a PCR Petition, arguing that trial counsel was ineffective for failing to conduct an adequate investigation, and that newly discovered evidence indicated Petitioner's innocence. The State argued the petition was untimely, and failed to qualify for consideration under the exceptions to the timeliness rules.

The PCR Court denied Petitioner's ineffective assistance of counsel claim as delinquent, and deferred ruling on the remaining claims until completion of discovery and a motion to amend to clarify the claims.

Petitioner then filed an Application to Amend and an Amended Memorandum. The Amended Memorandum argued that the events of the shooting as related by Falcon based on Munoz's statements were inconsistent with the evidence at the scene as demonstrated by subsequent experiments by crime scene investigators, including the inability of Munoz to conceal himself in the small backseat, and to exit through the passenger front door without creating more of a blood trail. The State argued in response that the experiments were not newly discovered evidence, could have been developed with reasonable diligence, were merely impeachment and would not have altered the outcome of trial.

On October 24, 2007, the PCR court adopted the State's arguments and dismissed the Petition

> **(1) Ground 3: Equal Protection Claim** - Petitioner's Ground 3 challenges the refusal of the Arizona Court of Appeals to remand the case back to the trial court for transcripts certified to be accurate, edited and corrected and instead relying upon the uncertified "rapid transcripts." Petitioner contends that this violated both his equal protection and due process rights under the *Fourteenth Amendment*. Respondents concede that the due process claim was fairly presented on direct appeal, but contend that Petitioner never asserted an equal protection claim to the Arizona Courts. Petitioner replies that the factual basis is part and parcel of the due process claim, and that the equal protection portion was fairly presented in his Opening Brief on direct appeal by quoting a portion of the Arizona case, *Matter of Hendrix, 145 Ariz. 345, 349, 701 P.2d 841 (1985)*, which in turn cited *Griffin v. Illinois, 351 U.S. 12, 76 S. Ct. 585, 100 L. Ed. 891 (1956)*. Petitioner contends *Griffin* is an equal protection case, and quoting the Arizona Supreme Court's citation of it was sufficient to raise the equal protection claim. Petitioner also contends that in the area of indigent appeals, the two clauses of the *Fourteenth Amendment* are interconnected.

The fact that the factual basis for Petitioner's due process and equal protection claims is the same is inapposite. A claim has been fairly presented to the state's highest court only if petitioner has described *both* the operative facts *and* the federal legal theory on which the claim is based. *Kelly v. Small, 315 F.3d 1063, 1066 (9th Cir. 2003).*

Nor was Petitioner's incidental quotation of *Griffith* sufficient to raise an equal protection claim. Petitioner's brief was explicitly limited to asserting a due process right under the Federal constitution.

> **(3) Ground 5: Actual Innocence** - In his Ground 5, Petitioner argues that he has newly discovered evidence of his actual innocence and therefore is held in violation of the *Fourteenth Amendment*. Respondents concede that Petitioner asserted a newly discovered evidence claim to the trial court in his first PCR proceeding, but argue he did not assert it as a federal claim. In his Reply, Petitioner argues that Grounds 5 and 6 (Ineffective Assistance for failure to investigate and discover the evidence) should be construed together and Ground 5 should thus not be deemed unexhausted.

Even if this claim were properly exhausted, "[c]laims of actual innocence based on newly discovered evidence have never been held to state a ground for federal habeas relief absent an independent constitutional violation occurring in the underlying state criminal proceeding...This rule is grounded in the principle that federal habeas courts sit to ensure that individuals are not imprisoned in violation of the Constitution-not to correct errors of fact." *Herrera v. Collins, 506 U.S. 390, 400-401, 113 S. Ct. 853, 122 L. Ed. 2d 203 (1993).*

The Ninth Circuit rejected a similar argument in *Rose v. Palmateer, 395 F.3d 1108 (9th Cir. 2005)*, where the court found that the petitioner did not fairly present a *Fifth Amendment* claim to the state courts when the claim was merely discussed as one of several issues handled ineffectively by counsel. "While [the ineffective assistance and underlying constitutional claim are] admittedly related, they are distinct claims with separate elements of proof, and each claim should have been separately and specifically presented to the state courts." *395 F.3d at 1112.* The *Rose* court noted that ineffective assistance of counsel claims could be disposed of without reaching the merits of the underlying constitutional claim, if, for example, the court found no prejudice because the outcome of the trial was not affected, or that counsel had made a reasonable tactical decision to not pursue the claim.

Here, Petitioner's ineffective assistance of counsel claim was disposed of by the state courts as untimely. Thus, the state courts had no cause to examine either the merits of the ineffective assistance claim itself, nor any constitutional claim underlying it.

Moreover, Petitioner did not assert the failure to raise a Federal Due Process due process/actual innocence claim in connection with   his ineffective assistance claim. Rather, he simply argued that counsel was
ineffective in not discovering the evidence on which he now relies to assert an actual innocence claim. Thus,
even if the Arizona courts had reached the merits of the ineffective assistance claim, they would not have
thus reached the instant due process claim.

Accordingly, the undersigned finds that the claim in Ground 5 was not fairly presented in Petitioner's PCR
proceeding, nor otherwise. Therefore, this claim was not properly exhausted.

D. GROUND 1: VAGUENESS

In his Ground 1, Petitioner argues that on its face and   as applied to Petitioner, the Arizona statute under
which Petitioner received a natural life sentence, the 1997 version of *A.R.S. § 13-703*, violates Petitioner's right to
due process under the *Fourteenth Amendment* because the statute is unconstitutionally vague by providing no
standards for sentencing and allows for an arbitrary application by Arizona trial and appellate judges.

Respondents argue that the Arizona Court of Appeals rejection of this claim on direct appeal was not contrary to nor an unreasonable application of applicable federal law, but was a reasonable application of the
decision in *Harmelin v. Michigan, 501 U.S. 957, 994, 111 S. Ct. 2680, 115 L. Ed. 2d 836 (1991)*.

Petitioner replies that the Arizona Court of Appeals wrongly focused on the "fair warning" flavor of
vagueness, and ignored his sole argument based upon the "arbitrary application" flavor and thus misapplied
federal law.

Arizona Court's Decision - On direct appeal, Petitioner argued:

> In 1993, [*Ariz. Rev. Stat. §] 13-703* was amended to its current form. It states that a defend-
> ant convicted of first degree murder will receive one of three specified sentences: death, natu-
> ra11ife in prison, or 25 years in prison. The death sentencing provisions of *13-703* are not at is-
> sue in this appeal.
>
> The problem with *ARS 13-703* is that it gives the trial judge no standards to use in determin-
> ing whether to impose the 25 year sentence or natural life.
>
> * * *
>
> A previous vagueness challenge to *ARS 13-703* argued the general vagueness argument, that
> *ARS 13-703* cannot be understood.
>
> * * *
>
> The appellant is making a different vagueness argument...
>
> * * *
>
> Instead, we have a criminal law which states two different punishments, one far more se-
> vere than the other, with no standards to guide the trial judge   in determining which sentence
> is appropriate.

In disposing of this claim, the Arizona Court of Appeals observed that in *State v. Wagner, 194 Ariz. 310,
311, 982 P.2d 270, 271 (1999)* the Arizona Supreme Court had disposed of a challenge to the statute based on
a lack of fair notice. The appellate court went on to observe, however, that *Wagner* had also rejected a claim
that the Constitution required sentencing guidelines to assist judges in selecting among sentencing options
(with the exception of the death penalty). Appellate counsel had conceded at oral argument that *Wagner* was
controlling law on the issue, and the appellate court relied upon it to dispose of the claim.

Mandate for Sentencing Guidelines - Petition argues that the Arizona court's decision was an unreasonable application of federal law because: (1) it relied on *Harmelin*, which is a cruel and unusual punishment case
not concerned with vagueness; and (2) the court incorrectly applied the "fair warning" standards to an "arbitrary application" claim.

Applicability of *Harmelin* - In *Harmelin*, the Supreme Court rejected a cruel and unusual punishment challenge to a mandatory natural   life sentence which was based upon the disproportionality of the sentence
and the lack of consideration of mitigating factors. With regard to the latter, the Court refused to extend its
"individualized capital sentencing doctrine" to a mandatory natural life sentence. *501 U.S. at 995-996.*

In Petitioner's case, the Arizona Court of Appeals did not . The appellate court found itself bound by the holding of *Wagner* and in reliance on it disposed of Petitioner's claim. *Wagner*, in turn, addressed the substance of the due process challenge to a standard-less imposition of a life sentence:

> Because appellant has no constitutional right to sentencing guidelines in a non-capital proceeding, the lack of guidelines for imposing a sentence of life or natural life does not violate appellant's right to due process or equal protection under the law. *See Harmelin, 501 U.S. at 994, 111 S.Ct. at 2701* (rejecting a claim that the Constitution requires a state "to create a sentencing scheme whereby life in prison without possibility of parole   is simply the most severe of a range of available penalties that the sentencer may impose after hearing evidence in mitigation and aggravation"); *United States v. LaFleur, 971 F.2d 200, 211-12 (9th Cir.1991)* (holding that the Constitution does not require an individual assessment of the appropriateness of a life sentence).

Wagner, 194 Ariz. at 313-314, 982 P.2d at 273-274.

Thus, *Wagner*, and consequently the Arizona Court in this case, improperly relied upon the *Eighth Amendment* decision in *Harmelin* to reject a due process/vagueness challenge to a sentencing statute.

However, the Arizona Courts' erroneous application of *Harmelin* does not automatically justify relief. Rather, Petitioner is entitled to relief only if the Court's decision is "contrary to or an unreasonable application of" Supreme Court law.

Contrary To - The Arizona Court of Appeals' decision was not contrary to Supreme Court law.

The Supreme Court has instructed that a state court decision is "contrary to" clearly established federal law "if the state court applies a rule that contradicts the governing law set forth in [Supreme Court] cases or if the state court confronts a set of facts that are materially indistinguishable   from a decision of [the Supreme] Court and nevertheless arrives at a result different from [its] precedent." *Lockyer v. Andrade, 538 U.S. 63, 73, 123 S. Ct. 1166, 155 L. Ed. 2d 144 (2003)* (internal quotation marks omitted).

Here, the rule applied did not contradict Supreme Court law. Petitioner points to no Supreme Court law which holds that the vagueness doctrine of due process precludes unguided judicial selection between various non-death penalty sentences. The last time the Supreme Court addressed any similar due process claim was in *McGautha v. California, 402 U.S. 183, 91 S. Ct. 1454, 28 L. Ed. 2d 711 (1971)*.

In *McGautha*, the Supreme Court addressed sentencing statutes, not under the *Eight Amendment*'s ban on cruel and unusual punishment, but under the vagueness mandate of the *Due Process Clause*.

> We consider first McGautha's and Crampton's common claim: that the absence of standards to guide the jury's discretion on the punishment issue is constitutionally intolerable. To fit their arguments within a constitutional frame of reference petitioners contend that to leave the jury completely at large to impose or withhold the death penalty as it see fit is fundamentally lawless and therefore violates the basic command of the *Fourteenth Amendment* that no   State shall deprive a person of his life without due process of law.

402 U.S. at 208. The Court ultimately rejected the claim:

> In light of history, experience, and the present limitations of human knowledge, we find it quite impossible to say that committing to the untrammeled discretion of the jury the power to pronounce life or death in capital cases is offensive to anything in the Constitution.

Id. "The Court refused to find constitutional dimensions in the argument that those who exercise their discretion to send a person to death should be given standards by which that discretion should be exercised." *Furman v. Georgia, 408 U.S. 238, 247, 92 S. Ct. 2726, 33 L. Ed. 2d 346 (1972)*.

Just one year after *McGautha*, the Court decided in *Furman* that a standards-less imposition of the death penalty was a violation of the *Eight Amendment*. In reliance on *Furman*, the Court vacated the judgment in *McGautha*, and remanded it for consideration under *Furman. Crampton v. Ohio, 408 U.S. 941, 92 S. Ct. 2873,*

33 L. Ed. 2d 765 (1972). "Thus, what had been approved under the *Due Process Clause of the Fourteenth Amendment* in *McGautha* became impermissible under the *Eighth* and *Fourteenth Amendments* by virtue of the judgment in *Furman.*" *Lockett v. Ohio, 438 U.S. 586, 599, 98 S. Ct. 2954, 57 L. Ed. 2d 973 (1978).* *See also Ford v. Wainwright, 752 F.2d 526, 534, n. 7 (1985),* overruled on other grounds, *477 U.S. 399, 106 S. Ct. 2595, 91 L. Ed. 2d 335 (1986)* ("*McGautha* ...was decided on the basis of the *Fourteenth Amendment* and not on *Eighth Amendment* grounds. In *Furman*...the Court recognized and began to explicate the *Eighth Amendment* parameters of capital sentencing."). Here, not only does Petitioner not assert an *Eight Amendment* claim, but he was not subjected to a death penalty.

Petitioner points to no Supreme Court decision since *McGautha* which adopts a contrary conclusion under due process, either as to death penalty cases or in the less formidable context of less-than-death sentences. The undersigned has found none.

Nor has Petitioner shown that the Arizona Court confronted "a set of facts that are materially indistinguishable from a decision of [the Supreme] Court and nevertheless arrive[d] at a result different from [its] precedent." *Lockyer, 538 U.S. at 73.* Indeed, *McGautha* is the closest due process case, and the Arizona decision arrived at the same result.

Unreasonable Application - Nor has Petitioner shown that the Arizona decision was an unreasonable application of Supreme Court law.

Distinguishing between an unreasonable and an incorrect application of federal law, the Court in *Williams v. Taylor, 529 U.S. 362, 120 S. Ct. 1495, 146 L. Ed. 2d 389 (2000)* clarified that an incorrect application is insufficient to justify relief. Distinguishing between an unreasonable and an incorrect application of federal law, the *Williams* Court clarified that even if the federal habeas court concludes that the state court decision applied clearly established federal law incorrectly, relief is appropriate only if that application is also objectively unreasonable. *Id. at 410-411.* "A state court's decision can involve an "unreasonable application" of federal law if it either (1) correctly identifies the governing rule but then applies it to a new set of facts in a way that is objectively unreasonable, or (2) extends or fails to extend a clearly established legal principle to a new context in a way that is objectively unreasonable.*" Anthony v. Cambra, 236 F.3d 568, 578 (9th Cir. 2000).*

The first branch - correct rule, unreasonable application - -doesn't apply. The Arizona Court simply selected the wrong rule.

The second branch - unreasonable failure to apply rule in new context - - doesn't apply either. In this regard, it is important to remember that "it is   the state court's decision, as opposed to its reasoning, that is judged under the 'unreasonable application' standard." *Merced v. McGrath, 426 F3d 1076, 1081 (9th Cir. 2005).* Here, the Arizona court's reasoning was flawed - - it chose the wrong precedent - - but there is no clearly established Federal law that was applicable and called for a decision different from that reached by the Arizona court. Indeed, *McGautha* mandated the very decision they reached.

Thus, despite the erroneous reliance on *Harmelin,* the Arizona court's decision was neither contrary to nor an unreasonable application of Supreme Court law.

"Fair Warning" v. "Arbitrary Application" - Finally, Petitioner argues that§ 2254's limitation on habeas relief is met because the Arizona court improperly applied a "fair warning" analysis to Petitioner's "arbitrary application" claim.

As recognized in *Anderson v. Morrow, 371 F.3d 1027 (9th Cir. 2004),* the due process proscription of vague statues encompasses both a "notice test" and an "arbitrary enforcement test." The "notice test" is concerned with whether "the statutory language is 'sufficiently precise to provide comprehensible notice' of the prohibited conduct." *Id. at 1032.*   The "arbitrary enforcement test" is concerned with the kind of statute that "does not provide explicit standards to those who apply them, so as to avoid arbitrary and discriminatory enforcement."

Here, the Arizona Court of Appeals' decision quoted those portions of *Wagner* that focused on notice, *i.e.* that "a person of ordinary intelligence can easily determine the range of punishment he or she faces for committing first degree murder." (quoting *Wagner, 194 Ariz. at 313, 982 P.2d at 273*).)

To the extent that the Arizona court failed to address the issue raised by Petitioner (e.g. arbitrary enforcement), it's decision could be considered erroneous or even unreasonable.

However, Petitioner fails to offer any Supreme Court precedent which extends the vagueness prohibition against arbitrary enforcement to the sentencing context.

Petitioner points to *Grayned v. City of Rockford, 408 U.S. 104, 108, 92 S. Ct. 2294, 33 L. Ed. 2d 222 (1972)* for the proposition that the vagueness doctrine prohibits statutes that lack "explicit standards for those who apply them." However, *Grayned* was not concerned with discretion in sentencing, but in prosecution decisions under a disturbing-the-peace statute. Petitioner points to no cases extending the vagueness doctrine past the prosecution stage to sentencing.

Ninth Circuit jurisprudence indicates that the Supreme Court has never done so. For example, in *Bradway v. Cate, 588 F.3d 990 (9th Cir. 2009)*, the Court noted the inapplicability of the *Eighth Amendment* vagueness jurisprudence to a life sentence, and concluded that no Supreme Court cases had addressed due process vagueness claims based upon a failure to narrow offenses subject to more severe penalties, where the penalties were less than the death penalty. *Id. at 992-993*. In *U.S. v. Johnson*, the Ninth Circuit observed that "[u]nconstitutional vagueness challenges to the Sentencing Guidelines have been questioned as theoretically unsound." *130 F.3d 1352, 1354 (9th Cir. 1997)* (citing *U.S. v. Wivell, 893 F.2d 156, 159-60 (8th Cir. 1990)* (vagueness doctrine does not mandate sentencing guidelines). As recently as 2006, the Ninth Circuit was required to simply assume "that a vagueness argument focused exclusively on sentencing, rather than on criminal conduct giving rise to the sentence, is cognizable." *U.S. v. Hungerford, 465 F.3d 1113 (9th Cir. 2006)*.

Again, because Petitioner fails to show that there is Supreme Court law that mandates relief, this Court cannot find that the Arizona court's decision to deny relief was "contrary to or an unreasonable application of" such law.

Therefore, Petitioner's Ground 1 is without merit and must be denied.

E. *APPRENDI*: Ground 2

In his Ground 2, Petitioner argues that his right to a jury trial under the *Sixth Amendment* and the *Fourteenth Amendments* was violated because the aggravating factor that supported Petitioner's natural life sentence was not found by a jury as required by *Apprendi v. New Jersey*. Respondents argue that no fact was necessary to be found to justify the judge's choice between a natural life sentence and a life sentence with possibility for parole. Petitioner responds that to avoid being unconstitutionally arbitrary, the judge's choice must be supported by an aggravating factor, and that the only ones authorized are those in *Ariz. Rev. Stat. § 13-703(F)*.

Petitioner's claim is without merit.

Apprendi mandated that: "Other than the fact of a prior conviction, any fact that increases the penalty for a crime beyond the prescribed statutory maximum must be submitted to a jury, and proved beyond a reasonable doubt." *530 U.S. 466 at 490, 120 S. Ct. 2348, 147 L. Ed. 2d 435*.

The applicable statute provided:

> A. A person guilty of first degree murder as defined in § 13-1105 shall suffer death or imprisonment in the custody of the state department of corrections for life as determined and in accordance with the procedures provided in subsections B through G of this section. If the court imposes a life sentence, the court may order that the defendant not be released on any basis for the remainder of the defendant's natural life. An order sentencing the defendant to natural life is not subject to commutation or parole, work furlough or work release. If the court does not sentence the defendant to natural life, the defendant shall not be released on any basis until the completion of the service of twenty-five calendar years if the victim was fifteen or more years of age and thirty-five years if the victim was under fifteen years of age.

Ariz. Rev. Stat. § 13-703(A) (1999). The plain import of this statute is that outside a death penalty (which did require fact finding on aggravating factors) the judge was required to sentence the first degree murder to life in prison, but had discretion to designate it as with or without parole. The statute provided no prerequisites to exercising that discretion. "In *Ariz. Rev. Stat. § 13-703(A)*, the Arizona legislature explicitly authorizes a sentence of natural life upon a conviction for first degree murder without the need for any further factual findings."

"The *Sixth Amendment* does not prevent judges from 'exercis[ing] discretion-taking into consideration various factors relating both to offense and offender-in imposing a judgment within the range prescribed by statute.' " *Butler v. Curry, 528 F.3d 624, 643 (9th Cir. 2008) (quoting Apprendi, 530 U.S. at 481).*

> We have never doubted the authority of a judge to exercise broad discretion in imposing a sentence within a statutory range. ...For when a trial judge exercises his discretion to select a specific sentence within a defined range, the defendant has no right to a jury determination of the facts that the judge deems relevant.

U.S. v. Booker, 543 U.S. 220, 233, 125 S. Ct. 738, 160 L. Ed. 2d 621 (2005).

Petitioner attempts to bring the statute within the ambit of *Apprendi* jurisprudence by arguing that the statute would be unconstitutional if some limits on   discretion were not read into the statute. This claim has been rejected in connection with Petitioner's Ground 1 (vagueness).

Moreover, even if Petitioner could make out such a claim, it would not permit a bootstrapping of an *Apprendi* claim. The sentencing statute would simply be void for vagueness.

Even if the statute were not simply void for vagueness, Petitioner proffers no rationale for his assumption that the limits that would be inscribed would be those that required specific factual findings, let alone the factors in *§ 13-703(F)*, which are referenced in the subsection solely as those which the sentencing court "shall consider." The only mandate for a finding of such an aggravating factor is as a condition of imposing "a sentence of death." *Ariz. Rev. Stat. § 13-703(E) (1999).*

This claim is without merit.

REASON WHY REMEDY IS HOLLOW

The Arizona Attorney General fails to notify the federal courts that there is a systemic problem in the Arizona system where prosecutors engage in misconduct and state courts refuse to do anything. Federal courts fail to consider the systemic problems with the Arizona judicial system when reviewing claims. If they consider systemic problems with the system there would be no convictions.

PROSECUTORIAL MISCONDUCT

> **Blaine Kyle McNeese, Petitioner, v. Charles Ryan, Arizona Attorney General, Respondents. CIV 12-00962 PHX FJM (MEA)UNITED STATES DISTRICT COURT FOR THE DISTRICT OF ARIZONA**
> **(Text modified for emphasis)**

THE POSITION OF THE COURTS

A grand jury indictment returned December 18, 2008, charged Petitioner with one count of theft of at least $25,000, one count of forgery, and one count of identity theft. The charges were based on the events of September 30, 2003, during which time Petitioner was an officer with the Arizona Department of Public Safety ("DPS").   The jury accepted the prosecution's theory of the case: Petitioner had arranged with a limousine driver   that, acting in his capacity as a DPS officer, Petitioner would "pull over" the limousine on a particular date at a particular time while the driver was transporting particular passengers who would be carrying a large sum of cash. Petitioner would cite and arrest the driver and search the vehicle pursuant to the arrest, removing $45,000 in cash that Petitioner knew the passengers would have in the limousine. Petitioner used the name of another DPS officer on the citation and he and the limousine driver split the $45,000. The passengers reported the loss of the money, leading to the investigation. Petitioner resigned from the DPS in November of 2003.

In June 2005, Detectives Vern Alley and Larry Landers were investigating the robbery of $40,000 in cash from the passengers of a limousine whose driver was arrested during a traffic stop conducted by Petitioner on September 30, 2003. The detectives went to Petitioner's home to confront him with the evidence regarding Petitioner's participation in the robbery. The detectives discussed the matter with Petitioner and his wife. During that conversation with the detectives Petitioner admitted that he had coordinated the traffic stop with the limousine driver and that he had obtained cash from the car. Petitioner also stated that he "got $20,000 out of it." Petitioner later engaged in a "freetalk" with detectives; the detectives testified at Petitioner's trial that he admitted to the crimes during this "freetalk." Attached to the state's sentencing recommendation as Exhibit 4 is a transcript of a portion (pages 32 through 42) of the "freetalk."

On January 7, 2010, after four days of trial, a jury convicted Petitioner of all three counts alleged in the indictment. However, the jury found that the theft was based on a value of less than $25,000, rendering that offense a class 3 felony as opposed to the class 2 felony charged in the indictment. The evidence introduced at trial included phone records indicating Petitioner and the limousine driver had spoken by phone on 79 occasions in the four months prior to the robbery and sixteen times on the date of the robbery.

On February 9, 2010, the trial court sentenced Petitioner to an aggravated term of six years imprisonment pursuant to his conviction on the theft charge and to an aggravated term of three years imprisonment pursuant to his conviction on the charge of identity theft. Petitioner was sentenced to the presumptive term of 2.5 years imprisonment pursuant to his conviction for forgery. The trial court ordered that the forgery and identity theft sentences be served concurrently to each other and consecutively to the sentence imposed for theft.

Petitioner took a timely direct appeal of his convictions and sentences. In his direct appeal Petitioner asserted that the trial court abused its discretion when it permitted the use of his "free talk" statements for impeachment purposes; that the prosecutor engaged in misconduct when he referred to a "free talk agreement" in direct examination and closing argument; and that the trial court erred in admitting a copy of the traffic citation issued to the limousine driver during the robbery into evidence after the state had destroyed the original.

The Arizona Court of Appeals denied relief in a decision entered June 21, 2011. The appellate court reviewed Petitioner's first claim for fundamental error, under state law. The court held that, although the trial court erred by permitting the state to use Petitioner's statements during a "free talk" with police to impeach the testimony of Petitioner's wife at trial, the error was not fundamental. The court noted that Petitioner had argued that "his state and federal constitutional rights were violated in the heading for this issue in his opening brief," but that Petitioner had failed "to provide citation to any authority or argument" for the claim. Accordingly, citing *Arizona v. Moody, 208 Ariz. 424, 452 n.9, 94 P.3d 1119, 1147 (2004)*, the court held Petitioner had "abandoned these claims." The state appellate court analyzed Petitioner's claim of prosecutorial misconduct under state law and held that the prosecutor's statements in closing argument did not constitute fundamental error. The state court further held that, under state law, the trial court's admission of a photocopy of the citation on which Petitioner had forged the name of a fellow DPS officer was not reversible error.

Petitioner sought review of the Arizona Court of Appeals' decision by the Arizona Supreme Court, which denied review on January 10, 2012.

Petitioner initiated a state action for post-conviction relief pursuant to Rule 32, Arizona Rules of Criminal Procedure, on May 18, 2010, while his direct appeal was pending. On June 16, 2010, Petitioner filed a motion "to withdraw [his] notice of post-conviction relief without prejudice so that it [could] be filed at a later date." The trial court dismissed the Rule 32 action without prejudice on August 3, 2010.

On July 15, 2011, Petitioner initiated a second Rule 32 action. The state trial court appointed counsel to represent Petitioner in his Rule 32 proceedings. On January 3, 2012, Petitioner's appointed counsel informed the trial court that he had reviewed the trial and appellate proceedings and was "unable to find any claims for relief to raise in post-conviction relief proceedings." On May 12, 2012, the Rule 32 action was dismissed for Petitioner's failure to timely file a pro per pleading by February 21, 2012, as ordered by the state trial court.

In his federal habeas action Petitioner asserts:

1. His right to due process of law was violated because the state used Petitioner's statements during a "free talk" to impeach his wife's trial testimony;

2. The prosecutor committed misconduct by referring to Petitioner's "free talk" in direct examination and closing argument;

3. The trial court erred by admitting a photocopy of a traffic citation at trial after the state had destroyed the original;

4. The two detectives who testified at Petitioner's trial "perjured themselves" by testifying that Petitioner admitted to the crimes of conviction.

1. Petitioner contends his right to due process was violated because the state used Petitioner's statements during a "free talk" to impeach his wife's trial testimony and because the state never "disclosed a copy of the 'freetalk.'"

In his direct appeal Petitioner asserted the trial court erred by allowing the introduction of statements he made during a "freetalk" to be used to impeach his wife's trial testimony. When discussing the merits of this claim the state court noted that, although Petitioner had stated in the heading of this section of his brief that his state and federal constitutional rights were violated by this error, Petitioner did not argue anywhere in the brief that these rights were violated, nor did he cite to any legal opinion so holding. Accordingly, the state court found Petitioner had abandoned any claim that this error by the trial court violated his state or constitutional rights.

The state court then reviewed the argument pursuant to state law and concluded that although the trial court erred, the error was not fundamental because it did not permeate the proceedings and deny Petitioner a fair trial, *inter alia*, given the "overwhelming" evidence of guilt.

Petitioner did not provide the state court the opportunity to review the merits of the federal constitutional claim presented in his *section 2254* petition. The state court decided the merits of the claim based solely on state law. Accordingly, Petitioner has procedurally defaulted this claim in the state courts. Because the state court's decision is an adequate and independent basis for declining to consider the merits of the federal habeas claim, the Court need not consider the merits of the claim absent a showing of cause and prejudice or that a fundamental miscarriage of justice will occur.

In his reply to the answer to his petition Petitioner contends:

> The Petitioner's claims are not procedurally barred.... Claims 1 through 3 were handled by a state appointed attorney []. He followed all appropriate rules and applications for the petitioner's state appeals. ... Since the Petitioner is not an attorney and has limited experience with the law the Petitioner assumes all the correct procedures were followed. If this is not the case the Petitioner should not be responsible.

With regard to the merits of his claim, Petitioner contends that the use of the "freetalk" violated Petitioner's *Fifth Amendment* rights because it was plain error and prejudicial and in violation of the Arizona state rules regarding admission of evidence and his right to not be forced to incriminate himself. Petitioner asserts repeatedly that because "the state never turned over a copy of Petitioner's 'freetalk'", that the "trial court erred by allowing the state to attempt to impeach Petitioner's wife with the 'freetalk," resulting in a violation of his constitutional rights. Petitioner further contends that he never voluntarily confessed to the alleged crimes. Petitioner alleges that the two detectives had a "vendetta" against him and lied and fabricated evidence to make him look guilty.

Although a habeas petitioner need not recite "book and verse on the federal constitution" to fairly present a claim to the state courts, *Picard v. Connor, 404 U.S. 270, 277-78, 92 S. Ct. 509, 512-13, 30 L. Ed. 2d 438 (1971)*, they must do more than present the facts necessary to support the federal claim. See *Anderson v. Harless, 459 U.S. 4, 6, 103 S. Ct. 276, 277, 74 L. Ed. 2d 3 (1982)*.

> A claim is not "fairly presented" if the state court "must read beyond a petition or a brief ...
> in order to find material" that alerts it to the presence of a federal claim. *Baldwin, 541 U.S. at*

32, 124 S. Ct. 1347 (concluding that a petitioner does not "fairly present" an issue for exhaustion purposes when the appellate judge can only discover the issue by reading a lower court opinion in the case).

Wooten v. Kirkland, 540 F.3d 1019, 1025 (9th Cir. 2008).

A "general appeal to a constitutional guarantee," such as due process, is insufficient to achieve fair presentation. *Shumway v. Payne, 223 F.3d 982, 987 (9th Cir. 2000).* Similarly, a federal claim is not exhausted merely because its factual basis was presented to the state courts on state law grounds--a "mere similarity between a claim of state and federal error is insufficient to establish exhaustion." *Id., 223 F.3d at 988* (quotations omitted); see also *Picard, 404 U.S. at 275-77.*

2. Petitioner contends the prosecutor committed misconduct by referring to Petitioner's "free talk" in direct examination and closing argument.

Petitioner presented a claim based on these facts to the Arizona state court in his direct appeal. The state court analyzed this claim pursuant to state law and held that the prosecutor's statements in closing argument did not constitute fundamental error. The state court examined the claim for fundamental error because Petitioner's counsel had not objected to the statements at trial as prosecutorial misconduct. [5] The appellate court specifically found that there was no evidence that the prosecutor was "reading" from the "freetalk" during closing argument, but concluded that the "objectionable statements appear to be the State's somewhat overzealous characterizations of Defendant's admissions to Detectives A and L as well as to some of the other evidence introduced at trial....." The appellate court also concluded that any erroneously admitted statements were not prejudicial in light of the weight of the evidence against Petitioner. Counsel did object to the statements as assuming facts not in evidence.

Petitioner is not entitled to federal habeas relief on this claim for the reasons stated with regard to his first claim for habeas relief. Petitioner did not present any federal constitutional claim to the Arizona Court of Appeals in his direct appeal with regard to the arguments raised in his second claim for federal habeas relief. When raising this claim in the state courts Petitioner's brief did not state any federal claim and did not cite any federal constitutional provision or any federal case law. Petitioner has procedurally defaulted this claim in the state courts. Because he has not shown cause for nor prejudice arising from his default of this claim, nor has Petitioner established a fundamental miscarriage of justice as that term is defined in federal habeas law, he is not entitled to relief on this claim.

3. Petitioner asserts the trial court erred by admitting a photocopy of a traffic citation at trial after the state had destroyed the original.

The state appellate court reviewed this assertion pursuant to state law, as a claim that the trial court erred in the admission of evidence. The appellate court concluded that the trial court did not abuse its discretion in admitting the evidence because the state had provided sufficient evidence of authenticity regarding the copies.

Relief on this claim is not warranted for the reasons cited with regard to Petitioner's first two claims for relief. Petitioner did not properly exhaust this claim in the state courts because he did not present a federal constitutional claim to the state courts when discussing this alleged error. When raising a similar claim in the state courts Petitioner's brief did not cite any federal constitutional provision or any federal case law. Petitioner has procedurally defaulted this claim in the state courts. Because he has not shown cause for nor prejudice arising from his default of this claim, nor has Petitioner established a fundamental miscarriage of justice will occur absent review of the claim, he is not entitled to relief on this claim.

4. The two detectives "perjured themselves" by testifying that Petitioner admitted to the crimes and to other acts.

In his reply to the answer to his petition, Petitioner allows that he did not present this claim to the state courts. Petitioner asserts that he did not present the claim to the state courts because his counsel in his direct appeal advised him that the claim was not likely to succeed.

Petitioner did not properly exhaust this claim in the state courts. Petitioner contends: "[C]ounsel ... had all the information in relationship to Ground 4 and stated that I did not have a colorful claim. Since my claim in

Ground 4 is one of the main causes that the Petitioner was convicted I believe that *Edwards v. Carpenter, 529 U.S. 446, 451, 120 S. Ct. 1587, 146 L. Ed. 2d 518 (2000)* applies." Petitioner contends that failure to review this claim will result in a fundamental miscarriage of justice, notwithstanding that the state court found the error was not fundamental.

The ineffective assistance of appellate counsel is not sufficient cause to excuse the procedural default of a claim unless the habeas petitioner exhausted an ineffective assistance of appellate counsel claim in the state courts, which Petitioner has not done. Additionally, counsel's failure to raise what counsel considers to be a losing argument is not deficient performance and is generally not prejudicial.

Petitioner has not shown cause for nor prejudice arising from his procedural default of this claim. Additionally, no fundamental miscarriage of justice will occur absent consideration of this claim because there is sufficient evidence that Petitioner was not factually innocent. Although Petitioner alleges numerous legal errors in his habeas pleadings he does not argue his factual innocence nor discuss a plausible theory regarding the other evidence introduced against him at trial.

REASONS WHY REMEDY IS HOLLOW

Though the Arizona Attorney General is aware that prosecutors in Arizona commit perjury and misconduct to convict with State courts refusing to take corrective action it refuses to notify federal courts of this.

RICKY NAPIER, Petitioner, v. CHARLES L. RYAN and ARIZONA ATTORNEY GENERAL, Respondents. CIV 09-02386 PHX ROS (MEA) UNITED STATES DISTRICT COURT FOR THE DISTRICT OF ARIZONA (Text modified for emphasis)

THE POSITION OF THE COURT

A Maricopa County grand jury indictment returned March 23, 2005, charged Petitioner with one count of first-degree murder, one count of aggravated assault, one count of first-degree burglary, and one count of armed robbery. It was alleged Petitioner shot to death a person who failed to provide change for Petitioner's purchase of twenty dollars-worth of crack-cocaine with a fifty dollar bill.

Prior to Petitioner's trial the state petitioned the trial court to grant use immunity to the victim's brother in exchange for his testimony at Petitioner's trial. After conducting a hearing, the trial court granted the requested immunity. Additionally, prior to trial the state alleged aggravating circumstances other than prior convictions.

At his trial Petitioner testified that he shot the victim in self-defense and the jury was given a self-defense instruction. Petitioner was found guilty by a jury on March 24, 2006.

On April 28, 2006, Petitioner was sentenced to a term of life in prison with the possibility of parole after 25 years pursuant to his conviction for first degree murder. Petitioner was sentenced to a concurrent presumptive term of 7.5 years imprisonment pursuant to his conviction for aggravated-assault. Petitioner was sentenced to a concurrent presumptive term of 7.5 years imprisonment pursuant to his conviction for first-degree-burglary and to a presumptive concurrent term of 10.5 years imprisonment on the armed-robbery conviction.

Petitioner took a direct appeal of his convictions and sentences. Petitioner was appointed counsel to represent him in his direct appeal. Petitioner's appointed counsel filed notice that she had "found no arguable question of law" to raise in the direct appeal "that is not frivolous." The Arizona Court of Appeals granted an extension of time for Petitioner to file a *pro se* brief and denied Petitioner's subsequent motion to change attorneys.

Petitioner's *pro se* brief in his direct appeal raised fifteen claims for relief.

1. Petitioner alleged his rights were violated because he was forced to wear a stun vest at trial and because officers threatened to shock Petitioner for no reason, citing to Gonzalez v. Pliler. Petitioner also alleged that jurors observed him in handcuffs in a courtroom hallway and that the jury observed a courtroom office assault Petitioner.

2. Petitioner alleged he was entitled to relief from his convictions because the victim's brother gave perjured testimony because he was in the country illegally; the brother was using and selling drugs; a blood test indicated the   brother had used crack cocaine; the brother admitted while testifying at Petitioner's trial that he had repeatedly lied to investigators; the brother failed to identify Petitioner as the perpetrator of the crimes at a line-up; the brother received immunity from potential drug possession charges arising from the incident in return for his testimony against Petitioner; at the time of Petitioner's trial, there were fifteen counts of armed robbery pending against the victim's brother. Petitioner cites to Pennsylvania case and Arizona Rules of Criminal Procedure. Does not mention the United States Constitution or reference any constitutional right.

3. Petitioner asserted he was entitled to relief from his convictions based on recently-passed state legislation regarding the burden of proof in a case wherein the defendant asserted self-defense. Petitioner argued the new burden of proof scheme should be applied retroactively to his case. Petitioner asserted that nothing in the United States Constitution prohibited the application of the new legislation to his case, citing the United States Supreme Court opinions in Apprendi and Blakely.

4. Petitioner maintained that the judgment against him   should be modified because there was insufficient evidence introduced at his trial to find him guilty of the charges against him. Petitioner did not cite to the United States Constitution or any federal case when asserting this argument.

5. Petitioner asserted the trial court erred by giving an incorrect instruction to the jury regarding intoxication. Petitioner alleged that Petitioner, the victim, and the victim's brother had all used drugs at the time of the crime. Petitioner did not reference the United States Constitution or any federal constitutional right in this section of his appellate brief and cited only to state court opinions in support of this argument.

6. Petitioner asserted the trial court erred by failing to give the jury an instruction regarding Arizona's "invitees law."

7. Petitioner maintained there was insufficient evidence to find him guilty on the charge of first-degree murder. Petitioner alleged that only a "scintilla" of circumstantial evidence supported the jury's verdicts. Petitioner cited to In re Winship and Jackson v. Virginia when maintaining he was entitled to relief on this basis. Petitioner asserted that the victim's brother's testimony was insufficient   evidence to support his conviction because the witness was intoxicated on crack cocaine at the time of the murder and because the witness failed to identify Petitioner as the perpetrator of the crimes in a line-up after the crimes.

8. Petitioner argued that the crimes were not properly investigated for forensic evidence. Petitioner did not cite to any federal case law or reference any federal constitutional right in raising this claim.

9. Petitioner alleged the trial court erred by allowing a gruesome photo of the victim to be displayed for thirty minutes on a large screen visible to the jury, despite the fact that the identity of the victim was not at issue. Petitioner asserted this error violated state law and his federal right to due process of law.

10. Petitioner maintained the trial court erred by limiting the cross-examination of the victim's brother to show this witness' lack of credibility. Petitioner argued this error violated his right to confront the witnesses against him, citing Crawford v. Washington.

11. Petitioner maintained the trial court erred by failing to instruct the jury on the lesser charge of manslaughter. Petitioner cited only to state law in asserting this claim   for relief.

12. "Rational Intellect of Statements". Petitioner alleged that at the time he was interviewed regarding the crimes he was in withdrawal from prescribed medications for anxiety and methadone and he had not slept in 35 hours. Petitioner did not reference any federal constitutional right or cite to any state or federal case when raising this claim for relief.

13. Petitioner asserted there was insufficient evidence to sustain his conviction on the charge of aggravated assault. Petitioner did not reference any federal constitutional right or cite to any federal case when raising this claim for relief.

14. Petitioner asserted there was insufficient evidence to sustain his conviction on the charge of first-degree burglary. Petitioner cited to In re Winship and Jackson v. Virginia when raising this claim. Petitioner asserted that the victim's brother's testimony was insufficient evidence to sustain his conviction be-

cause the witness was intoxicated on crack cocaine at the time of the murder and because the witness was awaiting trial on fifteen charges of aggravated robbery and was in the country illegally.

15. Petitioner asserted there was insufficient evidence to sustain his conviction on the charge of armed robbery. Petitioner cited to In re Winship and Jackson v. Virginia when raising this claim for relief. Petitioner asserted that the victim's brother's testimony was insufficient evidence because the witness' testimony that Petitioner took money from the victim's pockets was contradicted by a detective's testimony that money was found in the victim's pockets.

The Arizona Court of Appeals affirmed Petitioner's convictions and sentences in a memorandum decision filed June 21, 2007. The Arizona Court of Appeals reviewed the record on appeal for fundamental error. The Court of Appeals also specifically discussed and denied Petitioner's claims that his statements to investigators were involuntary; that he was mentally insufficient to stand trial; the witnesses' testimony was not credible; there was insufficient evidence of his guilt to sustain his convictions; he was forced to wear a stun belt and vest at his trial; the state was allowed to leave a gruesome picture of the victim before the jury for a half-hour; that the recent affirmative defense legislation applied to his case. The Court of Appeals stated Petitioner had not filed a supplemental pro per brief, which is in the record before this Court. The Court of Appeals evaluated the seven claims for relief raised in Petitioner's successive motions for new counsel in his appeal, filed after his appointed counsel had filed a pleading indicating she could find no meritorious issues to raise on Petitioner's behalf.

The appellate court subsequently summarily denied Petitioner's motion for reconsideration of the decision denying relief. Petitioner did not seek review of the appellate court's denial of relief in the Arizona Supreme Court.

On August 20, 2007, Petitioner initiated an action for post-conviction relief in the Maricopa County Superior Court, pursuant to Rule 32, Arizona Rules of Criminal Procedure. Petitioner was appointed counsel to represent him in his Rule 32 proceedings. In his Rule 32 action Petitioner argued the alleged use of an anonymous jury.

The Maricopa County Superior Court denied relief in Petitioner's Rule 32 action, finding his argument lacked of merit. Petitioner sought review of this decision. The Arizona Court of Appeals summarily denied review .

On December 21, 2009, Petitioner filed a federal habeas petition, raising seven claims for relief. Respondents contend that Petitioner procedurally defaulted three of his habeas claims in the state courts. Respondents assert that the other habeas claims may be denied because the Arizona Court of Appeals' decision denying those claims was not clearly contrary to nor an unreasonable application of federal law.

D. Petitioner's claims for relief

1. Petitioner's first claim for relief is "involuntariness of incriminative statements (sic)".

In the section of his habeas petition specifying facts in support of his first claim for relief, Petitioner asserts that he was not competent during his interrogation because he was in extreme pain and because he is mentally deficient. Petitioner contends that he was not competent to assist in his own defense during his interrogation. Petitioner does not cite to any provision of the United States Constitution that he believes was violated by these actions.

In his direct appeal Petitioner raised a claim similar to his first habeas claim, regarding the alleged involuntariness of Petitioner's statements to police officers investigating the crimes of conviction. However, when raising this claim in his direct appeal Petitioner did not cite to any provision of the federal constitution.

Petitioner did not "fairly present" his first federal habeas claim to the state courts as alleging the violation of a federal constitutional right. Arizona's rules regarding timeliness and the presentation of claims bar Petitioner from properly exhausting this claim at this time. Accordingly, the Court should not consider the merits of this claim absent a showing of cause and prejudice.

Petitioner has not filed a traverse to the respone to his petition. Petitioner has not shown cause for, nor prejudice arising from his procedural default of this claim. Accordingly, habeas relief may not be awarded on this claim.

2. Petitioner contends that he was denied his *Sixth Amendment* right to a fair trial because the jury was improperly instructed regarding the "right to use force in the defense of property and crime prevention."

Petitioner   failed to properly exhaust this claim by fairly presenting it to the Arizona Court of Appeals in a procedurally correct manner in his direct appeal. Petitioner raised an arguably similar claim in his pro se brief in his direct appeal, however, he did not cite any provision of the federal constitution nor did he assert the trial court's error violated his *Sixth Amendment* rights.

Petitioner did not "fairly present" his second federal habeas claim to the state courts as alleging the violation of a federal constitutional right. Arizona's rules regarding timeliness and the presentation of claims bar Petitioner from properly exhausting this claim at this time. Petitioner has not shown cause for, nor prejudice arising from his procedural default of this claim. Accordingly, habeas relief may not be awarded on this claim.

3. Petitioner alleges that he is entitled to relief because the victim's brother gave perjured testimony in exchange for immunity.

Petitioner asserts the victim's brother gave perjured testimony in return for immunity. Petitioner maintains the conclusion that the brother committed perjury is supported by the brother's testimony that he lied to police investigating the crimes.   Petitioner also alleges the brother gave inconsistent statements to police during the investigation. Petitioner also contends that the trial court improperly prohibited the defense from asserting that the brother's testimony was not believable because he had been charged with other felonies and was in the country illegally.

Petitioner failed to properly exhaust this claim by fairly presenting it to the Arizona Court of Appeals in a procedurally correct manner in his direct appeal. Petitioner raised an arguably similar claim in his pro se brief in his direct appeal, however, he did not cite any provision of the federal constitution. Petitioner echoed some of the facts he alleges in this claim in the state court in the context of his argument that there was insufficient evidence to support his convictions because this witness' testimony was perjured or unreliable, as discussed infra.

Petitioner did not "fairly present" his third federal habeas claim to the state courts as alleging the violation of a federal constitutional right. Arizona's rules regarding timeliness and the presentation of claims bar Petitioner from properly exhausting this claim at this time. Petitioner has not shown cause   for, nor prejudice arising from his procedural default of this claim. Accordingly, habeas relief may not be awarded on this claim.

4. Petitioner asserts he is entitled to relief from his convictions because there was insufficient evidence to find him guilty of the crimes.

Petitioner argues that, because the state's case against him was predicated on the brother's victim's testimony, which he asserts was perjured, there was insufficient evidence to find him guilty on the counts of conviction. Petitioner contends "the State's whole case was [based on the testimony of Gasp[e]r" whose "credibility and reliability ... should in no way be enough" to support Petitioner's conviction on all four counts.

Petitioner raised this claim in his direct appeal. The Arizona Court of Appeals denied relief on this claim, enumerating the reasons why a reasonable jury could conclude that Petitioner was guilty beyond a reasonable doubt.

The Arizona Court of Appeals' determination that there was sufficient evidence to find Petitioner guilty on all the counts of conviction was not clearly contrary to federal law.

"[T]he *Due Process Clause* protects the accused against conviction   except upon proof beyond a reasonable doubt of every fact necessary to constitute the crime with which he is charged." *In re Winship, 397 U.S. 358, 364, 90 S. Ct. 1068, 1073, 25 L. Ed. 2d 368 (1970)*. To determine whether sufficient evidence was introduced at trial to support a habeas petitioner's conviction, the Court must decide if, "viewing the evidence in the light most favorable to the prosecution, any rational trier of fact could have found the essential elements of the crime beyond a reasonable doubt." *Jackson v. Virginia, 443 U.S. 307, 319, 99 S. Ct. 2781, 2789, 61 L. Ed. 2d 560 (1979)*. See also *McDaniel v. Brown, 558 U.S. 120, 130 S. Ct. 665, 673, 175 L. Ed. 2d 582 (2010)*; *McMillan v. Gomez, 19 F.3d 465, 468-469 (9th Cir. 1994)*.

Under this standard, a federal habeas court faced with a record of historical facts that supports conflicting inferences must presume--even if it does not appear affirmatively in the record--that the trier of fact resolved any such conflicts in favor of the prosecution, and must defer to that resolution. *Jackson, 443 U.S. at 326, 99 S. Ct. at 2793*. See also *McDaniel, 130 S. Ct. at 673*.

> [I]t is the province of the jury to resolve conflicts in the testimony, to weigh the evidence, and to draw reasonable inferences from basic   facts to ultimate facts.[] As the Ninth Circuit has explained, The question is not whether we are personally convinced beyond a reasonable doubt. It is whether rational jurors could reach the conclusion that these jurors reached.[] While mere suspicion or speculation cannot be the basis for creation of logical inferences... [c]ircumstantial evidence and inferences drawn from it may be sufficient to sustain a conviction.

Atwood v. Schriro, 489 F. Supp. 2d 982, 1002-03 (D. Ariz. 2007) (internal citations and quotations omitted).

Petitioner bears the burden of proving that the record is so totally devoid of evidentiary support for the challenged conviction as to violate due process. See *Crow v. Eyman, 459 F.2d 24, 25 (9th Cir. 1972)*. Circumstantial evidence is sufficient to support a petitioner's guilty verdict. *Jackson, 443 U.S. at 324-25, 99 S. Ct. at 2792*; *Jones v. Wood, 207 F.3d 557, 563 (9th Cir. 2000)* (finding sufficient evidence to support a murder conviction when the evidence was almost entirely circumstantial and relatively weak); *Sera v. Norris, 400 F.3d 538, 547 (8th Cir. 2005)*. In reviewing a sufficiency of the evidence claim, a federal habeas court must defer to the trier of   fact with respect to issues of conflicting testimony, weight of the evidence, and the credibility of the witnesses. *Jackson, 443 U.S. at 319, 99 S. Ct. at 2789*.

Petitioner does not allege that he did not shoot the victim, but asserts that he acted in self-defense. At his trial, Petitioner testified that he acted in self-defense and the victim's brother testified Petitioner did not act in self-defense. The jury heard the testimony and rendered a verdict in accordance with its determination of credibility. Because the issue of evidentiary sufficiency involved witness credibility, the state court's determination that there was sufficient evidence to find Petitioner guilty was not clearly contrary to federal law nor an unreasonable application of federal law.

5. Petitioner contends the trial court committed fundamental error in his criminal proceedings because the jury observed him wearing a stun belt and vest. Petitioner asserts he had a constitutional right to be free of restraint during his trial.

In his fifth habeas claim, Petitioner argues that fundamental error occurred during his trial "because he had to wear a stun belt and vest in front of the jury" which "took away the defendant's   presumption of innocen[ce] until[] proven guilty in the eyes of the jury..." Petitioner asserts that use of the belt and vest were "in no way warranted".

Petitioner raised this claim in his direct appeal. The Arizona Court of Appeals rejected the claim on the grounds that Petitioner failed to object to the use of the belt or vest at trial. The appellate court also found Petitioner had not argued or show prejudice from the alleged error on appeal. The appellate court determined Petitioner's ability to communicate with counsel was not actually impacted and that the record failed to show the jury was aware of any use of restraints. This decision was not clearly contrary to federal law nor an unreasonable application of federal law.

All of the federal cases which discuss habeas relief based on a shackling claim state that, to succeed on this type of claim, the petitioner must show that the physical restraints 'had substantial and injurious effect or influence in determining the jury's verdict..." *Rhoden v. Rowland, 172 F.3d 633, 636 (9th Cir. 1999)*. See also *Holbrook v. Flynn, 475 U.S. 560, 568-69, 106 S. Ct. 1340, 1345, 89 L. Ed. 2d 525 (1986)*. To be entitled to habeas relief on this claim the District Court must conclude that the jury saw or was aware of the restraint and that the restraint was not justified by state interests. See *Ghent v. Woodford, 279 F.3d 1121, 1132 (9th Cir. 2002)*. Additionally, for unjustified restraint to rise to the level of a constitutional trial error, Petitioner must establish that he suffered prejudice as a result of the restraint. See id.; *Williams v. Woodford, 384 F.3d 567, 592-93 (9th Cir. 2004)*; *Gonzalez v. Pliler, 341 F.3d 897, 903 (9th Cir. 2003)*. See also *Dyas v. Poole, 317 F.3d 934, 936-37 (9th Cir. 2003)*.

Petitioner has not established that the jury saw the restraints, that he was unable to communicate with his counsel as a result of the restraints, or that he was otherwise prejudiced by the restraints. See *Williams, 384 F.3d at 592-93; Packer v. Hill, 291 F.3d 569, 583 (9th Cir. 2002)* (concluding no prejudice resulted from the defendant's leg brace when no juror interviewed after trial remembered seeing a leg brace on the defendant); *Rich v. Calderon, 187 F.3d 1064, 1069 (9th Cir. 1999)*. Accordingly, the state court's conclusion that Petitioner's constitutional rights were not violated by the use of the restraints is not clearly   contrary to federal law and Petitioner is not entitled to habeas relief on this claim.

6. Petitioner argues that his right to a fair trial was violated because "gruesome photographs of victim Carlos" were allegedly "left on a big screen for thirty to forty minutes during the trial[.]"

Petitioner states that, because he did not contest the victim's identity or the fact of the shooting, the pictures of the victim exhibited to the jury carried "no value," and that the pictures were "highly inflammatory," and, consequently, that showing the pictures prejudiced the jury.

Generally, the admissibility of evidence is a matter of state law which is not cognizable in a federal habeas proceeding. See, e.g., *Estelle, 502 U.S. at 67--68, 112 S. Ct. at 479-80; Middleton v. Cupp, 768 F.2d 1083, 1085 (9th Cir. 1985)*. Standing alone, the failure to comply with state rules of evidence is not a sufficient basis for granting federal habeas relief, i.e., such a failure is not equivalent to a deprivation of the federal constitutional right to due process of law. See, e.g., *Jammal v. Van de Kamp, 926 F.2d 918, 919--20 (9th Cir. 1991)*. A due process violation occurs only if there was no permissible inferences   that the jury could draw from the evidence. *Id., 926 F.3d at 920*.

To rise to the level of a constitutional violation, the introduced evidence must be of such quality as necessarily prevents a fair trial. Id., quoting *Kealohapauole v. Shimoda, 800 F.2d 1463, 1465 (9th Cir. 1986)*.

> The essence of our inquiry under the *Fifth, Sixth*, and *Eighth Amendments*, as applied to the states under the *Fourteenth Amendment*, is whether the admission of the photographs rendered the proceedings fundamentally unfair. See *Jackson v. Shanks, 143 F.3d 1313, 1322 (10th Cir.)* ("[D]ue process arguments relating to the admissibility of the victims' ... autopsy photos ... will not support habeas relief 'absent fundamental unfairness so as to constitute a denial of due process of law.'" (quoting *Martin v. Kaiser, 907 F.2d 931, 934 (10th Cir. 1990)))*... "[W]e approach the fundamental fairness analysis with 'considerable self-restraint.' *Jackson, 143 F.3d at 1322* (quoting *United States v. Rivera, 900 F.2d 1462, 1477 (10th Cir. 1990)* (en banc)). .... Given the probative nature of the photographs, the gruesome character of the crime itself, and the wealth of additional evidence supporting defendant's convictions, the   admission of the photographs was not so unduly prejudicial as to render the proceedings against petitioner fundamentally unfair. See *Jackson, 143 F.3d at 1322*. Consequently, petitioner is not entitled to relief on this ground.

> *Smallwood v. Gibson, 191 F.3d 1257, 1275 (10th Cir. 1999)*.

Although Petitioner asserts the photographs were admitted solely to inflame the jury, there was at least one permissible inference the jury could draw from the photographs, i.e., premeditation. Accordingly, the admission of the autopsy photographs did not violate Petitioner's right to due process of law and Petitioner is not entitled to federal habeas relief on the merits of this claim. See *Gerlaugh v. Lewis, 898 F. Supp. 1388, 1409--10 (D. Ariz. 1995)* (holding the autopsy photographs at issue were not so inflammatory or prejudicial as to render the trial fundamentally unfair).

7. Petitioner argues that the "recent amendments to Arizona's affirmative defense and justification statutes apply to his offenses, due to the circumstances of his case."

Petitioner asserted in his direct appeal that he was entitled to a new trial applying the recently-changed system for allocating the burden of proof in a case wherein   the issue of self-defense was raised. In his direct appeal Petitioner asserted federal law did not prohibit the retroactive application of the state statute to provide relief from his convictions.

In response to Petitioner's claim on direct appeal, the Arizona Court of Appeals followed the Arizona Supreme Court's interpretation of the state law and found the statutory changes inapplicable to Petitioner's case:

> Napier appears to argue that recent amendments to Arizona's affirmative defense and justification statutes apply to his criminal offenses which were committed before the effective date of the new statutes. Our supreme court has already held that these amendments, shifting the burden of proof to the State to disprove such defenses, do not apply to crimes committed before the statutory amendments' effective date of April 24, 2006. *Garcia v. Browning [(State of Arizona)], 214 Ariz. 250, 254, ¶ 20, 151 P.3d 533, 537 (2007).* Napier's offenses were committed on or about the [date of] March 13, 2005. The changes in the criminal code do not apply here.

Petitioner committed the crimes enumerated in the indictment on or about March 13, 2005, and, accordingly, his case   was not pending when the statute was changed on April 24, 2006. However, even if state law did render the statutory changes retroactive to Petitioner's case, an alleged violation of a state's own criminal law does not present a cognizable federal habeas claim.

REASONS WHY REMEDY IS HOLLOW

Aware that in Arizona prosecutors use as a matter of routine practice perjured testimony to convict and police take statements when defendants are medicated unable to know what they are saying, the Attorney General concealed this evidence.

> **James E. Young, Petitioner, v. Charles L. Ryan, Arizona Attorney General, Respondents. No. CV 13-02624 PHX GMS (MEA) UNITED STATES DISTRICT COURT FOR THE DISTRICT OF ARIZONA**
> **(Text modified for emphasis)**

THE POSITION OF THE COURT

On December 8, 2000, Petitioner was indicted on one count of first degree murder, which indictment alleged Petitioner caused the premeditated death of his estranged common-law wife on October 17, 2000. Petitioner was apprehended and arrested on this charge on June 13, 2001. Petitioner was represented by retained counsel at his criminal trial. A jury found Petitioner guilty as charged. On March 15, 2002, pursuant to this conviction, Petitioner was sentenced to a term of natural life imprisonment.

Petitioner took a timely direct appeal of his conviction and sentence. On January 30, 2003, the Arizona Court of Appeals affirmed Petitioner's conviction but remanded his case for resentencing, having found that Petitioner was incorrectly sentenced pursuant to *Arizona Revised Statutes § 13-702* rather than *section 13-703*. On January 28, 2005, Petitioner was re-sentenced to a term of life imprisonment with the possibility of parole after 25 years.

Before he was resentenced Petitioner initiated a state action for post-conviction relief pursuant to *Rule 32*, Arizona Rules of Criminal Procedure. Although the action was initially dismissed as premature, on November 19, 2004, on Petitioner's motion, the trial court reinstated Petitioner's *Rule 32* action. Petitioner was represented by counsel in his *Rule 32* proceedings. In his *Rule 32* action Petitioner asserted, *inter alia*, that his trial counsel was ineffective because of her deteriorating health during his trial and her continuing use of prescription drugs for her deteriorating health during his trial. Petitioner also asserted that phone records admitted at his trial were incorrect. In an order entered December 12, 2008, the state trial court granted post-conviction relief "on the grounds of unconstitutional ineffective assistance of counsel." The state trial court vacated Petitioner's conviction and sentence, reinstated the original charge against Petitioner, and ordered a new trial.

A jury found Petitioner guilty as charged after a second trial on the charge of first degree murder. Petitioner filed a motion seeking a new trial asserting that the verdict was contrary to the weight of the evidence, that he was subjected to prosecutorial misconduct, and that the trial court's evidentiary rulings violated Petitioner's right to due process of law. After hearing argument on the motion for new trial, the trial court denied the motion.

On December 3, 2010, Petitioner was again sentenced to a term of life imprisonment with the possibility of parole after 25 years, and given credit for 3,461 days of pre-sentence incarceration.

Petitioner took a timely direct appeal of his second conviction and sentencing. Petitioner argued that the trial court erred when it denied Petitioner's motions to dismiss the charges against him or remand the matter to the grand jury because the prosecution had presented false or misleading testimony to the grand jury. Petitioner also asserted that the trial court erred when it denied Petitioner's motion for a new trial. Petitioner alleged that he was entitled to a new trial because there was insufficient evidence to support his conviction. Petitioner further maintained he was entitled to a new trial because the prosecutor engaged in misconduct, including a failure to provide the defense with the substance of testimony presented to the jury and the prosecutor's repeated referral to Petitioner's silence in her closing argument. Petitioner further asserted that the trial court's cumulative errors deprived him of a fundamentally fair trial.

Thirteen days after Petitioner's opening brief in his direct appeal was docketed Petitioner filed a *pro per* motion to withdraw the brief, arguing that he was "aware that he will forever be barred if all issues not listed in this opening brief." The Arizona Court of Appeals denied the motion to withdraw the brief and instructed Petitioner that his counsel "need not raise every issue on appeal requested by appellant" and that, "after the conclusion of this appeal," if Petitioner believed that his appellate counsel was ineffective, he could "file a petition for post-conviction relief pursuant to the *Arizona Rule of Criminal Procedure 32*."

The Arizona Court of Appeals affirmed Petitioner's conviction and sentence in a memorandum decision entered July 10, 2012. *Inter alia*, noting that a conviction may rest on circumstantial evidence, the Court of Appeals stated: "Our review of the evidence finds it more than sufficient to permit a finder of fact to conclude beyond a reasonable doubt that Young murdered S.C." The court further found that Petitioner had raised two distinct claims of prosecutorial misconduct. With regard to Petitioner's argument that the prosecutor failed to disclose the content of a witness' testimony as required by *Rule 15.1*, Arizona Rules of Criminal Procedure, the appellate court found no abuse of discretion in allowing this testimony. The Court of Appeals also concluded "there [was] nothing improper in a prosecutor commenting on silence that is not *Miranda*-induced," noting "there was nothing improper in the prosecutor reminding the jury that Young made efforts to avoid the police following the murder..." The appellate court informed Petitioner that a petition for review to the Arizona Supreme Court was due on or before August 14, 2012. On August 24, 2012, because no petition for review had been filed, the Arizona Court of Appeals issued a mandate in Petitioner's direct appeal.

On August 28, 2012, Petitioner filed a *pro per* motion in the Arizona Court of Appeals "advising court of due process of law. Violation of Appellant's appeal by court & court appointed counsel," alleging that the state trial courts and the prosecutors of abusing their power and disregarding the rules of the court. Respondents aver that the Arizona Court of Appeals did not rule on this motion.

On March 11, 2013, Petitioner filed a notice pursuant to *Rule 32*, Arizona Rules of Criminal Procedure, acknowledging that it was untimely. Petitioner alleged in his *Rule 32* notice:

> State has tried Defendant in violation of Double [Jeopardy] Clause since Judge Contes reversed conviction after finding of Grand Jury Indictment was based on False misleading statements of fact by Det. Laird. Prosecutorial misconduct continued prosecution misconduct. Police malfeasence (sic), fraud, perjury. Falsifing (sic) evidence by state, selective prosecution, judicial bias & prejudice. State attorney threatening and intimidation defence (sic) witness Valerie Smith on CD. Judge Contes violated Rules of Court & letter of law to protect 2 other Judges.

The state trial court interpreted these claims as an allegation that Petitioner's conviction and sentence were obtained in violation of his constitutional rights, i.e., his right to be free of double jeopardy, as a claim of prosecutorial misconduct, a claim of police misconduct and perjury, and a claim of judicial bias and prejudice.

On April 2, 2013, the trial court dismissed Petitioner's *Rule 32* action as untimely because it was not filed within thirty days of the issuance of a final order or mandate of the appellate court in a direct appeal; in this matter the mandate was issued August 24, 2012, and the *Rule 32* notice received March 11, 2013. The court noted that Petitioner had not asserted a claim which could be properly stated in an untimely or successive *Rule 32* proceeding.

On May 24, 2013, Petitioner filed a *pro per* motion for reconsideration of the trial court's decision in his *Rule 32* action, asking permission to file an untimely *Rule 32* petition and seeking the appointment of counsel. Petitioner argued that his *Rule 32* action was untimely because he is not an attorney and because he was "unaware of the Rules concerning time frames for filing a notice, of his intention to file a *Rule 32- PCR* appeal." On August 9, 2013, the state trial court denied the motion for reconsideration, finding that Petitioner had raised no cognizable basis for reconsideration, that he was not entitled to advisory counsel to pursue an untimely *Rule 32* proceeding, and that his "claim of actual innocence is a conclusory statement unsupported by demonstrated facts, sworn testimony or required evidence."

In his federal habeas petition docketed December 23, 2013, Petitioner asserts he is factually and actually innocent of the crime of conviction, that he was subjected to double jeopardy, and that the prosecutor engaged in misconduct, depriving Petitioner of his right to due process of law. Petitioner further contends that exculpatory evidence was destroyed and that witnesses provided perjured testimony at his trial. Petitioner also alleges that he was denied his right to the effective assistance of trial counsel. Petitioner maintains he is "not a lawyer and ha[s] no legal training or understanding of law or rules."

Respondents assert: "This Court should dismiss, with prejudice, the remainder of Petitioner's habeas petition because: it is untimely; it does not raise claims that are cognizable in federal habeas; and all but two of Petitioner's subclaims are unexhausted..."

II Statute of limitations

The petition seeking a writ of habeas corpus is barred by the applicable statute of limitations found in the Antiterrorism and Effective Death Penalty Act ("AEDPA"). The AEDPA imposed a one-year statute of limitations on state prisoners seeking federal habeas relief from their state convictions. See, e.g., *Doe v. Busby, 661 F.3d 1001, 1011 (9th Cir. 2011); Espinoza Matthews v. California, 432 F.3d 1021, 1025 (9th Cir. 2005); Lott v. Mueller, 304 F.3d 918, 920 (9th Cir. 2002)*. The one-year statute of limitations on habeas petitions generally begins to run on "the date on which the judgment became final by conclusion of direct review or the expiration of the time for seeking such review." *28 U.S.C. § 2244(d)(1)(A)*. See also *Doe, 661 F.3d at 1011*.

Petitioner's conviction became final on August 14, 2012, when the time expired for seeking review by the Arizona Supreme Court of the Arizona Court of Appeals' decision denying relief in Petitioner's direct appeal. The one-year statute of limitations regarding Petitioner's claims for federal habeas relief began to run on August 14, 2012, and expired on August 13, 2013. Petitioner's federal habeas action, docketed on December 23, 2013, is not timely filed.

The AEDPA provides that a petitioner is entitled to tolling of the statute of limitations during the pendency of a "properly filed application for state post-conviction or other collateral review with respect to the pertinent judgment or claim." *28 U.S.C. § 2244(d)(2)*. See also *Artuz v. Bennett, 531 U.S. 4, 8, 121 S. Ct. 361, 363-64, 148 L. Ed. 2d 213 (2000); Stewart v. Cate, 757 F.3d 929, 934-35 (9th Cir.), cert. denied, 135 S. Ct. 341, 190 L. Ed. 2d 187 (2014); Harris v. Carter, 515 F.3d 1051, 1053 (9th Cir. 2008)*. "The time during which a properly filed application for State post conviction or other collateral review with respect to the pertinent judgment or claim is pending shall not be counted toward" the limitations period. *28 U.S.C. § 2244(d)(2)*. A state post-conviction petition is "clearly pending after it is filed with a state court, but before that court grants or denies the petition." *Chavis v. Lemarque, 382 F.3d 921, 925 (9th Cir. 2004)*. However, a state petition that is not filed within the state's required time limit is not "properly filed" and, therefore, the petitioner is not entitled to statutory tolling of the federal statute of limitations during the time such a petition is "pending" in the state courts. See *Pace v. DiGuglielmo, 544 U.S. 408, 413, 125 S. Ct. 1807, 1811-12, 161 L. Ed. 2d 669 (2005)*. "When a postconviction petition is untimely under state law, 'that [is] the end of the matter' for purposes of § 2244(d)(2)." *Id., 544 U.S. at 414, 125 S. Ct. at 1812*.

Petitioner's untimely state action for post-conviction relief pursuant to *Rule 32*, Arizona Rules of Criminal Procedure, did not toll the statute of limitations because the state court determined it was untimely as a matter of state law. See *Allen v. Siebert, 552 U.S. 3, 5-6, 128 S.Ct. 2, 3-4, 169 L. Ed. 2d 329 (2007); Cross v. Sisto, 676 F.3d 1172, 1176 (9th Cir. 2012).*

In his reply to the answer to his petition, Petitioner asserts that evidence was not provided to the grand jury and that this evidence was discovered eight years after the grand jury issued the original indictment. Petitioner alleges that the County Attorney and the Phoenix Police Department withheld evidence from the defense and that DNA testing was not performed on some evidence. Petitioner alleges that he was convicted as a result of cumulative prosecutorial misconduct, including "witness tampering" and "witness intimidation." Petitioner asserts his ability to take an appeal of his conviction and sentences was hindered when he was denied transcripts and copies of pleadings. Petitioner alleges he was subjected to police malfeasance and that evidence favorable to him was improperly suppressed. Petitioner alleges that a police detective who testified in his grand jury proceedings was later terminated by the police department and found to have committed acts of fraud. Petitioner maintains he was subjected to judicial bias and prejudice. Petitioner further contends that he could not timely pursue post-conviction relief because he was not informed by his counsel or the courts as to the deadline for pursuing this avenue of relief.

Petitioner has not stated an adequate basis for equitable tolling of the statute of limitations. Compare *Holland, 130 S. Ct. at 2564; Porter, 620 F.3d at 961* (noting the circumstances of cases determined before and after Holland). A petitioner's pro se status, ignorance of the law, and lack of legal representation during the applicable filing period do not constitute circumstances justifying equitable tolling because such circumstances are not "extraordinary." See, e.g., *Chaffer, 592 F.3d at 1048-49; Waldron-Ramsey, 556 F.3d at 1011-14; Rasberry v. Garcia, 448 F.3d 1150, 1154 (9th Cir. 2006); Shoemate v. Norris, 390 F.3d 595, 598 (8th Cir. 2004).* The vicissitudes of prison life are not "extraordinary" circumstances that make it impossible to file a timely habeas petition. See, e.g., *Ramirez v. Yates, 571 F.3d 993, 997 (9th Cir. 2009).* Although Petitioner contends he was not informed by his counsel or the courts as to the deadlines for pursuing post-conviction relief pursuant to *Rule 32*, Arizona Rules of Criminal Procedure, the record indicates that Petitioner was informed of the requirements of this rule.

The Ninth Circuit Court of Appeals has held that a petitioner is entitled to tolling of the statute of limitations if they can establish that they are actually innocent of the crimes of conviction. See *Lee, 653 F.3d at 934.*

> "Actual innocence, if proved, serves as a gateway through which a petitioner may pass whether the impediment is a procedural bar ... [or] expiration of the statute of limitations." *McQuiggin v. Perkins,[], 133 S. Ct. 1924, 1928, 185 L. Ed. 2d 1019,[] (2013).* When an otherwise time-barred habeas petitioner "presents evidence of innocence so strong that a court cannot have confidence in the outcome of the trial unless the court is also satisfied that the trial was free of non-harmless constitutional error," the Court may consider the petition on the merits. See *Schlup v. Delo, 513 U.S. 298, 115 S. Ct. 851, 130 L. Ed. 2d 808,* [] (1995). The Supreme Court has recently cautioned, however, that "tenable actual-innocence gateway pleas are rare." *McQuiggin, 133 S. Ct. at 1928.* "[A] petitioner does not meet the threshold requirement unless he persuades the district court that, in light of the new evidence, no juror, acting reasonably, would have voted to find him guilty beyond a reasonable doubt." *Id.*

Stewart, 757 F.3d at 937-38.

Petitioner's argument of "actual innocence" is predicated on the assertion that there was insufficient evidence, as a matter of law, to sustain his conviction. Petitioner has not made a showing of any new evidence. The phone records which Petitioner asserts are exculpatory were previously considered by the state trial court and resulted, in part, in Petitioner's retrial. The accuracy of the records and the legitimacy and credibility of the record evidence and the investigative efforts was thoroughly challenged on cross-examination in Petitioner's second trial. Petitioner does not present evidence of the existence of suppressed exculpatory evidence, other than Petitioner's own conclusory statement regarding the existence of this evidence and its alleged suppression. Accordingly, Petitioner is not entitled to tolling of the statute of limitations based on the theory of actual innocence.

Because the habeas action was not filed within the statute of limitations and Petitioner has not stated a proper basis for equitable tolling of the statute of limitations, the Court need not consider the merits of his claims.

The Arizona Court of Appeals found relief on the merits of the claims raised in Petitioner's *Rule 32* action was barred by Petitioner's failure to comply with the provisions of *Rule 32.9(c)*, Arizona Rules of Criminal Procedure, which require:

> The petition or cross-petition for review shall comply with the form requirements of *Rule 31.12* of these rules and contain a caption setting forth the name of the appellate court, the title of the case, a space for the appellate court case number, the trial court case number and a brief descriptive title. An original and seven copies of the petition and an original and one copy of the appendix, if any, shall be filed if review is being sought in the Supreme Court. An original and four copies of the petition and an original and one copy of the appendix, if any, shall be filed if review is being sought in the Court of Appeals. An original and one copy shall be filed if review is being sought in the superior court. The parties shall be designated as in the trial court proceedings. The petition or cross-petition shall not exceed 20 pages, exclusive of the appendix, shall not have a cover or be bound, but shall be fastened with a single staple in the upper left corner, and shall contain the following:
>
> (i) Copies of the trial court's rulings entered pursuant to *rules 32.6(c), 32.8(d)* and *32.9(b)*.
>
> (ii) The issues which were decided by the trial court and which the defendant wishes to present to the appellate court for review.
>
> (iii) The facts material to a consideration of the issues presented for review.
>
> (iv) The reasons why the petition should be granted. In capital cases all references to the record in the trial court shall be supported by an appendix, with appropriate copies of the portions of the record which support the petition. The petition shall not incorporate any document by reference, except the appendices. If the appendices exclusive of the trial court's rulings exceed 15 pages in length, such appendices shall be fastened together separately from the petition and the copies of the trial court's rulings.

Review of the merits of a procedurally defaulted habeas claim is required if the petitioner demonstrates review of the merits of the claim is necessary to prevent a fundamental miscarriage of justice. See *Dretke v. Haley, 541 U.S. 386, 393, 124 S. Ct. 1847, 1852, 158 L. Ed. 2d 659 (2004); Schlup v. Delo, 513 U.S. 298, 316, 115 S. Ct. 851, 861, 130 L. Ed. 2d 808 (1995); Murray v. Carrier, 477 U.S. 478, 485-86, 106 S. Ct. 2639, 2649, 91 L. Ed. 2d 397 (1986)*. A fundamental miscarriage of justice occurs only when a constitutional violation has probably resulted in the conviction of one who is factually innocent. See *Murray, 477 U.S. at 485-86, 106 S. Ct. at 2649; Thomas v. Goldsmith, 979 F.2d 746, 749 (9th Cir. 1992)* (showing of factual innocence is necessary to trigger manifest injustice relief). To satisfy the "fundamental miscarriage of justice" standard, a petitioner must establish by clear and convincing evidence that no reasonable fact-finder could have found him guilty of the offenses charged. See *Dretke, 541 U.S. at 393, 124 S. Ct. at 1852; Wildman v. Johnson, 261 F.3d 832, 842-43 (9th Cir. 2001)*.

The only claims properly exhausted in the state courts were the claims Petitioner presented to the Arizona Court of Appeals in his direct appeal, i.e., that there was insufficient evidence to sustain Petitioner's conviction and that prosecutorial misconduct deprived him of his right to due process of law. With regard to these claims, the state appellate court found: "Our review of the evidence finds it more than sufficient to permit a finder of fact to conclude beyond a reasonable doubt that Young murdered S.C. The court further found that Petitioner had raised two distinct claims of prosecutorial misconduct. With regard to Petitioner's argument that the prosecutor failed to disclose the content of a witness' testimony as required by *Rule 15.1*, Arizona Rules of Criminal Procedure, the appellate court found no abuse of discretion in allowing this testimony. The Court of Appeals also concluded "there [was] nothing improper in a prosecutor commenting on silence that is not *Miranda-* induced," noting "there was nothing improper in the prosecutor reminding the jury that Young made efforts to avoid the police following the murder..."

Petitioner's claim that he was subjected to double jeopardy was raised and denied based on procedural grounds in Petitioner's *Rule 32* action. Petitioner's assertion that he was denied his right to the effective assistance of trial counsel was not raised in the state courts and, because he may not now raise that claim in the state courts the claim is precluded. Petitioner did not properly exhaust these federal habeas claims in the state courts by fairly presenting them to the state courts in a procedurally correct manner.

As noted *supra*, in reply to the answer to his petition, which answer asserts Petitioner procedurally defaulted some of his claims in the state courts, Petitioner asserts, *inter alia*, that his ability to take an appeal of his conviction and sentences was hindered when he was denied transcripts and copies of pleadings and that he could not timely pursue post-conviction relief because he was not informed by his counsel or the courts as to the deadline for pursuing this avenue of relief.

Because Petitioner failed to properly exhaust these claims and has not shown cause for, nor prejudice arising from his default of the claims, the Court should not consider the merits of the claims.

B. Petitioner's prosecutorial misconduct claim

With regard to Petitioner's argument that the prosecutor failed to disclose the content of a witness' testimony as required by *Rule 15.1*, Arizona Rules of Criminal Procedure, the appellate court found no abuse of discretion in allowing this testimony. The Court of Appeals also concluded "there [was] nothing improper in a prosecutor commenting on silence that is not *Miranda*-induced," noting "there was nothing improper in the prosecutor reminding the jury that Young made efforts to avoid the police following the murder..."

On habeas review of a prosecutorial misconduct claim, the Court may grant relief only if the misconduct rises to the level of a due process violation--not because the Court might disapprove of the prosecutor's behavior. *Towery v. Schriro, 641 F.3d 300, 306 (9th Cir. 2010)*. See also *Sechrest v. Ignacio, 549 F.3d 789, 807 (9th Cir. 2008)*.

> When a petitioner makes a claim of prosecutorial misconduct, the touchstone of due process analysis... is the fairness of the trial, not the culpability of the prosecutor. On habeas review, [the Court's] role is to determine whether the conduct was so egregious as to render the entire trial fundamentally unfair.

Serra v. Michigan Dep't of Corr., 4 F.3d 1348, 1355 (6th Cir. 1993) (citation and internal quotation marks omitted).A constitutional violation arising from prosecutorial misconduct does not warrant habeas relief if the error is harmless. See *Sandoval v. Calderon, 241 F.3d 765, 778 (9th Cir. 2000)*. When a state court has found a constitutional error to be harmless beyond a reasonable doubt, a federal court may not grant habeas relief unless the state court's determination is objectively unreasonable. See *Mitchell v. Esparza, 540 U.S. 12, 17-18, 124 S.Ct. 7, 11-12, 157 L. Ed. 2d 263 (2003); Cooper v. Brown, 510 F.3d 870, 921 (9th Cir. 2007)*. Although the Arizona Court of Appeals did not specifically address whether Petitioner's federal due process rights were violated, it found that the prosecutor's alleged misconduct did not contribute to the verdict. This decision was not clearly contrary to nor an objectively unreasonable application of federal law. See *Towery, 641 F.3d at 307*.

In this matter, Petitioner did not allege in the state courts that evidence was suppressed, but instead argued that the prosecutor erred by not timely disclosing the content of the proffered testimony in violation of a local rule of criminal procedure. Such an error does not rise to the level of a due process violation because Petitioner's counsel was still able to cross-examine the witness.

Petitioner also asserted that he was denied his right to due process because the prosecutor commented to the jury of Petitioner's pre-Miranda silence. The state court did not err in finding Petitioner's right to due process was not violated in this regard. The Supreme Court recently held that prosecutors may use a defendant's pre-arrest silence as substantive evidence of his guilt if the defendant did not expressly invoke his right to remain silent. See *Salinas v. Texas, 133 S.Ct. 2174, 2179, 2184, 186 L. Ed. 2d 376 (2013)*. In this matter Petitioner evaded police knowing that he was a suspect in the death of S.C. The Circuit Courts of Appeal have concluded that a prosecutor's reference to a defendant's pre and post arrest, pre-Miranda statements does not violate the defendant's constitutional rights. See *Buckner v. Polk, 453 F.3d 195, 208 (4th Cir. 2006)*; *Bland v. Sirmons, 459 F.3d 999, 1023 (10th Cir. 2006)*. See also *Jenkins v. Anderson, 447 U.S. 231, 238, 100 S.Ct. 2124, 2129, 65 L. Ed. 2d 86 (1980)*; *United States v. Beckman, 298 F.3d 788 (9th Cir. 2002)*. The prosecutor's comments to this effect were not a violation of Petitioner's right to be free of self-incrimination or due process and the state court did not err in so holding.

REASONS WHY REMEDY IS HOLLOW

As a matter of practice Arizona prosecutors conceal evidence and tamper with witnesses/evidence to convict. State courts refuse to do anything and the Attorney General conceals this evidence of a systemic problem from federal courts.

Khalil Shakur, Petitioner, v. Charles Ryan, Arizona Attorney General, Respondents. CIV 11-02169 PHX FJM (MEA)UNITED STATES DISTRICT COURT FOR THE DISTRICT OF ARIZONA
(Text modified for emphasis)

THE POSITION OF THE COURT

In a direct complaint entered August 13, 2007, Petitioner, named as Eric Thomas, was charged by a grand jury indictment with one count of trafficking in the identity of another. On September 14, 2007, a preliminary hearing was ordered. Petitioner and a co-defendant were charged with selling a debit card to two undercover police officers for $80.

On September 18, 2007, a grand jury indictment was returned charging Petitioner with one count of trafficking in the identity of another. That same date the state moved to vacate the preliminary hearing, which motion was granted.

On December 12, 2007, the state amended the indictment to allege Petitioner had previously been convicted of seven felonies. Petitioner was tried before a jury, which found him guilty as charged on February 7, 2008. The state initially alleged a 2007 pending charge for possession of marijuana and a 1997 conviction for aggravated assault, in addition to two convictions for possession of narcotics in 1992 and 1988, and four other convictions occurring between 1979 and 1986. Two pre-trial settlement conferences were conducted with two different commissioners and at both conferences Petitioner indicated he was not interested in a plea agreement regardless of the sentence he faced if found guilty.

At sentencing, in return for the state recommending a "super-mitigated" sentence, Petitioner stipulated that he had two prior convictions. The trial court sentenced Petitioner to an "exceptionally mitigated" sentence of 10.5 years in prison.

Petitioner took a timely direct appeal of his conviction and sentence. On October 23, 2008, Petitioner's appointed appellate counsel informed the Arizona Court of Appeals that counsel had found no legitimate argument to raise on Petitioner's behalf. Counsel averred to the Court of Appeals that he had contacted Petitioner "soliciting suggested issues," and that Petitioner had identified the following issues that he wished to raise on appeal:

1. Petitioner's rights were violated when his preliminary hearing was vacated and his case presented to the grand jury;
2. Petitioner's right to the effective assistance of counsel was violated;
3. Petitioner's constitutional rights were violated by the state's selective and vindictive prosecution; and
4. Petitioner's constitutional rights were violated by prosecutorial misconduct.

Petitioner was given the opportunity to file a supplemental brief in his direct appeal but did not file a pro se brief.

On June 23, 2009, the Arizona Court of Appeals affirmed Petitioner's conviction and sentence in a memorandum decision addressing each of the issues related by Petitioner's appointed counsel. The Arizona Court of Appeals also addressed, inter alia, whether there was sufficient evidence to convict Petitioner and whether the jury had been properly empanelled and instructed. Petitioner did not seek review of this decision by the Arizona Supreme Court.

Petitioner initiated an action for state post-conviction relief pursuant to *Rule 32, Arizona Rules of Civil Procedure*, on September 9, 2009. Petitioner was appointed counsel to represent him in his Rule 32 proceedings. On May 24, 2010, counsel informed the trial court that she could find no colorable claim to present on Petitioner's behalf.

On July 21, 2010, Petitioner filed a supplemental petition. On August 19, 2010, Petitioner filed a second supplemental petition, which the trial court struck without prejudice because it did not comply with *Rule 32.5, Arizona Rules of Criminal Procedure*.

On September 22, 2010, Petitioner filed a third supplemental petition in his Rule 32 action, alleging:

1. The state had "misled" the grand jury by presenting hearsay testimony rather than "first hand" testimony;

2. The state violated Petitioner's rights by depriving him of a preliminary hearing;

3. He was denied   his right to the effective assistance of counsel. Petitioner alleged his counsel failed to challenge the grand jury proceedings, failed to adequately present Petitioner's motion for a voluntariness hearing, failed to inform Petitioner of his right to have grand jury transcripts, and failed to object on conflict of interest grounds to the commissioner who conducted Petitioner's settlement conference and a trial management conference; and

4. Ineffective assistance of counsel, with regard to establishing Petitioner's historical priors.

On February 16, 2011, the state Superior Court dismissed Petitioner's action for post-conviction relief. The trial court found Petitioner's claims of ineffective assistance of counsel were not colorable and that Petitioner's remaining claims were precluded under *Rule 32.2(a)(2), Arizona Rules of Criminal Procedure*, because they had been finally adjudicated on appeal.

In his federal habeas action Petitioner asserts that his constitutional rights were violated by prosecutorial misconduct (Ground One), the denial of his right to a preliminary hearing (Ground Two), prosecutorial misconduct and ineffective assistance of counsel with   respect to Petitioner's prior convictions (Ground Three), and ineffective assistance of counsel during his trial and appellate proceedings (Ground Four).

Respondents contend that Grounds One, Three, and Four of Petitioner's habeas claims have not been properly exhausted in state court, and therefore, are procedurally barred. Respondents assert habeas relief should not be granted on Ground Two of the petition because the Arizona court's conclusion that Petitioner was not denied his federal constitutional rights by the termination of the preliminary hearing upon Petitioner's indictment was not clearly contrary to nor an unreasonable application of federal law.

1. Petitioner contends   that his rights were violated by "Prosecutorial Misconduct: misleading the Grand Jury to Indict."

Respondents assert this claim is procedurally barred because Petitioner failed to properly exhaust his claim either on direct appeal or in a properly-filed action for state post-conviction relief. Respondents contend that, although Petitioner's appointed appellate counsel noted in an "Anders" brief that Petitioner believed his "constitutional rights" were violated by "prosecutorial misconduct," Petitioner did not provide the court with any factual basis for this claim because Petitioner did not file a pro per brief in his direct appeal.

A petitioner must present to the state courts the "substantial equivalent" of the claim presented in federal court. *Picard v. Connor, 404 U.S. 270, 278, 92 S. Ct. 509, 513-14, 30 L. Ed. 2d 438 (1971); Libberton v. Ryan, 583 F.3d 1147, 1164 (9th Cir. 2009)*. Full and fair presentation requires a petitioner to present the substance of his claim to the state courts, including a reference to a federal constitutional guarantee and a statement of facts that entitle the petitioner to relief. See *Scott v. Schriro, 567 F.3d 573, 582 (9th Cir. 2009); Lopez v. Schriro, 491 F.3d 1029, 1040 (9th Cir. 2007)*.

Although   a habeas petitioner need not recite "book and verse on the federal constitution" to fairly present a claim to the state courts, *Picard, 404 U.S. at 277-78, 92 S. Ct. at 512-13*, they must do more than present the facts necessary to support the federal claim. See *Anderson v. Harless, 459 U.S. 4, 6, 103 S. Ct. 276, 277, 74 L. Ed. 2d 3 (1982)*. Petitioner never even presented the facts necessary to support this claim to the state court in a direct appeal. Accordingly, because the factual and legal predicate for this claim was not fairly presented to the state court in Petitioner's direct appeal, Petitioner has procedurally defaulted this claim. *Rose, 395 F.3d at 1111.*

To the extent Petitioner raised the factual and constitutional basis for this habeas claim in his action for state post-conviction relief, the state court found the issue precluded because it was decided on the merits in Petitioner's direct appeal. The state court concluded that, as a matter of fact, Petitioner was not subjected to either prosecutorial vindictiveness nor was he subjected to prosecutorial misconduct. The state court did not discuss nor cite to federal cases discussing the United States Constitution when denying these claims.

To constitute an adequate and independent state procedural ground sufficient to support a state court's finding of procedural default, "a state rule must be clear, consistently applied, and well-established at the time of [the] petitioner's purported default." *Lambright v. Stewart, 241 F.3d 1201, 1203 (9th Cir. 2001).* A state rule is considered consistently applied and well-established if the state courts follow it in the "vast majority of cases." *Scott, 567 F.3d at 580,* quoting *Dugger v. Adams, 489 U.S. 401, 417 n.6, 109 S. Ct. 1211, 1221 n.6, 103 L. Ed. 2d 435 (1989).* The Ninth Circuit Court of Appeals has held that "federal courts should not insist upon a petitioner, as a procedural prerequisite to obtaining federal relief, comply[] with a rule the state itself does not consistently enforce." *Id., 567 F.3d at 581-82,* quoting *Siripongs v. Calderon, 35 F.3d 1308, 1318 (9th Cir. 1994).* It is Respondents' burden to prove the rule cited and relied upon by the state court in denying relief was clear, consistently applied, and well-established at the time the rule was applied to Petitioner's case. Id.

As noted supra, the Arizona Rules of Criminal Procedure regarding timeliness, waiver, and the preclusion of claims have been found to be clear, consistently applied, and well-established at the time the rules were applied to Petitioner's state action for post-conviction relief. See *Stewart, 536 U.S. at 860, 122 S. Ct. at 2581* (holding Arizona's state rules regarding the waiver and procedural default of claims raised in attacks on criminal convictions are adequate and independent state grounds for affirming a conviction and denying federal habeas relief on the grounds of a procedural bar). Therefore, to the extent that it can be found that Petitioner properly presented this habeas claim to the state court in his Rule 32 action, the state court found relief on the merits of the claim procedurally barred by operation of the state rules of criminal procedure. Additionally, Petitioner did not seek review of the Superior Court's denial of relief by the Arizona Court of Appeals. Therefore, Petitioner did not fairly present this habeas claim to the state's "highest court" in a procedurally correct manner.

In response to the answer to his habeas petition, Petitioner asserts that he could not properly pursue his habeas claims in the state courts because his appellate counsel's performance was deficient, i.e., counsel failed to raise and properly present the issues in Petitioner's direct appeal. Petitioner also asserts that his transfer to a prison in Colorado prevented him from filing a pro per brief in his direct appeal. Petitioner also contends that he was denied his right to the effective assistance of post-conviction counsel, asserting that his appointed post-conviction counsel had a conflict because all public defendants' counsel are conflicted with regard to their representation of defendants in Rule 32 proceedings.

Petitioner has not established cause for nor prejudice arising from his procedural default of this habeas claim. Nor has Petitioner established that a fundamental miscarriage of justice will occur if the merits of this claim are not considered.

2. Petitioner claims that he was denied his "right to have a preliminary hearing," arguing that the trial court's failure to afford Petitioner such a hearing "clearly circumvents the *United States Constitution Amendment Fourth* (14)-due process of law, as well as both the Arizona claims." In his traverse Petitioner states that he was subjected to prosecutorial misconduct by the denial of his "right" to a preliminary hearing.

Petitioner alleges that he was denied his right to a preliminary hearing, which constituted prosecutorial misconduct and a violation of his right to due process of law. Petitioner raised similar claims in his direct appeal. The Arizona Court of Appeals denied relief on this claim, stating:

First, Shakur's rights were not violated when the court vacated his preliminary hearing upon indictment by the grand jury on the same charge. The United States Constitution, Arizona Constitution, Arizona statutes and *Ariz. R. Crim. P. 5.1* do not grant the defendant an absolute right to a preliminary hearing. A preliminary hearing is only required when a person is prosecuted for a felony by information rather than indictment. See *Ariz. Const. art. 2, § 30*. The preliminary hearing may be waived pursuant to *Ariz. R. Crim. P. 5.1(b)* by written waiver signed by the defendant and an attorney or when the charges are dismissed upon return of a grand jury indictment. See *State v. Gonzales, 111 Ariz. 38, 42, 523 P.2d 66, 70 (1974)* (holding the defendant has no right to choose whether the State proceeds by either indictment or information). Here, the court vacated Shakur's preliminary hearing upon return of the grand jury's   indictment on the same charge. Thus, the superior court did not fundamentally err by vacating the preliminary hearing.

The state court's decision was not clearly contrary to federal law. The *Due Process Clause of the United States Constitution* does not require indictment by a grand jury, although it clearly requires some pretrial screening of criminal charges. See *Cooksey v. Delo, 94 F.3d 1214, 1217 (8th Cir. 1996)*. However, the federal courts have uniformly concluded that "a preliminary hearing before a magistrate is not a federal constitutional right which, if denied, requires a petitioner's release on habeas corpus." *Pappillion v. Beto, 257 F. Supp. 502, 503 (S.D. Tex. 1966)*. See also *Murphy v. Beto, 416 F.2d 98, 100 (5th Cir. 1969)*.

Petitioner was not deprived of a constitutional right because he was not afforded a complete preliminary hearing, and, accordingly, relief may be denied on this claim because it is not cognizable in a *section 2254* action.

3. Petitioner asserts that he was subjected to "prosecutorial misconduct" and denied his right to the effective assistance of counsel because the state alleged prior convictions that Petitioner contends could not properly   be used to enhance his sentence.

Respondents argue that Petitioner did not fairly present this claim to the state courts in a procedurally correct manner and that the claim has been defaulted.

Petitioner did not file a pro per brief in his direct appeal. Accordingly, Petitioner did not allege that he was denied his federal constitutional right to a fair trial or due process of law based on the prosecutor alleging prior convictions which Petitioner asserts could not be used to enhance his sentence. Petitioner did not "fairly present" this claim to the state's highest court in a procedurally correct manner.

Additionally, even if Petitioner properly presented this claim in his state action for post-conviction relief, Petitioner did not seek review by the Arizona Court of Appeals of the trial court's decision denying relief pursuant to Rule 32, Arizona Rules of Criminal Procedure. Therefore, the claim was not "fairly presented" to the state's "highest court" in a procedurally correct manner and the claim has been procedurally defaulted.

As noted supra, Petitioner has not shown cause for nor prejudice arising from his procedural default of this claim. Petitioner has not established that a fundamental   miscarriage of justice will occur absent a consideration of the merits of the claim. Therefore, the claim does not warrant the granting of relief.

4. Petitioner contends that he was denied his right to the effective assistance of counsel.

Petitioner raised an ineffective assistance of counsel claim in his first Rule 32 proceedings.

To state a claim for ineffective assistance of counsel, a habeas petitioner must show both that his attorney's performance was deficient and that the deficiency prejudiced the petitioner's defense. See *Strickland v. Washington, 466 U.S. 668, 687, 104 S. Ct. 2052, 2064, 80 L. Ed. 2d 674 (1984)*. The petitioner must overcome the strong presumption that counsel's conduct was within the range of reasonable professional assistance required of attorneys in that circumstance. See *id., 466 U.S. at 687, 104 S. Ct. at 2064*. To establish prejudice, the petitioner must establish that there is "a reasonable probability that, but for counsel's unprofessional errors, the result of the proceeding would have been different." *Strickland, 466 U.S. at 694, 104 S. Ct. at 2068*. See also, e.g., *Harrington v. Richter, 131 S. Ct. 770, 786-88, 178 L. Ed. 2d 624 (2011)*. Counsel's performance will be held constitutionally   deficient only if the defendant proves their actions "fell below an objective standard of reasonableness," as measured by "prevailing professional norms." *Strickland, 466 U.S. at 688, 104 S. Ct. 2052.* See also *Cheney v. Washington, 614 F.3d 987, 994-95 (9th Cir. 2010).*

To establish prejudice, the petitioner must establish that there is "a reasonable probability that, but for counsel's unprofessional errors, the result of the proceeding would have been different." *Strickland, 466 U.S. at 694, 104 S. Ct. at 2068.* See also, e.g., *Cheney, 614 F.3d at 994.* Therefore, to succeed on an assertion his counsel's performance was deficient because counsel failed to raise a particular argument, either in his trial proceedings or in his appeals, the petitioner must establish the argument was likely to be successful, thereby establishing that he was prejudiced by his counsel's omission. See *Tanner v. McDaniel, 493 F.3d 1135, 1144 (9th Cir. 2007); Weaver v. Palmateer, 455 F.3d 958, 970 (9th Cir. 2006).* "It is not enough for the defendant to show that the errors had some conceivable effect on the outcome of the proceeding." *Strickland, 466 U.S. at 693, 104 S. Ct. at 2067.* Accordingly, prejudice from   [*30] counsel's allegedly deficient performance is less likely when the case against the defendant is strong. See, e.g., *Wong v. Belmontes, 558 U.S. 15, 130 S. Ct. 383, 390-91, 175 L. Ed. 2d 328 (2009); Avila v. Galaza, 297 F.3d 911, 923-24 (9th Cir. 2002); Goodwin v. Johnson, 632 F.3d 301, 311 (6th Cir. 2011).* It is Petitioner's burden to establish both that his counsel's performance was deficient and that he was prejudiced thereby. See, e.g., *Wong, 130 S. Ct. at 384-85 (2009).*

"Surmounting Strickland's high bar is never an easy task." *Padilla v. Kentucky, 559 U.S. 356, 130 S. Ct. 1473, 1485, 176 L. Ed. 2d 284 (2010),* quoted in *Harrington, 131 S. Ct. at 788.* However, the Court must apply an extremely deferential standard of review with regard to Strickland claims presented by a state habeas petitioner. See *Harrington, 131 S. Ct. at 785* ("A state court must be granted a deference and latitude that are not in operation when the case involves review under the Strickland standard itself.").

> Establishing that a state court's application of Strickland was unreasonable under § 2254(d) is all the more difficult. The standards created by Strickland and § 2254(d) are both "highly deferential," *id., at 689, 104 S.Ct. 2052; Lindh v. Murphy, 521 U.S. 320, 333, n.7, 117 S.Ct. 2059, 138 L.Ed.2d 481 (1997),*   [*31] and when the two apply in tandem, review is "doubly" so, *Knowles, 556 U.S., at 123, 129 S.Ct. at 1420.* The Strickland standard is a general one, so the range of reasonable applications is substantial. *556 U.S., at 123, 129 S. Ct. at 1420.* Federal habeas courts must guard against the danger of equating unreasonableness under Strickland with unreasonableness under § 2254(d). When § 2254(d) applies, the question is not whether counsel's actions were reasonable. The question is whether there is any reasonable argument that counsel satisfied Strickland's deferential standard.

Harrington, 131 S. Ct. at 788.

The state court thoroughly examined Petitioner's claims regarding ineffective assistance of counsel presented in his state Rule 32 action and denied relief on this claim. The state court concluded that no alleged incident of deficient performance was prejudicial with regard to the outcome of Petitioner's criminal proceedings.

This decision was not clearly contrary to nor an unreasonable application of *Strickland.* The Court notes that Petitioner's counsel was prepared to try the issue of his prior felonies.. Additionally, as noted by the state court, the sentencing agreement   to stipulate to two prior historical felony convictions in return for receiving a super-mitigated sentence was extremely beneficial to Petitioner. The state alleged seven prior felony convictions and, if proved, Petitioner faced a considerably longer term of imprisonment.

REASONS WHY REMEDY IS HOLLOW

In Arizona prosecutors present false evidence as a matter of routine to indict and convict and this is why they decline preliminary hearings. Arizona courts allow this practice because with preliminary hearings most convictions would not be. The Attorney General fails to disclose this to federal courts.

**MARQUIS LEE JOHNSON, Petitioner - Appellant, v. ARIZONA ATTORNEY GEN-
ERAL; et al., Respondents - Appellees. No. 07-16849 UNITED STATES COURT OF
APPEALS FOR THE NINTH CIRCUIT
(Text modified for emphasis)**

THE POSITION OF THE COURT

Johnson contends that his appellate counsel was ineffective for failing to raise on direct appeal the various claims of prosecutorial misconduct and trial court error that he raises in his *§ 2254* petition. Johnson admits in his petition that counsel told him she had reviewed his suggested claims and found them to be without merit, and Johnson has not demonstrated that any of these claims were viable on direct appeal. Accordingly, Johnson has failed to meet his burden of showing that appellate counsel was deficient for declining
to raise his suggested claims on direct appeal, or that he suffered prejudice as a result. *See Strickland v.
Washington, 466 U.S. 668, 688, 694, 104 S. Ct. 2052, 80 L. Ed. 2d 674 (1984); see also Smith v. Robbins, 528
U.S. 259, 288, 120 S. Ct. 746, 145 L. Ed. 2d 756 (2000)* (noting that the presumption that appellate counsel
acted reasonably will generally be overcome only when claims not raised are clearly stronger than those presented). The state court's decision rejecting Johnson's ineffective assistance of counsel claim was therefore
not contrary to, nor an unreasonable application of, clearly established federal law. *See 28 U.S.C. § 2254(d);
see also Strickland, 466 U.S. at 694.*

Because Johnson has not set forth any specific facts that, if proven, would entitle him to relief, he has not
shown that he is entitled to an evidentiary hearing. *See Gonzalez v. Pliler, 341 F.3d 897, 903 (9th Cir. 2003).*

REASONS WHY THE REMEDY IS HOLLOW

Arizona prosecutors have a well documented and established practice of engaging in misconduct to convict
and defense lawyers refuse to raises these issues. Bothe the state courts and the Arizona Attorney General
are aware of this matter but decline to take any action.

**HANS G. HIGGINS, Petitioner, v. CHARLES RYAN, ARIZONA ATTORNEY GENERAL,
Respondents.
CIV 09-00345 PHX PGR (MEA) UNITED STATES DISTRICT COURT FOR THE DISTRICT
OF ARIZONA
(Text modified for emphasis)**

THE POSITION OF THE COURT

On June 12, 2006, Petitioner was indicted by a grand jury on one count of theft of a means of transportation and one count of unlawful flight from a law-enforcement vehicle. The indictment was later amended to
allege Petitioner had six prior felony convictions, in 1984, 1987, 1990, and 1992.

The state filed an amended allegation of historical priors on December 12, 2006.. On December 18, 2006,
Petitioner's counsel filed a motion to strike this pleading because it was not timely. The state trial court held a
hearing on the motion on December 20, 2006. The court took the motion under advisement at that time and
set a trial date for January 2, 2006.. It would appear from the record in this matter that the motion was denied but it is unclear from the record before the Court when the motion was denied.

Petitioner's first trial on the 2006 charges, in January of 2007, ended in a mistrial resulting from a hung
jury. Petitioner filed a special action in the Arizona Court of Appeals and the Arizona Supreme Court asserting
the trial judge erred by denying his motion for a directed verdict and that there was insufficient evidence to
find he had driven the allegedly stolen vehicle. The Arizona Court of Appeals and the Arizona Supreme
Court declined jurisdiction over the special action.

Petitioner's second trial in March of 2007 resulted in a twelve-member jury finding Petitioner guilty on
both counts charged in the indictment. At a sentencing hearing conducted December 7, 2007, the trial court
denied Petitioner's motion for a new trial. The trial court found Petitioner had three prior felony convictions
for aggravated driving under the influence. At the hearing Petitioner's counsel argued for the mitigation of

Petitioner's sentence based on his history of substance abuse, mental illness, and physical ill-health. Counsel noted that Petitioner's prior felony convictions occurred in 1994, which was relatively remote in time to the crimes of conviction.

After consideration of the evidence and the statements made at the hearing, the state trial court sentenced Petitioner to a mitigated term of 7.5 years imprisonment pursuant to his conviction for theft of means of transportation. Petitioner was also sentenced to a concurrent super-mitigated term of three years imprisonment pursuant to his conviction for unlawful flight from a law-enforcement vehicle.

Petitioner filed a timely notice of appeal with regard to his convictions and sentences. On May 23, 2008, Petitioner's appointed counsel filed a brief pursuant to Anders v. California and Arizona v. Clark, asserting they could find no meritorious issues to raise on Petitioner's behalf. Petitioner's counsel also filed a motion for an extension of the time allowed for Petitioner to file a *pro se* brief in his direct appeal. On May 28, 2008, the Arizona Court of Appeals granted the motion and set a deadline of July 7, 2008, for Petitioner to file a brief in his direct appeal. The premise of Petitioner's special action after his first trial was that the state had produced no evidence that Petitioner had driven the allegedly stolen vehicle. After his conviction, Petitioner's appointed appellate counsel's statement of facts in his Anders brief notes that, during the second trial, a witness "pointed out defendant in court as the man he saw driving the victim's vehicle on the date in question."

In his pro se brief in his direct appeal Petitioner made arguments with regard to errors which occurred in his first trial. Petitioner asserted the trial court erred by denying his motion to strike the state's amended allegation of historical prior felony convictions. Petitioner also argued that the prosecutor misled the jury during closing argument by misstating the law, and further argued that the trial court should have granted a judgment of acquittal under *Arizona Rule of Criminal Procedure 20*.

The Arizona Court of Appeals affirmed Petitioner's conviction in a memorandum decision. The court rejected Petitioner's arguments regarding errors in his first trial as moot:

> Appellant alleges in his supplemental brief that the trial court erred at multiple points during the first trial. Appellant argues that the State's allegation of historical priors was untimely and violated *Rule 16.1(b)* of the Arizona Rules of Criminal Procedure. Appellant also argues that misstatements of law to the jury by the State during the first trial prejudiced the jury, leading to the hung jury that resulted in a mistrial. Appellant's first trial ended in a mistrial, and thus, resulted in no conviction or sentence, which has the limited procedural effect of a vacated conviction. Because Appellant only raises issues from the first trial, such issues are moot. See *State v. Fritz, 157 Ariz. 139, 141, 755 P.2d 444, 446 (App. 1988)* (noting that any issue concerning a vacated conviction and sentence is moot).

Petitioner sought review of the Court of Appeals' decision by the Arizona Supreme Court. On January 13, 2009, the Arizona Supreme Court summarily denied review. The trial court appointed counsel. Appointed counsel filed a motion for extension of time and a request for the reporter's transcript o On September 3, 2008, Petitioner filed a notice of post conviction relief pursuant to Arizona Rule of Criminal Procedure 32f the proceeding that occurred on December 20, 2006. Thereafter Petitioner's appointed post-conviction counsel filed a notice stating she could find no meritorious issues to raise on Petitioner's behalf.

Petitioner filed a pro se petition. See Arizona v. Hans Higgins, S-0700-CR-2006131161 (docket available through public access to case information). The public docket indicates the state trial court denied post-conviction relief on or about November 24, 2009. Id. Petitioner evidently asserted in his post-conviction action that his federal constitutional rights were violated because three prior felony convictions were improperly "allowed." The state court found that Petitioner's federal claims were precluded by *Rule 32.2* because they were not raised in Petitioner's direct appeal. There is no indication in the public docket, nor does Petitioner assert, that he appealed the decision denying Rule 32 relief to the Arizona Court of Appeals.

On February 18, 2009, Petitioner filed the pending federal habeas petition in which he raises one "count" for relief which encompasses several allegations of constitutional error. Petitioner's "count" for relief asserts the violation of his rights pursuant to the "*5th, 8th,* and *14th Amendments to the United States Constitution.*"

Petitioner contends he has been subjected to a miscarriage of justice and double jeopardy. Petitioner contends that, therefore, his detention is improper. Petitioner asserts that, on the opening date of his first trial the prosecutor filed an untimely amended allegation of Petitioner's historical prior felonies. Petitioner argues that this constituted procedural error and violated the Arizona Rules of Criminal Procedure. Petitioner further alleges that the   filing of the amended allegation of prior felonies was done out of spite for Petitioner's decision not to plead guilty. Petitioner asserts the untimely amendment exposed him to a lengthier sentence and resulted in a jury of twelve, rather than eight individuals, pursuant to Arizona law. Petitioner maintains that, had his first trial not been marred by these errors, he would have been tried before eight jurors and he would have been acquitted. Petitioner further alleges the Arizona Court of Appeals erred by concluding that these claims were moot because his first trial resulted in a mistrial.

In his federal habeas petition Petitioner also alleges that he was deprived of due process because, during his second trial, a witness made a mistaken identification of Petitioner as the perpetrator of the charged crimes.

In response to the habeas petition, Respondents maintain that Petitioner did not properly exhaust his claims in the state courts. Respondents also argue:

> ...Petitioner has alleged only a violation of state law surrounding the timeliness of the State's disclosure that Petitioner had prior felony convictions that the State would use to seek an enhanced sentence. Although   Petitioner strongly believes that the prosecutor lied to the trial judge when she defended the late disclosure, no attribute of Petitioner's claim--the timing of the disclosure, the reasons for the timing of the disclosure, or the actual sentence imposed--concerns federal law, rendering the allegations noncognizable in this Court.

state court. See, e.g., id., *541 U.S. at 33, 124 S. Ct. at 1351.*

Full and fair presentation requires a petitioner to present the substance of his claim to the state courts, including a reference to a federal constitutional guarantee and a statement of facts that entitles the petitioner to relief. See *Scott v. Schriro, 567 F.3d 573, 582 (9th Cir. 2009); Lopez v. Schriro, 491 F.3d 1029, 1040 (9th Cir. 2007)*, cert. denied, *552 U.S. 1224, 128 S. Ct. 1227, 170 L. Ed. 2d 140 (2008).*   [*12] Although a habeas petitioner need not recite "book and verse on the federal constitution" to fairly present a claim to the state courts, *Picard, 404 U.S. at 277-78, 92 S. Ct. at 512-13*, they must do more than present the facts necessary to support the federal claim. See *Anderson v. Harless, 459 U.S. 4, 6, 103 S. Ct. 276, 277, 74 L. Ed. 2d 3 (1982).*

D. Petitioner's claims for relief

Petitioner did not properly exhaust any of his federal habeas claims in the state courts. In his action for post conviction relief Petitioner did assert that his right to due process was violated by an improper witness identification. However, Petitioner did not present this claim to the Arizona Court of Appeals. The record before the Court does not indicate that Petitioner appealed the state Superior Court's decision denying post-conviction relief to the Arizona Court of Appeals. Because the time for doing   so has expired, this claim is procedurally defaulted.

In his direct appeal Petitioner argued that the state trial court erred during his first trial. Petitioner alleged claims factually similar to those stated in his habeas petition, asserting the trial court's mistakes constituted "fundamental error." In his direct appeal Petitioner emphasized that the improper acts violated state law, rather than his federal constitutional rights. A petitioner's "general appeal to a constitutional guarantee," such as due process, is insufficient to achieve fair presentation. See *Shumway v. Payne, 223 F.3d 982, 987 (9th Cir. 2000)*. Similarly, a federal claim is not exhausted merely because its factual basis was presented to the state courts on state law grounds-a "mere similarity between a claim of state and federal error is insufficient to establish exhaustion." *Id., 223 F.3d at 988*. A claim is not "fairly presented" if the state court must read beyond a brief to find material that alerts it to the presence of a federal claim. See *Wooten v. Kirkland, 540 F.3d 1019, 1025 (9th Cir. 2008)*. Accordingly, as federal constitutional claims the habeas claims were not exhausted in Petitioner's direct appeal.

Petitioner arguably raised his federal claims regarding errors in the first trial in his action for post-conviction relief. However, in his action for post-conviction relief Petitioner did not pursue the claims to the Arizona Court of Appeals, i.e., he did not provide the opportunity for the state's "highest court" to evaluate the merits of his federal constitutional claims.

Petitioner has not shown cause for, nor prejudice arising from his procedural default of all of his claims stating violation of his federal constitutional rights. Accordingly, relief may not be granted on these claims.

Additionally, to the extent Petitioner might have asserted the violation of a federal constitutional right in his direct appeal, those claims were denied based on the Arizona Court of Appeals' conclusion that the claims were moot pursuant to Arizona law. The District Courts are not to review habeas claims presented to a state court if the decision of that state court denying rests on a state ground that is both independent of the federal claim and adequate to support that judgment. See, e.g., *Cook v. Schriro, 538 F.3d 1000, 1028-29 (9th Cir. 2008); Amos v. Scott, 61 F.3d 333, 338 (5th Cir. 1995)*. The procedural bar doctrine proscribes federal habeas review of a claim when the state court declined to address the petitioner's federal constitutional claim because the petitioner failed to meet a state procedural requirement with regard to the proper exhaustion of the claim in the state courts. See *Coleman, 501 U.S. at 729-30, 111 S. Ct. at 2553-54; Pitts v. Anderson, 122 F.3d 275, 278 (5th Cir. 1997)*. If the Court finds an independent and adequate state procedural ground, "federal habeas review is barred unless the prisoner can demonstrate cause for the procedural default and actual prejudice, or demonstrate that the failure to consider the claims will result in a fundamental miscarriage of justice." *Noltie v. Peterson, 9 F.3d 802, 804-05 (9th Cir. 1993)*. Petitioner has not established cause and prejudice nor has he established that a fundamental miscarriage of justice has occurred.

The undersigned further concludes that Petitioner's double jeopardy claim may be denied on the merits notwithstanding any failure to properly procedurally exhaust this claim in the state courts. See, e.g., *Arizona v. Washington, 434 U.S. 497, 505, 98 S. Ct. 824, 830, 54 L. Ed. 2d 717 (1978)* (explaining that while a prosecutor is generally entitled to only one opportunity to require an accused to stand trial, a retrial after a mistrial due to manifest necessity does not violate the protections of constitutional double jeopardy). "It is well-established that retrial following a hung jury does not constitute double jeopardy." *Wilson v. Belleque, 554 F.3d 816, 830 (9th Cir. 2009)*.

Furthermore, as noted by Respondents, a state prisoner may obtain a writ of habeas corpus only upon a showing that he is being held in violation of the Constitution, laws, or treaties of the United States. See *28 U.S.C. § 2254(a) (1994 & Supp. 2009); Engle v. Isaac, 456 U.S. 107, 119, 102 S. Ct. 1558, 1567, 71 L. Ed. 2d 783 (1982)*. Federal habeas relief is not available for alleged errors in the interpretation or application of state law, including a state's rules of criminal procedure See *Estelle v. McGuire, 502 U.S. 62, 67-68, 112 S. Ct. 475, 480, 116 L. Ed. 2d 385 (1991); Middleton v. Cupp, 768 F.2d 1083, 1085 (9th Cir. 1985)*.

To the extent that Petitioner asserts his convictions were obtained in violation of his right to due process because his first trial was improper conducted pursuant to Arizona statutory law or rules of criminal procedure, Petitioner has not stated a claim for federal habeas relief. See *Souch v. Schaivo, 289 F.3d 616, 623 (9th Cir. 2002)*. Although Petitioner asserts that his right to due process was violated because the state engaged in misconduct resulting in a hung jury rather than an acquittal, the characterization of this claim in this fashion does not render it cognizable on federal habeas review. See *Cacoperdo v. Demosthenes, 37 F.3d 504, 507 (9th Cir. 1994); Dellinger v. Bowen, 301 F.3d 758, 765 (7th Cir. 2002)*.

REASONS WHY REMEDY IS HOLLOW

There is a systemic problem in Arizona as they did in this case to present false witnesses to convict as courts allow this. Exhaustion of remedies in the Arizona Courts is futile for they have a well documented trend of condoning these practices. The Arizona Attorney General fails to bring this to federal court attention.

> **Robert Gonzalez, Petitioner, vs. Charles Ryan, et al., Respondents. No. CV-08-658-TUC-FRZ-DTF**
> **UNITED STATES DISTRICT COURT FOR THE DISTRICT OF ARIZONA (text modified for emphasis)**

THE COURTS DECISION

Gonzalez was convicted in two separate jury trials, for shooting at Mark Humo and Officer Lewis, in incidents that occurred two weeks apart. The following factual summary of the crimes is taken from the Arizona Court of Appeals' opinion, construing all facts in favor of the prosecution:

> On the evening of November 3, 2001, the victim, M[ark Humo] was outside of the apartment he shared with his girlfriend, A[lyssa Preciado], and A[lyssa's] three children, one of whom was fathered by Gonzalez. Carrying a firearm, Gonzalez approached M[ark] and asked about his daughter. The two men began to argue and A[lyssa] came outside to help defuse the situation. After a contentious exchange, Gonzalez shot M[ark] four times. Although M[ark] was seriously injured, the injuries were not fatal. Gonzalez then fled.
>
> About two weeks later on November 19, 2001, police attempted to serve Gonzalez with an arrest warrant in connection with the November 3 incident. For the arrest, they initiated a "dynamic takedown," meaning that they would have their weapons drawn. The officers waited in a strategic location, and when the supervising officer spotted Gonzalez, he announced "Tucson Police" and ordered Gonzalez to get on the ground. Gonzalez drew a handgun and fired four shots at one of the other officers, L[ewis], who was not seriously injured. The supervising officer then fired and hit Gonzalez, which subdued him and allowed the officers to arrest him.

As to the first event, Gonzalez was convicted of attempted first degree murder, three counts of aggravated assault and two counts of endangerment. He was convicted of attempted first degree murder, aggravated assault and disorderly conduct as to the second shooting. The longest sentences imposed were two, consecutive eighteen-year terms for the attempted murders.

Respondents concede that Gonzalez's December 12, 2008 petition, which initiated this federal habeas action, was within the statute of limitations. The Court first addresses Respondents' arguments that Claims 2, 3, 6 (in part), 7, 8/13, 9, 14, 15 (in part), 16 (in part), and 17 (in part) are procedurally defaulted and then turns to the merits of the remaining claims. Claim 8 challenges the reasonable doubt instruction given at Gonzalez's first trial. Claim 13 alleges the identical instruction given in Gonzalez's second trial. The parties address the claims simultaneously in their briefing.

Fair Presentation

Claims 7 and 8/13, and 6, 15, 16 and 17 (in part)

Respondents contend Gonzalez did not present the factual basis for Claims 7 and 8/13, and Claims 6, 15, 16 and 17 (in part).

Petitioner did not raise Claim 7, alleging prosecutorial misconduct during Trial I, on direct appeal or in his PCR petition. He does not dispute this in his reply brief. Petitioner concedes that Claims 8/13, which alleges that the reasonable doubt jury instructions at his first and second trials relieved the state of its burden of proof, were not raised in state court. Thus, Claims 7 and 8/13 were not fairly presented.

In Claim 6, Gonzalez alleges the trial court denied him a fair trial by precluding three witnesses, Gabriel Villa Escusa, Myrna Canez and Joe Duran. Respondents argue that the allegations as to Escusa and Canez were not fairly presented. In his reply brief in this Court, Gonzalez acknowledged Respondents' argument on exhaustion but did not respond to it. A review of Gonzalez's appellate brief reveals that he did not contest the exclusion of Escusa or Canez on appeal thus, these portions of Claim 6 were not fairly presented.

Claim 15 alleges nine instances of prosecutorial misconduct during the closing argument of Trial II: (a) emphasizing that premeditation can be any length of time; (b) stating that purchasing a gun is a substantial step toward committing first degree murder; (c) vouching for Officers Lewis and Blue; (d) arguing that Gonzalez had been dishonest and had a motive to lie; (e) referencing Gonzalez's prior conviction, which was not yet final; (f) asking the jury not to let Gonzalez "get away with it"; (g) arguing that Gonzalez resisted arrest because he knew he would be imprisoned for a very long time if arrested for his prior crime; (h) arguing that defense counsel did not know what Gonzalez was going to say on the stand and "concocted a story at the last second"; and (i) arguing that Officer Blue needed to move the police car after the shooting due to criminal activity in the area connected to Gonzalez. Respondents argue that only subclaims (e), (h) and (i) were presented on direct appeal. Gonzalez did not argue to the contrary and his appellate brief reveals that subclaims (a) to (d), (f) and (g) were not fairly presented on appeal .Gonzalez's assertion of prosecutorial misconduct on other grounds were not sufficient to exhaust all of the subclaims. *See Kelly v. Small, 315 F.3d 1063, 1069 (9th Cir. 2002)* (satisfying the requirement that "a federal habeas petitioner [must] provide the state courts with a 'fair opportunity' to apply controlling legal precedent to the facts bearing upon his constitutional claim," requires presenting the state courts with the operative facts) (quoting *Harless, 459 U.S. at 6*), *overruled on other grounds by Robbins v. Carey, 481 F.3d 1143 (9th Cir. 2007)*.

Respondents allege that twelve of Petitioner's fifteen allegations of ineffective assistance of counsel (IAC) were not fairly presented in state court. In Claim 16(A), Gonzales alleges he was denied effective assistance at Trial I because counsel failed to: (1) object to a preliminary jury instruction that misstated the presumption of innocence; (2) object sufficiently to evidence that Gonzalez was a gang member; (3) object to Detective Mark Cassel testifying as a ballistics expert; (4) object to testimony about a mug shot taken prior to either of the shootings at issue in the trial or challenge the reliability of that identification; (5) challenge the endangerment charge; (6) produce witness Gabriel Villa Escusa to impeach State witness Alyssa Preciado; (7) obtain a ballistics expert to counter (a) Detective Cassel's testimony, and (b) the endangerment counts; and (8) challenge the State's closing argument stating that the victim had four bullet wounds when he only had two. In Claim 16(B), Gonzales alleges he was denied effective assistance at Trial II because counsel failed to: (1) object to Officer Blue's testimony that Gonzalez heard and acknowledged the officer's identification and warning; (2) object to evidence on whether it is a violation of police procedure for an officer to not announce his presence; (3) object to the prosecutor asking how many times Gonzalez carried a weapon; (4) object to the prosecutor asking why Gonzalez did not contact the police if he knew there was a warrant for his arrest; (5) object to the prosecutor asking if Gonzalez turned himself in; (6) object to Detective Danny Donogean calling the incident an aggravated assault and referring to the victims; and (7) submit a limiting instruction on the use of the prior conviction.

Respondent contends the following IAC claims from Trial I were not raised in the PCR petition, (1), (2), (3), (5), (6) and (7)(b), and that none of the claims from Trial II were raised. Gonzalez does not dispute this argument (Doc. 21 at 71-72) and a review of his PCR petition reveals that these claims were not fairly presented (Doc. 18, Exs. G, H). *See Kelly, 315 F.3d at 1069* (requiring fair presentation of the operative facts); *Carriger v. Lewis, 971 F.2d 329, 333-34 (9th Cir. 1992)* (treating distinct failures by trial counsel as separate claims for exhaustion and procedural default); *Matias v. Oshiro, 683 F.2d 318, 319-20 & n.1 (9th Cir. 1982)* (finding no fair presentation of eight grounds of IAC not raised in state court); *cf. Strickland v. Washington, 466 U.S. 668, 690, 104 S. Ct. 2052, 80 L. Ed. 2d 674 (1984)* (requiring identification of the specific "acts or omissions" of counsel and a determination of whether those acts are outside the range of competent assistance).

Respondents contend that Gonzalez failed to fairly present two parts of Claim 17: the State failed to give notice of the aggravating factors for sentencing (subpart (B)(2)) and his counsel was ineffective at sentencing (subpart (C)). Gonzalez does not dispute this assertion and a review of his appellate brief and the PCR petition (Doc. 18, Exs. B, G) establish that he did not fairly present those portions of Claim 17.

The Court finds that Gonzalez failed to fairly present in state court Claims 6 (as to Escusa and Canez), 7, 8/13, 15 (a) to (d), (f) and (g), 16(A) (1), (2), (3), (5), (6) and (7)(b), 16(B), 17(B)(2), and 17(C).

Claims 2, 3, 9 and 11 as Based on Federal Law

Respondents contend that, although Gonzalez raised the factual basis of Claims 2, 3 and 9 in state court, he did not allege that these claims were based on federal law. With respect to Claim 2, on direct appeal, Gonzalez argued only that denial of a *Willits* instruction deprived him of a fair trial. Gonzalez contends the claim was fairly presented because "the factual scenario suggesting bad faith, loss of exculpatory evidence and favorable inferences from the loss of the evidence, all make it clear that Petitioner was alleging violations of his *Sixth* and *Fourteenth Amendment* rights, depriving him of a fair trial." However, "[i]f a habeas petitioner wishes to claim that an evidentiary ruling at a state court trial denied him the due process of law guaranteed by the *Fourteenth Amendment*, he must say so, not only in federal court, but in state court." *Duncan v. Henry, 513 U.S. 364, 366, 115 S. Ct. 887, 130 L. Ed. 2d 865 (1995)*. A general assertion accompanied by factual inferences that a defendant was deprived of a fair trial does not fairly present a federal constitutional claim. *See Casey v. Moore, 386 F.3d at 913; Johnson v. Zenon, 88 F.3d 828, 830 (9th Cir. 1996)*.

On direct appeal, Gonzalez alleged the factual basis of Claim 3 - that he was prejudiced by admission of evidence of his gang affiliation. Again, he did not cite a federal basis for this claim, he argued only that admission of this evidence denied him a fair trial. This is insufficient for fair presentation. *See Casey v. Moore, 386 F.3d at 913; Johnson v. Zenon, 88 F.3d at 830*.   Gonzalez argues that his reliance on *Arizona Rule of Evidence 404(a)* was sufficient for fair presentation because it prohibits the same evidence as *Federal Rule of Evidence 404(a)*. The Federal Rules of Evidence have no applicability in state court and, therefore, provide no basis for relief for a state criminal defendant. Further, the rules of evidence are not synonymous with a federal constitution right. More importantly, the Supreme Court has explicitly rejected the argument that similarity between the state claim alleged in state court and an unasserted federal claim satisfies the exhaustion requirement. *Duncan v. Henry, 513 U.S. 364, 366, 115 S. Ct. 887, 130 L. Ed. 2d 865 (1995)*.

In state court, Petitioner alleged the factual basis of Claim 9, that the trial court should not have admitted Gonzalez's prior conviction as impeachment..) However, he argued only that admission of that evidence was an abuse of discretion and violated the state evidentiary rules. Gonzalez does not contend he presented a federal claim to the Arizona Court of Appeals, but he argues that Claim 9 is exhausted because he raised the federal constitutional basis of this claim in his Petition for Review to the Arizona   Supreme Court. While his assertion is accurate ,exhaustion requires properly raising and fairly presenting a claim at every appropriate state court level. *See Casey v. Moore, 386 F.3d at 915-16, 918* (raising a claim for the first time to the highest court on discretionary review does not satisfy the fair presentation requirement). In Arizona, a petition for review to the supreme court is a vehicle only to raise issues previously presented to the court of appeals. *Ariz. R. Crim. P. 31.19(c)*. Therefore, raising claims for the first time to the appellate court was insufficient to fairly present any claims to the Arizona state courts.

In Claim 11, Gonzalez argues the trial court violated his right to due process by denying a duress instruction. Respondents indicated that Gonzalez fairly presented this claim in state court as one based on federal law. The Court finds this conclusion to be erroneous.   In his PCR petition, Gonzalez questioned whether the trial court was "at fault" for not allowing a duress instruction, and he argued that he was entitled to a duress instruction under Arizona law. Although Gonzalez cited two federal court cases,   they did not analyze a federal constitutional issue. Rather, both *United States v. Johnson, 956 F.2d 894, 897-905 (9th Cir. 1992)*, *superseded in part by U.S. Sentencing Guidelines Manual § 3E1.1(b)* (1992), and *United States v. LaFleur, 971 F.2d 200, 204-06 (9th Cir. 1991)*, were direct review cases assessing duress as a defense under federal criminal law. Citation to these federal cases, which did not analyze the due process claim Gonzalez now raises, was insufficient to fairly present this claim to the state court. *See Castillo v. McFadden, 399 F.3d 993, 1001 (9th Cir. 2004)*.   In this Court, Respondents argued that the state court found this claim precluded because it was, or could have been, raised on direct appeal. Again, the Court finds this assessment erroneous because the PCR court did not address this claim at all. However, because Respondents asserted procedural default with respect to this claim, although on a different ground, and Petitioner had an opportunity to respond to that argument and assert cause and prejudice and miscarriage of justice, the Court finds it proper to address a different basis for procedural default. *See Vang v. Nevada, 329 F.3d 1069, 1073 (9th Cir. 2003)*   (finding district court can raise procedural default sua sponte under appropriate circumstances); *cf. Day v. McDonough, 547 U.S. 198, 209, 126 S. Ct. 1675, 164 L. Ed. 2d 376 (2006)* (holding that district courts may sua sponte consider the timeliness of a habeas petition, just as circuit courts have held can be done for other affirmative defenses such as procedural default).

The Court finds Gonzalez failed to fairly present Claims 2, 3, 9 and 11.

Procedural Default

Gonzalez asks that the Court allow him to return to state court with any claims it determines are unexhausted. Respondents argue that the claims not yet fairly presented in state court are not unexhausted but, rather, technically exhausted and procedurally defaulted. Thus, the next step is for the Court to assess whether Petitioner presently has an available remedy in state court for these claims. *See Coleman v. Thompson, 501 U.S. at 735 n.1; Ortiz v. Stewart, 149 F.3d at 931.*

All of the claims found not to have been fairly presented could have been raised on appeal or in Gonzalez's first PCR petition, therefore, if he were to raise them in a successive PCR petition they would be found waived and untimely under *Rules 32.2(a)(3)* and *32.4(a)* of the Arizona Rules of Criminal Procedure. This is confirmed by the fact that Gonzalez does not argue he meets any of the exceptions to preclusion set forth in the Arizona Rules of Criminal Procedure -- defendant's sentence has expired, newly discovered material evidence probably would have changed the verdict or sentence, failure to timely file an appeal or PCR notice was not defendant's fault, a significant change in the law would probably change the conviction or sentence, or by clear and convincing evidence no reasonable fact-finder would have found defendant guilty. *Ariz. R. Crim. P. 32.1(d), (e), (f), (g), (h), 32.2(a), 32.2(b).*

Gonzalez's only basis for arguing that he has a remedy available in state court is that the claims, in particular his IAC claims, are of such constitutional magnitude that they can be raised in a subsequent collateral proceeding. The Comment to *Rule 32.2* provides that when a claim is of "sufficient constitutional magnitude" that personal knowledge is required to waive the constitutional right at issue, a *Rule 32.2(a)(3)* waiver requires the state to show the right was "knowingly, voluntarily and intelligently" waived. Review of the claims at issue suggest they do not arise out of fundamental constitutional rights requiring personal waiver, and Petitioner has not attempted to demonstrate otherwise. *See Stewart v. Smith, 202 Ariz. 446, 449-50, 46 P.3d 1067, 1070-71 (2002)* (citing as examples of rights requiring personal waiver, right to counsel and right to a jury trial by twelve persons). With respect to IAC claims, the Arizona Supreme Court has explicitly held that, regardless of the facts underlying the claim, if IAC has been raised in a PCR proceeding any subsequent IAC claim is precluded. *Id. at 450, 46 P.3d at 1071.* Because Gonzalez's claims are not based on constitutional rights requiring personal waiver and he does not meet any of the preclusion exceptions, he presently does not have a remedy available in state court. Therefore, Claims 2, 3, 6 (in part), 7, 8/13, 9, 11, 15 (in part), 16 (in part), and 17 (in part) are technically exhausted but procedurally defaulted. Petitioner argues, to the contrary, that IAC claims can be raised in a subsequent PCR proceeding, pursuant to *Rule 32.2.* In support he cites *State v. Spreitz, 190 Ariz. 129, 945 P.2d 1260 (1997).* That case is inapposite on this issue and stated only that it would address IAC claims on direct appeal in the event they were meritless. *Id. at 146, 945 P.2d at 1277.* In *Stewart v. Smith*, the Arizona Supreme Court cited its subsequent ruling, on Spreitz's petition for review from denial of PCR, for the proposition that all IAC claims should be resolved in one proceeding to avoid piecemeal litigation. *202 Ariz. at 449, 46 P.3d at 1070* (citing *State v. Spreitz, 202 Ariz. 1, 39 P.3d 525 (2002)).*

Because these claims are not unexhausted as asserted by Gonzalez, and there is not a remedy available in state court, a stay as requested by Gonzalez is not appropriate. *Cf. Rhines v. Weber, 544 U.S. 269, 273-74, 125 S. Ct. 1528, 161 L. Ed. 2d 440 (2005)* (allowing a stay while a petitioner exhausts claims in state court only as to claims that are truly unexhausted).

Claim 14

In Claim 14, Gonzalez alleges the police destroyed exculpatory evidence in violation of his right to due process and a fair trial. Respondents concede that Gonzalez fairly presented this claim in a supplemental PCR petition. Respondents argue, however, that the PCR court found this claim waived for failure to raise it on appeal and that it is procedurally defaulted. To the contrary, the PCR court did not mention this claim specifically and did not find any claims waived for failure to raise them on appeal. Because Gonzalez fairly presented Claim 14 and it was not barred by the state court, the Court will address it on the merits.

Cause and Prejudice

Gonzalez contends there is cause and prejudice to overcome any defaults found by the Court. Ordinarily "cause" to excuse a default exists if a petitioner can demonstrate that "some objective factor external to the defense impeded counsel's efforts to comply with the State's procedural rule." *Coleman, 501 U.S. at 753.* Gonzalez argues that the cause for failure to exhaust the claims is ineffective assistance of trial and appellate counsel.

Before ineffectiveness may be used to establish cause for a procedural default, it must have been presented to the state court as an independent claim. *Murray v. Carrier, 477 U.S. 478, 489, 106 S. Ct. 2639, 91 L. Ed. 2d 397 (1986)*. Petitioner did not allege in his PCR petition that his trial or appellate counsel were ineffective for failing to raise any claims. Ineffectiveness claims regarding counsel are now foreclosed in state court by *Arizona Rule of Criminal Procedure 32.2(a)(3) and 32.4(a)*. Because the Arizona state courts have   not had a fair opportunity to rule on Petitioner's ineffectiveness claims alleged as cause, and Petitioner may not exhaust these claims now, they are technically exhausted but procedurally defaulted. *See Gray, 518 U.S. at 161-62; Coleman, 501 U.S. at 735 n.1*. Therefore, Petitioner's allegations of ineffective trial and appellate counsel cannot constitute cause to excuse the default. *See Edwards v. Carpenter, 529 U.S. 446, 453, 120 S. Ct. 1587, 146 L. Ed. 2d 518 (2000)* (ineffective counsel as cause can itself be procedurally defaulted).

Additionally, a failure to exhaust did not occur at the trial court level. Rather, to the extent Gonzalez failed to exhaust claims it is based on a failure to raise or federalize the claims on direct appeal or in the PCR proceeding. Therefore, any conduct on the part of trial counsel cannot serve as cause for the failure to properly exhaust the claims in state court.

To the extent Gonzales is asserting that his pro se status at the time he filed his PCR petition is cause for his failure to raise claims in that proceeding, that argument has been rejected. *See Hughes v. Idaho State Bd. of Corrections, 800 F.2d 905, 909 (9th Cir. 1986)* (holding illiteracy was not cause for pro se petitioner's   failure to raise a claim in state court).

Because Petitioner has not established cause to overcome the default, the Court need not analyze prejudice. *Thomas v. Lewis, 945 F.2d 1119, 1123 n.10 (9th Cir. 1991)*.

Miscarriage of Justice

Gonzalez argues generally that it would be a miscarriage of justice for the Court not to review his defaulted claims. If a petitioner cannot meet the cause and prejudice standard, the Court still may hear the merits of procedurally defaulted claims if the failure to hear the claims would constitute a "fundamental miscarriage of justice." *Schlup v. Delo, 513 U.S. 298, 314-15, 115 S. Ct. 851, 130 L. Ed. 2d 808 (1995)*. To demonstrate a fundamental miscarriage of justice based on factual innocence of the crime, the petitioner must show that "a constitutional violation has probably resulted in the conviction of one who is actually innocent." *Id. at 327*. To establish the requisite probability, the petitioner must show that "it is more likely than not that no reasonable juror would have found petitioner guilty beyond a reasonable doubt." *Id*. The Supreme Court has characterized the exacting nature of an actual innocence claim as follows:

> [A] substantial claim that constitutional error has caused the   conviction of an innocent person is extremely rare. . . . To be credible, such a claim requires petitioner to support his allegations of constitutional error with new reliable evidence -- whether it be exculpatory scientific evidence, trustworthy eyewitness accounts, or critical physical evidence -- that was not presented at trial. Because such evidence is obviously unavailable in the vast majority of cases, claims of actual innocence are rarely successful.

Id. at 324; see also *House v. Bell, 547 U.S. 518, 538, 126 S. Ct. 2064, 165 L. Ed. 2d 1 (2006)*.

Gonzalez has not argued that he is actually innocent of the crimes nor has he attempted to meet this standard. Critically, he does not identify any "new evidence" that would establish his innocence. Petitioner fails to establish that there will be a fundamental miscarriage of justice if the Court does not consider his defaulted claims.

Conclusion

Gonzalez did not fairly present in state court Claims 2, 3, 6 (in part), 7, 8/13, 9, 11, 15 (in part), 16 (in part), and 17 (in part). He does not presently have a remedy available in state court for these claims. The claims are technically exhausted but procedurally defaulted. Petitioner has not established cause and prejudice to   overcome the default or that a fundamental miscarriage of justice will result if the Court does not review these claims.

MERITS

The Court reviews the exhausted claims on the merits, Claims 1, 4, 5, 6 (as to Duran), 10, 12, 14, 15(e), (h) and (i), 16(A) (4), (7)(a) and (8), 17(A), and 17(B)(1).

Claim 1 (Trials I and II)

Gonzalez alleges that the jury instruction on premeditation, used at both trials, relieved the state of its burden of proving actual reflection, which violated the *Sixth Amendment* and amounted to structural error. At each trial, the court gave the following instruction:

> Premeditation means that the defendant acts with either the intention or the knowledge that he will kill another human being, when such intention or knowledge precedes the killing by any length of time to permit reflection. It is this period of time that distinguishes second degree murder from first degree murder. Proof of actual reflection is not required, but an act is not done with premeditation if it is the instant effect of a sudden quarrel or heat of passion.

(RT 5/23/02 at 172-73; RT 10/11/02 at 21-22.) The Arizona Court of Appeals found that this instruction was erroneous because the state is required to prove reflection; however, it found the error harmless and denied the claim. That ruling was based on *State v. Thompson, 204 Ariz. 471, 480, 65 P.3d 420, 429 (2003)*, in which the Arizona Supreme Court found erroneous a premeditation instruction, such as that given in Gonzalez's trials, that stated "actual reflection is not required."

Due process requires that the state prove every element of a crime beyond a reasonable doubt. *In re Winship, 397 U.S. 358, 364, 90 S. Ct. 1068, 25 L. Ed. 2d 368 (1970); Sandstrom v. Montana, 442 U.S. 510, 520-21, 99 S. Ct. 2450, 61 L. Ed. 2d 39 (1979)*. Petitioner's allegation is that the premeditation jury instruction relieved the prosecution of the burden of proving actual reflection beyond a reasonable doubt. Further, Gonzalez argues this error is structural and not subject to a harmless error analysis. Respondents do not dispute the instruction given was erroneous, but they contend the error was harmless.

The Supreme Court has rejected Gonzalez's argument, based on *Sullivan v. Louisiana, 508 U.S. 275, 113 S. Ct. 2078, 124 L. Ed. 2d 182 (1993)*, that this type of error is structural and not subject to harmless error review. *See Neder v. United States, 527 U.S. 1, 10-11, 119 S. Ct. 1827, 144 L. Ed. 2d 35 (1999)*. An improper instruction as to one element of an offense, whether it is omitted or improperly stated, is subject to harmless error analysis. *Id. at 9*. Thus, the question is "whether it appears 'beyond a reasonable doubt that the error complained of did not contribute to the verdict obtained.'" *Id. at 15* (quoting *Chapman v. California, 386 U.S. 18, 24, 87 S. Ct. 824, 17 L. Ed. 2d 705 (1967))*.

Trial I

As discussed by the appellate court, there was ample evidence of premeditation:

> [A] week before shooting M[ark], Gonzalez had called A[lyssa] and had told her that he blamed M[ark] for the fact that Gonzalez could not see his daughter. On the night of the shooting, Gonzalez arrived at M[ark]'s apartment carrying a weapon. Gonzalez immediately asked about his daughter, which resulted in an argument culminating in Gonzalez's shooting M[ark]. And the instruction given properly covered any defense that the shooting was the instant effect of a sudden quarrel.

Additionally, during the several minutes of verbal argument, Mark Humo and Alyssa Preciado asked Gonzalez to put down the gun and "fight like a man," but Humo never touched Gonzalez prior to the shooting. Gonzalez suggests that when he told Humo he would be back that Humo escalated the confrontation by moving closer and challenging him to take care of things right then. Although there was a confrontation between the two men, it was not sudden but was precipitated by Gonzalez appearing with a gun to confront Humo. The fact that Gonzalez suggested he was going to leave, but did not, supports reflection before acting to shoot Humo not a lack of reflection as Gonzalez argues. Additionally, Gonzalez shot at Humo after he turned and tried to run away. These facts, along with all the evidence presented at trial, demonstrate that the shooting was premeditated.

Further, Gonzalez argued two defenses to the charge of attempted first degree murder, neither of which was tied to whether the shooter actually reflected. One, Gonzalez argued that there was not proof beyond a reasonable doubt that he was the shooter. This defense was not impacted at all by the erroneous premeditation instruction. Second, Gonzalez argued that the shooting was not premeditated because it was the instant effect of a sudden quarrel. The instruction accurately represented that an act was not premeditated if it was impulsive, the instant effect of a sudden quarrel. Again, this defense was not impacted by the erroneous language in the instruction. The jury's verdict indicates they clearly rejected both of these defenses.

Because the trial evidence established that the shooting was premeditated, and Gonzalez's defense was not compromised by the erroneous portion of the instruction, it appears beyond a reasonable doubt that the error did not contribute to the verdict. Thus, the error was harmless and the Arizona Court of Appeals' denial of this claim was not an objectively unreasonable application of federal law.

Trial II

In the second trial, the appellate court found sufficient evidence of premeditation was presented and not rebutted: "Gonzalez testified that he had purchased the gun about a week before the incident. Gonzalez also testified that he had shot L[ewis] in self-defense, admitting that he had intentionally fired his gun at L[ewis] knowing that by pulling the trigger he would likely kill him."

The thrust of defense counsel's closing argument was that Gonzalez acted in self defense, not that there was a lack of premeditation. Counsel did argue briefly that Gonzalez did not have time to premeditate. (*Id.* at 97.) However, this was contrary to Gonzalez's trial testimony:

> Q. As far as this officer, sir, you were afraid Sergeant Lewis was going to shoot you, so you decided to pull your trigger and shoot him first?
> A. Yes.
> . . . .
> Q. You were shooting at the person in the truck, were you not, sir?
> A. Yes, I was.
> Q. So that was your intention, whether it be to defend yourself or not was to shoot the person inside that truck.
> Correct, sir?
> A. Yes.
> . . . .
> Q. So is it fair to say, you knew when you pointed that gun at the person in the truck and you pulled the trigger, you knew that that would kill the person in the truck.
> Did you not, Mr. Gonzalez?
> A. Yeah, I knew that.

Gonzalez testified that he did not shoot at Officer Blue because he thought by the time he could take out his gun and turn to shoot him, that he would have gotten shot, and there was a girl nearby and he was afraid he would hit her. He also stated that he had seen Officer Lewis in his truck and thought that if he turned around to shoot at Officer Blue, then Officer Lewis would have shot him. Gonzalez's testimony reveals clearly he knew that firing his weapon at Officer Lewis would kill him. He reflected upon this knowledge prior to pulling the trigger, enough to decide not to shoot at Officer Blue but to aim his weapon at Officer Lewis with that knowledge.

Gonzalez argues that there was no time to reflect and that firing his weapon was merely a natural reaction in the face of being accosted by unknown armed men, which amounted to a sudden quarrel or heat of passion. First, his trial testimony recited above establishes that he reflected before shooting his weapon. Whether he knew that he was shooting at an officer is irrelevant to the element of premeditation. Second, his counsel's closing argument did not suggest the shooting was the instant effect of a sudden quarrel. Further, the instruction accurately represented that an act was not premeditated if it was impulsive, the instant effect of a sudden quarrel. Thus, it is clear the jury did not find the shooting to be the result of a sudden quarrel.

Because the trial evidence established that the shooting was premeditated, and Gonzalez's defense was not compromised by the erroneous portion of the instruction, it appears beyond a reasonable doubt that the error did not contribute to the verdict. Thus, the error was harmless and the Arizona Court of Appeals' denial of this claim was not an objectively unreasonable application of federal law.

Claim 4 (Trial I)

Gonzalez alleges that he was denied due process and a fair trial by the admission of 9-millimeter shell casings from his car.

Prior to trial, Gonzalez moved to preclude evidence regarding two 9-millimeter shell casings found in his car after the Humo shooting. The State argued that the casings were relevant because they could be associated with the .38-caliber bullet found in the Humo shooting. At that time, Detective Cassel informed the court that there was a revolver that could shoot 9-millimeter and .38-caliber rounds. The judge denied the motion to preclude. Gonzalez intermingles within this claim arguments about the ineffectiveness of his counsel regarding this evidence. This is a separate claim (Claim 16(A)(7)(a)), therefore, the Court does not address those arguments within the discussion of Claim 4.

Detective Denogean testified at trial that he found two 9-millimeter shell casings in Gonzalez's car after the Humo shooting and that those casings were associated with a semiautomatic weapon. Detective Cassel testified that the bullet removed from Humo was a .38-caliber, which could be fired by a revolver or a semiautomatic weapon, including a 9-millimeter. He stated that it was possible for a .38-caliber bullet to be associated with a 9-millimeter casing. Detective Cassel testified that he could not tell whether the 9-millimeter casings found in the car came from a revolver or a semiautomatic gun. He also testified that he could not tell if the .38-caliber bullet recovered from Humo's body was associated with one of the 9-millimeter casings found in the car, nor could he tell if the bullet was fired by a revolver or semiautomatic weapon.

The court of appeals denied this claim finding that:

> Although the evidence at trial did not establish whether the weapon that injured M[ark] was a .38-caliber or a nine-millimeter weapon, the state's expert testified that a particular type of revolver uses both kinds of bullets interchangeably. Thus, the presence of the nine-millimeter shell casings in Gonzalez's car was marginally relevant to the issue of whether he had shot M[ark].

This Court may only grant habeas relief on a claim alleging erroneous admission of evidence if the evidence "rendered the trial fundamentally unfair" in violation of due process. *Kealohapauole v. Shimoda, 800 F.2d 1463, 1466 (9th Cir. 1986); Estelle v. McGuire, 502 U.S. 62, 70, 112 S. Ct. 475, 116 L. Ed. 2d 385 (1991); Jammal v. Van de Kamp, 926 F.2d 918, 919 (9th Cir. 1991).* The United States Supreme Court has "very narrowly" defined the category of infractions that violate the due process test of fundamental fairness. *Dowling v. United States, 493 U.S. 342, 352, 110 S. Ct. 668, 107 L. Ed. 2d 708 (1990).*

Gonzalez argues that the shell casings were the only physical evidence used to establish a connection between him and the shooting. With further investigation, Gonzalez argues that he may be able to prove that the 9-millimeter shell casings and the bullet recovered from Humo's body have no relation to one another. In light of this possibility, he argues that admission of this evidence was highly prejudicial.

Gonzalez argues that the prosecutor highlighted the evidence of the casings in closing arguments. In her initial closing argument, the prosecutor did not mention the 9-millimeter casings. Defense counsel, however, made the following argument regarding the casings in her closing argument:

> Casings. If the casings are related to this case and I'm not suggesting to you the casings may not be related to the case. If the casings that are found in Robert Gonzalez's car are somehow related to this shooting, then do you want those fingerprinted to see, is Robert Gonzalez con-

nected to the casings? Now, are the casings connected? Well, again, physical evidence by - physical testing by a criminal lab would have told you that.

It seems that the State's theory is that it's a revolver that shot Mr. Humo, both from Mr. Humo saying it's a revolver and the fact that there are no casings found at the scene. And there's no evidence of the shooter gathering up casings at the scene. There were no casings found at the scene. A semiautomatic weapon would fire bullets and they would expect that the casings would be expected to be seen in the parking lot of the Preciado apartment complex.

It would be nice to know whether the casings that are in the car are related to a revolver or not, because if all the evidence is that the casings that the shooter had were from a revolver and there are casings in Robert Gonzalez's car that are for a revolver, then   that is a step for you to say, Robert Gonzalez did it. And equally, the fact that you don't know the answer to that is one of the reasonable doubts you should have in this case.

You know from the testimony I elicited from Detective Cassel that if it's a semiautomatic, there's going to be two ejector marks on the casings, such as ballistics could look at those casings, and be able to tell if it's a semiautomatic or revolver.

Detective Cassel can't look at the casings himself, just by looking at them, eyeballing them and be able to tell if they are revolver or a semiautomatic, but an expert could tell whether there are ejector marks on them.

In response to the defense attorney's argument, in her closing rebuttal, the prosecutor argued:

Fingerprint the shell casings. Fingerprint the shell casings could have proven that Robert Gonzalez touched some shell casings in his car, nothing more than that. We didn't have the gun, Ladies and Gentlemen. He wasn't stupid enough to leave the gun in his car when he parked it behind the house on Knox Street that night without the gun. We couldn't prove these shell casings came from the weapon, couldn't prove these shell casings came   from the same bullet that was taken from Humo.

All that would have proven was that Robert Gonzalez' fingerprints were on the shell casings, which are found in Robert Gonzalez' car. It's just a red herring.

Detective Cassel's testimony established only that the 9-millimeter casings and the .38-caliber bullet that hit Humo could be associated with each other and both could be associated with the same gun. Contrary to Gonzalez's argument review of the prosecutor's closing argument reveals that she did not rely on, or even mention, that the casings and the bullet were consistent with one another. Gonzalez argues that he can demonstrate that the bullet could not have been directly linked to the shell casing. Even if true, as found by the state courts, the shell casings were marginally relevant because they could be compatible with a gun that could have shot the .38-caliber bullet recovered from Humo.

Even if the shell casings were not relevant, their admission did not render Gonzalez's trial fundamentally unfair. In the end, the defense relied on them more than the prosecution to argue there was reasonable doubt as to whether Gonzalez was the shooter.   The admission of the shell casings was not critical evidence linking Gonzalez to the shooting. The critical evidence was that three eye witnesses identified Gonzalez as the shooter and/or his car as present at the shooting. In the face of that evidence, the casings had no impact on the verdict and did not violate his right to due process. At a minimum, the Arizona Court of Appeals' decision denying this claim was not objectively unreasonable.

Petitioner requests discovery and an evidentiary hearing regarding this claim. It is self-evident that when reviewing a claim of trial court error regarding admission of evidence, this Court reviews the evidence that was before the trial court at the time it made the decision. There is no material factual dispute requiring an evidentiary hearing, see *Townsend v. Sain*, 372 U.S. 293, 312-13, 83 S. Ct. 745, 9 L. Ed. 2d 770 (1963), *overruled in part by Keeney v. Tamayo-Reyes*, 504 U.S. 1, 112 S. Ct. 1715, 118 L. Ed. 2d 318 (1992), *and limited by §* 2254(e)(2), because this is strictly a record-based claim. Because Claim 4 must be decided based on the state court record, neither discovery nor an evidentiary hearing is warranted.

Claim 5 (Trial I)

Gonzalez alleges he was denied the right to present a complete defense by the trial court's preclusion of impeachment testimony of Humo. Specifically, Gonzalez wanted to establish that Humo had warrants out for his arrest, which the state refrained from serving on him, he had tattoos indicating gang membership, and he had prior convictions. Respondents fail to acknowledge the third part of this claim regarding Humo's prior convictions. Review of Gonzalez's appellate brief indicates this portion of the claim was not fairly presented in state court. Regardless, the Court will address this part of the claim because it is meritless. *See 28 U.S.C. § 2254(b)(2).*

Legal Standard

Due process provides a defendant the right to a fair opportunity to present a defense to the State's accusations. *Chambers v. Mississippi, 410 U.S. 284, 294, 93 S. Ct. 1038, 35 L. Ed. 2d 297 (1973).* When these rights are restricted in a way that deprives a defendant of a fair trial in violation of due process, he is entitled to relief. *Id. at 302* (trial court excluded "critical evidence"). However, a defendant does not have "an unfettered right to offer testimony that is incompetent, privileged, or otherwise inadmissable under standard rules of evidence." *Taylor v. Illinois, 484 U.S. 400, 410, 108 S. Ct. 646, 98 L. Ed. 2d 798 (1988).* States have the power to "exclude evidence through the application of evidentiary rules that themselves serve the interests of fairness and reliability," and judges have wide latitude to exclude evidence that is "marginally relevant" or would cause confusion of the issues. *Crane v. Kentucky, 476 U.S. 683, 689-90, 106 S. Ct. 2142, 90 L. Ed. 2d 636 (1986)* (citing *Delaware v. Van Arsdall, 475 U.S. 673, 679, 106 S. Ct. 1431, 89 L. Ed. 2d 674 (1986); Chambers, 410 U.S. at 302*).

Warrants

Prior to trial, defense counsel moved to introduce evidence that Humo had outstanding misdemeanor warrants for his arrest and he was not being arrested on them as a benefit for his testimony. The prosecutor attested to the court that she had no knowledge of the warrants prior to defense counsel bringing them to her attention and that Humo was not receiving any benefit for his testimony. The trial court denied the request because Gonzalez had not established the prosecution knew about the warrants. The court of appeals found the trial court was within its discretion to deny admission of the warrants because the prosecutor avowed that she first learned of the warrants from Gonzalez's motion in limine. The court found Gonzalez's argument -- that Humo was not being arrested on the warrants as a benefit for his testimony -- was based entirely on conjecture and the evidence was properly precluded.

In this Court, Gonzalez again argues he should have been allowed to introduce the warrants for Humo's arrest because they demonstrated he was receiving a benefit for his testimony. The state court found that Gonzalez had not demonstrated that Humo was receiving any benefit. This Court must defer to the factual findings of the state courts. *28 U.S.C. § 2254(e)(1).* Because Humo was not receiving any benefit from his testimony, there was no basis to admit the outstanding misdemeanor warrants. Preclusion of Humo's arrest warrants did not render Gonzalez's trial unfair in violation of due process.

Claim 6 (Trial I)

Gonzalez alleges the trial court's preclusion of witness Joe Duran as a sanction for late disclosure violated his right to due process under the *Fourteenth Amendment* and compulsory process under the *Sixth Amendment.*

Gonzalez's counsel represented to the trial court that Duran was disclosed as a witness in a pretrial statement, however, the defense was not able to serve him with a subpoena and hear what he had to offer as testimony until ten days before trial. They were not able to interview him until the day before trial, at which time the prosecutor was not available. Counsel represented that Duran would testify that "he overheard Mr. Gonzalez's side of a conversation. He picked up the phone, it was Alyssa, he handed the phone to Mr. Gonzalez. Then he overheard Mr. Gonzalez's portion of a conversation where it appeared to him Mr. Gonzalez was getting upset because of the things Ms. Preciado was saying." The court found the relevance of Duran's testimony "very tenuous," and granted the motion to preclude due to the late disclosure and inability for the prosecution to prepare.

The court of appeals found that Duran's proposed testimony demonstrated only that Gonzalez was angry at Preciado It held that its relevance was not vital and "very tenuous." Further, because the defense was able to cross-examine Preciado regarding her relationship with Gonzalez, the court found he was not prejudiced by the preclusion.

A defendant has the right to a fair opportunity to present a defense to the State's accusations, including calling witnesses on his behalf, based on the *Due Process Clause of the Fourteenth Amendment* and the *Compulsory Process Clause of the Sixth Amendment*. *Chambers, 410 U.S. at 294*; *Taylor, 484 U.S. at 408-09*. However, judges have wide latitude to exclude evidence that is "marginally relevant." *Crane, 476 U.S. at 689-90* (citing *Van Arsdall, 475 U.S. at 679*; *Chambers, 410 U.S. at 302*). Further, the deprivation of a particular witness's testimony does not violate either the *Sixth* or *Fourteenth Amendment* unless the defendant makes a showing that the witness's testimony was material and favorable. *See United States v. Valenzuela-Bernal, 458 U.S. 858, 867, 872, 102 S. Ct. 3440, 73 L. Ed. 2d 1193 (1982)*.

Gonzalez fails to demonstrate that Duran's testimony was material. He asserts that Duran would have testified that Preciado had animosity against Gonzalez and this led her to accuse him of the shooting. (Doc. 1 at 48.) A review of the proffer made in state court indicates that Gonzalez's characterization overstates Duran's personal knowledge. As found by the appellate court, Duran heard only Gonzalez's side of a conversation, which indicated Gonzalez was upset. Duran could not hear Preciado's portion of the conversation and Gonzalez has proffered no basis to believe Duran could support his defense that Preciado wrongly accused Gonzalez because of her anger at him. Because this evidence was not material, its exclusion did not violate Gonzalez's constitutional rights.

Claim 16(A) (Trial I)

Gonzales alleges he was denied effective assistance of counsel at his first trial because trial counsel failed to: (4) object to testimony about a mug shot taken prior to either of the shootings at issue in the trial or to challenge the reliability of that identification; (7) obtain a ballistics expert; and (8) challenge the State's closing argument stating that the victim had four bullet wounds when he only had two.

Legal Standard

The governing federal law standard for claims of ineffective assistance of counsel is set forth in *Strickland v. Washington, 466 U.S. 668, 686, 104 S. Ct. 2052, 80 L. Ed. 2d 674 (1984)*, which recognizes a right to "effective assistance of counsel" arising under the *Sixth Amendment*. The *Strickland* standard for IAC has two components. A defendant must first demonstrate that counsel's performance was deficient, *i.e.*, that counsel made errors so serious that counsel was not functioning as the "counsel" guaranteed a defendant by the *Sixth Amendment*. *466 U.S. at 687*. It requires the defendant to show that counsel's conduct "fell below an objective standard of reasonableness." *Id. at 687-88*. Counsel's performance is strongly presumed to fall within the ambit of reasonable conduct unless petitioner can show otherwise. *Id. at 689-90*. Second, a defendant must show that the mistakes made were "prejudicial to the defense," that is, the mistakes created a "reasonable probability that, but for [the] unprofessional errors, the result of the proceeding would have been different." *Id. at 694*.

Subclaim 4

Gonzalez alleges that his counsel failed to object to the use of a mug shot taken before the shooting of Humo, in October 2001, which was shown to witness Miguel Camarena. Gonzalez alleges that testimony regarding this photo informed the jury that he had a prior conviction and that the admission of the photographic identification was unreliable.

The prosecutor showed Camarena a photograph, Exhibits 37 and 37A (enlarged), and asked if he recognized the person.) He identified the person as the driver of the car, who was the person that shot Humo. Camarena testified that no one ever asked him to pick the shooter out of a photographic line up. Initially,

Camarena stated that he did not recognize anyone in the courtroomHe later identified Gonzalez as the driver and shooter on November 3, 2001.

At a bench conference, Gonzalez's counsel did not object to the prosecutor having Detective Cassel identify and lay the foundation for admission of the photograph. Defense counsel requested only that the actual date of the photograph not be elicited, so the jury would not hear it was taken prior to the shooting;   the prosecutor agreed to that limitation. Detective Cassel testified that the photograph of Gonzalez was taken near in time, within three to four weeks of the offense. The blown-up version of the photograph, Exhibit 37A, was admitted without objection.

The PCR court denied this claim finding that the photograph was relevant for identification purposes because Gonzalez's appearance was markedly different at the time of trial. Further, the court found that Gonzalez had not shown any prejudice from its admission.

In this Court, Gonzalez has not demonstrated that he was prejudiced by counsel's action with respect to the photograph. Contrary to his argument, admission of a mug shot from "near in time" to the shooting did not inform the jury that Gonzalez had a prior conviction. A booking photo does not equate to a conviction. Further, the jury could have thought the photo was affiliated with the case currently before them, the Humo shooting.

Gonzalez has not shown that if counsel had objected the photograph would have been precluded. Additionally, although Gonzalez argues that counsel should have requested an identification   hearing, he does not articulate the steps necessary to win such a motion nor explain why such a motion would have been successful. His failure to demonstrate that, if counsel had acted as he alleges she should have, the action would have been successful, precludes a finding of prejudice. *See Kimmelman v. Morrison, 477 U.S. 365, 375, 106 S. Ct. 2574, 91 L. Ed. 2d 305 (1986)* (petitioner most prove an issue is meritorious to establish counsel failed to act competently); *Wilson v. Henry, 185 F.3d 986, 990 (9th Cir. 1999)* (citing *Morrison, 477 U.S. at 373-74*). Further, he has not established that if the photograph had not been admitted there is a reasonable probability he would not have been convicted. Initially, Camarena identified Gonzalez's car, which was affiliated with the shooting, and later in his testimony he identified Gonzalez as the shooter. Humo and Preciado also identified Gonzalez as the shooter. The PCR court's denial of this claim was not an objectively unreasonable application of *Strickland.*

Subclaim 7(a)

Gonzalez alleges counsel was ineffective for failing to obtain a ballistics expert to counter the testimony of Detective Cassel regarding the 9-millimeter shell casings. The PCR court denied this claim finding   that Gonzalez had not called Detective Cassel's testimony into question and, without the evidence of the casings in his car, there was sufficient evidence from Humo and Preciado to connect him to the shooting.

Resolution of this claim is driven by the Court's analysis as to Claim 4. As found above, in light of the eyewitness testimony in this case, the admission of the casings and the related testimony had no impact on the verdict. Therefore, Gonzalez was not prejudiced by his counsel's failure to obtain expert testimony to counter the evidence regarding the casings found in his car. The PCR court's denial of this claim was not an objectively unreasonable application of *Strickland.*

Petitioner requests discovery and an evidentiary hearing with respect to this claim. He seeks to present the evidence he contends counsel should have developed and presented at trial. To establish a right to either discovery or an evidentiary hearing, Petitioner must demonstrate that, if allowed to fully develop the facts he alleges, he will be entitled to relief. *See Bracy v. Gramley, 520 U.S. 899, 908-09, 117 S. Ct. 1793, 138 L. Ed. 2d 97 (1997); Townsend, 372 U.S. at 312-13.* Because the Court has determined that Petitioner   is not entitled to relief on this claim based on his allegations, there is no basis for discovery or an evidentiary hearing.

Subclaim 8

Petitioner alleges his counsel was ineffective for failing to challenge the prosecutor's closing argument, in which she stated that Humo had four bullet wounds when in fact he was only shot twice. The PCR court denied this claim finding that Gonzalez had not established how correcting this discrepancy would have impacted the verdict.

The information before the Court does not establish with certainly how many times Humo was shot. In the grand jury proceeding, Detective Michael Carroll testified that Humo was hit with two bullets. At trial, Humo testified that he was shot four times, once in the left side of his ribs and then three in his left butt area.

Petitioner argues that it was a critical failure of counsel not to clarify the number of bullet wounds Humo suffered because the additional bullets supported the prosecutor's argument that the crime was attempted first degree murder. The Court disagrees. It is undisputed that Gonzalez fired at least four shots because Humo was struck at least   twice and two bullets were lodged in the wall of the apartment building. Further, it is undisputed that Gonzalez fired at Humo after he turned and was attempting to run away. Whether Gonzalez struck him two or four times is irrelevant to the elements for attempted first degree murder. The PCR court's finding that Petitioner had not established prejudice was not objectively unreasonable.

Claim 14 (Trial II)

Gonzalez alleges he was denied due process and a fair trial by   police destruction of exculpatory evidence. Specifically, Officer Blue moved his car prior to the investigation of the shooting. As discussed in the procedural default section above, Gonzalez fairly presented this claim in a supplemental PCR brief. The PCR court did not address it. Therefore, the Court reviews the claim *de novo*. *See Pirtle v. Morgan, 313 F.3d 1160, 1167 (9th Cir. 2002)*.

In *Arizona v. Youngblood, 488 U.S. 51, 58, 109 S. Ct. 333, 102 L. Ed. 2d 281 (1988)*, the Court held that absent a showing of bad faith on the part of the police, "failure to preserve potentially useful evidence does not constitute a denial of due process of law." The duty to preserve evidence is limited to "evidence that might be expected to play a significant role in the suspect's defense," which requires that the "evidence must both possess an exculpatory value that was apparent before the evidence was destroyed, and be of such a nature that the defendant would be unable to obtain comparable evidence by other reasonably available means." *California v. Trombetta, 467 U.S. 479, 488-89, 104 S. Ct. 2528, 81 L. Ed. 2d 413 (1984)*. The bad faith requirement of *Youngblood* hinges on whether the government had knowledge of the exculpatory value of the evidence before its destruction. *See United States v. Cooper, 983 F.2d 928, 931 (9th Cir. 1993)*.

Gonzalez argues that Officer Blue was very experienced and, therefore, knew his car would be part of the investigation and moving it would amount to destruction of evidence. Petitioner explained that "[t]he location of Officer Blue at the time of the shooting became extremely important when it was the Defendant's and other witnesses' testimony that he was shooting from behind the open door of his vehicle, located in the middle of the road." There was conflicting testimony about whether Officer Blue remained behind his door or immediately stepped into full view as he exited his car. Petitioner fails to explain how the exact location of Officer Blue's car would have helped establish whether he was behind his door when he began shooting.

Although Petitioner does not discuss the significance of Officer Blue's location, presumably the issue was whether Gonzalez had a good view of Officer Blue prior to the shooting, such that he should have known he was a police officer. That point turns out not to be critical, as conceded by defense counsel in closing arguments. She emphasized that even if Officer Blue was not behind his door,   that Officer Blue himself stated that he fired his weapon from behind a tall truck, which would have obscured him being fully seen. As counsel stated, the more critical factor was whether Officer Blue identified himself and Gonzalez knew he was a police officer. Similarly, Officer Blue testified that he announces himself because a person might not otherwise know he was a police officer. The jury concluded beyond a reasonable doubt that Gonzalez knew or should have known that the victim, Officer Lewis, was a peace officer on official duty. Thus, Officer Blue's location did not play a "significant role in the suspect's defense." Further, the exact location of his car is a distinct, irrelevant, matter from Officer Blue's location in relation to the car when he exited his vehicle and when he shot his weapon. Finally, Petitioner has not demonstrated bad faith because, regardless of Officer Blue's experience, he could not have known when he moved his car that there would later be a conflict in the testimony at trial, which could have been resolved if he had not moved his car. Thus, the exact location of his car did not   have apparent exculpatory value.

Petitioner has failed to establish that he was denied due process by Officer Blue moving his vehicle prior to investigation of the crime scene.

REASON WHY REMEDY IS HOLLOW

In Arizona the type of misconduct described above is very common and state courts refuse to ensure they are not repeated. In their win at all costs approach the Arizona Attorney general fails to bring this structural deficiencies in the system to the attention of federal courts.

FAILURE TO CONDUCT ANDERS REVIEW

Jose Lewis Bosquez, Petitioner, v. Charles L. Ryan, et al., Respondents.No. CV-13-01714-PHX-PGR (BSB) UNITED STATES DISTRICT COURT FOR THE DISTRICT OF ARIZONA
(text modified for emphasis)

A. Charges, Guilty Plea, and Sentencing

On June 23, 2010, Petitioner was indicted in Maricopa County Superior Court case number CR2010-013094-001 on the following charges: (1) conspiracy to commit aggravated robbery, a class three dangerous felony (Count One); (2) armed robbery, a class two dangerous felony (Count Two); (3) kidnapping, a class two dangerous felony (Count Three); (4) theft of a means of transportation, a class three dangerous felony (Count Four); (5) first degree murder, a class one dangerous felony (Count Five); (6) trafficking in stolen property in the second degree, a class three felony (Count Six); (7) two counts of hindering prosecution in the first degree, class three felonies (Counts Seven and Nine); and (8) tampering with physical evidence, a class six felony (Count Eight).

The State later alleged that Petitioner committed the offenses while on release. The State also alleged several aggravating circumstances, including the infliction or threatened infliction of serious physical injury, the use or threatened use or possession of a deadly weapon or dangerous instrument (a gun), the presence of an accomplice, that the offenses were committed in an especially heinous, cruel or depraved manner, and that the offenses were committed as consideration for the receipt, or in the expectation of the receipt, of anything of pecuniary value.

On February 28, 2012, Petitioner pleaded guilty to Counts One through Six of the indictment. Before the sentencing hearing, Petitioner's counsel filed a mitigation report with the trial court. During the sentencing hearing on May 25, 2012, the court heard aggravation and mitigation evidence before sentencing Petitioner to seven-and-one half years' imprisonment (presumptive) on Count One, ten-and-one-half-years' imprisonment (presumptive) on Count Two, ten-and-one-half years' imprisonment (presumptive) on Count Three, seven-and-one-half years' imprisonment (presumptive) on Count Four, natural life (aggravated) on Count Five, and three-and-one-half years' imprisonment on Count Six. The court ordered that Petitioner's sentences run concurrently.

B. Post-Conviction Proceedings

1. First Post-Conviction (Rule 32 of-right) Proceeding

By pleading guilty, Petitioner waived his right to a direct appeal under Arizona law. *See Ariz. Rev. Stat. § 13-4033(B)*. Petitioner, however, retained the right to seek review in an "of-right" proceeding pursuant to *Rule 32* of the Arizona Rules of Criminal Procedure. *See Ariz. R. Crim. P. 32.1* and *32.4*. On June 28, 2012, Petitioner filed a timely notice of post-conviction relief in the trial court pursuant to *Rule 32*. On July 12, 2012, the trial court appointed post-conviction counsel. On November 17, 2012, post-conviction counsel filed a petition for relief arguing that Petitioner's sentence of natural life imprisonment violated *Miller v. Alabama,* U.S. , 132 S. Ct. 2455, 183 L. Ed. 2d 407 (2012), because the trial court failed to give him an "individualized sentencing." On February 19, 2013, the court denied post-conviction relief, concluding that the trial court had considered mitigating evidence during sentencing and that Petitioner's claim was not "colorable

2. Second Post-Conviction Proceeding

On March 4, 2013, Petitioner filed a second notice of post-conviction relief alleging ineffective assistance of trial counsel. On March 18, 2013, the court dismissed the second notice of post-conviction relief because it was untimely and did not raise a claim that could be raised in an untimely or successive *Rule 32* petition. (citing *Ariz. R. Crim. P. 32.1(d), (e), (f), (g),(h)* and *Ariz. R. Crim. P. 32.4(a)*).)

3. Appeal of Post-Conviction Proceedings

Petitioner then filed a "Delayed Petition for Review" in the Arizona Court of Appeals. The notice of filing the petition for review is dated April 26, 2013 in a hand written notation. However, the notice is file-stamped received by the court on May 10, 2013. In the delayed petition for review, Petitioner stated that he sought review of the trial court's decision entered on "2/14/2013" and challenged his sentence under *Miller*. On May 20, 2013, the appellate court dismissed the delayed petition for review as untimely. The court stated that:

> A review of the record in this matter indicates that the trial court dismissed the petition for post-conviction relief on *March 18, 2013*, and the petition for review was not filed until May 10, 2013. . . . Whether petitioner was without fault for the untimely filing is a question of fact. The trial court may, "after being presented with proper evidence, allow a late filing" if it finds that petitioner was not responsible for the untimely filing.

In this order, the appellate court did not identify that Petitioner had filed two post-conviction proceedings. Based on the appellate court's reference to the March 18, 2013 dismissal of the post-conviction proceeding, it appears that the appellate court considered the delayed petition for review to relate to Petitioner's second post-conviction proceeding that was dismissed on March 18, 2013. The delayed petition for review, however, stated that Petitioner sought review of the trial court's February 14, 2013 decision, and it raised the same claim asserted in the first petition for post-conviction relief (a *Miller* claim), not the second petition for post-conviction relief (ineffective assistance of trial counsel). The trial court's order denying review of the first petition for post-conviction relief is dated February 14, 2013 and filed February 19, 2013.

Nonetheless, even if Petitioner had intended for the delayed petition for review to be an appeal from the trial court's February 19, 2013 denial of his first petition for post-conviction relief, the delayed petition for review would have been untimely under *Rule 32.9(c)* (whether it was considered filed on the date it was signed, April 26, 2013, or the date it was filed, May 10, 2013) because it was filed more than thirty days after the court's February 19, 2013 decision. *See Ariz. R. Crim. P. 32.9(c)* (providing that a petition for review must be filed within thirty days of the final decision of the trial court on the petition for post-conviction relief).

C. Petition for Writ of Habeas Corpus

On August 20, 2013, Petitioner filed a petition for writ of habeas corpus in this Court asserting several claims. Ground One, the only remaining ground for relief, asserts that Petitioner's natural life sentence violates *Miller*. In their supplemental brief Respondents argue that habeas corpus review of this claim is procedurally barred. Despite the opportunity to do so, Petitioner has not filed a supplemental brief to support his Petition, or responded to Respondents' supplemental brief, and the deadlines to do so have passed.

III. Procedural Bar Applied to Petitioner's Claim in Ground One

In Ground One, Petitioner argues that his natural life sentence violates *Miller*. Petitioner presented this claim in his first petition for post-conviction relief, his Rule 32 of-right proceeding. On February 19, 2013, the court denied post-conviction reliefPetitioner did not immediately appeal the denial of his first-petition for post-conviction relief. Rather, on March 4, 2013, Petitioner filed a second notice of post-conviction relief alleging ineffective assistance of trial counsel, but not raising a *Miller* claim. On March 18, 2013, the court dismissed the second notice of post-conviction relief as untimely.

Petitioner then filed a "Delayed Petition for Review" in the Arizona Court of Appeals. The delayed petition for review states that Petitioner seeks review of the trial court's decision entered on "2/14/2013" and raises a claim under *Miller*. Thus, it appears that Petitioner may have intended to appeal the trial court's February 2013 denial of his first petition for post-conviction relief, which also raised a *Miller* claim. On May 20, 2013, the appellate court dismissed the delayed petition for review as untimely. (As previously noted, the appellate court's order denying the delayed petition referred to the March 18, 2013 dismissal of the second post-conviction proceeding, and thus it appears that the appellate court considered the delayed petition for review to relate to Petitioner's second post-conviction proceeding.

Nonetheless, whether Petitioner was attempting to appeal the denial of his first or second petition for post-conviction relief, the delayed petition for review asserted the *Miller* claim that Petitioner presents in Ground One of the pending Petition. The appellate court found review of that claim precluded because the petition for review was untimely filed. As noted in Section I.B.3, regardless of whether the delayed petition for review sought review of the first or second post-conviction proceeding, it was untimely under *Rule 32.9(c)* because it was filed more than thirty days after the court's February 19, 2013 and March 18, 2013 decisions. *See Ariz. R. Crim. P. 32.9* (providing that a petition for review must be filed within thirty days of the final decision of the trial court on the petition for post-conviction relief).

In the May 20, 2013 order, the appellate court stated that whether "petitioner was without fault for the untimely filing [of his petition for review] is a question of fact." The court further stated that "[t]he trial court may 'after being presented with proper evidence, allow a late filing' if it finds that petitioner was not responsible for the untimely filing." (*Id.*) (citing *State v. Pope, 130 Ariz. 253, 635 P.2d 846, 848 (1981)*

In their Supplemental Brief, Respondents state that there is nothing in the state trial court record or docket indicating that Petitioner returned to the state trial court to determine the responsibility for his untimely petition for review. Respondents filed a copy of the docket sheet in Petitioner's criminal case. The Court has reviewed the docket sheet and agrees that it does not reflect that Petitioner returned to the state trial court for further proceedings after the appellate court's May 20, 2013 order. There is no indication that Petitioner sought a determination in the state court of whether he was without fault for the untimely petition for review under *Rule 32.1(f)*. On July 10, 2013, the court of appeals sent the trial court a certified copy of the order dismissing the appeal.

Thus, the Arizona Court of Appeals court found that Petitioner's failure to comply with *Rule 32.9(c)*'s deadlines for filing a petition for review from the denial of post-conviction relief precluded consideration of his *Miller* claim, the same claim asserted in Ground One of the pending Petition. Petitioner did not seek further review of that decision. Additionally, there is no evidence that Petitioner returned to the state trial court to determine whether he was without fault for the untimely filing of his petition for review. Accordingly, federal habeas corpus review of Ground One is barred because *Rule 32.9(c)* is an independent and adequate state law ground. *See Simmons v. Schriro, 187 Fed. App'x 753, 754 (9th Cir. 2006)* (holding that Arizona's procedural rules, including its timeliness rules, are "clear" and "well-established"); *Miloni v. Schriro, 2006 U.S. Dist. LEXIS 39191, 2006 WL 1652578, *5 (D. Ariz. Jun. 7, 2006)* (concluding that a procedural ruling based on *Rule 32.9(c)* is adequate).

Moreover, it would be futile for Petitioner to return to the state court to try to properly exhaust Ground One because a successive petition for post-conviction relief would be untimely, and this claim would be precluded from *Rule 32* review because it could have been raised in Petitioner's prior post-conviction proceeding. *See Ariz. R. Crim. P. 32.2(a)(3) and 32.4(a); see also State v. Bennett, 213 Ariz. 562, 146 P.3d 63, 67 (2006)* ("As a general rule, when [claims] are raised, or could have been raised, in a *Rule 32* post-conviction proceeding, subsequent claims [] will be deemed waived and precluded.") (internal quotation omitted). Additionally, Petitioner's claim does not implicate the exceptions to the timeliness or preclusion rules referred to in *Rule 32.4(a)* and *Rule 32.2(b)*, which include being held in custody after the imposed sentence expired, the presentation of newly discovered material facts that probably would have changed the verdict or sentence, the failure to file a timely notice of post-conviction relief or a notice of appeal that was not the defendant's fault, a change in the law, or the petitioner's actual innocence. *See Ariz. R. Crim. P. 32.1(d), (e), (g) and (h).*

Although, as the Court noted in the March 10, 2015 Order (Doc. 18), Petitioner could attempt to qualify for *Rule 32.1(f)'s* exception to the timeliness and preclusion rules by showing that the failure to file a timely petition for review in the Arizona Court of Appeals was without fault on his part, there is no evidence that Petitioner returned to state court to try to make such a showing. Additionally, even if Petitioner could still return to state court to try to make this showing, Petitioner has not presented any evidence showing that the failure to file a notice of appeal within the prescribed time was without fault on his part. *See Ariz. R. Crim. P. 32.1(f).* Accordingly, Ground One is procedurally defaulted and barred from federal habeas corpus review unless Petitioner establishes "cause and prejudice" or a "fundamental miscarriage of justice" to overcome the procedural bar. *See Coleman, 501 U.S. at 749.* For the reasons below, Petitioner has not established a basis to overcome the procedural bar.

A. Fundamental Miscarriage of Justice

A federal court may review the merits of a procedurally defaulted claim if the petitioner demonstrates that failure to consider the merits of that claim will result in a "fundamental miscarriage of justice." *Schlup v. Delo, 513 U.S. 298, 327, 115 S. Ct. 851, 130 L. Ed. 2d 808 (1995).* The standard for establishing a *Schlup* procedural gateway claim is "demanding." *House v. Bell, 547 U.S. 518, 538, 126 S. Ct. 2064, 165 L. Ed. 2d 1 (2006).* The petitioner must present "evidence of innocence so strong that a court cannot have confidence in the outcome of the trial." *Schlup, 513 U.S. at 316.* Under *Schlup*, to overcome the procedural hurdle created by failing to properly present his claims to the state courts, a petitioner "must demonstrate that the constitutional violations he alleges "ha[ve] probably resulted in the conviction of one who is actually innocent," such that a federal court's refusal to hear the defaulted claims would be a 'miscarriage of justice.'" *House, 547 U.S. at 555-56* (quoting *Schlup, 513 at 326, 327*)). To meet this standard, a petition must present "new reliable evidence -- whether it be exculpatory scientific evidence, trustworthy eyewitness accounts, or critical physical evidence -- that was not presented at trial." *Schlup, 513 U.S. at 324.* The petitioner has the burden of demonstrating that "it is more likely than not that no reasonable juror would have convicted him in light of the new evidence." *Id. at 327.*

"[A] convincing showing of actual innocence [as applied in *Schulp*] enable[s] habeas petitioner's to overcome a procedural bar to consideration of the merits of their constitutional claims." *McQuiggin v. Perkins, U.S. , 133 S. Ct. 1924, 1928, 185 L. Ed. 2d 1019 (2013)* (holding "that actual innocence, if proved serves as a gateway through which a petitioner may pass whether the impediment is procedural bar, as it was in *Schlup . . .*, or expiration of the statute of limitations."). However, even if a petitioner can satisfy the *Schlup* gateway, this "does not by itself provide a basis for [habeas] relief." *Schlup, 513 U.S. at 315.* Instead, the gateway merely enables the petitioner "to have [an] otherwise barred constitutional claim considered on the merits." *Id.* (internal quotations omitted).

Petitioner does not rely on *Schlup* to overcome the procedural bar to review of his claim asserted in Ground One. In Ground One, Petitioner asserts that his natural life sentence violates *Miller*. This claim does not satisfy the fundamental miscarriage of justice exception. *See Johnson v. Knowles, 541 F.3d 933, 937 (9th Cir. 2008)* (concluding "that the miscarriage of justice exception is limited to those extraordinary cases where the petitioner asserts his innocence and establishes that the court cannot have confidence in the contrary finding of guilt."); *Vernes v. Acton, 2008 U.S. Dist. LEXIS 67169, 2008 WL 4104161, at *4 (D. Mont. Sept. 3, 2008)* (stating that "[b]y definition, genuine remorse and sentencing disparity cannot amount to a "fundamental miscarriage of justice" within the meaning of *Schlup*."); *Hughes v. Schriro, 2007 U.S. Dist. LEXIS 3866, 2007 WL 163074, at *6 (D. Ariz. Jan. 18, 2007)* (noting that the petitioner did not assert that he was actually innocent, and finding that the fundamental miscarriage of justice exception did not apply to the petitioner's claims that his sentence might have been mitigated if the court had known he was ill). Thus, Petitioner has not met *Schlup's* high standard and this exception does not excuse the procedural bar to federal habeas corpus review of Ground One.

B. Cause and Prejudice

A federal court may review the merits of a procedurally defaulted claim if a petitioner establishes "cause" and "prejudice." *Coleman, 501 U.S. at 750.* To establish "cause," a petitioner must establish that some objective factor external to the defense impeded his efforts to comply with the state's procedural rules. *Teague, 489 U.S. at 298.* A showing of "interference by officials," constitutionally ineffective assistance of counsel, or "that the factual or legal basis for a claim was not reasonably available" may constitute cause. *Murray, 477 U.S. at 488.*

"Prejudice" is actual harm resulting from the constitutional violation or error. *Magby v. Wawrzaszek, 741 F.2d 240, 244 (9th Cir. 1984).* To establish prejudice, a habeas petitioner bears the burden of demonstrating that the alleged constitutional violation "worked to his actual and substantial disadvantage, infecting his entire trial with error of constitutional dimensions." *United States v. Frady, 456 U.S. 152, 170, 102 S. Ct. 1584, 71 L. Ed. 2d 816 (1982)* (emphasis in original); *see Thomas v. Lewis, 945 F.2d 1119, 1123 (9th Cir. 1991).* If petitioner fails to establish cause for his procedural default, then the court need not consider whether petitioner has shown actual prejudice resulting from the alleged constitutional violations. *Smith v. Murray, 477 U.S. 527, 533, 106 S. Ct. 2661, 91 L. Ed. 2d 434 (1986).*

2. Ineffective Assistance of Post-Conviction Counsel

Petitioner does not assert the ineffective assistance of post-conviction counsel as cause for his procedural default. Additionally, as Respondents note in their Supplemental Brief Petitioner cannot rely on the Supreme Court's recent decision in *Martinez v. Ryan, U.S. , 132 S. Ct. 1309, 1315, 182 L. Ed. 2d 272 (2012),* to argue that the ineffective assistance of post-conviction counsel (in his second post-conviction proceeding) for failing to file timely a notice of appeal constitutes cause for the procedural default of Ground One.

The ineffective assistance of counsel may constitute cause for failing to properly exhaust claims in state court and excuse procedural default. *Ortiz v. Stewart, 149 F.3d 923, 932 (9th Cir. 1998).* However, ordinarily, to meet the "cause" requirement, the ineffective assistance of counsel must amount to an independent constitutional violation. *Id.* Accordingly, when no constitutional right to an attorney exists (such as in a post-conviction proceeding), ineffective assistance will not amount to cause excusing the state procedural default. *Id.* The Supreme Court has held that "[t]here is no constitutional right to an attorney in state post-conviction proceedings. Consequently, a petitioner cannot claim constitutionally ineffective assistance of counsel in such proceedings." *Coleman v. Thompson, 501 U.S. 722, 752, 111 S. Ct. 2546, 115 L. Ed. 2d 640 (1991)* (citations omitted). Thus, in *Coleman*, the Court held that the ineffectiveness of post-conviction counsel also could not establish cause to excuse a failure to properly exhaust state remedies and procedural default on a claim. *Id.*

However, in *Martinez v. Ryan, U.S. , 132 S. Ct. 1309, 1315, 182 L. Ed. 2d 272 (2012),* the Supreme Court established a limited exception to this general rule. The Court held that the ineffective assistance of post-conviction counsel "at initial-review collateral review proceedings" -- while not stating a constitutional claim itself -- may establish cause to excuse procedural default of claims of ineffective assistance of trial counsel when a post-conviction proceeding represents the first opportunity under state law for a petitioner to litigate such claims. *Id. at 1315.* In *Nguyen v. Curry, 736 F.3d 1287, 1296 (9th Cir. 2013),* the Ninth Circuit held that the *Martinez* standard for cause applies to all *Sixth Amendment* ineffective-assistance claims that have been procedurally defaulted by ineffective counsel in the initial-review state-court collateral proceeding. *(Id.)*

Because the *Martinez* cause standard applies only to defaulted ineffective assistance of counsel claims, it does not apply to Petitioner's *Miller* claim raised in Ground One. Accordingly, Petitioner cannot rely on *Martinez* and he has not shown cause for his failure to properly present his *Miller* claim to the state courts. Therefore, the Court does not consider whether Petitioner can establish prejudice. *See Smith v. Murray, 477 U.S. 527, 533, 106 S. Ct. 2661, 91 L. Ed. 2d 434 (1986)* (stating that the court does not need to consider prejudice when the petitioner does not demonstrate cause).

3. Ineffective Assistance of Rule 32 of-Right Counsel

The Court could assume that if Petitioner had filed a supplemental brief, he may have argued that counsel in his first post-conviction proceeding, a Rule 32 of-right proceeding, was ineffective for failing to file a timely notice of appeal. Petitioner's first post-conviction proceeding was a Rule 32 of-right proceeding, which the Ninth Circuit has recognized as a "form of direct review." *See Summers v. Schriro, 481 F.3d 710, 717 (9th Cir. 2007)* (concluding "that Arizona's Rule 32 of-right proceeding for plea-convicted defendants is a form of direct review within the meaning of *28 U.S.C. § 2244(d)(1)(A)*."). Accordingly, Petitioner had the right to the effective assistance of counsel in his Rule 32 of-right proceeding. *See Ramon v. Ryan, 2010 U.S. Dist. LEXIS 93037, 2010 WL 3564819, at *11 (D. Ariz. Jul. 23, 2010)* (a defendant has a right to the effective assistance of counsel in a Rule-32 of right proceeding in Arizona) (citing *Evitts v. Lucey, 469 U.S. 387, 396, 105 S. Ct. 830, 83 L. Ed. 2d 821 (1985)*).

However, a claim of ineffective assistance of counsel to establish "cause" in this context is itself subject to the exhaustion requirements. *Murray, 477 U.S. at 492; Edwards v. Carpenter, 529 U.S. 446, 120 S. Ct. 1587, 146 L. Ed. 2d 518 (2000)*. In other words, before an allegation of ineffective assistance of counsel may be used to establish cause for a procedural default, it must have been presented to the state court as an independent claim. *Edwards, 529 U.S. at 451-53*. Here, Petitioner never exhausted a claim of ineffective assistance of Rule 32 of-right counsel because he never presented that issue to the state courts. Consequently, even if Petitioner had asserted this argument, he cannot rely on the alleged ineffective assistance of Rule 32 of-right counsel to establish cause for the default of Ground One.

For these reasons, Petitioner has not established a basis to overcome the procedural bar to federal habeas corpus review of Ground One. However, in an abundance of caution, Section IV, below, addresses the merits of Petitioner's claim in Ground One. *See 28 U.S.C. § 2254(b)(2)* (stating that "[a]n application for a writ of habeas corpus may be denied on the merits, notwithstanding the failure of the applicant to exhaust the remedies available in the courts of the State."). This review establishes that Ground One lacks merit and should be dismissed.

IV. Review of Petitioner's Claim in Ground One

A. Federal Review of Claims Adjudicated on the Merits in State Court

If a habeas petition includes a claim that was "adjudicated on the merits in State court proceedings," federal court review of that claim is limited by *§ 2254(d)*. Under *§ 2254(d)(1)*, a federal court cannot grant habeas corpus relief unless the petitioner shows: (1) that the state court's decision "was contrary to" federal law as clearly established in the holdings of the United States Supreme Court at the time of the state court decision, *Greene v. Fisher, U.S. , 132 S. Ct. 38, 43, 181 L. Ed. 2d 336 (2011)*; or (2) that it "involved an unreasonable application of" such law, *§ 2254(d)(1)*; or (3) that it "was based on an unreasonable determination of the facts" based on the record before the state court. *28 U.S.C. § 2254(d)(2); Harrington v. Richter, 562 U.S. 86, 100, 131 S. Ct. 770, 178 L. Ed. 2d 624 (2011)*. This standard is "difficult to meet." *Richter, 562 U.S. at 102*. It is also a "highly deferential standard for evaluating state court rulings, which demands that state court decisions be given the benefit of the doubt." *Woodford v. Visciotti, 537 U.S. 19, 24, 123 S. Ct. 357, 154 L. Ed. 2d 279 (2002)* (per curiam) (citation and internal quotation marks omitted). When evaluating state court decisions on habeas review, federal courts look through summary or unexplained higher state court opinions to the last reasoned decision on the claim. *Robinson v. Ignacio, 360 F.3d 1044, 1055 (9th Cir. 2004)*.

To determine whether a state court ruling was "contrary to" or involved an "unreasonable application" of federal law, courts look exclusively to the holdings of the Supreme Court that existed at the time of the state court's decision. *Greene, 132 S. Ct. at 44*. A state court's decision is "contrary to" federal law if it applies a rule of law "that contradicts the governing law set forth in [Supreme Court] cases or if it confronts a set of facts that are materially indistinguishable from a decision of [the Supreme Court] and nevertheless arrives at a result different from [Supreme Court] precedent." *Mitchell v. Esparza, 540 U.S 12, 14, 124 S. Ct. 7, 157 L. Ed. 2d 263 (2003)* (citations omitted).

A state court decision is an "unreasonable application of" federal law if the court identifies the correct legal rule, but unreasonably applies that rule to the facts of a particular case. *Brown v. Payton, 544 U.S. 133, 141, 125 S. Ct. 1432, 161 L. Ed. 2d 334 (2005)*. "A state court's determination that a claim lacks merit precludes federal habeas relief so long as 'fairminded jurists could disagree on the correctness of the state court's decision.'" *Richter, 562 U.S. at 101* (citing *Yarborough v. Alvarado, 541 U.S. 652, 664, 124 S. Ct. 2140, 158 L. Ed. 2d 938 (2004)*). "[E]valuating whether a rule application was unreasonable requires considering the rule's specificity. The more general the rule, the more leeway courts have in reaching outcomes in case-by-case determination." *Richter, 562 U.S. at 101.*

Federal courts may also grant habeas corpus relief when the state-court decision "was based on an unreasonable determination of the facts in light of the evidence presented in the State court proceeding." *28 U.S.C. § 2254(d)(2).* "Or, to put it conversely, a federal court may not second-guess a state court's fact-finding process unless, after review of the state-court record, it determines that the state court was not merely wrong, but actually unreasonable." *Taylor v. Maddox, 366 F.3d 992, 999 (9th Cir. 2004), abrogated on other grounds, Murray v. Schriro, 745 F.3d 984, 1000 (9th Cir. 2014); see Pollard v. Galaza, 290 F.3d 1030, 1033, 1035 (9th Cir. 2002)* (the statutory presumption of correctness applies to findings by both trial courts and appellate courts). Additionally, a state court's findings of fact are presumed to be correct. *28 U.S.C. § 2254(e)(1).* A petitioner may rebut this presumption with "clear and convincing evidence." *Id.*

When a state court decision is deemed to be contrary to or an unreasonable application of clearly established federal law or based on an unreasonable determination of the facts, a petitioner is not entitled to habeas corpus relief unless the erroneous state court ruling also resulted in actual prejudice as defined in *Brecht v. Abrahamson, 507 U.S. 619, 637, 113 S. Ct. 1710, 123 L. Ed. 2d 353 (1993). See Benn v. Lambert, 283 F.3d 1040, 1052 n.6 (9th Cir. 2002).* "Actual prejudice" means that the constitutional error at issue had a "substantial and injurious effect or influence in determining the jury's verdict." *Brecht, 507 U.S. at 631.* "The *Brecht* harmless error analysis also applies to habeas review of an error with respect to sentencing, in other words the test is whether such error had a 'substantial and injurious effect' on the sentence." *Hernandez v. La-Marque, 2006 U.S. Dist. LEXIS 62636, 2006 WL 2411441, at *3 (N.D. Cal., Aug.18, 2006)* (citing *Calderon v. Coleman, 525 U.S. 141, 145-47, 119 S. Ct. 500, 142 L. Ed. 2d 521 (1998)* (finding sentencing error harmless because even if the evidence of three prior convictions was insufficient, petitioner was not prejudiced by the court's consideration of those convictions because it found four other prior convictions that would have supported the petitioner's sentence)). The Court will consider Plaintiff's claim in Ground One under this standard.

B. Petitioner is not Entitled to Habeas Corpus Relief

In Ground One, Petitioner asserts that his natural life sentence violates the Supreme Court's decision in *Miller v. Alabama, U.S., 132 S. Ct. 2455, 183 L. Ed. 2d 407 (2012),* because he was denied an "individualized sentencing." In *Miller,* the Court held that "mandatory life without parole for those under the age of 18 at the time of their crimes violates the *Eighth Amendment's* prohibition on 'cruel and unusual punishments.'" *Miller, 132 S. Ct. at 2460.* Respondents state that *Miller* applies to this case. The Supreme Court issued *Miller* on June 25, 2012, one month after Petitioner's sentencing hearing. However, because Petitioner's convictions and sentences were not yet final on direct review, *Miller* applies to his proceedings, regardless of whether *Miller* should be retroactively applied. *See Teague v. Lane, 489 U.S. 288, 109 S. Ct. 1060, 103 L. Ed. 2d 334 (1989)* (new constitutional rules of criminal procedure will not be applicable to those cases that have become final before new rules are announced, unless they fall within exception to general rule).

Petitioner presented this sentencing claim to the trial court in his first petition for post-conviction relief. The court rejected this claim because it found that the trial court "did consider [Petitioner's] age, lack of maturity, and all of the other mitigation proffered by the [Petitioner] when it imposed the natural life sentence. Therefore, the Court finds that the [Petitioner] fails to set forth a colorable claim." Petitioner has not shown that the state court's decision is based on an unreasonable determination of the facts, or that it is contrary to or based on an unreasonable application of *Miller. See 28 U.S.C. § 2254(d).* Accordingly, he is not entitled to habeas corpus relief.

In *Miller,* the Supreme Court held that the "*Eighth Amendment* forbids a sentencing scheme that mandates life in prison without the possibility of parole for juvenile offenders." *132 S. Ct. at 2469.* The Court explained that "[m]andatory life without [the possibility of] parole for a juvenile precludes consideration" of the defendant's "chronological age and its hallmark features," the defendant's "family and home environment," the "circumstances of the [underlying] homicide offense," the fact that the offender "might have been charged and convicted of a lesser offense if not for incompetencies associated with youth," and "the possibility of rehabilitation." *Id. at 2468.* The Court stated that the *Eighth Amendment* requires that "a judge or jury must have the opportunity to consider mitigating circumstances before imposing the harshest penalty possible for juveniles." *Id. at 2475.*

As the state court found, Petitioner is not entitled to relief under *Miller* because the trial court considered Petitioner's youth and other mitigating circumstances before imposing a sentence of life without parole. During the sentencing hearing, the court heard argument from defense counsel about mitigating circumstances, including support of friends and family, a dysfunctional childhood, prenatal exposure to drugs, childhood homelessness, mental health issues, the use of illegal drugs, his age at the time of the offense (seventeen), and evidence that he was functioning at a lower level than his chronological age. The trial court also heard from Petitioner who apologized for his actions and said that he believed he could change. The trial court acknowledged that it considered all of the aggravation and mitigation evidence. The trial court then sentenced Petitioner to a term of natural life imprisonment on Count Five, the first-degree murder conviction. The court explained its reasoning for the sentence, stating:

> I am mindful when I impose a sentence, I'm instructed by law to consider a couple of things. I'm to look at the nature and circumstances of the offense, the character and background of the accused. When I look at the nature and circumstances of this offense, I'm morally offended. I can imagine no greater horror in life than to be locked in a trunk for a long period of time, to die from the elements.
>
> When I look at your character and background, you shouldn't have had the experience growing up that you've had. It was clearly mitigated. But now I look at you today and I look at what you've done since you've become an adult. I think, is this man damaged goods? Is this man somebody who's going to continue to terrorize society like you did in this case? Those are the questions I have to answer imposing this sentence.
> * * *
> Regarding Count 5. After reviewing all of the materials, everything in aggravating and mitigation, it is the determination of this Court you should never be released. Thereby, I impose a term of natural life. No credit for time served.

(*Id.* at 28-29, 32.) The record reflects that the trial court considered Petitioner's "chronological age and its hallmark features," and other mitigating circumstances before imposing a natural life sentence. *see Miller, 132 S. Ct. at 2468.* Thus, Petitioner's natural life sentence did not violate the Supreme Court's pronouncement in *Miller. See Bell v. Uribe, 748 F.3d 857, 869 (9th Cir. 2014)* (assuming, without deciding, that a habeas corpus petitioner's *Miller* claim was not defaulted and that *Miller* applied retroactively and concluding that because the sentencing judge considered mitigating and aggravating factors "under a [California] sentencing scheme that affords discretion and leniency, there is no violation of *Miller.*"); *Ramos v. Wipson, 2014 U.S. Dist. LEXIS 92670, 2014 WL 3130036, at *14-15 (C.D. Cal. June 4, 2014)* (relying on *Bell* to support a conclusion that because the trial court considered argument on whether it should impose a life sentence or a twenty-five-years-to-life sentence and exercised its direction and made its sentencing decision after considering those arguments, no *Miller* violation occurred and, under the AEDPA, the court must defer to the trial court's determination of petitioner's sentencing claim).

Accordingly, Petitioner cannot show that the state court's rejection of his *Miller* claim was contrary to, or involved an unreasonable application of, clearly established Supreme Court law, or that it was based on an unreasonable determination of the facts. *See 28 U.S.C. § 2254(d).* Therefore, Petitioner is not entitled to habeas corpus relief on this claim.

REASONS WHY THE REMEDY IS HOLLOW

Whenever the legislature changes the law it is understood that it did not do so with a vengeance but that everybody should benefit from the change. Realizing the fact that federal habeas review is restricted, Arizona courts refuse to afford all persons benefit of changes in law. It is the duty of the judicial branch to ensure that the "evolving standards of decency" applies to all. For administrative inconvenience and due to overzealousness the state courts and Attorney General decline to do so.

<u>GUILTY PLEAS</u>

Marc Allen Clark, Petitioner, vs. Charles L. Ryan, et al., Respondents. No. CV-14-8112-PCT-DGC (JZB) UNITED STATES DISTRICT COURT FOR THE DISTRICT OF ARIZONA
(text modified for emphasis)

A. FACTS OF THE CASE

On November 18, 2006, Prescott Valley police officers began an investigation of the murder of victim Michael Sirois. As a part of the investigation, officers learned that Petitioner helped clean a car containing the victim's blood. On November 19, 2006, officers obtained a search warrant to search Petitioner's residence for evidence of drug-related offenses. After a search of the residence, police seized methamphetamine and paraphernalia consistent with drug trafficking. On November 24, 2006, Petitioner was indicted for offenses committed on November 18 and 19, 2006.

On April 16, 2007, Petitioner was in a vehicle that was stopped by police. After a search of the vehicle, officers found drug paraphernalia and a handgun. On April 24, 2007, an information was filed for offenses committed on April 16, 2007.

B. TRIAL COURT PROCEEDINGS

On April 24, 2007, Petitioner pleaded guilty, pursuant to a six-page plea agreement, to three felonies arising out of the two indictments and the information. Specifically, Petitioner pleaded guilty to Hindering Prosecution, a class 3 felony (CR 2006-1517); Possession of Dangerous Drugs for Sale, a class 2 felony (CR 2006-1519); and, Weapons Misconduct (Prohibited Possessor), a class 4 felony (CR 2007-040492J/CR 2007-0622). The plea agreement stipulated "that Defendant shall receive a term of imprisonment of 15 calendar years." Petitioner avowed that he had five prior felony convictions. Petitioner initialed each page and signed the agreement on the final page. This stipulation was hand written into the plea agreement. Petitioner asserts he was unaware of the provision.

During the plea hearing, the trial court reviewed the charges, the agreement, the statutory maximums, Petitioner's rights, and the facts of the offenses. During the colloquy, defense counsel advised the court that a 15-year term of imprisonment had been added into the agreement.

> COUNSEL: Mr. Clark and I talked about what his options are with reference to his liability if he were to go to trial on all these cases and how much he would be looking at.
>
> I think he understand the significant benefit by entering into this plea agreement. The plea agreement speaks to a stipulated term, at least 15 calendar years. That provision was put in there by the State and agreed to and he understands that -- well, he understands that this is what he wants to do, he wants to do it today to wrap all these matters up. We talked about that.

> THE COURT: That's your desire, sir?
> THE DEFENDANT: Yes, sir.

Petitioner does not contest the validity of his plea, instead he contends he was unaware of the 15-year stipulation. He requests the Court "order a sentence reduction from 15 years to the original agreed on sentence of 10 years."

On June 28, 2007, Petitioner was sentenced to 15 years' imprisonment for the Possession of Dangerous Drugs For Sale charge, to run concurrently with terms of seven and three years' imprisonment for the other two charges. Petitioner acknowledged in writing that he had 90 days in which to file a Notice of Post-Conviction Relief.

C. PETITIONS FOR POST-CONVICTION RELIEF

On October 31, 2011, Petitioner filed a notice for Post-Conviction Relief. Petitioner alleged that he agreed to a 10-year term of imprisonment, but instead the agreement was "altered" by the prosecutor "to include a stipulated 15 (fifteen) year termPetitioner argued that he had "no access to case law" and did not have a "true copy of my authentic record."

On November 21, 2011, the PCR court dismissed Petitioner's PCR petition. The court found that Petitioner had been advised of the 90-day deadline and further found "that the reasons offered by the Defendant as to why he did not file his Notice of Post-Conviction Relief in a timely manner are not sufficient for the Court to accept a late filing."

On May 15, 2013, the Arizona Court of Appeals denied review of the trial court's dismissal order. On October, 23, 2013, the Arizona Supreme Court denied Petitioner's petition for review.

A. THE PETITION IS UNTIMELY.

1. Time Calculation

The AEDPA imposes a one-year limitation period, which begins to run "from the latest of . . . the date on which the judgment became final by the conclusion of direct review or the expiration of the time for seeking such review." *28 U.S.C. § 2244(d)(1)(A)*.

Having entered into a plea agreement, Petitioner was sentenced on June 28, 2007. Petitioner had 90 days from that date to timely file an "of-right" petition for post-conviction relief. *Ariz. R.Crim. P. 32.4(a)* ("In a *Rule 32* of-right proceeding, the notice must be filed within ninety days after the entry of judgment and sentence"). Because no petition was filed within that time in Superior Court, Petitioner's judgment became final on September 26, 2007. *See 28 U.S.C. § 2244(d)(1)(A); Gonzalez v. Thaler, 132 S.Ct. 641, 656, 181 L. Ed. 2d 619 (2012)* ("with respect to a state prisoner who does not seek review in a State's highest court, the judgment becomes 'final' under § 2244(d)(1)(A) when the time for seeking such review expires").

The one-year statute of limitations on Petitioner's habeas action expired on September 26, 2008, unless statutorily or equitably tolled.

2. Statutory Tolling

The AEDPA provides for tolling of the limitations period when a "properly filed application for State post-conviction or other collateral relief with respect to the pertinent judgment or claim is pending." *28 U.S.C. § 2244(d)(2)*. In Arizona, post-conviction review is pending once a notice of post-conviction relief is filed. *See Isley v. Arizona Dep't of Corr., 383 F.3d 1054, 1056 (9th Cir. 2004). See also Ariz. R. Crim. P. 32.4(a)* ("A proceeding is commenced by timely filing a notice of post-conviction relief with the court in which the conviction occurred.").

The statute of limitations was not tolled by Petitioner's October 31, 2011 Notice of Post-Conviction Relief. This filing was not a "properly filed" state action for post-conviction relief. Once the AEDPA limitations period expires, a subsequently filed state post-conviction proceeding cannot restart the statute of limitations. *See Ferguson v. Palmateer, 321 F.3d 820, 823 (9th Cir. 2003)* (noting that an application for state post-conviction relief filed after expiration of the AEDPA statute of limitations did not reinitiate the limitations period).

Accordingly, statutory tolling does not apply.

3. Equitable Tolling

"A petitioner who seeks equitable tolling of AEDPA's 1--year filing deadline must show that (1) some 'extraordinary circumstance' prevented him from filing on time, and (2) he has diligently pursued his rights. *Holland v. Florida, 560 U.S. 631, 649, 130 S.Ct. 2549, 177 L.Ed.2d 130 (2010)." Luna v. Kernan, 784 F.3d 640, 646 (9th Cir. 2015)*. The petitioner bears the burden of showing that equitable tolling should apply. *Espinoza-Matthews v. California, 432 F.3d 1021, 1026 (9th Cir. 2005)*. Equitable tolling is only appropriate when external forces, rather than a petitioner's lack of diligence, account for the failure to file a timely habeas action. *Chaffer v. Prosper, 592 F.3d 1046, 1048-49 (9th Cir. 2010)*. Equitable tolling is to be rarely granted. *See, e.g.,*

Waldron--Ramsey v. Pacholke, 556 F.3d 1008, 1011 (9th Cir. 2009). Petitioner must show that "the extraordinary circumstances were the cause of his untimeliness and that the extraordinary circumstances made it impossible to file a petition on time." *Porter v. Ollison, 620 F.3d 952, 959 (9th Cir. 2010).* "Indeed, 'the threshold necessary to trigger equitable tolling [under AEDPA] is very high, lest the exceptions swallow the rule.'" *Miranda v. Castro, 292 F.3d 1063, 1066 (9th Cir. Cal. 2002)* (quoting *Marcello, 212 F.3d at 1010*).

Here, Petitioner asserts equitable tolling should be granted because he "could NOT obtain all the unaltered records from the attorney in a timely fashion thus delaying my filing of a notice for a *Rule 32*." Petitioner asserts that the "U.S. Supreme Court made two rulings in 2012 regarding ineffective assistance of counsel dealing with plea agreements" and he "was in the process of filing his first Petition for Post-Conviction Relief during that time of the new rulings." Petitioner has not established that equitable tolling should apply in this case.

Petitioner's claim that he could not obtain the records of his case did not prevent him from filing a timely Petition. The information contained in this Petition was available to the Petitioner in 2007. Petitioner was aware of the simple nature of his claim and was able to file a Petition. *See Waldron--Ramsey, 556 F.3d at 1014* (stating that petitioner "could have prepared a basic form habeas petition and filed it to satisfy the AEDPA deadline."); *United States v. Battles, 362 F.3d 1195, 1198 (9th Cir. 2004)* (even without access to his case file, petitioner must "at least consult his own memory of the trial proceedings."). Petitioner's claim that Supreme Court rulings in 2012 delayed his Petition does not explain, at a minimum, the delay from 2007 to 2012. Petitioner has not satisfied his burden of showing that equitable tolling should apply.

REASONS WHY REMEDY IS HOLLOW

Arizona has a systemic problem where defense counsel with the affirmative assistance of prosecutors and judges have pleas entered into by affirmative deception. Though the appellate courts and Arizona Attorney General's staff have knowledge of this fact they decline to take corrective action.

**Claude Raymond Dove, Petitioner -vs- Charles L. Ryan, et al., Respondents
CV-08-1914-PHX-MHM (JRI) UNITED STATES DISTRICT COURT FOR THE DISTRICT
OF ARIZONA
(text modified for emphasis)**

THE POSITION OF THE COURT

1. Case 16160

Petitioner was indicted in Maricopa County Superior Court case number CR2004-016160 on one count of possession of cocaine for sale, and one count of possession with intent to use drug paraphernalia. The state filed allegations of historical priors, alleging a series of three prior convictions, and an allegation that the offense was committed while on released on bond. The Maricopa County Public Defender was appointed as counsel and on January 31, 2005 Petitioner proceeded to trial to the court and was found guilty on Count One, the Class 2 Felony. No verdict was entered on the Class 6 paraphernalia charge, and Petitioner successfully moved to dismiss the paraphernalia count.

Petitioner proceeded to sentencing on July 15, 2005. The court found four prior felony convictions, and sentenced Petitioner to 14 years imprisonment, concurrent with the sentence in the other pending case, CR2004-017353.

2. Case 17353

Petitioner   was indicted in Maricopa County Superior Court case number CR 2004-017353 on one count of transportation of cocaine for sale. The state filed allegations of historical priors, alleging a series of four prior convictions (including case CR2004-016160). The Maricopa County Public Defender was appointed as counsel , and on January 325, 2005 Petitioner proceeded to trial to a jury and was found guilty.

Petitioner proceeded to sentencing on July 28, 2005. The court found four prior felony convictions, and sentenced Petitioner to 14 years imprisonment, concurrent with an identical sentence in the other pending case, CR2004-016160.

3. Plea Negotiations and Burden of Proof on Prior Convictions

Settlement Conference - Prior to trial, on October 8, 2004, a consolidated settlement conference was held in both cases. The conference began with the judge reviewing the charges and noting that the State had alleged "two prior felony convictions." In reviewing the potential sentencing on the felony charges, the judge stated:

> if you're convicted at trial and the State   proves the prior felony convictions, **and the State would have to prove those at the trial beyond a reasonable doubt**, the absolute minimum prison sentence for each of the Class 2 felonies is 10.5 years. The standard minimum is 14 years.

(*Id.* at 2-3 (emphasis added).)

The court went on to discuss the sentencing on the other charges, and the State's offer to allow Petitioner to plead to just the two class two felonies with an agreement to cap the sentence at concurrent presumptive sentences. The court went on to explain the sentencing effect of the proffered plea:

> So the maximum you'd be facing would be nine-and-a-quarter years for everything all wrapped up instead of 35 years on each of the Class 2 felonies. These occurred on separate occasions, so you could be sentenced to consecutive sentences if you're convicted of all this at a trial or trials, and the judge would be able to do that.

(*Id.* at 4.)

Priors Trial - At the bench trial on the historical priors, the State proffered evidence of four prior convictions. A trial was held on the priors, with the defense opposing two as stale and asserting that the state had failed   to meet its burden of proving all but one of the others beyond a reasonable doubt. During the course of the proceeding, defense counsel argued that the State was required to prove the priors beyond a reasonable doubt, and that the State had failed to do so because fingerprints were provided only with respect to a single prior, and the use of a "pen pack" was improperly replied upon to prove the balance. The Arizona Court of Appeals described the "pen pack" as including "a certified 'Automated Summary Record' which summarized Dove's prior convictions and sentences, a certified prior conviction record, a series of photographs of Dove, a complete set of Dove's fingerprints. and a certification that all of these documents came from Dove's DOC master record file." The judge disagreed on the burden of proof, but eventually recessed to research the matter. Eventually, the judge determined that the "the burden of proof on historical convictions is clear and convincing."

The judge found that the state had "proved that the defendant has actually four prior felony convictions by clear and convincing   evidence." Nonetheless, Petitioner was sentenced on the basis of "two historical prior convictions" (*id.* at 33), which was sufficient to trigger the enhanced sentencing.

B. CONSOLIDATED PROCEEDINGS ON DIRECT APPEAL

Petitioner filed notices of appeal in both cases. New counsel was appointed. The appeals were consolidated, and a combined Opening Brief was filed by counsel, asserting insufficient evidence of the prior felony convictions, and abuse of discretion in failing to consider mitigating factors. The Arizona Court of Appeals rejected both claims, and affirmed Petitioner's sentences. Petitioner did not seek further review, and the mandate was issued on July 7, 2006.

C. CONSOLIDATED PROCEEDINGS ON POST-CONVICTION RELIEF

In both cases, Petitioner then filed Notice of Post-Conviction Relief. The Office of the Public Defender was appointed to represent Petitioner, and the proceedings were consolidated. Petitioner   filed a PCR Petition raising a single claim of ineffective assistance of counsel, asserting that trial counsel had incorrectly advised

Petitioner during plea negotiations on the state's burden of proof on prior convictions. Petitioner cited no federal authority in support of his Petition. The Petition was summarily denied on December 8, 2006.

Petitioner filed through counsel a Petition for Review, again raising the single claim of ineffective assistance of trial counsel. Petitioner cited a single federal authority, *U.S. v. Day, 969 F.2d 39 (3rd Cir. 1992)* for the proposition that relief on the claim was available even if Petitioner received a fair trial. The Arizona Court of Appeals summarily denied review. Petitioner then filed a *pro se* Petition for Review by the Arizona Supreme Court . Petitioner again raised the same claim of ineffective assistance. The Arizona Supreme Court summarily denied review.

c. Application to Petitioner's Claims

Ineffective Assistance - In his Ground One, Petitioner argues that he received ineffective assistance of counsel based upon counsel's advice on the state's burden of proof to prove the prior conviction. Petitioner asserted the factual basis of this claim at each level of his PCR proceeding. In asserting these claims, Petitioner never explicitly referenced the federal constitution in support of this claim. However, the state and federal cases cited by Petitioner were plainly founded upon federal constitutional law.

Petitioner cited *State v. Donald*), where the Arizona court held that "once the State engages in plea bargaining, the defendant has a *Sixth Amendment right* to be adequately informed of the consequences before deciding whether to accept or reject the offer." *198 Ariz. 406, 413, 10 P.3d 1193, 1200 (Ariz. App.2000)* (emphasis added). The reference to the *Sixth Amendment*, as well as the *Donald* court's reliance upon *Strickland v. Washington, 466 U.S. 668, 104 S. Ct. 2052, 80 L. Ed. 2d 674 (1984)*, *id.*, and myriad other federal ineffective assistance cases, makes clear that the court was applying federal constitutional law. While the Arizona Constitution does provide for a comparable right to counsel in criminal proceedings, that provision is located in *Article 2, Section 24 of the Arizona Constitution*. Ariz.Rev.Stat. *Const. Art. 2 § 24* ("the accused shall have the right to appear and defend in person, and by counsel"). Moreover, amendments to the Arizona Constitution are engrossed in the Constitution, and are not identified as sequential amendments. See generally Ariz.Rev.Stat. Const. Thus the *Donald* court's reference to the "*Sixth Amendment*" was a plain indication of the federal nature of their analysis.

Petitioner also cited *U.S. v. Day, 969 F.2d 39 (3rd Cir. 1992)*, which was founded upon a defendant's "*Sixth Amendment* right not just to counsel, but to 'reasonably effective assistance' of counsel."

Respondents incorrectly argue that these citations were not sufficient because the state court was required to "read beyond the petition to be alerted to the federal claim." ((citing *Baldwin v. Reese, 541 U.S. 27, 32, 124 S. Ct. 1347, 158 L. Ed. 2d 64 (2004)*).) *Baldwin* did not involve a brief which cited applicable authorities without explicitly naming the constitutional guarantee. Rather, *Baldwin* involved an appellate brief which made no connection to the petitioner's constitutional claim, and the state appellate court could "discover that claim only by reading lower court opinions in the case." *541 U.S. at 31.* Petitioner did not leave the Arizona Court of Appeals to go sift through his other briefs to find his federal claim. Respondents fail to refer this Court to the portions of *Baldwin* where the Court went on to explicate the ways in which a federal claim could be raised:

> A litigant wishing to raise a federal issue can easily indicate the federal law basis for his claim in a state-court petition or brief, for example, by citing in conjunction with the claim the federal source of law on which he relies   or a case deciding such a claim on federal grounds, or by simply labeling the claim "federal."

541 U.S. at 32.

Here, Petitioner did just that. He "cit[ed] in conjunction with the claim . . . .a case deciding such a claim on federal grounds." *Id.* In fact he cited more than one such case, and offered no other basis for seeking review.

Respondents also complain that this was mere "drive-by citation," citing *Castillo v. McFadden, 399 F.3d 993, 1003-03 (9th Cir. 2004).* The *Castillo* court described the nature of their petitioner's purported presentation of his federal due process claim:

The conclusion of Castillo's brief did no better in fairly presenting a federal due process claim to the Arizona Court of Appeals. The brief's parting sentence asserted that "[t]he gross violations of Appellant's *Fifth*, *Sixth*, and *Fourteenth Amendment* rights requires [sic] that his convictions and sentences be reversed and that he be granted a new trial consistent with due process of law." This conclusory, scattershot citation of federal constitutional provisions, divorced from any articulated federal legal theory, was the first time Castillo's brief used the words "due process" or "*Fifth Amendment*."

Castillo, therefore, left the Arizona Court of Appeals to puzzle over how the *Fifth*, *Sixth*, and *Fourteenth Amendments* might relate to his three foregoing claims.

399 F.3d at 1002. Here, Petitioner did not offer some scattershot of citations in a concluding paragraph of his brief. Rather, in the heart of his brief he cited two cases, each based upon the *Sixth Amendment* right to effective assistance of counsel, each involving the same factual scenario (*i.e.* failure by counsel to properly advise on a plea offer), and Petitioner made specific arguments connected to each case. Instead of a drive-by spraying of citations, Petitioner drew a sniper's bead on authorities which plainly established the federal nature of his claims.

Moreover, Respondents ignore the explicit direction in *Castillo* about the efficacy of citations to case law:

> Consistent with the recognition that state and federal courts are jointly responsible for interpreting and safeguarding constitutional guarantees, we have held that citation to either a federal or state case involving the legal standard for a federal constitutional violation is sufficient to establish exhaustion.

399 F.3d at 999.

Similarly, in their Answer in chief, Respondents argue that "the habeas petitioner must cite in state court to the specific constitutional guarantee upon which he wishes to base his claim in federal court." ((citing *Tamalini v. Stewart*, 249 F.3d 895, 898 (9th Cir. 2001)). *Tamalini* did not mandate an explicit reference to a specific constitutional guarantee. To the contrary, *Tamalini* involved a situation where the petitioner had explicitly asserted *Sixth Amendment* ineffective assistance claims throughout his state briefs and to the district court, and then on habeas appeal attempted to convert his claims to ones asserting denials of due process and equal protection. *Tamilini* made no reference to the efficacy of citing to case authorities dealing with federal constitutional claims. To the extent that *Tamilini* could somehow be read to infer Respondents proposition, such inference would have been nullified in light of the explicit language in *Baldwin* and *Castillo*.

The undersigned finds that Petitioner fairly presented his ineffective assistance claim.

2. Standard for Ineffective Assistance

Generally, claims of ineffective assistance of counsel are analyzed pursuant to *Strickland v. Washington*, 466 U.S. 668, 104 S. Ct. 2052, 80 L. Ed. 2d 674 (1984). In order to prevail on such a claim, Petitioner must show: (1) deficient performance - counsel's representation fell below the objective standard for reasonableness; and (2) prejudice - there is a reasonable probability that, but for counsel's unprofessional errors, the result of the proceeding would have been different. *Id. at 687-88*. Although the petitioner must prove both elements, a court may reject his claim upon finding either that counsel's performance was reasonable or that the claimed error was not prejudicial. *Id. at 697*.

3. Application to Petitioner's Claim

Respondents contend that this clam is without merit because: (1) the erroneous advice on the burden of proof on prior convictions came after the plea agreement expired; (2) there is no evidence to support Petitioner's contention that the erroneous advice affected his decision to reject the plea offer, because Petitioner rejected the plea on the basis that it would result in a nine year sentence. Moreover, Respondents contend that the state court's decision must be upheld because the result reached was not objectively unreasonable.

Method of Applying *Strickland* Unreasonable - However, a tenable   conclusion is not the only the hallmark of an objectively reasonable decision. As recognized in *Nunes v. Mueller, 350 F.3d 1045 (9th Cir. 2003)*, "[u]nder the AEDPA standard of review, it is entirely appropriate-even necessary-that federal courts ask whether the state court applied correct legal principles (in this case, the *Strickland* analysis) in an objectively unreasonable way, an inquiry that requires analysis of the state court's *method* as well as its result." *Id. at 1054* (citations omitted, emphasis in original). The *Nunes* court found that the California court had applied *Strickland* unreasonably because it summarily rejected the petitioner's claim of ineffectiveness in a rejected plea despite the fact that the Petitioner had "clearly made out a prima facie case of ineffective assistance of counsel under *Strickland.*" (*Id.*)

Here, the trial court rejected Petitioner's ineffective assistance claim on the basis that Petitioner "failed to present a colorable claim for relief." As a result, Petitioner was not permitted an evidentiary hearing, and the court did not evaluate the evidence underlying his claims.

However, Petitioner's assertion that trial counsel   rendered defective advice and resulted in his rejection of a plea he would have otherwise accepted, laid out an ineffective assistance claim under *Strickland*. No other fact need have been alleged to make out such a claim.

An Arizona PCR petition is not required, under the Arizona Rules of Criminal Procedure to contain conclusive evidence supporting a claim nor even all evidence a petitioner hopes to present in support of his claim.

> A defendant is entitled to an evidentiary hearing when he presents a colorable claim, that is a claim which, if defendant's allegations are true, might have changed the outcome. When doubts exist, "a hearing should be held to allow the defendant to raise the relevant issues, to resolve the matter, and to make a record for review."

State v. Watton, 164 Ariz. 323, 328, 793 P.2d 80, 85 (1990) (internal citations omitted). The PCR court was "obligated to treat his factual allegations as true." *State v. Jackson, 209 Ariz. 13, 15-16, 97 P.3d 113, 115-116 (App. 2004). See also State v. Richmond, 114 Ariz. 186, 194, 560 P.2d 41, 49 (1976), overruled on other grounds, State v. Salazar, 173 Ariz.399, 416, 844 P.2d 566, 583 (1992)* ("To be colorable, a claim has to have   the appearance of validity, i.e., if the defendant's allegations are taken as true, would they change the verdict?").

The evidentiary requirements for supporting a petition are far from strenuous:

> Facts within the defendant's personal knowledge shall be noted separately from other allegations of fact and shall be under oath. Affidavits, records, or other evidence currently available to the defendant supporting the allegations of the petition shall be attached to it.

Ariz. R. Crim. P. 32.5.

Here, Petitioner made out essentially the same allegations as the petitioner in *Nunes*:

> With Nunes' claims being taken at face value as the state court claimed it had done, the factual scenario was (1) that Nunes' attorney gave him the wrong information and advice about the state's plea offer and (2) that if Nunes had instead been informed accurately, he would expressly have taken the bargain.

350 F.3d at 1054. The only difference in Petitioner's allegations were that the claimed error was not on the plea offer itself, but on the alternatives to that offer. Despite those allegations, the Arizona court concluded that Petitioner had failed to make out a colorable claim. "With the state court having purported   to evaluate [Petitioner's] claim for sufficiency alone, it should not have required [Petitioner] to prove his claim without affording him an evidentiary hearing." *Nunes, 350 F.3d at 1054.* Refusing to do so was an objectively unreasonable application of *Strickland.*

However, while an unreasonable application of Supreme Court law is necessary to habeas relief, it is not sufficient. Petitioner must still show to this Court that his claim is meritorious.   In *Nunes*, the district court had concluded that the ineffective assistance claim was meritorious, and thus the dispute on appeal focused on whether the requirements of *28 U.S.C. § 2254(d)* had been met.

Defective Performance - Petitioner contends that he rejected the plea offer of a maximum of 9.25 years in prison based upon trial counsel's advice that the state would have to prove his prior convictions "beyond a reasonable doubt" and that the evidence they had available, *i.e.* the ADC "pen pack" would not meet that burden. As it turned out, some three months before Petitioner's settlement conference, the Arizona Court of Appeals had determined that the actual burden of proof was "clear and convincing." *See State v. Cons, 208 Ariz. 409, 94 P.3d 609 (App. 2004)* (decided July 22, 2004).

Timing of Advice - Respondents contend that the erroneous advice came after the plea offer had already expired. They point to the fact that the only time this advice was given on the record was at the sentencing proceedings in July, 2005, long after the plea offer purportedly had expired. (Suppl. Ans. #16 at 14.) They argue that Petitioner "rejected" the offer at the settlement conference on October 8, 2004. At the settlement conference, the prosecutor agreed to extend the deadline for excepting the offer through the following Monday. It is not clear to the undersigned that the plea was "rejected." The transcript simply reveals that Petitioner declined to accept it at the time of the hearing. The conclusion of the hearing was:

> THE COURT: I take it you don't want to accept it today?
> THE DEFENDANT: No, No.
> THE COURT: All right. Have a nice weekend.
> THE DEFENDANT: All right. You, too.

However, the advice need not have been on the record to support Petitioner's claim. *See Nunes, 350 F.3d at 1055, n.6* (observing the tension between *Strickland* and a rule requiring evidence beyond a defendant's own statement). Petitioner points to the fact that prior to Petitioner's declining to accept the plea offer, the trial judge had advised Petitioner, without correction by trial counsel, that "the State would have to prove [the prior felony convictions] at trial beyond a reasonable doubt. Corroboration of Petitioner's allegations flows from the fact that counsel continued to argue the erroneous position at sentencing. Nonetheless, the undersigned is not prepared to finally determine the timing (or even the existence) of such advice without an evidentiary hearing to evaluate Petitioner's credibility, and without any testimony by trial counsel.

Regardless, this Court need not resolve the timing issue to resolve Petitioner's claim.

Prejudice - Petitioner must not only show deficient performance, but prejudice. To establish prejudice from incorrect advice resulting in rejection of a plea offer, Petitioner "must show that there is a reasonable probability that he would have accepted the plea agreement had he received accurate advice from his attorney." *Hoffman v. Arave, 455 F.3d 926, 941-942 (9th Cir. 2006), judgment vacated in part on other grounds by Arave v. Hoffman, 552 U.S. 117, 128 S.Ct. 749, 169 L. Ed. 2d 580 (2008).* Respondents argue that Petitioner would have rejected the plea offer even with the correct advice, pointing to his aversion to going "to prison for nine years, signing my life away for nine years."

Of course, in his verified Petition and in his verified Supplemental Reply, Petitioner avows that "[h]ad petitioner been furnished accurate information before and at his Settlement Conference Hearing, this petitioner would have accepted the State's Plea Offer." However, this Court is not obligated to accept Petitioner's bare, after-the-fact assertion, but is required to evaluate all the circumstances. *Cf. Hill v. Lockhart, 474 U.S. 52, 59, 106 S. Ct. 366, 88 L. Ed. 2d 203 (1985)* (court required to assess likelihood of different decision in instance where plea *accepted* on basis of bad advice).

Plea Range - The plea offer provided for Petitioner to plead to the two Class 2 felony charges with one prior felony conviction, dismiss the Class 6 paraphernalia charge, and stipulate to concurrent sentences capped at the presumptive. That resulted in an effective sentencing range of **4.5 to 9.25 years**, with a presumptive concurrent sentence of **9.25 years**.

Assumed Range - Petitioner claims that he was led to believe that if he rejected the plea offer and was convicted, he would face sentencing on the basis of only one prior felony. With just one prior conviction, Petitioner would have faced sentences of 4.5 to 23.25 years on each Class 2 felony, and .75 to 2.75 years on the Class 6 felony, which if consecutive would be a sentencing range of **5.25 to 49.25 years**, with a presumptive concurrent sentence of **9.25 years**. Arizona courts have discretion to select either consecutive or concurrent sentences. *State v. Garza, 192 Ariz. 171, 174-175, 962 P.2d 898, 901-901 (1998).*

Actual Range - Finally, based upon the finding of two or more priors, Petitioner ultimately faced a sentencing range of 10.5 to 35 years on each Class 2 felony, and 2.25 to 5.75 years on the Class 6 felony, for an effective range of **12.75 to 75.75 years**, with a concurrent presumptive sentence of **15.75 years**.

Given the disparity between the assumed sentencing range at trial and the actual range, and the lack of disparity between the offered plea sentencing range and the assumed trial range, it is not unreasonable to believe that a defendant might elect trial under the assumed trial sentencing range, but would have chosen the plea had he known the actual sentencing range.

That is particularly so where, as here, the defendant believed there were substantive defenses to be exploited at trial. For example, at the settlement conference, Petitioner, counsel and the court discussed the potential for a motion to suppress, and an entrapment defense. Petitioner goes to some lengths to explain why there was no assertion by him or counsel of the lack of evidence on the prior convictions, arguing that to do so would have alerted the prosecution to the weakness in their evidence on the priors while they still had time to shore it up. That explanation is plausible, but does not alter the undersigned's conclusions.

Based solely upon the foregoing, the undersigned might be able to conclude that there is a reasonable probability that but for counsel's erroneous advice Petitioner would have accepted the plea offer.

However, by the time that trial was prepared to begin, Petitioner had experienced a change of heart and was seeking to revive the plea offer. Other than the proximity of trial, the only thing that had changed was Petitioner's loss of his suppression motion. Petitioner (and, based upon his arguments at sentencing, counsel) continued to believe at that time that the priors required proof beyond a reasonable doubt. This suggests that the burden of proof issue was at least not the sole basis for declining the plea offer.

Moreover, the record reflects that Petitioner and counsel were not focused on the potential exposure at trial, but were preoccupied with the belief that the prosecutor was being unusually harsh in his dealings with Petitioner, and that a better plea offer could eventually be obtained. That was a centerpiece of Petitioner's explicit reasoning in declining the plea at the settlement conference:

THE DEFENDANT: . . . It was like nine people that has been arrested at the same time as I was, and none of them have gotten nine years for the little rock they had. People have gone home on probation.

THE DEFENDANT: . . .But yet you want to lock me away forever. But people who have pounds, tons of cocaine are getting probation. I don't think it's fair.

THE COURT: Well, let me interrupt you, Mr. Dove, because your argument isn't with me. Your argument is with them. I understand I asked you if you had any questions, but they control the plea offer that they make. I can't tell the State what to offer you, and this is the best they are offering. And if they don't --

MR. TERPSTRA [defense counsel]: I'm sorry, judge. I think it should be clear, as I have told your Honor and Mr. Dove, and the record should be clear, the things Mr. Dove is saying I have brought to the attention of [the prosecutor] Mr. Yost. And the names he's given me of the other people arrested, I followed up on and talked to their attorneys and brought it to the attention of Mr. Yost to show just these things.

THE DEFNDANT: Okay, I understand what you just said. But if they are so bad on drug offenders, why the people that got arrested with me went home on probation? If they so bad on drug offenders, they should be locked up along with me. That's all I am saying. I just think there is favoritism being played here. Something is going on here.

Even at the time of trial, it was suggested that the reason for the rejection of the plea was not based upon an evaluation of the plea versus trial, but on the belief that a better plea would be offered.

> MR. TERPSTRA: . . . We had a settlement conference previously with Judge Howser [sic] and Mr. Dove rejected the offer at that time. We've had a further discussion, myself and Mr. Yost and Mr. Dove about trying to make an improvement on the offer. Mr. Yost has consistently not be [sic] willing to improve on the offer that had been extended.
>
> Today, the morning of trial, Mr. Dove expressed to me that he would like to take that offer, would like to take that plea bargain as it had been offered. I explained to him, as he knew, the deal had been off the table. I also told him that we could try and get it back.

> THE WITNESS [Petitioner]: Yes. I really don't have no excuse for what I did, I was suffering from a disease. I'm not a drug seller at all, I was hooked on crack cocaine. I didn't quite under-stand what was going on because it was a sting operation that got a lot of smokers off the street, like ten of us got   locked up the same day. **All the people that got locked up, the most any of them got was three years or probation and they wanted me to do nine years, that's why I didn't want to take the plea bargain.** I thought they would give me three years, too. The rest of the people involved was smoking drugs just like me and they got three years and two years and they want to give me nine years.
>
> I would like to take, if I could, take the plea bargain now because if I lose, I'm going to get more than nine years so --

At sentencing, trial counsel pursued this line so far as to suggest that the individual prosecutor, Mr. Yost, had some special animus in these types of cases that resulted in unfavorable plea offers. Counsel argued that most similar cases resulted in much more favorable plea offers. He argued that in another case he defended in which the same prosecutor had prosecuted, a similar offer had been made by Mr. Yost.

> MR. TERPSTRA: . . . Same offer, plead to nine and a quarter years or prior with class two with a prior and he didn't budge from that offer either. . . . Never budged from the offer.
>
> Went to a different prosecutor, settlement   conference, easily dropped another prior, pled without a prior, got a super mitigated sentence three years after Mr. Yost was off the case.
>
> THE COURT: Was there a settlement conference in this case?
>
> MR. TERPSTRA: Absolutely, before Judge Hauser. Mr. Yost never budged from the offer.
>
> I don't think Mr. Yost is a bad guy. When he says he was reasonable, I never believe that Mr. Dove, compared to other defendants or circumstances of this case should have got the offer that he did but that was the offer and clearly it was better than losing at trial.
>
> Clearly he did reject it and he was let out of custody in November by Judge Hicks on both cases and Mr. Yost says he's not numb to certain things. He's certainly numb to the situation that someone that does have an addiction like Mr. Dove and how they process information. He's not the same person as you or me, come on dummy, nine and a quarter versus 15. If you reject it, how could you be so stupid. Look at the obvious differences --
>
> THE COURT: I don't know what you're saying, is he not competent?
>
> MR. TERPSTRA: He's perfectly competent. He doesn't view reality in the same ways. He's desperate. **He kept believing through the whole thing it would get   better**, I'm telling him --

All of this suggests that Petitioner's rejection of the plea was not a weighing of the plea versus the poten-tial outcomes at trial (and thus dependent upon counsel's defective advice on the priors), but was instead based upon a weighing of the plea against the potential that a better plea would eventually be forthcoming. Testimony from counsel or Petitioner at any habeas evidentiary hearing would have to be weighed against these statements on the record, and Petitioner suggests no reason to believe they would eliminate the reasonableness of a decision to rely instead upon the inferences from the existing record.

Given the record of the proceedings in this case, the undersigned cannot conclude that there is a reasonable probability that the defective advice made the difference in Petitioner's decision to let the plea offer pass unaccepted.

REASONS WHY THE REMEDY IS HOLLOW

In Arizona the Arizona Attorney general and courts are aware that defense counsel as a matte of routine give inaccurate advice as to plea agreements and very often this advice results in the defendant rejecting the plea.

KURT B. WILLIAMS, Petitioner - Appellant, v. DORA B. SCHRIRO; ARIZONA ATTORNEY GENERAL, Respondents - Appellees.No. 07-16537, No. 08-15864 UNITED STATES COURT OF APPEALS FOR THE NINTH CIRCUIT (text modified for emphasis)

THE POSITION OF THE COURT

(1) Williams contends that the prosecutor's plea bargaining position -- including a plea offer acceptance deadline -- and ancillary actions violated his constitutional rights and deprived him of effective assistance of counsel as a matter of "clearly established Federal law, as determined by the Supreme Court of the United States." *28 U.S.C. § 2254(d)(1); see also Lockyer v. Andrade, 538 U.S. 63, 71-76, 123 S. Ct. 1166, 1172-75, 155 L. Ed. 2d 144 (2003); Williams v. Taylor, 529 U.S. 362, 412-13, 120 S. Ct. 1495, 1523, 146 L. Ed. 2d 389 (2000); Moses v. Payne, 555 F.3d 742, 754 (9th Cir. 2009).* We disagree. In the first place, no clearly established Supreme Court law indicates that Williams has a general constitutional right to discovery, or to a plea bargain, or that a prosecutor is required to facilitate his consideration of the prosecution's plea bargaining positions or offers, or that a prosecutor cannot take a harsh or unpleasant position, including revocation of the plea offer. [4] Beyond that, the record shows that the prosecutor did, indeed, give a good deal of information to defense counsel. In short, the prosecutor's plea bargaining actions and inactions did not violate clearly established Supreme Court law.

But, says Williams, the prosecutor's position somehow denied him effective assistance of counsel because, as a matter of clearly established Supreme Court law, it was highly unlikely that any lawyer would provide effective assistance of counsel to his client under the circumstances. *See United States v. Cronic, 466 U.S. 648, 658, 104 S. Ct. 2039, 2046, 80 L. Ed. 2d 657 (1984).* We disagree. What Williams overlooks is the fact that counsel had time to investigate and to counsel him on his choices. *See id. at 649, 666-67, 104 S. Ct. at 2041, 2051; see also Wright v. Van Patten, 552 U.S. 120, 128 S. Ct. 743, 746, 169 L. Ed. 2d 583 (2008),* (per curiam) (holding that no clearly established Supreme Court law indicated that an appearance of counsel by telephone at a plea hearing made it unlikely that counsel could be effective). Defense counsel's comfort level does not define the prosecutor's obligations.

Williams does not assert any particular instance in which counsel *was* ineffective and, thus, does not actually attempt to meet the general standard for claims of ineffective assistance of counsel. *See Strickland v. Washington, 466 U.S. 668, 687-88, 104 S. Ct. 2052, 2064, 80 L. Ed. 2d 674 (1984).*

In short, the state courts did not violate clearly established Supreme Court law when they found no violation of a constitutional right, despite Williams' claim that he should have had further time to consider a plea offer (maybe even to accept it) rather than having to go to trial for his crime. *See Weatherford, 429 U.S. at 561, 97 S. Ct. at 846* (noting the novelty of an argument "that constitutional rights are infringed by trying the defendant rather than accepting his plea of guilty.").

(2) Williams also asserts that the district court erred when it did not permit him to amend his habeas corpus petition to allege prosecutorial vindictiveness. The district court denied the motion to amend on the basis that the proposed amendment would be futile. *See Bonin v. Calderon, 59 F.3d 815, 845 (9th Cir. 1995).* We agree with Williams that the district court's given reason - his failure to plead the very language of *28 U.S.C. § 2254(d)* rendered his pro se claim futile -- was incorrect. *See Mayle v. Felix, 545 U.S. 644, 649, 125 S.*

Ct. 2562, 2566, 162 L. Ed. 2d 582 (2005); Woods v. Carey, 525 F.3d 886, 889-90 (9th Cir. 2008). However, we can affirm on any ground supported by the record, and on this record it is pellucid that Williams' claim of prosecutorial vindictiveness was futile. *See Nunes v. Ramirez-Palmer, 485 F.3d 432, 441-42 (9th Cir. 2007)* (setting out the burdens for prosecutorial vindictiveness claims). Moreover, Williams did not spell out any persuasive justification for his untimely attempt to amend. *See Bonin, 59 F.3d at 845*.

REASONS WHY REMEDY IS HOLLOW

In Arizona acting in concert with defense counsel, prosecutors often are able to act vindictively and provide inaccurate information as to plea agreements. Though the Arizona Attorney General and courts are aware of this fact they condone this practice.

> **JAMES EARL FOX, Petitioner - Appellant, v. CHARLES L. RYAN; STATE OF ARIZONA ATTORNEY GENERAL, Respondents - Appellees. No. 09-15834 UNITED STATES COURT OF APPEALS FOR THE NINTH CIRCUIT**
> **(Text modified for emphasis)**

THE POSITION OF THE COURT

Fox turned down a favorable plea   deal and, after he was convicted by a jury and sentenced to 27 years in custody, moved for post-conviction relief, arguing that his trial counsel was ineffective for failing to warn him that his sentences on the multiple counts could be consecutive. What occurred following the state court's grant of post-conviction relief was unusual. The post-conviction court vacated Fox's sentence of 15.75 years for trafficking in stolen property and 11.25 years for attempted trafficking, both sentences to run consecutively--but the court did not vacate his convictions following a jury trial. The court then conducted a plea colloquy where Fox pleaded guilty to a count of which he had already been convicted, which conviction was still valid. When the state post-conviction court subsequently realized it made a mistake, it vacated the "second" guilty plea and resentenced Fox on the original convictions so that the 15.75 year term and the 11.25 year term would run concurrently. The end result of the court's actions is that Fox's total sentence was reduced from 27 years to 15.75 years.

The state appellate court's determination that the *Double Jeopardy Clause* was not violated by the court's *sua sponte* vacatur   of the "second," accepted guilty plea, followed by its resentencing Fox pursuant to the original convictions, was reasonable. *See 28 U.S.C. § 2254(d)(1)*. There is currently a split of authority in the circuits as to whether jeopardy automatically attaches in every case immediately upon a court's acceptance of a guilty plea. *See United States v. Patterson, 406 F.3d 1095, 1100 (9th Cir. 2005)* (Kozinski, C.J., dissenting from denial of rehearing en banc) (discussing circuit split on this issue). As the Supreme Court has told us, divergent treatment by different circuit courts may "[r]eflect[] the lack of guidance from [the Supreme] Court." *Carey v. Musladin, 549 U.S. 70, 76, 127 S. Ct. 649, 166 L. Ed. 2d 482 (2006)*. That is the case here: there is no clearly established federal law as established by the Supreme Court on this issue. *See 28 U.S.C. § 2254(d)(1)*. Further, the reinstatement of convictions on charges of which Fox had already been found guilty by a jury beyond a reasonable doubt, followed ultimately by a *reduction* in his overall sentence, does not implicate any of the purposes of the *Double Jeopardy Clause* as stated in *Ohio v. Johnson, 467 U.S. 493, 501, 104 S. Ct. 2536, 81 L. Ed. 2d 425 (1984)*. The district court properly declined to grant habeas   on this issue.

REASONS WHY REMEDY IS HOLLOW

Arizona courts and the Attorney General aware of the systemic problem that prosecutors with defense counsel and state judges act in concert to cause pleas be entered into without being fully informed correctly, continue with the practice.

> **MIGUEL ANGEL PLATERO DIAZ, Petitioner, v. CHARLES RYAN and ARIZONA ATTORNEY GENERAL, Respondents. CIV 09-00725 PHX MHM (MEA)UNITED STATES DISTRICT COURT FOR THE DISTRICT OF ARIZONA**

(Text modified for emphasis)

THE POSITION OF THE COURT

A Maricopa County grand jury indictment issued May 26, 2006, in docket number CR2006-121919, charged Petitioner and a co-defendant with one count of burglary in the first degree, seven counts of aggravated assault, one count of assisting a criminal street gang, and one count of impersonating a peace officer.. The charges arose from a home invasion that occurred on or between April 21 and 22, 2006.

A settlement conference in CR2006-121919 and another case   wherein Petitioner was the sole defendant, CR2006-140056, was set for November 14, 2006. Docket number CR2006-140056 involved charges of possession of marijuana for sale, possession or use of marijuana, and misconduct involving weapons. In Petitioner's settlement conference memoranda he acknowledged possession of a large amount of marijuana and that a weapon was found during the execution of a search warrant at his home. Petitioner also acknowledged that, in docket number CR2006-121919, the home invasion crime, the "State has a cooperating co-defendant who places the defendant at the scene. The rest of the evidence against the defendant is somewhat circumstantial."

In the settlement conference memorandum Petitioner averred he had no prior felony convictions. Petitioner acknowledged he had been offered a plea agreement that provided he would plead guilty to one count of burglary in CR2006-121919 and be sentenced to a term of seven to 21 years imprisonment. The plea offer provided the sentence for burglary would run concurrently with that imposed in CR2006-140056, in which Petitioner would plead guilty to one count of possession   of marijuana for sale. The settlement conference memorandum states:

> The Defendant is not adamantly adverse to a plea but he and his family understandably have reservations about the range which is up to 21 years in prison. No individuals were seriously injured in the home invasion and the defense does not believe the Defendant would necessarily receive more than 21 years after trial, however, does acknowledge some form of stacked sentences is a possibility.

On November 14, 2006, pursuant to a written plea agreement signed that same day, Petitioner pled guilty in CR2006-121919 to one count of burglary in the first degree. The plea agreement provided Petitioner was "giving up [his] right to a determination of probable cause, to a trial by jury ... [his] right to jury determination of aggravating factors beyond a reasonable doubt, and right to appeal." The written plea agreement provided the presumptive term of imprisonment for burglary was 10.5 years and that the maximum sentence was 21 years. The plea agreement stipulated that Petitioner's sentence would not exceed 16 years imprisonment.

In the state's sentencing   memorandum it argued Petitioner's sentence should be aggravated based on the emotional, physical, and financial harm to the victims, and the presence of an accomplice. The state also asserted Petitioner was a threat to public safety, and argued there were a lack of mitigating factors. The sentencing memorandum also alleged Petitioner was a documented member of a street gang involvement and provided general information regarding gang activity.

A sentencing hearing was conducted February 8, 2007.. Two of the victims from the home invasion testified regarding the impact of that crime. Petitioner's counsel presented mitigation evidence at the sentencing hearing, asserting Petitioner's lack of an adult criminal record and the fact that he had relinquished his ties to a street gang weighed in favor of leniency. In response, the state maintained that, under the circumstances of the case, Petitioner was not deserving of any leniency.

Before sentencing Petitioner, the state court asked if he was satisfied with his counsel's representation, to which question Petitioner responded, "Yes, sir." The trial court then found the following aggravating circumstances with regard to the burglary conviction: Petitioner was a documented gang member; the crime was committed for pecuniary gain; there were multiple victims; the extreme emotional and financial harm to the victims; the physical injuries suffered by the victims; and the presence of one or more accomplices. The trial court determined that the aggravating circumstances substantially outweighed the mitigating circumstances and sentenced Petitioner to serve a term of 16 years imprisonment pursuant to his conviction for burglary. The court sentenced Petitioner to a concurrent term of seven years imprisonment in CR2006-140056 pursuant to his conviction for possession of marijuana for sale.

On March 21, 2007, Petitioner initiated a timely state action for post-conviction relief pursuant to Rule 32, Arizona Rules of Criminal Procedure. In Arizona this is the first appeal "as of right" for defendants who plead guilty and thereby waive their right to a direct appeal. Accordingly, Petitioner was appointed counsel to represent him in his post conviction proceedings. After reviewing the record, Petitioner's appointed counsel notified the state trial court that he was unable to find any claims for relief to raise on Petitioner's behalf.

On November 14, 2007, Petitioner filed a *pro per* brief asserting he was entitled to post-conviction relief because his right to a fair trial was violated when the trial court imposed an improper aggravated sentence. Petitioner also asserted Arizona's sentencing scheme was unconstitutional because it mandated that judges, rather than a jury, find the existence of aggravating sentencing factors. Additionally, Petitioner asserted he was denied his right to the effective assistance of counsel because his trial counsel failed to properly advise him regarding the plea agreement. Petitioner asserted his counsel assured Petitioner his sentence would not be greater than the presumptive sentence, i.e., 10.5 years imprisonment. Petitioner also alleged his counsel was ineffective for failing to object to the sentence imposed by the trial court at the time Petitioner was sentenced.

The state trial court summarily dismissed Petitioner's action for post-conviction relief, finding he had "failed to show any colorable claim for post-conviction relief." Petitioner sought review of this decision by the Arizona Court of Appeals, which denied review on January 21, 2009. Petitioner did not seek review of this decision by the Arizona Supreme Court.

In his federal habeas action Petitioner asserts he is entitled to relief because he was denied his right to the effective assistance of counsel. Petitioner also argues he was unconstitutionally sentenced to an aggravated term of imprisonment in violation of his *Sixth* and *Fourteenth Amendment* rights. Petitioner also contends his sentence for burglary must be vacated because he was sentenced pursuant to a state statute that violates the United States Constitution.

D. Petitioner's claims for relief

1. Petitioner asserts he is entitled to relief because he was denied his right to the effective assistance of counsel during his plea and sentencing proceedings.

Petitioner contends his counsel's performance was deficient because counsel assured Petitioner he would receive the presumptive sentence, i.e., 10.5 years imprisonment. Petitioner also argues his counsel was ineffective for failing to lodge a contemporaneous objection to Petitioner's sentence went it was imposed by the trial court. Petitioner properly exhausted these ineffective assistance of counsel claims in the state courts by asserting the claims before the Arizona Court of Appeals in his state action for post-conviction relief. The state courts' determination that Petitioner's constitutional right to the effective assistance of counsel was not violated was not clearly contrary to federal law.

Petitioner has not established that he was prejudiced by any alleged error in his counsel's prediction of the sentence ultimately imposed by the state trial court. The record in this matter, *inter alia* Petitioner's state trial court criminal case settlement conference memorandum, indicates Petitioner was entirely aware of the fact that his guilty plea could result in a maximum sentence of 21 years imprisonment. Petitioner was also alerted to the potential consequences of his guilty plea, i.e., a statutory maximum sentence of 21 years imprisonment and a maximum sentence of 16 years imprisonment pursuant to the plea agreement, by the state trial court before the court accepted Petitioner's plea.

Even if defense counsel did inaccurately predict the sentence ultimately imposed this alleged deficiency would not, as a matter of law, constitute unconstitutionally ineffective assistance of counsel. See *Womack v. McDaniel, 497 F.3d 998, 1003-04 (9th Cir. 2007)* (holding a petitioner is not unconstitutionally prejudiced by their counsel's inaccurate predictions as to a sentence if the petitioner was informed of the potential sentence by a written plea agreement).

Petitioner also contends his counsel was ineffective because counsel did not object to the sentence imposed by the trial court. The state courts' determination that Petitioner's counsel's performance was not deficient nor prejudicial in this regard was not clearly contrary to federal law. To succeed on an assertion his counsel's performance was deficient because counsel failed to raise a particular argument the petitioner must establish the argument was likely to be successful, thereby establishing that he was prejudiced by his counsel's omission. See *Tanner v. McDaniel, 493 F.3d 1135, 1144 (9th Cir.)*, cert. denied, *552 U.S. 1068, 128 S. Ct. 722, 169 L. Ed. 2d 565 (2007)*; *Weaver v. Palmateer, 455 F.3d 958, 970 (9th Cir. 2006)*, cert. denied, *552 U.S. 873, 128 S. Ct. 177, 169 L. Ed. 2d 120 (2007)*. A defendant has no constitutional right to compel counsel to raise particular objections if counsel, as a matter of professional judgment, decides not to raise those objections. See *Jones v. Barnes, 463 U.S. 745, 751, 103 S. Ct. 3308, 3312, 77 L. Ed. 2d 987 (1983)* (declining to promulgate "a per se rule that the client, not the professional   advocate, must be allowed to decide what issues are to be pressed"). Because an argument that the sentence imposed was not in accordance with the plea agreement or the United States Constitution would not be successful, Petitioner's *Sixth Amendment* rights were not violated by his counsel's failure to object to his sentence.

2. Petitioner also argues he was unconstitutionally sentenced to an aggravated term of imprisonment in violation of his *Sixth* and *Fourteenth Amendment* rights.

Petitioner asserts his sentence violated the plea agreement because the plea agreement stated that all "enhancements" would be "dismissed" and, he asserts, he was sentenced to an "enhanced" term of imprisonment. Petitioner alleges the enhancements were used to sentence him to a prison term above the "maximum sentence of 10.5 years" allowed by the plea agreement.

Respondents contend Petitioner did not properly exhaust this claim by raising the same legal issue in the state courts in Petitioner's Rule 32 action. Respondents further argue:

> Furthermore, Petitioner is clearly confusing aggravation of a sentence with enhancement of a sentence. Petitioner's sentence was aggravated, not enhanced. Thus, Petitioner's claim   is not only unexhausted, but also factually irrelevant.
>
> Petitioner's sentence was not enhanced under *A.R.S. § 13-604* as no historical prior felonies were used to sentence Petitioner. Rather Petitioner's sentence was aggravated to a term of 16 years' imprisonment under *A.R.S. § 13-702(C)*. Petitioner's sentencing range of a minimum sentence of 7 years, a presumptive sentence of 10.5 years, and a maximum sentence of 21 years was for a first offense class 2 dangerous felony. Thus, *A.R.S. § 13-604* is inapplicable to Petitioner's case.

In his *pro se* brief in his state action for post-conviction relief, Petitioner asserted that his sentence was improper because it was aggravated based on facts found by a judge rather than a jury. Accordingly, Petitioner's second claim for habeas relief as it is stated in the petition appears to be factually incorrect and procedurally defaulted. Additionally, the crux of Petitioner's second claim for relief is an argument in effect subsumed by his third claim for relief, i.e., that Petitioner's sentence was improperly aggravated.

3. Petitioner contends his sentence for burglary must be vacated because he was sentenced pursuant to a state statute   that violates the United States Constitution.

Petitioner alleges that Arizona's sentencing scheme violates the *Sixth*, *Eighth*, and *Fourteenth Amendments to the United States Constitution*. Petitioner contends the statutes violates the Constitution because they require a judge, rather than a jury, to find factors used to aggravate a convicted defendant's sentence. Petitioner argues that because the statutes require a judge, rather than a jury, to find aggravating factors, the statutes violate the *Sixth Amendment* right to a jury trial.

Petitioner arguably raised this claim in his state action for post-conviction relief, asserting both that his sentence violated the United States Supreme Court's opinion in Blakely v. Washington and that *subsection 702(B)* and *subsection 702(C)* are unconstitutional. In his state action for post-conviction relief Petitioner argued the United States Constitution was violated by Arizona's determination that one Blakely-compliant factor was sufficient to aggravate a defendant's sentence when the other factors were found by a judge rather than a jury. The Arizona state courts' denial of relief on Petitioner's claim that his sentence violates his   federal constitutional right to a determination by a jury of each factual element of the crime charged was not clearly contrary to federal law.

Petitioner was sentenced to a term of imprisonment above the presumptive term but below the maximum term. However, Petitioner's sentence was "aggravated" based on factors admitted by Petitioner, including the presence of an accomplice.

In *Blakely v. Washington, 542 U.S. 296, 303-04, 124 S. Ct. 2531, 2537-38, 159 L. Ed. 2d 403 (2004)*, the United States Supreme Court determined that a defendant in a criminal case is entitled to have a jury determine beyond a reasonable doubt any fact that increases his sentence beyond the "statutory maximum," unless the fact was admitted by the defendant or was based on a prior conviction. The United States Supreme Court clarified that the term "statutory maximum" was to be interpreted as the presumptive sentence, or the presumptive sentence given the facts as found by the jury or admitted by the defendant, rather than the maximum statutory sentence allowed. See *Allen v. Reed, 427 F.3d 767, 772 (10th Cir. 2005)* ("In other words, the relevant 'statutory maximum' is not the maximum sentence a judge may impose after finding additional facts, but the maximum he may impose without any additional findings.").

However, the maxim of *Blakely* does not provide relief to a defendant when the facts supporting the sentence enhancement are established by a plea of guilty or admitted by the defendant. Accordingly, the Arizona state courts' decision that Petitioner's *Sixth Amendment* right to have a jury find each fact used to aggravate his sentence was not clearly contrary to federal law.

In *Arizona v. Martinez, 210 Ariz. 578, 115 P.3d 618 (2005)*, the Arizona Supreme Court considered the impact of Blakely on Arizona's sentencing statutes. In Arizona, the statutory maximum sentence in a case where no Blakely-compliant or Blakely-exempt aggravating factors are present is the presumptive term. See *210 Ariz. at 583, 115 P.3d at 623*. However, because an Arizona defendant may receive an aggravated sentence based on a single aggravating factor, see *Arizona Revised Statutes Annotated § 13-702(B)*, a single Blakely-compliant or Blakely-exempt aggravating factor establishes the facts "legally essential" to punishment. See *Arizona v. Martinez, 210 Ariz. 578, 115 P.3d 618 (2005)*; *Arizona v. Henderson, 210 Ariz. 561, 115 P.3d 601 (2005)*. The sentencing scheme iterated in Martinez was upheld upon review by the United States Supreme Court. See *Martinez v. Arizona, 546 U.S. 1044, 126 S. Ct. 762, 163 L. Ed. 2d 592 (2005)*.

Because an Arizona defendant may receive an aggravated sentence based on a single aggravating factor, see *Arizona Revised Statutes Annotated § 13-702(B)*, the federal courts have concluded that if a single Blakely-compliant or Blakely-exempt aggravating factor establishes the facts "legally essential" to punishment, a defendant's constitutional right to a jury trial is not violated by the fact that other factors were found in the context of sentencing the defendant. See, e.g., *Stokes v. Schriro, 465 F.3d 397, 402-03 (9th Cir. 2006)*.

Arizona's response to Blakely as explained in Martinez has been found to be not clearly contrary to federal law. See *Cunningham v. California, 549 U.S. 270, 294 n.17, 127 S. Ct. 856, 871 n.17, 166 L. Ed. 2d 856 (2007)* (finding California's sentencing process unconstitutional and analyzing the Colorado Supreme Court's response to Blakely in *Colorado v. Lopez, 113 P.3d 713, 716 (Colo. 2005)*; Colorado's Lopez decision is materially similar to the Arizona Supreme Court's Martinez opinion); *Stokes, 465 F.3d at 402-03* (holding "the Arizona state courts' interpretation of these [sentencing] provisions does not contradict clearly established federal law"). Accordingly, the Arizona court's decision denying this claim in Petitioner's direct appeal was not clearly contrary to federal law and Petitioner is not entitled to relief on this claim.

REASONS WHY REMEDY IS HOLLOW

Arizona judges help prosecutors and defense counsel misrepresent the potential sentences when they have people plead guilty and though the Arizona Attorney General has knowledge of this fact, refuses to notify federal courts of this.

RICHARD K. BLASDEL, Petitioner/Appellant, v. CHARLES RYAN, Respondent/Appellee. 2 CA-HC 2003-0006 COURT OF APPEALS OF ARIZONA, DIVISION TWO, DEPARTMENT A(Text modified for emphasis)

THE POSITION OF THE COURTS

Richard Blasdel, an inmate of the Department of Corrections (DOC), appeals from the trial court's dismissal of his petition for writ of habeas corpus and the subsequent denial of his motion for reconsideration. We review a trial court's ruling on a petition for writ of habeas corpus for an abuse of discretion. *Long v. Ariz. Bd. of Pardons & Parole, 180 Ariz. 490, 885 P.2d 178 (App. 1994).* The warden is correct that habeas corpus relief is appropriate only when a prisoner is entitled to absolute release. *See A.R.S. § 13-4131(A); Long.* But we conclude Blasdel may be correct that he is entitled to immediate release. Accordingly, we remand the case for an evidentiary hearing on his petition.   We note that   the trial court improperly ordered the name of the respondent in Blasdel's petition changed from Charles Ryan, the warden of the prison in which Blasdel was incarcerated, to "State of Arizona, Department of Corrections." The proper respondent in a habeas corpus petition, however, is the person charged with detaining the petitioner, not the institution. *See A.R.S. §§ 13-4122, 13-4125.*

On November 29, 1993, a superior court judge in Maricopa County sentenced Blasdel in four separate cases. The judge imposed concurrent prison terms of seven years, 7.5 years, and ten years and a consecutive, ten-year prison term. According to Blasdel's petition for writ of habeas corpus, he was granted parole on the seven-year sentence on March 19, 1996, effective September 1996, to begin serving his consecutive sentence. Blasdel alleged that both his seven-year and 7.5-year sentences had expired and that he had reached his earned release credit date on the ten-year, concurrent sentence on August 28, 2000. Blasdel also alleged that he had appeared before the Board of Executive Clemency on April 8, 2002, and had been granted parole on the ten-year, consecutive sentence, effective September 16, 2002, to   a detainer from an Indiana sheriff. In the argument attached to his petition, Blasdel alleged that, five days before his scheduled release date, DOC authorities conducted an audit of his records and discovered DOC had erroneously certified him for parole in 1996 on the shortest concurrent sentence instead of the longest. As a result, DOC refused to release Blasdel and declared both paroles he had been granted void. Blasdel's petition followed.

Blasdel argues that DOC had no authority to retroactively rescind the paroles he had been granted and that all his sentences have since expired, entitling him to immediate release. The warden responds, however, that the trial court properly dismissed Blasdel's petition for writ of habeas corpus because the March 1996 grant of parole was invalid and he is properly serving his consecutive sentence. Although we agree with the warden that DOC's error in structuring the order of Blasdel's sentences did not divest DOC of authority to keep him in custody, *see McKellar v. Arizona State Department of Corrections, 115 Ariz. 591, 566 P.2d 1337 (1977),* we do not agree that Blasdel was required to serve his concurrent, ten-year sentence in full because he waived the right to parole on it.

Under *A.R.S. § 31-201.01(A)*, the director of DOC "shall hold in custody all persons sentenced to the department under the law and shall hold such persons for the term directed by the court, subject to law." Because he committed his offenses before January 1, 1994, Blasdel was required to serve a minimum of half his concurrent sentences. *See A.R.S. § 41-1604.09(D) and (I).* Because his longest concurrent sentence was ten years, he was required to serve a minimum of five years. Thus, we reject Blasdel's argument that the warden had authority to release Blasdel to parole improperly granted on the seven-year sentence after he had served only three and one-half years of his sentences. *See McKellar* (corrections authorities properly took erroneously released prisoner into custody and returned him to prison to serve balance of required minimum sentence); *State v. Deddens, 112 Ariz. 425, 542 P.2d 1124 (1975)* (warden who improperly releases prisoner can be held in contempt even if acting in good-faith reliance on attorney general's interpretation of law).

We also reject Blasdel's argument that no Arizona statute governs how DOC should structure an inmate's multiple, concurrent sentences. Implicit in the language of *§ 41-1604.09(D)*--that a "prisoner's earliest parole eligibility occurs when the prisoner has served one-half of his sentence" unless a greater minimum sentence is mandated--is the requirement that the prisoner serve one-half of the longest concurrent sentence before becoming eligible for parole. We thus agree with the warden that DOC was entitled to correct its error in having certified Blasdel for parole on his shortest concurrent sentence.

We find no merit to Blasdel's claim that the Ninth Circuit Court of Appeals overruled *McKellar* in *McQuillion v. Duncan, 342 F.3d 1012 (9th Cir. 2003)*. The Ninth Circuit's ruling that the district court had properly granted an inmate's petition for writ of habeas corpus was based on the appellate court's earlier conclusion in *McQuillion v. Duncan, 306 F.3d 895 (9th Cir. 2002)*, that the inmate had acquired a liberty interest in a previously granted parole date under the language of California's parole statutes, language that paralleled the statutory parole scheme at issue in *Greenholtz v. Inmates of Nebraska Penal & Correctional Complex, 442 U.S. 1, 99 S. Ct. 2100, 60 L. Ed. 2d 668 (1979)*. Arizona's statutes contain no such language. Thus, neither *McQuillion* decision supports Blasdel's claim.

That does not end our inquiry, however. The warden argues that the Board of Executive Clemency's granting of parole in March 1996 and April 2002 was rescinded after DOC discovered its error in calculating the order in which Blasdel must serve his sentences. The warden failed to establish, however, that the Board rescinded its grant of parole.

In his response to Blasdel's petition, the warden produced a letter from DOC to the Board explaining DOC's error in having certified Blasdel for parole in March 1996 and April 2002 and asking the Board to review its granting of parole as follows:

> Therefore, it is requested that the Board of Executive Clemency review the Parole grant and allow the Parole to Consecutive sentence granted to begin on the eligibility date of February 28, 1998, and the Parole granted on CR#2001014672 on April 8, 2002 to his Detainer is null and void.

The warden did not produce any document from the Board rescinding Blasdel's parole, simply asserting in his response that "the Board [had] rescinded the parole declaration." In making that assertion, the warden apparently relied on an affidavit by a DOC time computation program specialist who stated that, "on September 16, 2002, the Arizona Board of Executive Clemency did null and void the grant to the detainer." And the letter DOC sent Blasdel stated both that "a review by the Board of Executive Clemency to your consecutive sentence has been requested" and that "your parole to consecutive sentence granted on Mary [sic] 19, 1996 is null and void." The letter did not mention the parole granted in April 2002.

Blasdel asserts that DOC lacked the authority to rescind his parole, noting that *§ 41-1604.09(D)* provides that "the entire parole process shall be rescinded" if an inmate DOC has certified as eligible for parole fails to remain in a parole eligible classification "until the date of release on parole." The process to which the statute refers is DOC's certification five months before the prisoner's earliest eligibility date that the prisoner is eligible for parole. *§ 41-1604.09(D)*. That process period had long since passed by September 2002 when DOC purported to rescind the parole Blasdel had been granted in May 1996.

Moreover, *A.R.S. § 31-402(A)* grants the Board of Executive Clemency "exclusive power to pass upon and recommend . . . paroles." *See also A.R.S. § 31-411(D)* ("If parole is granted, the prisoner shall remain on parole unless the board revokes the parole . . . ."). In addition, the warden's assertion on appeal that DOC had "certified Blasdel to appear before the Board" is not supported by DO C's letter to him purportedly declaring his parole void. Nothing in that letter suggests he could appear before the Board to address the rescission of his parole. Therefore, we agree with Blasdel that it is unclear whether his parole was ever lawfully rescinded. Certainly, the trial court had no evidence that it had been.

The printout DOC gave Blasdel shortly after he began serving his sentences in late 1993 listed the correct length of each of those sentences and correctly stated that the parole eligibility release date for his ten-year, concurrent sentence was February 28, 1998, exactly five years after the date his sentences began. Yet DOC inexplicably twice certified him for parole calculated on the wrong sentence and later purported without authority to declare void the parole he had been granted more than six years previously. And after Blasdel objected to his loss of parole by filing his petition, the warden asserted, but only by way of a one-sentence paragraph in the time computation program specialist's affidavit, that he had waived any future parole on his ten-year, concurrent sentence by having "appeared and waived the hearing" on November 7, 2002.

The warden repeatedly states that Blasdel waived the right to be paroled on his concurrent, ten-year sentence at a November 2002 hearing before the Board of Executive Clemency. As a result, the warden contends Blasdel could not begin serving his consecutive sentence until he had fully served his ten-year, concurrent sentence on February 28, 2003. And, the warden asserts, Blasdel will not be eligible for parole on the consecutive sentence until March 2009 because he must serve at least two-thirds of that sentence. Although the Board of Executive Clemency's board hearing results of November 7, 2002, contains the notation "appeared and waive d," we do not believe that cryptic conclusion may stand under the facts of this case.

In *McKellar*, the supreme court addressed the arguments of an inmate who had been prematurely released from prison and who had returned to his parents' home, obtained a   job, applied to reenter college, and received treatment for his substance abuse problems. As the supreme court put it, "[i]n short, he conducted himself as a model parolee for two and one-half months." *McKellar, 115 Ariz. at 592, 566 P.2d at 1338*. The court did not hesitate in concluding that DOC had not lost jurisdiction of the inmate despite its having prematurely released him. But, the court held, because the inmate "ha[d] committed no wrong, . . . [t]he state's error [could] not . . . work to [the inmate's] further detriment since he was in no way at fault." *Id. at 593-94, 566 P.2d at 1339-40*. The court thus ordered that DOC credit the inmate with the time when he had been illegally paroled.

The same was true in *Schwichtenberg v. State, 190 Ariz. 574, 951 P.2d 449 (1997)*. The inmate there was erroneously released because DOC was somehow unaware he still had a consecutive sentence to serve. After ten years, the inmate petitioned for a certificate of absolute discharge, but DOC ordered him to report to prison to serve the consecutive sentence. After his petition for special action was denied in superior court on the ground he was partially to blame for his premature release, the   inmate eventually appealed his case to the supreme court. Applying the *McKellar* theory, the supreme court ruled that the inmate was not at fault and was entitled to credit for the time he had been free. Because that time exceeded the length of his consecutive sentence, the supreme court concluded that he was not required to return to prison.

We conclude that theory is applicable to Blasdel. No one disputes that he is not to blame for any errors in calculating the dates he became eligible for parole. Nor is it disputed that he was twice certified as eligible for parole in recognition of his "adherence to the rules of [DOC] and continual willingness to volunteer for or successful participation in a work, educational, treatment or training program" as required by *§ 41-1604.09(B)* and *(C)*. In addition, Blasdel was entitled to be paroled on his concurrent sentences to serve his consecutive sentence. *See Cawley v. Ariz. Bd. of Pardons & Paroles, 145 Ariz. 387, 701 P.2d 1195 (App. 1984), aff'd, 145 Ariz. 380, 701 P.2d 1188 (1985); State v. LaBarre, 125 Ariz. 497, 610 P.2d 1058 (App. 1980)*.

Under the *McKellar* theory, Blasdel was entitled to retroactive parole to his consecutive sentence   effective February 28, 1998, once DOC discovered its error. Because he was required to serve two-thirds of his consecutive sentence, and because he had been awarded presentence incarceration credit of 266 days on that sentence, he would have been entitled to be paroled on the consecutive sentence to his Indiana detainer in March 2004. Considering the uncertainty of his legal status in November 2002 in the wake of DOC's audit and its sudden announcement after six years that it had twice wrongly submitted his name for parole, we reject the warden's assertion that Blasdel "appeared and waived" his right to be paroled from his ten-year concurrent sentence to his ten-year consecutive sentence.

Based on the difference between eligibility for parole in March 2004 and eligibility in March 200 9, we find no support in the record for the trial court's conclusion that Blasdel's sentence was not affected by DOC's erroneous calculations. We acknowledge, however, that Blasdel was not eligible for immediate release at the time the trial court ruled on his petition. We reverse the court's dismissal of the petition for writ of habeas corpus and remand the case for the court to conduct an evidentiary   hearing on Blasdel's entitlement to immediate parole. We point out, how ever, that nothing precludes the warden from promptly recertifying Blasdel for parole to his Indiana detainer, which would obviate the need for an evidentiary hearing and avoid further delay in releasing Blasdel.

REASONS WHY REMEDY IS NOT HOLLOW

The ADOC has a well documented practice of not releasing inmates when they should and this is a rare situation when the court released the inmate.

Michael Joe Murdaugh, Petitioner, vs. Charles L. Ryan, et al., Respondents.
No. CV 09-831-PHX-FJM UNITED STATES DISTRICT COURT FOR THE DISTRICT OF ARIZONA

THE POSITON OF THE COURT

Petitioner was convicted and sentenced to death for the 1995 murder of David Reynolds. The following facts concerning the crime are based on the Arizona Supreme Court's opinion in *State v. Murdaugh, 209 Ariz. 19, 22-26, 97 P.3d 844, 847-51 (2004)*, and this court's review of the record.

On June 26, 1995, Petitioner's girlfriend, Rebecca Rohrs, met the victim, David Reynolds, at a gas station. Rohrs told Reynolds that she was looking for a job and Reynolds indicated he might be able to help her. Rohrs gave Reynolds a copy of her resumé and the two exchanged phone numbers. At some point in the conversation, Reynolds offered to pay Rohrs for oral sex. Rohrs declined and went home.

When Rohrs arrived at the home she shared with Petitioner, she told him what had happened at the gas station. Petitioner decided to teach Reynolds a lesson and instructed Rohrs to contact Reynolds and invite him to the house.

Rohrs paged Reynolds and invited him to party with her and her friend, Betty Gross. Reynolds returned the page. While Rohrs was talking to Reynolds, Petitioner stood nearby and told her what to say. After the call, Petitioner and a friend, Jesse Dezarn, left to buy methamphetamine. They instructed Rohrs and Gross to page them as soon as Reynolds arrived. Petitioner also told them to make sure Reynolds did not leave before he returned.

Approximately fifteen minutes after Reynolds arrived, Petitioner and Dezarn entered the house brandishing firearms. Petitioner shouted at Reynolds, demanding to know why he thought that he could treat Rohrs "like a whore." Petitioner continued to yell at Reynolds while Gross and Rohrs left the house to remove anything of value from Reynolds' van. Reynolds remained in the house with Dezarn and Petitioner, both of whom continued to wave their guns. Petitioner ordered Reynolds to empty his pockets onto the coffee table. Reynolds had about $200 in cash. At some point in the evening Petitioner took the money.

While Rohrs and Gross were unloading the van, Petitioner went outside and reprimanded them for not wearing gloves. He told them that they had left fingerprints on everything and asked, "Do you know what I am going to have to do now?" Petitioner instructed Gross and Rohrs to wipe the equipment clean of fingerprints and to put everything back in Reynolds' van. Reynolds likely heard this exchange.

Petitioner returned to the house and at his request Rohrs brought him a baseball bat. He asked Rohrs if she would like to take a swing at Reynolds' head. She declined. Petitioner also told Gross to take a swing at Reynolds, but she too refused.

At about 11:30 p.m., after Rohrs, Petitioner, Dezarn, and Gross ate dinner, Petitioner led Reynolds to the garage. Dezarn, still armed with a firearm, walked behind Reynolds. Inside the garage, Petitioner ordered Reynolds into the trunk of his Buick so that he could "figure things out." Throughout the night, Petitioner, Dezarn, Gross, and Rohrs returned to the garage to take methamphetamine.

In the early morning hours of the next day, Dezarn and Petitioner agreed that they needed to get rid of Reynolds' van. They decided to "ditch" it near Whitman Cemetery. Petitioner led the way in his truck while Dezarn followed in Reynolds' van. They abandoned the van on Cemetery Road and began driving back to Petitioner's house. On the way, they stopped for gas in Whitman and ran into an acquaintance named Ron Jesse. They asked Jesse for drugs, and all three returned to Petitioner's house. From there, Dezarn and Jesse left to get more methamphetamine with the money Petitioner had taken from Reynolds.

After Dezarn and Jesse returned with the drugs, they and Petitioner locked themselves in the garage to shoot up. While in the garage, Petitioner told Jesse what happened to Rohrs at the gas station and that he had Reynolds locked in the trunk.

At about 8:30 a.m., Petitioner opened the door to the garage and allowed Gross and Rohrs to join him, Dezarn, and Jesse to take more drugs. When Petitioner opened the trunk to show Jesse that Reynolds was there, Reynolds stated that he needed to relieve himself. Petitioner let Reynolds out of the trunk and took him to the corner of the garage to urinate. While Reynolds' back was turned, Petitioner struck him in the head with a nylon meat tenderizer. Reynolds fell to the floor. Petitioner picked up a jack hammer spike and continued to hit him in the face and head. The attack caused three major crushing blows to Reynolds' skull, resulting in his death. At some point, Petitioner placed a bag over Reynolds' head.

Petitioner left Reynolds lying face down in the garage with the bag tied over his head. He instructed Gross and Rohrs to sprinkle horse manure over Reynolds' body and on the blood surrounding his body. The body was left in this condition for the rest of the day.

At some point after the murder Jesse attempted to leave Petitioner's home but was unable to do so because of a locked gate. When Petitioner arrived to unlock the gate he threatened Jesse, stating that if Jesse told anyone what had happened in the garage he would "kill [Jesse] last and peel the skin off his children." Petitioner then opened the gate and allowed Jesse to leave.

Around the time of the murder, Petitioner realized that he and Dezarn had left items in the van that would show it belonged to Reynolds. Petitioner directed Dezarn and Rohrs to remove the items. Dezarn retrieved Reynolds' pagers, wallet, and identification papers and returned to Petitioner's house with Rohrs.

Later that evening, Petitioner and Dezarn loaded Reynolds' body into Petitioner's horse trailer. Petitioner told Rohrs to clean up the blood in the garage. He then packed to go on a camping trip, leaving some time after midnight.

Once at his campsite, Petitioner dismembered Reynolds' body in an effort to prevent its identification. First, he cut off Reynolds' head and hands. He then removed the finger pads from the hands and pulled all of Reynolds' teeth. He threw the teeth and finger pads out the window of his truck as he drove along a forest service road. He then buried the head and hands in one shallow grave and the torso in another. He returned to his campsite, where he placed several calls to Rohrs using Reynolds' cell phone.

The police, having been notified by Reynolds' family of his disappearance, obtained copies of Reynolds' cell phone records. They discovered that on June 26 Reynolds had made several calls to his company and his girlfriend, and that he had also called Rohrs five times. Officers contacted Rohrs on June 28, and she told them that she had Reynolds' business card and was willing to come to the Sheriff's Office to look at a photograph of Reynolds. Rohrs never went to the Sheriff's Office to make the identification. On June 29, the police discovered that Reynolds' cell phone had been used to make several additional calls to Rohrs on June 28.

On June 29, police located Reynolds' van. They found his work boots in the vehicle and discovered that his cell phone was missing. They learned that the most recent calls from the cell phone originated from the Flagstaff area. The same day, the police were contacted by a resident of Whitman who told them that a murder had taken place in Petitioner's garage. After contacting another witness, the police interviewed Ron Jesse, who told them that he had witnessed Reynolds' murder.

During their phone conversations, Rohrs told Petitioner that the police were tracking the calls he made with Reynolds' cell phone. Petitioner left his campsite and called Rohrs from a pay phone. She told him that she had been contacted by the police but had not told them anything. Petitioner broke Reynolds' cell phone into pieces and disposed of it, along with Reynolds' wallet and papers, near Reynolds' body. Back at the campsite, Petitioner was cleaning one of his horse's hooves when his knife slipped and severely cut his leg. He went to the Yavapai Regional Medical Center for treatment.

On June 30, 1995, the police obtained a search warrant for Petitioner's home and garage. They found blood stains covered with horse manure on the garage floor.

The Maricopa County Sheriff's Office notified other law enforcement agencies that they were looking for Petitioner. The Yavapai County Sheriff's Office called the investigators and informed them that Petitioner was in the emergency room at the Yavapai Regional Medical Center. The investigators asked the Yavapai authorities to impound Petitioner's vehicle and then went to the hospital to contact Petitioner.

Detective Griffiths of the Maricopa County Sheriff's Office spoke with hospital personnel, confirming that Petitioner had not been given any pain medication. He then met with Petitioner at approximately 8:55 p.m. on June 30. He read Petitioner the *Miranda* warnings and Petitioner agreed to answer questions. Petitioner asked whether his garage had been cleaned. When informed that it had not, he responded, "Then you have enough to do me in." He then described Reynolds' murder and provided Detective Griffiths with a detailed map and directions to the campsite. He also told Griffiths where to find Reynolds' body and personal effects. Police located the body the next day.

The detectives also questioned Petitioner about the murder of Douglas Eggert, which had occurred earlier in 1995 and bore similarities to the Reynolds murder. Petitioner admitted that he had killed Eggert by beating him to death with a meat tenderizer and then throwing the body into a canal.

On January 10, 2000, Petitioner pled guilty to the kidnapping, robbery, and first degree murder of Reynolds. He also pled guilty to the kidnapping and first degree murder of Eggert. The State and Petitioner agreed that he would receive a life sentence for the murder of Eggert. Petitioner also acknowledged that his guilty plea to the Eggert murder would be used as an aggravating factor in the Reynolds case.

At sentencing, the trial court found that the State had proved two aggravating circumstances with respect to the Reynolds murder: that Petitioner had been convicted of another offense for which a sentence of life imprisonment or death was imposable, pursuant to *A.R.S. § 13-703(F)(1)*, and that he committed the murder in an especially heinous, cruel, or depraved manner under *§ 13-703(F)(6)*. Although Petitioner waived the presentation of mitigating evidence, the trial court found eight nonstatutory mitigating circumstances, based primarily on the effects of Petitioner's drug abuse, personality disorder, and paranoia. The court determined, however, that these circumstances were not sufficiently substantial to outweigh the aggravating factors, and sentenced Petitioner to death.

On direct appeal to the Arizona Supreme Court, Petitioner raised two claims in his opening brief. First, he argued that *Ring* error was not harmless. Second, he contended that his plea agreement was "not enforceable" because he could not have knowingly and voluntarily waived his rights when he was not informed that he had a right to a jury determination of his sentence under *Ring. Id.* at 11-13. The Arizona Supreme Court rejected these claims. *Murdaugh, 209 Ariz. at 28-33, 97 P.3d at 853-58. Ring v. Arizona, 536 U.S. 584, 122 S. Ct. 2428, 153 L. Ed. 2d 556 (2002),* invalidated the capital sentencing scheme under which aggravating factors were found by a judge rather than a jury.

At oral argument before the Arizona Supreme Court, Petitioner raised two new claims: that the delay in his case constituted cruel and unusual punishment and that he had been incompetent to plead guilty. *Id. at 26, 97 P.3d at 851.* The Arizona Supreme Court, after reviewing the claims for fundamental error and finding none, deemed both claims waived. *Id. at 26-27, 97 P.3d at 851-52.* The court affirmed Petitioner's convictions and death sentence. *Id. at 37, 97 P.3d at 862.*

Petitioner filed an Amended Petition for Post-Conviction Relief ("PCR") on November 4, 2005, raising 12 claims. The PCR court held an evidentiary hearing on Petitioner's claim of ineffective assistance of counsel at sentencing. The court denied the claim and dismissed the remaining claims, the majority of which challenged Petitioner's competence to plead guilty and waive mitigation, as precluded or not colorable. Petitioner filed a petition for review, which the Arizona Supreme Court summarily denied. Petitioner then commenced proceedings in this court.

Petitioner sets forth 20 claims in his habeas petition. Respondents concede that 10 claims are properly exhausted in whole or in part. They contend that Claims 5, 6, 9, 10, 11, 13, 14, 17, 19, and 20 are procedurally barred. Petitioner seeks evidentiary development with respect to all but two of his claims. Respondents contend that Petitioner is not entitled to evidentiary development. The court will first address, as necessary, the procedural status and merits of Petitioner's claims. The court will then consider Petitioner's requests for evidentiary development.

Petitioner's principal claims are based on his assertion that his guilty pleas and waiver of the presentation of mitigating evidence were not valid due to his mental incompetence. In addition, according to Petitioner, both defense counsel and the trial court failed to take Petitioner's incompetence into account in allowing him to plead guilty and waive mitigation. The Court will first discuss the claims relating to Petitioner's guilty pleas.

A. Guilty Pleas: Claims 8-11

Petitioner contends that he was mentally incompetent to enter a knowing, voluntary, and intelligent guilty plea, that defense counsel performed ineffectively in handling the issue, and that the trial court failed to make an adequate competency determination before accepting the guilty pleas.

Background

At trial and sentencing Petitioner was represented by Jess Lorona, pursuant to Lorona's contract with the Maricopa County Office of Court Appointed Counsel ("OCAC"). Lorona was assisted by co-counsel (first Patricia Gitre, then Peter Claussen), investigators (Stella Salinas and Jeff Bachtle), and a mitigation specialist (first Holly Wake, then Linda Christianson).

On November 20, 1998, at the request of defense counsel, the trial court ordered that Petitioner undergo a competency screening evaluation "in preparation for a possible Change of Plea." On December 9, 1998, Dr. Jack Potts, a forensic psychiatrist, conducted the evaluation. Dr. Potts reviewed the court's minute entry ordering the evaluation, a police report regarding the Reynolds murder, a copy of the indictment, and Petitioner's Correctional Health Services medical records.

According to Dr. Potts, Petitioner was "fully alert and oriented to his name, our location, and the general reason for our interview." Petitioner's thought processes were "goal-directed and intact throughout" and there was "absolutely no evidence that he was suffering from perceptual disturbances such as auditory or visual hallucinations during the time of [the] evaluation." Petitioner denied having any "special powers," his memory was "grossly intact for both recent and remote events," his "cognitive abilities appeared to be consistent with that of the general population, if not slightly above average," and "his abilities to abstract and conceptualize appeared to be grossly intact."

Dr. Potts noted that Petitioner had "some beliefs that may be considered 'fringe.'" Petitioner described having "out of body experiences." He claimed to have knowledge of the Buddhist monk killings in Phoenix. Petitioner also informed Dr. Potts that he believed he was "being monitored through telephone wiretaps and surveillance." Petitioner was concerned that when he underwent leg surgery while incarcerated, "a location transmitting device had been implanted in his skull"; he wanted to get a CT scan or skull x-ray to confirm this suspicion. Dr. Potts noted, however, that "when questioned further, the defendant said these concerns and knowledge of surveillance activities" had "nothing to do with his taking a plea."

Dr. Potts determined that Petitioner understood the charges against him, was aware of his constitutional rights, knew that the prosecution would be seeking the death penalty, and understood the ramifications of pleading guilty. Petitioner maintained that he was "not desirous of putting his family or the alleged victim's families through the trauma of a trial."

Dr. Potts opined that Petitioner would likely be found competent. His "initial impression" was that Petitioner's "belief systems do not impact on his rational or factual understanding of the proceedings he is facing, his ability to effectively assist his attorney, or his understanding of waiving his rights by entering a plea."

However, while noting that Petitioner had never evidenced "any major mental illness" to the court or to the attorneys, Dr. Potts explained that Petitioner had a long history of "abusing methamphetamine" and might suffer from "a paranoid delusional disorder secondary to his past use." Therefore, Dr. Potts recommended that Petitioner's competency be evaluated further, out of concern that Petitioner's paranoia might impair his judgment and could prompt him to plead guilty whether or not doing so was in his best interest.

On December 10, 1998, the trial court granted Petitioner's motion for a competency determination and transferred the case to a Commissioner for further Rule 11 proceedings. The court appointed Drs. John Scialli, a psychiatrist, and Scott Sindelar, a clinical psychologist, to examine Petitioner and evaluate his competency to stand trial or plead guilty. The doctors were ordered to evaluate Petitioner's "present competency," including whether he was "able to understand the nature and object of the proceeding" and "able to assist in [his] defense." They were also instructed to address "whether mental illness, defect or disability has substantially impaired [Petitioner's] ability to make a competent decision concerning a waiver of rights and to have a rational, as well as factual understanding of the consequences of entering a plea of guilty," and whether Petitioner understood the constitutional rights he would give up by pleading guilty.

Dr. Sindelar examined Petitioner on January 19, 1999. He determined that Petitioner was "competent to stand trial," "able to understand the nature of the proceedings against him," and "currently able to assist counsel in the preparation of his defense." Dr. Sindelar noted that Petitioner had a "long history of multiple substance abuse," including intravenous injection of methamphetamine. Nonetheless, Dr. Sindelar believed that Petitioner could make a competent decision concerning the waiver of his rights and that he had a "factual and a rational understanding of the consequences of pleading guilty." Petitioner "appeared very knowledgeable about his alternatives and the reasons for his choices." His "thought content was logical and connected except when he attempted to convince [Dr. Sindelar] that he might have an electronic device implanted in his skull"; according to Dr. Sindelar, this "content sounded delusional." However, Dr. Sindelar did not believe this delusion affected Petitioner's competency or his "ability to help his attorney."

Dr. Scialli examined Petitioner and also concluded that he was competent to stand trial and to plead guilty. Dr. Scialli interviewed Petitioner on January 12, 1999. He reviewed police reports from Petitioner's offenses, medical records from Correctional Health Services, Dr. Potts' pre-screening report, and news stories regarding the charges against Petitioner. Dr. Scialli noted that Petitioner had one prior "known psychiatric contact," an incident in 1978 when Petitioner was briefly hospitalized in Indiana while intoxicated with amphetamines. In 1997, while incarcerated on the present charges, Petitioner had informed jail staff that he was depressed, suicidal, and had a sleep disorder. No medication was prescribed at the time, but subsequently he was diagnosed with anxiety disorder and prescribed anti-anxiety medication. Dr. Scialli indicated that he had spoken to Petitioner's ex-wife, who said that Petitioner "had been making comments about the CIA for around the year prior to his incarceration," and that Petitioner believed a tracking device had been implanted in his leg.

Dr. Scialli determined that Petitioner was "criminally competent to stand trial," explaining that Petitioner was able to "understand the nature of the proceedings against him" and "assist counsel in the preparation of his own defense." Although Petitioner possessed the "fringe" beliefs noted by Dr. Potts, Dr. Scialli found "no evidence of illogical thoughts, delusions or hallucinations." Dr. Scialli also found that Petitioner's beliefs did not interfere with his reasoning ability.

According to Dr. Scialli, if Petitioner "chooses to plead guilty, mental illness has not substantially impaired [his] ability to make a competent decision concerning waiver of rights, and to have a rational, as well as factual, understanding of the consequences of pleading guilty." Petitioner was aware of the details of his plea agreement, which he had discussed with counsel; he specifically acknowledged to Dr. Scialli that he would still "get the death penalty even with the plea deal." Petitioner's motivation for accepting the plea deal was that "death row has a better quality of life" than that of the general prison population, and that he wanted to "spare others from the stress of a trial." He also believed that the outcome would be the same whether he pled guilty or went to trial. Dr. Scialli found "nothing illogical" about Petitioner's reasoning. When Dr. Scialli explained "possible defense and/or mitigating factors" available in a trial, Petitioner indicated that he was "not previously aware of these things" but even with that information he would still choose to plead guilty.

Finally, Dr. Scialli discussed Petitioner's desire to obtain an x-ray to identify the tracking device he believed was in his skull, and the possible effect of this desire on his decision to plead guilty. Petitioner told Dr. Scialli that when he discussed the plea agreement with Lorona, Lorona told him he would get the x-ray if he signed the agreement. Dr. Scialli found that Petitioner's discussion of the issue was "done in a logical way, notwithstanding no information from his attorney as to whether the skull x-ray had been discussed when discussing the plea agreement." Dr. Scialli found that Petitioner's beliefs about the implant did not "interfere[] with his ability to enter a plea of guilty" and concluded that "[w]hat was more convincing was that the defendant said that he would still enter a plea(s) of guilty even if getting an x-ray were not part of the deal." Dr. Scialli also noted that Petitioner would "drop" the issue if he received an x-ray and it showed no evidence of an implant. According to Dr. Scialli, "This sort of reasoning is not typical of a paranoid delusion."

On January 26, 1999, the parties stipulated to a determination of Petitioner's competency based on Dr. Sindelar and Dr. Scialli's reports. The Commissioner found Petitioner competent to stand trial, concluding that he was "competent in assisting counsel in his own defense, and making rational decisions reference the handling of this matter." The Commissioner then remanded the case to the trial court for a status conference.

On February 1, 1999, the State filed a motion requesting that the court order Correctional Health Services to provide Petitioner with a skull x-ray. The prosecutor stated that the x-ray would "reassure [Petitioner] that no tracking device exists" and "alleviate any potential coercive allegations raised at any future plea proceedings.". The court granted the State's motion and ordered Correctional Health Services to perform a skull x-ray.

On May 3, 1999, Lorona orally requested that Petitioner be sent back to Dr. Potts for an additional Rule 11 competency evaluation; the court granted the request. Thereafter, the court granted a number of continuances for Dr. Potts to complete the evaluation.

Dr. Potts visited Petitioner again on August 19, 1999, eight months after his initial interview, and found that Petitioner "continues to present as he has." Dr. Potts again opined that Petitioner was "very well aware of the charges he is facing" and "well aware that he has been offered a plea agreement wherein, on at least one of the cases he would be sentenced to life, and in the other case, he might receive the death penalty." Dr. Potts noted that Petitioner continued to desire testing to "see if there is an implant in his brain." Petitioner had already undergone a CT scan, which was "reported as negative," but, "as is not uncommon with paranoid individuals," Petitioner believed that the results might have been doctored and now wanted an MRI. As discussed below, the record presented during the PCR proceedings indicates that on July 30, 1999, jail staff discovered that Petitioner had cut himself on his left wrist and elbow and on the top of both feet. He was escorted on his own power to the jail clinic where he received stitches. After assuring staff that he would not harm himself further, he returned to his cell. Petitioner stated that he was upset over the anniversary of his father's death. Staff also found a "suicide note."

Although Petitioner still believed he had a tracking device in his head, Dr. Potts stated that Petitioner did not "believe that the implant has anything to do with the legal proceedings he is facing." Dr. Potts also noted that Petitioner continued to claim knowledge of the Buddhist temple murders but opined that those beliefs did not "impact on his offenses or the proceedings he is presently facing."

Dr. Potts found that Petitioner was "continuing to experience paranoid beliefs and delusions secondary to his past amphetamine abuse," noting that it is not uncommon for such symptoms to persist "even for years after the cessation of amphetamines." He reiterated that Petitioner's presentation was "consistent with delusions secondary to past chronic methamphetamine abuse." Dr. Potts indicated, based on the information he had, that Petitioner had functioned "relatively well" before he became an addict. He concluded that it was likely that Petitioner's methamphetamine use "greatly contributed to the alleged offenses having occurred."

Dr. Potts again determined that Petitioner fully appreciated the rights he would waive by pleading guilty and that Petitioner was "capable of weighing various options." He noted that one of Petitioner's stated reasons for entering a guilty plea was to spare the victims' families additional suffering. According to Dr. Potts, a more extensive competency evaluation was not warranted, because Petitioner's delusions were "relatively circumscribed" and seemed to have little if any bearing on the proceedings.

On October 8, 1999, Lorona informed the trial court that Dr. Potts had again found Petitioner competent and did not recommend any further competency proceedings. The trial court denied the defense motion for a full competency evaluation.

Petitioner's change of plea hearing occurred on January 10, 2000. The trial court questioned Petitioner to determine whether he understood the proceedings. The court asked Petitioner about his age, education level, whether he had difficulty reading or understanding English, and whether he was taking any medications. Petitioner informed the court that he had taken Klonopin for anxiety and Elavil for back pain.. He stated that the medications helped him to understand the proceedings and that he understood "everything very clearly."

The court asked Petitioner if his attorney had discussed the plea agreement with him; Petitioner stated that he had. The court then informed Petitioner of the charges against him and the potential sentence on each charge. Petitioner stated that he understood all of the charges and possible sentences. When asked if any promises or guarantees had been made to him in exchange for his pleas, Petitioner replied, "None at all."

Petitioner expressed a desire that the court and the State avoid speaking to the media about the offenses, but indicated that he had received no guarantees   from anyone regarding media coverage.

The court asked Petitioner if he had signed each of the plea agreements because he "understood them and agreed with them." Petitioner responded, "Yes, ma'am." When the court asked Petitioner if there was anything in the agreements that he did not understand, Petitioner replied, "No, ma'am."

The court then informed Petitioner that he had a right to a separate jury trial in each of his cases, in which the "obligation would be on the state to prove [his] guilt to a jury beyond a reasonable doubt as to each count in each case." Petitioner stated that he understood that right. The court told Petitioner that if the case went to trial, the State would call witnesses and his attorney could cross-examine those witnesses and call witnesses on Petitioner's behalf. The court informed Petitioner that he could choose whether or not to testify at trial and if he chose not to testify the jury could not use his silence against him. *Id.* Petitioner stated that he understood those rights.

Petitioner pled guilty to kidnapping and first degree murder in the Eggert case and aggravated robbery, kidnapping, and first   degree murder in the Reynolds case. As the prosecutor described the factual bases of the charges, Petitioner occasionally interrupted to correct what he considered to be factual errors. When the court questioned him regarding the factual bases of the charges, Petitioner again answered the questions clearly and offered corrections. The trial court found that Petitioner's guilty pleas were knowing, intelligent, and voluntary.

On appeal, during oral argument before the Arizona Supreme Court, Petitioner's appellate counsel asserted for the first time that Petitioner had been incompetent to plead guilty. *Murdaugh, 209 Ariz. at 27, 97 P.3d at 852*. Because Petitioner did not raise the claim in his opening brief, the court reviewed the claim only for fundamental error, concluded there was none, and found the claim waived. *Id.* The court explained:

> In this case, the trial judge found that Murdaugh was competent to plead guilty and that there was a sufficient factual basis to support the plea. The judge questioned Murdaugh directly about his agreement with the State, and Murdaugh responded that he understood both the nature and the consequences   of his plea. He also told the judge that he was not under the influence of alcohol at the time of the plea and that the drugs he was taking to control anxiety and back pain did not impair his ability to understand the plea proceedings. In addition, Murdaugh stated that his attorney had gone over all the terms of the plea agreement with him and that he fully understood the implications of the plea.
>
> The trial judge did not inquire further into whether Murdaugh was mentally competent to enter the plea agreement. A year before the plea proceedings, however, Drs. Sindelar and Scialli had evaluated Murdaugh's competency to stand trial. Relying on the reports prepared by these doctors, the court had found Murdaugh competent to stand trial. Dr. Potts re-evaluated Murdaugh approximately four months before he entered into his plea agreements. Murdaugh's counsel informed the court that Dr. Potts did not recommend any further competency evaluation. From this we can infer that Dr. Potts found Murdaugh competent to understand the proceedings and assist in his defense. Finally, neither Murdaugh nor his trial counsel raised any claim, either during the change of plea or during the sentencing hearing,   that Murdaugh may have been incompetent to plead guilty.
>
> Viewing this evidence in the light most favorable to sustaining the trial court's decision, reasonable evidence supports the trial court's finding that Murdaugh was competent to enter a plea of guilty and that he entered the plea knowingly, intelligently, and voluntarily.

(1) Claim 8

Petitioner alleges that trial counsel performed ineffectively by failing to ensure that his guilty pleas were knowing, intelligent, and voluntary and by inducing him to plead guilty by making promises based on his delusions. Respondents concede this claim is exhausted.

Clearly established federal law

Claims of ineffective assistance of counsel are governed by the principles set forth in *Strickland v. Washington, 466 U.S. 668, 104 S. Ct. 2052, 80 L. Ed. 2d 674 (1984)*. To prevail under *Strickland*, a petitioner must show that counsel's representation fell below an objective standard of reasonableness and that the deficiency prejudiced the defense. *Id. at 687-88.*

The inquiry under *Strickland* is highly deferential and "every effort [must] be made to eliminate the distorting effects of hindsight, to reconstruct the circumstances of counsel's challenged conduct, and to evaluate the conduct from counsel's perspective at the time." *Id. at 689; see Wong v. Belmontes, 130 S. Ct. 383, 384, 175 L. Ed. 2d 328 (2009)* (per curiam); *Bobby v. Van Hook, 130 S. Ct. 13, 16, 175 L. Ed. 2d 255 (2009)* (per curiam). Thus, to satisfy *Strickland*'s first prong, a defendant must overcome "the presumption that, under the circumstances, the challenged action might be considered sound trial strategy." *Id.* "The test has nothing to do with what the best lawyers would have done. Nor is the test even what most good lawyers would have done. We ask only whether some reasonable lawyer at the trial could have acted, in the circumstances, as defense counsel acted at trial." *Id. at 687-88.*

With respect to *Strickland*'s second prong, a petitioner must affirmatively prove prejudice by "show[ing] that there is a reasonable probability that, but for counsel's unprofessional errors, the result of the proceeding would have been different. A reasonable probability is a probability sufficient to undermine confidence in the outcome." *Strickland, 466 U.S. at 694.*

Because an ineffective assistance of counsel claim must satisfy both prongs of *Strickland*, the reviewing court "need not determine whether counsel's performance was deficient before examining the prejudice suffered by the defendant as a result of the alleged deficiencies." *Id. at 697*. Therefore, "if it is easier to dispose of an ineffectiveness claim on the ground of lack of sufficient prejudice . . . that course should be followed." *Id.*

Under the AEDPA, this Court's review of the state court's rulings on Petitioner's ineffective assistance claims is subject to another level of deference. *Bell v. Cone, 535 U.S. 685, 698-99, 122 S. Ct. 1843, 152 L. Ed. 2d 914 (2002); see Knowles v. Mirzayance, 129 S. Ct. 1411, 1420, 173 L. Ed. 2d 251 (2009)* (noting that a "doubly deferential" standard applies to *Strickland* claims under the AEDPA). Therefore, to prevail on this claim, Petitioner must make the additional showing that the PCR court, in ruling that trial counsel was not ineffective, applied *Strickland* in an objectively unreasonable manner. *28 U.S.C. § 2254(d)(1).*

Analysis

Petitioner sets forth a number of specific challenges to Lorona's performance. He alleges that counsel spent insufficient time working on the case, did not visit him regularly in jail, and did not consult with him. He contends that his "paranoid and disturbed" behavior should have alerted Lorona to "possible mental health and competency issues." He argues that Lorona failed to provide defense experts with information regarding his interactions with Petitioner. He claims that Lorona did not personally review the plea agreement with him. Finally, he asserts that Lorona induced him to plead guilty by promising that he would receive a head x-ray.

The PCR court rejected these allegations of ineffective assistance, finding that Petitioner's guilty plea was knowing and voluntary and noting that Petitioner appeared coherent and rational in his interactions with the trial court and assured the court that he "understood the proceedings as well as the consequences." This ruling was neither contrary to nor an unreasonable application of *Strickland*, nor was it based on an unreasonable determination of the facts. Petitioner's allegations, some of which are contrary to the record, are insufficient to establish that Lorona performed at a constitutionally ineffective level with respect to Petitioner's guilty pleas.

First, far from ignoring signs that Petitioner had mental health issues, Lorona secured examinations from three experts, all of whom found Petitioner competent to plead guilty. The court rejects Petitioner's assertion that Lorona performed ineffectively by failing to argue that Petitioner was incompetent to enter a plea. Drs. Potts, Scialli, and Sindelar examined Petitioner and "provided detailed, reasoned reports which contained their individual opinions that [he] was competent." *Moran v. Godinez, 57 F.3d 690, 699-700 (9th Cir. 1994).* Because Lorona was "entitled to rely on these reports," it was unnecessary for him to investigate the issue further. *Id. at 700.*

In *Taylor v. Horn, 504 F.3d 416, 438-39 (3d Cir. 2007)*, the Third Circuit held that the petitioner could show neither deficient performance nor prejudice based on counsel's failure to request a competency examination. Prior to his guilty plea, the petitioner had been found competent by two experts. *Id. at 421.* The court determined that "counsel's interactions with Taylor - paired with both the . . . reports concluding that Taylor was competent - were sufficient for counsel to reasonably forego a competency hearing." *Id. at 438.* In addition, because there was no reasonable probability that the petitioner was incompetent, counsel's failure to request a competency   hearing was not prejudicial. *Id. at 439.* Similarly, in Petitioner's case, there were "sufficient indicia of competence," *id. at 438*, such that Lorona's failure to pursue an argument that Petitioner was incompetent to plead guilty did not constitute deficient performance and did not result in prejudice.

Also unavailing is Petitioner's assertion that Lorona failed to provide the Rule 11 experts with records necessary for their evaluations. Although Dr. Potts stated in his pre-screening competency report that he did not receive any information from the defense, investigator Jeff Bachtle recalled delivering documents about Petitioner's background to Dr. Potts. At the evidentiary hearing before the PCR court on Petitioner's claims of ineffective assistance of counsel, Dr. Potts testified that he spoke with Lorona concerning the pre-screening evaluation but could not remember if they had further contact, nor could he recall if Bachtle had provided him with additional records.. Dr. Scialli testified that while he received no materials from defense counsel, he had enough information before him to make a determination.. Neither Dr.   Potts nor Dr. Scialli suggested that their evaluations were compromised due to a lack of documentary evidence.

Next, Petitioner fails to show that Lorona performed ineffectively with respect to Petitioner's desire for a head x-ray. Petitioner himself indicated to Drs. Potts and Scialli that an x-ray was not a necessary condition of his guilty plea. In addition, prior to pleading guilty Petitioner received an x-ray at the State's request.. Therefore, Lorona's promise of an x-ray did not serve as an inducement for Petitioner's plea.

Petitioner's complaints about counsel's lack of effort and infrequent jail visits are not sufficient to establish ineffective assistance of counsel. Although Lorona only visited Petitioner in jail five or six times over the course of his representation, he spoke to Petitioner on the phone two to three times every week and discussed the case with Petitioner during court appearances. In addition, defense investigator Bachtle visited Petitioner in jail more than 20 times and spoke with him on the phone several times a week. The mitigation specialists also had contact with   Petitioner in jail.

Even if Lorona's infrequent jail visits constituted deficient performance, "the mere fact that counsel spent little time with [petitioner] is not enough under *Strickland,* without evidence of prejudice or other defects." *Bowling v. Parker, 344 F.3d 487, 506 (6th Cir. 2003).* While Petitioner alleges generally that Lorona had a duty to engage in more frequent personal contact with him, he has provided "no explanation how additional meetings with his counsel, or longer meetings with his counsel, would have led to new or better theories of advocacy or otherwise would have created a 'reasonable probability' of a different outcome." *Hill v. Mitchell, 400 F.3d 308, 325 (6th Cir. 2005); see Lenz v. Washington, 444 F.3d 295, 302-03 (4th Cir. 2006).*

Petitioner argues that the numerous delays in the proceedings reflect the extent of Lorona's other commitments and his lack of focus on Petitioner's case. However, the record indicates that Lorona requested continuances primarily to prepare for trial, because discovery was not complete, because the parties were attempting to settle the case, or because reports from the defense experts were   not yet available. Other continuances were requested by the State. Moreover, it was Petitioner's express desire that Lorona "stretch out" the case for "as long as possible."

Likewise, Petitioner's contention that Lorona did not discuss the plea agreement with him are not well-founded. During the PCR evidentiary hearing, Bachtle testified that Lorona, who had already reviewed the plea agreement with Petitioner, requested that he go to the jail and again discuss the agreement with Petitioner. Lorona testified that either he or co-counsel went to the jail to review the plea agreement with Petitioner. Lorona also discussed the agreement with Petitioner while they were together in court. Moreover, after being presented with the plea agreement, Petitioner wrote Lorona a letter discussing changes he would like made and concluding, "Get these matters taken care of and I will then sign the plea deals to avoid the trauma of trials on my own and the victim's families." Such statements are   inconsistent with the assertion that Petitioner was unfamiliar with the terms of the plea agreement.

It is clear that from an early point in the case Petitioner expressed a desire to plead guilty in order to spare his and the victims' families the ordeal of a trial. For example, on April 18, 1996, Bachtle wrote a memo to Lorona noting that "Petitioner stated that he does NOT want to go to trial regarding his murder charges. He does NOT want to bring the victims family or his own family into court to listen to the allegations pertaining to the victim's death."

The Ninth Circuit recently reiterated that "prejudice does not generally exist when a defendant chooses to plead guilty." *Smith v. Mahoney, 596 F.3d 1133, 1146 (9th Cir. 2010)* (citing *Lambert v. Blodgett, 393 F.3d 943, 980 (9th Cir. 2004)*; *Langford v. Day, 110 F.3d 1380, 1383-84 (9th Cir. 1996)*). Petitioner, like the defendants in *Langford* and *Smith*, "strongly and repeatedly insisted on pleading guilty and seeking the death penalty." *Langford, 110 F.3d at 1386*. He was "determined and unequivocal in his decision to plead guilty," *id. at 1388*, consistently citing as the reason for his plea a desire to spare the families the trauma of a trial. As the court stated in *Smith*, "In such cases, where 'the defendant has his own reasons for pleading guilty,' relief is not warranted." *596 F.3d at 1147* (quoting *McMann v. Richardson, 397 U.S. 759, 767, 90 S. Ct. 1441, 25 L. Ed. 2d 763 (1970)*).

Conclusion

Petitioner wanted to plead guilty, and the uncontradicted opinions of the mental health experts indicated that he was competent to do so. Lorona's performance was neither deficient nor prejudicial. Therefore, the PCR court's rejection of this claim was not objectively unreasonable and Petitioner is not entitled to relief. Claim 8 is denied.

(2) Claims 9, 10, and 11

In Claim 9, Petitioner alleges that his guilty pleas were not knowing, intelligent, or voluntary because they were the product of his paranoid beliefs, safety fears, and promises by counsel. In Claim 10, he alleges that the trial court erred when it failed to conduct an adequate competency determination to ensure that he was competent to plead guilty. In Claim 11, Petitioner asserts that he was incompetent to plead guilty, resulting in a waiver of his right to trial that was not knowing, intelligent, and voluntary. Petitioner also alleges that appellate counsel was ineffective in failing to properly raise the issue of Petitioner's competency to plead guilty.

Procedural status

Respondents assert that these claims are procedurally barred. With respect to Claim 9, Respondents contend that Petitioner failed to present the federal basis of the claim to the Arizona Supreme Court in his petition for review and therefore the claim is unexhausted.

Petitioner raised Claim 9 in his PCR petition, alleging violations of the *Eighth* and *Fourteenth Amendments* and citing *Boykin v. Alabama, 395 U.S. 238, 89 S. Ct. 1709, 23 L. Ed. 2d 274 (1969)*. The PCR court rejected the claim:

> Defendant next claims that his plea of guilty and decision to waive mitigation was involuntary because it was the product of false promises and threats.
>
> In the colloquy for his change of plea, defendant told the trial court that there were no other promises made to him, and that his decision to plead guilty was not the result of any threat. Defendant specifically advised the trial court that his decision was voluntarily made.
>
> As stated previously, the trial court carefully questioned defendant about his awareness of the content of mitigation and his right to present it, and determined that his decision to waive mitigation was knowingly and voluntarily made.
>
> IT IS ORDERED dismissing defendant's fourth claim summarily pursuant to *Rule 32.6(c)*.

In his petition for review, Petitioner argued that his "guilty plea was invalid because he was mentally incompetent, because the plea was not knowing, intelligent and voluntary, because there was an inadequate determination of his competence to waive fundamental constitutional rights (*see supra*, Claim 2), and because improper promises were made to Murdaugh by Lorona in order to induce him to plead guilty." PR at 28.

Petitioner argues that his reference to Claim 2, which challenged his competence to waive mitigation and cited the federal constitution and case law, was sufficient to present the federal basis of this claim.

The court agrees that Petitioner fairly presented the federal basis of the claim to the state court, and will consider Claim 9 on its merits.

Respondents also contend that Claim 10 is precluded and procedurally barred. The court again disagrees.

In his PCR petition, Petitioner for the first time raised the claim that the trial   court erroneously failed to conduct a competency determination. The PCR court found the claim precluded under *Rule 32.2(a)(1), (2),* and *(3)* because it "was raised, or could have been raised on appeal." The court alternatively held:

> [T]here was no need for further competence determination. The record is devoid of any evidence suggesting defendant's decision to plead guilty was based on anything other than his expressed desire to spare the victim's family and his family from a trial. Dr. Scialli and Dr. Sindelar specifically stated in their reports that defendant was able to assist counsel in preparation of a defense.
>
> It is clear from the colloquy at the change-of-plea hearing, and from the mental health evaluations, that defendant understood the nature of the proceedings against him, that he was able to assist counsel, and that he understood the constitutional rights he would be giving up by pleading guilty. This claim, thus, fails to state a colorable claim for relief, and is summarily dismissed pursuant to *Rule 32.6(c).*

The PCR court's procedural ruling, that the claim was raised or could have been raised, is ambiguous. It fails to distinguish a claim previously raised, which is exhausted, from a claim waived because it was not raised previously. The ruling, therefore, does not function as an adequate bar to federal review. *See Valerio v. Crawford, 306 F.3d 742, 774-75 (9th Cir. 2002)* (en banc); *Koerner v. Grigas, 328 F.3d 1039, 1049-50 (9th Cir. 2003); Ceja v. Stewart, 97 F.3d 1246, 1253 (9th Cir. 1996).* The court will consider Claim 10 on its merits.

Finally, Respondents contend that Claim 11, challenging Petitioner's competence to plead guilty, is procedurally barred. Here, the court agrees.

Petitioner raised this claim during oral argument before the Arizona Supreme Court. The court, finding no fundamental error, deemed the claim waived. *Murdaugh, 209 Ariz. at 26, 97 P.3d at 851.* Petitioner raised the claim again in his PCR petition. The PCR court found it precluded under *Rule 32.2(a)(1) and (3)* because it could have been raised on direct appeal. The court alternatively denied the claim as not colorable for the reasons set forth in Claim 10 above. The fact that the PCR court alternatively discussed the   merits of the claim does not affect the application of *Rule 32.2(a)(3)* because the court "explicitly invoke[d] a state procedural bar as a separate basis for decision." *Harris, 489 U.S. at 264 n.10.*

This preclusion ruling rests on an independent and adequate state procedural bar. *See Smith, 536 U.S. at 860; Ortiz, 149 F.3d at 931-32.* Therefore, Claim 11 is procedurally barred, absent a showing of cause and prejudice or a fundamental miscarriage of justice.

Petitioner alleges ineffective assistance of appellate counsel as cause for his default of the claim. While properly exhausted in state court, the allegation that appellate counsel was ineffective is itself meritless because, for the reasons set forth below, Petitioner cannot show that he was prejudiced by appellate counsel's handling of the competence issue. Therefore, Petitioner's default of this claim is not excused by appellate counsel's performance. *Carrier, 477 U.S. at 492* ("Attorney error short of ineffective assistance of counsel does not constitute cause for a procedural default"). Nor has Petitioner established that a fundamental miscarriage of justice would result from the court's failure to consider Claim 11 on the merits. *See Schlup, 513 U.S. at 327.*

Clearly established federal law

Due process requires that a defendant be competent to plead guilty. *Pate v. Robinson, 383 U.S. 375, 384-85, 86 S. Ct. 836, 15 L. Ed. 2d 815.* The standard for competence to plead guilty is the same as the standard for competence to stand trial. *Godinez v. Moran, 509 U.S. 389, 396, 399-401, 113 S. Ct. 2680, 125 L. Ed. 2d*

321 (1993). The defendant must have "sufficient present ability to consult with his lawyer with a reasonable degree of rational understanding," together with "a rational as well as factual understanding of the proceedings against him." *Dusky v. United States, 362 U.S. 402, 80 S. Ct. 788, 4 L. Ed. 2d 824 (1960)* (per curiam); *see Boag v. Raines, 769 F.2d 1341, 1343 (9th Cir. 1985).*

Due process also requires a court to conduct a competency hearing on its own motion when "a reasonable judge would be expected to have a *bona fide* doubt as to the defendant's competence." *Moran, 57 F.3d at 695; see Amaya-Ruiz v. Stewart, 121 F.3d 486, 489 (9th Cir. 1997).* A bona fide doubt exists if there is "substantial evidence of incompetence." *Id.* "Although no particular facts signal incompetence, suggestive evidence includes a defendant's demeanor before the trial court, previous irrational behavior, and available medical evaluations." *Id.* A state court's competency determination is entitled to a presumption of correctness on federal habeas review and may be overturned only if it is not "fairly supported by the record." *Demosthenes v. Baal, 495 U.S. 731, 735, 110 S. Ct. 2223, 109 L. Ed. 2d 762 (1990)* (per curiam); *see Franklin v. Luebbers, 494 F.3d 744, 750 (8th Cir. 2007); Dennis ex rel. Butko v. Budge, 378 F.3d 880, 891- 92 (9th Cir. 2004).* In reviewing whether a state trial judge was required to conduct a competency hearing, a habeas court may consider only the evidence that was before the judge. *See McMurtrey v. Ryan, 539 F.3d 1112, 1118 (9th Cir. 2008)* (citing *Williams v. Woodford, 384 F.3d 567, 604 (9th Cir. 2004)).* As Respondents note, there is no support for Petitioner's argument that this court must make an "independent decision on the question of competence"

For a guilty plea to be valid, the defendant must not only be competent, but the plea must be "knowing and voluntary." *Godinez v. Moran, 509 U.S. at 400; see Brady v. United States, 397 U.S. 742, 748, 90 S. Ct. 1463, 25 L. Ed. 2d 747 (1970).* The plea must "represent[] a voluntary and intelligent choice among the alternative courses of action open to the defendant." *Hill v. Lockhart, 474 U.S. 52, 56, 106 S. Ct. 366, 88 L. Ed. 2d 203 (1985)* (quoting *North Carolina v. Alford, 400 U.S. 25, 31, 91 S. Ct. 160, 27 L. Ed. 2d 162 (1970)).* A plea is voluntary when a defendant is informed of and waives his privilege against self-incrimination, his right to trial by jury, and his right to confront witnesses. *Boykin, 395 U.S. at 243.* A plea is coerced and void if it was "induced by promises or threats which deprive it of the character of a voluntary act." *Machibroda v. United States, 368 U.S. 487, 493, 82 S. Ct. 510, 7 L. Ed. 2d 473 (1962); see Doe v. Woodford, 508 F.3d 563, 570 (9th Cir. 2007).*

A habeas petitioner bears the burden of establishing that his guilty plea was not voluntary and knowing. *See Parke v. Raley, 506 U.S. 20, 31-34, 113 S. Ct. 517, 121 L. Ed. 2d 391 (1992); Little v. Crawford, 449 F.3d 1075, 1080 (9th Cir. 2006); Miles v. Dorsey, 61 F.3d 1459, 1472 (10th Cir. 1995).* Findings by the judge accepting the plea "constitute a formidable barrier in any subsequent collateral proceedings. Solemn declarations in open court carry a strong presumption of verity." *Blackledge v. Allison, 431 U.S. 63, 74, 97 S. Ct. 1621, 52 L. Ed. 2d 136 (1977); see Doe v. Woodford, 508 F.3d at 571-72.*
Analysis

1. Competence

Petitioner argues that he was not competent to plead guilty and that appellate counsel performed ineffectively by failing to properly raise the issue , and that the trial court failed to make an adequate competency determination . The record does not support these claims.

The Ninth Circuit has noted that "[i]n cases finding sufficient evidence of incompetency, the petitioners have been able to show either extremely erratic or irrational behavior during the course of trial . . . or lengthy histories of acute psychosis and psychiatric treatment." *Boag, 769 F.2d at 1344; see Drope v. Missouri, 420 U.S. 162, 180, 95 S. Ct. 896, 43 L. Ed. 2d 103 (1975).* Petitioner has made neither showing.

In *Boag,* evidence of the petitioner's mental condition included five suicide attempts, repeated head injuries, bizarre behavior, alcoholism, the report of a prison psychiatrist made four months before trial that the petitioner had sociopathic personality disturbance and anti-social reaction, and a state judge's comment made six months before trial that the petitioner needed intensive psychiatric treatment. *769 F.2d at 1343.* The Ninth Circuit found that "these facts, taken as a whole, do not raise a substantial doubt as to Boag's competency" such that the trial court was required to order a competency hearing. *Id.*

In *Amaya-Ruiz,* the Ninth Circuit rejected the petitioner's claim that the trial court erroneously failed to determine that he was incompetent. *121 F.3d 486.* Amaya-Ruiz had been evaluated by two mental health professionals and found competent to stand trial. *Id. at 489.* Subsequently, he appeared to exhibit a lack of understanding of the legal proceedings and engaged in irrational behavior, including speaking in a loud voice at inappropriate times during the proceedings and acting in a disruptive manner at sentencing. *Id. at 489-90.* He also had attempted suicide, and records indicated that he was "prone to deep depression" and was taking medication. *Id. at 492.* The trial court refused to order an additional competency examination, and sentenced the defendant to death. *Id. at 491-92.*

The Ninth Circuit affirmed, explaining that "[t]hese events were insufficient to cause the state trial court to have a bona fide doubt as to Amaya-Ruiz's competency." *Id. at 491.* The court noted that the "state trial court previously had ordered two evaluations and the doctors opined Amaya-Ruiz was competent to stand trial. The evaluations suggested Amaya-Ruiz was malingering and had chosen a strategy of noncooperation. . . . Further, while his behavior may not have been rational at times, his behavior was not so extreme as to require an additional evaluation." *Id.* The Ninth Circuit also rejected the argument that a competency evaluation was required when the trial court discovered that the petitioner had been taking psychiatric medication. *Id. at 493.* The court noted that the trial judge, in making his determination that another evaluation was unnecessary, "had observed Amaya-Ruiz throughout the pretrial and trial proceedings" and "also had the benefit of two evaluations which indicated Amaya-Ruiz was a competent malingerer." *Id.*

By contrast, in *McMurtrey* the Ninth Circuit held that the petitioner's due process rights were violated by the trial court's failure to hold a hearing because there was sufficient evidence to raise a bona fide doubt concerning his competence to stand trial. *539 F.3d at 1127.* Defense experts noted that the McMurtrey had a history of head injuries and psychological problems, had a "spotty memory" which could impede his ability to assist counsel, and was subject to seizures and hallucinations. *Id. at 1119.* Prior to trial McMurtrey was moved to a psychiatric hospital due to suicidal ideation and a psychotic breakdown; a defense psychiatrist opined that he was incompetent to stand trial due to anxiety and memory problems. *Id. at 1121.* However, the state's psychological expert concluded that McMurtrey was competent to stand trial, basing his opinion on an hour-long interview. *Id. at 1121-22.* While incarcerated McMurtrey received high doses of a variety of anti-psychotic and anti-anxiety medications; as a result he repeatedly became physically ill during the trial. *Id. at 1122-23.* The record also showed that he exhibited erratic and volatile behavior in jail, and at sentencing he responded irrationally to the judge's questions. *Id.* at 1124-45.

Similarly, in *Maxwell v. Roe, 606 F.3d 561, 568-69 (9th Cir. 2010),* the petitioner was unable to control his behavior in jail or in court. He was involuntarily committed several times before and during trial. *Id. at 569-74.* His treating doctors described him as "actively psychotic" and "unable to function." *Id. at 573.* The trial judge was aware that Maxwell had a history of mental illness and was being treated with a "panoply" of antipsychotic drugs at the time of trial, which took place largely in his absence. *Id. at 570-71.* Finally, there was "substantial evidence that Maxwell's mental condition had significantly deteriorated since the initial pretrial competency examination." *Id. at 575.* The Ninth Circuit held that the failure to order a competency hearing violated due process, and the state appellate court made an unreasonable factual determination in finding that the petitioner was not entitled to such a hearing. *Id. at 576. See also Torres v. Prunty, 223 F.3d 1103, 1109-10 (9th Cir. 2000)* (holding that a competency hearing was required where defendant believed his attorney was part of a conspiracy against him, threatened to assault his attorney, insisted on being handcuffed, and continually disrupted the trial until he was removed from the courtroom).

In Petitioner's case, the trial court could not have been expected to have a bona fide doubt about his competence to plead guilty. First, as recounted above, three court-appointed experts evaluated Petitioner and concluded that he was competent to stand trial and plead guilty. While noting Petitioner's fringe beliefs, they each found that he was not otherwise delusional, was able to think rationally, and comprehended his legal situation and options. There was no evidence that Petitioner's condition had deteriorated by the time of his guilty pleas. Furthermore, unlike the petitioners in *Amaya-Ruiz* and *McMurtrey,* Petitioner's conduct before the judge was never irrational or inappropriate. Judge Hutt observed Petitioner's courtroom demeanor on a number of occasions and heard his cogent answers during the plea colloquy.

Finally, the record revealed only one previous hospitalization for Petitioner. This occurred in 1978 when Petitioner was temporarily deemed incompetent after "a transitory psychotic episode influenced by drug ingestion, most likely amphetamines." He was subsequently found competent, with "no serious emotional distress," "unimpaired" reality testing, logic, and memory, "no indications of systematic delusions" or "hallucinatory experiences," and "no evidence of an active psychosis."

Under these circumstances, the trial court was not required to conduct a more thorough competency determination before accepting Petitioner's guilty pleas. Therefore, Claim 10 is without merit.

Petitioner likewise fails to meet his burden with respect to his claim that he was incompetent when he entered his plea. The record reflects that the state court's competency determination was reasonable and fairly supported by the record, including the Rule 11 reports and the trial judge's personal observations of Petitioner. Petitioner has failed to rebut that determination by clear and convincing evidence. Therefore, his claim that he was not competent to plead guilty must fail. *See Demosthenes v. Baal, 495 U.S. at 735; Dennis ex rel. Butko v. Budge, 378 F.3d at 891-92; Hunter v. Bowersox, 172 F.3d 1016, 1021 (8th Cir. 1999).*

Because the claim that Petitioner was not competent lacks merit, appellate counsel's failure to raise the issue in his opening brief did not prejudice Petitioner and cannot constitute ineffective assistance. This conclusion is also supported by the Arizona Supreme Court's discussion of Petitioner's competence and the trial court's handling of the issue. *Murdaugh, 209 Ariz. at 27, 97 P.3d at 852.* Claim 11 is without merit.

2. Knowing, intelligent, and voluntary

Petitioner argues that his mental problems and promises made by counsel rendered his guilty pleas involuntary Again, the record does not support this claim.

There has never been any evidence that Petitioner lacked the requisite rational and factual understanding of the proceedings. Three experts opined that Petitioner, notwithstanding his fringe beliefs, was competent to plead guilty. Petitioner's plea colloquy, described above, further supports the conclusion that his plea was knowing and voluntary. Petitioner informed the trial court that he understood the plea agreements and was aware of the rights he was waiving, that no promises or threats had been made, and that there was a factual basis for his guilty pleas.. Petitioner's declaration that his plea was knowing and voluntary carries "a strong presumption of verity." *Blackledge v. Allison, 431 U.S. at 74.* In addition, as recounted above, there were no false promises regarding a head x-ray, and he did not insist on an x-ray as a condition of his pleas. Instead, the record shows that Petitioner was motivated to plead guilty by his desire to avoid a trial that would traumatize his and the victims' families. Petitioner attached to his motion for evidentiary development a "psychological summary" prepared in 2009 by Dr. Robert Smith. Dr. Smith concluded that Petitioner "is of at least average intelligence and has a full comprehension of the legal process." While stating that additional time was required to complete a "psychosocial history, diagnostic workup and full mental health examination," Dr. Smith's "diagnostic impressions" of Petitioner included delusional disorder, substance dependence, and narcissistic traits. He also opined that trial counsel should have obtained an additional mental health evaluation upon Petitioner's decision to waive mitigation.

Petitioner's case parallels the issues addressed in *Hunter v. Bowersox, 172 F.3d 1016 (8th Cir. 1999).* There, the petitioner pled guilty to two counts of first degree murder. The trial court found that the plea was knowing, intelligent, and voluntary. *Id. at 1018.* Court-ordered mental health evaluations, performed both before and after the plea hearing, found the petitioner competent, concluding that he "functioned at bright-average intelligence, understood the charges against him and the options available to him, was capable of entering a voluntary and intelligent plea, and had chosen to plead guilty because he wished to take responsibility for his participation in the crime and did not want to spend the rest of his life in prison." *Id. at 1021.* The petitioner subsequently moved to withdraw his plea, arguing that the effects of cocaine withdrawal and the conditions under which he was held in administrative segregation rendered him incapable of entering a knowing and voluntary plea. *Id. at 1022.* The trial court denied relief, as did the post-conviction court, the state supreme court, and the federal district court on habeas review. *Id. at 1018-22.* The Eighth Circuit affirmed, explaining that "the state courts' findings are entitled to the presumption of correctness, and that these findings fully support the determination that Hunter's plea of guilty was voluntary, knowing, and intelligent." *Id. at 1022*. In particular, the court noted that the petitioner's plea colloquy belied any claim that his cocaine addiction or the conditions of his confinement caused him to plead guilty. *Id. at 1022-23*.

Similarly, in Petitioner's case, the record fully supports the state courts' determination that Petitioner's guilty pleas were knowing and voluntary. Petitioner is unable to rebut the presumption that the this determination was correct.

Conclusion

Petitioner was competent to plead guilty. His pleas were knowing and voluntary. The decisions [*70] of the state court rejecting these claims were based on reasonable factual determinations and the reasonable application of federal law. Claims 9, 10, and 11 are therefore denied.

B. Mitigation Waiver: Claims 4-7

Petitioner contends that his mental health issues rendered him incompetent to waive the presentation of mitigation evidence, that defense counsel performed ineffectively in handling the issue of Petitioner's competence and by failing to present mitigating evidence at sentencing, and that the trial court failed to make an adequate competency determination before accepting the waiver.

(1) Sentencing proceedings

In preparation for sentencing, Lorona retained an addictionologist, Dr. Charles Shaw, and a psychiatrist, Dr. James Deming, to examine Petitioner for mitigation purposes. Dr. Shaw met with Petitioner for four and a half hours on December 12, 2000, discussing Petitioner's history of substance abuse as well as his family background and the details of the murders. Dr. Shaw opined that "Petitioner had the signs and symptoms of paranoid schizophrenia along with a substance induced mood disorder." He concluded: "I strongly recommend that [Petitioner] have a psychiatric evaluation. I believe he will be found schizophrenic and needs appropriate treatment."

Dr. Deming conducted a 12-hour personal interview of Petitioner, reviewed numerous documents, including Petitioner's medical records, and prepared a lengthy report dated August 27, 2001. Dr. Deming diagnosed Petitioner with delusional disorder of a mixed type with grandiose, jealous, and persecutory features; a history of polysubstance abuse and dependence which may have created a permanent organic brain syndrome; and post-concussion syndrome resulting from numerous severe head injuries beginning at age 17. Dr. Deming's report included detailed discussions of Petitioner's family background, drug use, and medical history, and emphasized the role Petitioner's paranoia and delusions played in the murders.

Petitioner initially indicated that he did not wish to present mitigating evidence. He changed his mind briefly before finally deciding that he would waive mitigation. Before his final decision, Petitioner told defense investigator Bachtle that he believed Dr. Potts would testify on his behalf for mitigation purposes, to the effect that at the time of the murders Petitioner could not control his actions because of his addiction to methamphetamine. On November 22, 2000, Petitioner wrote to Lorona requesting that he "[g]et my Rolodex from property siezed [sic] by deputies from my house. Need to have it to give Lisa [Christianson, the mitigation specialist] a more complete and accurate list of people to contact on my behalf. Has names and phone numbers of people I know are not listed in any directories." Petitioner also asked Lorona to look into hiring a neuropsychologist, because another death row inmate had undergone neuropsychological testing to explain his outbursts of "sudden violence."

In addition, Petitioner requested that Lorona obtain a "complete list of all states that have an interstate compact with Arizona." Petitioner reasoned:

> If we pull this off and I do get natural life, then I want you to request a court order for a D.O.C. transfer out of Arizona. I do not want to spend 5 to 7 years in SMU 1 or 2, as this is where I will be sent upon transfer from here to D.O.C. Because my crimes will give me a 5-5 score going in. Being out of State will also allow my sons to get on with their lives much easier.

Petitioner also discussed the fact that Lorona rarely visited him in jail, adding:

> Anyway, what I'm getting at here is this: we both knew going in that this was a loser because of witnesses, and I know you have done as I've asked in trying to stretch it out as long as possible. I don't want to do anything to tarnish your name or abilities in any way. But if I tell the Judge of the sparse visits would somehow help my mitigation [sic], I think we should discuss this face to face. It's well known around the courthouse that you don't visit clients in this jail very often. This was told to me by a deputy that's been there for 35 years, I'm sure you know "Cookie," Roy Cook, he's the one who said you're a good attorney, "but have a bad rap when it comes to visits." I still want you to keep putting off the sentencing date as long as is possible.
>
> What ya need to do is set aside some time to come down here and talk to me. Things have changed in my life and we need to kick Mary Barry's ass on mitigation. I'm going to have Lisa try to get people to write letters on my behalf to present to the Judge as to my character before Becky and meth took over my life. So please come down here. Maybe we can pull it off.

In a another letter, Petitioner further detailed his desire to serve a natural life sentence out of state:

> I need info on interstate compacts so if by some miracle Lisa can get me life I don't want to do it here. I've had 43 years of this heat and that's enough for me. I want to go North, Idaho, Wyoming, Montana, Colorado, Nevada. Not Utah or Oregon, they're as bad as here from what I've learned. Anyway get back to me. I think about you every time I get one of these Snoopy the Lawyer toons.

In late August and early September 2001, Petitioner decided that he did not want to present mitigating evidence, and directed Lorona not to provide copies of Lisa Christianson's mitigation report or Dr. Deming's evaluation to the prosecution.

At a status conference on September 7, 2001, Lorona informed the court that Petitioner believed his life was in danger in jail and feared that a life sentence would be the equivalent of the death penalty for him because of the difficulties he had with other inmates. Petitioner had urged Lorona to ask the prosecution to allow him to serve his time out of state. Lorona had discussed this with the prosecutor, who refused the request. The court subsequently confirmed that it did not have the power to order the Department of Corrections to place Petitioner out of state.

Lorona told the court that, given these circumstances, Petitioner did not want the defense team to "put on any mitigation at all." Lorona noted that he had obtained complete reports from Drs. Deming and Shaw and a report from his mitigation specialist, but Petitioner did not want these offered as evidence or filed in the record. Lorona explained that if the court could not guarantee Petitioner an out-of-state sentence, he wanted the death penalty so that he could be placed on death row.

The trial court informed Petitioner that if he did not present mitigation evidence, the court would "order the State to give me what they have," and would "seek it from any source that is legitimately available to the Court and require the State to provide it." The prosecutor stated that he would "willingly, whether the court orders me or not, turn over all information that I have that appears to me to be mitigating on the part of Mr. Murdaugh because I believe I have a duty to do so and I'd be happy to do that in this situation." However, the prosecutor reminded the court that he was actively seeking the death penalty in spite of any mitigating evidence.

Petitioner then addressed the court and explained his understanding of the proceedings:

> In my six years with being in Madison Street Jail I know how everything works. I know the steps that are followed. I have had several friends that have gone through death penalty cases and gotten the death penalty, and several who have gone through death penalty cases and got natural life.

I have also known some who have been sent out of state on interstate compact with that request coming from the Department of Corrections. And I recently learned that you do not have the power to send me out of state without the approval of the Department of Corrections.

In a motion filed immediately before the mitigation hearing, Lorona objected to the presentation of any mitigating evidence on Petitioner's behalf, explaining that Petitioner was fully aware of the mitigating evidence that the defense team had collected. Lorona also requested that the court determine whether Petitioner was competent to waive mitigation. Lorona noted that he faced an ethical dilemma because Petitioner did not want him to present any mitigation, while he believed he had an obligation to argue against a death sentence.

At the outset of the mitigation hearing on September 28, 2001, Lorona again asked the court to determine whether Petitioner was competent to waive his right to present mitigating evidence. Lorona noted that "some time" had passed since Petitioner's Rule 11 evaluations, when the court determined that he was competent to plead guilty and assist counsel; since that time Petitioner had been evaluated by defense experts and by an expert for the State, Dr. Gina Lang. Lorona also informed the court that based on his contact and discussions with Petitioner, and Lisa Christianson's interactions with Petitioner, he believed that Petitioner was competent to make a decision about the presentation of mitigating evidence.

The court stated that it would first make a determination as to Petitioner's competence to waive mitigation; it would then determine whether to accept the waiver. The State called Dr. Lang to testify regarding Petitioner's competence. Her testimony also addressed potential mitigating circumstances.

Dr. Lang, a forensic psychologist who regularly performed Rule 11 competency evaluations, testified that she met with Petitioner for approximately 11 or 12 hours on three separate days during the week before the hearing. She also reviewed the reports of Drs. Potts, Sindelar, Scialli, and Deming; information from Correctional Health Services regarding Petitioner's medical history; his written communications with jail personnel and his disciplinary record; and police reports from the crimes. Dr. Lang was aware that Drs. Scialli, Sindelar, and Potts had found Petitioner competent. Based on her recent contact with Petitioner, she did not disagree with their assessments and believed that Petitioner's condition had not changed since their evaluations.

Dr. Lang conducted a general psychological evaluation of Petitioner "to determine his psychological and intellectual functioning." Although the examination was not specifically a competency evaluation, Dr. Lang observed nothing to indicate that Petitioner was incompetent.. Petitioner had no difficulty performing the psychological tests that she asked him to complete. He appeared to understand the nature of the proceedings and the roles of the various parties involved, and there was no indication that he was mentally unable to make a decision concerning the charges against him.

Dr. Lang administered an IQ test and the Minnesota Multiphasic Personality Inventory ("MMPI"). Petitioner scored a 106 on the IQ test, placing him high in the average range. *Id.* at 46. Dr. Lang diagnosed Petitioner with antisocial personality disorder, based on his MMPI results and his history of violent, aggressive, and illegal activities, and with polysubstance abuse. Dr. Lang noted no impairments in Petitioner's cognitive functioning. She found no evidence that he was suffering from delusions when she interviewed him or at the time of the crime. Although Petitioner mentioned his belief that the CIA was tracking him, Dr. Lang concluded that his behavior during the offense, including luring the victim to Petitioner's residence, was inconsistent with having paranoid delusional disorder. Instead, Petitioner offered Dr. Lang a different explanation for leading Reynolds to his home - that Reynolds needed to be taught a lesson for propositioning Petitioner's girlfriend. Dr. Lang noted that this explanation "is not consistent with delusional process." *Id.* at 49. Petitioner also told Dr. Lang that he initially considered beating Reynolds and then releasing him but got carried away.

Petitioner was able to recall the crime in detail, and during the offenses he displayed logic, decision-making, and planning skills. According to Dr. Lang, this was consistent with Petitioner having "perfectly fine" cognitive functioning during the offense. Moreover, Dr. Lang concluded that Petitioner's capacity to appreciate the wrongfulness of his conduct or conform his conduct with the requirements of the law was not impaired, because he engaged in behaviors during the offense that demonstrated his understanding of the law. For example, he attempted to evade capture by disposing of Reynolds' vehicle and by mutilating Reynolds' body to hide its identity.

Dr. Lang noted that Petitioner used methamphetamine on the day of the Reynolds murder, which would likely have caused feelings of euphoria, power, and energy; it also could have led him to become aggressive and paranoid. Petitioner told Dr. Lang that he believed the methamphetamine may have contributed to his getting carried away while beating Reynolds.

Based on Dr. Lang's testimony and the reports the trial court had previously reviewed, the court found that Petitioner was "competent to assist counsel, to understand the nature of these proceedings," and to "waive the right to mitigation" and "the right to present evidence."

At that point, the court took a break to review the caselaw and decide whether it could compel the defense to present mitigating evidence. After the break the court ruled that because Lorona had conducted a mitigation investigation and shared the resulting information with Petitioner, Petitioner had made a knowing and intelligent waiver of the presentation of mitigating evidence. The court then addressed Petitioner directly to determine whether he wished to waive mitigation:

> COURT: Did you discuss the matters with your counsel, the information that was produced as a result of the mitigation search?
> DEFENDANT: I have copies of everything. And I have read everything.
> COURT: And knowing what that information is do you desire not to present that evidence on your own behalf?
> DEFENDANT: Yes, ma'am. That is my wish.
> COURT: You understand this is a capital case?
> DEFENDANT: Yes, ma'am.
> COURT: And that until I have all of the pieces, I don't know what I have. And that any evidence may be considered. And any evidence would be considered by this Court. There is no evidentiary standard for mitigation evidence. By that I mean the Rules of Evidence are relaxed. And it is not as though I would not consider certain matters. I would consider everything. Do you understand that?
> DEFENDANT: Yes, ma'am.
> COURT: To your knowledge was this investigation as complete as it could reasonably be?
> DEFENDANT: Yes, I believe so.
> COURT: And is it your desire that counsel not present this evidence in this hearing?
> DEFENDANT: That is true.

Lorona then informed the court that Petitioner did not even want him to submit the doctors' reports and other mitigating evidence to the court as an offer of proof to be sealed for future use. The court continued:

> [T]his Court further finds that there is no failure of counsel to uphold his duty to the defendant. The Court finds that there has been no ineffective assistance of counsel in preparing for sentencing; that the preparation of counsel has allowed the client to make a knowing and intelligent waiver and not simply a tactical waiver.
>
> And that where the waiver is knowing and intelligent the Court will not compel the defendant to testify. He has a *Fifth Amendment* right not to testify. He has that right not to testify directly or indirectly through other means. Therefore, the Court will not require counsel to seal, as in the manner of an offer of proof, what that evidence might have been.
>
> This Court will not guess what the weight of that evidence might have been on the decision that this Court will make. Rather it is the obligation of the Court to determine that the waiver was knowing and intelligent and that the assistance of counsel has been of an appropriate level.
>
> And having made those determinations in the affirmative, there is no further basis to seal those items.

The court   confirmed with Petitioner that by not sealing the items, they would be omitted from the record. Petitioner stated that he understood.

The court then asked the State to present mitigating evidence on Petitioner's behalf. The prosecutor reminded the trial court that Petitioner and his co-defendants were using methamphetamine at the time of the Reynolds murder. The prosecutor offered materials from Petitioner's previous Rule 11 evaluations. Lorona did not object because the Rule 11 reports had already been admitted. The prosecutor also sought to introduce biographical information about Petitioner gathered by the mitigation specialist, hospital records from Indiana and Arkansas, and Dr. Deming's report. Lorona advised the court that Petitioner wanted him to object to the admission of that evidence.

The court ruled that Petitioner's "meaningful waiver and assertion of privacy" would be violated if it were to admit and consider evidence that the prosecutor had obtained from the defense through discovery. The court concluded that it would consider the Rule 11 evaluations but not the items   prepared by defense experts and the mitigation specialist. The State then presented testimony from Dr. Lang in support of possible mitigating circumstances.

On October 24, 2001, Lorona filed a sentencing memorandum challenging the aggravating factors advocated by the state and arguing in support of the (G)(1) mitigating factor. Lorona contended that Petitioner's capacity to appreciate the wrongfulness of his conduct or to conform his conduct to the requirements of the law was significantly impaired because at the time of the crime he had been using methamphetamine continuously and had been "up for several days." In accordance with Petitioner's wishes, however, Lorona restricted his sentencing memorandum to information that was already part of the record.

On October 30, the parties again appeared in court. Lorona informed the judge that he had "done some more research about [his] duties and obligations" and had decided that it was his "duty, obligation as a lawyer, to argue for life." He stated that he would not "advocate the death penalty on [Petitioner's] behalf, no matter what."

At the conclusion of the hearing, the judge allowed   Petitioner to address the court. Petitioner made the following statement regarding his waiver of mitigation and his desire for the death penalty:

> I wanted the Court to know that I have been a supporter of the death penalty all of my life, and raised my sons with that knowledge, as well. In fact, I wish the death penalty were expanded to cover what it use [sic] to in the form of rapists and child molesters. That is my belief.
>
> And I don't think that me being in this situation would change that belief. And it hasn't.
>
> And I am asking the Court to go ahead and proceed, and give me the death penalty, because I do not desire life in prison.
>
> My children, my two sons, have grieved for six years already with me being in here. And my circumstances where I have been in solitary lockdown for six years with very little contact.
>
> And I want the grieving to end for my own family.

Petitioner then discussed the circumstances of the murders. He informed the court that in the interim between the Eggert and Reynolds murders, he and Becky Rohrs had broken up and she had stayed with Betty Gross. According to Petitioner, during that time Rohrs was free to contact the police about   the Eggert murder. Petitioner also explained that he had killed Eggert because Eggert had threatened his stepdaughter and a woman he was dating, and that Rohrs had agreed with his plan to kill Eggert. Petitioner further noted that during the Reynolds kidnapping and murder, all of his co-defendants had the opportunity to release Reynolds when Petitioner was not present. He also contended that his co-defendants had lied about details of the Reynolds murder during their testimony..

(2) Postconviction proceedings

In his PCR petition, Petitioner raised a claim of ineffective assistance of counsel consisting of numerous specific allegations. The PCR court held a lengthy evidentiary hearing, focusing on Petitioner's allegation that counsel performed ineffectively with respect to Petitioner's competence to waive mitigation.

Drs. Scialli and Potts testified about their competency evaluations of Petitioner. Both stated that a person's competence can change over time. Dr. Scialli testified that a different assessment would be required to measure competency to waive mitigation as opposed to competency to stand trial. He would have recommended that Petitioner undergo a new evaluation prior to his waiver of mitigation. Neither Dr. Scialli nor Dr. Potts had contact with Petitioner after December 1999.

Dr. Potts noted in his December 1999 competency evaluation that Petitioner's delusional beliefs had not changed from the time of his first competency screening. When questioned about Petitioner's "attempted suicide," which occurred prior to the December 1999 evaluation, Dr. Potts testified that information regarding the incident would have been "helpful to know" in making a determination as to Petitioner's competence to waive mitigation. Dr. Potts stated that he had no "independent recollection" of what collateral information he received from Lorona, but noted that there was no evidence in his file indicating that he been informed about Petitioner's suicide attempt prior to the second evaluation.

Dr. Lang also testified. She stated that she was not specifically asked to evaluate Petitioner's competence to waive mitigation.. She testified, however, that according to her evaluation Petitioner's mental condition did not affect his decision-making processes. Dr. Lang indicated that in evaluating Petitioner prior to sentencing she had reviewed collateral material including his jail disciplinary and medical records. She could not recall whether that material included reports about Petitioner's suicide attempt.

Holly Wake, who preceded Linda Christianson as Petitioner's mitigation specialist, testified about her relationship with Lorona and Petitioner. She stated that Lorona was "nonaccessible" and that she resigned from the defense team out of frustration with Lorona's lack of involvement in the case. She acknowledged, however, that her resignation letter referred only to Petitioner's refusal to cooperate with her investigation. Wake also testified that Petitioner expressed paranoid thoughts about government agents monitoring his activities. Petitioner's ex-wife told Wake that after his father's death Petitioner's mental condition had deteriorated greatly due to his methamphetamine addiction.

Lisa Christianson likewise testified about her work with Lorona and her relationship with Petitioner. Christianson stated that she took over Petitioner's case from Wake, who had quit because she found Petitioner "extremely difficult to work with." During her involvement in the case, Christianson received correspondence from Lorona directing her to investigate Petitioner's chronic methamphetamine use. She also received numerous letters from Lorona asking her to contact him and requesting that she investigate various aspects of Petitioner's case.

Christianson testified that she informed Petitioner about the meaning of mitigation and explained how the presentation of mitigating evidence could help him. Petitioner, however, was reluctant to provide her with information about his family, making it difficult for her to contact family members. During their conversations, Christianson "was constantly trying to encourage [Petitioner]," explaining "the importance of presenting" evidence about his paranoid mental state and its effect on his conduct and "how that was relevant and how the judge needed to know that." Nonetheless, Petitioner remained "adamant about the fact that this information couldn't get out, because not only would he be at risk, but he would be risking his family." In addition to concern for his family's safety, Petitioner also indicated to Christianson that he had experienced difficulties with jail staff and other inmates and "thought his life was in danger if he was required to serve in the general population in the Arizona Department of Corrections"; therefore "he would rather be sentenced to death and he would not allow mitigation to be presented if he could not be guaranteed an out-of-state transfer."

Despite Petitioner's reluctance, Christianson conducted a mitigation investigation, during which she obtained Petitioner's medical records and contacted Drs. Shaw and Deming to evaluate Petitioner. Christianson then wrote a mitigation report, the contents of which she discussed with Petitioner.

Christianson also testified that she was concerned about Petitioner's lack of access to defense counsel and her own difficulty in contacting Lorona. However, she did inform Lorona that there was strong mitigation evidence.

Jeff Bachtle, the defense investigator, also described his work with Lorona and Petitioner. Bachtle testified that the defense operated as a team, and that he was the person who received discovery and reviewed issues with Petitioner at the jail. Bachtle, Lorona, co-counsel Gitre, and sometimes the mitigation specialist met regularly to discuss Petitioner's defense and to ensure that the expert witnesses received the documents they needed to evaluate Petitioner. Bachtle visited Petitioner in the jail more than 20 times.

Bachtle explained that Petitioner had numerous problems with other inmates and had been labeled a "snitch" by co-defendant Dezarn. Petitioner told Bachtle that his cellmate once tried to shank him. Given the troubles he was experiencing in jail, Petitioner wanted to plead guilty and get the death penalty because he would have a longer life on death row. Petitioner also indicated that he "didn't want his family's name to be drug through the mud. Didn't want the victim's family to be drug through the mud or relive the death of a family member." In addition, Petitioner did not want mitigation specialist Wake "talking to his family and digging into his past" and was "very adamant" that no one talk to his mother. Instead, Petitioner wanted the death penalty so that his family could move on with their lives.

Bachtle described Petitioner as "very demanding" and heavily involved in the proceedings, providing details of the case and asking to review evidence. Petitioner called Bachtle three to four times each week and sometimes several times a day. According to Bachtle, Petitioner was able to "understand and comprehend" their conversations.

Bachtle testified that Lorona always addressed his concerns and suggestions quickly. Bachtle did not perceive any "breakdown of duties" on the defense team; rather, "[e]veryone had a job to do, and to the best of my knowledge, they all did their job." Bachtle stated that Lorona never told him not do to do something on Petitioner's case because it would be too expensive or time-consuming.

Lorona testified at the evidentiary hearing. He believed that Petitioner's decision to waive mitigation was knowing and voluntary "based upon what he told me and the rationale he gave me." He also felt that Petitioner's "justification was reasonable." Petitioner's "vehement" desire not to present mitigation caused an "ethical dilemma" for Lorona, who felt he had a "duty to put on mitigation." Thus, although he complied with Petitioner's instructions not to present the reports of Shaw, Deming, or Christianson, Lorona submitted a sentencing memorandum on Petitioner's behalf.

Lorona testified that, based on the findings of Drs. Potts, Scialli, and Sindelar, he had no reason to believe that Petitioner was incompetent. He also did not believe, based on those reports, Dr. Lang's evaluation, and his personal contact with Petitioner, that Petitioner's competence had diminished from the time of the Rule 11 examinations. Although Lorona only visited Petitioner in jail five or six times, he spoke to Petitioner on the phone approximately two to three times each week, communicated by mail, and had contact with Petitioner during court appearances. Lorona further testified that he, along with Wake and Christianson, explained the concept of mitigation to Petitioner, who appeared to understand. He also stated that he provided the Rule 11 examiners with whatever information they requested.

Lorona reiterated that when Petitioner decided to plead guilty, he also wanted to receive the death penalty. Given Petitioner's desire to plead guilty, Lorona recognized that sentencing would be the central issue in the case and to that end he retained a mitigation specialist at an earlier point than was typical in capital cases. Lorona testified that he was "always focused on mitigation."

It was Petitioner's desire for the death penalty that prompted Lorona to move for the Rule 11 examinations. Petitioner explained to Lorona that he wanted to spare his family and the victims' families the pain of a trial and was tired of having problems with inmates in the jail. According to Lorona, Petitioner was aware that the trial judge had never sentenced a defendant to death; thus, because Petitioner wanted "to ensure that he would receive the death penalty," he "compelled [Lorona] to voir dire Judge Hutt to ensure that she would give him the death penalty."

Lorona acknowledged that throughout the case Petitioner expressed fringe beliefs about the CIA and the Buddhist temple murders. However, these beliefs were circumscribed and had not altered or expanded since the time of the Rule 11 examinations. Petitioner did not appear to have acquired any delusions beyond those he had at the time he was found competent in 1999.

Lorona also noted that there was a period when Petitioner expressed a desire to investigate and present mitigating evidence. Subsequently, however, Petitioner changed his mind and again decided to waive mitigation.

Following the evidentiary hearing, the PCR court denied Petitioner's ineffective assistance of counsel claim. The court concluded that Petitioner had not proved that he was prejudiced by counsel's performance:

> The procedure that Judge Hutt used to determine that defendant's decision to waive mitigation was knowing, intelligent, and voluntary was recently upheld by the United States Supreme Court in *Schriro v. Landrigan, 550 U.S. 465, 127 S. Ct. 1933, 167 L. Ed. 2d 836 (2007)*. Moreover, defendant's understanding of the significance of mitigation and certainty about not presenting any was no less clear or   unequivocal than was upheld in *Schriro. Id. at 1942*. Because defendant offered no testimony at the Rule 32.8 hearing, no evidence was proffered, presented, or [sic] to show that defendant was precluded, deluded, truncated, tricked, cajoled, or threatened into waiving mitigation.
>
> Interspersed throughout defense counsel's Rule 32 pleadings and Rule 32.8 presentation is the stated and implied argument that the strongest proof of defendant's incompetence is that he waived mitigation. The fallacy of this argument is the case law that recognizes that a defendant who decides to waive mitigation can still be competent and, in fact, has the right to waive mitigation even over his counsel's better judgment. As stated by the United States Supreme Court, neither *Wiggins v. Smith, 539 U.S. 510, 123 S. Ct. 2527, 156 L. Ed. 2d 471 (2003)*, nor *Strickland* addresses the situation in which a client interferes with counsel's effort to present mitigating evidence to a sentencing court. *Schriro, at 1942*. More significantly, the Supreme Court held "that a defendant who refused to allow the presentation of any mitigating evidence could not establish *Strickland*   prejudice based on his counsel's failure to investigate further mitigating evidence." *Schriro, at 1942*.
>
> While defendant's Rule 32 counsel have attacked Mr. Lorona's performance as deficient, they have provided no new evidence that would have caused Judge Hutt to re-consider her weighing of aggravating factors and mitigating circumstances, and finding that death was the appropriate sentence. Similarly, they have provided no new evidence that would have caused the Supreme Court to re-consider their *de novo* weighing of aggravating factors and mitigating circumstances, and finding that death was the appropriate sentence.
>
> . . . .
>
> In the present case, no new mitigating evidence was proven or proffered. No evidence, no affidavit, no testimony was proffered at the Rule 32.8 hearing by defendant that he was duped, tricked, misinformed, misled, deluded, or coerced by Mr. Lorona or by his mental condition at any time before sentencing into waiving mitigation or forbidding Mr. Lorona from presenting mitigation.
>
> In their Closing Brief, defense counsel state, "In light of the mitigation evidence that could have been presented but was not, there is a reasonable probability that [defendant] would not have been sentenced to death." To the extent that defendant's Rule 32 claim is that trial counsel failed to more effectively present mitigation at the time of the 1995 murders, the claim is insufficient. Both Judge Hutt and the Supreme Court considered the mental health experts' reports touching on defendant's 1995 state of mind despite defendant's objection to do so.
>
> There was no evidence presented or proffered at the Rule 32.8 hearing that defendant's 1995 mental condition deprived him of the ability to differentiate right from wrong. As stated recently in *State v. Boggs, 218 Ariz. 325, 185 P.3d 111 (2008)*, without a causal link between the murders and a defendant's mental health issues, these mitigating circumstances are entitled to

less weight. *Boggs,* ¶ 96; *See also, Belmontes v. Ayers, 529 F.3d 834, 861-64 (9th Cir. 2008)* (inadequacy of habeas counsel's mitigating circumstances evidence)

CONCLUSION

Defendant has failed to produce evidence that his competence at the time of waiving mitigation had deteriorated from the time when Doctors Sindelar, Scialli, and Potts deemed him competent at the time of his change of plea. Nothing in the record, or evidence presented during the evidentiary hearing shows that defendant's delusions or belief system changed from the time of his competency evaluations to the time of sentencing.

On each occasion that defendant and Judge Hutt interacted directly, defendant was responsive and appropriate. Defendant repeatedly assured the trial court at both the plea and sentencing that he understood the proceedings as well as the consequences.

The trial court found that defendant was competent at the time he decided to waive mitigation. The trial court found that defendant's decision to waive mitigation was knowingly and voluntarily made. No evidence has been presented to undermine the trial court's findings. A competent defendant has the right to ignore the intelligent advice of his counsel.

Because defendant has failed to meet the prejudice prong of *Strickland,* any comment by this Court regarding trial counsel's performance would be dicta.

(3) Claim 4

Petitioner alleges that trial counsel performed at a constitutionally ineffective level with respect to Petitioner's competency to waive mitigation and the investigation and presentation of mitigating evidence. Respondents concede that this claim is exhausted.

Clearly established federal law

The right to effective assistance of counsel applies not just to the guilt phase but "with equal force at the penalty phase of a bifurcated capital trial." *Silva v. Woodford, 279 F.3d 825, 836 (9th Cir. 2002)* (quoting *Clabourne v. Lewis, 64 F.3d, 1373, 1378 (9th Cir. 1995)).* In assessing whether counsel's performance was deficient under *Strickland,* the test is whether counsel's actions were objectively reasonable at the time of the decision. *Strickland, 466 U.S. at 689-90.* The question is "not whether another lawyer, with the benefit of hindsight, would have acted differently, but 'whether counsel made errors so serious that counsel was not functioning as the counsel guaranteed the defendant by the *Sixth Amendment.*'" *Babbitt v. Calderon, 151 F.3d 1170, 1173 (9th Cir. 1998)* (quoting *Strickland, 466 U.S. at 687).*

With respect to prejudice at sentencing, the *Strickland* Court explained that "[w]hen a defendant challenges a death sentence . . . the question is whether there is a reasonable probability that, absent the errors, the sentencer . . . would have concluded that the balance of aggravating and mitigating circumstances did not warrant death." *466 U.S. at 695.* In *Wiggins v. Smith, 539 U.S. 510, 534, 123 S. Ct. 2527, 156 L. Ed. 2d 471 (2003),* the Court noted that "[i]n assessing prejudice, we reweigh the evidence in aggravation against the totality of available mitigating evidence." The totality of the available evidence includes "both that adduced at trial, and the evidence adduced in the habeas proceeding." *Id. at 536* (quoting *Williams v. Taylor, 529 U.S. at 397-98).* Recently, the Court reiterated that "*Strickland* places the burden on the defendant, not the State, to show a 'reasonable probability' that the result would have been different." *Belmontes, 130 S. Ct. at 390-91.*

Analysis

Petitioner raises numerous specific allegations in support of Claim 4. He contends that Lorona "should have been aware of facts" that would have raised a reasonable doubt about Petitioner's competency to waive mitigation; misled the court by representing that he "had enough interactions with [Petitioner] and knowledge of his delusional disorder to opine on his competency"; did not "explain the concept of mitigating evidence to Petitioner or attempt to dissuade him from waiving mitigation evidence"; failed to secure an independent competency evaluation; failed to provide the court-appointed mental health experts with "relevant documents and information regarding his relationship with his client and his client's delusions"; failed to secure a "complete social history of Petitioner"; presented mitigation in a "half-hearted manner"; and "successfully bur[ied] substantial evidence regarding competency and mitigation." Petitioner asserts that he was prejudiced because, if counsel had presented more evidence regarding Petitioner's mental problems, he likely would have been found incompetent and received a life sentence.

None of these allegations entitle Petitioner to relief. The record does not support the contention that Lorona was unaware of or misrepresented Petitioner's mental condition, that Petitioner was not competent to waive mitigation, that his waiver was not knowing and voluntary, or that the defense team did not investigate and prepare a case in mitigation.

As an initial matter, there is no dispute that a defendant may waive the presentation of mitigating evidence. In *Blystone v. Pennsylvania,* the United States Supreme Court held that no constitutional violation occurred when a defendant was allowed to waive all mitigation evidence after repeated warnings from the judge and advice from counsel. *494 U.S. 299, 306, 110 S. Ct. 1078, 108 L. Ed. 2d 255 & n.4 (1990).*

Petitioner's primary contention is that trial counsel performed ineffectively by failing to argue that Petitioner was not competent to waive mitigation. He asserts that as a result of this failure, his waiver was not knowing and intelligent. These arguments are unpersuasive.

As previously noted, the standard for competence to stand trial, plead guilty, or waive the right to counsel is whether the defendant has "sufficient present ability to consult with his lawyer with a reasonable degree of rational understanding" along with "a rational as well as factual understanding of the proceedings against him." *Dusky, 362 U.S. at 402; see Godinez v. Moran, 509 U.S. at 396, 399-401.* While some courts have used this standard to determine competency to waive mitigation, *see Wood v. Quarterman, 491 F.3d 196, 204 (5th Cir. 2007); Coleman v. Mitchell, 244 F.3d 533, 545 (6th Cir. 2001),* the Supreme Court in *Landrigan* explained that it has "never imposed an 'informed and knowing' requirement upon a defendant's decision not to introduce evidence" and has "never required a specific colloquy to ensure that a defendant knowingly and intelligently refused to present mitigating   evidence." *Landrigan, 550 U.S. at 479.*

As previously recounted, when Petitioner decided to plead guilty, Lorona moved for an evaluation of his competency. Following Dr. Potts' pre-screening competency evaluation, two court appointed experts evaluated Petitioner. Drs. Scialli and Sindelar determined that Petitioner was competent while noting his fringe beliefs and his chronic methamphetamine addiction. Immediately before Petitioner pled guilty, Lorona moved for a third competency evaluation. Dr. Potts found that there had been no changes since his last evaluation and concluded that Petitioner was competent to weigh his options and assist his attorney. Dr. Potts further opined that Petitioner's delusions and paranoia were circumscribed and had minimal bearing on the proceedings.

When Petitioner decided to waive mitigation, Lorona requested that the court make a determination of his competence even though Lorona believed that Petitioner was competent. In making this request Lorona noted that Petitioner had already been found competent by three court-appointed experts and by Dr. Lang and that, based on his and the defense team's contact with Petitioner, there was no basis to question his [*106] competency. Lorona did not perform ineffectively in making this representation to the court. He was entitled to rely on the findings of the experts in reaching his opinion of Petitioner's competence. *See Moran v. Godinez, 57 F.3d at 699-700* ("Because counsel could rely on the psychiatrists' reports that Moran was competent to stand trial, it was unnecessary for them to investigate his competence to plead guilty, waive counsel or forego the presentation of mitigating evidence."), *superceded on other grounds by AEDPA; see also Taylor v. Horn, 504 F.3d at 438-39* (rejecting claim that counsel performed ineffectively in not seeking competency evaluation where counsel reasonably relied on two expert evaluations reports finding defendant competent); *Galowski v. Berge, 78 F.3d 1176, 1182 (7th Cir. 1996)* (counsel not ineffective for failing to seek a competency hearing when defense expert determined defendant was competent). Lorona also had a duty of candor to the court and recognized that the competency issue had to be addressed in light of Petitioner's insistence on waiving mitigation. Counsel's actions in this regard were not unreasonable.

Moreover, the record does not support Petitioner's assertion   that he was in fact incompetent to waive mitigation. Dr. Shaw's report did not address the competence issue at all. Dr. Deming, on whose findings Petitioner primarily relies for his claim that he was incapable of knowingly and voluntarily waiving mitigation, did not evaluate Petitioner's competence but prepared his report for mitigation purposes, with a focus on Petitioner's compromised mental functioning at the time of the murdersBy contrast, Drs. Potts, Scialli, and Sindelar had evaluated Petitioner concerning his competence to waive his rights and assist his attorney. In addition, Dr. Lang, who examined Petitioner immediately before his waiver and who was familiar with legal competency standards, opined that Petitioner was competent, as she had detected no changes in his mental status since the prior evaluations. Dr. Lang found no evidence that Petitioner was incompetent or that his cognitive functioning was impaired.

The contents of Dr. Deming's mitigation report do not alter this court's conclusion that Petitioner was competent to waive mitigation. Dr. Deming diagnosed Petitioner with delusional disorder, substance abuse and dependence, and post-concussion disorder. However, these findings are consistent with those of the Rule 11 experts concerning the scope and nature of Petitioner's delusions,), and fail to suggest that Petitioner did not have a "a rational as well as factual understanding of the proceedings against him." *Dusky, 362 U.S. at 402*.

Dr. Deming found that Petitioner's "cognitive functioning" was "intact revealing above-average I.Q. by estimate, with a quick flow of thoughts, and no hesitation in answering questions." He noted that Petitioner's memory was "intact for immediate, recent, and remote events, even with incredible detail and sophistication of memory." Petitioner was able to interpret proverbs "with abstraction and the capability for objectivity," and was "oriented to person, place, and situation." There was "no evidence of any suicidal ideation" and "no acute auditory or visual hallucinations." Dr. Deming noted Petitioner's "tremendous social skills," stating that he was a "natural leader, with good confidence in his ability to talk and direct other people's behavior." He found that Petitioner was "acutely interested in making sure he understands where people are, where they are going, and how they relate to him at all times." In sum, Dr. Deming's report is not inconsistent with any of the previous evaluations, none of which establish that Petitioner lacked the mental capacity to offer a knowing and voluntary waiver of the presentation of mitigating evidence.

Likewise there is no evidence that Petitioner's decision to waive mitigation was uninformed. Prior to Petitioner's waiver, members of the defense team interacted with him on a regular basis. Lorona spoke to Petitioner on the telephone two to three times a week and discussed the case with him during court appearances. Bachtle, the defense investigator, routinely visited Petitioner at the jail. The mitigation specialists began their investigation in 1997, met with Petitioner regularly, and explained their role in his defense. In addition, Lorona retained Drs. Shaw and Deming to evaluate Petitioner for mitigation purposes; they both prepared reports discussing Petitioner's background, drug problems, and mental state. Linda Christianson also prepared a mitigation report.

The record further belies Petitioner's contention that as a result of counsel's deficiencies, Petitioner was unfamiliar with the concept of mitigation. Petitioner's letters to Lorona and Bachtle demonstrate that he understood the nature and purpose of mitigating information. He wrote that he believed Lorona's infrequent jail visits could be used as evidence of ineffective assistance and might prove mitigating. During the period before his final decision to waive mitigation, Petitioner recognized the importance of contacting friends and family members to speak on his behalf, and in being evaluated by experts to show that he might be prone to "sudden violence" or that his methamphetamine addiction caused him not to understand what he was doing when he committed the murders. Bachtle wrote a memo to Lorona dated August 30, 1999, in which he noted, "According to Murdaugh, Dr. Potts will testify at his mitigation hearing that he could NOT control his actions because of the heavy methamphetamine addiction."

In his colloquy with the court, Petitioner stated that he had received and reviewed all of the mitigating information, that he believed the information was complete, but that he did not want any of it presented. The court found that Petitioner knowingly and intelligently waived his right to present mitigating evidence. The court also determined that "there is no failure of counsel to uphold his duty to the defendant" and "no ineffective assistance of counsel in preparing for sentencing" and that "the preparation of counsel has allowed the client to make a knowing and intelligent waiver and not simply a tactical waiver."

Moreover, Petitioner cannot prove that he was prejudiced by counsel's failure to seek an additional mental health examination prior to Petitioner's waiver. Petitioner presented no evidence at the PCR evidentiary hearing demonstrating that the trial court's findings as to his waiver of mitigation or the court's sentencing decision would have been any different if Lorona had sought a new expert evaluation. Likewise Petitioner has offered no evidence demonstrating that his competence had actually deteriorated following the evaluations of Drs. Potts, Scialli, and Sindelar.

Petitioner also contends that counsel failed to investigate and prepare a case in mitigation and that this failure prejudiced the defense. Besides being rendered moot by Petitioner's decision not to offer mitigating evidence (discussed below), this allegation is not supported by the record. Lorona did not fail to pursue a mitigation case or conduct only a truncated investigation. Instead, with the aid of a mitigation specialist, he undertook a full-scale investigation, gathering background information and retaining mental health experts. Linda Christianson, in preparing her mitigation report, met with Petitioner 10 times, reviewed his medical and military records, interviewed his mother, sister, sons, and girlfriend, and contacted other family members who refused to be interviewed.

Lorona was prepared to present the results of this investigation in the form of Christianson's mitigation report and the evaluations performed by Drs. Deming and Shaw. However, it was the admission of this evidence, along with the supporting jail and hospital records, to which Petitioner specifically objected. Thus, when the prosecutor attempted to offer Dr. Deming's report to the court for purposes of mitigation, Petitioner directed Lorona to object and to prevent any information in the report from being entered into evidence.

Nevertheless, the trial court at sentencing reviewed for mitigation purposes the Rule 11 competency evaluations, Dr. Lang's testimony, and other evidence in the record. Based on that information, the court found that Petitioner's paranoia, mental problems, and drug abuse constituted mitigating circumstances. However, balanced against these mitigating circumstances were two weighty aggravating factors. Petitioner had been convicted of a separate first degree murder. The killing of Reynolds was especially heinous or depraved; the crime was senseless, the victim was helpless, and Petitioner mutilated the victim's body. *See Van Hook, 130 S. Ct. at 20* (finding defendant could not prove prejudice from counsel's failure to present more mitigating evidence given strong aggravating circumstances "[o]n the other side of the scales"). Given the strength of the aggravating factors, Petitioner's knowing and voluntary waiver of the mitigating information uncovered by counsel, and the trial court's consideration of the available mitigating evidence, Petitioner cannot show that he was prejudiced by Lorona's performance at sentencing.

Furthermore, as the PCR court noted, relief on Claim 4 is foreclosed by the holding in *Landrigan, 550 U.S. 465, 127 S. Ct. 1933, 167 L. Ed. 2d 836*. Petitioner cannot establish prejudice from counsel's performance at sentencing because he waived the presentation of mitigating evidence and thereby prevented the trial court from hearing the mitigating information procured by Lorona and the defense team.

In *Landrigan,* the petitioner refused to allow defense counsel to present the testimony of his ex-wife and birth mother as mitigating evidence. He also interrupted as counsel tried to proffer other evidence and told the Arizona trial judge that he did not wish to present any mitigating evidence and to "bring on" the death penalty. The court sentenced him to death and the sentence was affirmed on direct appeal. *State v. Landrigan, 176 Ariz. 1, 859 P.2d 111 (1993).* The PCR court rejected Landrigan's request for a hearing and denied his claim that counsel was ineffective for failing to conduct further investigation into mitigating circumstances, finding that he had instructed counsel at sentencing not to present any mitigating evidence at all. Landrigan then filed a federal habeas petition. The district court denied the petition and refused to grant an evidentiary hearing because Landrigan could not make out a colorable claim of ineffective assistance of counsel. A panel of the Ninth Circuit affirmed. *Landrigan v. Stewart, 272 F.3d 1221 (9th Cir. 2001).* The en banc Ninth Circuit reversed, holding that counsel's performance at sentencing was ineffective. *441 F.3d 638 (9th Cir. 2006).* According to the court, Landrigan's "last-minute decision could not excuse counsel's failure to conduct an adequate investigation prior to sentencing." *Id. at 647.* The court then reiterated its view "that a lawyer's duty to investigate [mitigating circumstances] is virtually absolute, regardless of a client's expressed wishes." *Id.*

The Supreme Court reversed. *Schriro v. Landrigan, 550 U.S. 465, 127 S. Ct. 1933, 167 L. Ed. 2d 836.* The Court held that the district court did not abuse its discretion in failing to hold an evidentiary hearing on Landrigan's claim of sentencing-stage ineffectiveness and that the court was within its discretion in denying the claim based on Landrigan's unwillingness to present mitigation evidence. *Id. at 481*.

Landrigan establishes the standard for evaluating a sentencing-stage ineffective assistance claim brought by a petitioner who directed counsel not to offer a case in mitigation. "If [the petitioner] issued such an instruction, counsel's failure to investigate further could not have been prejudicial under *Strickland*." *Id. at 475; see Owens v. Guida, 549 F.3d 399, 406 (6th Cir. 2008)* ("a client who interferes with her attorney's attempts to present mitigating evidence cannot then claim prejudice based on the attorney's failure to present that evidence"); *see also Taylor v. Horn, 504 F.3d at 455* (no *Strickland* prejudice where petitioner refused to allow presentation of mitigating evidence); *Wood v. Quarterman, 491 F.3d at 203* ("Neither the Supreme Court nor this court has ever held that a lawyer provides ineffective assistance by complying with the client's clear and unambiguous instructions to not present evidence."); *Lovitt v. True, 403 F.3d 171, 179 (4th Cir. 2005)* ("Lovitt is correct to insist that a client's decision in this regard should be an informed one. At the same time, Lovitt's lawyers were hardly ineffective for incorporating their client's wishes into their professional judgment."); *Rutherford v. Crosby, 385 F.3d 1300, 1313-14 (11th Cir. 2004)* ("[U]nder *Strickland* the duty is to investigate to a reasonable extent . . . and that duty does not include a requirement to disregard a mentally competent client's sincere and specific instructions about an area of defense and to obtain a court order in defiance of his wishes."); *Jeffries v. Blodgett, 5 F.3d 1180, 1198 (9th Cir. 1993)* ("[C]ounsel for Jeffries had been prepared to present evidence in mitigation and had discussed with Jeffries the ramifications of failing to present the evidence. Accordingly, counsel did not deprive Jeffries of effective assistance in acquiescing in the latter's considered decision."). Because Petitioner unambiguously instructed Lorona not to present a case in mitigation, he was not prejudiced by Lorona's failure to disobey his instructions.

Conclusion

Petitioner has not demonstrated that trial counsel performed at a constitutionally ineffective level in his handling of the issue of Petitioner's competence to waive mitigation or in the investigation and presentation of mitigating evidence. The record does not support the allegation that Lorona failed to take Petitioner's mental state into account or that he neglected his duties in preparing for sentencing. Further, no prejudice existed because Petitioner chose not to present mitigating evidence.

"A defendant cannot be permitted to manufacture a winning [ineffective assistance of counsel] claim by sabotaging her own defense, or else every defendant clever enough to thwart her own attorneys would be able to overturn her sentence on appeal." *Owens, 549 F.3d at 412* (citing *Landrigan, 550 U.S. at 475-76*). This principle applies to Petitioner's case.

The PCR court's rejection of this claim did not represent an unreasonable application of clearly established federal law as set forth in *Strickland* and *Landrigan*. Therefore, Claim 4 is denied.

(4) Claims 5, 6, and 7

In Claim 5, Petitioner alleges that the trial court failed to make an adequate determination of his competence to waive mitigation. In Claim 6, he alleges that he was incompetent when he waived mitigation and therefore the waiver was not knowing and voluntary. Respondents contend that these claims are procedurally defaulted and barred. In Claim 7, Petitioner alleges that ineffective assistance of appellate counsel excuses any default of Claim 5 or 6. Respondents concede that Claim 7 is exhausted.

Petitioner raised these claims in his PCR petition. The PCR court found Claims 5 and 6 precluded under *Ariz. R. Crim. P. 32.2(a)(1)* and *(3)* because they could have been raised on direct appeal. The court alternatively held:

> [T]he record demonstrates that defendant was aware of the mitigation evidence that could be presented through Dr. Deming and Dr. Shaw, and the mitigation specialist, but that he decided not to present it after reviewing it. The trial court found that defendant's decision to waive the presentation of mitigating evidence was voluntary, knowing, and intelligent, and that he was competent to make that decision at the time.

Moreover, even in the absence of defendant's presentation, the trial court, as it was obliged to do, considered and found mitigation nonetheless. Defendant's claim, therefore, is not colorable, and is summarily denied pursuant to *Rule 32.6(c)*.

The PCR court's determination that the claims had been waived constitutes an adequate state procedural bar. *See Smith, 536 U.S. at 860; Ortiz, 149 F.3d at 931-32; see also Harris, 489 U.S. at 264 n. 10.*

However, as noted, Petitioner alleges   ineffectiveness of appellate counsel as cause to excuse the default. To establish ineffective assistance of counsel on appeal, Petitioner must show that counsel's performance was deficient and that the deficiency resulted in prejudice. *Strickland, 466 U.S. at 687; Evitts v. Lucey, 469 U.S. 387, 396, 105 S. Ct. 830, 83 L. Ed. 2d 821 (1985)* (recognizing the right to effective assistance of counsel for a first appeal as of right). To establish prejudice, Petitioner must show that there is a "reasonable probability" that, absent counsel's errors, the result of the appeal would have been different. *Strickland, 466 U.S. at 694; see Smith v. Robbins, 528 U.S. 259, 285-86, 120 S. Ct. 746, 145 L. Ed. 2d 756 (2000); Neill v. Gibson, 278 F.3d 1044, 1057 (10th Cir. 2001)* ("When considering a claim of ineffective assistance of appellate counsel for failure to raise an issue, we look to the merits of the omitted issue."); *Bailey v. Newland, 263 F.3d 1022, 1033-34 (9th Cir. 2001)*. Thus, the court will assess the merits of Claims 5 and 6 to determine whether, if they had been raised on appeal, there is a reasonable probability they would have been successful.

Petitioner contends in Claim 5 that the trial court failed to make an adequate determination that he was competent   to waive mitigation. The court disagrees. At the time of the waiver, the trial court had no information supporting a bona fide doubt about Petitioner's competence and therefore was not obligated to undertake a more thorough competency determination.

The court had been provided with three Rule 11 reports indicating that Petitioner was competent to stand trial and plead guilty. The court further heard the testimony of Dr. Lang, who opined that Petitioner was competent to waive mitigation. Lorona also informed the court that he had no reason to question Petitioner's competence.

As discussed above, Petitioner did not exhibit "extremely erratic or irrational behavior during the course of trial." *Boag, 769 F.2d at 1344.* To the contrary, the trial judge had observed Petitioner in court over a period of several years. He consistently engaged in rational colloquies with the court, including at the time of his guilty pleas and when he waived mitigation. Petitioner did not have a "lengthy histor[y] of acute psychosis and psychiatric treatment." *Id.* Instead, the record indicated only one previous hospitalization for mental health issues, an incident caused by drug abuse and resolved as the effects   of the drugs dissipated. Finally, the court again notes that under *Landrigan,* even assuming that a waiver of mitigating evidence must be knowing and voluntary, no specific colloquy was needed to establish a valid waiver. *550 U.S. at 479.*

Petitioner's arguments in Claim 6, alleging that he was incompetent when he waived mitigation, are equally unavailing. As set forth above, it is Petitioner's burden to prove incompetence. He has failed to meet that burden. The record reflects that the state court's competency determination was not unreasonable, and Petitioner has failed to rebut that determination with clear and convincing evidence. Therefore, his claim that he was incompetent to waive mitigation must fail. *See Demosthenes v. Baal, 495 U.S. at 735.*

Based on this analysis, Claim 7, alleging ineffective assistance of appellate counsel due to counsel's failure to raise Claims 5 and 6 on appeal, is without merit. Because the underlying claims are meritless, Petitioner was not prejudiced by appellate counsel's failure to raise them. Therefore, appellate counsel's performance does not excuse the default. *Carrier, 477 U.S. at 492.* Claims 5, 6, and 7 are denied.

C. Conflict of Interest: Claims   12 and 13

In Claim 12, Petitioner alleges that trial counsel labored under an unconstitutional conflict of interest because he represented Petitioner pursuant to a flat-fee contract with the OCAC. He makes the same argument in Claim 13 with respect to appellate counsel. Respondents contend that only the *Sixth Amendment* aspect of Claim 12 is exhausted and that Claim 13 is procedurally barred because Petitioner failed to state a federal basis for the claim in his petition for review to the Arizona Supreme Court. (Doc. 38 at 157-58, 161.) Because Claim 13, like Claim 12, is plainly meritless, the Court will deny both claims on the merits without addressing their procedural status.

Petitioner raised these claims in his PCR petition. The PCR court rejected them as not colorable, explaining, with respect to trial counsel's alleged conflict of interest:

> Defendant seeks Rule 32 relief claiming that inadequate public financing of his trial counsel created a conflict of interest with his attorney. He argues that the funding structure for indigent representation created a Hobson's Choice for his attorney - do less than what the case required for the money paid, or do what the case required, some of which would be uncompensated.
>
> Funding in defendant's case, as with every other indigent defendant in Maricopa County not represented by a public defender, was administered by the Office of Court Appointed Counsel (hereinafter OCAC). As with every other indigent defendant in Maricopa County not represented by a public defender, defendant's counsel was paid by a fixed fee contract with the OCAC. Defendant claims that the amount of the fixed fee contract is inadequate on its face, and deprived counsel of the ability to adequately represent him.
>
> Defendant provides no factual support for the claim, or specifies anything counsel did not do for defendant because of insufficient compensation. His claim cynically assumes that any attorney will only represent his client to the extent he is paid. Defendant's claim also requires this Court to find that OCAC's authorized pay scale is inadequate as a matter of law. There is no legal support for such a claim.

Using the same analysis, the court rejected Petitioner's claim that appellate counsel's performance was affected by a financial conflict of interest.

The PCR court's ruling was not contrary to or an unreasonable application of clearly established federal law, nor was it based on an unreasonable determination of the facts.

To be entitled to relief on these claims, Petitioner must show that the fee arrangement constituted an actual conflict of interest. "Under this standard, an actual conflict is a conflict that affected counsel's performance - as opposed to a mere theoretical division of loyalties." *United States v. Wells, 394 F.3d 725, 733 (9th Cir. 2005)* (quoting *Mickens v. Taylor, 535 U.S. 162, 171, 122 S. Ct. 1237, 152 L. Ed. 2d 291 (2002)); see Cuyler v. Sullivan, 446 U.S. 335, 348, 100 S. Ct. 1708, 64 L. Ed. 2d 333 (1980)).* The Ninth Circuit has explained that "to show adverse effect, a defendant need not demonstrate prejudice - that the outcome of his trial would have been different but for the conflict - but only that some plausible alternative defense strategy or tactic might have been pursued but was not and that the alternative defense was inherently in conflict with or not undertaken due to the attorney's other loyalties or interests." *Id. at 733* (quotation omitted) (holding that a fee arrangement by which co-defendant paid defendant's attorney did not adversely affect attorney's performance).

Petitioner has not met this standard. He has shown at most that the flat fee arrangement constituted a theoretical conflict of interest. In *Williams v. Calderon, 52 F.3d 1465, 1473 (9th Cir. 1995)*, the petitioner argued that "the fact that payment for any investigation or psychiatric services could have come from counsel's pocket forced counsel to choose between Williams' interests and his own." *Id.* The court "discern[ed] in this situation no conflict of constitutional dimension," explaining that "[a]ll Williams alleges is the same theoretical conflict that exists between an attorney's personal fisc and his client's interests in any pro bono or underfunded appointment case. Such arrangements, without more, do not require *Sixth Amendment* scrutiny." *Id.;* see *Bonin v. Calderon, 59 F.3d 815, 827 (9th Cir. 1995)* (no actual conflict based on counsel's substitution as retained counsel depriving defendant of state-funded investigators and expert witnesses and requiring attorney to pay for any investigative experts out of his own pocket); *United States v. Stitt, 552 F.3d 345, 350-51 (4th Cir. 2008)* (petitioner failed to show fee arrangement had adverse effect on counsel's performance where there was no showing that hiring out-of-state investigation was plausible, objectively reasonable strategy); *Hand v. Secretary, Dept. Of Corrections, 305 Fed.Appx. 547, 550 (11th Cir. 2008)* (state court did not unreasonably apply clearly established federal law by finding no prejudice where defense counsel represented defendant on a fixed fee with all costs and expenses to be paid by counsel).

Petitioner has failed to show that the fixed-fee arrangement had an adverse effect on counsel's performance. Petitioner asserts that the contract hindered Lorona's performance and prevented him from retaining defense experts. Notwithstanding the contract, however, the record shows that Lorona hired investigators who worked on Petitioner's case throughout the guilt phase, hired a mitigation specialist early in the case, and was assisted by co-counsel.

During the PCR evidentiary hearing, Lorona acknowledged a dispute with OCAC concerning his fees in Petitioner's case but testified that it did not affect his representation. With respect to his statement that he did not hire an independent   expert to evaluate Petitioner's competency to waive mitigation because he believed that the OCAC would not have paid for it, Lorona clarified that he felt the OCAC would not have permitted him to hire an expert who was not on the office's approved list. Defense investigator Bachtle testified that he never perceived any breakdowns on the defense team, and that everyone on the team performed his or her job properly. Bachtle further stated that Lorona never directed him to curtail his investigation based on cost.. While other witnesses, including mitigation specialist Christianson, opined that Lorona neglected his duties, there was no indication that these alleged deficiencies were due to funding issues. In sum, Petitioner has not demonstrated that any plausible alternative strategy or tactic was foregone due to funding issues.

The same analysis applies to appellate counsel. While Petitioner criticizes the brief prepared by appellate counsel, he offers no evidence tying its alleged inadequacies to any funding issues.

Claims 12 and 13 are without merit and will be denied.

D. Presentation of Mitigating Evidence: Claims 14, 15, and   16

Petitioner raises several claims based on the trial court's order directing the prosecutor to present mitigating evidence. In Claim 14, Petitioner alleges that he was denied his right to conflict-free representation because "the advocate who presented mitigating evidence" was also "charged with securing the . . . death sentence." In Claim 15, he alleges that he received ineffective assistance based on trial counsel's failure to challenge the court's order. In Claim 16, he alleges ineffective assistance of appellate counsel based on counsel's failure to raise the issue on appeal. Respondents concede that Claims 15 and 16 are exhausted but contend that Claim 14 is procedurally defaulted. Regardless of the procedural status of Claim 14, it is meritless, as are Claims 15 and 16.

As noted above, Petitioner waived mitigation and directed Lorona not to present any evidence. In response, the trial court directed the prosecution to offer any mitigating evidence it possessed. Petitioner's challenges to this process are unfounded.

Arizona law specifically provides for the presentation of mitigating evidence by the State. As set forth in *A.R.S. § 13-703(C)*:

> At   the penalty phase of the sentencing proceeding that is held pursuant to section 13-703.01, the prosecution or the defendant may present any information that is relevant to any of the mitigating circumstances included in subsection G of this section, regardless of its admissibility under the rules governing admission of evidence at criminal trials.

Similarly, *A.R.S. § 13-703(G)* states in relevant part, "The trier of fact shall consider as mitigating circumstances any factors proffered by the defendant or the state that are relevant in determining whether to impose a sentence of less than death." Therefore, if defense counsel had objected to the court's order, such an objection would not have been sustained.

Moreover, Petitioner cannot prove that he was prejudiced by counsel's performance, given that he waived the presentation of any mitigation evidence. A successful objection by Lorona simply would have prevented the presentation of the evidence offered by the prosecution. There was not a reasonable probability of a different sentence if counsel had managed to forestall the presentation of additional mitigating information. Appellate counsel did not perform ineffectively by failing to   raise this meritless issue. Claims 14, 15, and 16 are denied.

E. *Ring* Error: Claims 1 and 2

(1) Claim 1

Citing *Ring v. Arizona, 536 U.S. 584, 122 S. Ct. 2428, 153 L. Ed. 2d 556 (2002)* ("*Ring II*"), Petitioner alleges that he was denied the right to a jury trial in violation of the *Sixth* and *Fourteenth Amendments.* He asserts that the denial of his right to be sentenced by a jury constituted structural error and requires "reversal of his death sentence and a remand for resentencing." He also contends that the Arizona Supreme Court erred in its application of the harmless error standard because it was "unreasonable to find that a rational juror could not view the aggravating and mitigating evidence differently than the trial judge and find that a life sentence was appropriate." Respondents concede that the claim is exhausted.

Harmless error standard

In *Ring II*, the United State Supreme Court invalidated Arizona's judge-only capital sentencing scheme by holding that a jury must determine the existence of facts rendering a defendant eligible for the death penalty. *536 U.S. at 609.* Subsequently, the Arizona Supreme Court, in *State v. Ring ("Ring III"), 204 Ariz. 534, 552, 65 P.3d 915, 933 (2003)*, held that the *Sixth Amendment* "does not require automatic reversal of a death sentence imposed under [Arizona's] former sentencing statutes." Instead, relying on *Neder v. United States, 527 U.S. 1, 8, 119 S. Ct. 1827, 144 L. Ed. 2d 35 (1999)*, and *Arizona v. Fulminante, 499 U.S. 279, 306-07, 111 S. Ct. 1246, 113 L. Ed. 2d 302 (1991)*, the court held that it would review capital sentences under the harmless error standard. *Id. at 552-53, 65 P.3d at 933-34.* Noting that it had "repeatedly rejected" the argument that *Ring* error is structural, the Arizona Supreme Court applied the harmless error test in evaluating Petitioner's death sentence. *Murdaugh, 209 Ariz. at 29-30, 97 P.3d at 854-55.* This was not contrary to or an unreasonable application of clearly established federal law.

A structural error is a "defect affecting the framework within which the trial proceeds, rather than simply an error in the trial process itself." *Fulminante, 499 U.S. at 310.* Structural error affects "the entire conduct of the trial from beginning to end." *Id. at 309.* The "very limited class of cases" in which structural error has been found feature "such defects as the complete deprivation of counsel or trial before a biased judge," which "necessarily render a criminal trial fundamentally unfair or an unreliable vehicle for determining guilt or innocence." *Neder, 527 U.S. at 8* (finding that a jury instruction omitting an element of the offense does not constitute structural error).

The United States Supreme Court has never held that *Ring* error is included in that limited class of cases. In *Ring II* itself, the Court declined to "reach the State's assertion that any error was harmless because a pecuniary gain finding was implicit in the jury's guilty verdict." *536 U.S. at 609 n.7; see id. at 621* (Justice O'Connor dissenting) ("I believe many of these challenges will ultimately be unsuccessful . . . because the prisoners will be unable to satisfy the standards of harmless error."). Subsequently, in *Schriro v. Summerlin*, holding that *Ring II* did not apply retroactively, the Court rejected claims that *Ring II* was either a substantive ruling or a "watershed rule[] of criminal procedure implicating the fundamental fairness and accuracy of the criminal proceeding," explaining that it could not "confidently say that judicial factfinding so *seriously* diminishe[s] accuracy that there is a large risk of punishing conduct the law does not reach." *542 U.S. 348, 355-356, 124 S. Ct. 2519, 159 L. Ed. 2d 442 (2004)* (interior quotations omitted).

As the Arizona Supreme Court explained in *Ring III, 204 Ariz. at 545, 554-55, 65 P.3d at 926, 935-36*, the holding in *Ring II* was preceded by, and premised on, the ruling in *Apprendi v. New Jersey*, which held that "any fact that increases the penalty for a crime beyond the prescribed statutory maximum must be submitted to a jury, and proved beyond a reasonable doubt." *530 U.S. 466, 490, 120 S. Ct. 2348, 147 L. Ed. 2d 435 (2000).* There is no question that *Apprendi* errors are subject to harmless error analysis. *See Washington v. Recuenco, 548 U.S. 212, 218-22, 126 S. Ct. 2546, 165 L. Ed. 2d 466 (2006)* (holding that *Apprendi* errors are reviewed for harmlessness using the framework of *Neder*); *see also United States v. Zepeda-Martinez, 470 F.3d 909, 910 (9th Cir. 2006).*

The Arizona Supreme Court did not unreasonably apply Supreme Court precedent when it determined that harmless error was the appropriate standard of review. *Ring* error does not affect the framework within which the trial proceeds or the entire conduct of the trial, but only the trial process itself. The court properly found that *Ring* error, like the failure to instruct a jury on an element of the offense, was not so fundamental that it necessarily rendered Petitioner's capital sentence unfair or unreliable.

IV. EVIDENTIARY DEVELOPMENT

Petitioner seeks evidentiary development with respect to Claims 2-19. (Doc. 51.) Respondents oppose the request. For the reasons set forth below, the court finds that Petitioner is not entitled to evidentiary development.

A. Standards

(1) Discovery

Rule 6(a) of the Rules Governing Section 2254 Cases provides that "[a] judge may, for *good cause,* authorize a party to conduct discovery under the Federal Rules of Civil Procedure, and may limit the extent of discovery." *Rule 6(a), Rules Governing § 2254 Cases*, 28 U.S.C. foll. *§ 2254* (emphasis added). Thus, unlike the usual civil litigant in federal court, a habeas petitioner is not entitled to discovery "as a matter of ordinary course," *Bracy v. Gramley, 520 U.S. 899, 904, 117 S. Ct. 1793, 138 L. Ed. 2d 97 (1997); see Campbell v. Blodgett, 982 F.2d 1356, 1358 (1993),* nor should courts allow him to "use federal discovery for fishing expeditions to investigate mere speculation," *Calderon v. United States Dist. Ct. for the N. Dist. of Cal. (Nicolaus), 98 F.3d 1102, 1106 (9th Cir. 1996); see also Rich v. Calderon, 187 F.3d 1064, 1067 (9th Cir. 1999)* (habeas corpus is not a fishing expedition for petitioners to "explore their case in search of its existence") (quoting *Aubut v. State of Maine, 431 F.2d 688, 689 (1st Cir. 1970)).* Whether a petitioner has established "good cause" for discovery under *Rule 6(a)* requires a habeas court to determine the essential elements of the petitioner's substantive claim and evaluate whether "specific allegations before the court show reason to believe that the petitioner may, if the facts are fully developed, be able to demonstrate that he is . . . entitled to relief." *Bracy, 520 U.S. at 908-09* (quoting *Harris v. Nelson, 394 U.S. 286, 300, 89 S. Ct. 1082, 22 L. Ed. 2d 281 (1969)).*

(2) Evidentiary Hearing / Expansion of the Record

Historically, the district court had considerable discretion to hold an evidentiary hearing to resolve disputed issues of material fact. *See Townsend v. Sain, 372 U.S. 293, 312, 318, 83 S. Ct. 745, 9 L. Ed. 2d 770 (1963), overruled in part by Keeney v. Tamayo-Reyes, 504 U.S. 1, 112 S. Ct. 1715, 118 L. Ed. 2d 318 (1992), and limited by § 2254(e)(2); Baja v. Ducharme, 187 F.3d 1075, 1077-78 (9th Cir. 1999); Rule 8, Rules Governing § 2254 Cases*, 28 U.S.C. foll. *§ 2254* (providing that the district court judge shall determine if an evidentiary hearing is required). That discretion is significantly circumscribed by *§ 2254(e)(2)* of the AEDPA. *See Baja, 187 F.3d at 1077-78.*

Section 2254 provides that:

> If the applicant has failed to develop the factual basis of a claim in State court proceedings, the court shall not hold an evidentiary hearing on the claim unless the applicant shows that -
> (A) the claim relies on -
> (I) a new rule of constitutional law, made retroactive to cases on collateral review by the Supreme Court, that was previously unavailable; or
> (ii) a factual predicate that could not have been previously discovered through the exercise of due diligence; and

> (B) the facts underlying the claim would be sufficient to establish by clear and convincing evidence that but for constitutional error, no reasonable factfinder [*182] would have found the applicant guilty of the underlying offense.

28 U.S.C. § 2254(e)(2) (emphasis added). The Supreme Court has interpreted *subsection (e)(2)* as precluding an evidentiary hearing in federal court if the failure to develop a claim's factual basis is due to a "lack of diligence, or some greater fault, attributable to the prisoner or the prisoner's counsel." *Williams, 529 U.S. at 432.* A hearing is not barred, however, when a petitioner diligently attempts to develop the factual basis of a claim in state court and is "thwarted, for example, by the conduct of another or by happenstance was denied the opportunity to do so." *Id.; see Baja, 187 F.3d at 1078-79* (allowing hearing when state court denied opportunity to develop factual basis of claim).

When the factual basis for a particular claim has not been fully developed in state court, the first question for a district court is whether the petitioner was diligent in attempting to develop the factual record. *See Baja, 187 F.3d at 1078* (quoting *Cardwell v. Greene, 152 F.3d 331, 337 (4th Cir. 1998)).* The diligence assessment is an objective one, requiring a determination of whether a petitioner "made a reasonable attempt, in light   of the information available at the time, to investigate and pursue claims in state court." *Williams, 529 U.S. at 435.* For example, when there is information in the record that would alert a reasonable attorney to the existence and importance of certain evidence, the attorney "fails" to develop the factual record if he does not make reasonable efforts to sufficiently investigate and present the evidence to the state court. *See id. at 438-39, 442; Alley v. Bell, 307 F.3d 380, 390-91 (6th Cir. 2002)* (lack of diligence because petitioner knew of and raised claims of judicial bias and jury irregularities in state court, but failed to investigate all the factual grounds for such claims).

The petitioner bears the "burden of showing he was diligent in efforts to develop the facts supporting [his claims]." *Williams, 529 U.S. at 440.* Absent unusual circumstances, diligence requires that a petitioner "at a minimum, seek an evidentiary hearing in state court in the manner prescribed by state law." *Id. at 437; see Bragg v. Galaza, 242 F.3d 1082, 1090 (9th Cir.)* (finding no diligence because petitioner neither requested an evidentiary hearing in the trial court nor filed a state habeas petition),   *amended on denial of reh'g, 253 F.3d 1150 (9th Cir. 2001).* The mere request for an evidentiary hearing, however, may not be sufficient to establish diligence if a reasonable person would have taken additional steps. *See Dowthitt v. Johnson, 230 F.3d 733, 758 (5th Cir. 2000)* (failed to present affidavits of family members that were easily obtained without court order and with minimal expense); *Koste v. Dormire, 345 F.3d 974, 985-86 (8th Cir. 2003)* (no effort to develop the record or assert any facts to support claim); *McNair v. Campbell, 416 F.3d 1291, 1299-1300 (11th Cir. 2005)* (no development of evidence available through himself, family members and literature, and no appeal of denial of funds and hearing); *Cannon v. Mullin, 383 F.3d 1152, 1177 (10th Cir. 2004)* (lack of diligence if petitioner does not proffer "evidence that would be readily available if the claim were true.").

In sum, if this court determines that Petitioner has not been diligent in establishing the factual basis for his claims in state court, then the court may not conduct a hearing unless the petitioner satisfies one of § 2254(e)(2)'s narrow exceptions. If, however, Petitioner has not failed to develop the factual   basis of a claim in state court, the court will then proceed to consider whether a hearing is appropriate or required under the criteria set forth by the Supreme Court in *Townsend. 372 U.S. 293, 83 S. Ct. 745, 9 L. Ed. 2d 770; see Baja, 187 F.3d at 1078* (quoting *Cardwell, 152 F.3d at 337); Horton, II v. Mayle, 408 F.3d 570, 582 n.6 (9th Cir. 2005).*

Pursuant to *Townsend,* a federal district court *must* hold an evidentiary hearing in a § 2254 case when: (1) the facts are in dispute; (2) the petitioner "alleges facts which, if proved, would entitle him to relief;" and (3) the state court has not "reliably found the relevant facts" after a "full and fair evidentiary hearing," at trial or in a collateral proceeding. *Townsend, 372 U.S. at 312-13; cf. Hill v. Lockhart, 474 U.S. 52, 60, 106 S. Ct. 366, 88 L. Ed. 2d 203 (1985)* (upholding the denial of a hearing when petitioner's allegations were insufficient to satisfy the governing legal standard); *Turner v. Calderon, 281 F.3d 851, 890 (9th Cir. 2002)* (petitioner entitled to an evidentiary hearing only if he alleges "facts that, if proven, would entitle him to relief") (quoting *Tapia v. Roe, 189 F.3d 1052, 1056 (9th Cir. 1999)); Bashor v. Risley, 730 F.2d 1228 (9th Cir. 1984)* (hearing not required when claim   must be resolved on state court record or claim is based on non-specific conclusory allegations).

In any other case in which diligence has been established, the district court judge "has the power, constrained only by his sound discretion, to receive evidence bearing upon the applicant's constitutional claim." *Townsend, 372 U.S. at 318.* However, if a "habeas applicant was afforded a full and fair hearing by the state court resulting in reliable findings, [the judge] may, and ordinarily should, accept the facts as found in the hearing." *Id.*

Rule 7 of the Rules Governing Section 2254 Cases authorizes a federal habeas court to expand the record to include additional material relevant to the petition. The purpose of *Rule 7* "is to enable the judge to dispose of some habeas petitions not dismissed on the pleadings, without the time and expense required for an evidentiary hearing." Advisory Committee Notes, *Rule 7, 28 U.S.C. foll. § 2254; see also Blackledge v. Allison,*

431 U.S. 63, 81-82, 97 S. Ct. 1621, 52 L. Ed. 2d 136 (1977). When expansion of the record is sought, the court must assess whether the materials submitted are relevant to resolution of the petition.

Section 2254(e)(2), as amended by the AEDPA, limits a petitioner's ability to present new evidence through a *Rule 7* motion to expand the record to the same extent that it limits the availability of an evidentiary hearing. *See Cooper-Smith v. Palmateer, 397 F.3d 1236, 1241 (9th Cir. 2005)* (applying *§ 2254(e)(2)* to expansion of the record when intent is to bolster the merits of a claim with new evidence) (citing *Holland v. Jackson, 542 U.S. 649, 652-53, 124 S. Ct. 2736, 159 L. Ed. 2d 683 (2004)* (per curiam)). Thus, when a petitioner seeks to introduce new affidavits and other documents never presented in state court, for the purpose of establishing the factual predicate of a claim, he must either demonstrate diligence in developing the factual basis in state court or satisfy the requirements of *§ 2254(e)(2)(A) & (B)*. However, when a petitioner seeks to expand the record for other reasons, such as to cure omissions in the state court record, *see Dobbs v. Zant, 506 U.S. 357, 359, 113 S. Ct. 835, 122 L. Ed. 2d 103 (1993)* (per curiam), establish cause and prejudice, or demonstrate diligence, the strictures of *§ 2254(e)(2)* do not apply. *See Boyko, 259 F.3d 781, 790 (7th Cir. 2001).*

B. Discussion

At the outset the court finds that evidentiary development is not appropriate for Claims 2 and 16-19 because they are record based, involve purely legal issues, or are plainly meritless. As the Supreme Court explained in *Landrigan*, "if the record refutes the applicant's factual allegations or otherwise precludes habeas relief, a district court is not required to hold an evidentiary hearing. The Ninth Circuit has recognized this point in other cases, holding that 'an evidentiary hearing is not required on issues that can be resolved by reference to the state court record.'" *550 U.S. at 474* (quoting *Totten v. Merkle, 137 F.3d 1172, 1176 (1998)*). We next address Petitioner's request for evidentiary development with respect to the remaining claims.

(1) Discovery

Petitioner seeks to depose members of the defense team, including lead counsel (Lorona), co-counsel (Gitre and Claussen), the investigators (Salinas and Bachtle), the mitigation specialists (Wake and Christianson), and appellate counsel (Michael Reeves and Michael Tafoya). He also seeks depositions from Drs. Potts, Sindelar, Scialli, Lang, and Deming; the prosecutor, Mark Barry; the trial judge, Judge Hutt; attorneys Mike Terribile, who testified at the PCR evidentiary hearing regarding funding issues, and Larry Hammond, who testified as a "*Strickland* expert"; individuals listed in Lorona's correspondence with the OCAC; and detention employees who had contact with Petitioner during his incarceration.

Petitioner requests the issuance of a subpoena for records from the OCAC relevant to the representation of Petitioner, including the contracts, billing records, payment records, and disciplinary records of trial and appellate counsel, as well as all correspondence between the OCAC and trial and appellate counsel; disciplinary records from the State Bar of Arizona for trial and appellate counsel; any documentation of communication, including but not limited to emails, letters, and phone calls between appellate counsel and any persons who may have worked with them on Petitioner's case; and disciplinary records from the State Bar of Arizona for Mark Barry and any other prosecutor involved in the sentencing phase of Petitioner's case.

Petitioner seeks a subpoena directed at the Office of the Maricopa County Attorney demanding "that the office produce its entire file relating to [Petitioner's case], or at least in regard to the presentation of mitigation or mitigation rebuttal, in order to discover evidence of the prosecutor's awareness of his divided loyalties and the level of preparation he took in preparing his mitigation presentation." He also seeks a subpoena directed to the offices of Dr. Michael Bayless, Dr. Lang's employer at the time of her mitigation hearing testimony.

Finally, Petitioner seeks the issuance of interrogatories to appellate counsel requesting information concerning the staff who may have worked with them on Petitioner's case and anyone else who may have knowledge about their representation of Petitioner. He requests that interrogatories be issued to the prosecutor and Dr. Lang. He even requests a "direct interrogatory to the Arizona Supreme Court regarding what sealed evidence they did or did not review in determining mitigation

As noted, to determine whether good cause for discovery exists, the court must first determine the essential elements of Petitioner's substantive claims. *Bracy, 520 U.S. at 908-09.* Petitioner requests discovery with respect to Claims 2, 3, and 5-16. The court, having identified the elements of these claims above, must assess whether the requested discovery would lead to the development of facts that may entitle Petitioner to relief. For the   reasons set forth below, the Court finds that it would not.

Petitioner cannot show good cause with respect to much of the requested discovery because it is not relevant to his claims. *See Stephens v. Branker, 570 F.3d 198, 213 (4th Cir. 2009)* (petitioner's "discovery request is deficient because - although he has identified specific information sought - he has not demonstrated that such discovery would result in him being entitled to habeas relief on the conflict claim"). For example, in pursuing his ineffective assistance claims , Petitioner seeks trial and appellate counsel's bar records and records from the OCAC. However, counsel's conduct in other matters is not relevant to their performance during Petitioner's trial and appeal. In determining whether counsel's performance was deficient, the only issue is the reasonableness of counsel's conduct "on the facts of the particular case, viewed as of the time of counsel's conduct." *Strickland, 466 U.S. at 690*; *see Babbitt, 151 F.3d at 1173-74.* Therefore, the development of additional facts regarding counsel's past conduct in other cases cannot "show reason to believe" that Petitioner is entitled to relief on any   of his ineffective assistance claims. *Bracy, 520 U.S. at 908-09.* The same analysis applies to Petitioner's conflict of interest claims Petitioner cannot explain how additional information about the OCAC's funding situation is relevant to the issue of whether trial or appellate counsel labored under an actual, as opposed to a theoretical, conflict of interest. *Cf. Wallace v. Ward, 191 F.3d 1235, 1245-46 (10th Cir. 1999)* (district court did not abuse discretion in denying discovery where conflict of interest claims were general and conclusory).

Petitioner also fails to demonstrate that there are any contested facts the discovery of which would bear on the merits of his claims. This is true with respect to Petitioner's request to depose Judge Hutt. The record is complete concerning the trial court's handling of Petitioner's guilty plea and waiver of mitigation There are no contested facts underlying these "procedural incompetence" claims because the relevant facts about Petitioner's mental capacity were those in the judge's possession at the time she accepted his plea and waiver and upon which she was required to make her determination of competence.   *Cf. Boyde v. Brown, 404 F.3d 1159, 1165 n.6 (9th Cir. 2005)* (citing *Davis v. Woodford, 384 F.3d 628, 644-45 (9th Cir. 2004)).* The same is true for the prosecutor and his presentation of evidence at the mitigation hearing ; the only material facts are those found in the record of the hearing. The prosecutor had no duty to further investigate mitigating evidence, especially when Petitioner himself waived the presentation of any mitigation.

Petitioner's claims of ineffective assistance of appellate counsel are likewise resolvable on the record. *See Gray v. Greer, 800 F.2d 644, 647 (7th Cir. 1985)* ("it is the exceptional case" where a claim of appellate ineffective assistance "could not be resolved on the record alone"). Moreover, because the underlying claims are without merit, Petitioner cannot establish prejudice notwithstanding any additional information discovered concerning the quality of appellate counsel's representation.

Petitioner's request for evidentiary development of Claim 3 through an interrogatory to the Arizona Supreme Court regarding what mitigating evidence the court considered is also denied. Such information is not relevant to Petitioner's   claim that the court applied an unconstitutional nexus requirement to its review of Petitioner's capital sentence. Moreover, Petitioner has no right to invade the decision-making process of a court that is not otherwise of record.

A final consideration warrants a finding that Petitioner has not established good cause for his discovery requests, including his request to depose the defense team and various mental health and legal experts in support of his claims that he was incompetent to plead guilty and waive mitigation. Petitioner had the opportunity to gather this information in state court during the PCR proceedings just two years ago. In fact, he previously deposed many of these individuals, who also testified at the evidentiary hearing, including Lorona, Gitre, Bachtle, Christianson, Wake, and Drs. Potts, Scialli, and Lang. Other individuals, such as jail employees, could have been deposed during the PCR proceedings. Under these circumstances, Petitioner cannot demonstrate good cause for additional discovery from the same individuals concerning the same issues. *See Smith v. Gibson, 197 F.3d 454, 459 (10th Cir. 1999)* (discovery may be inappropriate if the petitioner had an opportunity   [*195] to conduct discovery and to develop evidence during the state post-conviction proceedings); *cf. Jones v. Wood, 114 F.3d 1002, 1009 (9th Cir. 1997)* (finding good cause for discovery existed "particularly given that there was never any hearing for the ineffective assistance claim at the state-court level").

Petitioner's discovery requests are deficient because he has made "no showing that the information sought is material to the merits" of any of his claims. *Stephens, 570 F.3d at 213*. Accordingly, Petitioner's requests for discovery are denied.

(2) Expansion of Record / Evidentiary Hearing

Petitioner requests expansion of the record and/or an evidentiary hearing with respect to each of his claims. He seeks to expand the record with declarations from lead counsel Lorona ; appellate counsel Reeves; mitigation specialist Christianson; mitigation specialist Mary Durand ; managing court reporter, Denise Sanders Couvaras ; Dr. Sindelar ; and individuals familiar with Petitioner's defense team, mental illness, drug abuse, background, and the circumstances surrounding the crime. He seeks to expand the record to include a police report regarding a prior drug possession incident, military records obtained by Holly Wake and the Office of the Federal Public Defender, and junior high and high school, as well as photographs from Petitioner's suicide attempt, and jail visitor logs . Petitioner also seeks to include Lorona's state bar disciplinary record; the transcript of an interview of investigator Bachtle dated 7/11/05 ;Dr. Robert Smith's curriculum vitae and psychological summaries ; and the transcript of Reeves' oral argument before the Arizona Supreme Court on June 1, 2004.

Along with expansion of the record, Petitioner seeks an evidentiary hearing to hear testimony from Lorona, Claussen, Gitre, Reeves, Tafoya, Dr. Smith, Dr. Deming, Dr. Potts, Dr. Sindelar, Dr. Scialli, Dr. Lang, Dr. Shaw, Mark Barry, Judge Hutt, Michael Terribile, Larry Hammond, Stella Salinas, Holly Wake, Linda Christianson, Mary Durand, an expert on the legal issues surrounding competency in capital cases, an expert on the legal issues surrounding voluntariness, a "legal expert . . . and an expert in psychological ethical issues to address the problems with Dr. Lang's role in the case," and Petitioner's family and friends

According to Petitioner, his trial and appellate counsel will each testify about the various ways in which their performance was deficient; the defense investigator and mitigation specialists will testify about Lorona's "lack of effort"; the Rule 11 experts will testify that their examinations did not assess Petitioner's competency to waive mitigation; Drs. Smith and Deming will testify that Petitioner was incompetent to waive mitigation; Terribile and Hammond will testify about the funding problems of capital attorneys in Maricopa County; and the proposed new experts, medical and legal, will testify in accordance with the allegations advanced in Petitioner's habeas claims.

Respondents contend that Petitioner is not entitled to expansion of the record or an evidentiary hearing because he did not diligently develop the facts of his claims in state court. This court agrees.

As discussed above, Petitioner sought an evidentiary hearing in state court, and a hearing was granted with respect to his claim of ineffective assistance of trial counsel. The court finds that Petitioner, acting with reasonable diligence during the PCR proceedings, could have gathered all of the materials contained in his request to expand the record. While Petitioner complains that funding difficulties impeded PCR counsel's efforts, he makes no showing that such problems prevented him from obtaining declarations from trial and appellate counsel and members of the defense team. *See Ward v. Hall, 592 F.3d 1144, 1159-63 (11th Cir. 2010)* (rejecting argument that budget problems were responsible for petitioner's inability to develop claims in state court where he was "afforded approximately three years to secure affidavits and witness testimony prior to his state habeas evidentiary hearings and managed to submit numerous exhibits and affidavits during course of his hearings, including affidavit testimony from family members, friends, acquaintances, and former jurors"); *Roberts v. Dretke, 381 F.3d 491, 500-01 (5th Cir. 2004)* (finding that "no action by the state habeas court prevented Roberts from seeking an affidavit . . . despite fact that the state habeas court could have been more helpful with regards to funding and holding an evidentiary hearing"); *Dowthitt, 230 F.3d at 758* ("Dowthitt's arguments that lack of funding prevented the development of his claims are also without merit. Obtaining affidavits from family members is not cost prohibitive.").

Similarly, PCR counsel acting with reasonable diligence   could have obtained Petitioner's school and military records, information concerning his prior drug charge, jail visitor logs, and photographs of his suicide attempt. All of this information was readily available.

In addition, as noted above, the majority of the proposed witnesses testified during the PCR evidentiary hearing. Nothing prevented Petitioner from questioning any of these witnesses, and Petitioner had the opportunity to make any relevant inquiries at that time. To the extent Petitioner wants to develop additional facts through the testimony of the same witnesses, he has not demonstrated that he diligently attempted to develop such facts in state court. If he intends to present the same testimony in federal court that he presented in state court, he has failed to demonstrate that the state hearing was not full and fair or that the state court failed to reliably find the relevant facts. *Townsend, 372 U.S. at 318.*

Petitioner also seeks to call a number of witnesses who did not testify at the PCR evidentiary hearing. These include appellate counsel, a legal expert, Judge Hutt, the prosecutor, and Drs. Smith and Deming. Along with Petitioner's failure to exercise diligence in   developing the factual bases of his claims in state court, he has also failed to identify any relevant disputed facts the resolution of which requires an evidentiary hearing. Petitioner's competence to plead guilty, while disputed now, was the subject of contemporaneous mental health evaluations which all reached the same conclusion. His competency to waive mitigation - along with other issues associated with counsel's performance at sentencing - was the subject of the extensive evidentiary hearing in state court. With respect to these issues, Petitioner "has not established that an evidentiary hearing would produce evidence more reliable or more probative than the medical records and expert opinion" that already are part of the record before this Court. *Griffin v. Johnson, 350 F.3d 956, 966 (9th Cir. 2003); see Totten v. Merkle, 137 F.3d at 1176.*

In *Landrigan,* the Supreme Court explained that the criteria for determining whether an evidentiary hearing is required must take into account the AEDPA's deferential standard of review:

> In deciding whether to grant an evidentiary hearing, a federal court must consider whether such a hearing could enable an applicant to prove the factual allegations, which, if true, would entitle the applicant to federal habeas relief. Because the deferential standards prescribed by § 2254 control whether to grant habeas relief, a federal court must take into account those standards in deciding whether an evidentiary hearing is appropriate.
>
> It follows that if the record refutes the applicant's factual allegations or otherwise precludes habeas relief, a district court is not required to hold an evidentiary hearing.

550 U.S. at 474 (citations and footnoted omitted).

Application of this standard highlights the deficiencies of Petitioner's request for an evidentiary hearing. The reasonableness of the state court's decisions rejecting Petitioner's claims is not undermined by the factual allegations advanced in Petitioner's motion. These allegations simply restate the arguments made in state court and in the habeas petition. Thus, even if a hearing would produce evidence in support of the allegations, Petitioner would not be entitled to relief.

Finally, Petitioner cannot meet the exceptions to the diligence requirement of *28 U.S.C. § 2254(e)(2),* according to which he must show that his claims rely on a new rule of constitutional made retroactive to cases on collateral review by the Supreme Court or that he could not have previously discovered the factual predicate of his claims through due diligence, and that the facts underlying the claims would establish that but for constitutional error, no reasonable factfinder would have found him guilty of the Reynolds murder. Therefore, Petitioner is not entitled to expand the record or to an evidentiary hearing on his claims.   The court also rejects Petitioner's assertion that he is entitled to evidentiary development because the new evidence "does not fundamentally alter the nature of the claim presented in state court." (*See, e.g.,* Doc. 51 at 30.) Petitioner's argument appears to conflate the exhaustion requirements of *§ 2254(b)(1)(A)* with the diligence requirements of *§ 2254(e)(2).* These are two separate inquiries. *See, e.g., Winston v. Kelly, 592 F.3d 535, 551 (4th Cir. 2010); Richey v. Bradshaw, 498 F.3d 344, 352 (6th Cir. 2007); Lopez v. Schriro, 491 F.3d 1029, 1040, 1041 n.8 (9th Cir. 2007).*

REASONS WHY REMEDY IS HOLLOW

"Federal courts sitting in habeas are not an alternative forum for trying facts and issues which a prisoner made insufficient effort to pursue in state proceedings." *Williams v. Taylor, 529 U.S. at 437*. Petitioner's motion for evidentiary development seeks to use these habeas proceedings to re-litigate his challenges to his guilty pleas, waiver of mitigation, and sentencing proceedings, as well as the outcome of his direct appeal and the postconviction proceedings. The facts and evidence Petitioner now wishes to present could "have been previously discovered through the exercise of due diligence," *§ 2254(e)(2)(A)(ii)*, and because Petitioner has not alleged the existence of disputed relevant facts that would entitle him to relief under the deferential standards of the AEDPA, *Landrigan, 550 U.S. at 474*, his requests for evidentiary development are denied.

The Arizona Attorney General is aware that in Arizona the prosecutor, defense counsel and judge act in concert to elicit false factual basis to plead guilty and refuse to presenting mitigating evidence. Counsel has divided loyalty, loyal to the prosecutor not client.

John Edward Sansing, Petitioner, vs. Charles L. Ryan et al., Respondents.
No. CV-11-1035-PHX-SRB UNITED STATES DISTRICT COURT FOR THE DISTRICT OF ARIZONA (Text modified for emphasis)

THE POSITION OF THE COURTS

In September 1998, Petitioner pled guilty to the first-degree murder, kidnapping, armed robbery, and sexual assault of Trudy Calabrese. The Arizona Supreme Court summarized the facts as follows:

On February 24, 1998, the defendant called the Living Springs Church and requested delivery of a food box for his family. He gave the church secretary his name and home address for the delivery. The defendant then telephoned his wife, Kara Sansing, at work several times, primarily to discuss how to obtain more crack cocaine for the two of them to smoke. During these calls, the defendant informed his wife that he had obtained some crack cocaine, that he had smoked some of it and was saving the rest for her. He also told her that he had called a church and arranged for delivery of some food. When Kara Sansing returned home at approximately 3:20 p.m., the couple smoked the remaining crack cocaine. The defendant, in the presence of his four children, informed Kara of his plan to rob the person who came from the church with the food boxes so he could purchase more crack cocaine.

Trudy Calabrese left the Living Springs Church in her truck at approximately 4:00 p.m. She arrived at the Sansing home shortly thereafter, parked in front of the house, and delivered two boxes of food. Ms. Calabrese chatted with Kara Sansing in the kitchen while the defendant signed a receipt for the delivery. Before Ms. Calabrese could leave, the defendant grabbed her from behind and threw her to the dining room floor. Aided by his wife and with his children watching, the defendant bound her wrists while she cried, "Lord, please help me" and, "I don't want to die, but if this is the way you want me to come home, I am ready," and repeatedly asked the defendant's children to call the police. The defendant instructed his children to go into the living room and watch television.

Using a club, the defendant struck Ms. Calabrese in the head several times with force sufficient to break the club into two pieces and render her temporarily unconscious. Leaving her on the dining room floor, the defendant took her keys and moved her truck to a business parking lot nearby. At some point before he returned, Ms. Calabrese regained consciousness. Upon his return, the defendant dragged her into his bedroom and sexually assaulted her. Kara Sansing, who witnessed the rape, testified that she heard the defendant and Ms. Calabrese speaking during the rape. The defendant then fatally stabbed her in the abdomen three times with a kitchen knife. During the attack, the defendant placed a sock in Ms. Calabrese's mouth and secured two plastic bags over her head with additional cords and a necktie. According to the medical examiner, she lived several minutes after being stabbed. After the murder, the defendant left the bedroom and went to look out the dining room window to make certain no one had observed his actions.

The defendant then removed Ms. Calabrese's jewelry and left her body in his bedroom, covered with laundry, for several hours. The defendant engaged in two separate drug transactions shortly after the murder. First, he telephoned a drug dealer and arranged to trade the victim's rings for crack cocaine. Later, he arranged to trade her necklace for more crack cocaine.

Later in the evening, Pastor Becker from Living Springs Church called the Sansing home looking for Ms. Calabrese and spoke to the defendant. The defendant, giving a false address, told the pastor that she had never arrived.

Late that night, the defendant dragged Ms. Calabrese from the bedroom to the backyard and placed her body in a narrow space between the back of his shed and the fence. He covered her with a piece of old carpeting and other debris. At least three of the four Sansing children saw the body behind the shed. At some point, the defendant washed the bloody club and hid the clothes he had used to cover her body in a box in the bedroom.

The next day, searchers found Ms. Calabrese's truck in a parking lot near the Sansing home. Inside, they found a piece of paper with the Sansings' correct address. The police went to the Sansing home and the victim's body behind the shed. The defendant, who had driven to his sister's house, admitted to her that he and his wife had killed Ms. Calabrese. Eventually, the defendant's father telephoned the police and reported the defendant's location. The defendant knew the police were coming and did not attempt to flee. When the police arrived, he submitted to custody peacefully and without resistance.

State v. Sansing, 200 Ariz. 347, 351-52, 26 P.3d 1118, 1122-23 (2001) (Sansing I).

In September 1999, Maricopa County Superior Court Judge Ronald S. Reinstein held a sentencing hearing to determine the existence of aggravating and mitigating circumstances. The court found that the State had proven beyond a reasonable doubt that Petitioner committed the crime in the expectation of pecuniary gain, *A.R.S. § 13-703(F)(5)* and that Petitioner committed the murder in an especially cruel, heinous, or depraved manner, *A.R.S. § 13-703(F)(6)*. The court further found that Petitioner had failed to prove any statutory mitigating circumstances under *A.R.S. § 13-703(G)*, but that he had established five non-statutory mitigating circumstances: (1) impairment from the use of crack cocaine; (2) a difficult childhood; [*7] (3) acceptance of responsibility and remorse; (4) lack of education; and (5) family support. Weighing the sentencing factors, the court determined that the proven mitigation was not sufficiently substantial to outweigh the aggravation and sentenced Petitioner to death.

On appeal, the Arizona Supreme Court struck the pecuniary gain aggravating factor but nonetheless affirmed. *Sansing I, 200 Ariz. at 355-56, 26 P.3d at 1126-27*. Subsequently, the United States Supreme Court decided *Ring v. Arizona, 536 U.S. 584, 122 S. Ct. 2428, 153 L. Ed. 2d 556 (2002)*, holding that Arizona's aggravating factors are an element of the offense of capital murder and therefore must be found by a jury. The Court granted Petitioner's petition for certiorari, vacated the Arizona Supreme Court's judgment, and remanded for further consideration in light of *Ring. Sansing v. Arizona, 536 U.S. 954, 122 S. Ct. 2654, 153 L. Ed. 2d 830 (2002)* (mem.). On remand, the state court determined that the lack of jury findings as to aggravation constituted harmless error in Petitioner's case. *State v. Sansing, 206 Ariz. 232, 77 P.3d 30 (2003) (Sansing II).* The Supreme Court denied a petition for certiorari. *Sansing v. Arizona, 542 U.S. 939, 124 S. Ct. 2906, 159 L. Ed. 2d 816 (2004).*

Petitioner then sought post-conviction relief in state court, raising six claims for relief. In July 2008, the trial court dismissed five of the claims as meritless or procedurally precluded. It held a four-day evidentiary hearing on the remaining claim, which alleged ineffective assistance of counsel at sentencing, and ultimately denied relief in July 2010. The Arizona Supreme Court summarily denied a petition for review in May 2011, and Petitioner thereafter initiated these habeas corpus proceedings. Petitioner complains that he was directed to file his habeas petition prior to expiration of the statute of limitations under *28 U.S.C. § 2244(d)* and that he therefore "reserves the right to amend this petition any time before the one year statutory deadline expires without being required to meet the strict requirements for amendment imposed by *Mayle v. Felix, 545 U.S. 644, 125 S. Ct. 2562, 162 L. Ed. 2d 582*." Because Petitioner did not seek to amend his petition, either before expiration of the limitations period or after, this issue is moot.

DISCUSSION

I. DENIAL OF JURY TRIAL

Petitioner contends that he was denied his *Sixth Amendment* right to a jury determination on the factors that rendered him eligible for capital punishment, in violation of *Ring v. Arizona.* He argues that this denial amounted to structural error and, therefore, the Arizona Supreme Court's decision to review for harmless error was contrary to or an unreasonable application of controlling federal law. Petitioner further contends that, even if subject to harmless error review, the Arizona Supreme Court's finding of harmlessness was contrary to federal law and based on an unreasonable determination of the facts.

A. Harmless Error Standard

In *Ring,* the United States Supreme Court invalidated Arizona's judge-only capital sentencing scheme by holding that a jury must determine the existence of facts rendering a defendant eligible for the death penalty. *536 U.S. at 609.* Subsequently, the Arizona Supreme Court, in *State v. Ring, 204 Ariz. 534, 552, 65 P.3d 915, 933 (2003)* ("*Ring III*"), held that the *Sixth Amendment* "does not require automatic reversal of a death sentence imposed under [Arizona's] former sentencing statutes." Instead, relying on *Neder v. United States, 527 U.S. 1, 8, 119 S. Ct. 1827, 144 L. Ed. 2d 35 (1999)*, and *Arizona v. Fulminante, 499 U.S. 279, 306-07, 111 S. Ct. 1246, 113 L. Ed. 2d 302 (1991)*, the court held that it would review capital sentences under the harmless error standard. *Id. at 552-53, 65 P.3d at 933-34.* Having rejected the argument that *Ring* error is structural, the Arizona Supreme Court applied the harmless error test in evaluating Petitioner's death sentence. *Sansing II, 206 Ariz. at 235, 77 P.3d at 33.* This was not contrary to or an unreasonable application of clearly established federal law.

A structural error is a "defect affecting the framework within which the trial proceeds, rather than simply an error in the trial process itself." *Fulminante, 499 U.S. at 310.* Structural error affects "the entire conduct of the trial from beginning to end." *Id. at 309.* The "very limited class of cases" in which structural error has been found feature "such defects as the complete deprivation of counsel or trial before a biased judge," which "necessarily render a criminal trial fundamentally unfair or an unreliable vehicle for determining guilt or innocence." *Neder, 527 U.S. at 8* (finding that a jury instruction omitting an element of the offense does not constitute structural error).

The United States Supreme Court has never held that *Ring* error is included in that limited class of cases. In *Ring* itself, the Court declined to "reach the State's assertion that any error was harmless because a pecuniary gain finding was implicit in the jury's guilty verdict." *536 U.S. at 609 n.7; see id. at 621* (Justice O'Connor dissenting) ("I believe many of these challenges will ultimately be unsuccessful . . . because the prisoners will be unable to satisfy the standards of harmless error."). Subsequently, in *Schriro v. Summerlin,* holding that *Ring* did not apply retroactively, the Court rejected claims that *Ring* was either a substantive ruling or a "watershed rule[] of criminal procedure implicating the fundamental fairness and accuracy of the criminal proceeding," explaining that it could not "confidently say that judicial factfinding so *seriously* diminishe[s] accuracy that there is a large risk of punishing conduct the law does not reach." *542 U.S. 348, 355-356, 124 S. Ct. 2519, 159 L. Ed. 2d 442 (2004)* (internal quotations omitted).

As the Arizona Supreme Court explained in *Ring III, 204 Ariz. at 545, 554-55, 65 P.3d at 926, 935-36,* the holding in *Ring* was preceded by, and premised on, the ruling in *Apprendi v. New Jersey,* which held that "any fact that increases the penalty for a crime beyond the prescribed statutory maximum must be submitted to a jury, and proved beyond a reasonable doubt." *530 U.S. 466, 490, 120 S. Ct. 2348, 147 L. Ed. 2d 435 (2000).* There is no question that *Apprendi* errors are subject to harmless error analysis. *See Washington v. Recuenco, 548 U.S. 212, 218-22, 126 S. Ct. 2546, 165 L. Ed. 2d 466 (2006)* (holding that *Apprendi* errors are reviewed for harmlessness using the framework of *Neder*); *see also United States v. Zepeda-Martinez, 470 F.3d 909, 910 (9th Cir. 2006).*

The Arizona Supreme Court did not unreasonably   apply Supreme Court precedent when it determined that harmless error was the appropriate standard of review. *Ring* error does not affect the framework within which the trial proceeds or the entire conduct of the trial, but only the trial process itself. The state court properly found that *Ring* error, like the failure to instruct a jury on an element of the offense, was not so fundamental that it necessarily rendered Petitioner's capital sentence unfair or unreliable.

B. Harmless Error Analysis

On direct appeal, the Arizona Supreme Court rejected Petitioner's argument that it could not determine beyond a reasonable doubt that no jury would find the mitigating circumstances sufficient to call for leniency. *Sansing, 206 Ariz. at 241, 77 P.3d at 39.* Petitioner argues that the state court's harmless error analysis was unreasonable and contrary to Supreme Court law.

Relevant Facts

Petitioner pled guilty on September 18, 1998, to all of the charged offenses. The plea agreement provided that Petitioner could be sentenced on the first-degree murder count to life imprisonment for a minimum of 25 years, life imprisonment without the possibility of release, or death. In a written factual   basis statement accompanying the plea, Petitioner admitted that he planned to rob the victim before her arrival and that he struck her in the head with a wooden stick after detaining her in his home. He also admitted that the victim was conscious after he returned from moving her vehicle and that he "knowingly engaged" in sexual intercourse with her without her consent while she was bound and tied. Petitioner further stated that the victim was blindfolded, gagged, and had two plastic bags placed over her head, and that he stabbed her in the abdomen.

Sentencing Proceedings

Sentencing took place one year after entry of the guilty plea. In its presentencing memorandum, the State urged the trial court to find three aggravating factors: the (F)(5) pecuniary gain factor, the (F)(6) heinous, cruel, or depraved factor, and the (F)(2) prior serious offense factor. (ROA doc. 96 at 7-31.) At the aggravation/mitigation hearing, the State proffered testimony from Detective Joseph Petrosino, Dr. Mark Fischione, and Kara Sansing, Petitioner's wife. In addition, the parties jointly stipulated to admission of audio/video taped interviews of Petitioner's four children as well as statements   made by the children to a counselor, Dr. Carol Ainley, in lieu of calling the children as witnesses. The parties also stipulated to the admission of statements made by Petitioner to a reporter, Victoria Harker, as well as DNA test results from (1) a vaginal swab of the victim indicating the presence of Petitioner's semen, and (2) a carpet swatch from Petitioner's home indicating the presence of the victim's blood.

Det. Petrosino described the crime scene, including the numerous items that covered the victim's body when it was found behind a shed in Petitioner's backyard. He also described discovering in Petitioner's home a broken piece of a wooden club in a sink cabinet and a rusty boning knife later identified by Kara Sansing as the one used by Petitioner to stab Trudy Calabrese. Dr. Fischione testified concerning the victim's numerous injuries. He opined that she died as a result of multiple stab wounds to her abdomen and blunt force head trauma. He further testified that it was possible Calabrese regained consciousness after receiving the head injuries but he "doubt[ed] it."

Kara Sansing, who pled guilty to first-degree murder in exchange for a life sentence with the possibility of release after 25 years, testified to the events surrounding Calabrese's death. On the day of the murder, Petitioner called her at work several times and at one point said he had obtained and smoked some crack cocaine. After returning home from work, Kara smoked crack and waited with her husband for Calabrese to arrive less than an hour later. She testified that her children could see her and Petitioner tie up the victim, who kicked and struggled against the bindings and pleaded not to be hurt. Calabrese also repeatedly asked the Sansing children to call 911 and became unconscious when Petitioner struck her in the head with a wooden club. Petitioner then moved Calabrese's truck and upon returning dragged her to a bedroom and raped her. Kara also testified that she heard Calabrese speak with Petitioner during the sexual assault. Afterward, Petitioner stabbed Calabrese with a knife and then used her jewelry to twice buy crack from dealers who came to the house in the hours following the murder. Kara also testified that she had been   married to Petitioner for 14 years and that he was not acting normal that day compared to previous times he took drugs.

Each of Petitioner's children reported to investigators that their father grabbed the victim from behind and held her down while their mother helped tie her up. In her report, Dr. Ainley stated that Petitioner's 12-year-old son saw his father hit Calabrese with a wooden pole and that his parents would not let him help her. Dr. Ainley further stated that this son suffers from severe guilt at having followed his father's direction to find an extension cord to bind the victim. Petitioner's ten-year-old son described seeing his father break a stick on Calabrese's head and wash one of the pieces before stashing it under the sink. The children further told investigators that the victim prayed to God for help and asked them to call 911. Dr. Ainley also relayed that each of the children reported seeing the victim in the bedroom under a pile of clothes and again the next day behind the shed. In addition, two of the children told Dr. Ainley   that their parents regularly used drugs.

The parties stipulated that Victoria Harker, a reporter for the Arizona Republic, would testify that Petitioner told her in January 1999 that he had not planned to rob or harm the victim prior to her arrival at his house but decided to end her suffering after raping and beating her so badly. Petitioner also denied to Harker that his children witnessed the attack but conceded that they may have seen Calabrese tied up and that she had regained consciousness after he moved her truck. Petitioner told Harker that once he attacked the victim he "had to finish it up because I was going to jail anyway. . . . Once you start something, you just can't stop."

During the mitigation portion of the presentencing hearing, Petitioner proffered statements and testimony from four witnesses: his wife Kara, his sister Patsy Hooper, his mother Glenda Singh, and his brother Allan Sansing. Petitioner also made a statement, and the parties stipulated that Petitioner was arrested peaceably at his sister's house after their father called the police.

Kara Sansing pleaded with the court to spare her husband's life. She reiterated her previous testimony that Petitioner was not acting normal, even under the influence of drugs, on the day of the murder. Patsy Hooper testified about the close bond she shared with Petitioner, whom she said was the baby of the family and loved by all. She described the struggles he and his wife endured trying to raise four children and how Petitioner visited her to confess the crime and wait to be arrested after she asked their father to call the police. She begged the court to spare his life, noting that her brother was willing to take responsibility for what he had done while on drugs and that his children would suffer if he was sentenced to death

Petitioner's mother stated that she had been a single mother, who worked hard as a waitress to make enough money to feed and house her family. She said her son and his wife had been going to church and were doing well until drugs took over Petitioner's life. She acknowledged the wrongfulness of Petitioner's conduct, but asked that his life be spared for the sake of his children. Petitioner's brother told the court that despite not being a close family, he loved his brother and hoped his life would be spared. He said that Petitioner was not a monster, that drugs led Petitioner to commit such a horrific crime, and that life imprisonment would be sufficient punishment because Petitioner was tormented daily by the knowledge of what he did to the victim and her family. He further said that he lived in the same room with Petitioner from age five to 15 and that Petitioner did not have a violent side despite their hard life.

Petitioner concluded the presentence hearing with a lengthy statement. He began with an apology to the victim's family for his "really terrible" and "awful" acts. "[A]s I have said many times before to the media and also to the Court, that what I have done deserves the death penalty but I ask for mercy from the Court to spare my life and give me a chance to prove myself as a human being, not as a monster that people make me out to be." Petitioner acknowledged essentially asking for the death penalty at one point in the process but realized after speaking with a jail psychiatrist that it would be better for his wife and children   if his life was spared. Next, Petitioner addressed the victim's husband directly and again apologized for the nightmare he created. Petitioner said he had been praying for the Calabrese family and that he pled guilty to spare them additional pain. Petitioner then addressed his own family, saying he did not "blame no one or nothing in my past to lead to what I had done." He remarked that everyone knew he had problems with drugs and wished the family "could have taken some actions to get me the help I needed." However, he also acknowledged he "would have refused it because drugs meant the world" to him. Petitioner apologized for the pain he caused his family, emphasized his love for them, and asked them to go along with his desire to donate his organs should he be sentenced to death. Finally, Petitioner addressed his wife, stating that he probably would have hurt her had she not gone along with his attack on the victim, that he was to blame for letting drugs take over his life, and that he loved her deeply. In conclusion, Petitioner told the judge he was a new person now that he was off of drugs and asked that his life be spared for the sake of his loved ones.

Prior to sentencing, a mitigation specialist employed by the defense provided a notebook of materials to the judge. These included a letter reporting Petitioner's social history, numerous photographs, school records, and articles about crack cocaine and marijuana. The report provided details of Petitioner's genetic background, developmental years, and criminal background. It stated that between the ages of six and ten, Petitioner was exposed to weekly domestic abuse, fueled by his mother's and stepfather's alcohol abuse. It further stated that at age 14 Petitioner was sent to a juvenile corrections facility for breaking into a school while on probation and that testing there found him to be functioning in the borderline IQ range. Available school records indicated that Petitioner failed classes and quit school shortly after ninth grade. The report described Petitioner's abusive relationship with his wife and their drug addiction, asserting that they attempted to quit and sought help from family members and their church but relapsed shortly before the offense. According to the mitigation specialist, at the time of the murder, Petitioner and his wife had been on a four-day crack cocaine binge. In conclusion, the report asked the court to sentence Petitioner to life without the possibility of parole based on his genetics, childhood environment, cooperation with authorities, genuine remorse, and the influence of drugs during the offense.

In a presentencing memorandum, defense counsel refuted application of the State's alleged aggravating factors and urged the trial court to find that the proffered mitigation outweighed any aggravation. With regard to statutory mitigating factors, counsel argued that Petitioner's capacity to appreciate the wrongfulness of his conduct or to conform his conduct to the requirements of law was significantly impaired by the abuse of alcohol and crack cocaine. *See A.R.S. § 13-703(G)(1).* Counsel also argued that Petitioner's 31 years of age was a mitigating factor under *§ 13-703(G)(5)* because he lacked intelligence, as indicated by his poor academic history and the "lack of planning" and "unsophisticated approach" to the crime. (ROA doc. 97 at 15.) In the event the court did not find the existence of significant impairment and age under *(G)(1)* and *(G)(5)*, counsel asked the court to nonetheless find them to be non-statutory mitigating factors.

Defense counsel also urged numerous other non-statutory mitigating factors, asserting that Petitioner had a difficult childhood, grew up in a dysfunctional family, and witnessed significant abuse during his formative years. Counsel noted Petitioner's low intelligence and lack of education. Counsel argued that Petitioner did not have a violent character or history and would not likely be a future danger, especially in the controlled setting of a prison; that Petitioner's pleading guilty and accepting responsibility demonstrated that he had potential for rehabilitation; and that as a result of Petitioner's reflection on his actions he was committed to changing his behavior for the better. Counsel emphasized that Petitioner's family loved and supported him, despite what he had done, and that Petitioner's children in particular would be devastated if he were sentenced to death. Counsel also noted that the victim's husband had not requested the death penalty and that her ten-year-old daughter expressly asked that Petitioner not be sentenced to death

Finally, counsel addressed Petitioner's remorse, observing that Petitioner "has accepted full responsibility for his conduct and expressed deep and genuine remorse for his actions almost from the beginning of this litigation." Counsel continued:

> This was never a part of any strategy to seek leniency from this Court. As counsel told the Court at the time of the change of plea in September of 1998, John Sansing told his lawyers at their second visit, just a few days after his arrest, that "There isn't going to be a trial . . . I am responsible for what I have done . . . I'm not going to put the victim's family or my children through a trial."

>From that day forward, John Sansing expressed a desire to public [sic] apologize to the victim's family and plead guilty to what he had done. It was counsel undersigned who delayed the process until September of 1998, so that they could investigate the case and properly advise the defendant of his options. John Sansing on numerous occasions expressed his frustration with his counsel about the delay in going to court and pleading guilty.

Counsel undersigned has had numerous conversations   with John Sansing since February of 1998. We believe that his remorse and acceptance of responsibility are complete and absolutely genuine. He has spoken with deep regret about the pain and suffering that he has caused the Calabrese family and the trauma that he has caused to his own children.

In support, counsel appended to their memorandum the transcript from a November 1998 sentencing status conference during which Petitioner apologized for his actions, explained why he pled guilty, minimized his wife's involvement, and stated that he was willing to accept the death penalty. Counsel concluded by noting that Petitioner's level of remorse and acceptance of responsibility were, in their experience, unique for this type of case and asked that these factors be given substantial mitigating weight.

Prior to sentencing Petitioner sent two letters to the trial judge. In the first, Petitioner requested an opportunity to speak with his wife about their children and to physically say goodbye to her and other family members. He also noted his willingness to accept the death penalty if the court believed that to be the appropriate punishment.   In the second, Petitioner requested that his sentencing be postponed a few days while he figured out how to donate his organs.

A presentence report (PSR) was also prepared by the court's probation department. On the advice of counsel, Petitioner declined to discuss his background, substance abuse issues, or the offense, and the PSR writer noted that defense counsel would be providing that information directly to the court. The PSR did include a statement from Petitioner's sister, Patsy Hooper, who opined that drugs influenced Petitioner's actions and that he was remorseful. In addition, the victim's husband stated that he would agree with any sentence the judge chose to hand down.

Sentencing took place on September 30, 1999. Prior to imposition of sentence, Petitioner made another statement, again apologizing, expressing remorse, and asking that his organs be donated if sentenced to death. The court indicated that it had considered the evidence presented at the aggravation/mitigation hearing, the parties' written memoranda, and the written mitigation materials proffered by the defense. The court also indicated that it had not considered   any information contained in the PSR or any victim impact statements in determining the existence or nonexistence of aggravating factors, but did consider the PSR to determine the existence of mitigating circumstances.

Regarding aggravation, the trial court rejected the State's argument that Petitioner's contemporaneous convictions for kidnapping, sexual assault, and robbery of the victim constituted a prior "serious offense" for purposes of *A.R.S. § 13-703(F)(2)*. However, the court agreed with the State that the evidence established beyond a reasonable doubt that Petitioner committed the offense for pecuniary gain under *§ 13-703(F)(5)* and that the murder was committed in an "especially heinous, cruel, or depraved" manner under *§ 13-703(F)(6)*. For the latter, the court found both *(F)(6)* prongs--that the killing was cruel as well as heinous and depraved.

In finding that the murder was especially cruel, the court first determined that the victim "suffered unimaginable mental anguish during the approximately one hour or more that she was held hostage prior to her death." Citing the testimony of Kara Sansing, as well as the Sansing children's statements to   the police and Dr. Ainley, the court found that the victim had prayed to God and pleaded with them to call 911. The court further noted that both Petitioner, in an interview with a newspaper reporter, and his wife stated that the victim had regained consciousness before Petitioner raped her. This also established "beyond a reasonable doubt that Trudy Calabrese suffered extraordinary mental anguish, including uncertainty as to her ultimate fate."

Second, the court found cruelty based on its determination that the victim consciously suffered severe physical pain prior to her death and that the defendant knew or should have known she would suffer. In support, the court referenced ligature wounds and bruises on the victim's wrists and ankles, defensive wounds to her hands, trauma to her face, and "two deep blows to the back her head, which caused bruising of the brain and hemorrhaging." Although the court agreed the victim likely passed out from the head blows, it found that she regained consciousness before the rape and was then stabbed three times in the abdomen with a rusty knife. Citing the medical examiner's testimony, the court found that it would have taken several minutes to die from the loss of blood caused by the stab wounds. Finally, the court referenced Petitioner's own statement to a reporter that he killed the victim to end her suffering as proof she was consciously suffering severe physical pain.

In finding that the murder was committed in an especially heinous or depraved manner, the court determined that Petitioner inflicted gratuitous violence, that the victim was helpless, and that the killing was senseless. *See State v. Gretzler, 135 Ariz. 42, 659 P.2d 1 (1983)* (identifying factors to be considered in determining whether a killing is heinous or depraved). In finding gratuitous violence, the court stated that Petitioner hit the victim "so hard with the club that it broke in two pieces. He hogtied her ankles and wrists and brutally sexually assaulted her. Finally, he stabbed her, not once but three times, even grinding the rusty butcher knife into her as witnessed by Kara Sansing." As to the other factors, the court stated that the victim "was rendered utterly and completely helpless by the defendant's surprise attack" and that the killing was senseless because it "was completely unnecessary in order for the defendant to accomplish his goal of robbing Trudy."

Turning to mitigation, the court found it likely that Petitioner was impaired or affected by his crack cocaine usage at the time of the murder. However, it did not find that this established by a preponderance of the evidence that Petitioner's capacity to appreciate the wrongfulness of his conduct or to conform his conduct to the requirements of the law was *significantly* impaired, pursuant to A.R.S. § 13-703(G)(1). In making this determination, the court noted that Petitioner "devised and carried out a plan to lure a Good Samaritan to his home and then rob her," consciously sought to hide her truck, and concealed her body to avoid detection. The court also rejected the *(G)(5)* age factor, finding that Petitioner was a 31-year-old married father of four who had been living an adult lifestyle for many years.

With regard to non-statutory mitigating factors, the court again declined to find that Petitioner had established age as a mitigator and ruled that the victim's daughter's recommendation of leniency was not a mitigating circumstance. The court also found that Petitioner had failed to prove by a preponderance of the evidence that he had changed his life, would not be a future danger, or had potential for rehabilitation.

In support of mitigation, the court determined that although Petitioner did not establish significant impairment under *(G)(1)*, Petitioner's capacity to conform his conduct to the law's requirements was somewhat impaired by his use of crack cocaine. The court also found that Petitioner had proven by a preponderance of the evidence that he had a difficult childhood and family background. In support, the court noted that Petitioner's parents were divorced shortly after his birth, he had virtually no relationship with his father, his early developmental years were chaotic, his mother married three more times, and when he was six to ten years of age, his mother and stepfather abused alcohol and he was exposed to weekly episodes of domestic abuse by his stepfather upon his mother. (*Id.* at 20-21.) Although the court found the existence of a difficult childhood as a mitigating factor, it determined this circumstance was not entitled to significant mitigating weight due to the lack of a causal link between Petitioner's background and the crime.

The court further found as mitigating that Petitioner had accepted responsibility for his actions, was genuinely remorseful, and entered a guilty plea to avoid putting the victim's family and his children through a trial. In addition, the court found that Petitioner presented sufficient evidence to establish a lack of education, but determined this had only minimal mitigating weight. Finally, the court found that Petitioner established by a preponderance of the evidence that he had the love and support of his family but assigned it only minimal weight because it did not prevent Petitioner from committing the crime or victimizing his own children.

In determining that the proven mitigation did not outweigh the aggravation, the court considered the mitigating circumstances both individually and cumulatively. It further found that even considering all of the proposed mitigating factors, they would be insufficient to call for leniency "when balanced against the especially cruel manner in which defendant murdered Trudy Calabrese." The court explained:

The infliction of such grotesque, emotional and physical pain to a woman who, with all the hate, violence and lack of compassion we see, stood out like a shining light, as a true Samaritan, is shockingly evil. Throughout her ordeal, enveloped in defendant's drugged out and twisted plan of greed and violence, Trudy Calabrese kept her faith in God to the end.

The surprise attack on this good woman, followed by being beaten with a club defendant eventually broke in two on her head, then brutally stripped of her dignity as she was raped, and finally being stabbed three times, all together resulted in a terror-filled and horrible murder.

On appeal, the Arizona Supreme Court found insufficient evidence to establish that the murder was committed "to facilitate the taking of or ability to retain items of pecuniary value." *Sansing I, 200 Ariz. at 354, 26 P.3d at 1125.* However, on independent review after striking the pecuniary gain aggravating factor, it found that the murder was especially cruel and that the mitigation was insufficient to call for leniency.

Harmless Error Review

In conducting its harmless error review following *Ring,* the Arizona Supreme Court considered the (F)(6) aggravating factor found at sentencing and upheld on appeal--that the murder was committed in an especially heinous, cruel, or depraved manner. The court explained that the State needed to prove only one of the (F)(6) elements. *Sansing II, 206 Ariz. at 235, 77 P.3d at 33.*

The court first determined that cruelty was established in three independent ways: (1) the victim suffered mental anguish, as evidenced by the victim's defensive wounds, pleas for help, and attempts to resist the attack; (2) the victim suffered both mental and physical suffering when she was raped while her arms and legs were bound; and (3) the victim endured physical pain, as demonstrated by the multiple injuries to her head and abdomen, none of which caused immediate death. *Id. at 235-36, 77 P.3d at 33-34.* The court rejected Petitioner's argument that the evidence was inconclusive as to whether the victim was conscious during all portions of the attack, citing Petitioner's own admissions, including to a reporter, as well as his wife's testimony. *Id. at 237, 77 P.3d at 35.* The court concluded beyond a reasonable doubt that any reasonable jury would have found that the murder was committed in an especially cruel manner, and it was thus harmless error for the trial court to have determined the existence of this aggravating factor.

The court then determined that heinousness and depravity were established by "[o]verwhelming and uncontroverted evidence" that Petitioner inflicted gratuitous violence upon a helpless victim. *Id.* It concluded that the "rape, facial wounds, neck ligatures, gagging, blind-folding, and grinding of the knife constitute[d] violence beyond that necessary to kill," and that the victim, having been bound by both her wrists and ankles, which were then tied together, was helpless to defend herself. *Id. at 238, 77 P.3d at 36.* The court found beyond a reasonable doubt that any reasonable jury would have concluded that Petitioner inflicted gratuitous violence upon a helpless victim and that consequently the murder was especially heinous.

Next, the court considered whether the mitigating evidence was sufficiently substantial to call for leniency. The court first assessed the evidence concerning *A.R.S. § 13-703(G)(1),* which provides a mitigating circumstance where "[t]he defendant's capacity to appreciate the wrongfulness of his conduct or to conform his conduct to the requirements of law was significantly impaired, but not so impaired as to constitute a defense to prosecution." *Id. at 239, 77 P.3d at 37.* Like the trial court, the supreme court found that this factor had not been proved:

No reasonable jury would have concluded that Sansing met his burden to establish that his ability to control his behavior or his capacity to appreciate the wrongfulness of his conduct was significantly impaired. Sansing presented no expert testimony to support his assertion that his use of cocaine impaired either his capacity to control his conduct or his capacity to appreciate the wrongfulness of his actions. He therefore failed entirely to show any causal nexus between his alleged drug use and impairment.

Sansing also presented only minimal testimony about his drug use on the day of the murder. Kara testified that Sansing telephoned her while she was work at approximately 1:30 p.m. During this conversation, Sansing informed her that he had purchased some crack cocaine. He told her that he had smoked some of the crack but was saving the rest for her. Kara testified that she could tell he had ingested the crack from the sound of his voice. She testified that when she returned home from work several hours later, Sansing was not "acting normal." However, she also testified that Sansing's actions were thought out and that he was not acting as if he were in a trance.

That evidence is insufficient to establish, by a preponderance of the evidence, that Sansing's capacity to control his behavior was significantly impaired. First, Kara did not quantify how much crack Sansing used. Moreover, no reasonable jury would conclude that Kara's testimony that Sansing was not acting himself was sufficient to establish that his capacity was significantly impaired.

Furthermore, Sansing's deliberate actions refute his impairment claim and establish that the drug use did not overwhelm Sansing's ability to control his conduct. Kara testified that Sansing planned to rob the person who delivered the food. Additionally, Sansing contacted two different churches in his attempt to lure an unsuspecting victim to his home.

Sansing's impairment argument fails on yet another basis. Sansing admitted and stipulated to facts that leave no doubt that he attempted to avoid detection. After beating and hog-tying Trudy, Sansing left and moved her truck away from the apartment. When Pastor Becker called the Sansing home, inquiring about Trudy's whereabouts, Sansing gave him a false address and told him that Trudy never arrived. Additionally, Sansing's ten-year-old son told the police Sansing washed blood from the club that he used to strike Trudy. These steps, which can only be regarded as part of an attempt to avoid detection, negate any possibility that a reasonable jury would find that Sansing's capacity to appreciate the wrongfulness of his conduct was significantly impaired.

Id. at 239-40, 77 P.3d at 37-38 (citations omitted). The court further found beyond a reasonable doubt that any reasonable jury would have rejected Petitioner's age as a statutory mitigating circumstance.

The court then proceeded to examine the non-statutory mitigating circumstances found by the trial court. For the same reasons the court determined that the (G)(1) impairment factor would not have been found, the court reasoned that no reasonable jury could have accorded Petitioner's impairment more than minimal weight as a non-statutory mitigating factor. *Id. at 240-41, 77 P.3d at 38-39.* The court further concluded that although a jury "might have concluded that Sansing established a difficult, although not abusive, childhood and lack of education," it would have accorded these factors only minimal weight because Petitioner had failed to demonstrate any causal link between them and the crime. *Id. at 241, 77 P.3d at 39.* Next, the court assumed that "a reasonable jury would have accorded some weight to Sansing's family's love and support and to the fact that he accepted responsibility for his crime." *Id.* Lastly, the court determined that no reasonable jury could have given more than minimal weight to Petitioner's claim that he presents no future threat and that a jury could not have considered the victim's daughter's request that he be given a life sentence because such evidence is not proper mitigation.

The Arizona Supreme Court concluded its harmless error review as follows:

The evidence leaves no doubt that Sansing murdered Trudy Calabrese in an especially cruel, heinous, or depraved manner. The brutality of this murder clearly sets it apart from the norm of first degree murders. Collectively, the mitigating evidence is minimal at most. We conclude beyond a reasonable doubt that any reasonable jury would have concluded that the mitigating evidence was not sufficiently substantial to call for leniency. Accordingly, we hold the [*Ring*] violation constituted harmless error.

Analysis

Petitioner is entitled to relief on this aspect of Claim 1 only if the Arizona Supreme Court's ruling was "in conflict with the reasoning or the holdings of [Supreme Court] precedent" or if it "applied harmless-error review in an 'objectively unreasonable' manner." *Mitchell v. Esparza, 540 U.S. 12, 17, 18, 124 S. Ct. 7, 157 L. Ed. 2d 263 (2003)* (per curiam) (quoting *Lockyer v. Andrade, 538 U.S. 63, 75-77, 123 S. Ct. 1166, 155 L. Ed. 2d 144 (2003)); see also Fry v. Pliler, 551 U.S. 112, 119, 127 S. Ct. 2321, 168 L. Ed. 2d 16 (2007)* ("In *Mitchell v. Esparza*, we held that, when a state court determines that a constitutional violation is harmless, a federal court may not award habeas relief under § 2254 unless *the harmlessness determination itself* was unreasonable."). He is not entitled to relief if the state court "simply erred" in concluding that the *Ring* error was harmless. *Esparza, 540 U.S. at 18.*

Petitioner first argues that the Arizona Supreme Court's determination that the victim was conscious, upon which he asserts its finding of cruelty rests, was based upon an unreasonable determination of the facts. (Doc. 35 at 42-44.) He contends that the evidence was inconclusive in light of the medical examiner's doubt about the victim regaining consciousness after the head injuries, the alleged unreliability of Kara Sansing's statements, and questions concerning the voluntariness of the written factual basis supporting Petitioner's plea. (*Id.*) However, the latter two allegations are based on evidence that was not part of the record on appeal to the Arizona Supreme Court. Under AEDPA, this Court must consider whether the state court's decision "was based on an unreasonable determination of facts *in light of the evidence presented in the State court proceeding.*" 28 U.S.C. § 2254(d)(2) (emphasis added); see also Pinholster, 131 S. Ct. at 1398-99 (limiting review under § 2254(d)(1) "to the record that was before the state court that adjudicated the claim on the merits").

Petitioner alleges that Kara Sansing's statement to police regarding an exchange between Petitioner and the victim during the rape is "completely unbelievable." He acknowledges, however, that evidence of the actual exchange was not admitted during the sentencing proceeding. During her testimony, Kara initially denied hearing the victim speak and was then impeached with her statement to police concerning the fact the victim had spoken. However, in doing so, the prosecutor directed her not to repeat the content of the conversation she overheard. That this evidence was not before the state court is confirmed by Petitioner's motion for evidentiary development, in which he seeks to expand the record to include Kara Sansing's statement to police, arguing it is relevant to demonstrate the unreliability of her testimony regarding consciousness. Similarly, Petitioner's allegation concerning involuntariness of the factual basis of his plea was not developed until his state PCR proceedings and thus was not before the Arizona Supreme Court when it conducted its harmless error review. Accordingly, the Court does not consider either of these allegations in determining under AEDPA the reasonableness of the state court's ruling.

Looking at the record that was before the state court, this Court cannot say that its finding of fact as to consciousness was objectively unreasonable. Petitioner admitted in the factual basis for the plea that the victim was conscious when he raped her and also stipulated that he told a reporter the victim had regained consciousness when he returned from moving her truck. Petitioner's wife also testified that she heard the victim speak during the rape, and Petitioner told the reporter that he decided to kill the victim because she was suffering. The Arizona Supreme Court considered the medical examiner's speculation about the victim's consciousness but found the direct evidence uncontroverted. This was not an unreasonable determination of fact.

Moreover, Arizona law provides that a victim need not be conscious for "each and every wound" inflicted for cruelty to apply. *Sansing, 206 Ariz. at 235, 77 P.3d at 33* (citation omitted). There is no dispute that Trudy Calabrese was conscious when she was grabbed from behind, thrown to the ground, and hogtied. She sustained numerous defensive wounds and other injuries during her struggle, pleaded for help, and prayed to God. The Arizona Supreme Court's finding of cruelty based on the victim's mental anguish as to her fate while she struggled with her attackers was not objectively unreasonable. This alone was sufficient under state law to sustain the cruelty factor, regardless of whether the victim was conscious during the rape and stabbing.

Petitioner further contends that the court's cruelty analysis is unreasonable when compared with its decisions in other *Ring*-remand cases. However, to the extent that his argument is based on a comparison with the analyses undertaken in other cases, Petitioner's critique of the Arizona Supreme Court's cruelty finding in his case is unavailing. The fact that the court did not find cruelty beyond a reasonable doubt in other cases, each of which involved distinct facts and circumstances, does not demonstrate that the same court's ruling in Petitioner's case was objectively unreasonable.

Petitioner next argues that the Arizona Supreme Court unreasonably found that the murder was especially heinous. He asserts that the evidence was insufficient to establish beyond a reasonable doubt that Petitioner inflicted gratuitous violence because "it was impossible to determine which of the three stab wounds were fatal." However, the state court's determination was not based solely on the stab wounds. Rather, it cited the numerous injuries sustained by the victim, including to her forehead, left orbital region, and mouth, as well as the rape, neck ligatures, gagging, blindfolding, and grinding of the knife as constituting violence beyond that   necessary to kill. *Sansing, 206 Ariz. at 238, 77 P.3d at 36.* The state court's finding as to gratuitous violence was not based on an unreasonable determination of the facts in light of the evidence.

Lastly, Petitioner criticizes the court's assessment of the mitigating evidence. This criticism is unwarranted. The Supreme Court in *Ring* held only that a jury must determine the aggravating factors in a capital case that render a person eligible for the death penalty; it did not require jury determination of the ultimate sentence. Therefore, the Arizona Supreme Court's review of *Ring* error was complete when it determined beyond a reasonable doubt that no rational jury would have found that the (F)(6) aggravating factor had not been proved. *Cf. Butler v. Curry, 528 F.3d 624, 648-49 (9th Cir. 2008)* (reviewing *Apprendi* violation for harmless error by asking whether jury would have found aggravating factor rendering defendant eligible for increased sentence). To the extent the Arizona Supreme Court chose to include review of mitigation as part of its harmless error analysis, it did so as a matter of state law. Furthermore, the court's review of the mitigating evidence, while not required by   *Ring*, was thorough, and its assessment of the evidence was not objectively unreasonable. Petitioner's argument that the court improperly imposed a causal nexus on its consideration of the mitigating evidence is discussed as part of Claim 7 in Section IV.A below.

C. Conclusion

The Arizona Supreme Court did not unreasonably apply United States Supreme Court precedent when it determined that harmless error was the appropriate standard of review for *Ring* error. In addition, the state court's harmless error analysis in this case neither conflicted with controlling Supreme Court law nor was applied in an objectively unreasonable manner. Because Petitioner is precluded from relief by § 2254(d), the Court declines to expand the record to include new evidence allegedly refuting the state court's finding as to the consciousness of the victim when she was sexually assaulted and stabbed.

II. VOLUNTARINESS OF PLEA

In Claim 8, Petitioner argues that his guilty plea was not knowing, intelligent, or voluntary because the written factual basis established an aggravating factor and he did not waive his privilege against self-incrimination for the penalty phase. He asserts that he was unaware his admission   concerning the victim's consciousness would be used to establish cruelty under *A.R.S. § 13-703(F)(6)* and that the trial court failed to explain the consequences this admission would have at sentencing.

Relevant Facts

Petitioner's written plea agreement included a summary of the rights waived by pleading guilty, including the privilege against self-incrimination. The signed plea agreement did not give Petitioner any benefits in terms of sentencing, but did provide that the State would dismiss charges filed against Petitioner in a separate action. Before accepting Petitioner's plea, the court first determined that Petitioner was mentally competent. The court then engaged Petitioner in a personal colloquy that included ascertaining whether Petitioner had read and understood the plea agreement, including the paragraph setting forth the constitutional rights he was giving up by pleading guilty. Although not apparent on the face of the agreement, Respondents assert that this separate matter involved four counts of child abuse.

After Petitioner entered his guilty plea, the court read the factual basis signed by Petitioner and counsel, asking if the facts were true and if the statement accurately recounted the offense; Petitioner replied affirmatively to both inquiries. The prosecutor then sought to orally add several additional facts, including that the victim suffered severe blows to the head, that semen found inside the victim was determined to contain DNA matching Petitioner, and that a different charitable organization had delivered a food box to Petitioner's home the day before the offense. Petitioner disputed only the latter assertion that he had received an earlier food box.

In his PCR petition, Petitioner argued that he would not have pled guilty had he understood the sentencing consequences of the factual admissions accompanying the plea. In support, he appended an affidavit attesting that at the time of the plea he was unaware that (1) the State would have to prove aggravating factors to render him eligible for the death penalty; (2) the victim's consciousness would be relevant to a finding of cruelty; and (3) the admission regarding consciousness was not a necessary component of the guilty plea. Petitioner also denied   that the victim was in fact conscious after he moved her truck and claimed that he lied about this fact because he feared being attacked by other inmates for having sexually assaulted the victim and thought "it would be better if she was conscious during my assault."

The state PCR court denied relief without explanation, stating that the claim failed to present "a material issue of fact or law." The Arizona Supreme Court summarily denied review.

Analysis

When a state court does not explain its reasons for denying relief, a reviewing habeas court must determine what arguments or theories could have supported the state court's decision and "then it must ask whether it is possible fairminded jurists could disagree that those arguments or theories are inconsistent with the holding in a prior decision" of the Supreme Court. *Harrington v. Richter, 131 S. Ct. 770, 786, 178 L. Ed. 2d 624 (2011)*. The burden is on Petitioner to show "there was no reasonable basis for the state court to deny relief." *Id. at 784*.

Due process requires that a defendant's guilty plea be voluntary and intelligent. *Boykin v. Alabama, 395 U.S. 238, 242, 89 S. Ct. 1709, 23 L. Ed. 2d 274 (1969)*. Because a guilty plea waives the rights against self-incrimination, to trial by jury, and to confront one's accusers, its acceptance requires that the accused "has a full understanding of what the plea connotes and of its consequence." *Id. at 244*. "Among other circumstances, a plea of guilty can be voluntary only if it is 'entered by one fully aware of the *direct* consequences' of his plea." *Carter v. McCarthy, 806 F.2d 1373, 1375 (9th Cir. 1986)* (quoting *Brady v. United States, 397 U.S. 742, 755, 90 S. Ct. 1463, 25 L. Ed. 2d 747 (1970)*) (emphasis in original). This includes being advised of the "range of allowable punishment" that will result from the plea. *U.S. ex rel. Pebworth v. Conte, 489 F.2d 266, 268 (9th Cir. 1974)*.

The Ninth Circuit has held that "although a defendant is entitled to be informed of the direct consequences of the plea, the court need not advise him of all the possible collateral consequences." *Torrey v. Estelle, 842 F.2d 234, 235 (9th Cir. 1988)* (internal quotation omitted). "The distinction between a direct and collateral consequence of a plea turns on whether the result represents a definite, immediate and largely automatic effect on the range of the defendant's punishment." *Id. at 236* (internal quotation omitted). Under this standard, direct   consequences include a mandatory parole term, ineligibility for parole, and the maximum punishment provided by law. IA consequence is generally "collateral" if it does not derive automatically as a result of the plea, but rather results from some discretionary decisionmaking proceeding, such as whether a defendant's sentences may run consecutively or the possibility of parole revocation.

Petitioner argues that the failure to inform him of the sentencing-related consequences attendant to his admission in the plea's factual basis renders the plea involuntary. However, the trial court's aggravation findings were not a *direct* consequence of the plea, but rather the result of a separate, discretionary proceeding during which Petitioner retained all his constitutional rights and the burden was on the prosecution to establish aggravating factors beyond a reasonable doubt. Petitioner did not admit the existence of the (F)(6) aggravating factor in his plea, and the trial court was under no obligation to find this factor proven beyond a reasonable doubt. That Petitioner admitted facts from which the judge ultimately found the (F)(6) factor is not the same as stipulating to the existence   of the factor. *Cf. Adams v. Peterson, 968 F.2d 835, 839 (9th Cir. 1992)* (en banc) ("A stipulation to facts from which a judge or jury may *infer* guilt is simply not the same as a stipulation *to* guilt, or a guilty plea."). Because Petitioner's plea had only collateral consequences on the aggravation phase of sentencing, no constitutional violation arose out of the court's failure to advise Petitioner of the possibility he would be found eligible for the death penalty as a result of the admissions contained in the plea's factual basis. Petitioner has failed to show that there was no reasonable basis for the state court to deny relief on this claim.

III. INEFFECTIVE ASSISTANCE OF COUNSEL

Petitioner contends that he was denied his *Sixth Amendment* right to the effective assistance of counsel when counsel failed to investigate and present mitigating evidence (Claim 2), investigate and rebut the (F)(6) "heinous, cruel, or depraved" aggravating factor (Claim 3), and properly advise him about the consequences of his plea, stipulated factual basis, and sentencing stipulation (Claim 4). Petitioner also asserts cumulative prejudice from counsel's alleged deficient performance (Claim 5).

A. Failure to Investigate and Present Mitigating Evidence

Petitioner alleges that sentencing counsel failed to competently investigate and present substantial mitigating evidence. He further alleges that counsel failed to select competent mental health and substance abuse experts and provide them with his social history. Petitioner argues that competent experts would have explained how mental disorders and substance abuse played a role in the commission of the offense and, consequently, would have established the (G)(1) substantial impairment mitigating factor. (Doc. 35 at 53.) Respondents concede exhaustion except to the extent Petitioner alleges that counsel was ineffective for failing to retain a neuropsychologist. It appears to this Court from its review of the PCR record, including the evidence and arguments presented during the state court evidentiary hearing, that the entirety of Claim 2 was exhausted.

Relevant Facts

Petitioner was represented at sentencing by Maricopa County Deputy Public Defenders Emmet Ronan and Sylvina Cotto. During PCR proceedings, Petitioner alleged that counsel provided constitutionally ineffective representation by failing to investigate and present substantial mitigating evidence and failing to provide Petitioner's social history to competent mental health and substance abuse experts. The PCR court found this to be a colorable claim and held a four-day evidentiary hearing in January 2010.

At the hearing, Petitioner called as witnesses two of his siblings, four experts, trial counsel Ronan, and mitigation specialist Pamela Davis. The State presented testimony from a psychologist. In addition, the parties stipulated to admission of deposition transcripts, in lieu of live testimony, from co-counsel Cotto and a mental health expert who evaluated Petitioner before sentencing. The parties also agreed to the admission of numerous exhibits, including the 1989 American Bar Association Guidelines for the Appointment and Performance of Counsel in Death Penalty Cases (ABA Guidelines), pre-sentencing psychological reports, post-conviction expert reports, and a 1986 psychological evaluation.

Evidence Regarding Counsel's Investigation

Mitigation specialist Davis testified that she began working as a non-capital mitigation specialist for the Maricopa County Public Defender in 1991, after having worked more than   five years in adult probation departments. Before being recruited by Ronan to assist in Petitioner's case, she had worked on only one capital case. Davis recalled meeting frequently with Petitioner at the jail and traveling to Alabama, Nevada, and Utah to interview family members and obtain records. Davis said she did not meet with any of the experts retained by counsel to evaluate Petitioner and did not know whether they were given any of the background information she had compiled. However, Davis also testified that at the time she began working on Petitioner's case in 1998, mitigation specialists were not commonly used in capital cases and she believed her role was to compile a written social history for presentation to the court, not to recommend experts to counsel. Trial counsel Ronan also testified that in 1999 the concept of a capital mitigation specialist was new in his public defender office.

Petitioner's brother, Allen Sansing, and one of his sisters, Susan Mitchell, testified that they recalled meeting jointly with Davis in Alabama prior to Petitioner's sentencing. Allen told Davis about his mother's alcohol abuse, methods of discipline, husbands, and problems the children encountered with their stepfathers. Likewise, Susan told Davis everything she believed was important about their upbringing, including Petitioner's drug use and their mother's neglect and beatings.

In addition to investigating Petitioner's social history, trial counsel consulted three mental health experts. Dr. Sara Hill, a clinical psychologist, was asked to determine Petitioner's competency to stand trial or plead guilty. In her report, Dr. Hill noted that Petitioner said he had a long history of using marijuana, was on probation for a drug charge prior to the murder, and went from smoking marijuana to smoking crack cocaine, which he was doing "all day long at the time of his arrest." She found Petitioner to be "quite conversant in discussing legal matters" and "unequivocally competent to stand trial." She further found that Petitioner had a history of antisocial behaviors, but required more background information to make a diagnosis of antisocial personality disorder.

Dr. Katherine Menendez, a psychologist, evaluated Petitioner "for the purpose of establishing learning capacity and the presence of a learning disorder." In the background section of her report, Dr. Menendez described Petitioner as saying that his mother had "treated him well," that he recalled only one incident of harsh physical discipline from his first stepfather, that he had a "normal" early family life, and that he had been an "average" student. Petitioner reported that he began smoking crack cocaine at age 28 and became "very paranoid, violent and hypersexual." Dr. Menendez determined that Petitioner had a full scale IQ of 80, which is below average, but that he did not appear to have a "pronounced, significant learning disorder." She also diagnosed Petitioner with cocaine abuse in remission and an antisocial personality disorder.

Lastly, defense counsel enlisted the assistance of Dr. Susan Parrish, a psychologist specializing in neuropsychological testing and post-traumatic stress disorder. Dr. Parrish retained notes from her presentence interview with Petitioner, but could not recall whether she performed any tests, made a diagnosis, or prepared a report. However, she believed she was asked to meet with Petitioner to determine whether he displayed any obvious psychological difficulties and that "nothing jumped out at me that he had any difficulties" such as an "obvious neuropsychological symptom" that would have justified more testing or that needed to be pursued.

Trial counsel Ronan had few specific recollections of his conversations with the experts and did not know whether he had provided Petitioner's social history to Dr. Hill or school records to Dr. Menendez. He testified that it was his usual custom and practice to provide background information to consulting experts, but acknowledged statements in Dr. Menendez's report about Petitioner's upbringing, such as being an average student and getting along well with his mother, that contradicted information compiled by Davis. Although he had no recall of speaking with Dr. Menendez, Ronan testified that he did not consider a diagnosis of antisocial personality disorder to be mitigating and "[b]ased on the report as I have now seen it, I would not see any reason to call her." (He also acknowledged that evidence concerning an antisocial personality disorder generally opens the door for prosecutors to proffer evidence of bad acts consistent with that diagnosis. Regarding Dr. Parrish, Ronan believed it likely she found nothing helpful after meeting with Petitioner because otherwise he would have had her prepare a report and testify at the sentencing hearing. He also would have consulted with others types of experts if Dr. Parrish had made such a recommendation.

Regarding Petitioner's drug use, Ronan believed the information that Petitioner had purchased $750 of crack cocaine in the four days prior to the offense was presented to the sentencing judge in Davis's mitigation report. Ronan did not know whether Dr. Parrish had relayed to counsel that Petitioner told her he had spent $2,000 during the same time period, as reflected in her interview notes. In response to a question as to why he did not enlist and present testimony from experts in child development and pharmacology, Ronan said he had no recollection of why those types of experts were not utilized:

> [M]y best guess is that I felt that Judge Reinstein, with his background and experience would understand the information that was going to be presented in Pam Davis's letter, that with his background and experience he understood the nexus between substance abuse and the commission of crimes, substance abuse and dysfunctional childhood, and those types of things, and that it was simply going to be a question of whether he found that significant enough as a mitigating factor to outweigh the aggravate [sic] factors.

In hindsight, he would not have made the same decisions on how mitigation evidence was presented to the sentencing judge.

In her deposition, co-counsel Cotto said that her representation was limited to drafting the aggravation section of the presentencing memorandum and that Ronan was teaching her how to handle a capital case. She recalled that Ronan was "very clear" that the mitigation investigation "needed to begin from the very onset." Cotto had no recollection of meeting with experts but, after reviewing Dr. Menendez's report, did not believe her diagnosis of antisocial personality disorder was mitigating. She recalled meeting with Ronan to "discuss things as they developed and trying to figure out what could be useful or not" and also recalled discussing Dr. Parrish, but had no specific recollection of what was said.

Petitioner's *Strickland* expert, Vicki Liles, testified that counsel's failure to provide experts with background information, retain a substance abuse expert, and engage a psychologist to "pull all [the background information] together" fell below the standard of care for a capital defense attorney at the time of Petitioner's sentencing. She further opined that antisocial personality disorder is mitigating and that counsel was ineffective for failing to present that diagnosis at sentencing. In addition, Liles suggested that counsel was ineffective for failing, in light of Petitioner's substance abuse, to obtain a neuropsychological examination at the start of the case because a brain can "heal and can repair itself."

At the time of Petitioner's offense, Liles was employed by the Maricopa County Public Defender but had no involvement in Petitioner's case because she had a "more generalized caseload at that time." She recalled that   sometime in 1998 or 1999, her office formed a major felony unit comprised of three attorneys, including Ronan. When Petitioner was sentenced in 1999, Liles had tried only one capital case through sentencing and that was as second chair in an effort to become qualified to serve as lead counsel in a capital case. In a declaration proffered to the PCR court, Liles opined that "it was standard practice to use the services of a mitigation specialist in capital representation in 1998 and 1999" and that the "specialist would then locate and suggest the participation of necessary experts." However, at the PCR hearing, she acknowledged that under the 1989 ABA Guidelines in effect at the time a "mitigation specialist wasn't really required as part of the defense team."

Mitigation Evidence

Petitioner's brother Allen and sister Susan testified at the PCR hearing. Each described their mother as a self-centered woman, who showed no love or affection, who on occasion abandoned and regularly neglected their basic needs, and who routinely hit them with belts and sticks for perceived infractions. They also reported that   their mother drank heavily, had numerous failed marriages, and frequently fought with her husbands. One of their stepfathers liked to pick fights and beat up on Allen and Petitioner. Each saw Petitioner begin to use marijuana and inhalants when he was around 10 or 11 years of age. Allen left home at age 17, when Petitioner was about 11, and Susan left home and moved in with Allen when she was 14 and Petitioner was 13.

Petitioner also presented testimony from three new experts. Dr. Paul Miller, a developmental psychologist, interviewed Petitioner, Allen, and Petitioner's sister Patsy. Based on these interviews as well as Davis's mitigation report, Davis's notes, and Petitioner's school records, Miller prepared a 60-page developmental assessment report that examined the nature of the risk factors to which Petitioner was exposed as a child and the relationship of those factors to later negative outcomes, such as conduct disorders and drug abuse. In summary, Dr. Miller opined that various life stressors, including parental neglect, harsh discipline, exposure to domestic violence, maternal alcohol abuse, frequent changes in residences and maternal marital relationships, and extreme poverty led Petitioner to use drugs as a coping mechanism. Because he focused only on Petitioner's adolescent development, Dr. Miller had no opinion on the role Petitioner's risk factors played in the offense.

Dr. Edward French, a pharmacologist, testified regarding the physiological effects of cocaine. Although Petitioner did not tell him the amount of crack cocaine he consumed prior to the offense, Dr. French opined that Petitioner was in a cocaine-induced psychosis when he attacked and killed the victim. As support for this conclusion, Dr. French cited statements made by Petitioner that (1) his heart was racing so fast during the offense that he thought he would die (classic physiological effect of cocaine); (2) he believed the victim knew his intentions based on an innocuous gesture to his wife (evidence of paranoia); and (3) he had "no conscious there" during the attack (indicating a break in reality). In conclusion, Dr. French stated that drugs "hijack the brain," cause "pronounced behavioral and cognitive changes," take over the behavior of an individual, and diminish the ability "to process   information correctly." On cross-examination, Dr. French acknowledged that he was not qualified to diagnose mental disease or defects and that the information about the effects of cocaine included in the mitigation specialist's report to the sentencing judge was accurate.

Dr. Richard Lanyon, a forensic and clinical psychologist, also testified. On the basis of record review, interviews, and psychological testing, Dr. Lanyon prepared a lengthy report in which he concluded that Petitioner's profile "suggests the likelihood of a significant anxiety disorder, depression, and thought disorder" but "does not indicate antisocial characteristics or the likelihood of impulsive acting-out." He determined that Petitioner has a full scale IQ of 87, placing him in the low-average range of intelligence. He also found no suggestion of impaired functioning due to brain damage.

With regard to the offense, Dr. Lanyon opined it was highly probable that, as a result of a cocaine-induced delusional psychotic state as well as a paranoid personality disorder, Petitioner's capacity to appreciate   the wrongfulness of his conduct or to conform his conduct to the requirements of the law was significantly diminished. Similar to Dr. French, Dr. Lanyon based this opinion on the "serious and pivotal cognitive distortion" that the victim knew he was going to do something to her. According to Petitioner's account to Dr. Lanyon, he made a hand gesture to his wife signifying that the victim's purse was not in her truck, that there was "no way anyone could read that to mean anything," but nonetheless he "became convinced that the [victim] somehow knew what it was and was going to, therefore, turn him in."

> He has a delusion she knows exactly what he intends to do, and, in fact, these thoughts are in his mind and it suggests that he feels very guilty about them, then he becomes delusional that she knows exactly what's going on, it's in her mind, too, and he then finds himself in these unusual physiological reactions which signal, to me, are a likelihood of a cocaine induced psychosis, which a major aspect of that is delusions.

Dr. Lanyon opined that this paranoid delusion caused Petitioner to enter into a severely abnormal mental state,   as evidenced by Petitioner's statements that "[i]t was not me" and that he had no thoughts or feelings when he attacked her. Rather, there was "[c]omplete blackness. I stepped into a hole . . . everything's dark." Petitioner told Dr. Lanyon that he had no control over the initial attack and that his subsequent actions were done out of panic. In Dr. Lanyon's opinion, Petitioner remained in a psychotic state while taking deliberate actions not to get caught. Regarding antisocial personality disorder, Dr. Lanyon declined to make such a diagnosis, but acknowledged there were "enough symptoms or characteristics" to put him into that category. Finally, Dr. Lanyon concluded that Petitioner's cocaine use was a product of the extreme dysfunction in his childhood environment and thus "the effects of his childhood environment can also be considered to be a causal factor in significantly diminishing his capacity to appreciate the wrongfulness of his conduct or to conform his conduct to the requirements of law."

The State presented Dr. Michael Bayless in rebuttal. Dr. Bayless determined that Petitioner has a   full scale IQ of 88 and found no indication of neurological impairment. In his report, Dr. Bayless concluded that Petitioner has a personality disorder not otherwise specified, with antisocial and obsessive compulsive traits. He changed his diagnosis to an antisocial personality disorder after reviewing a 1986 psychological evaluation conducted as part of a diagnostic evaluation for the Utah Department of Corrections. In that report, clinical psychologist Dr. Donald Long diagnosed Petitioner, then 18 years old, with a conduct disorder and extreme emotional immaturity. He also derived an abstract IQ of 89.

Dr. Bayless's interview notes reveal that Petitioner relayed essentially the same story regarding the offense as he told to Drs. French and Lanyon, namely that he made a motion to his wife to indicate "there's nothing [in the victim's truck]," that the victim "saw and got spooked and said I've got to go," and that when she turned toward the door, "the darkness came over me, heart racing, and I grabbed her in bear hug." The notes also reported Petitioner as saying that he "crossed   line--blackness clearing--on probation, hit her with wooden pole." Dr. Bayless testified that when he asked Petitioner why he raped her, Petitioner smiled and gestured in a way that angered Dr. Bayless, who interpreted the gesture to mean "seeing a vaginal area would make me do such a thing." In relaying this impression, Dr. Bayless stated that the victim's dress had flown up. On cross-examination, Dr. Bayless acknowledged that the victim had not been wearing a dress and that his notes did not include this aspect of Petitioner's statement, but that he remembered it "precisely" and despite the inaccuracy concerning her clothing was "what [Petitioner] said to me."

Addressing antisocial personality disorders, Dr. Bayless testified that such a disorder would not render a person incapable of knowing right from wrong or from having the ability to control his or her conductRather, "it's choice issues"--such individuals know what's right, know what is acceptable, but choose not to act appropriately. He further testified that the "central feature of a substance induced psychotic disorder   are hallucinations and delusions that are due to the direct physiologic effects of [the] substance" and that in this case Petitioner "knew exactly what was going on. He was not seeing things. He was not hearing voices. He was not delusional." Dr. Bayless concluded that Petitioner was "fully aware of what he was doing" when he committed the offense and "knew it was wrong."

> He explained to me, he talked about it very clearly. He remembered the essence of what had taken place. He was very much focused. He was very much in reality when we talked about what happened on the day of the offense.
>
> Look, there is no indication that he was suffering from any psychosis. There is no indication that he did not know what he was doing. There is no indication that cocaine played a role in his behavior, his choices at the time. Was he high on cocaine? He had done some cocaine. But was he at a point where now he did not know what he was doing? No.
>
> His voluntary intoxication at that time was voluntary intoxication, but he was not at a level that he did not know what he was doing. Pure and simple. He knew why he moved the car. He knew why he put a blanket over her stomach when he   stabbed her. He knew what he was doing when he raped her. He said to me specifically: I'm going to make this look--I wanted to make this look like she was raped in a robbery. He said that to us specifically, that he thought that before he did it. I don't know what all the fight is about.

State Court Ruling

Following the hearing and submission of post-hearing memoranda, the state PCR court denied relief in a 15-page ruling..) After setting forth in detail the standard for relief under *Strickland v. Washington, 466 U.S. 668, 104 S. Ct. 2052, 80 L. Ed. 2d 674 (1984)*, the court addressed the credibility of the expert opinions. It found that much of "Dr. French's opinions were based on speculation about the quantity of cocaine that was used by the Defendant." It further found that Dr. Lanyon's opinions "were less than persuasive." Specifically the court wrote:

> Dr. Lanyon believed that Sansing's statement to him that everything went black and blank was a strong indication of psychosis. [Footnote 20: Sansing's trial attorney testified at the evidentiary hearing that he does not ever recall Sansing saying this to him. If Sansing had said this to him, he would have followed up on these statements.] However, Dr. Lanyon's opinions were contradicted by Dr. Michael Bayless (a psychologist called by the state) and several versions of the facts of the crime provided by Sansing in which he remembers many details after the alleged "going black" episode. Dr. Bayless opined that the Defendant suffered from a classic anti-social personality disorder, that Sansing was high on cocaine at the time of the crime, but that he knew what he was doing was wrong. Significantly, Sansing smiled as he described to Dr. Bayless the reason why he committed the rape: he saw Trudy Calabrese's vaginal area. Sansing also described that he placed a blanket over Trudy to stab her so as to avoid blood splatter. This court finds the testimony of Dr. Bayless to be the more credible and more persuasive.

Addressing *Strickland*'s performance prong, the PCR court noted that trial counsel had consulted with three different mental health experts, one of whom diagnosed Petitioner with an antisocial personality disorder and another who recalled no issues that required further testing. The court noted that although Ronan could not recall what information he supplied to Dr. Menendez, he did not doubt supplying her with any available records, as was his standard practice. The court further noted Ronan's belief that proffering evidence of an antisocial personality disorder as mitigation would have opened the door to the prosecution submitting evidence of Petitioner's other violent, antisocial acts. "This type of 'double-edged' mitigation evidence would be more detrimental than helpful, and making a strategic decision to avoid damaging a case for mitigation despite losing a slim advantage cannot be unreasonable." Regarding counsel's failure to utilize expert witnesses, the court credited Ronan's belief that the trial judge's background and experience would allow him to understand the nexus between Petitioner's difficult childhood, his drug use, and the murder.

In conclusion, the court stated:

> [T]he issue presented is whether Sansing's counsel performed deficiently, or rather, unreasonably based on the information he knew at the time, and based on the extent of his investigations and reliance on medical and mental health experts. Based on the factual accounts from the evidentiary hearing, counsel appears to have acted reasonably, even though no expert witnesses were called during the mitigation phase to attempt to create a causal nexus between Sansing's drug usage, tough childhood and antisocial personality disorder and the crime. This court finds that the testimony of Dr. Paul Miller regarding the Defendant's abusive childhood was duplicative of the investigation of Pamela Davis. The court further finds that the proposed expert testimony such as that offered by Drs. French and Lanyon regarding the effects and nexus between Defendant's cocaine use and the commission of the crime to be speculative and unpersuasive. The evidence of a "cocaine-induced psychosis" is speculative at best. Many of the facts upon which Dr. Lanyon based his testimony were quite effectively disputed by Dr. Michael Bayless. Dr. Bayless' opinions (including those disputing that any psychosis existed at the time of the crime given Sansing's detailed memory of what had occurred) were far more credible and reasonable. More importantly, [trial counsel] did not call expert witnesses for strategic or tactical reasons. I find no deficient performance by trial counsel.

Turning to *Strickland*'s prejudice prong, the court found that, even assuming counsel performed deficiently in failing to investigate and call experts, Petitioner had failed to demonstrate a reasonable probability of a different outcome. First, it concluded that, in light of his attempts to avoid prosecution, expert testimony connecting his dysfunctional upbringing to the offense would not have established that he was unable to appreciate the wrongfulness of his actions or to conform his conduct to the requirements of the law. Specifically, the court noted that Petitioner moved the victim's truck, lied and gave false information when asked about the victim's whereabouts, and hid the body. Analogizing to decisions by the Arizona Supreme Court in other capital cases, the PCR court concluded that each of these actions "was performed in order to elude suspicion and avoid prosecution" and "clearly demonstrated that he fully appreciated the wrongfulness of his conduct."

Similarly, the court found that expert testimony concerning cocaine intoxication would not have established that he was unable to conform his conduct to the requirements of the law due to drug impairment at the time of the offense. Again referencing a state supreme court case, the court noted that most of the testimony about Petitioner's drug use was derived from Petitioner himself. Because of Petitioner's "motive to fabricate self-serving testimony," this evidence would have been met with skepticism. The court also observed that although "no expert testified about Sansing's tough childhood, drug use, anti-social personality disorders or a causal nexus between his personality disorder and the crime, the *factual information* regarding Sansing's difficult childhood, his drug use, and the crime was presented to the sentencing judge." Finally, the court found that the murder was "horribly cruel" and that even if all of the proffered mitigating circumstances were proven, no reasonable jury would find the mitigation sufficiently substantial to outweigh the aggravation.

Controlling Law

As recognized by the state court, claims of ineffective assistance of counsel are governed by the principles set forth in *Strickland*. To prevail, a petitioner must show that counsel's representation fell below an objective standard of reasonableness and that the deficiency prejudiced the defense. *466 U.S. at 687-88.*

The inquiry under *Strickland* is highly   deferential and "every effort [must] be made to eliminate the distorting effects of hindsight, to reconstruct the circumstances of counsel's challenged conduct, and to evaluate the conduct from counsel's perspective at the time." *Id. at 689; see Wong v. Belmontes, 558 U.S. 15, 130 S. Ct. 383, 384, 175 L. Ed. 2d 328 (2009)* (per curiam); *Bobby v. Van Hook, 558 U.S. 4, 130 S. Ct. 13, 16, 175 L. Ed. 2d 255 (2009)* (per curiam). Thus, to satisfy *Strickland*'s first prong, a defendant must overcome "the presumption that, under the circumstances, the challenged action might be considered sound trial strategy." *Id.* "The test has nothing to do with what the best lawyers would have done. Nor is the test even what most good lawyers would have done. We ask only whether some reasonable lawyer at the trial could have acted, in the circumstances, as defense counsel acted at trial." *Id. at 687-88.*

With respect to *Strickland*'s second prong, a petitioner must affirmatively prove prejudice by "show[ing] that there is a reasonable probability that, but for counsel's unprofessional errors, the result of the proceeding would have been different. A reasonable probability is a probability sufficient to undermine confidence in the outcome." *Strickland, 466 U.S. at 694.* "When   a defendant challenges a death sentence . . . the question is whether there is a reasonable probability that, absent the errors, the sentencer . . . would have concluded that the balance of aggravating and mitigating circumstances did not warrant death." *466 U.S. at 695.* In *Wiggins v. Smith,* the Court further noted that "[i]n assessing prejudice, we reweigh the evidence in aggravation against the totality of available mitigating evidence." *539 U.S. 510, 534, 123 S. Ct. 2527, 156 L. Ed. 2d 471 (2003); see also Mayfield v. Woodford, 270 F.3d at 928.* The "totality of the available evidence" includes "both that adduced at trial, and the evidence adduced" in subsequent proceedings. *Wiggins, 539 U.S. at 536* (quoting *Williams v. Taylor, 529 U.S. 362, 397-98, 120 S. Ct. 1495, 146 L. Ed. 2d 389 (2000)).*

Under the AEDPA, this Court's already-deferential review of trial counsel's performance is subject to another level of deference under § 2244(d) and is thus "doubly" deferential. *Richter, 131 S. Ct. at 788* (quoting *Knowles v. Mirzayance, 556 U.S. 111, 129 S. Ct. 1411, 1420, 173 L. Ed. 2d 251 (2009)).* Therefore, to establish entitlement to relief, Petitioner must make the additional showing that the PCR court, in ruling that trial counsel was not ineffective, applied *Strickland* in an objectively   unreasonable manner. In making this determination, "the question is not whether counsel's actions were reasonable," but "whether there is any reasonable argument that counsel satisfied *Strickland*'s deferential standard." *Id.* Because the *Strickland* standard is a general one, "the range of reasonable applications is substantial." *Id.*

Analysis

Petitioner first asserts that the PCR court made no findings of fact nor reached any conclusions of law on his allegations concerning counsel's failure to investigate and to present Petitioner's social history to the experts, and that he is thus entitled to *de novo* review on these claims. However, it is apparent from the record that the court at least implicitly ruled on these allegations when it stated that "the issue presented is whether Sansing's counsel performed deficiently, or rather, unreasonably based on the information he knew at the time, and based on the extent of his investigations and reliance on medical and mental health experts." In addition, the court described the extent of counsel's investigation and noted counsel's testimony regarding his standard practice with respect to providing background information to experts.   In the absence of a clear indication that the state court declined to reach the merits of Petitioner's claim, this court "must assume that the state court has decided all the issues." *Murdoch v. Castro, 609 F.3d 983, 990 n.6 (9th Cir. 2010)* (en banc) (plurality opinion); *see Muth v. Frank, 412 F.3d 808, 815 (7th Cir. 2005)* ("An adjudication on the merits is perhaps best understood by stating what it is not: it is not the resolution of a claim on procedural grounds."); *see also Miller-El v. Cockrell, 537 U.S. 322, 347, 123 S. Ct. 1029, 154 L. Ed. 2d 931 (2003)* (noting that "a state court need not make detailed findings addressing all the evidence before it"); *Delgado v. Lewis, 223 F.3d 976, 982 (9th Cir. 2000)* (holding that "Federal habeas review is not *de novo* when the state court does not supply reasoning for its decision"). The court also described Petitioner's claim as failing "to fully investigate and develop possible mitigating factors, because expert witnesses were not presented," failing "to utilize an expert to explain his difficult childhood and polysubstance abuse," failing "to establish a causal nexus between Sansing's upbringing, antisocial personality disorder and the crime," failing to consult "with an expert in cocaine addiction," and failing "to produce an expert to develop the causal nexus between his substance abuse and the crime."

Addressing review under § 2254(d), Petitioner argues that the PCR court unreasonably applied *Strickland* in finding neither deficient performance nor prejudice. He further asserts that the state court's decision was based on the following seven instances of "unreasonable" factual determinations:

(1) The court's implicit determination that Ronan provided background information to Dr. Menendez, despite the discrepancies between her report and the available information concerning Petitioner's academic performance and relationship with his mother;

(2) The court's adoption of Dr. Bayless's account that Petitioner raped the victim because he saw her vaginal area when her dress flew up, despite the fact the victim had not been wearing a dress, Petitioner had not relayed seeing her vaginal area in any of his previous statements about the offense, and the absence of this alleged statement in Dr. Bayless's report and interview notes.

(3) The court's determination that Dr. Bayless was more credible than Petitioner's experts, in light of Dr. Bayless's testimony the victim was wearing a dress, his assertion that Petitioner suffered from no mental illness despite antisocial personality disorder being identified in the DSM as a mental illness, his unfounded assertions concerning the cost and amount of cocaine used by Petitioner, and his unprofessional personal feelings against Petitioner;

(4) The court's determination that Dr. French's opinion was based upon speculation about the quantity of cocaine used by Petitioner, despite Dr. French testifying that his opinion was not based on the amount of drugs Petitioner consumed;

(5) The court's finding that trial counsel chose to not offer the diagnosis of antisocial personality disorder as a mitigating factor because it could have opened the door to damaging rebuttal evidence, given that Ronan did not expressly testify he made such a decision in Petitioner's case, only that he agreed generally that prior bad acts would be part of the calculus an attorney would consider in deciding whether to present evidence of an antisocial personality disorder;

(6) The court's finding that Dr. Miller's report was duplicative of that prepared by the mitigation specialist, given that as a developmental psychologist Dr. Miller's report "goes much further" than Davis's investigation and had a different purpose; and

(7) The court's finding that trial counsel made a tactical decision not to present expert witnesses, given that Ronan had no recollection of why he did not do so.

Under the standard set forth in § 2254(d)(2), a state court decision "based on a factual determination will not be overturned on factual grounds unless objectively unreasonable in light of the evidence presented in the state-court proceeding." *Miller-El, 537 U.S. at 340 (2003); see Taylor v. Maddox, 366 F.3d 992, 999 (9th Cir. 2004)* ("[A] federal court may not second-guess a state court's fact-finding process unless, after review of the state-court record, it determines that the state court was not merely wrong, but actually unreasonable."). A state court's factual determination "is not unreasonable merely because the federal habeas court would have reached a different conclusion in the first instance." *Wood v. Allen, 558 U.S. 290, 130 S. Ct. 841, 849, 175 L. Ed. 2d 738 (2010).* "This is a daunting standard--one that will be satisfied in relatively few cases." *Taylor, 366 F.3d at 1000.*

Counsel's Performance

After reviewing the entirety of the record, this Court concludes that the state court reasonably determined that Ronan made a tactical decision, after conducting a reasonable investigation, not to present evidence of an antisocial personality disorder or to utilize expert witnesses to testify concerning Petitioner's difficult childhood, drug addiction, and cocaine intoxication at the time of the offense.

The evidence at the PCR hearing established that counsel consulted three different experts. Dr. Hill's report indicated that she was retained to determine Petitioner's competency to stand trial or plead guilty. Dr. Menendez's report stated that she was asked to determine whether Petitioner suffered from a learning disability. Neither counsel nor Dr. Parrish could recall her role in the case, but given her specialization in neuropsychology and post-traumatic stress disorder, it is not unreasonable to conclude that she was on the lookout for problems in these areas.

In addition, counsel enlisted a mitigation specialist to investigate and prepare a detailed social history report. According to Davis's report, she had extensive personal interviews with Petitioner and his wife, mother, father, stepmother, brother, three sisters,   and several aunts and uncles. She described Petitioner's positive relationship with the only significant male figure in his life--a maternal grandfather who died unexpectedly when Petitioner was seven years old. She relayed that between the ages of six and 14, Petitioner lived in a very unstable home, that his mother went through a succession of relationships with men, none of which were positive or supportive, that they lived in poverty, and that Petitioner's mother did not permit his father to have contact with Petitioner and his siblings. Davis recounted that Petitioner's mother "forbid her children to play outside or have friends in their home" and that there was one instance when a welfare worker arrived unannounced and found their living conditions to be "unacceptable." Describing Petitioner's mother's marriage to her second husband, when Petitioner was between the ages of six and ten, Davis reported that Petitioner's stepfather was an extremely abusive alcoholic, who would spend the weekends drinking and fighting with his wife. During these times, Petitioner and his siblings would be denied food and sleep until the fighting ended for the night, and Petitioner's mother would forbid   her children from eating or going to bed until a fight was resolved. The mitigation report also detailed Petitioner's juvenile criminal history, poor academic record, drug use beginning in the fifth grade, relationship with Kara Sansing, adult criminal history, and crack cocaine addiction.

Petitioner argues it was unreasonable for the court to implicitly find that Ronan provided this background information to Dr. Menendez. However, while Dr. Menendez's report contains some factual discrepancies compared to the information gathered by mitigation specialist Davis, this Court cannot say that the state court's finding was objectively unreasonable in light of Ronan's testimony concerning his standard practice of providing available background materials to experts and his having no reason to believe he did not follow this practice in this case. Because Dr. Menendez did not testify at the PCR hearing, there is no way to know whether she was given background materials but for whatever reason neglected to review them. Nor is there anything in the record to suggest that counsel failed to provide Petitioner's social history to Drs. Hill and Parrish; Dr. Hill did not testify and Dr. Parrish had   no specific recollection.

In addition, Petitioner does not allege that any of the experts requested additional information, *see Hendricks v. Calderon, 70 F.3d 1032, 1038 (9th Cir. 1995)* (holding that counsel does not have a duty to provide an expert with information necessary to reach a mental health diagnosis in the absence of a specific request to do so), or that the absence of any particular information precluded an accurate evaluation of Petitioner's mental state, *see Crittenden v. Ayers, 624 F.3d 943, 965 (9th Cir. 2010)* (noting that none of the experts suggested that additional background information or testing was necessary to accurately evaluate the defendant's mental health). Nor does Petitioner assert how additional background information would have affected any of the expert's conclusions.

Petitioner argues that it was unreasonable for the court to find that Ronan made a strategic decision not to offer the diagnosis of antisocial personality disorder as a mitigating factor. However, the record supports the state court's finding that Ronan likely concluded that the antisocial personality disorder diagnosed by Dr. Menendez would have harmed more than helped the mitigation case.   Although Ronan could not recall whether he considered presenting evidence of Petitioner's antisocial personality disorder, he testified that in his opinion such a diagnosis is not mitigating. He also testified that evidence of an antisocial personality disorder generally opens the door for prosecutors to present evidence of prior bad acts consistent with that diagnosis. Based on this testimony, it was not unreasonable for the state court to conclude that Ronan made a strategic decision in Petitioner's case not to call Dr. Menendez as a witness at sentencing.

Nor was it unreasonable for the state court to determine that the strategy itself was reasonable. *Cf. Crittenden, 624 F.3d at 968 n.15* (finding that counsel made tactical decision supported by adequate investigation to keep evidence of antisocial personality disorder away from sentencing jury). The Ninth Circuit has repeatedly observed that evidence of an antisocial personality disorder may be potentially more harmful than helpful. *See, e.g., Daniels v. Woodford, 428 F.3d 1181, 1204, 1210 (9th Cir. 2005)* (suggesting that evidence the defendant may have been a sociopath was aggravating); *Beardslee v. Woodford, 358 F.3d 560, 583 (9th Cir. 2004)* (acknowledging that an antisocial personality diagnosis can be damaging); *Clabourne v. Lewis, 64 F.3d 1373, 1384 (9th Cir. 1995)* (noting that mental health records omitted from the sentencing hearing "hardly turned out to be helpful" because they indicated that the defendant had an antisocial personality, not a thought disorder). Here, evidence of Petitioner's antisocial personality disorder would have opened the door to Petitioner's history of antisocial behavior, including violence against his wife, involvement of his children in other illegal activities, and other past crimes. Thus, this case differs from *Stankewitz v. Wong, 698 F.3d 1163, 1174 (9th Cir. 2012)*, where the court found that evidence of an antisocial personality would not have had a significant adverse impact because the prosecution had "already painted a grim picture of Stankewitz's violent, antisocial tendencies" and the jury had "heard next to nothing about Stankewitz's traumatic childhood."

Petitioner also argues that the state court unreasonably determined that Ronan made a strategic decision not to present expert witnesses to establish a nexus between Petitioner's commission of the offense and his substance abuse and dysfunctional upbringing. Information about Petitioner's dysfunctional upbringing, past substance abuse, and cocaine use at the time of the crime were presented to the judge through the mitigation specialist's report. Although Ronan had difficulty remembering his exact thought process, he speculated that he presented the mitigation case without experts because he believed the sentencing judge had the background and experience to understand the connection between Petitioner's background, drug abuse, and the crime. This was sufficient evidence from which the state court could reasonably conclude that counsel made a strategic decision.

Moreover, it was not objectively unreasonable for the state court to find that Ronan acted reasonably in not utilizing expert witnesses to establish a nexus between Petitioner's dysfunctional upbringing, drug abuse, and the crime. *See Hurles v. Ryan, No. 08-99032, 706 F.3d 1021, 2013 U.S. App. LEXIS 1305, 2013 WL 219222 (9th Cir. Jan. 18, 2013)* (finding that "counsel did not perform below the objective standard of care when she did not establish a causal nexus between Hurles's mental conditions and the crime" because Supreme Court precedent did not require such a showing). The connection between Petitioner's difficult childhood and drug addiction "was neither complex nor technical. It required only that the [judge] make logical connections of the kind a layperson is well equipped to make." *Wong v. Belmontes, 558 U.S. 15, 130 S. Ct. 383, 388, 175 L. Ed. 2d 328 (2009); see Fairbank v. Ayers, 650 F.3d 1243, 1253 (9th Cir. 2011)* (finding no ineffectiveness from counsel's failure to utilize an expert to link substance abuse and abusive childhood to the defendant's behavior during the crime); *see also Raley v. Ylst, 470 F.3d 792, 803 (9th Cir. 2006)* (noting that "the link between suffering abuse as a child and later committing abusive acts is not so esoteric as to be beyond the understanding of a lay jury"); *Nields v. Bradshaw, 482 F.3d 442, 455-56 (6th Cir. 2007)* (finding no ineffectiveness from counsel's failure to have an expert testify about the causal relationship between the defendant's alcoholism and his behavior on the night of the murder). In hindsight Ronan questioned whether he made the right decision on how the mitigation evidence was presented. However, this is insufficient to establish deficient performance under *Strickland*'s highly deferential standard.

In light of the record developed in state court, the Court concludes that the state court's finding of no deficient performance was based on neither an unreasonable application of *Strickland* nor an unreasonable determination of fact. Ronan could not recall many of the specifics of his decision-making process; however, there was sufficient other evidence in the record to support the state court's findings. *See Greiner v. Wells, 417 F.3d 305, 326 (2nd Cir. 2005)* ("Time inevitably fogs the memory of busy attorneys. That inevitability does not reverse the *Strickland* presumption of effective performance."); *see also Richter, 131 S. Ct. at 790* ("Although courts may not indulge *post hoc* rationalization for counsel's decisionmaking that contradicts the available evidence of counsel's actions, neither may they insist counsel confirm every aspect of the strategic basis for his or her actions.") (internal quotation omitted). Counsel undertook a reasonable investigation and made strategic decisions about the evidence to proffer in mitigation and how that evidence would be presented. "A disagreement with counsel's tactical decisions does not prove that the representation was constitutionally deficient." *Cox v. Ayers, 613 F.3d 883, 893 (9th Cir. 2010).*

Prejudice

In ultimately concluding that Petitioner was not prejudiced by any of counsel's alleged deficiencies, the state court made numerous findings, including that Dr. Bayless was more credible than Dr. Lanyon, that the opinions of Drs. French and Lanyon regarding a cocaine-induced psychosis were speculative and unpersuasive, that the proposed expert testimony would not have established that Petitioner's ability to appreciate the wrongfulness of his actions or to conform his conduct to the law's requirements was substantially impaired, that Dr. Miller's report was duplicative of that prepared by the mitigation specialist, and that the factual information regarding Petitioner's difficult childhood and drug abuse was before the sentencing judge.

Petitioner takes issue with the state court's credibility determinations concerning the experts, but federal courts have "no license to redetermine credibility of witnesses whose demeanor has been observed by the state trial court, but not by them." *Marshall v. Lonberger, 459 U.S. 422, 434, 103 S. Ct. 843, 74 L. Ed. 2d 646 (1983).* Even if reasonable minds reviewing a record might disagree about a witness's credibility, "on habeas review that does not suffice to supersede the trial court's credibility determination." *Rice v. Collins, 546 U.S. 333, 341-42, 126 S. Ct. 969, 163 L. Ed. 2d 824 (2006).* Rather, "so long as 'fairminded jurists could disagree' on the correctness" of the state court's credibility findings, Petitioner cannot demonstrate that these findings were objectively unreasonable. *Richter, 131 S. Ct. at 786* (citing *Yarborough v. Alvarado, 541 U.S. 652, 664, 124 S. Ct. 2140, 158 L. Ed. 2d 938 (2004)).*

Petitioner argues that it was objectively unreasonable for the PCR court to find that Petitioner committed the rape after seeing the victim's vaginal area because Dr. Bayless failed to document this alleged statement in his report or notes, Petitioner never made such an assertion in his other numerous statements about the offense, and the victim was not wearing a dress. In making this finding, the state court concluded that Dr. Bayless was a credible witness. Because as discussed next it was not objectively unreasonable for the state court to credit Dr. Bayless's testimony, none of Petitioner's alleged grounds are sufficient to overturn the state court's determination that Petitioner raped the victim after seeing her vaginal area. Moreover, the state court's reference to Petitioner's alleged sexual arousal played no significant role in its ultimate findings concerning counsel's representation. Petitioner had also reported both to Dr. Bayless and other experts that he raped the victim in order to make it look like she had been raped during a robbery. And it was this fact, separate from Petitioner's alleged arousal, that formed the basis of Dr. Bayless's opinion that Petitioner was fully aware of his actions when he committed the offense.

In a related argument, Petitioner asserts that it was objectively unreasonable for the state court to find Dr. Bayless more credible than Drs. Lanyon and French. However, this is a classic credibility determination to which this Court must defer so long as "fairminded jurists could disagree." *Richter, 131 S. Ct. at 786.* The essence of Petitioner's experts' testimony was that Petitioner entered a cocaine-induced psychotic state when Petitioner irrationally concluded that the victim could read his mind and was going to report him to the police. They based their conclusion on not only Petitioner having been on a crack binge for days, but also on his describing having "no conscious there" and experiencing "blackness" when he initiated the attack on Calabrese. However, as noted by the state court, trial counsel did not recall Petitioner ever telling him that he had no control over his actions and that counsel would have followed up on such a statement. It is also noteworthy that in interviews with the post-conviction experts Petitioner said the victim never regained consciousness. This change in narrative, in the face of his stipulated plea, his wife's testimony, and his statement to a reporter concerning the victim's consciousness, casts some doubt on the veracity of his newly-claimed lack of control. Regardless, Dr. Bayless testified that a cocaine-induced psychosis requires hallucinations and delusions and that in this case Petitioner was not delusional but knew exactly what he was doing as evidenced by Petitioner's logical and deliberate actions. In light of the competing experts' opinions and the evidentiary record, it was not objectively unreasonable for the state court to credit Dr. Bayless's testimony over that of Drs. Lanyon and French.

Petitioner also complains that the state court unreasonably determined that the testimony of Dr. Miller regarding Petitioner's difficult childhood was duplicative of that reported   by mitigation specialist Davis because Dr. Miller's report examined the nature of the risk factors that Petitioner was exposed to as a child, "such as abuse, neglect, parental alcoholism, multiple marriages and divorces, and violent, aggressive behavior between adults in the home." He further asserts that Davis was unqualified to opine whether Petitioner's "background contributed to psychological conditions or was a causal factor in the commission of the offense." However, Dr. Miller rendered no such opinion, testifying only that the identified risk factors increase the probability a child will someday engage in criminal activity. He expressly declined to offer an opinion about what role Petitioner's risk factors may have played in the offense or to assess Petitioner's psychological condition. In addition, Dr. Miller's report is based in large measure on Davis's mitigation report and her interview notes. It was not objectively unreasonable for the state court to find that Dr. Miller's contributions were largely duplicative of mitigation specialist Davis.

After careful review of the record, the Court concludes that it was not objectively unreasonable   for the PCR court to find no reasonable probability of a different outcome had counsel presented expert testimony concerning cocaine intoxication and connecting Petitioner's dysfunctional upbringing to his drug addiction and to the offense. The testimony at the PCR hearing of Petitioner's siblings and Dr. Miller was largely duplicative and cumulative of the information contained in the mitigation specialist's report. The sentencing judge found, based on Davis's report, that Petitioner had established a difficult childhood as a mitigating factor. Similarly, the sentencing judge found as a nonstatutory mitigating factor that Petitioner was somewhat impaired by crack cocaine at the time of the offense. Petitioner argues that expert testimony would have shown that he was in a cocaine-induced psychosis and thus *substantially* impaired under *A.R.S. § 13-703(G)(1)*, but the PCR court found otherwise. This was not an unreasonable determination in light of the evidence of Petitioner's planning, deliberate actions to conceal the crime, and his detailed memory of what occurred. Specifically, it was not unreasonable to find that Petitioner had the ability to appreciate the wrongfulness of his actions   based on his discussing a plan to rob the victim before she arrived at the house, moving the victim's truck, lying to her church about her whereabouts and his home address, washing the stick used to bludgeon her head, and hiding the body.

Conclusion

In determining that Petitioner's *Sixth Amendment* right to the effective assistance of counsel was not violated by counsel's alleged deficiencies in investigating and presenting mitigating evidence, the PCR court neither unreasonably applied *Strickland* nor unreasonably determined the facts in light of the evidence developed in state court. Because Petitioner is precluded from relief by *§ 2254(d)*, the Court declines to permit discovery, expansion of the record, and an evidentiary hearing on Claim 2.

REASONS WHY REMEDY IS HOLLOW

In Arizona defense lawyers fail to repeatedly investigate and present mitigating evidence. The courts decline to take any action to ensure this is not done.

BIBILIOGRAPHY

Cases

ANDREW J. ALLERDICE, Petitioner - Appellant, v. CHARLES L. RYAN, Director of the Arizona Department of Corrections, and ARIZONA ATTORNEY GENERAL, Respondents - Appellees. No. 08-17281 UNITED STATES COURT OF APPEALS FOR THE NINTH CIRCUIT 120

ANGEL MENDOZA LOPEZ, Petitioner, v. CHARLES L. RYAN and ARIZONA ATTORNEY GENERAL, Respondents.CIV 09-0536 PHX NVW (MEA) UNITED STATES DISTRICT COURT FOR THE DISTRICT OF ARIZONA...99

ARTIS GIPSON, Petitioner - Appellant, v. CHARLES RYAN and STATE OF ARIZONA ATTORNEY GENERAL, Respondents - Appellees. No. 10-15792 UNITED STATES COURT OF APPEALS FOR THE NINTH CIRCUIT 25

Blaine Kyle McNeese, Petitioner, v. Charles Ryan, Arizona Attorney General, Respondents. CIV 12-00962 PHX FJM (MEA)UNITED STATES DISTRICT COURT FOR THE DISTRICT OF ARIZONA 143

Boy White, Petitioner, v. Charles Ryan, Arizona Attorney General, Respondents. 46

Charles Anthony McDonald, Petitioner, vs. Charles L. Ryan, et al., Respondents..............................101

Claude Raymond Dove, Petitioner -vs- Charles L. Ryan, et al., Respondents 191

David Martinez Ramirez, Petitioner, vs. Charles L. Ryan, et al., Respondents. 26

DEMONT OSHAUN HILL, Petitioner, v. CHARLES L. RYAN, TERRY GODDARD, Respondents. CIV 09-01597 PHX MHM (MEA) UNITED STATES DISTRICT COURT FOR THE DISTRICT OF ARIZONA 21

DEWEY DERALD GULLICK, Petitioner - Appellant, v. BOCK, Deputy Warden; STATE OF ARIZONA ATTORNEY GENERAL, Respondents - Appellees. No. 10-15409 UNITED STATES COURT OF APPEALS FOR THE NINTH CIRCUIT...20

FRANK ROQUE, Petitioner, v. CHARLES L. RYAN and ARIZONA ATTORNEY GENERAL, Respondents. CIV 08-02154 PHX PGR (MEA)UNITED STATES DISTRICT COURT FOR THE DISTRICT OF ARIZONA.....................62

George Russell Kayer, Petitioner, vs. Charles L. Ryan, et al., Respondents. 78

HANS G. HIGGINS, Petitioner, v. CHARLES RYAN, ARIZONA ATTORNEY GENERAL, Respondents. 164

James E. Robinson, Petitioner, vs. Charles L. Ryan, et al., Respondents...22

James E. Young, Petitioner, v. Charles L. Ryan, Arizona Attorney General, Respondents. No. CV 13-02624 PHX GMS (MEA) UNITED STATES DISTRICT COURT FOR THE DISTRICT OF ARIZONA 153

JAMES EARL FOX, Petitioner - Appellant, v. CHARLES L. RYAN; STATE OF ARIZONA ATTORNEY GENERAL, Respondents - Appellees. No. 09-15834 UNITED STATES COURT OF APPEALS FOR THE NINTH CIRCUIT ..200

Jeffrey A. Herald, Petitioner, v. Charles L. Ryan, Arizona Attorney General, Respondents. No. CV 14-2188 PHX DLR (MEA) UNITED STATES DISTRICT COURT FOR THE DISTRICT OF ARIZONA 11

John Calvin Neuendorf II, Petitioner, v. Charles L. Ryan, et al., Respondents. 18

John Edward Sansing, Petitioner, vs. Charles L. Ryan et al., Respondents. 245

JOHNNY RAY WASHINGTON, Petitioner - Appellant, v. CHARLES L. RYAN, Director, AZ Department of Corrections and STATE OF ARIZONA ATTORNEY GENERAL, Respondents - Appellees.No. 08-17039 UNITED STATES COURT OF APPEALS FOR THE NINTH CIRCUIT...9

Jose Lewis Bosquez, Petitioner, v. Charles L. Ryan, et al., Respondents.No. CV-13-01714-PHX-PGR (BSB) UNITED STATES DISTRICT COURT FOR THE DISTRICT OF ARIZONA..181

Khalil Shakur, Petitioner, v. Charles Ryan, Arizona Attorney General, Respondents. CIV 11-02169 PHX FJM (MEA)UNITED STATES DISTRICT COURT FOR THE DISTRICT OF ARIZONA 159

KURT B. WILLIAMS, Petitioner - Appellant, v. DORA B. SCHRIRO; ARIZONA ATTORNEY GENERAL, Respondents - Appellees.No. 07-16537, No. 08-15864 UNITED STATES COURT OF APPEALS FOR THE NINTH CIRCUIT...120, 199

Marc Allen Clark, Petitioner, vs. Charles L. Ryan, et al., Respondents. No. CV-14-8112-PCT-DGC (JZB) UNITED STATES DISTRICT COURT FOR THE DISTRICT OF ARIZONA 189

MARQUIS LEE JOHNSON, Petitioner - Appellant, v. ARIZONA ATTORNEY GENERAL; et al., Respondents -

www.ingramcontent.com/pod-product-compliance
Lightning Source LLC
Chambersburg PA
CBHW051752200326
41597CB00025B/4525